Harnessing
MicroStation 95

Harnessing MicroStation 95

G.V. Krishnan

James E. Taylor

Delmar Publishers

an International Thomson Publishing company I(T)P®

Albany • Bonn • Boston • Cincinnati • Detroit • London • Madrid
Melbourne • Mexico City • New York • Pacific Grove • Paris • San Francisco
Singapore • Tokyo • Toronto • Washington

NOTICE TO THE READER

Cover images courtesy of Bentley Systems, Incorporated. Raytraced images rendered with MicroStation Masterpiece.

Delmar Staff:
Publisher: Bob Lynch
Associate Editor: Sandy Clark
Developmental Editor: Peg Gantz
Project Editor: Karianne Simone
Production Manager: Larry Main
Art & Design Coordinator: Mary Beth Vought

COPYRIGHT © 1997
By Delmar Publishers
An International Thomson Publishing Company

The ITP logo is a trademark under license

Printed in the United States of America

For more information, contact:

Delmar Publishers
3 Columbia Circle, Box 15015
Albany, New York 12212-5015

International Thomson Publishing Europe
Berkshire House
168–173 High Holborn
London, WC1V 7AA
England

Thomas Nelson Australia
102 Dodds Street
South Melbourne, 3205
Victoria, Australia

Nelson Canada
1120 Birchmount Road
Scarborough, Ontario
Canada M1K 5G4

International Thomson Editores
Campos Eliseos 385, Piso 7
Col Polanco
11560 Mexico D F Mexico

International Thomson Publishing GmbH
Königswinterer Strasse 418
53227 Bonn
Germany

International Thomson Publishing Asia
221 Henderson Road
#05–10 Henderson Building
Singapore 0315

International Thomson Publishing Japan
Hirakawa-cho Kyowa Building, 3F
2-2-1 Hirakawa-cho
Chiyoda-ku, 102 Tokyo
Japan

    3 4 5 6 7 8 9 XXX 02 01 00 99 98 97

Library of Congress Cataloging-in-Publication Data

Krishnan, G. V.
    Harnessing MicroStation 95 / G.V. Krishnan, James E. Taylor,
Robert A. Rhea.
    p.   cm.
    Includes index.
    ISBN 0-8273-8048-8
    1. Computer-aided design—Computer programs. 2. MicroStation.
I. Taylor, James E. II. Rhea, Robert A. III. Title.
TA174.K745 1997   96-17792
620'.0042'02855369—dc20   CIP

•

CONTENTS

DEDICATION

HATS OFF!

bhuvana
avinash
kavitha

dorothy

•
INTRODUCTION

Harnessing MicroStation 95 gives you the necessary skills to get going with a very powerful CAD program—MicroStation 95. We have created a comprehensive book providing information, references, instructions, and exercises for people of varied skill levels, disciplines, and requirements for applying this powerful design/drafting software.

Now in its 2nd edition, *Harnessing MicroStation 95* was written and updated as a comprehensive tool for the novice and the experienced MicroStation user, both in the classroom and on the job.

Readers immediately gain a broad range of knowledge of the elementary CAD concepts necessary to complete a simple design. We do not believe the user should be asked to wade through all components of every command or concept the first time that command or concept is introduced. Therefore, we have set up the early chapters so that fundamentals are covered and practiced extensively to better prepare them for the more advanced topics covered later in the book.

Harnessing MicroStation 95 is intended to be both a classroom text and a desk reference. If you are already a user of MicroStation Version 4 or Version 5, you will see an in-depth explanation provided in the corresponding chapters for all the new features for MicroStation 95. Features introduced in MicroStation 95 give personal computer-based CADD even greater depth and breadth.

Chapter 1—Getting Started The beginning of this chapter describes the hardware you need to get started with MicroStation. The balance of this chapter explains how to start MicroStation 95 in DOS, Windows 3.1, and the Windows 95 operating system; the salient features of dialog, settings boxes, and MicroStation application window; input methods, design plane and working units, saving changes and exiting the design file, and a summary of the enhancements in MicroStation 95.

Chapters 2 and 3—Fundamentals Introduces all the basic element placement and manipulation commands needed to draw a moderately intricate design. All commands are accompanied by examples. Ample exercises are designed to give students the chance to test their level of skill and understanding.

Chapter 4—AccuDraw and SmartLine An in-depth explanation is provided for the two new tools introduced in MicroStation 95.

Chapter 5—Menu Placing Groups of Elements Introduces all the manipulation commands available to manipulate groups of elements including element selection and fence manipulation.

Chapter 6—Placing Text, Data Fields, and Tags An in-depth explanation is provided in placing text by various methods, placement of data fields and tags.

Chapter 7—Element Modification Introduces various methods available in modification of elements. All commands are accompanied by Examples.

Chapter 8—Measurement and Dimensioning Introduces various measurement commands and detailed explanation is provided for dimensioning including dimension settings.

Chapter 9—Plotting Introduces all the features related to plotting.

Chapter 10—Cells and Cell Libraries Introduces the powerful set of tools available in MicroStation for creating and placing symbols, called cells, and storing them in Cell Libraries. The tools permit you to group elements under a user-determined name and perform certain manipulation commands on the group as though they were a single element.

Chapter 11—Patterning Introduces the set of tools available in MicroStation to place repeating patterns to fill regions in a design for various purposes.

Chapter 12—Reference Files One of the most powerful time-saving features of MicroStation is its ability to view other design files while you are working in your current design file. MicroStation lets you display the contents of up to 255 design files (although the default is set to 32 design files) while working in your current design file. This function is in the form of reference files. This chapter introduces all the powerful tools that are available to manipulate reference files.

Chapter 13—Special Features MicroStation provides some special features that are less often used than the commands described in Chapters 1 through 12, but provide added power and versatility. This chapter introduces several such features.

Chapter 14—MicroStation and Microsoft Windows This chapter explains all the available unique features in MicroStation running in Microsoft Windows 95.

Chapter 15—Customizing MicroStation Introduces several facets of customizing MicroStation such as creating multi-line definition, custom line styles, workspaces, creating and modifying tool boxes, tool frames, function key menus, installing fonts, and archive utility.

Chapter 16—3D Design and Rendering   This chapter provides an overview of the tools and specific commands available for 3D design.

In addition, **appendices** are included that provide valuable information to the user such as the MicroStation pull-down menu layout and available tool boxes and tool frames, tablet menu, list of key-in commands, list of alternate key-ins, primitive commands, and list of available seed files.

A sequence suitable for learning, ample exercises, examples, review questions, and thorough coverage of the MicroStation program should make *Harnessing MicroStation 95* a must for multiple courses in MicroStation, as well as self-learners, everyday operators on the job, and aspiring customizers.

ACKNOWLEDGMENTS

This book was a team effort. We are very grateful to many people who worked very hard to help create this book. We are especially grateful to the following individuals at Delmar Publishers whose efforts made it possible to complete the project on time: Mr. Robert Lynch, Publisher; Ms. Sandy Clark, Associate Editor; Ms. Karianne Simone, Project Editor; Ms. Peg Gantz, Development Editor; Ms. Jennifer Gaines, Production Coordinator; Mr. Larry O'Brien, Typesetter; Ms. Carol Micheli, Proofreader; and Mr. Elliott Simon, Copy Editor.

And, last but not least, special appreciation to Bentley Systems, Inc. for providing the MicroStation 95 software and technical help whenever we needed and also special thanks to Applications Techniques, Inc. for providing the Pizzaz Plus software to capture screen layout.

CHAPTER

1

GETTING STARTED

The beginning of this chapter describes the hardware you need to get started with MicroStation. If you need to set up the MicroStation program on the computer and you are not familiar with the computer operating system (files, drives, directories, operating system commands, etc.), you may wish to review Appendix C, DOS and File Handling, refer to the Installation Guide that comes with the program, and/or consult the dealer from whom you purchased MicroStation. Once the computer is set up, you will have at your disposal a versatile design and drafting tool that continues to grow in power with each new version.

The balance of this chapter explains how to start MicroStation and gives an overview of the screen layout and the salient features of dialog and settings boxes. Detailed explanations and examples are provided for the concepts and commands throughout the chapters that follow.

At the end of the chapter, a list of enhancements for MicroStation 95 is provided. If you are already a user of MicroStation Version 5, check the list to see the new and improved features in MicroStation 95. Throughout the book you will find in-depth explanations in the chapters corresponding to all the new features of MicroStation 95. Features introduced in MicroStation 95 give personal computer-based CADD even greater depth and breadth.

HARDWARE CONFIGURATION

The configuration of your system is a combination of the hardware and software you have assembled to create your system. Countless PC configurations are available. The goal for a new computer user should be to assemble a PC workstation that will not block future software and hardware upgrades.

To use MicroStation, your computer system must meet certain minimum requirements. Following are the minimum and recommended configurations for Micro-Station 95 PC:

- Intel-compatible PCs—80386 (with a math co-processor), 80486DX, Pentium or DEC Alpha Processor or PowerPC
- DOS, DOS with Microsoft Windows 3.1x, Microsoft Windows 95 operating system, Microsoft Windows NT operating system, IBM OS/2 Warp
- 8MB minimum, 16MB recommended (DOS); 16MB minimum, 24MB recommended (Windows 3.1x/Windows 95/Windows NT/IBM OS/2 Warp); 24MB minimum, 32MB recommended (PowerPC or DEC Alpha Windows NT)
- 200MB minimum hard disk (typical installation: 50MB)
- Input device: mouse or tablet (tablet on Windows 3.1x/95/NT requries vendor-supplied WINTAB driver)
- Supported graphics card (256 or more color card recommended for rendering)
- Dual screen graphics supported (Windows 3.1x/95/NT and OS/2 require vendor-supplied drivers)

Processors

Select the one that best suits your workload. The faster and more powerful the processor, the better MicroStation performs. Thus, the processor of choice is generally the most technologically advanced one available. With the availability of fast Pentium-based systems under $2,000, a good platform for MicroStation can be attained from a number of sources. Several manufacturers of RISC processors are introducing PC-compatible systems that can now run most DOS/Windows applications.

Memory

To run MicroStation, your computer must be equipped with at least 8MB of RAM (random-access memory). Depending on your MicroStation application 16MB of RAM or more may be required for optimal performance. If you are going to be using MicroStation in Windows 3.1, you may require 16MB to 24MB for the same level of performance. The availability of low-cost RAM has made this an easy upgrade for most MicroStation users.

Hard Drives

The hard disk is the personal computer's primary data storage device. A hard disk with at least 200MB capacity is required, but a larger capacity is advised. The hard disk accesses data at a rate of 12 milliseconds to 80 milliseconds. High performance is 30 milliseconds or faster, while 80 milliseconds is considered slow. Obviously, the faster the hard-disk drive, the more productive you will be with MicroStation.

Video Adapter and Display

As with any graphics program for PC CAD systems, MicroStation requires a video adapter capable of displaying graphics information. A video adapter is a printed circuit board that plugs into the central processing unit (CPU) and generates signals to drive a monitor. MicroStation supports a number of display options, ranging from low-priced monochrome setups to high-resolution color units. Some of the video display controllers can be used in combination, giving a two-screen display.

Input Devices

MicroStation supports several input device configurations. Data may be entered through the keyboard, a mouse, or a digitizing tablet with a cursor.

Keyboard The keyboard is one of the primary input methods. It can be used to enter commands and responses.

Mouse A mouse is used with the keyboard as a tracking device to move the crosshairs on the screen. MicroStation supports a two-button mouse and a three-button mouse (see Figure 1–1). As you move your pointing device around on a mouse pad or other suitable surface, the cursor will mimic your movements on the screen. It may be in the form of crosshairs when you are being prompted to select a point. Each of the buttons in the mouse is programmed to serve specific functions in MicroStation. See Table 1–1 for the specific functions that are programmed for the two- and three-button mice.

Digitizing Tablet A digitizer is literally an electronic drawing board. An internal wiring system forms a grid of fine mesh, which corresponds to the coordinate points on the screen. The digitizer works with a puck. When the user moves the puck across the digitizer, crosshairs follow on the screen. The number of buttons on a puck depends on the manufacturer. A puck usually has four buttons, as shown in Figure 1–2; each of the buttons on the puck is programmed to serve specific functions in MicroStation. If there are more than four buttons on the puck, the first four are preprogrammed. For example, when you place a line, the points are selected by

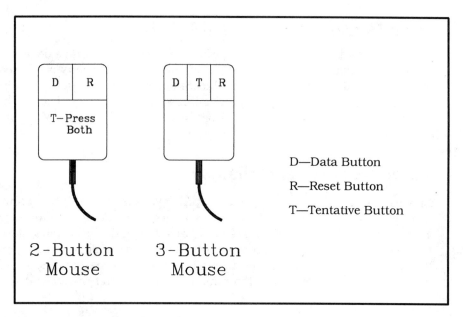

FIGURE 1–1   Pointing device—two-button mouse and three-button mouse.

Table 1–1. Button Functions on Two- and Three-Button Mice

	BUTTON POSITION	
BUTTON FUNCTION	**TWO-BUTTON MOUSE**	**THREE-BUTTON MOUSE**
Data button	Left (first button)	Left (first button)
Reset button	Right (second button)	Right (third button)
Tentative button	Left and right simultaneously	Center (second button)

pressing the designated Data button in two locations. Although the user's attention is focused on the screen, the points are actually selected on the coordinates of the tablet. The coordinates from the tablet are then transmitted to the computer, which draws the image of a line on your screen.

Another advantage of a tablet is the ability to use a tablet menu for command selection. Menus have graphic representations of the commands and are taped to the digitizing tablet's surface. The menu is attached or activated with the key-in **AM=** followed by that menu's specific name. See Appendix B for a detailed explanation of the menu attachment. The commands are chosen by placing the puck's crosshairs over the block that represents the command you want to use and pressing the designated command button. Another powerful feature of the tablet (not related to entering commands) is that it allows you to lay a map or other picture on the tablet

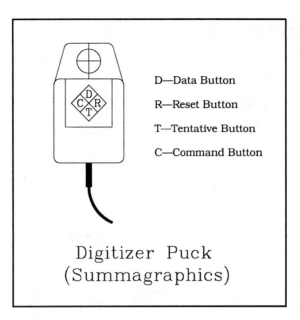

D—Data Button

R—Reset Button

T—Tentative Button

C—Command Button

Digitizer Puck
(Summagraphics)

FIGURE 1–2 Pointing device—digitizer puck.

Table 1–2. **Button Functions on the Four-Button Puck**

FUNCTION	FOUR-BUTTON PUCK
Data button	Top (yellow)
Reset button	Right (green)
Tentative button	Bottom (blue)
Command button	Left (white)

and trace over it with the puck. See Table 1–2 for the specific functions that are programmed for the four-button puck. Detailed explanations of the functions are given later in the chapter, in the section on Input Methods.

STARTING MICROSTATION 95

The look and feel of MicroStation 95 are the same whether you are running in DOS, Windows 3.1, or the Windows 95 operating system. A few additional features (such as Object Linking and Embedding) are provided for Windows 3.1 and Windows 95 that are not available for DOS.

To Start MicroStation 95 in DOS

Call up the USTATION batch by typing **USTATION** at the DOS prompt, and press ⏎ENTER .

> C:\>**USTATION** ⏎ENTER

MicroStation displays the MicroStation Manager dialog box similar to Figure 1–3.

> **NOTE:** Unless certain DOS paths and systems configurations are properly set up, you should not initiate the MicroStation program from a directory other than the one that the MicroStation files are in.

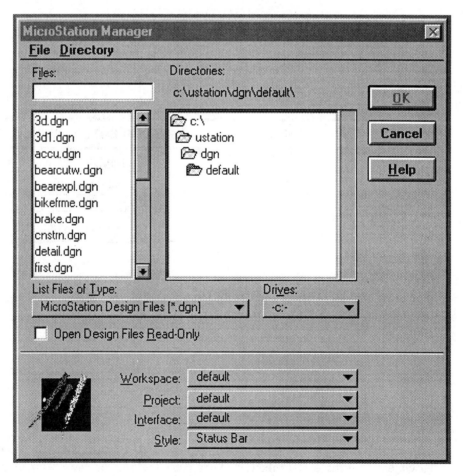

FIGURE 1–3 MicroStation Manager dialog box.

To Start MicroStation 95 in Windows 3.1

In the MicroStation 95 program group, double-click the MicroStation 95 icon. Micro-Station displays the MicroStation Manager dialog box similar to Figure 1–3.

To Start MicroStation 95 in the Windows 95 Operating System

Click the Start button, select the MicroStation 95 program group, and then select the MicroStation 95 program. MicroStation displays the MicroStation Manager dialog box similar to Figure 1–3.

> **NOTE:** All the screen captures shown in this textbook are taken from MicroStation 95 running in the Windows 95 operating system.

Before we start a new design file, let's discuss the important features of dialog boxes and settings boxes.

USING DIALOG BOXES AND SETTINGS BOXES

A dialog box is a special type of window displayed by MicroStation. Dialog boxes were designed to permit the user to perform many actions easily within MicroStation. Dialog boxes force MicroStation to stop and focus on what is happening in that dialog box only. You cannot do anything else in MicroStation until you close the dialog box. The MicroStation Manager is a good example of this type of dialog box.

In addition to dialog boxes, MicroStation provides settings boxes. Several settings boxes can be left on the screen while you work in other areas of MicroStation. For instance, the Lock Toggles settings box (see Figure 1–4) can be left open as long as you need. While it is open, you can turn the locks ON and OFF as you need and at the same time interact with other dialog boxes. To close the settings box, double-click the "–" symbol located in the top left corner of the settings box. If you are working in the Windows operating system, you can close by clicking on the "X" symbol located in the top right corner of the settings box.

When you move the cursor onto a dialog box or settings box, the cursor changes to a pointer. You can use the arrow keys on your keyboard to make selections, but it is much easier with your pointing device. Another way to make selections is via the keyboard equivalents.

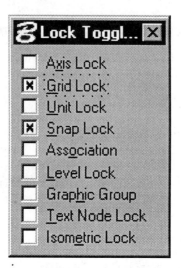

FIGURE 1-4 Lock Toggles settings box.

Title Bar and Menu Bar Item MicroStation displays the title of the dialog box or settings box in the Title bar, as shown in Figure 1–5. Below the Title bar, Micro-Station displays any available pull-down menus in the menu bar, as shown in Figure 1–5. In this case, two pull-down menus are available, File and Directory. Selecting from the list is a simple matter of moving the cursor down until the desired item is highlighted, then pressing the designated Pick (Data) button on the pointing device. If a menu item has an arrow to the right, it has a cascading submenu. To display the submenu, just click on the menu title. Menu items that include ellipses (...) display dialog boxes. To select these, just pick the menu item.

Label Item MicroStation displays the text (display only) to label the different parts of the dialog box or settings box, as shown in Figure 1–6.

Edit Field An edit field is an area that accepts one line of text entry. It normally is used to specify a name, such as a file name, including the drive and/or directory path or level name. Edit fields often make an alternative to selecting from a list of names when the desired name is not displayed in the list box. Once the correct text is keyed in, enter it by pressing [ENTER].

Moving the pointer into the edit field causes the text cursor to appear in a manner similar to the cursor in a word processor. If necessary, the text cursor, in combination with special editing keys, can help to facilitate changes to the text. You can see the text cursor and the pointer at the same time, making it possible to click the pointer on a character in the edit field and relocate the text cursor to that character. You can select a group of characters in the edit field to manipulate, for instance, or to delete

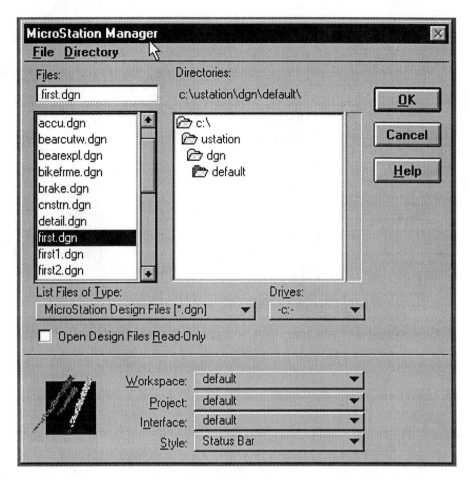

FIGURE 1–5 MicroStation Manager dialog box showing the Title bar and pull-down menus.

by highlighting the characters. This is accomplished by holding down the designated Pick button on your pointing device and dragging left or right. You can also use the right and left arrows on the keyboard to move the cursor right or left, respectively, across text without affecting the text.

List Boxes and Scroll Bars List boxes make it easy to view, select, and enter a name from a list of existing items, such as file names (see Figure 1–6). With the pointer, highlight the desired selection. The item, when clicked, will appear in the edit field. You can accept this item by clicking OK or by double-clicking on the item. List boxes are accompanied by scroll bars to facilitate moving long lists up and down in the list box. When you point and hold onto the slider box, you can move it up and down to cause the list to scroll. Pressing the up/down arrows causes the list to scroll up or down one item at a time.

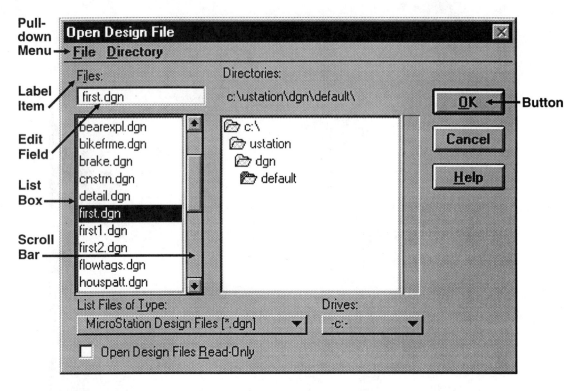

FIGURE 1–6 Dialog box.

Buttons Actions are initiated immediately when one of the various buttons is clicked (OK or Cancel, for example). If a button (such as the OK button in Figure 1–6) is surrounded by a heavy line, it is the default button, and pressing ⏎ is the same as clicking that button. Buttons with action that is not acceptable will be disabled; they will appear grayed out. Buttons with ellipses (...) will cause that action's own dialog box (subdialog) to appear.

Toggle Buttons A button that indicates an ON or OFF setting is also called a *check box* or *toggle button*. For instance, in Figure 1–7, the Axis, Grid, and Snap locks are set to ON and the remaining locks are set to OFF.

Option Button A list of items is displayed when you click on the option button menu, and only one item may be selected from the list, as shown in Figure 1–8.

Let's get on to the business of starting a new design file in MicroStation.

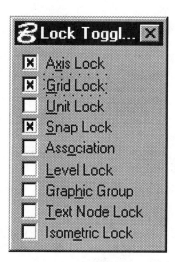

FIGURE 1-7   Toggle buttons.

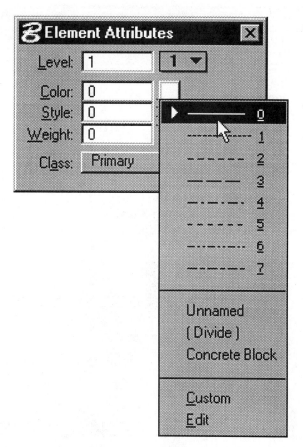

FIGURE 1-8   Option button menu.

BEGINNING A NEW DESIGN

To begin a new design, select the New... command from the pull-down menu File, as shown in Figure 1–9.

The Create Design File dialog box opens, as shown in Figure 1–10.

Select the appropriate seed file (more about this in the section on Seed Files), enter a name for your new design in the Name edit field, and click the OK button. The Create Design File dialog box is closed and control is passed to the MicroStation Manager. MicroStation by default highlights the name of the file you just created in the Files list box.

Before you click the OK button to open the newly created design file, make sure the appropriate Workspace, Project, and Interface are selected from the option menu located at the bottom of the MicroStation Manager dialog box.

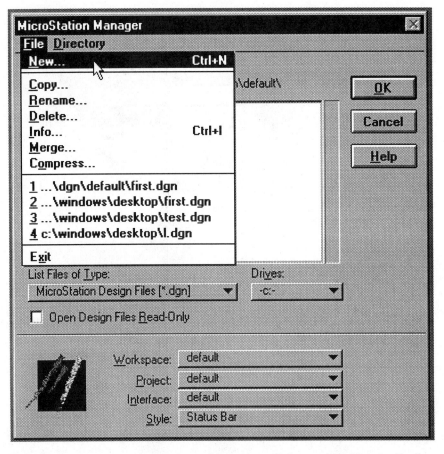

FIGURE 1–9   Invoking the New... command from the pull-down menu File.

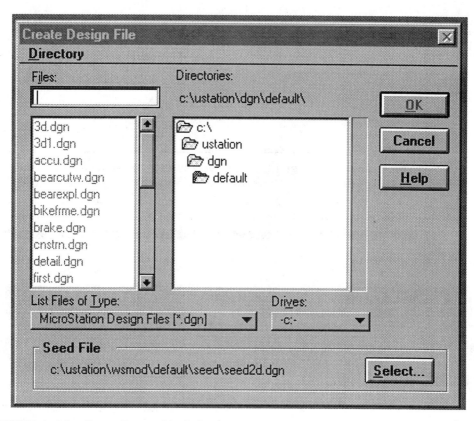

FIGURE 1-10 Create Design File dialog box.

A Workspace is a customized drafting environment that permits the user to set up MicroStation for specific purposes. You can set up as many workspaces as you need. A workspace consists of "components" and "configuration files" for both the user and the project. By default, MicroStation selects the default workspace. If necessary, you can create or modify an existing workspace. Refer to Chapter 15 for detailed description of creating or modifying workspace.

The selection of the project sets the location and names of data files associated with a specific design project. Refer to Chapter 15 for setting up the project. By default, MicroStation selects the default in the Project option menu.

The selection of the interface sets a specific look and feel of MicroStation's tools and general on-screen operation. If necessary, you can change the selection of the interface from the Interface option menu. MicroStation comes with discipline-specific interfaces: civil, architecture, mechanical, drafting, and mapping. In addition it has interfaces for previous versions (V4 and V5) and AutoCAD users. By default, MicroStation selects the default in the Interface option menu. Refer to Chapter 15 for detailed explanation on creating and modifying the MicroStation interface.

The Style option menu allows you to select whether to use the older Command Window (V4 and V5) method of communicating with MicroStation or the new Status bar. The default selection is the Status bar. Whichever style you select, MicroStation will remember it from session to session.

To open the new design file, click the OK button. Your screen will look similar to the one in Figure 1–11.

> **NOTE:** If the design file name you key-in is the same as the name of an existing file name, MicroStation displays an Alert Box asking if you want to replace the existing file. Click the OK button to replace, or Cancel to reissue a new file name.

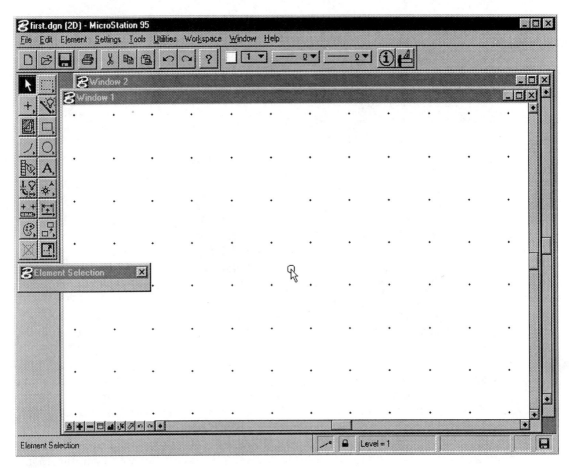

FIGURE 1–11 MicroStation Application Window.

File Names

The name you enter in the Name edit field will be the name of the file in which information about the design is stored. It must satisfy the requirements for file names as specified by the particular operating system on your computer. DOS and UNIX are the two most common operating systems.

File Names in DOS In PC-DOS™ and MS-DOS™ each design is a file with a "file specification." The file specification, or file spec, is the full name of the file. The file specification consists of a name and an extension. For example, in the file specification FLOOR.DGN, FLOOR is the file name and .DGN is the extension. File names are from one to eight characters and extensions can be a maximum of three characters. Names and extensions are separated by a period. Names may be made up of combinations of uppercase and lowercase letters, numbers, the underscore (_), the hyphen (-), and the dollar sign ($). DOS converts all of the characters to uppercase. No blank spaces are allowed in the name. Valid examples include:

> floor-1.dgn
> lab1.dgn
> $345-p.dgn
> PART_NO5.wrk

Examples of improper key names include:

> *test.dgn   *The asterisk is not a valid character.*
> nametoolong.dgn   *The name is too long (more than eight characters).*

When MicroStation prompts for a design name, just type in the file name and MicroStation will append the extension .DGN by default. For instance, if you respond to the design name as FLOOR1, then MicroStation will create a file with the file spec FLOOR1.DGN. If you need to provide a different extension, key-in the extension with the file name.

As you progress through the lessons, note how various functions ask for names of files. If MicroStation performs the file processing, it usually adds the proper default extension. If you use DOS, you should include the extension.

The Path If you want to create a new design file or edit a design file that is on a drive and/or directory other than the current drive/directory, you must furnish what is called the *path* to the design file as part of the file specification you enter. Specifying a path requires that you use the correct pathfinder symbols—the colon (:) and/or the backslash (\). The drive with a letter name (usually A through E) is identified as such by a colon, and the backslashes enclose the name of the directory where the design file is (or will be) located. Examples of path/key name combinations are as follows:

a:proj1	*The file proj1 in the working directory on drive A.*
b:\spec\elev	*The file elev in the \spec directory on drive B.*
\buil\john	*The file john in the \buil directory.*
ACME\doors	*The file doors in the working directory's ACME subdirectory.*
..\PIT\flange	*The file flange in the parent directory's PIT subdirectory.*

> *NOTE:* Instead of specifying the path as part of the design file name, select the appropriate drive and directory from the list box and then select the design file from the files list box. MicroStation Manager displays the current drive and path in the dialog box.

Seed Files

Each time you use MicroStation's Create New File utility, a copy is made of an existing "prototype," or "seed," file. If necessary, you can customize the seed file. In other words, you can control the initial "makeup" of the file. To do so, open an existing seed file, make the necessary changes in the settings of the parameters, and place elements such as title block, etc. Whenever you start a new design file, make sure to copy the appropriate seed file.

MicroStation programs come with several seed files. See Appendix G for a list of seed files and default working units. Depending on the discipline, use an appropriate seed file. For instance, if you plan to work on an architecture floor plan, then use the architecture seed file (SDARCH2D.DGN). When you open the Create Design file, MicroStation displays the name of the default seed file as shown in Figure 1–12. If necessary, you can change the default seed file by clicking the Select button. Micro-Station displays a list of available seed files as shown in Figure 1–13. Select the one you want from the list and click the OK button.

OPENING AN EXISTING DESIGN FILE

Whenever you want to open an existing design file in MicroStation, simply click the name of the file in the Files list box item of the MicroStation Manager dialog box, then click the OK button or double-click the name of the file. If the design file is not in the current directory, change to the appropriate drive and directory from the Directories list box, then select the appropriate design file. In addition, MicroStation displays the names (including the path) of the last four design files opened in the pull-down menu File as shown in Figure 1–14. If you need to open one of the four design files, click on the file name and MicroStation displays the design file.

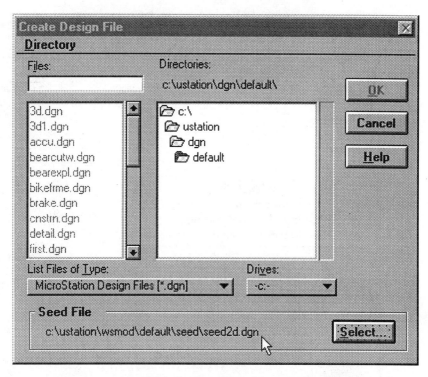

FIGURE 1-12   Create Design File dialog box displaying the name of the default seed file.

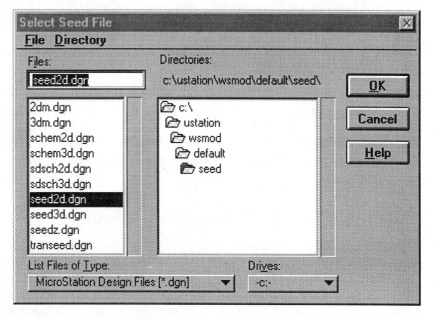

FIGURE 1-13   Select Seed File dialog box.

FIGURE 1–14 Pull-down menu File from the MicroStation Manager dialog box, displaying the names of the last four design files opened.

NOTE: You can also create a new design file or open an existing design file by selecting the New... or Open... command, respectively, from the pull-down menu File located in the MicroStation Application Window.

Opening a Design in Read-Only Mode

MicroStation allows you to open a design in read-only mode by turning ON the toggle button for Open Design Files Read-Only located in the MicroStation Manager dialog box. When the Read-Only option is chosen, MicroStation opens the active design file in a read-only state and displays a disk icon with a large red X in the lower right corner of the Application Window. Any changes you make to the design will not be saved as part of the design file.

MICROSTATION APPLICATION WINDOW

The MicroStation Application Window consists of pull-down menus (also called *menu bars*), the Status bar, tool frames, tool boxes, the Key-in window, and view windows with the View Control bar (see Figure 1–15).

Pull-down Menus

The MicroStation Application Window has a set of pull-down menus, as shown in Figure 1–15. Several tool boxes, dialog boxes, and settings boxes are available from the pull-down menus. To select one of the pull-down menus, select the name of the pull-down menu. MicroStation displays the list of options available. Selecting from the list is a simple matter of moving the cursor down until the desired item is highlighted and then pressing the Data button on the pointing device. If a menu item has an arrow to the right, it has a cascading submenu. To display the submenu, just

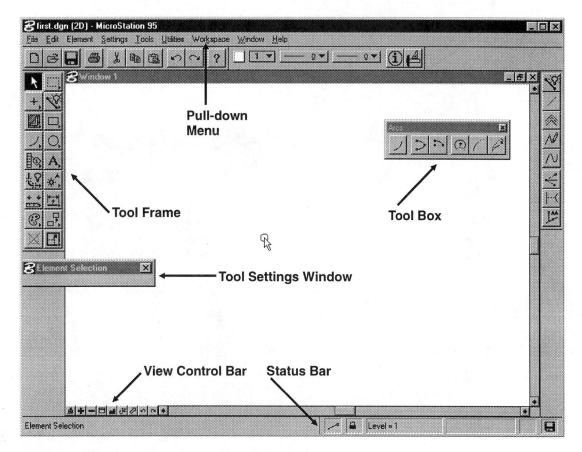

FIGURE 1–15   MicroStation Application Window.

select the name of the submenu. Menu items that include ellipses (...) display dialog boxes. When a dialog box is displayed, no other action is allowed until that dialog box is dismissed or closed.

The pull-down menu Tools displays the list of available tool boxes in MicroStation. To select one of the available tool boxes, just select the name of the tool box and it will be displayed on the screen. Check marks are placed in the Tools menu to indicate open tool boxes. Choosing an item in the pull-down menu Tools toggles the state of the corresponding tool box. If the tool box is closed, it opens; if the tool box is open, it closes. You can place the tool box anywhere on the screen by dragging it with your pointing device. There is no limit to the number of the tool boxes that can be displayed on the screen.

To open multiple tool boxes at the same time, open the Tool Boxes dialog box from:

| Pull-down menu | <u>T</u>ools > Tool <u>B</u>oxes... (or  + **T, B**) |

MicroStation displays the Tool Boxes dialog box, similar to Figure 1–16.

Select all the tool boxes to open by turning ON their check boxes, then click the OK button to close the dialog box. MicroStation displays the selected tool boxes.

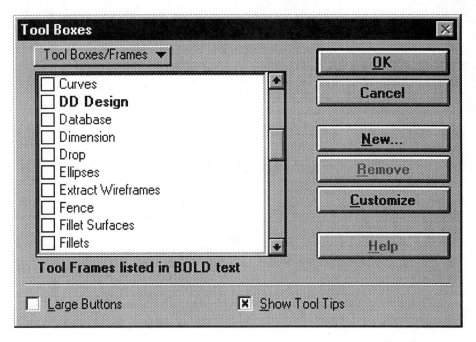

FIGURE 1–16 Tool Boxes dialog box.

If you are working with two monitors, you can drag the tool box to the second monitor. You can close the tool box by double-clicking on the "–" symbol located in the top left corner of the tool box if you are working in DOS. On the Windows 95 operating system you can close by clicking on the X located in the top right corner of the tool box. When you open the tool box, it is displayed at the same location where it was previously open.

Tool Frames and Tool Boxes

Tool frames hold tool boxes of related tools and display the icon for the most recently invoked tool within each tool box. MicroStation provides three tool frames: Main, 3D Tools, and DD Design. The most important one is the Main tool frame, shown in Figure 1–17. The Main tool frame provides access to the majority of MicroStation's drawing tools, including measurement and dimensioning tools. Consider always leaving the Main tool frame open while drawing.

Tool boxes consist of various tools. To access one of the tools from the tool box, click on the icon with the Data button and the appropriate command is invoked. To access one of the tools from a tool box in the tool frame, click, hold, and drag the pointer to the appropriate icon and release the pointer. The selected command is invoked.

FIGURE 1–17 Main tool frame.

If necessary, you can tear the tool box from the tool frame. To do so, select the appropriate tool box by pressing and holding the tool box, then drag it to anywhere on the screen and release it. Figure 1–18 shows the Linear Elements tool box taken out from the Main tool frame.

Resizing the Tool Box By clicking and dragging on the edge of the tool box you can change the shape of the tool box's window. Figure 1–19 shows the resizing of the Linear Elements tool box to three different layouts. The tools contained within will move to fill the new window shape. The resized version of any given tool box will be remembered by MicroStation from session to session.

Docking a Tool Box MicroStation allows you to dock a tool box to any edge of the MicroStation Application Window so it becomes part of the Application Window. Docking can happen on all four sides of the application window. And you can dock more than one tool box to each edge of the MicroStation Application Window. Figure 1–20 shows tool boxes docked on four sides of the Application Window. When a tool box is docked to the top edge of the Application Window it is most often referred to as a *tool bar*. For all practical purposes, a tool box and a tool bar are one and the same.

> **NOTE:** To override the docking feature, hold ⌨️ while dragging the tool box to the edge of the Application Window.

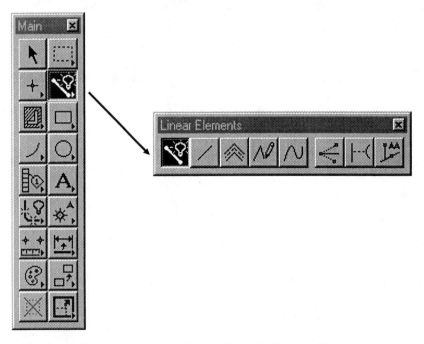

FIGURE 1-18 Linear Elements tool box taken out from the Main tool frame.

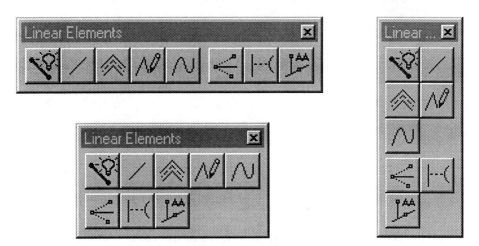

FIGURE 1-19 Linear Elements tool box resized to three different layouts.

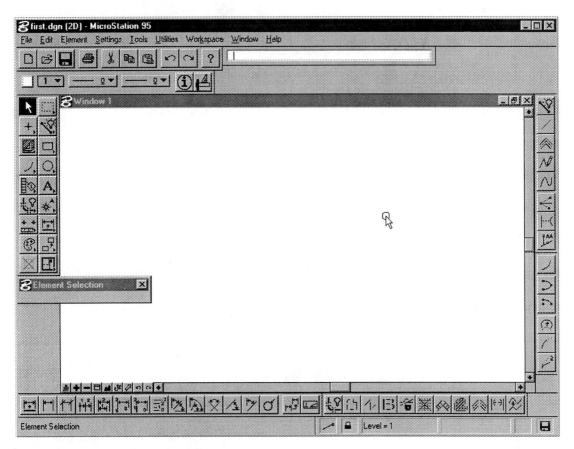

FIGURE 1-20 Docking of tool boxes.

FIGURE 1–21 Standard tool box.

Undocking a Tool Box To undock a tool box, grab part of the frame around the target tool box and drag it onto the main part of the MicroStation window. Once this is done, the tool box will return to its floating condition, or undragged.

Standard Tool Box (Also Called Standard Tool Bar) By default, the Standard tool box (see Figure 1–21) is docked just below the pull-down menu. The Standard tool box contains icons that enable quick access to many commonly used File and Edit pull-down menu items. Table 1–3 lists the tools available in the Standard tool box and the corresponding items in the pull-down menus.

Table 1–3. Tools Available in the Standard Tool Box

STANDARD TOOL BOX ITEM	PULL-DOWN MENU ITEM
New File	File > New...
Open File	File > Open...
Save Design	File > Save
Print	File > Print/Plot
Cut	Edit > Cut
Copy	Edit > Copy
Paste	Edit > Paste
Undo	Edit > Undo
Redo	Edit > Redo
Help	Help > Contents

Primary Tool Box (Also Called Primary Tool Bar) By default, the Primary tool box (see Figure 1–22) is docked along the side of the Standard tool box. The Primary tool box contains icons that provide access to the more frequently accessed element

FIGURE 1–22 Primary tool box.

symbology settings, along with two tools. Table 1–4 lists the tools available in the Primary tool box.

Table 1– 4.   Tools Available in the Primary Tool Box

PRIMARY TOOL BOX ITEM	FUNCTION
Active Color	Sets the active color
Active Level	Sets the active level
Active Line Style	Sets the active line style
Active Line Weight	Sets the active line weight
Analyze Item	Reviews information about an element
Start AccuDraw	Starts the AccuDraw tools

Tool Tips   When you move the pointer over any icon, MicroStation displays the tool tip, as shown in Figure 1–23. In addition, MicroStation displays a brief description of the function of the command in the Status bar. This is very helpful, especially when you are unfamiliar with which icon goes with which tool.

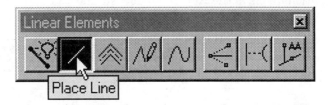

FIGURE 1–23   Invoking the Place Line command (with the display of the tool tip) from the Linear Elements tool box.

If necessary, you can disable the tool tips by turning off the option via the pull-down menu Help.

Tool Settings Window

Whenever you invoke a command, MicroStation displays the controls required for adjusting the settings in the Tool Settings window. For example, if the Place Arc tool is selected, the Method, Radius, Start Angle, and Sweep Angle options are displayed in the Tool Settings window, as shown in Figure 1–24. If the Tool Settings window is closed, it opens automatically when a tool with settings is selected.

FIGURE 1–24 Place Arcs tool box and Tool Settings window.

Key-in Window

Key-ins are typed instructions entered into the Key-in window to control Micro-Station. You can invoke any MicroStation command by typing the name of the command in full or in abbreviated form in the Key-in window. Open the Key-in window from:

Pull-down menu	Utilities > Key-in (or + **U**, **K**)

MicroStation displays the Key-in window similar to Figure 1–25.

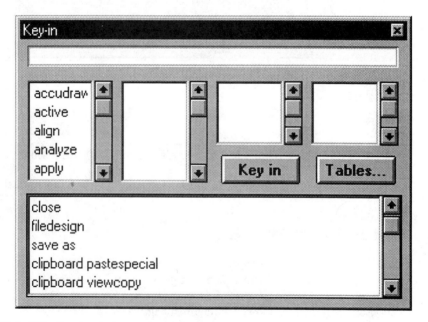

FIGURE 1–25 Key-in window.

As you type, the characters are matched to keywords in the list box below the Key-in window and are automatically selected in the list box. If it selects the right key-in command, press the **Spacebar** to complete the key-in, then click the Key-in button or press [ENTER] to enter the constructed key-in.

The list box in the Key-in window can also help you find and build key-ins. Scroll through the list of first words of key-ins in the left-most list box and select the keyword; it is then displayed in the key-in field. The subordinate, second-level keywords are shown in the key-in window's next list box. Select the desired keyword, and subsequently third-level keywords, if any, are shown. Select additional keywords, one per list box from left to right, until the desired key-in is constructed. To enter the constructed key-in, click the Key-in button or press [ENTER].

MicroStation stores submitted key-ins in a buffer so you can recall them and, if necessary, edit them. Press [↑] or [↓] on your keyboard repeatedly until the desired key-in text appears in the key-in field of the Key-in window. Make any necessary changes, if any. In addition, MicroStation lists the submitted key-ins in the list box at the bottom of the Key-in window, and you can select the desired key-in from that list box.

Status Bar

The Status bar, located at the bottom of the MicroStation Application Window, as shown in Figure 1–15, displays a variety of useful information, including prompts, messages, and the name of the selected tool.

The Status bar is divided into two sections, as shown in Figure 1–26.

Left-hand Section   The left-hand section of the Status bar shows the name of the selected command, followed by either a "greater than" symbol (>) or a colon (:) and message text. The message text that follows ">" is the selected command's prompts. For example, when you invoke the Place Line command, MicroStation prompts on the left side of the Status bar as follows:

Place Line > Enter first point

The command programs guide you step by step as you perform an operation with a command. The text that follows the colon is a message that indicates a possible problem.

FIGURE 1–26   *Status bar.*

In addition, as you move the pointer on the tools in a tool box, the name of the selected command and the associated message text are replaced with a description of the tool over which the pointer is located. This is intended as a form of online assistance.

Right-hand Section   The right-hand section of the Status bar consists of a series of fields. Following are the available fields, from left to right.

- The first field indicates the Snap Mode setting.
- The Locks icon in the second field allows you to open the Setting menu's Locks submenu. You can toggle the locks settings.
- The third field indicates the status of the current level.
- The fourth field indicates the count of the selected elements. If this field is blank, no elements are selected.
- The fifth field indicates whether there is a fence in the design. If this field is blank, no fence is placed.
- The last field indicates whether changes to the active design file are unsaved. If the field is blank, there are no unsaved changes. If the field has a red icon with an X through it, the active design file is open for "read-only" access.

When you enter a tentative point or request quantitative information, the fields in this section to the right of the Snap Mode field are temporarily replaced with a single message field. To restore the fields, press the Reset button or click anywhere in the Status bar.

View Windows

MicroStation displays the elements you draw in the view windows. The portion of the design that is displaying in the view window is referred to as a *view*. With this part of the screen, all of the various commands you enter will construct your design. As you progress, you can Zoom In and Zoom Out to control the design's display. You can also move the scroll bar located both on the right side and at the bottom to pan the design. A view typically shows a portion of the design, but may show it in its entirety, as in Figure 1–27.

Eight view windows can be open (ON) at the same time, and all view windows are active. This lets you begin an operation in one view and complete it in another. You can move a view window by pressing and holding the cursor on the Title bar and dragging it to anywhere on the screen. You can resize the display window by clicking and dragging on its surrounding border, and shrink and expand the window by clicking the push buttons located at the top right corner of the window. To close the view window, double-click the (–) symbol located at the top left corner of the view

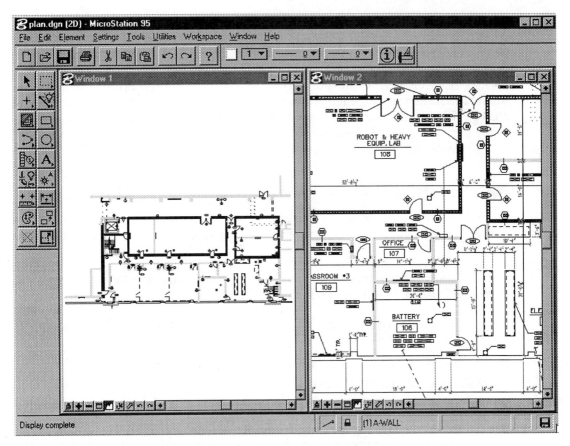

FIGURE 1–27   Two view windows displaying different portions of a design.

window in DOS. In the Windows operating system, you can close by clicking the X located at the top right corner of the view window.

MicroStation also provides a set of tools at the bottom left of the view window to control the view. View controls operate much like drawing tools; many even have "tool" settings. Detailed explanations of the View controls are provided in Chapters 2 through 5.

INPUT METHODS

Input method refers to the manner in which you tell MicroStation what command to use and how to operate the command. As mentioned earlier, the two most popular input devices are the mouse and the digitizing tablet, in addition to the keyboard.

Keyboard

To enter a command from the keyboard, simply key-in (type) the command name in the Key-in window and click the Key-in button or press ⌨ENTER. *Key-in* is the name given to the function of providing information via the keyboard to MicroStation. MicroStation key-in language is much like plain English. For example, keying-in **PLACE LINE** selects that line command; **DELETE ELEMENT** selects the delete command, and so on. See Appendix D for a list of the key-in commands available in MicroStation.

Pointing Devices

As mentioned earlier, MicroStation supports a two-button mouse, a three-button mouse, and a digitizer. Depending on your needs and hardware, select one of the three pointing devices.

Detailed explanations of the functions that are programmed to the pointing device buttons (mouse and digitizing tablet puck) follow.

Data Button (or Pick Button)   This is the most-used button on the mouse/puck. The Data button is used to:

Select a command from the pull-down menus and tool box.

Define location points in the design plane.

Identify elements that are to be manipulated.

In addition, it is used to accept tentative points, and generally tell the computer "yes" (accept) whenever it is prompted to do so. The Data button is also referred as the *Identify button* or the *Accept button*.

Reset Button   The Reset button enables you to stop the current operation and reset MicroStation to the beginning of the current command sequence. For instance, when you are in the Place Line command, a series of lines can be drawn by using the Data button. When you are ready to stop the sequence, press the Reset button. Micro-Station will stop the current operation and reset the Line sequence to the beginning. In addition, the Reset button also can reject a prompt, and generally tell the computer "no" (reject) whenever it is prompted to do so. The Reset button is also referred as the *Reject button*.

Tentative Button   The tentative point is one of MicroStation's most powerful features. The Tentative button enables you to place a tentative (temporary) point on the screen. Once you are happy with the location of the point, accept it with the Data button. In other words, the tentative point lets you try a couple of places before actually selecting the final resting point for the data point. The Tentative button also can snap to elements at specific locations—for instance, the center and four quadrants of a circle, when the Snap lock is turned to ON. For a detailed explanation, see Chapter 2.

Command Button The Command button is only available on the digitizer tablet puck and lets you choose commands from the tablet menu. To do so, look down the tablet menu, place the puck crosshairs in the box that represents the command you want to activate, then press the Command button. The corresponding command is invoked.

See Table 1–1 (page 1–4) and Table 1–2 (page 1–5) for the specific functions that are programmed for the two- and the three-button mouse and the four-button digitizer puck.

Cursor Menu

MicroStation has a cursor menu that can be made to appear at the location of the cursor by pressing the designated button on your pointing device. Two cursor menus are available, one for View Control commands and another for Snap Mode options.

To invoke the View Control Commands (Figure 1–28), press [SHIFT] + Reset button. The menu includes all the available commands for controlling the display of the design.

To invoke the Snap Mode options (Figure 1–29), press [SHIFT] + Tentative button. The menu includes all the available Snap Mode options. The reason the Snap Mode options are in such ready access will become evident when you learn the significance of these functions.

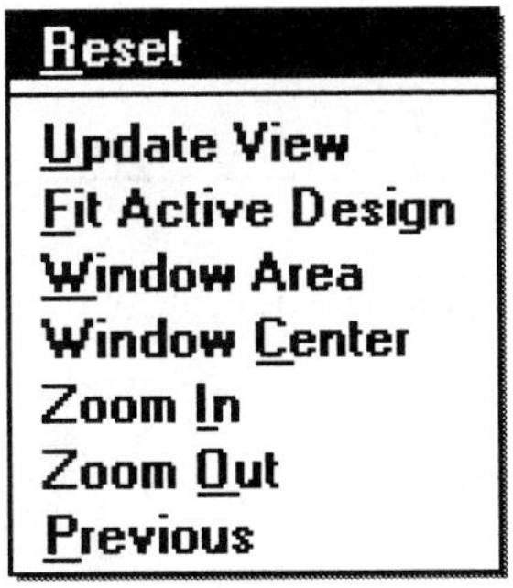

Reset

Update View
Fit Active Design
Window Area
Window Center
Zoom In
Zoom Out
Previous

Button Bar

Nearest
◆ Keypoint
Midpoint
Center
Origin
Bisector
Intersection
Tangent
Tangent From
Perpendicular
Perp From
Parallel
Through Point
Point On

FIGURE 1–28 Cursor menu ([SHIFT] + Reset button)—View Control commands.

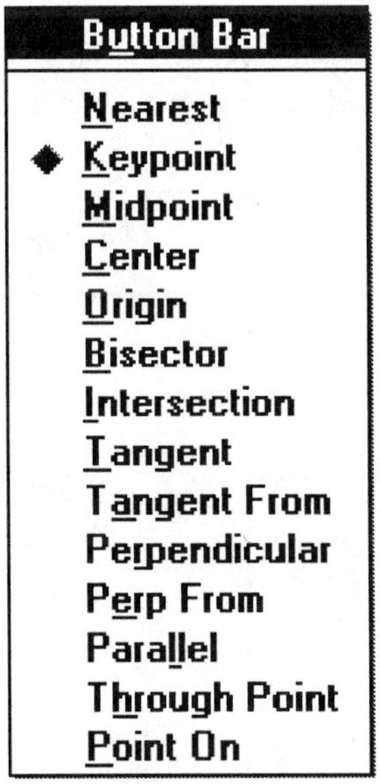

FIGURE 1–29 Cursor menu ([SHIFT] + Tentative button)—Snap Mode options.

THE DESIGN PLANE

In conventional drafting, the drawing is normally done to a certain scale, such as ¼″ = 1′-0″ or 1″ = 1′-0″. But in MicroStation, you draw full scale: All lines, circles, and other elements are drawn and measured as full size. For example, if a part is 150 feet long, it is drawn as 150 feet actual size. When you are ready to plot the part, MicroStation scales the design to fit a given sheet size. Alternatively, you can specify a scale factor to plot on a given sheet size.

Whenever you start a new two-dimensional design, you get a design plane—the electronic equivalent of a sheet of paper on a drafting table. The two-dimensional design plane is a large, flat plane covered with an invisible matrix grid consisting of 4,294,967,296 (2^{32}) by 4,294,967,296 (2^{32}) coordinate intersections along the X and Y axes. The distance between two adjacent points is one positional unit, or unit of resolution (UOR). The center of the design plane (2,147,483,648 by 2,147,483,648) is the global origin and is assigned coordinates (0,0), as shown in Figure 1–30. Any point to the right of the global origin has a positive X value; any point to the left has a negative X value. Any point above the global origin has a positive Y value; any point below has a negative Y value.

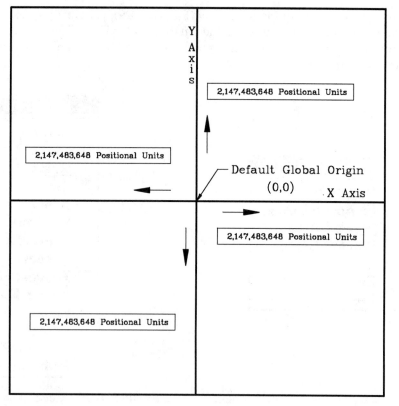

FIGURE 1–30   *X* and *Y* coordinates indicating the location of the global origin.

If necessary, you can change the location or coordinates of the global origin. For example, an architect might want all coordinates to be positive in value, he or she therefore sets the global origin at the bottom left corner of the design plane.

WORKING UNITS

As mentioned earlier, a design plane is divided into positional units (2^{32} by 2^{32}), but, at the same time, you can draw in "real world" units such as feet and inches, or meters and centimeters. These real-world units are called Working Units.

Working Units are comprised of Master or Major units (MU), Sub Units (SU), and working resolution or Positional Units (PU). The Master Unit is the largest unit being used in the design. The fractional parts of a Master Unit are called Sub Units. The number of Positional Units per Sub Unit is the working resolution. Working resolution determines both the precision with which elements are drawn and the working area of the design plane.

For example, you can draw a building floor plan specifying feet as Master Units, inches as Sub Units (12 parts make one Master Unit), and 1,600 Positional Units per Sub Unit. Adjacent data points can be entered as close as 1/1600 of an inch on a design plane stretching 223,696 feet ($4,294,967,296 \div 1600 \times 12$) in each dimension. Enough room for a whole city!

The working units can be assigned any value necessary to your work. You can define working area in terms of miles and quarters of a mile, meters and decimeters, inches and tenths of an inch, and so on. Working Units can be set to any real-world units. The number of Positional Units specified determines the value of the Sub Units.

When you wish to specify a distance, a radius, and so on, it is based on the Working Units. MicroStation has a standard syntax for doing this with the MU:SU:PU format. Each one of the three positions represents a value in relation to its respective unit. Whenever you key-in the value, make sure to use the colon (:) to separate Master Units, Sub Units, and Positional Units. Do *not* use the semicolon (;).

The following are the options available to key-in 3⅛ feet when the Working Units are set as feet for Master Units, inches for Sub Units, and 1,600 Positional Units per Sub Unit:

3.125	*In terms of feet, one need not specify SU and PU, since they are 0.*
3:1.50	*In terms of feet and inches.*
3:1:800	*In terms of feet, inches, Positional Units.*
0:37.50	*In terms of inches.*
3:⅛	*In terms of feet and inches in fractions.*

Whenever you start a new design, you need not set the Working Units if you used the appropriate seed file to create the new design file. To draw an architectural floor plan, you copy SDARCH2D.DGN (architectural seed file); then MicroStation sets the

Working Units to feet, inches, and 8,000 Positional Units. See Appendix G for a list of seed files and default Working Units available with MicroStation 95.

If necessary, you can make changes to the current Working Units. To do so, open the Design File Settings dialog box from:

Pull-down menu	Settings > Design File ... (or [ALT] + **S, D**)

MicroStation displays the Design File Settings box, similar to Figure 1–31.

Select Working Units in the Category list box. MicroStation displays the appropriate controls needed to Modify the Working Units Parameters (see Figure 1–31).

Enter the appropriate unit names in the Master Units edit box and Sub Units edit box located in the Units section of the dialog box. If necessary, change the number of Sub Units per Master Unit and the number of Positional Units per Sub Unit in the edit boxes provided in the Resolution section. Click the OK button to close the dialog box. MicroStation displays an Alert dialog box similar to the one shown in Figure 1–32. If you really want to make the changes, click the OK button to continue.

Make sure appropriate Working Units are set *before* you start drawing.

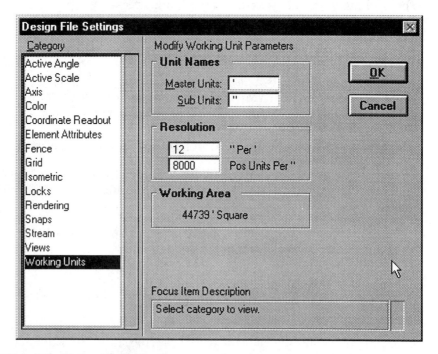

FIGURE 1–31 Design File Settings box.

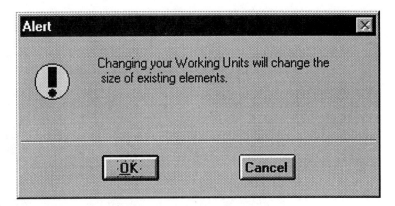

FIGURE 1–32   Alert dialog box.

> **NOTE:** Do not change the Working Units when you have already placed elements in the design. Changing the Working Units alters the size of existing elements.

SAVING CHANGES AND EXITING THE DESIGN FILE

Before we discuss how to place elements in the design file, let's discuss how to save the current design file. By default, MicroStation saves all elements in your design file as you draw them. There is no separate Save command. You can get out of your design file without doing the proper exit procedure and still not lose any work. Even if there is a power failure during a design session, you will get most of the design file back without significant damage.

If necessary, you can set the Immediately Save Design Changes toggle button to OFF. Then MicroStation provides a Save command in the pull-down menu File to save the design file. No other automatic save feature is provided. Whenever you want to save the design file, you have to invoke the Save command from the pull-down menu File.

To change the status of the toggle button for Immediately Save Design Changes, open the Preferences dialog box from:

| Pull-down menu | Workspace > Preferences... (or [ALT] + **K, P**) |

MicroStation displays the Preference dialog box similar to Figure 1–33.

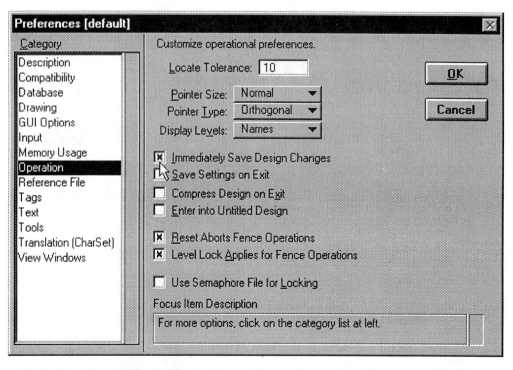

FIGURE 1–33 Preferences dialog box.

Select Operation option from the Category list box and set the toggle button to ON/OFF for Immediately Save Design Changes.

To save the current design file to a different file name, invoke the Save As command from:

| Pull-down menu | File > Save As... (or [ALT] + F, A) |

MicroStation displays the Save As dialog box. Select the directory where you want to save the design file, and key-in the name of the design file in the Files edit box. Click the OK button to save the file.

Saving the Design File Settings

To save the design file settings such as working units, grid spacing, view settings, etc. between sessions, you must explicitly save the settings. To do so, invoke the Save Settings command from:

Pull-down menu	File > Save Settings (or 🔲CTRL + **F** or 🔲ALT + **F, V**)
Key-in window	**Filedesign** (or **fi**) 🔲ENTER

MicroStation saves the current settings.

If you forget to save the settings, you will have to spend time adjusting the design and view settings to match what you had in place the last time you worked on the design.

To save automatically the settings on exiting the design file, set the toggle button for Save Settings on Exit to ON. By default it is set to OFF.

To change the status of the toggle button for Save Settings on Exit, open the Preferences dialog box from:

Pull-down menu	Workspace > Preferences... (or 🔲ALT + **K, P**)

MicroStation displays the Preferences dialog box. Select the Operation option from the Category list box, and set the toggle button to ON/OFF for Save Settings on Exit.

Exiting the MicroStation Program

To exit the MicroStation program and return to the operating system, invoke the Exit command from:

Pull-down menu	File > Exit (or 🔲ALT + **F, X**)
Key-in window	**Exit** (or **exi**) 🔲ENTER

MicroStation exits the program and returns to the operating system.

If, instead, you prefer to return to the MicroStation Manager dialog box, invoke the Close command from:

Pull-down menu	File > Close (or 🔲ALT + **F, C**)
Key-in window	**Close Design** (or **clo d**) 🔲ENTER

MicroStation returns to the MicroStation Manager dialog box.

GETTING HELP

When you are in a design file, MicroStation provides an online help facility available from the pull-down menu Help (see Figure 1–34). Online help is provided through the Help window, by specific topics, by searching for a text string within help topic names or help articles, or by browsing key-ins.

Contents

The Contents window lists the top-level topics, as shown in Figure 1–35. To see a list of more specific subtopics related to a topic in the list, select the topic. MicroStation displays a list of subtopics, and by selecting a subtopic, MicroStation displays the available help information on that topic. In addition, you can also search for a text string by clicking the Search button and MicroStation will display the Search settings box. Key-in the text string and click the Search button, and MicroStation will display the help available on the text string.

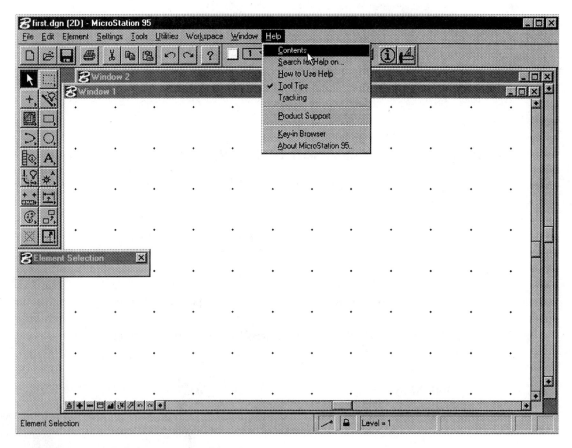

FIGURE 1–34 Pull-down menu Help.

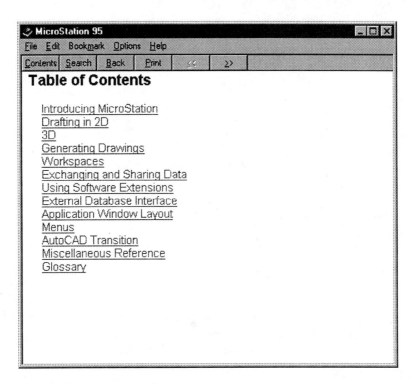

FIGURE 1–35   Help Contents window.

The MicroStation Help window also has a Topic option menu displaying the current topic's parent, its parent's topic, and so on, up to the Contents. Selecting any one of the topics moves you "up" to that level in the Help document. You can also display the Help file's previous article and next article by clicking the Previous (<<) and Next (>>) buttons.

Search for Help On...

Selecting this option opens the Search settings box, as shown in Figure 1–36, which is used to search for a text string in the open Help file. Type the first few letters of the word you are looking for in the edit field and press ENTER. MicroStation displays the Help information.

How to Use Help

This option opens the Help window that provides instructions for using online help.

Product Support

This option displays information about contacting MicroStation technical support.

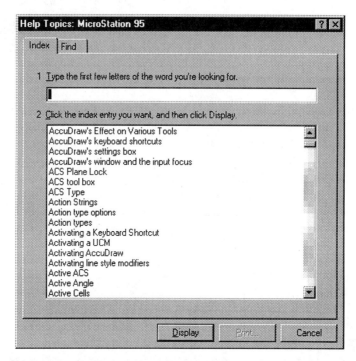

FIGURE 1–36   Search settings box.

Key-in Browser

This option opens the Key-in window, similar to the one shown in Figure 1–37. Refer to the section on the Key-in window, earlier in this chapter, for further details.

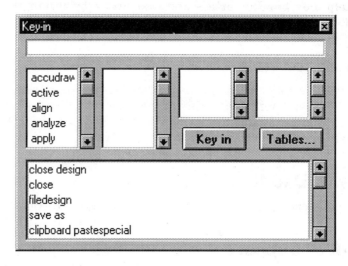

FIGURE 1–37   Key-in window.

ENHANCEMENTS IN MICROSTATION 95

Following are the enhancements that were added to MicroStation 95.

- True Microsoft Windows Application
- New look and feel in User Interface—Microsoft Office Compliant (includes resizable tool boxes)
- Tool Consolidation
- Four additional types of fences—circular fence, existing element into a fence, setting fence based on a view's current extents, fence to encompass the entire design file
- Modify Element, with a new set of options
- Change Text Attributes—selectively changing individual attributes
- Place Note—multiple lines of text
- Productivity enhancements in Reference Files
- Printing and plotting enhancements, including easy-to-create pen tables
- AccuDraw—the most versatile and powerful new tool
- SmartLine—composite drawing tool for placing linear elements
- Flags—annotation in a design file, with reminders or suggestions for future changes
- Cell Selector—new utility that allows access to cells from multiple cell libraries without attaching each library to your design file
- Archive Utility—utility that allows you to combine all of the resources needed to support the design file
- Animation Producer—new set of tools for producing keyframe animation sequences
- Enhancements in customizing MicroStation tools
- MicroStation BASIC—New programming tool

CHAPTER

2

FUNDAMENTALS I

OBJECTIVES

After completing this chapter, you will be able to:

- ✓ Draw lines, blocks, shapes, circles, and arcs.

- ✓ Drop blocks and shapes and delete elements.

- ✓ Precision Input

- ✓ View Control: zoom in, zoom out, window area, fit, pan, and update.

- ✓ Use drawing tools: grid, axis, units, and tentative snap.

- ✓ Set element symbology.

- ✓ Control and view levels.

- ✓ Match element attributes.

PLACEMENT COMMANDS

MicroStation provides various tools for drawing objects. The primary drawing element is the line, and the Place Line tool enables you to draw series of lines. In addition, MicroStation provides tools for drawing objects such as blocks, shapes, circles, arcs, polygons, ellipses, multi-lines, and curves. This section explains in detail the various tools for drawing lines, blocks, shapes, circles, and arcs.

Place Line

Invoke the Place Line command from:

Linear Elements tool box	Select the Place Line tool (see Figure 2–1).
Key-in window	**Place line** (or **pl li**) [ENTER]

MicroStation prompts:

> Place Line > Enter first point

Specify the first point by providing a data point via your pointing device (mouse or puck) or by precision input (more on this later). After you specify the first point, MicroStation prompts:

> Place Line > Enter end point *(Place a data point or key-in coordinates to define the end point of the line.)*

Specify the end of the line by placing a data point via your pointing device (mouse or puck) or by precision input. MicroStation repeats the prompt:

> Place Line > Enter end point

Place a data point via pointing device or by precision input to continue. To save time, the Place Line tool remains active and prompts for a new end point after each point you specify. When you have finished placing a series of lines, press the Reset button or invoke another tool to terminate the Place Line command.

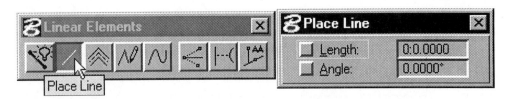

FIGURE 2–1   Invoking the Place Line command from the Linear Elements tool box.

When placing data points with your pointing device to draw a series of lines, a rubber band line is displayed between the starting point and the crosshairs. This helps you to see where the resulting line will go. In Figure 2–2 the dotted lines represent previous cursor positions. To specify the end point of the line, click the Data button. You can continue to place lines with the Place Line command until you press the Reset button or select another tool.

Place Line to a Specified Length To place a line to a specified length, select the Place Line tool in the Linear Elements tool bar and turn ON the toggle button for Length in the Tool Settings window. Key-in the distance in MU:SU:PU in the Length edit field. The prompts are similar to those for the Place Line command, and you can place any number of line segments of specified length.

Place Line at an Angle To place a line to a specified angle, select the Place Line tool in the Linear Elements tool bar and turn ON the toggle button for Angle in the Tool Settings window. Key-in the angle in the Angle edit field. The prompts are similar to those for the Place Line command, and you can place any number of line segments of specified angle.

If necessary, you can turn both of the toggle buttons ON for the Length and Angle; MicroStation allows you to place a line with a specific length and angle constrained.

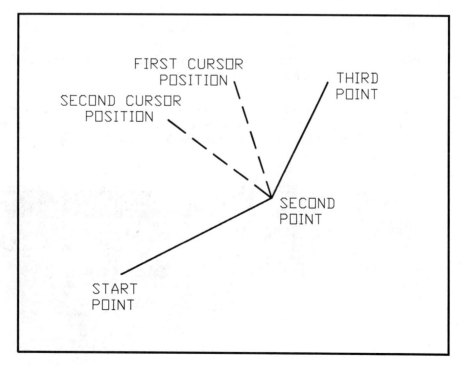

FIGURE 2–2 Placing data points with the cursor rather than with coordinates.

Place Block

MicroStation allows you to draw a rectangular block by two different methods: orthogonal and rotated.

Orthogonal Method The Place Block tool (orthogonal) allows you to place a rectangular block by selecting two points that define the diagonal corners of the shape. Place the two diagonal corners by specifying data points via your pointing device or by keying-in 2D coordinates (see later discussion on "Precision Input").

Invoke the Place Block (orthogonal) command from:

Polygons tool box	Select the Place Block tool and Orthogonal from the Method option menu located in the Tool Settings window (see Figure 2–3).
Key-in window	**Place Block Orthogonal (or pl bl or)** (ENTER)

MicroStation prompts:

> Place Block > Enter first point *(Place a data point or key-in coordinates to define the start point of the block.)*
> Place Block > Enter opposite corner *(Place a data point or key-in coordinates to define the opposite corner of the block.)*

A block is a single element, and element manipulation commands such as Move, Copy, and Delete manipulate a block as one element. If necessary, you can make a block into individual line elements with the Drop Line String tool.

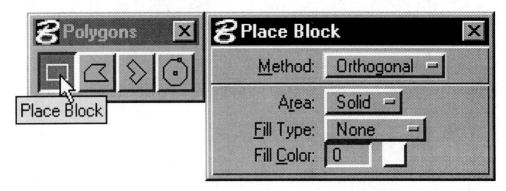

FIGURE 2–3 Invoking the Place Block (orthogonal) command from the Polygons tool box.

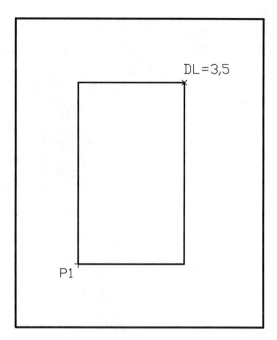

FIGURE 2-4   Placing a 3 × 5 block using the Place Block command.

For example, the following command sequence shows placement of a block that is 3 Master Units by 5 Master Units, as shown in Figure 2–4 using the Place Block (orthogonal) tool.

> Place Block > Enter first point *(Place a data point as shown in Figure 2–4.)*
> Place Block > Enter opposite corner **DL=3,5** [ENTER]

Rotated Method   The Place Block (rotated) tool allows you to place a rectangular block at any angle that is defined by the first two data points. The first data point defines the first corner of the block and the point the block rotates around. The second data point defines the angle of the block, and the third data point entered diagonally from the first defines the opposite corner of the block.

Invoke the Place Block (rotated) command from:

Polygons tool box	Select the Place Block tool and Rotated from the Method option menu located in the Tool Settings window (see Figure 2–5).
Key-in window	**Place Block Rotated** (or **pl bl ro**) [ENTER]

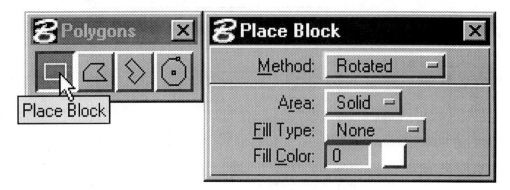

FIGURE 2–5 Invoking the Place Block (rotated) command from the Polygons tool box.

MicroStation prompts:

> Place Rotated Block > Enter first base point *(Place a data point or key-in coordinates to define the start point of the block.)*
> Place Rotated Block > Enter second base point *(Place a data point or key-in coordinates to define the angle of the block.)*
> Place Rotated Block > Enter diagonal point *(Place a data point or key-in coordinates to define the opposite corner of the block.)*

See Figure 2–6 for an example of placing a rotated block via the Place Block Rotated command by providing three data points.

Similar to an orthogonal block, a rotated block is also a single element.

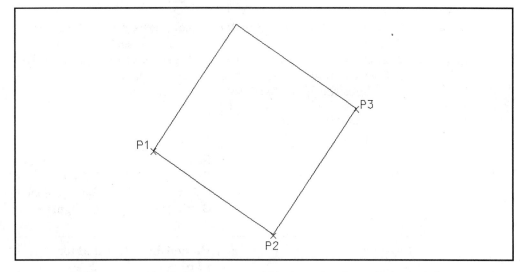

FIGURE 2–6 An example of placing a rotated block via the Place Block Rotated command.

Place Shape

The Place Shape command allows you to place a multisided shape defined by a series of data points (3 to 100) that indicates the vertices of the polygon. To complete the polygon shape, the last data point should be placed on top of the starting point. You can specify the starting point and subsequent points via absolute or relative coordinates (see "Precision Input," later) or by using your pointing device.

Invoke the Place Shape command from:

Polygons tool box	Select the Place Shape tool (see Figure 2–7).
Key-in window	**Place Shape** (or **pl sh**) [ENTER]

MicroStation prompts:

> Place Shape > Enter first point *(Place a data point or key-in coordinates to define the starting point of the shape.)*
> Place Shape > Enter vertex or Reset to cancel *(Place a data point or key-in coordinates to define the vertex, or press Reset button to cancel.)*

Continue placing data points. To complete the polygon shape, place the last data point on top of the starting point or click the Close Element button located in the Tool Settings window.

You can also draw a shape by constraining to Length and/or Angle by turning on the toggle button for Length: and for Angle:, appropriately located in the Tool Settings window.

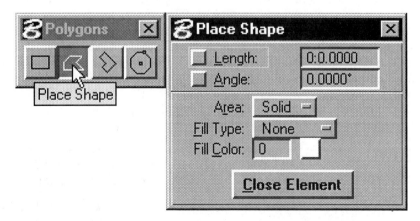

FIGURE 2–7   Invoking the Place Shape command from the Polygons tool box.

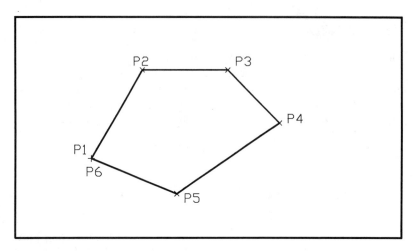

FIGURE 2-8   An example of placing a closed shape via the Place Shape command.

See Figure 2–8 for an example of placing a closed shape via the Place Shape command by providing six data points.

Similar to a block, a shape is also a single element. Element manipulation commands such as Move, Copy, and Delete manipulate the shape as one element. If necessary, you can make the shape into individual line elements with the Drop Line String tool.

> **NOTE:** Area and Fill type options are explained in Chapter 11 on Patterning.

Place Orthogonal Shape

The Place Orthogonal Shape tool allows you to create a multisided shape that has adjacent sides at right angles. As with Place Block Rotated, the first two points define the vertices of the orthogonal shape. The additional points define the corners of the shape. To complete the polygon shape, the last data point should be placed on top of the starting point. You can specify the starting point and subsequent points with absolute or relative coordinates (see "Precision Input," later) or by using your pointing device.

Invoke the Place Orthogonal Shape command from:

Polygons tool bar	Select the Place Orthogonal Shape tool (see Figure 2–9).
Key-in window	**Place Orthogonal Shape** (or **pl or sh**) ⏎

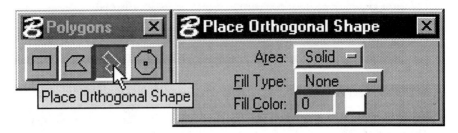

FIGURE 2-9 Invoking the Place Orthogonal Shape command from the Polygons tool box.

MicroStation prompts:

> Place Orthogonal Shape > Enter shape vertex *(Place a data point or key-in coordinates to define the start point of the shape.)*
> Place Orthogonal Shape > Enter shape vertex *(Place a data point or key-in coordinates to define the vertex.)*

MicroStation prompts for additional shape vertices. Continue placing data points. To complete the polygon shape, the last data point should be placed on top of the starting point.

Similar to a block, an orthogonal shape is also a single element. Element manipulation commands such as Move, Copy, and Delete manipulate the orthogonal shape as one element. If necessary, you can make the shape into individual line elements with the Drop Line String command.

See Figure 2–10 for an example of placing an orthogonal shape with the Place Orthogonal Shape command by providing nine data points.

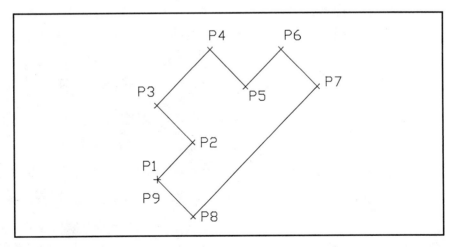

FIGURE 2–10 An example of placing an orthogonal shape with the Place Orthogonal Shape command.

> **NOTE:** Area and Fill type options are explained in Chapter 11 on Patterning.

Place Circle

MicroStation offers several methods for drawing circles. These include Place Circle By Center, Place Circle By Edge, and Place Circle By Diameter. The appropriate method is selected from the Method option menu located in the Tool Settings window.

Place Circle By Center With the Place Circle By Center tool, you can draw a circle by defining two points: the center point and a point on the circle.

Invoke the Place Circle By Center command from:

Ellipses tool box	Select the Place Circle tool and Center from the Method option menu located in the Tool Settings window (see Figure 2–11).
Key-in window	**Place Circle Center** (or **pl ci ce**) [ENTER]

MicroStation prompts:

Place Circle By Center > Identify Center Point *(Place a data point or key-in coordinates to define the center of the circle.)*
Place Circle By Center > Identify Point on Circle *(Place a data point or key-in coordinates to define the edge of the circle.)*

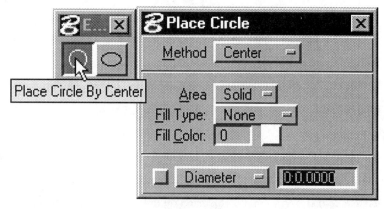

FIGURE 2–11   Invoking the Place Circle By Center command from the Ellipses tool box.

> **NOTE:** After you place the first data point, a dynamic image of the circle drags with the screen pointer.

To save time, the Place Circle By Center command remains active and prompts for a new center point. When you are finished placing circles, invoke another tool to terminate the Place Circle By Center command.

For example, the following command sequence shows placement of a circle with the Place Circle By Center tool (see Figure 2–12).

Place Circle By Center > Identify Center Point **XY=2,2** ENTER
Place Circle By Center > Identify Point on Circle **DL=1,0** ENTER

In the last example, MicroStation used the distance between the center point and the point given on the circle for the radius of the circle.

You can also place a circle by center by keying-in its diameter or radius. Select Diameter or Radius from the options menu located in the Tool Settings window, turn on the toggle button, key-in the value in MU:SU:PU format, then press ENTER or TAB. When the desired diameter/radius is entered using the MU:SU:PU format, a circle of that diameter/radius appears on the screen cursor. You will then be asked to identify the center point of the circle. Position your cursor where you want the center of the circle to be, and place a data point. Continue placing circles having the same diameter/radius, or press the Reset button to allow you to change the diameter/radius of the circle. If you do not wish to continue placing circles, invoke another tool to terminate the Place Circle By Center command.

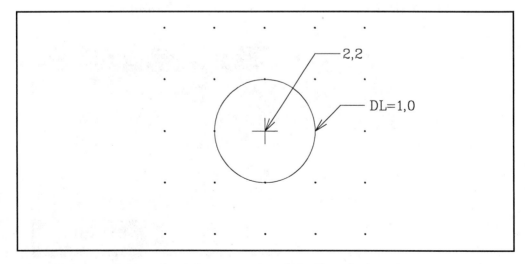

FIGURE 2–12   An example of placing a circle with the Place Circle By Center command.

Place Circle By Edge The Place Circle By Edge tool enables you to draw a circle by defining three data points on the circle.

Invoke the Place Circle By Edge command from:

Ellipses tool box	Select the Place Circle tool and Edge from the Method option menu located in the Tool Settings window (see Figure 2–13).
Key-in window	**Place Circle Edge** (or **pl ci ed**) ⏎

MicroStation prompts:

Place Circle By Edge > Identify Point on Circle *(Place a data point or key-in coordinates to define the first edge point of the circle.)*
Place Circle By Edge > Identify Point on Circle *(Place a data point or key-in coordinates to define the second edge point of the circle.)*
Place Circle By Edge > Identify Point on Circle *(Place a data point or key-in coordinates to define the third edge point of the circle.)*

For example, the following command sequence shows placement of a circle via the Place Circle By Edge tool (see Figure 2–14).

Place Circle By Edge > Identify Point on Circle **XY=2,3** ⏎
Place Circle By Edge > Identify Point on Circle **XY=3,2** ⏎
Place Circle By Edge > Identify Point on Circle **XY=2,1** ⏎

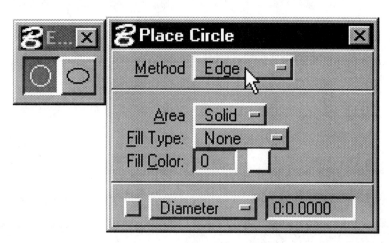

FIGURE 2–13   Invoking the Place Circle By Edge command from the Ellipses tool box.

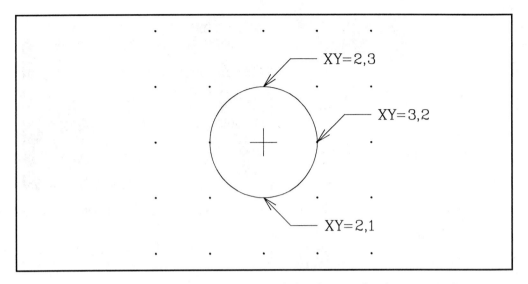

FIGURE 2-14   An example of placing a circle with the Place Circle Edge command.

You can also place a circle by edge by keying-in its diameter or radius. Select Diameter or Radius from the options menu located in the Tool Settings window, turn on the toggle button, key-in the value in MU:SU:PU format, then press [ENTER] or [TAB]. When the desired diameter/radius is entered in the MU:SU:PU format, MicroStation prompts for two data points, instead of three, to place a circle by edge.

Place Circle By Diameter   With the Place Circle By Diameter tool, you can draw a circle by defining two data points: two end points of the diameter.

Invoke the Place Circle By Diameter command from:

Ellipses tool box	Select the Place Circle tool and Diameter from the Method option menu located in the Tool Settings window (see Figure 2–15).
Key-in window	**Place Circle Diameter** (or **pl ci di**) [ENTER]

MicroStation prompts:

Place Circle By Diameter > Enter First Point on Diameter *(Place a data point or key-in coordinates to define the first end point of one of its diameters.)*
Place Circle By Diameter > Enter Second Point on Diameter *(Place a data point or key-in coordinates to define the second end point of one of its diameters.)*

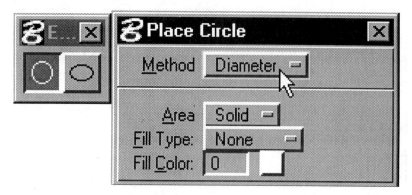

FIGURE 2–15 Invoking the Place Circle By Diameter command from the Ellipses tool box.

For example, the following command sequence shows placement of a circle via the Place Circle By Diameter tool (see Figure 2–16).

Place Circle By Diameter > Enter First Point on Diameter **XY=1,2** [ENTER]
Place Circle By Diameter > Enter Second Point on Diameter **XY=3,2** [ENTER]

Place Arc

Similar to placing circles, MicroStation offers two different methods for placing arcs: Place Arc By Center and Place Arc By Edge. The appropriate method is selected from the Method option menu located in the Tool Settings window.

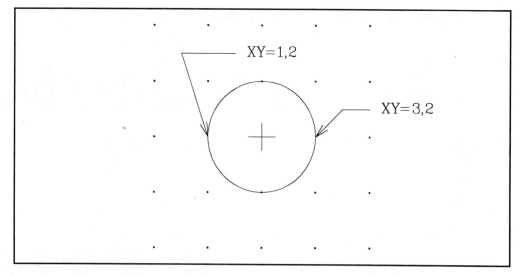

FIGURE 2–16 An example of placing a circle via the Place Circle By Diameter command.

Place Arc By Center The Place Arc By Center tool enables you to draw an arc defined by three points: the center point, the first arc end point, and the second arc end point.

Invoke the Place Arc By Center command from:

Arcs tool box	Select the Place Arc tool and Center from the Method option menu located in the Tool Settings window (see Figure 2–17).
Key-in window	**Place Arc Center** (or **pl ar ce**) [ENTER]

FIGURE 2–17   Invoking the Place Arc By Center command from the Arcs tool box.

MicroStation prompts:

> Place Arc By Center > Identify First Arc Endpoint *(Place a data point or key-in coordinates to define the first arc end point.)*
> Place Arc By Center > Identify Arc Center *(Place a data point or key-in coordinates to define the arc center.)*
> Place Arc By Center > Identify Second Arc Endpoint *(Place a data point or key-in coordinates to define the second arc end point.)*

> **NOTE:** After you place the first data point, a dynamic image of the arc drags with the screen pointer.

For example, the following command sequence shows placement of an arc with the Place Arc By Center tool (see Figure 2–18).

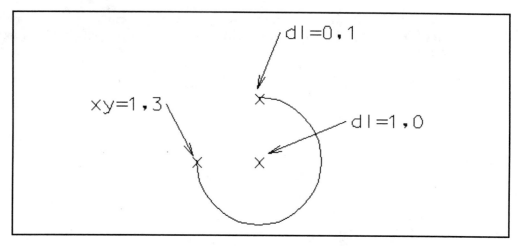

FIGURE 2-18   An example of placing an arc via the Place Arc By Center command.

Place Arc By Center > Identify First Arc Endpoint **XY=1,3** [ENTER]
Place Arc By Center > Identify Arc Center **DL=1,0** [ENTER]
Place Arc By Center > Identify Second Arc Endpoint **DL=0,1** [ENTER]

You can also draw an arc by center by keying-in its radius. To do so, turn on the toggle button for Radius located in the Tool Settings window, key-in the appropriate value in MU:SU:PU format in the Radius edit field, and press [ENTER] or [TAB]. The prompts are similar to those for the Place Arc By Center command, except the First Arc Endpoint and Second Arc Endpoint define the starting and ending directions of the arc.

Similarly, you can also constrain the Start Angle and Sweep Angle by keying-in appropriate angles in the respective edit fields. The MicroStation prompts depend on the number of constraints turned ON. For example, if Radius and Start Angle are preset, MicroStation prompts for the center point of the arc and the sweep angle; if Radius, Start Angle, and Sweep Angle are preset, MicroStation prompts only for the center of the arc.

Place Arc By Edge   The Place Arc By Edge tool allows you to draw an arc defined by three points on the arc.

Invoke the Place Arc By Edge command from:

Arcs tool box	Select the Place Arc tool and Edge from the Method option menu located in the Tool Settings window (see Figure 2–19).
Key-in window	**Place Arc Edge** (or **pl ar ed**) [ENTER]

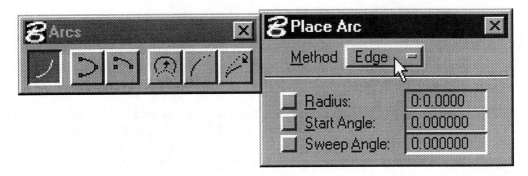

FIGURE 2–19   Invoking the Place Arc By Edge command from the Arcs tool box.

MicroStation prompts:

> Place Arc By Edge > Identify First Arc Endpoint *(Place a data point or key-in coordinates to define the first arc end point.)*
> Place Arc By Edge > Identify Point on Arc Radius *(Place a data point or key-in coordinates to define another point on the arc radius.)*
> Place Arc By Edge > Identify Second Arc Endpoint *(Place a data point or key-in coordinates to define the second arc end point.)*

For example, the following command sequence shows placement of an arc with the Place Arc By Center tool (see Figure 2–20).

> Place Arc By Center > Identify First Arc Endpoint **XY=1,2** [ENTER]
> Place Arc By Center > Identify Arc Center **XY=2,1** [ENTER]
> Place Arc By Center > Identify Second Arc Endpoint **XY=3,2** [ENTER]

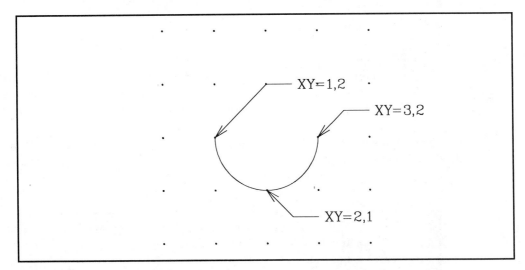

FIGURE 2–20   An example of placing an arc via the Place Arc By Edge command.

You can also draw an arc by edge by keying-in the radius. To do so, turn on the toggle button for Radius located in the Tool Settings window, key-in the appropriate value in MU:SU:PU format in the Radius edit field, and press ⏎ or ⭾. The prompts are similar to those for the Place Arc By Edge command, except the First Arc Endpoint and Second Arc Endpoint define the starting and ending directions of the arc.

Similarly, you can also constrain the Start Angle and Sweep Angle by keying in appropriate angles in the respective edit fields. The MicroStation prompts depend on the number of constraints turned ON. For example, if Radius and Start Angle are preset, MicroStation prompts for the First Arc Endpoint and Second Arc Endpoint. If Radius, Start Angle, and Sweep Angle are preset, MicroStation prompts only for the First Arc Endpoint.

DELETE ELEMENT

MicroStation not only allows you to draw easily, it also allows you to manipulate the elements you have drawn. Of the many manipulation commands available, the Delete Element command is probably the one you will use most often. Everyone makes mistakes, but MicroStation makes it easy to delete them.

Invoke the Delete Element command from:

Main tool box	Select the Delete Element tool (see Figure 2–21).
Key-in window	**Delete** (or **del**) ⏎

MicroStation prompts:

Delete Element > Identify element *(Identify the element to delete.)*
Delete Element > Accept/Reject (select next input) *(Click the Accept button to delete the selected element, select another element to delete, or click the Reject button to terminate the command sequence.)*

If you change your mind about deleting an element, press the Reject button. If you need to delete additional elements, identify one after another and accept them. The only way to get out of the Delete Element command is to invoke another command.

> **NOTE:** The Delete Element command deletes only one element at a time. If you need to delete a group of elements, use the Fence Delete command, explained in Chapter 5.

Delete Element

FIGURE 2–21   Invoking the Delete Element command from the Main tool frame.

DROP LINE STRING/SHAPE STATUS

The Drop Line String/Shape Status command causes blocks and shapes to separate into a series of connected individual line elements that can be manipulated as individual elements. Once a block or shape is dropped, it behaves as it is had been drawn with a Place Line command.

Invoke the Drop Line String/Shape Status command from:

Drop tool box	Select the Drop Line String/Shape Status tool (see Figure 2–22).
Key-in window	**Drop String** (or **dr str**) ⏎

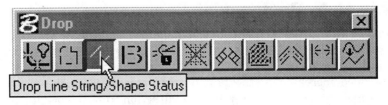

FIGURE 2–22   Invoking the Drop Line String/Shape Status command from the Drop tool box.

MicroStation prompts:

> Drop Line String/Shape Status > Identify element *(Identify the block or shape to be dropped.)*
>
> Drop Line String/Shape Status > Accept/Reject (select next input) *(Click the Accept button to accept, select another element to drop, or the Reject button to reject.)*

You can also identify another block or shape to drop with the second data point.

PRECISION INPUT

MicroStation allows you to draw an object at its true size and then make the border, title block, and other non-object-associated features fit the object. The completed combination is reduced (or increased) to fit the plotted sheet size you require when you plot.

Drawing a not-to-scale schematic does not take advantage of MicroStation's full graphics and computing potential. But even though the symbols and distances between them have no relationship to any real-life dimensions, the sheet size, text size, line widths, and other visible characteristics of the drawing must be considered to give your schematic the readability you desire. Some planning, including sizing, needs to be applied to all drawings.

When MicroStation prompts for the location of a point, instead of providing the data point with your pointing device, you can use three precision input commands that enable you to place data points precisely. Each of the commands allows you to key-in by coordinates, which include absolute rectangular coordinates, relative rectangular coordinates, and relative polar coordinates.

The rectangular coordinates system is based on specifying a point's location by giving its distances from two intersecting perpendicular axes for two-dimensional (2D) points or from three intersecting perpendicular planes for three-dimensional (3D) points. Each data point is measured along the X axis (horizontal) and Y axis (vertical) for two-dimensional design and along the X axis, Y axis, and Z axis (toward or away from the viewer) for three-dimensional design. The intersection of the axes, called the *origin* (XY=0,0), divides the coordinates into four quadrants for two-dimensional design, as shown in Figure 2–23.

Absolute Rectangular Coordinates

Points are located by Absolute Rectangular Coordinates at an exact X,Y intersection on the design plane in relation to the Global Origin. By default, the Global Origin is located at the center of the design plane, as shown in Figure 2–24. The horizontal distance increases in the positive X direction from the origin, and the vertical distance increases in the positive Y direction from the origin. To enter an absolute coordinate, key-in:

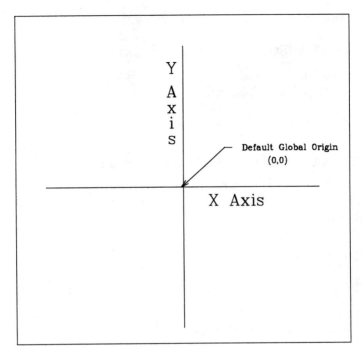

FIGURE 2-23 Two-dimensional coordinate system.

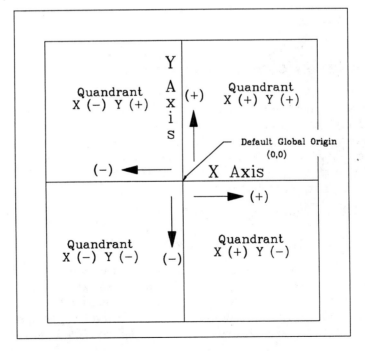

FIGURE 2-24 Showing Global Origin in a two-dimensional design.

XY=<X coordinate>,<Y coordinate> [ENTER]

or

POINT ABSOLUTE <X coordinate>,<Y coordinate> [ENTER]

The <X coordinate> and <Y coordinate> are the coordinates in MU:SU:PU in relation to the Global Origin. For example:

XY=2,4

Relative Rectangular Coordinates

Points are located by Relative Rectangular Coordinates in relation to the last specified position or point in MU:SU:PU, rather than in relation to the origin. This is similar to specifying a point as an offset from the last point you entered. To enter a Relative Rectangular Coordinate, key-in:

DL=<X coordinate>,<Y coordinate> [ENTER]

or

POINT DELTA <X coordinate>,<Y coordinate> [ENTER]

The <X coordinate> and <Y coordinate> are the coordinates in relation to the last specified position or point. For example, if the last point specified was XY=4,4, the key-in

DL=5,4

is equivalent to specifying the Absolute Rectangular Coordinates XY=9,8 (see Figure 2–25).

Relative Polar Coordinates

Relative Polar Coordinates are based on a distance from a fixed point at a given angle. In MicroStation, a Relative Polar Coordinate is determined by the distance and angle measured from the previous data point. By default, the angle is measured in a counterclockwise direction relative to the positive X axis. It is important to remember that points located by Relative Polar Coordinates are always positioned relative to the previous point, not to the Global Origin (0,0). To enter a Relative Rectangular Coordinate, key-in:

DI=<distance>,<angle> [ENTER]

or

POINT DISTANCE <distance>,<angle> [ENTER]

The <distance> and <angle> are specified in relation to the last specified position or point. The distance is specified in current working units (MU:SU:PU), and the direction is specified as an angle in degrees relative to the X axis. For example, to specify a point at a distance of 6.4 Master Units from the previous point and at an angle of 39 degrees relative to the positive X axis (see Figure 2–26), key-in:

DI=6.4,39

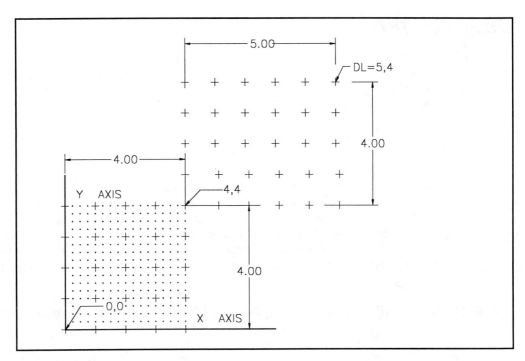

FIGURE 2–25   An example of placing a line by Relative Rectangular Coordinates.

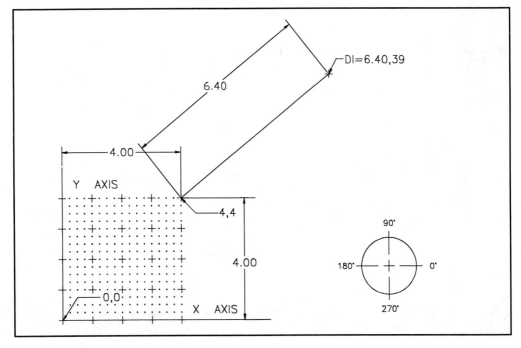

FIGURE 2–26   An example of placing a line by Relative Polar Coordinates.

VIEW CONTROL

There are many ways to view a drawing in MicroStation. With the View Control commands you can select the portion of the drawing to be displayed. By letting you see your drawing in different ways, MicroStation gives you the means to draw more quickly, easily, and accurately.

The commands explained in this section are utility commands; they make your job easier and help you to draw more accurately.

The View Control commands can be selected from the View Control Bar located on the lower left corner of the view window border, as shown in Figure 2–27, from the 2D View Control tool box (invoked from the pull-down menu Tools), as shown in Figure 2–28, or from the pop-up menu, as shown in Figure 2–29, that appears when you hold the 〔SHIFT〕 key and the Reset button at the same time. Selecting a View Control tool from the View Control Bar designates the view whose border contains the bar as

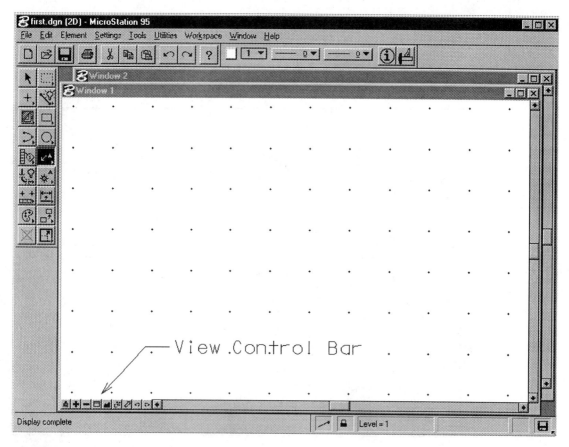

FIGURE 2–27 View Control Bar (lower left corner of the view window).

FIGURE 2–28   2D View Control tool bar.

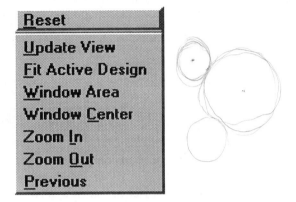

FIGURE 2–29   Pop-up menu.

the view on which to operate. If, instead, you select a View Control tool from the pop-up menu or from the 2D View Control tool box, then MicroStation prompts you to select a view window on which to operate.

Controlling the Amount of Display

The amount of information that can be displayed in a view can be controlled in a way similar to using a zoom lens on a camera. You can increase or decrease the viewing area, although the actual size of the object remains constant. As you increase the visible size of the object, you view a smaller area of the drawing in greater detail. As you decrease the visible size of the object, you view a larger area. This ability gives greater accuracy and detail.

MicroStation provides three commands that control the amount of information that can be displayed on the screen view: Zoom In, Zoom Out, and Window Area.

Zoom In   The Zoom In command increases the visible size of objects, allowing you to view a smaller area of the drawing in greater detail. The Zoom Ratio sets the factor by which the view is magnified, with the default value being set to 2. If necessary, you can change the Zoom Ratio between 1 and 50 by keying-in the appropriate value in the Tool Settings window.

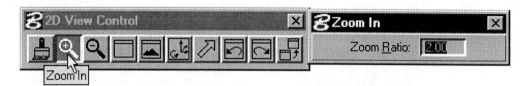

FIGURE 2–30 Invoking the Zoom In command from the 2D View Control tool bar.

Invoke the Zoom In command from:

2D View Control tool box	Select the Zoom In tool (see Figure 2–30).
Key-in window	**Zoom In Extended** (or **zo in ex**) [ENTER]

MicroStation prompts:

> Zoom In > Enter zoom center point

When you move the pointer in the view, a rectangular box is displayed that indicates the new view boundary. Place a data point to define the center of the area of the view window to be displayed (see Figures 2–31a and b). You may continue defining data points to magnify further, or you may invoke a new command.

Zoom Out The Zoom Out command decreases the visible size of objects, allowing you to view a larger area of the drawing. The Zoom Ratio sets the factor by which the view magnification is decreased, and the default value is set to 2. If necessary, you can change the Zoom Ratio between 1 and 50 by keying-in the appropriate value in the Tool Settings window.

Invoke the Zoom Out command from:

2D View Control tool bar	Select the Zoom Out tool (see Figure 2–32).
Key-in window	**Zoom Out Extended** (or **zo ou ex**) [ENTER]

MicroStation prompts:

> Zoom Out > Enter zoom center point

Place a data point to define the center of the area of the view window with the decreased magnification (see Figures 2–33a and b). You may continue defining data points to decrease magnification further, or you may invoke a new command.

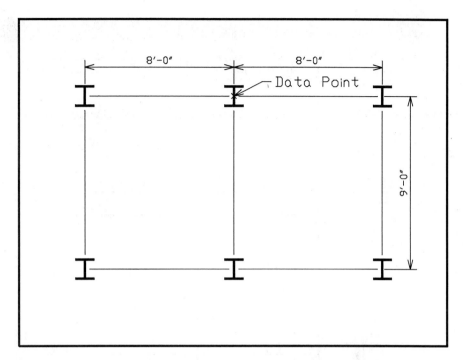

FIGURE 2–31a   The Design shown before the Zoom In command is invoked.

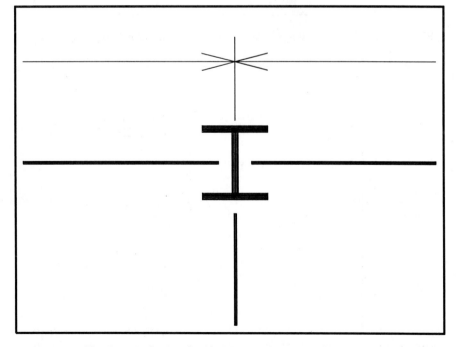

FIGURE 2–31b   The Design shown after the Zoom In command is invoked.

FIGURE 2–32   Invoking the Zoom Out command from the 2D View Control tool bar.

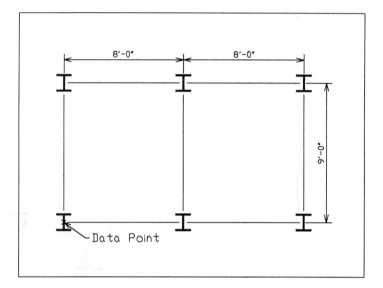

FIGURE 2–33a   The Design shown before the Zoom Out command is invoked.

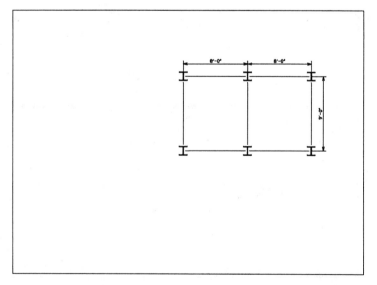

FIGURE 2–33b   The Design shown after the Zoom Out command is invoked.

FIGURE 2-34   Invoking the Window Area command from the 2D View Control tool bar.

Window Area The Window Area command allows you to specify an area of the design you wish to magnify by placing two opposite corner points of a rectangular window. The center of the area selected becomes the new display center, and the area inside the window is enlarged to fill the display as completely as possible. If necessary, you can change the destination window in the Tool Settings window.

Invoke the Window Area command from:

2D View Control tool bar	Select the Window Area tool (see Figure 2–34).
Key-in window	**Window Area Extended** (or **wi ar ex**) [ENTER]

MicroStation prompts:

> Window Area > Define first corner point *(A full screen crosshair appears. Place a data point or key-in coordinates to define the first corner point.)*
> Window Area > Define opposite corner point *(Place a data point or key-in coordinates to define the opposite corner point.)*

MicroStation updates the contents of the window in the destination window view (see Figures 2-35a and b). You may continue using the Window Area command by defining another area and displaying in the view, or you may select a new command.

Fit View

The Fit View command lets you see the entire design. In a plan view, it zooms to show the entire design drawn on the design plane.

Invoke the Fit View command from:

2D View Control tool bar	Select the Fit View tool (see Figure 2–36).
Key-in window	**Fit View Extended** (or **fit vi ex**) [ENTER]

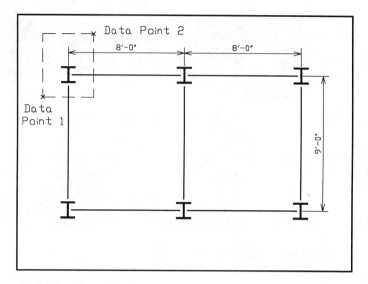

FIGURE 2–35a Design shown before the Window Area command is invoked.

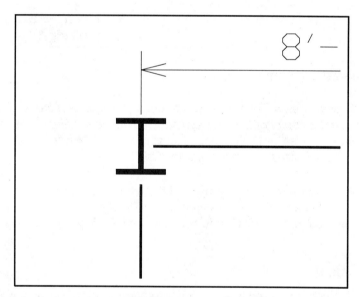

FIGURE 2–35b Design shown after the Window Area command is invoked.

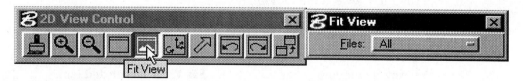

FIGURE 2–36 Invoking the Fit View command from the 2D View Control tool bar.

MicroStation prompts:

> Fit View > Select view to fit *(Place a data point anywhere in the view to display the design.)*

MicroStation updates, showing all elements in the design plane (see Figures 2-37a and b).

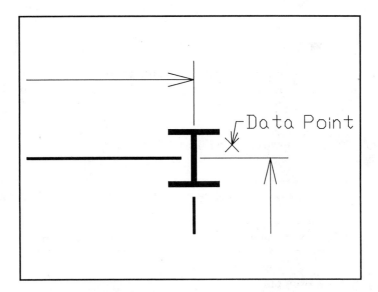

FIGURE 2–37a   Design shown before the Fit View command is invoked.

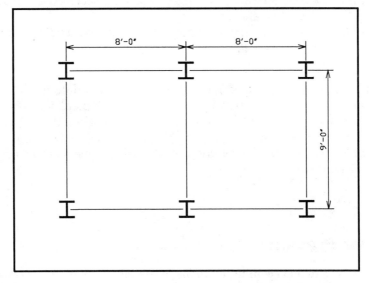

FIGURE 2–37b   Design shown after the Fit View command is invoked.

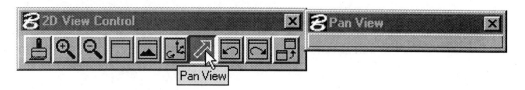

FIGURE 2–38   Invoking the Pan View command from the 2D View Control tool bar.

Pan View

The Pan View command lets you view a different portion of the design in the current view, without changing the magnification. You can move your viewing area to see details that are currently off-screen.

Invoke the Pan View command from:

2D View Control tool bar	Select the Pan View tool (see Figure 2–38).
Key-in window	**Pan View** (or **pan vi**) [ENTER]

MicroStation prompts:

> Pan View > Select view *(Place a data point to select the view to pan and to define the origin for panning.)*
> Pan View > Define amount of panning *(Place a data point to define the position where you want the origin to be displayed.)*

In addition, you can also perform dynamic panning: Hold the [SHIFT] key, press the Data button (the pointer location becomes the anchor point for panning), and drag the pointer in the direction to pan. When panning begins, the [SHIFT] key can be released. You can drag the pointer in any direction. Release the Data button to terminate the panning. The panning speed increases as the pointer is dragged farther away from the anchor point.

View Previous

The View Previous command displays the last displayed view. You can restore back up to the previous six views.

FIGURE 2–39   Invoking the View Previous command from the 2D View Control tool bar.

Invoke the View Previous command from:

| 2D View Control tool bar | Select the View Previous tool (see Figure 2–39). |
| Key-in window | **View Previous (or vi pre)** ⌨ENTER |

MicroStation prompts:

View Previous > Select view *(Place a data point in a view to restore the previous view.)*

View Next

The View Next command negates the view that was displayed by the View Previous command.

Invoke the View Next command from:

| 2D View Control tool bar | Select the View Next tool (see Figure 2–40). |
| Key-in window | **View Next (or vi ne)** ⌨ENTER |

MicroStation prompts:

View Next > Select view *(Place a data point in a view to negate the view that was displayed by the View Previous command.)*

FIGURE 2–40   Invoking the View Next command from the 2D View Control tool bar.

FIGURE 2–41   Invoking the Update View command from the 2D View Control tool bar.

Update View

The Update View command instructs the computer to redraw the on-screen image. You can use this command whenever you see an incomplete image of your design. If you delete an object on the display, there may be gaps in the outline of other elements it crossed or there may be grid dots that do not show up after deleting. If you update the display, the grid dots will be refreshed and all elements will be repainted.

Invoke the Update View command from:

2D View Control tool bar	Select the Update View tool (see Figure 2–41).
Key-in window	**Update View** (or **up**) ENTER

MicroStation prompts:

Update View > Select view *(Place a data point to update the view.)*

DRAWING EXERCISES 2–1 THROUGH 2–5

In Exercises 2–1 through 2–3, write down the coordinates necessary to draw the objects shown above the tables, then use the coordinates to draw the object. The coordinates are already entered in Exercise 2–1 as an example.

> ***NOTE:*** Do not draw the dimensions or text.

Exercise 2–1

Draw the object using absolute coordinate key-ins (**XY**=<x,y>).

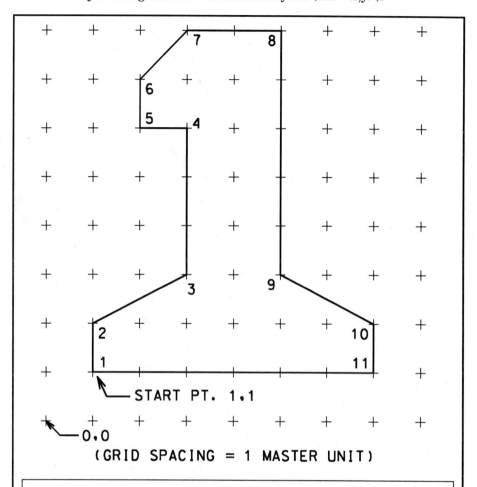

START PT. 1,1

0,0

(GRID SPACING = 1 MASTER UNIT)

ABSOLUTE COORDINATE EXERCISE

KEY IN THESE COORDINATES TO DRAW THE FIGURE.

1.	XY=1,1	7.	XY=3,8
2.	XY=1,2	8.	XY=5,8
3.	XY=3,3	9.	XY=5,3
4.	XY=3,6	10.	XY=7,2
5.	XY=2,6	11.	XY=7,1
6.	XY=2,7	1.	XY=1,1

Exercise 2–2

Draw the object using relative coordinate key-ins (**DL=<x,y>**).

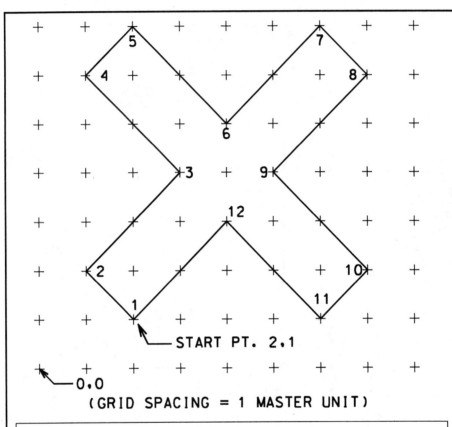

RELATIVE COORDINATE EXERCISE

1. ENTER THE COORDINATES IN THE TABLE BELOW.
2. KEY IN THE COORDINATES TO DRAW THE FIGURE.

1.	XY=2,1	7.	DL=
2.	DL=-1,1	8.	DL=
3.	DL=2,2	9.	DL=
4.	DL=	10.	DL=
5.	DL=	11.	DL=
6.	DL=	1.	DL=

Exercise 2-3

Draw the object using polar coordinate key-ins (**DI**=<x,y>).

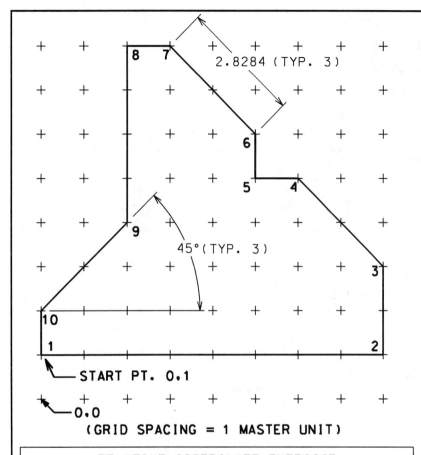

2.8284 (TYP. 3)

45°(TYP. 3)

START PT. 0.1

0.0

(GRID SPACING = 1 MASTER UNIT)

```
            RELATIVE COORDINATE EXERCISE
1. ENTER THE COORDINATES IN THE TABLE BELOW.
2. KEY IN THE COORDINATES TO DRAW THE FIGURE.

     1.    XY=0.1            7.    DI=
     2.    DI=8.0            8.    DI=
     3.    DI=2.90           9.    DI=
     4.    DI=              10.    DI=
     5.    DI=              11.    DI=
     6.    DI=               1.    DI=
```

In Exercises 2–4 and 2–5, select the best precision input method to use for each placement.

Exercise 2–4

Draw the gasket.

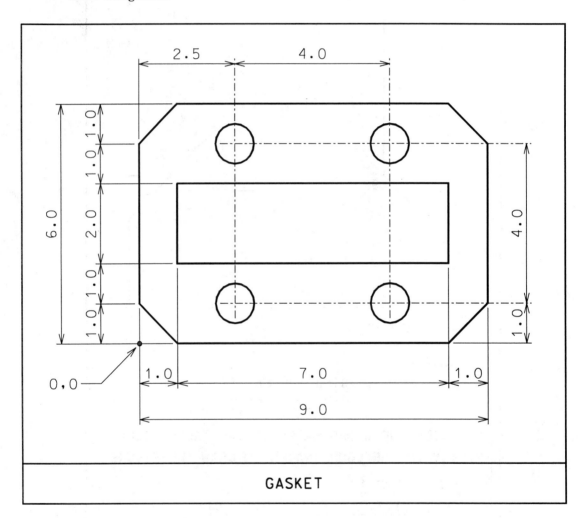

GASKET

Exercise 2–5
Draw the front elevation.

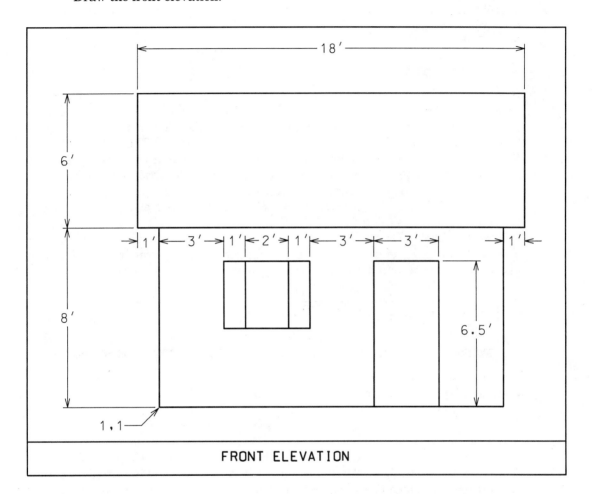

FRONT ELEVATION

DRAWING TOOLS

MicroStation provides several different drawing tools to make your drafting and design layout easier.

The Grid System

Grids are a visual tool for measuring distances precisely and placing elements accurately. MicroStation displays a grid system that is similar to a sheet of graph paper. You can turn the Grid display to ON or OFF as needed, and the spacing can be changed at any time. There are two types of grid systems. The first is the Grid Reference, which appears on your screen as a cross; by default the spacing between crosses is set to one Master Unit (MU). The second is the Grid Unit (GU), which appears as a dot on the screen; by default the spacing between dots is set to one Sub Unit (SU). The grid is just a drawing tool, not part of the drawing; it is for visual reference only and is never plotted. Grids serve two purposes; they provide a visual indication of distances and, with Grid lock set to ON, they force all data points to start and end on a grid point. This is useful for keeping lines straight, ensuring that distances are exact, and making sure all elements meet.

> **NOTE:** MicroStation overrides the Grid lock when you key-in the location of a point by precision input.

Grid Display The Grid display (visual) can be turned ON or OFF. If it is set to ON, then you can see the Grid display on the screen. MicroStation, by default, displays a maximum of 90 dots and 46 crosses. You may not see any crosses or dots if you zoom out farther. When it is set to OFF, the grid is not displayed. You can change the status of the Grid display from the View Attributes setting box. To change the status, invoke the View Attributes settings box by selecting View Attributes from the settings pull-down menu. The resulting settings box is similar to the one shown in Figure 2–42.

Make any necessary change to the Grid Display in the View Attributes settings box. If the button is depressed and has a dark center, the attribute is ON; if the button appears to be sticking out, the attribute is OFF. If you only want the attribute change applied to a specific view, pick the number of the view you want in the View Number (default is the current working view) options menu at the top of the settings box, then click the Apply button. If you want to turn ON the Grid display on all the open views, click the ALL button. (For a detailed explanation of Views and the View Attributes settings box, see Chapter 5.)

Grid Spacing When the Grid Display is turned ON, you will notice a series of evenly spaced dots and crosses. The grid consists of a matrix of dots with the reference

FIGURE 2-42 View Attributes settings box with the cursor position on Grid toggle.

crosses falling at equally spaced intervals. The spacing between both the grid dots and the reference crosses may be changed at any time to suit your drawing needs by marking appropriate changes to the Grid settings.

To set up grid units:

Pull-down menu	Settings > Design File... (or ⊞ + **S**, **D**) (see Figure 2–43).

MicroStation displays Design File Settings box similar to the one shown in Figure 2–44. Select Grid from the Category list, as shown in Figure 2–44, and MicroStation displays controls for adjusting the grid unit settings. In the settings box two edit fields are provided, one for Grid Master unit, the other one for Grid Reference. The Grid Master unit defines the distance between the grid units (dots) and is specified in terms of MU:SU:PU. By default, this is set for one sub-unit. If necessary, you can override the default spacing by keying-in in the edit field in terms of MU:SU:PU.

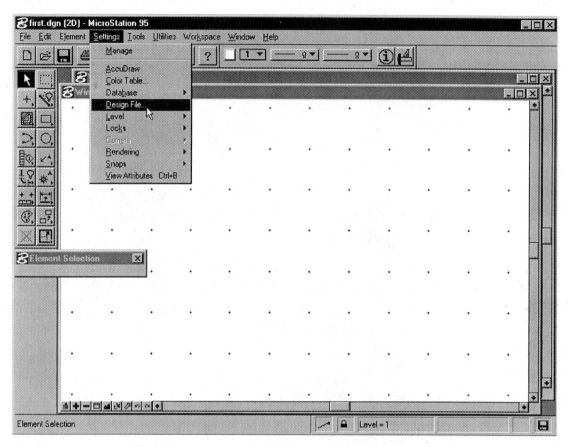

FIGURE 2–43 Invoking the Design File... from the pull-down menu settings.

The Grid Reference is set to define the number (integer) of grid units between the grid reference (crosses). For example, let's say the Grid Master unit is set up to .125 inches and you would like to have the distance between the Crossing be 0.5 inch. Then the Grid Reference has to be set to 4 (0.5"/.125"), as shown in Figure 2–44.

Figure 2–45 shows the screen display for the grid settings.

You can also set the Grid Master unit and the Grid Reference by keying-in at the key-in window. To set the Grid Master unit, key-in **GU=**<distance> and press ⏎. The Key-in window <distance> has to be specified in MU:SU:PU. To set the Grid Reference, key-in **GR=**<integer number> and press ⏎. The <integer number> is the number of grid units between the grid reference crosses. To keep the grid settings in effect for future editing sessions for the current design file, select Save Settings from the pull-down menu File.

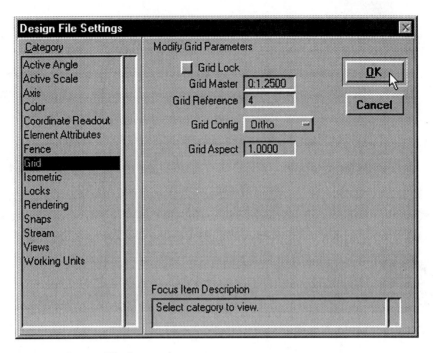

FIGURE 2–44   Design File Settings box.

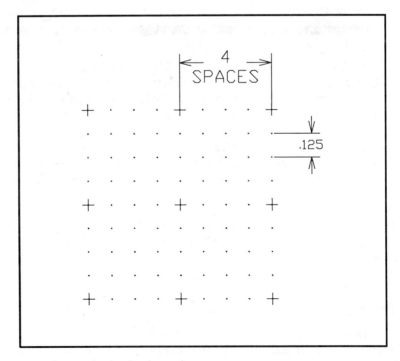

FIGURE 2–45   Screen display for the grid settings.

Grid Configuration MicroStation provides three choices to control the orientation of the Grid display: Orthogonal, Isometric, and Offset. The selection can be made from the Grid Settings box under the Configuration options menu. The Orthogonal option aligns the grid points orthogonally (default option). The Isometric option aligns the grid points isometrically. The Offset option offsets the rows by half the distance between horizontal grid points.

Grid Aspect Ratio (Y/X) The Grid Aspect Ratio edit field in the Grid Settings box allows you to set the ratio of vertical (Y) Grid points to horizontal (X) grid points. The default is set at 1.000.

Grid Lock The Grid Lock can be set to ON or OFF. When it is set to ON, Micro-Station forces all the data points to the grid marks. You cannot place a data point in between the grid dots. By setting the Grid Lock to ON, you can enter points quickly, letting MicroStation ensure that they are placed precisely. You can always override the Grid Lock by keying-in absolute or relative coordinate points.

When Grid Lock is set to ON, you can identify the elements that were drawn on the grid. To identify an element that is not on the grid, simply set the Grid Lock to OFF and try again.

> **NOTE:** The Grid Lock is effective regardless of the status of the Grid display. It still locks to grid points even if you cannot see the grid.

The Grid Lock can be turned ON or OFF (toggle) from the Grid Unit settings located in the Design File settings box. MicroStation displays the current status of the Grid Lock in the right-hand section of the Status bar. Click the OK button to close the Design File Settings box after making the appropriate changes for the grid settings.

You can also toggle the Grid Lock: (1) from the settings box that appears by clicking the lock icon located on the right-hand section of the Status box, (2) from the Settings pull-down menu's Lock's submenu, or (3) from the Lock Toggles settings box, as shown in Figure 2–46.

To keep the grid settings (including the Grid Lock setting) in effect for future editing sessions for the current design file, choose Save Settings from the pull-down menu File.

Axis Lock

The Axis Lock forces each data point to lie at an angle (or multiples of that angle) from the previous data point. If necessary, you can change the Axis Start Angle, which is relative to the X axis, and the Axis Increment angle.

FIGURE 2–46   Locks Toggles settings box.

To set up Axis Lock settings:

Pull-down menu	Settings > Design File... (or [ALT] + **S, D**)

MicroStation displays the Design File Settings box. Select Axis from the Category list and MicroStation displays controls for adjusting the Axis Lock settings. Key-in the appropriate Axis Start Angle in the Start Angle edit field and the Axis Increment angle in the Increment edit field. For example, whenever you want to draw horizontal or vertical lines, key-in an Axis Start Angle of 0 degrees and an Axis Increment angle of 90 degrees. Axis Start Angle and Axis Increment are only in effect when the Axis Lock is set to ON.

Snap Lock

The Snap Lock controls the placement of a tentative point at a specific point on an element, depending on the snap mode selected. Tentative snapping is a way of previewing a data point *before* it is actually entered in the design. Once a tentative point is placed in your design plane, a large cross appears to identify the tentative point. If it is snapped to an element, the element is highlighted and, in addition, MicroStation displays the absolute coordinates of the point selected in the right-hand side of the Status bar. If this is the point you wish to select, click the Accept button (same as the Data button) to confirm it. If, however, this is not the point you wish to select, move the cursor and click the tentative button again. This process of selecting another tentative point rejects the last tentative point and selects a new one highlighted by the large cross. Once you accept the tentative point with the Accept button, the large cross disappears. You may cancel the tentative point by clicking the Reset button.

A tentative point is placed by clicking the designated tentative button on your pointing device. For example, for a three-button mouse, click the middle button to place the tentative point; for a two-button mouse, press both buttons simultaneously to place a tentative point.

Snap Lock Mode As mentioned earlier, the Snap Lock controls the placement of a tentative point at a specific point on an element, depending on the snap mode selected. If the Snap Lock toggle is set to ON, you can snap to a specific point on an element, depending on the snap mode selected. For example, if you set the snap mode to Center and turn ON the Snap Lock, the tentative button snaps to the center of circles, blocks, lines, and segments of line strings. A tentative point can be placed while executing any MicroStation command that requests a point such as Line, Circle, Arc, Move, or Copy. If the Snap Lock toggle is set to OFF, tentative points do *not* snap to elements.

To set up Snap Lock settings:

Pull-down menu	Settings > Locks > Toggles (or ⌨ + **S, K, T**)
	Settings > Locks > Full (or (⌨ + **S, K, F**)

You can toggle the Snap Lock from either the Lock Toggles settings box or the Locks settings box, as shown in Figure 2–47.

Selecting a Snap mode You can select an active (default) snap mode that always stays in effect, and, when you occasionally need a different one, you can select an override snap mode that applies only to the next tentative point.

To set snap active (default) mode:

Pull-down menu	Settings > Locks > Full Select the desired snap mode from the Snap Mode option menu (see Figure 2–48).
Pull-down menu	Settings > Snaps > Button Bar Double-click the desired snap mode (see Figure 2–49).

You can also select the default snap mode from the pop-up Snap Mode menu. Hold down the ⌨ key and press the Tentative button—the pop-up Snap Mode appears as shown in Figure 2–50. While holding the ⌨ key, choose the desired Snap Mode by clicking on it.

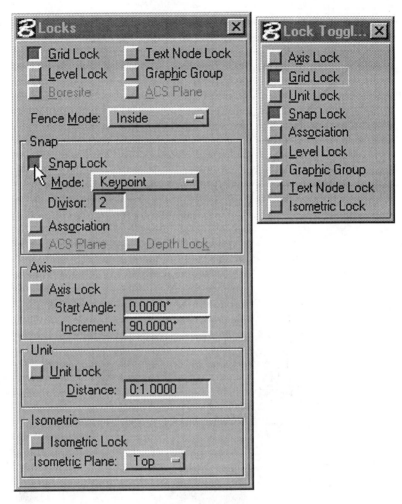

FIGURE 2–47   Lock Toggles and Locks settings boxes.

To set Snap override mode:

Pull-down menu	Settings > Snaps > Button Bar Then click the desired snap mode.
Pull-down menu	Settings > Snaps Then choose the desired Snap Mode override.

You can also select the override snap mode from the pop-up Snap Mode menu. Hold down the ⌈SHIFT⌋ key and press the Tentative button—the pop-up Snap Mode appears. Select the desired override snap mode from the Snap Mode menu.

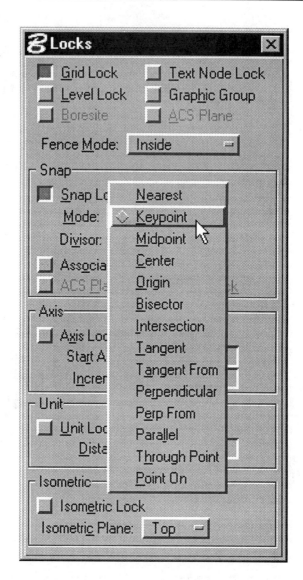

FIGURE 2-48   Lock settings box displaying the Snap Mode option menu.

FIGURE 2-49   Button bar.

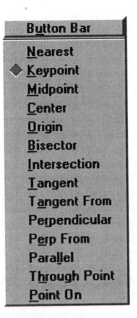

FIGURE 2-50   Pop-up Snap Mode menu.

MicroStation displays the snap mode icon that is in effect on the right-hand side of the status bar. Also, MicroStation displays a diamond-shaped object to the left of the default snap active mode in the menu. If an override mode is selected, then a square appears to the left of the default snap active mode and a diamond shape object appears to the left of the current override snap mode.

> **NOTE:** The number of snap modes included in the Snaps menu varies. The menu shows only the snap modes that are available for the active placement or manipulation command. Some commands do not allow all snap modes.

How to Use the Tentative Button To use the Tentative button in placing and manipulating elements:

1. Select the placement or manipulation tool.
2. Select the snap mode you want (these modes are described later).
3. Point to the element you want to snap to, and click the Tentative button.
4. Click the Data button to accept the tentative point.
5. Continue using snap modes and tentative points as necessary to complete the placement or manipulation.

For example, if you want to start a line in the exact center of a block, select the Place Line tool, set the snap mode to Center, then click the Tentative button on the block.

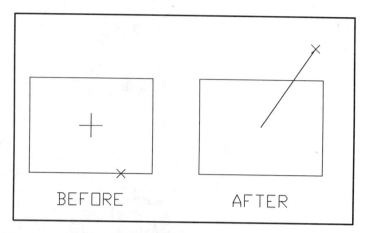

FIGURE 2-51 An example of a placement of the Tentative point.

The block is highlighted and a large tentative cross appears at the exact center of the block. Place a data point to start the line at the block center (see Figure 2–51).

Keep in mind the following points when you use the tentative button.

- You can only snap to elements when Snap Lock is ON.
- If Grid Lock is ON and the element you are trying to snap to is placed between grid points, the Tentative button may always snap to grid points rather than to the element you want. If that happens, turn OFF the Grid Lock.
- When the Tentative button snaps to an element, the element is highlighted and the tentative cross appears at the snap to point. If the cross appears on the snap point but the element is not highlighted, you did not snap to the element; you may have snapped to a grid point close to the point you wanted.
- When you press the Tentative button, MicroStation starts searching for elements in the area immediately around the screen pointer. It selects elements in the order they were placed in the design. If the element it finds is not the one you want, just click the Tentative button again and the next element is found; there is no need to move the screen pointer location or to press the Reset button. If the Tentative button cycles through all elements in the area without finding the one you want, move the screen pointer closer to the element and press the Tentative button again. For example: You placed a block, then placed a line starting very near one corner of the block. You need to snap to the end of the line for the next command, but the tentative point snaps to the corner of the block. Just click the Tentative button again, and it should snap to the end of the line. If the second snap also does not find the end of the line, move the screen pointer a little closer to it and snap again.
- You do not have to place the screen pointer exactly on the point of the element you want to snap to, just near it. In fact, to lessen the chance of snapping to the wrong element, it is best to move back along the element, away from other elements.

Types of Snap Modes Following are the available snap modes.

Keypoint mode Keypoint mode allows tentative points to snap to predefined keypoints on elements. For a line, it is the end points of the line; for a circle, it is the center and four quadrants; for a block, it is the four corners, and so on. See Figure 2–52 for snap points for various element types. To snap to a key point on an element, position the cursor close to the key point (make sure the Snap Lock is turned ON and the keypoint mode selected), and click the Tentative button. The tentative cross appears on the element's key point and the element highlights. If the tentative cross appears but the element does not highlight, you have not found the element's snap point. Press the Tentative button until the snap point is located, then press the Accept button.

The *keypoint snap divisor* works with the keypoint snap mode and allows you to select additional snap points on an element by defining a value that divides the element into a specific number of divisions or parts. For example, setting the keypoint snap divisor to 5 divides an element into five equal divisions. Figure 2–53 shows the keypoint snaps for different keypoint snap divisor values. The keypoint snap divisor can be set in the Locks settings box (Full) by keying-in the value in the Divisor edit field. You can also set the value by keying-in at the key-in window: **KY=**<number of divisors> and press [ENTER].

Nearest mode When active, the Nearest mode will place tentative points on any point of an element that is closest to the cursor. This rule remains the same among all element types, except as applied to text where the project point is the justification point. With the Nearest mode you are always certain that you can locate any point on any type of element. To pick a specific point on an element, position the cursor close to the point you want to select, ensure that the Snap Lock is set to ON and that

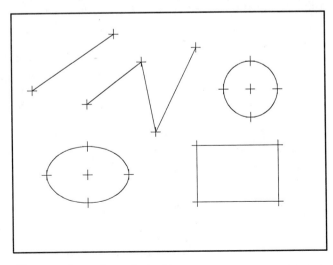

FIGURE 2–52 Keypoints for various element types.

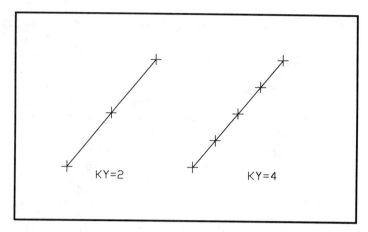

FIGURE 2-53   Examples for various keypoint snap divisor.

the Nearest mode is selected from the mode option menu. Press the Tentative button, and the tentative cross will appear at the closest point on the element as the element highlights. If the tentative cross appears but the element does not highlight, then you have not found the element. Press the Tentative button until a point is located, then press the Accept button.

Midpoint mode   The Midpoint mode, when active, will place tentative points at the midpoint of an element or segment of a complex element (see Figure 2–54). The point position varies with different types of elements.

It bisects a line, arc, or partial ellipse.

It bisects the selected segment of a line string, block, multisided shape, or regular polygon.

It snaps to the 180-degree (9 o'clock) position of a circle or an ellipse.

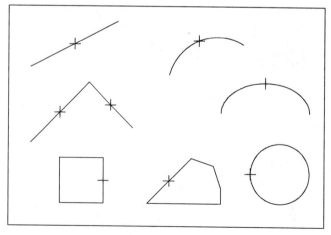

FIGURE 2-54   Midpoint for various element types.

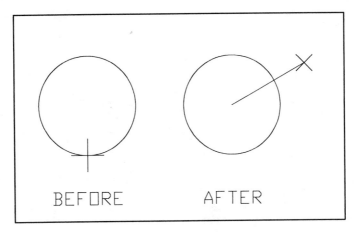

FIGURE 2-55   Example of snapping to the center of the circle.

Center mode   The Center mode causes tentative points to snap to the center of the space in the design occupied by an element (such as circle, block, or arc); see Figure 2–55.

Intersection mode   The Intersection mode causes tentative points to snap to the intersection of two elements. To find the intersection, snap to one of the intersecting elements. One or both of the elements may appear dashed while they are highlighted, but they return to normal appearance when you complete the command.

If the elements do not actually intersect, the tentative cross appears at the intersection of an imaginary extension of the two elements. If the two elements cannot be extended to an intersection, the message "Elements do not intersect" appears in the Status bar, and a tentative cross is not placed (see Figure 2–56).

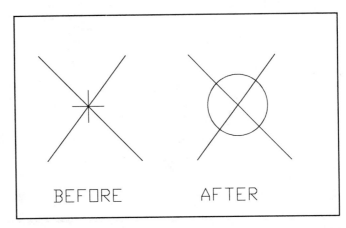

FIGURE 2-56   Example of snapping to the intersection of two elements in placing a circle.

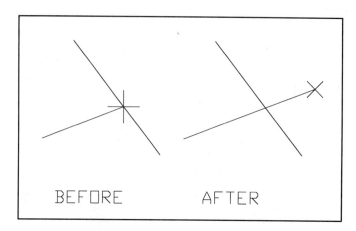

FIGURE 2-57 Example of snapping to a through point.

Through Point mode The Through Point mode causes tentative points to define a point on an existing element through which the element you are placing must pass (see Figure 2–57).

Tangent mode The Tangent mode forces the element you are creating to be tangent to a nonlinear element (such as a circle, ellipse, or arc). The actual point of tangency varies, depending on how you place the element (see Figure 2–58).

Tangent From mode The Tangent From mode forces the element you are placing to be tangent to an existing nonlinear element (such as a circle, ellipse, or arc) at the point where you placed the tentative point (see Figure 2–59).

Origin mode The Origin mode snaps to the center of an arc, circle, origin of the text, or cell.

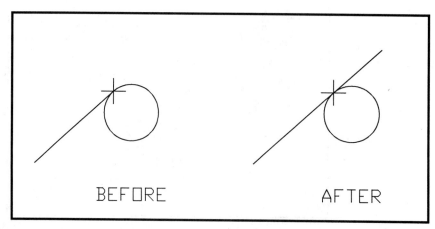

FIGURE 2-58 Example of snapping to a tangent point.

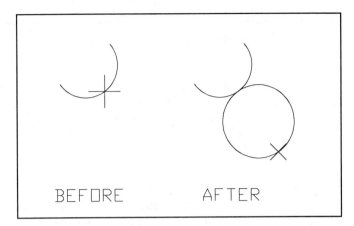

FIGURE 2–59   Example of snapping to a tangent of an existing nonlinear element.

Bisector mode The Bisector mode sets the snap mode to bisect an element; the snap point varies with different types of elements.

Perpendicular mode The Perpendicular mode forces the element to be perpendicular to an existing element. The actual perpendicular point depends on the way the element is placed.

Perpendicular From mode The Perpendicular From mode forces the element to be perpendicular to an existing element at the point where you place the tentative point.

Parallel mode The Parallel mode forces the line or segment of the line string to be parallel to a linear element.

Point On mode The Point On mode snaps to the nearest element (after you have entered the first point of element placement) and constrains the next data point to lie on a closed element or anywhere on a linear element's line.

ELEMENT ATTRIBUTES

There are four important attributes associated with placement of elements. The attributes includes level, color, line style, and line weight.

Levels

MicroStation offers a way to group elements on levels in a manner similar to a designer's drawing different parts of a design on separate transparent sheets. By stacking the transparent sheets one on top of another, the designer can see the complete drawing but can only draw on the top sheet. If the designer wants to show a customer only part of the design, he or she can remove from the stack the sheets that contain the parts of the design the customer does not need to see.

MicroStation supports the same functionality as the transparent sheets by providing you with 63 levels in each design file. For example, an architectural design in MicroStation might have the walls on one level, the dimensions on another level, electrical information on still another level, and so on. Separating parts of the design by level allows designers to turn on only the part they need to work on and to plot parts of the design separately.

You can only draw on one level at a time (the active level), but can turn ON or OFF the display of any number of levels except the active level in selected views. Elements on levels that are not displayed disappear from the view and cannot be plotted, but they are still in the design file. The same coordinate system and zoom factors apply to all levels. Levels are identified by numbers (1 through 63), and the right-hand side of the Status bar displays the number of the active level with LV=<level number>.

When you manipulate an element, the resulting manipulation takes place on the same level on which the element was placed. For instance, a copy of an element goes on the same level as the original element, regardless of what level is currently active. The Change Element Attributes command moves elements to different levels (discussed later).

Setting an Active Level As just mentioned, you can have only one active level at any time, and with most tools that is the level on which new elements are placed. The level number to which the Active Level is set is shown in the Status bar and in the Primary tool box.

To set the Active Level:

Primary tool box	Select the appropriate level number from Level option menu (see Figure 2–60).
Status bar	Click the Active Level field. The Set Active Level dialog box opens (see Figure 2–61). Select the appropriate level number and click the OK button to close the dialog box.
Key-in window	**LV**=<level number> ⏎

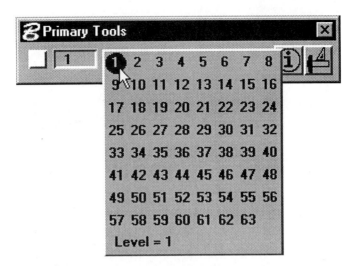

FIGURE 2-60 Primary tool box—Level option menu.

Controlling the Display of Levels The Level Display settings box controls the display of levels. You can control the display (ON or OFF) of one or more levels in one or more views.

To control the display of levels, open the View Levels settings box from:

Pull-down menu	Settings > Level > Display (or [ALT] + **S, L, D**)
Key-in window	**ON**=<level numbers> [ENTER] **OFF**=<level numbers> [ENTER]

FIGURE 2-61 Set Active Level dialog box.

FIGURE 2–62   View Levels settings box.

MicroStation displays the View Levels settings box as shown in Figure 2–62.

The settings box shows the number of each of the 63 total levels. The display of level numbers with a black background is set to ON, and the display of level numbers with a gray background is set to OFF. The View Number options menu at the top of the settings box displays the number of the view to which the level display settings apply. The View Number menu also allows you to change the number of the view displayed in the settings box (see Chapter 5 for a discussion on View setting).

The level number within a black circle is the current active level (the level on which all new elements are placed). The active level applies to all views.

To change the active level, double-click the level number you want to make active. Click once on a level number to toggle its display status between ON and OFF. To change the display status of a group of level numbers, drag the screen cursor across them while holding down the Data button on your pointing device.

> **NOTE:** Display of the active level cannot be turned OFF.

The Apply button applies the current level display settings (ON or OFF) to the selected view and applies the active level to all views. The All button applies the current level display settings (ON or OFF) and the active level to all views.

NOTE: The active level and the level display settings for each view remain in effect until you change them or exit from MicroStation. To keep them in effect for the next editing session, select Save Settings from the pull-down menu File.

Keeping Up with the Levels Keeping up with what level everything is on can be confusing. To help overcome the confusion, MicroStation provides a level symbology table. Use the table to specify unique combinations of display color, weight, and style for each level. When level symbology is turned ON, all elements display using the symbology assigned to the level on which the elements are placed, rather than their true symbology. Chapter 13 describes the level symbology table in detail. In addition, MicroStation allows you to assign a name to a level. For detailed explanation, see Chapter 15 on Customizing MicroStation.

Element Color

The color for an element is very helpful in enabling you to differentiate between the many elements on your design, especially when all the levels are displayed at one time. Before you place an element with a specific color, you have to select the active color.

To set the Active Color:

Primary tool box	Select the appropriate color tile from the Color option menu (see Figure 2–63).
Key-in window	**CO**=<name of the color or color number anywhere from 0 to 255>

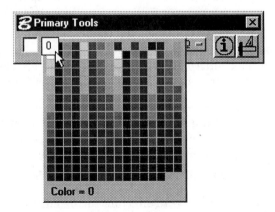

FIGURE 2–63 Primary tool box—Color option menu.

The actual colors shown depend on your monitor, graphics card, and what colors are defined in MicroStation's color table. Click on a color in the color palette to make it the active color.

> **NOTE:** Setting up the active color does not affect elements that are already in the design plane, unless the Change Element Attributes command (explained later in this chapter) is used.

To keep the active color in effect for future editing sessions for the current design file, select Save Settings from the pull-down menu File.

Element Line Style

Similar to color, MicroStation allows you to place elements with a specific line style (or line type). By default, MicroStation provides you with eight line styles (called internal line styles). In addition, MicroStation comes with numerous custom-made line styles. If necessary, you can change the custom-made line styles or add new ones. A detailed explanation for creating and modifying the custom-made line styles is given in Chapter 15.

Before you place an element with a specific line style, you have to make that line style an active line style.

To set the Active Line Style:

Primary tool box	Select the appropriate Line Style from the Line Style option menu (see Figure 2–64).
Key-in window	**LC**=<name of the line style or line style number> [ENTER]

If you need to use one of the custom line styles, select Custom from the Line Style option menu, and MicroStation displays the Line Styles settings box, as shown in Figure 2–65. Select one of the available line styles from the list.

> **NOTE:** Selecting a new active line style does not affect elements that already exist in the design plane, unless the Change Element Attributes command (explained later in the chapter) is used.

To keep the active line style in effect for future editing sessions for the current design file, select Save Settings from the pull-down menu File.

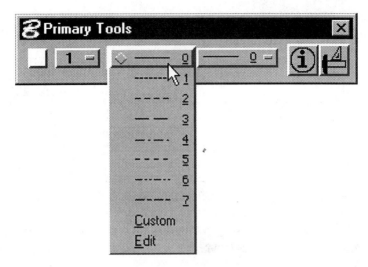

FIGURE 2–64   Primary tool box—Line Style option menu.

FIGURE 2–65   Listing of the customized line styles.

Element Line Weight

In MicroStation, weight refers to the width of the element. There are 32 line weights to choose from (numbered from 0 to 31), which is comparable to 32 different technical pens.

In drafting, the color, style, and even the weight (width) of the lines for creating elements in the design contribute to the "readability" or understanding of the design. For example, in a piping arrangement drawing, the line weight (width) for the pipe is the widest of all the lines on the drawing, to make the pipe stand out from the equipment, foundations, and supports.

To set the Active Element Line Weight:

Primary tool box	Select the appropriate Line Weight from the Line Weight option menu (see Figure 2–66).
Key-in window	**WT**=<line weight number anywhere from 0 to 32> [ENTER]

> **NOTE:** Setting up the active line weight does not affect elements that already exist on the design plane, unless the Change Element Attributes command (explained later in the chapter) is used.

To keep the active line weight in effect for future editing sessions for the current design file, select Save Settings from the pull-down menu File.

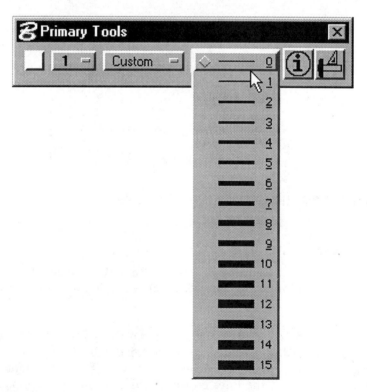

FIGURE 2-66   Primary tool box—Line Weight option menu.

Element Attributes Settings Box

The Element Attributes settings box lets you control the attributes of elements, such as level, color, line style, and line weight. Instead of using four different commands (level, color, line style, and line weight) to set up the attributes, use the Element Attributes settings box to do the same thing in one place.

To set the Element Attributes:

Pull-down menu	Settings > Design File...

MicroStation displays the Design File Settings box. Select Element Attributes from the Category list, as shown in Figure 2–67, and MicroStation displays the controls for adjusting the Element Attributes.

The Level edit field allows you to set the active level by keying-in the level number and pressing [ENTER] or [TAB].

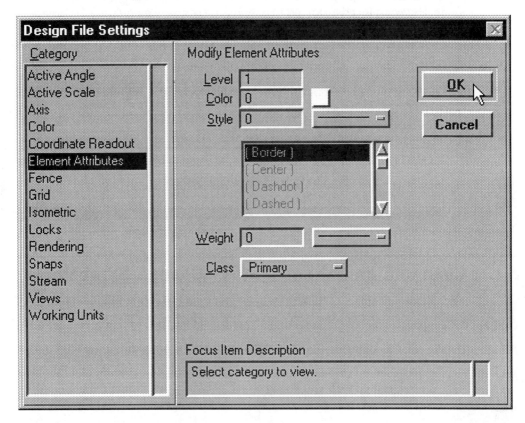

FIGURE 2–67 Design File Settings box—Element Attributes.

The Color edit field allows you to set the current active color either by keying in a numerical value in the Color edit field and pressing [ENTER] or by choosing a color, without regard for numerical values, from the color palette. To open the color palette, which represents the active color table, click the colored button located next to the Color edit field and select the appropriate color from the palette.

The Style edit field allows you to set the current active line style either by keying-in a numerical value in the Style edit field and pressing [ENTER] or by choosing a line style, without regard for numerical values, from the option menu located next to the Style edit field.

The Weight edit field allows you to set the current active line weight either by keying in a numerical value in the Weight edit field and pressing [ENTER] or by choosing a line weight, without regard for numerical values, from the option menu located next to the Weight edit field.

The Class option menu specifies the class of an element upon placement. Two options are available, Primary and Construction. Primary (default option) elements are the elements that comprise the design. Construction elements are placed in the design plane, then employed as an aid to placing the primary elements. You create geometric constructions with fundamental entities such as lines, circles, and arcs to generate intersections, end points, centers, points of tangency, midpoints, and other useful data that might take a manual drafter considerable time to calculate or hand-measure on the board. From these you can create primary elements using intersections or other data generated from the construction elements. When the design is complete, display of the construction elements can be turned OFF from the View Attributes settings box (see Chapter 5).

> **NOTE:** If construction elements are displayed in a plotted view, they also plot. Turn them OFF before creating a plot of the finished drawing.

Change Element Attributes—Change Symbology

The Change Element Attributes command enables you to change an element to the active element attributes (level, color, line style, line weight, and class).

Invoke the Change Element Attributes command from:

Change Attributes tool box	Select the Change Element Attributes tool (see Figure 2–68).

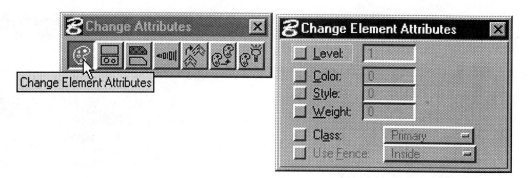

FIGURE 2-68 Invoking the Change Element Attributes command from the Change Attributes tool box.

Turn on the toggle button to Level, Color, Style, Weight and/or Class, and then make the necessary changes to the settings in the Tool Settings window. MicroStation prompts:

> Change Element Attributes > Identify element *(Identify the element to make the necessary changes to the attributes.)*

> Change Element Attributes > Accept/Reject *(Click the Data button to accept or click the Reject button to reject the changes.)*

Match Element Attributes

In addition to being able to change the attributes of an element to the active settings, you can, with the Match Element Attributes command, change the active attributes (level, color, style, and weight) to those that were in effect when an existing element was created. This command provides a quick way to return to placing elements with the same attributes as elements you placed earlier in the design.

Invoke the Match Element Attributes command from:

Change Attributes tool box	Select the Match Element Attributes tool (see Figure 2–69).

Turn on the toggle button to the Level, Color, Style, and/or Weight to which you want the element to match in the Tool Settings window. MicroStation prompts:

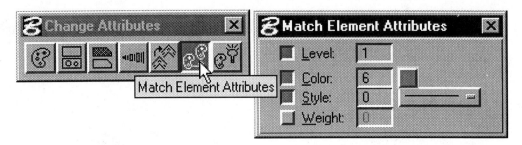

FIGURE 2-69   Invoking the Match Element Attributes command from the Change Attributes tool box.

Match Element Attributes > Identify element *(Identify the element to which you want to match the attributes.)*

Match Element Attributes > Accept/Reject *(Click the Data button to accept or click the Reject button to reject the changes.)*

REVIEW QUESTIONS

Write your answers in the spaces provided.

1. How many possible positions (positional units) are there in the X and Y directions of a 2D design file?

   _____

2. Define Master Units:

   _____

   _____

3. Define Sub Units:

   _____

   _____

4. Define Positional Units:

   _____

   _____

5. Name the command that will make individual elements from a shape.

   _____

6. Explain briefly the differences between the absolute rectangular coordinates and relative rectangular coordinates precision key-ins.

   _____

   _____

7. Name the three key-ins that are used in precision input for absolute rectangular coordinates, relative rectangular coordinates, and polar relative coordinates.

   _____

   _____

8. Explain briefly the difference between the Zoom In and Zoom Out commands.

   _____

   _____

9. Which command will get you closer to a portion of your design by a factor of 2?

   _____

10. Name the command that will Rebuild, Refresh, or Update your views.

    _____

11. When MicroStation displays the information regarding the size of an element or coordinates, it does so in the following format:

    _____:_____:_____

12. Panning lets you view _____

    _____ .

13. To pan in a view, hold the [SHIFT] key and press the _____ button.

14. If in a design file the Working Units are set up as inches, eighths, and 1600 positional units per eighth, what distance does 1:6:600 represent?

    _____

15. If in a design file the Working Units are set up as feet, inches, and 1600 positional units per inch, what Working Units expression is equivalent to 4'-0.3200"?

    _____

16. What is the purpose of the Grid lock?

    _____

17. The _____ settings box allows you to control the display of the grid.

18. The Grid Master unit defines the distance between the _____ and is specified in terms of _____:_____:_____ .

19. The Grid Reference is set to define the _____ .

20. If the button is depressed and has a dark center for the Grid Lock toggle in the Locks settings box, then the Grid Lock is _____ .

21. To keep the grid settings in effect for future editing sessions for the current design file, invoke the _____ command.

22. The Aspect Ratio edit field in the Grid settings box allows you to set the

    _____

23. Name the three menu options that are available to select the Snap mode.

    _____

24. Name four Snap modes available in MicroStation.

_____

25. Keypoint mode allows tentative points to snap to _____ .

26. The Midpoint mode snaps to the _____ position of a circle and an ellipse.

27. The Axis Lock forces each data point _____ .

28. List the four attributes associated with the placement of elements.

_____

_____

29. How many levels come with a new design file? _____

30. How many level(s) can be active at any time? _____

31. How many level(s) can you turn ON or OFF at any time in a specific view? _____

32. How many colors or shades of colors are available in the color palette? _____

33. What two-letter key-in makes a color active? _____

34. How many Line Styles (internal) are available in MicroStation? _____

35. In MicroStation, Line Weight refers to _____ .

36. How many line weights are available in MicroStation ? _____

37. Name the three methods by which you can place circles in MicroStation.

_____

38. If you wish to draw a circle by specifying three known points on the circle, invoke the _____ command.

39. The command related to placing arcs are in the _____ tool box.

40. The Place Arc Edge command places an arc by identifying _____ points on the arc.

PROJECT EXERCISE

This project exercise provides step-by-step instructions for creating the design shown in Figure P2–1. The intent is to guide you in applying the concepts and tools presented in Chapters 1 and 2. (Note that these instructions are not necessarily the most efficient way to draw the objects. Your efficiency will improve as you learn more commands in later chapters.)

In this project, you:

- Create a new design file.
- Set the working units and grid spacing.
- Draw the border using precision input.
- Use view commands to provide the optimum view window alignment for drawing.
- Draw the upper left object using precision input.
- Draw the upper right object using Grid Lock.
- Draw the lower left object using Axis Lock.
- Draw the lower right object via precision input and tentative snapping.

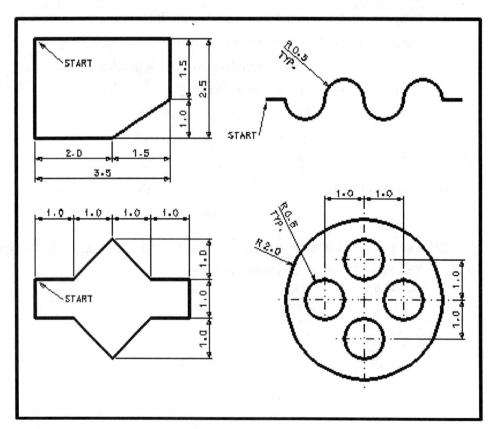

FIGURE P2–1 Completed project design.

NOTE: Do not draw the dimensions. Dimensioning is introduced in a later chapter.

NOTE: As you complete each step in the project procedures, place a check mark by the step to help you keep up with where you are in the project.

Create a Design File

This procedure has you start MicroStation and create a design file for the project design.

STEP 1:   Invoke the MicroStation program.

Example: Under Microsoft Windows 95, find the MicroStation program in the Start > Programs menu and select it.

STEP 2:   In the MicroStation Manager dialog box, select the New... option from the pull-down menu File to open the Create New Design File dialog box.

STEP 3:   If the "Seed File" area of the Create New Design File dialog box does not show SEED2D.DGN as the seed file, click the Select button and select SEED2D.DGN as the seed file.

STEP 4:   In the Create New Design File dialog box, type **CH2.DGN** as the name for the project design file in the Name edit field, then click the OK button to create the file and close the dialog box.

STEP 5:   In the MicroStation Manager dialog box, select the CH2.DGN file from the files list box and click the OK button to load the file in MicroStation.

Set the Working Units and Grid Spacing

This procedure presents the steps by which to:

- Set the working unit ratios to 10 subunits per Master Unit and 1000 Positional Units per subunit.
- Set the Grid spacing to 0.1 and the grid reference to 0.5.
- Set the Element Attributes.

STEP 1: In the MicroStation application window, select the Design File... option from the pull-down menu Settings.

STEP 2: In the Design File dialog box, select the Working Units category, and set the Working Units ratio as shown in Figure P2–2.

STEP 3: In the Design File dialog box, select the Grid category and set the Grid Units and Grid Reference as shown in Figure P2–3.

STEP 4: Click the OK button to close the Design file dialog box and keep the changes.

STEP 5: If an Alert box opens to tell you the Working Units are being changed, click its OK button to accept the changes.

STEP 6: Open the Element Attributes settings box by selecting Attributes from the pull-down menu Element. Set the Active Level to 10, Color to 1 (blue),

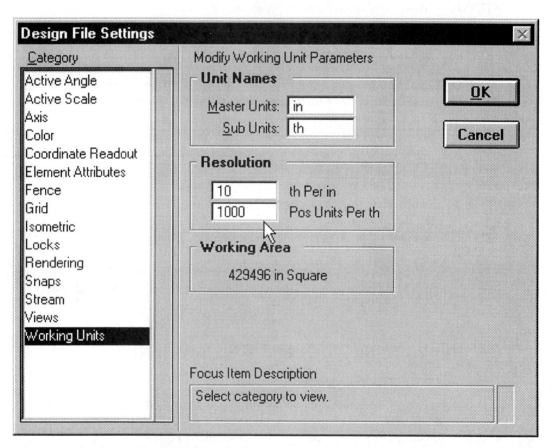

FIGURE P2–2 Design File dialog box—Working Units ratio setup.

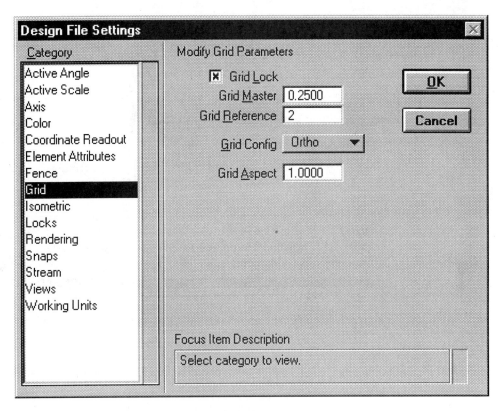

FIGURE P2–3   Design File dialog box—Grid Units setup.

Line Style to 0 (continuous), and Line Weight to 2, as shown in Figure P2–4.

STEP 7:   Select Save Settings from the pull-down menu File to save the settings of the Working Units, grid settings, and element attributes.

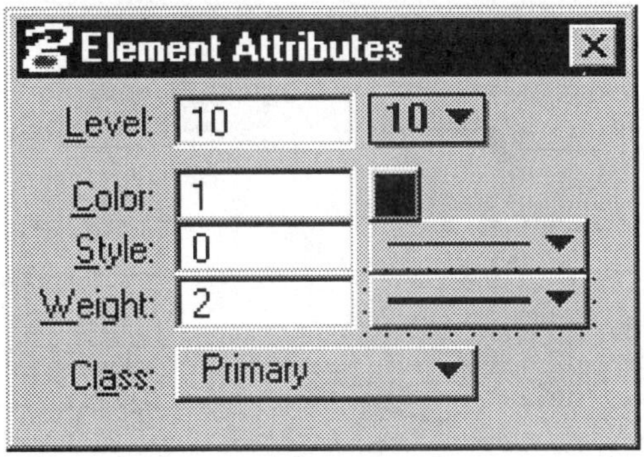

FIGURE P2–4   Element Attributes settings box.

Draw the Border via Precision Input

This procedure presents the steps for employing the XY absolute coordinates to draw the border and invoking the Fit View command to see the complete border outline in the view window.

STEP 1: Invoke the Place Block command from the Polygons tool box.

MicroStation prompts:

Place Block > Enter first point *(Click in the Key-in window's input field, key-in* **XY=0,0** *as shown in Figure P2–5 and press* [ENTER].*)*

> **NOTE:** If the Key-in window is not open, then select the Key-in... option from the pull-down menu Utilities to open the Key-in window.

Place Block > Enter opposite corner *(Key-in* **XY=12,10** *in the Key-in window and press* [ENTER].*)*

STEP 2: Invoke the Fit View command from the View Control bar to display the complete border outline in the selected view.

STEP 3: Invoke the Save settings from the pull-down menu File.

If the procedure was executed correctly, a rectangle should be seen in the view, as shown in Figure P2–6.

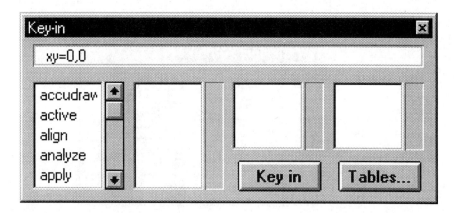

FIGURE P2–5 Key-in window.

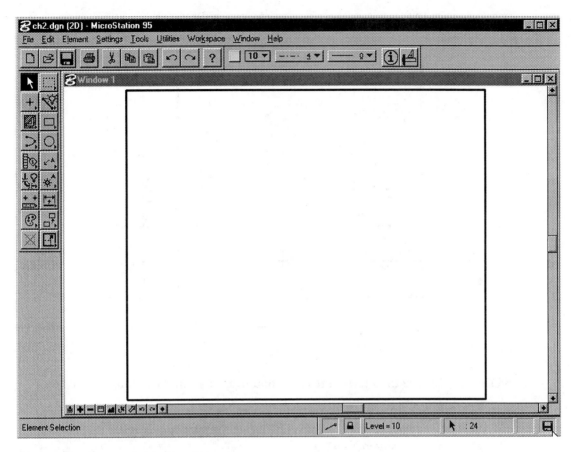

FIGURE P2-6 Completed border outline.

Draw the Upper Left Object via Precision Input

This procedure describes the steps required to draw the object in the upper left quadrant of the border, as shown in Figure P2–7. The figure is drawn with line elements using precision input. Drawing starts at the upper left corner and proceeds clockwise around the object.

STEP 1:   Invoke the Window Area command from the View Control bar (bottom left of the view window) to align the view window to show only the top left quadrant of the border area.

If the Element Attributes settings box is not open, open it by selecting Attributes from the pull-down menu Element. Set the Active Level to 2 and the Color to green.

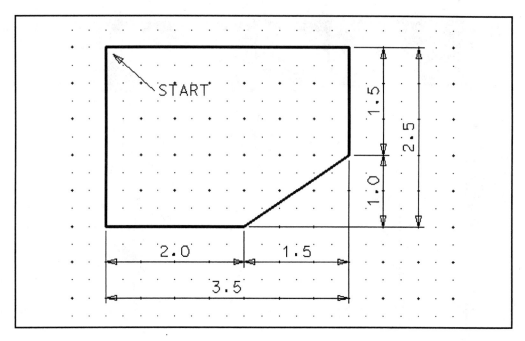

FIGURE P2–7 First object to draw.

STEP 2: Invoke the Place Line command from the Linear Elements tool box.

MicroStation prompts:

> Place Line > Enter first point *(Click in the Key-in window's input field, key-in* **XY=1,9.5**, *and press* ⏎*.)*
>
> Place Line > Enter end point *(Key-in* **DL=3.5,0** *in the Key-in window and press* ⏎*.)*
>
> Place Line > Enter end point *(Key-in* **DL=0,–1.5** *in the Key-in window and press* ⏎*.)*
>
> Place Line > Enter end point *(Key-in* **DL=–1.5,–1** *in the Key-in window and press* ⏎*.)*
>
> Place Line > Enter end point *(Key-in* **DL=–2,0** *in the Key-in window and press* ⏎*.)*
>
> Place Line > Enter end point *(Key-in* **DL=0,2.5** *in the Key-in window and press* ⏎*.)*

STEP 3: Invoke the Fit View command from the View Control bar to display the complete border outline in the selected view.

STEP 4: Invoke the Save settings from the pull-down menu File.

If the object was drawn correctly, it should match the object lines shown in Figure P2–7 and be located in the upper left quadrant of the border. If it was not drawn correctly, delete all of the object elements and repeat the procedure.

Draw the Upper Right Object Using Grid Lock

This procedure describes the steps required to draw the object in the upper right quadrant of the border, as shown in Figure P2–8. The figure is drawn with line and arc commands by snapping on grid points with the Grid lock set to ON.

STEP 1: Invoke the Window Area command from the View Control bar to align the view window to show only the top right quadrant of the border area.

STEP 2: Set the Grid lock to ON by selecting the Locks submenu from the pull-down menu Settings.

If the Element Attributes settings box is not open, open it by selecting Attributes from the pull-down menu Element. Set the Active Level to 3 and the Color to red.

STEP 3: Invoke the Save settings from the pull-down menu File.

STEP 4: Invoke the Place Line command from the Linear Elements tool box.

MicroStation prompts:

Place Line > Enter first point *(Click in the Key-in window's input field, key-in* **XY=6.5,8**, *and press* [ENTER].*)*
Place Line > Enter end point *(Drag the drawing cursor one Grid Reference (crosses) to the right, place a data point to end the line, and click the Reset button to terminate the command sequence.)*

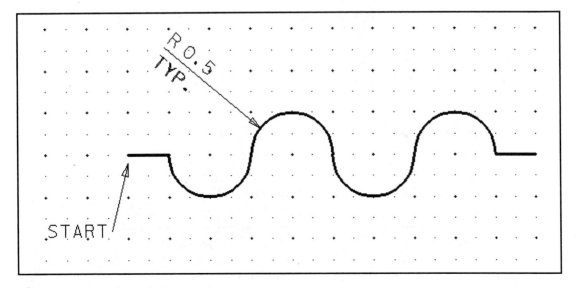

FIGURE P2–8   Second object to draw.

STEP 5: Invoke the Place Arc command from the Arcs tool box, and select the Center Method in the Tool Settings box.

MicroStation prompts:

> Place Arc By Center > Identify First Arc Endpoint *(Place the first data point at the right end of the line you just completed.)*
> Place Arc By Center > Identify Arc Center *(Place the arc center point one Grid Reference (cross) to the right.)*
> Place Arc By Center > Identify Second Arc Endpoint *(Place the end of the counterclockwise arc sweep one Grid Reference to the right of the center point.)*

STEP 6: Place the second arc:

- Start two Grid Reference points to the right of the first arc.
- Place the arc center one Grid Reference to the right of the first arc.
- Place the end of the counterclockwise arc sweep on the right end of the first arc.

STEP 7: Similarly, place the third and fourth arcs, as shown in Figure P2–8.

STEP 8: Invoke the Place Line command, and snap to the end of the fourth arc for the starting point of the line, ending one Grid Reference point to the right of the fourth arc.

STEP 9: Invoke the Fit View command from the View Control bar to display the complete border outline in the selected view.

STEP 10: Invoke the Save settings from the pull-down menu File.

If the object was drawn correctly, it should match the object lines shown in Figure P2–8 and be located in the upper right quadrant of the border. If it was not drawn correctly, delete all object elements and repeat the procedure.

Draw the Lower Left Object Using Axis Lock

This procedure describes the steps required to draw the object in the lower left quadrant of the border using the Place Shape command, as shown in Figure P2–9. The figure is drawn with the help of Axis and Grid locks.

> **NOTE:** The Axis lock isn't really necessary to draw this object. It is used only to illustrate how it allows drawing elements at specific angles without the need for precision input.

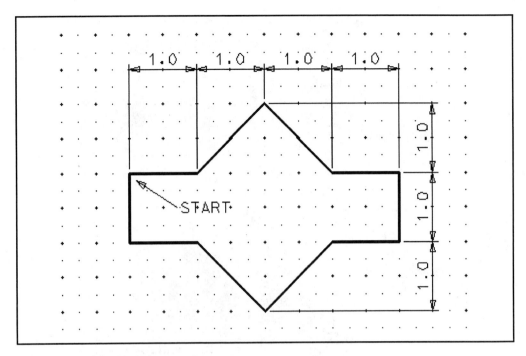

FIGURE P2–9   Third object to draw.

STEP 1:   Invoke the Window Area command from the View Control bar to align the view window to show only the bottom left quadrant of the border area.

STEP 2:   Open the full Locks settings box by selecting Full from the Locks sub-menu in the pull-down menu Settings.

STEP 3:   Set the Axis Lock fields to match those shown in Figure P2–10 and close the Locks settings box.

   If the Element Attributes settings box is not open, open it by selecting Attributes from the pull-down menu Element. Set the Active Level to 4 and the Color to blue.

STEP 4:   Invoke the Save settings from the pull-down menu File.

STEP 5:   Invoke the Place Shape command from the Polygons tool box.

   MicroStation prompts:

   Place Shape > Enter first point *(Click in the Key-in window's input field, key-in* **XY=1,2.5** *and press* ⏎*.)*
   Place Shape > Enter vertex or Reset to cancel *(Place the vertices as shown in Figure P2–9 by snapping to the grid reference points, and close the shape.)*

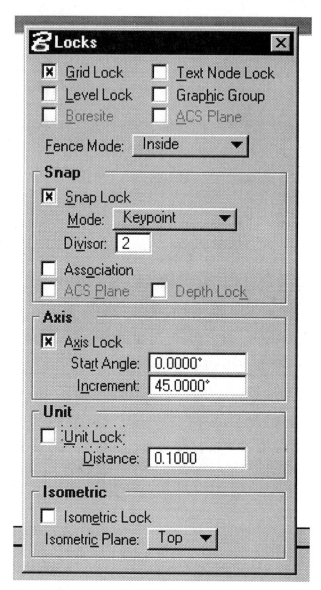

FIGURE P2–10   Axis Lock settings in the full Locks settings box.

STEP 6:   Invoke the Fit View command from the View Control bar to display the complete border outline in the selected view.

STEP 7:   Invoke the Save settings from the pull-down menu File.

If the object was drawn correctly, it should match the object lines shown in Figure P2–9 and be located in the lower left quadrant of the border. If it was not drawn correctly, delete all object elements and repeat the procedure.

Draw the Lower Right Object Using Tentative Snap

This procedure describes the steps required to draw the object in the lower right quadrant of the border as shown in Figure P2–11. Two major steps are involved: drawing the circles and then drawing the centerlines for the circles.

First, draw the circles:

STEP 1: Invoke the Window Area command from the View Control bar to align the view window to show only the bottom right quadrant of the border area.

STEP 2: Click the Snaps icon in the Status bar, and select Center mode by pressing [SHIFT].

If the Element Attributes settings box is not open, open it by selecting Attributes from the pull-down menu Element. Set the Active Level to 5 and the Color to white.

STEP 3: Invoke the Save settings from the pull-down menu File.

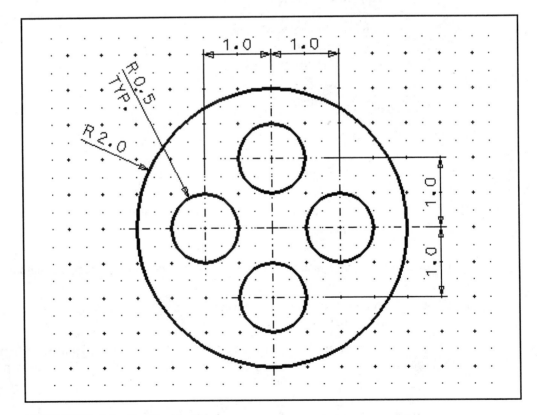

FIGURE P2–11   Fourth object to draw.

STEP 4: If the Key-in window is not open, open it from the pull-down menu Utilities.

STEP 5: Invoke the Place Circle command to place the large outer circle from the Ellipses tool box, select the Center Method in the Tool Settings window, set the Radius to 2 Master Units, and turn ON the toggle button for Radius.

MicroStation prompts:

Place Circle By Center > Identify Center Point *(Click in the Key-in window's input field, key-in* **XY=9.5,3** *and press* ⌨.*)*

STEP 6: To draw four small circles inside the large circle:

■ Change the Radius field to .5 Master Units, tentative snap anywhere on the large circle, key-in **DL=1,0** in the Key-in window, and press ⌨.
■ Tentative snap anywhere on the large circle, key-in **DL=0,1** in the Key-in window, and press ⌨.
■ Tentative snap anywhere on the large circle, key-in **DL=0,–1** in the Key-in window, and press ⌨.
■ Tentative snap anywhere on the large circle, key-in **DL=–1,0** in the Key-in window, and press ⌨.

Second, draw the centerlines:

STEP 1: If the Element Attributes settings box is not open, open it by selecting Attributes from the pull-down menu Element. Set the Active Level to 10, the Line Weight to 0, the Line Style to center, and the Color to yellow.

STEP 2: Click the Snaps icon in the Status bar, and select Keypoint mode by pressing ⌨.

STEP 3: Invoke the Place Line command from the Linear Elements tool box.

STEP 4: Draw the horizontal and vertical centerlines for the outer circle by drawing the part inside the circle:

■ Snap to the 180-degree point (9 o'clock position) and place a data point.
■ Snap to the 0-degree point (3 o'clock position) and place a data point.
■ Click the Reset button.

Figure P2–12 shows the way the object should appear now.

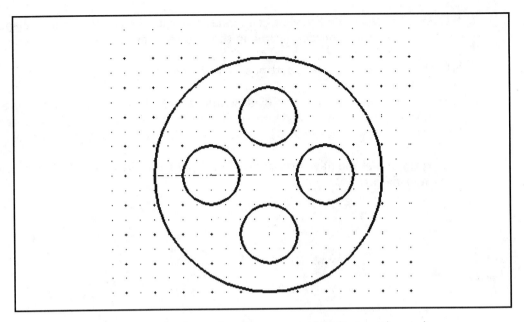

FIGURE P2–12   Lower right object after drawing part of the horizontal centerline.

- Snap to the 90-degree point (12 o'clock position) and place a data point.
- Snap to the 270-degree point (6 o'clock position) and place a data point.
- Click the Reset button.

STEP 5:   Complete the centerlines for the outer circle by adding lines outside the circle:

- Snap to the 0-degree point and draw a line one Grid Unit long to the right.
- Snap to the 90-degree point and draw a line one Grid Unit long straight up.
- Snap to the 180-degree point and draw a line one Grid Unit long to the left.
- Snap to the 270-degree point and draw a line one Grid Unit long straight down.

STEP 6:   Similarly, add the centerlines for the inner circles as shown in Figure P2–11.

> **NOTE:** MicroStation has a tool called Place Center Mark, available in the Dimension tool box, that places the centerlines by just identifying the circle. This is explained in detail in Chapter 8.

STEP 7:   Invoke the Fit View command from the View Control bar to display the complete border outline in the selected view.

STEP 8:   Invoke the Save settings from the pull-down menu File.

If the object was drawn correctly, it should match the object lines and centerlines shown in Figure P2–11 and be located in the lower right quadrant of the border. If it was not drawn correctly, delete all object elements and repeat the procedure.

Congratulations! You have just successfully applied several MicroStation concepts in creating a design.

DRAWING EXERCISES 2–6 through 2–10

Use the following table to set up the design files for Exercises 2–6 through 2–8.

SETTING	VALUE
Seed File	SEED2D.DGN2
Working Units	MU = IN, SU = 10 TH, PU = 1000
Grid	Master = .1, Reference = 10, Grid Lock ON
Object Elements	Color = 0, Level = 1, Style = 0, Weight = 1
Hidden Lines	Color = 0, Level = 1, Style = 3, Weight = 1
Centerlines	Color = 3, Level = 2, Style = 6, Weight = 0

Exercise 2–6   Crane pulley plate.

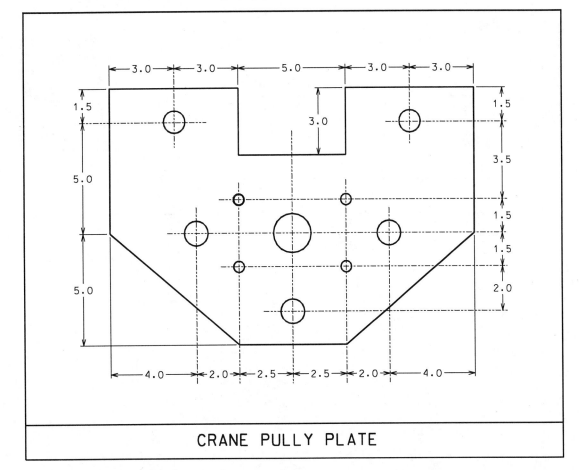

CRANE PULLY PLATE

Exercise 2–7 Pipe clamp.

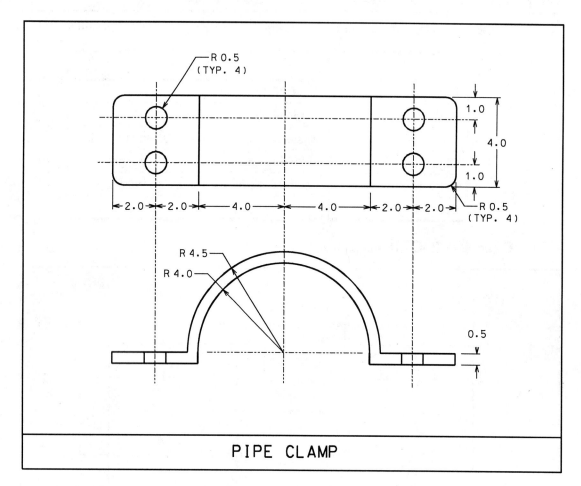

PIPE CLAMP

In Exercise 2–8, use the grid as a guide to drawing the diagram. The dimensions are provided to indicate the approximate size of the objects in the diagram.

Exercise 2–8   Flow diagram.

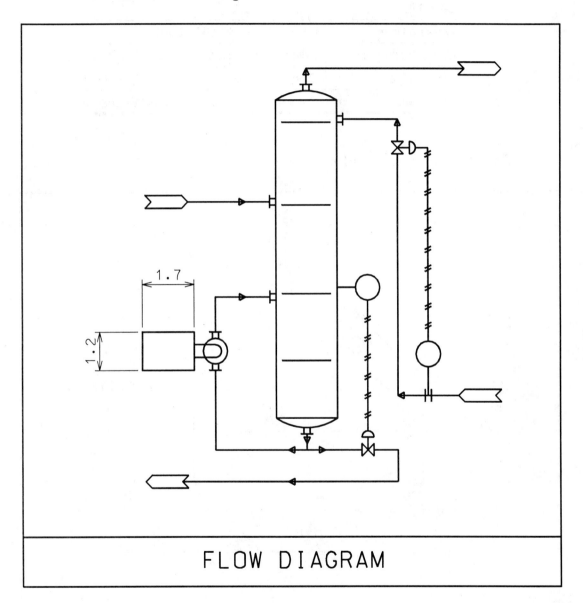

FLOW DIAGRAM

Use the following table to set up the design files for Exercises 2–9 and 2–10.

SETTING	VALUE
Seed File	SEED2D.DGN
Working Units	MU = ', SU = 12", PU = 8000
Object Elements	Color = 0, Level = 1, Style = 0, Weight = 1
Hidden Lines	Color = 0, Level = 1, Style = 3, Weight = 1
Centerlines	Color = 3, Level = 2, Style = 6, Weight = 0

Exercise 2–9   Foundation plan.

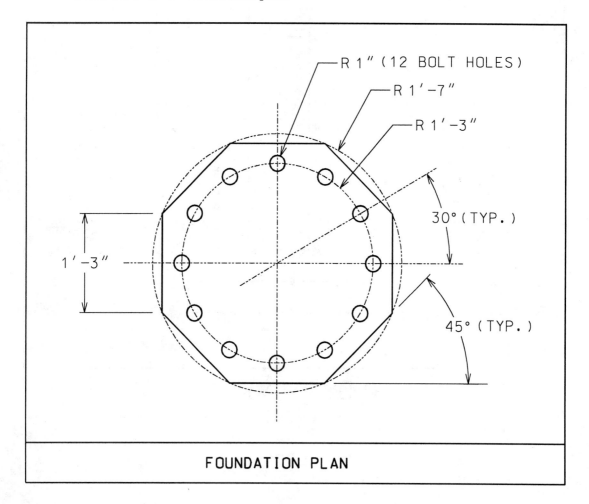

FOUNDATION PLAN

Exercise 2–10 Shop floor plan.

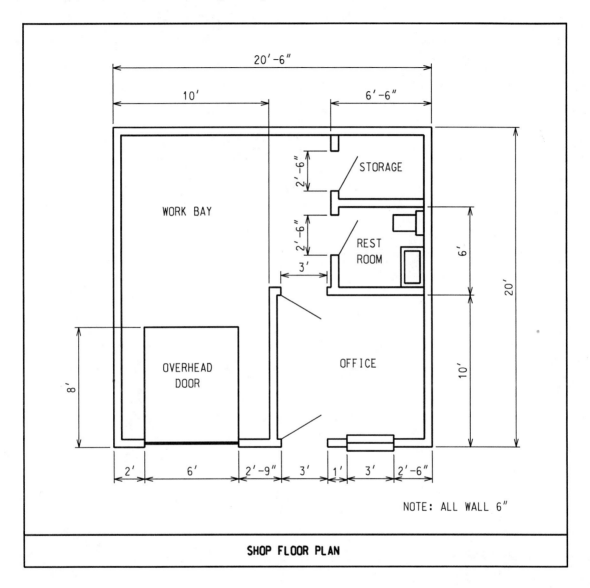

SHOP FLOOR PLAN

OBJECTIVES

After completing this chapter, you will be able to:

✓ Draw ellipses, polygons, point curves, curve streams, and multi-lines.

✓ Modify elements: fillets, chamfers, trim, and partial delete.

✓ Manipulate elements: move, copy, move and copy parallel, scale original and copy, rotate original and copy, mirror original and copy, and array.

✓ Use the Undo and Redo commands.

✓ Place text: via text parameters and by origin.

PLACEMENT COMMANDS

In this chapter, four more placement commands are explained: Ellipse, Curve (Place Point Curve and Place Curve Stream), and Multi-line commands. This adds to the placement commands already described in Chapter 2.

Place Ellipse

MicroStation offers two different methods for drawing an ellipse: Place Ellipse by Center and Edge and Place Ellipse by Edge Points. The appropriate method is selected from the Method option menu located in the Tool Settings window.

Place Ellipse By Center and Edge The Place Ellipse By Center and Edge tool lets you draw an ellipse by defining three points: the center point, one end of the primary (major) axis, and one end of the secondary (minor) axis.

Invoke the Place Ellipse By Center and Edge command from:

Ellipses tool box	Select the Place Ellipse tool and Center from the Method option menu located in the Tool Settings window (see Figure 3–1).
Key-in window	**Place Ellipse Center Constrained** (or **pl el ce co**) ENTER

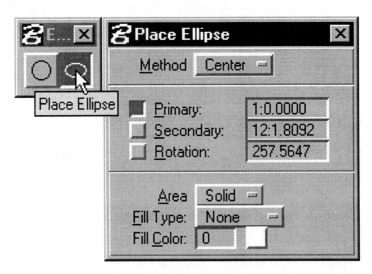

FIGURE 3–1   Invoking the Place Ellipse By Center and Edge command from the Ellipses tool box.

MicroStation prompts:

> Place Ellipse By Center and Edge > Identify Ellipse Center *(Place a data point or key-in coordinates to define the center of the ellipse.)*
> Place Ellipse By Center and Edge > Identify Ellipse Primary Radius *(Place a data point or key-in coordinates to define the one end of the primary axis.)*
> Place Ellipse By Center and Edge > Identify Ellipse Secondary Radius *(Place a data point or key-in coordinates to define the one end of the secondary axis.)*

For example, the following command sequence shows how to place an ellipse with the Place Ellipse by Center and Edge command (see Figure 3–2).

> Place Ellipse By Center and Edge > Identify Ellipse Center **XY=3,2** ⏎ENTER
> Place Ellipse By Center and Edge > Identify Ellipse Primary Radius **DL=2,0** ⏎ENTER
> Place Ellipse By Center and Edge > Identify Ellipse Secondary Radius **XY=3,3** ⏎ENTER

You can also place an ellipse by center and edge by keying-in the primary radius (constrained). To do so, turn ON the toggle button for Primary and key-in the value in MU:SU:PU format and press ⏎ENTER or ⏎TAB. MicroStation prompts you to identify the Ellipse Center and the Secondary Ellipse Radius. Similarly, you can also constrain the Secondary Radius and Rotation by turning ON the toggle button appropriately, keying-in the values in the edit fields, and pressing ⏎ENTER or ⏎TAB. MicroStation prompts depend on the number of constraints turned ON. For example, if the Primary and Secondary Radius are preset, MicroStation prompts you to identify the center and rotation data points. If the Primary Radius, Secondary Radius, and Rotation are preset, MicroStation prompts you to identify the ellipse center point.

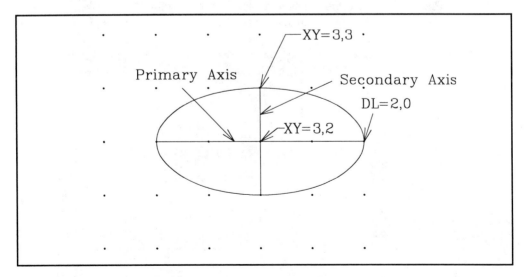

FIGURE 3–2   Example of placing an ellipse by means of the Place Ellipse by Center and Edge command.

Place Ellipse By Edge Points   The Place Ellipse By Edge Points tool enables you to draw an ellipse by defining three points on the ellipse.

Invoke the Place Ellipse By Edge Points command from:

Ellipses tool box	Select the Place Ellipse tool and Edge from the Method option menu located in the Tool Settings window (see Figure 3–3).
Key-in window	**Place Ellipse Edge Constrained** (or **pl el ed co**) ENTER

MicroStation prompts:

> Place Ellipse By Edge Points > Identify Point on Ellipse *(Place a data point or key-in coordinates to define the first point on the ellipse.)*
> Place Ellipse By Edge Points > Identify Point on Ellipse *(Place a data point or key-in coordinates to define the second point on the ellipse.)*
> Place Ellipse By Edge Points > Identify Point on Ellipse *(Place a data point or key-in coordinates to define the third point on the ellipse.)*

For example, the following command sequence shows how to place an ellipse with the Place Ellipse by Edge Points command (see Figure 3–4).

> Place Ellipse By Edge Points > Identify Point on Ellipse **XY=1,2** ENTER
> Place Ellipse By Edge Points > Identify Point on Ellipse **XY=3,3** ENTER
> Place Ellipse By Edge Points > Identify Point on Ellipse **DL=4,0** ENTER

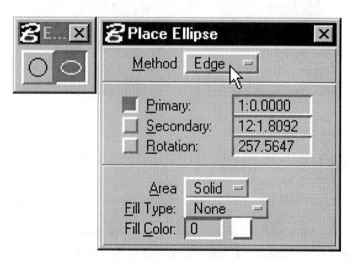

FIGURE 3–3   Invoking the Place Ellipse By Edge Points command from the Ellipses tool box.

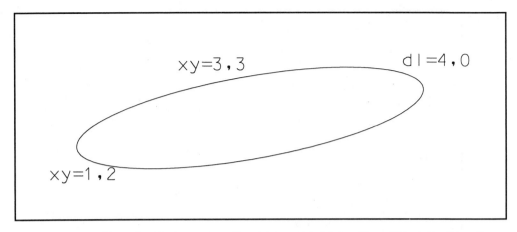

FIGURE 3-4 Example of placing an ellipse by means of the Place Ellipse By Edge Points command.

You can also place an ellipse by edge points by keying-in the primary radius (constrained). To do so, turn ON the toggle button for Primary, key-in the value in MU:SU:PU format, and press [ENTER] or [TAB]. MicroStation prompts you to identify the two edge points. Similarly, you can also constrain the Secondary Radius and Rotation by turning ON the toggle button appropriately, keying-in the values in the edit fields, and pressing [ENTER] or [TAB]. MicroStation prompts depend on the number of constraints turned ON. For example, if the Primary and Secondary Radius are preset, Micro-Station prompts you to identify an edge point and rotation data points. If the Primary Radius, Secondary Radius, and Rotation are preset, MicroStation prompts you to identify an edge point on the ellipse.

> **NOTE:** Similar to placing arcs, you can also place half and quarter ellipses. The commands are located in the Arcs tool box.

Place Polygon

You can place regular 2D polygons (all edges are equal length, all vertex angles are equal) with the Place Polygon command. The maximum number of sides is limited to 100. MicroStation provides three methods for placing regular polygons: Place Inscribed Polygon, Place Circumscribed Polygon, and Place Polygon by Edge. The appropriate method is selected from the Method option menu located in the Tool Settings window.

Place Inscribed Polygon The Place Inscribed Polygon tool places a polygon of equal length for all sides inscribed inside an imaginary circle (see Figure 3–5) having the same diameter as the distance across opposite polygon corners.

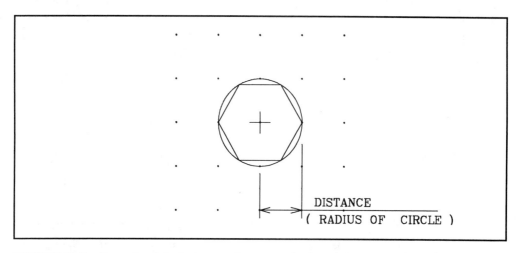

DISTANCE
(RADIUS OF CIRCLE)

FIGURE 3–5   Example of displaying a polygon inscribed inside an imaginary circle.

Invoke the Place Inscribed Polygon command from:

Polygons tool box	Select the Place Regular Polygon tool and Inscribed from the Method option menu located in the Tool Settings window (see Figure 3–6).
Key-in window	**Place Polygon Inscribed** (or **pl poly ins**) ⏎

Key-in the number of sides of the polygon and the radius of the imaginary circle in the Edges and Radius edit fields, respectively, located in the Tool Settings window. If you set the radius to 0, then you can define the radius graphically with a data point or you can key-in coordinates.

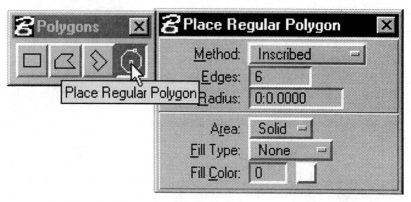

FIGURE 3–6   Invoking the Place Polygon Inscribed command from the Polygons tool box.

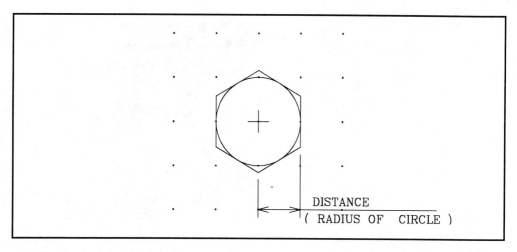

FIGURE 3-7   Example of displaying a polygon circumscribed around the outside of an imaginary circle.

MicroStation prompts:

> Place Inscribed Polygon > Enter point on axis *(Place a data point or key-in coordinates to define the center of the polygon.)*
> Place Inscribed Polygon > Enter first edge point *(Place a data point or key-in coordinates to define the radius of the imaginary circle, the polygon's rotation, and one vertex.)*

Place Circumscribed Polygon   The Place Circumscribed Polygon tool places a polygon circumscribed around the outside of an imaginary circle having the same diameter as the distance across the opposite polygon sides (see Figure 3–7).

Invoke the Place Circumscribed Polygon command from:

Polygons tool box	Select the Place Regular Polygon tool and Circumscribed from the Method option menu located in the Tool Settings window (see Figure 3–8).
Key-in window	**Place Polygon Circumscribed** (or **pl poly cir**) ⏎

Key-in the number of sides of the polygon and the radius of the imaginary circle in the Edges and Radius edit fields, respectively, located in the Tool Settings window. If you set the radius to 0, then you can define the radius graphically with a data point or you can key-in coordinates.

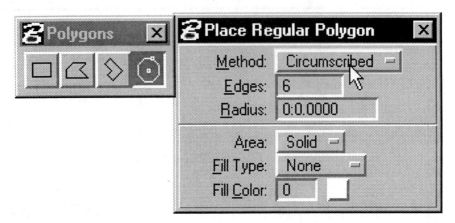

FIGURE 3-8 Invoking the Place Polygon Circumscribed command from the Polygons tool box.

MicroStation prompts:

> Place Circumscribed Polygon > Enter point on axis *(Place a data point or key-in coordinates to define the center of the polygon.)*
>
> Place Circumscribed Polygon > Enter radius or point on circle *(Place a data point or key-in coordinates to define the radius of the imaginary circle, the polygon's rotation, and one vertex.)*

Place Polygon By Edge The Place Polygon By Edge tool allows you to place a polygon by defining two end points of an edge of a polygon (see Figure 3–9).

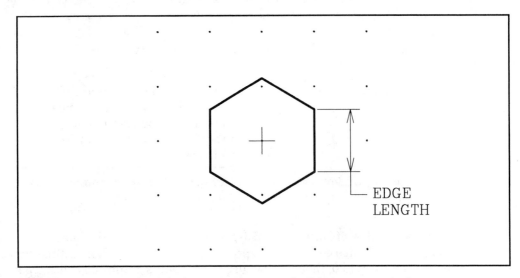

FIGURE 3-9 Example of displaying a polygon via the Edge option method.

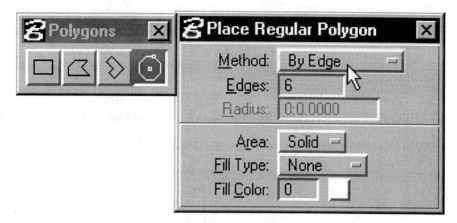

FIGURE 3–10   Invoking the Place Polygon by Edge command from the Polygons tool box.

Invoke the Place Polygon By Edge command from:

Polygons tool box	Select the Place Regular Polygon tool and Edge from the Method option menu located in the Tool Settings window (see Figure 3–10).
Key-in window	**Place Polygon Edge** (or **pl poly ed**) ⏎

Key-in the number of sides of the polygon in the Edges edit located in the Tool Settings window.

MicroStation prompts:

> Place Polygon by Edge > Enter first edge point *(Place a data point or key-in coordinates to define the vertex of the edge.)*
> Place Polygon by Edge > Enter next (CCW) edge point *(Place a data point or key-in coordinates to define the second edge point.)*

Place Point Curve

The Place Point Curve command can place a 2D (single-plane) curve element. This is accomplished by defining a series of data points the curve passes through. A curve element can have 3 to 97 vertices and is considered as one element. If more than 97 vertices are selected, MicroStation creates a complex chain consisting of one or more curved elements.

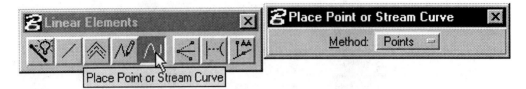

FIGURE 3–11   Invoking the Place Point Curve command from the Linear Elements tool box.

Invoke the Place Point Curve command from:

Linear Elements tool box	Select the Place Point or Stream Curve tool and Points from the Method option menu located in the Tool Settings window (see Figure 3–11).
Key-in window	**Place Point Curve** (or **pl po cur**) ⏎

MicroStation prompts:

Place Point Curve > Enter first point in curve string *(Place a data point or key-in coordinates to define the starting point of the curve.)*
Place Point Curve > Enter point or Reset to complete *(Place a data point or key-in coordinates to define the next vertex, or click the Reset button to complete.)*

At least three points are required to describe a curved element. Once you are through defining curve data points and/or key-in coordinates, press the Reset button to terminate the command sequence. See Figure 3–12 for an example of placing a curve by Place Point Curve command by providing five data points.

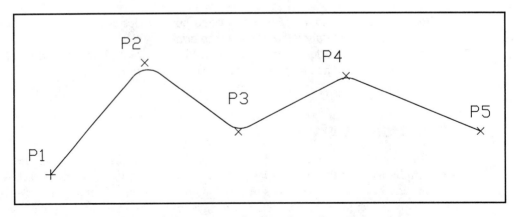

FIGURE 3–12   Example of placing an arc by Place Point Curve command.

Place Stream Curve

The Place Stream Curve command is used to place a curve stream that follows the movement of your cursor. As you move your input device, MicroStation records data points based on stream settings—active stream delta, active stream tolerance, active stream angle, and active stream area. A stream curve element can have 3 to 97 vertices. If more than 97 vertices are defined, MicroStation automatically creates a complex chain consisting of one or more curve elements.

Invoke the Place Curve Stream command from:

Linear Elements tool box	Select the Place Point or Stream Curve tool and Stream from the Method option menu located in the Tool Settings window (see Figure 3–13).
Key-in window	**Place Curve Stream** (or **pl cur str**) [ENTER]

MicroStation prompts:

Place Stream Curve > Enter first point in curve string *(Place a data point or key-in coordinates to define the starting point of the curve stream.)*

Place Stream Curve > Enter point or Reset to complete *(Move your cursor to define the curve stream. When you are finished, press the Reset button to complete the curve stream.)*

See Figure 3–14 for an example of placing a curve stream by means of the Place Curve Stream command.

FIGURE 3–13   Invoking the Place Stream Curve command from the Linear Elements tool box.

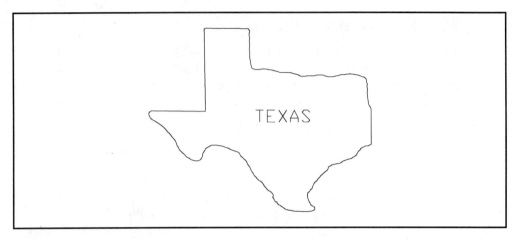

FIGURE 3-14 *Example of placing a curve stream by means of the Place Curve Stream command.*

Place Multi-line

With the Place Multi-line command you can draw multiple parallel line segments, which are considered as one element, similar to a curve drawn with the Place Point Curve tool. Multi-line can have as many as 16 separate lines of various line styles, weights, and colors, and the Place Multi-line tool allows you to draw a multi-line that is currently set as the active definition. If necessary, you can create or modify an existing multi-line definition with the help of the Multi-line settings box invoked from the pull-down menu Element. (Refer to Chapter 15 for a detailed description of creating or modifying an existing multi-line definition.)

Invoke the Place Multi-line command from:

Linear Elements tool box	Select the Place Multi-line tool (see Figure 3–15).
Key-in window	**Place Mline Constrained** (or **pl ml con**) ⏎

MicroStation prompts:

> Place Multi-line > Enter first point *(Place a data point or key-in coordinates to define the starting point of the multi-line.)*
> Place Multi-line > Enter vertex or Reset to complete *(Place a data point or key-in coordinates to define a vertex, or press the Reset button to complete.)*

Place Multi-line to a Specified Length To place a multi-line to a specified length, select the Place Multi-line tool in the Linear Elements tool bar and turn ON the

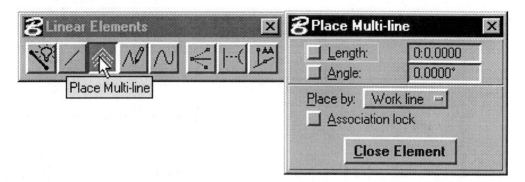

FIGURE 3-15 Invoking the Place Multi-line command from the Linear Elements tool box.

toggle button for Length in the Tool Settings window. Key-in the distance in MU:SU:PU in the Length edit field. The prompts are similar to those for the Place Multi-line command, and you can place any number of line segments of specified length.

Place Multi-line to an Angle To place a multi-line to a specified angle, select the Place Multi-line tool in the Linear Elements tool bar and turn ON the toggle button for Angle in the Tool Settings window. Key-in the angle in the Angle edit field. The prompts are similar to those for the Place Multi-line command, and you can place any number of line segments of specified angle.

If necessary, you can turn both of the toggle buttons ON for Length and Angle, and MicroStation allows you to place a multi-line with a specified length and angle constrained.

MicroStation has a set of tools to edit Multi-lines called Multi-line Joints. See Chapter 7 for details about using Multi-line Joints.

ELEMENT MODIFICATION

MicroStation not only allows you to place elements easily, but also allows you to modify them as needed. This section discusses four important tools that will make your job easier: Fillet, Chamfer, Trim, and Delete part of element.

Construct Circular Fillet

The Construct Circular Fillet tool joins two elements (lines, line strings, circular arcs, circles, or shapes), two segments of a line string, or two sides of a shape with an arc of a specified radius.

MicroStation constructs a circular fillet depending on the option selected from the Truncate option menu located in the Tools Settings window.

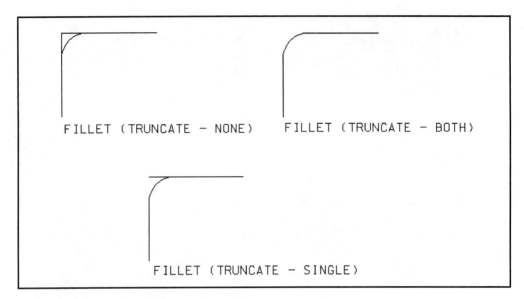

FILLET (TRUNCATE - NONE)   FILLET (TRUNCATE - BOTH)

FILLET (TRUNCATE - SINGLE)

FIGURE 3-16 *Examples of placing a fillet by three different truncate option methods.*

The None option places the fillet arc and at the same time does not truncate the selected sides. The Both option places the fillet arc and at the same time truncates at their point of tangency with the fillet. And the First option places the fillet arc and truncates the first side identified. See Figure 3–16 for examples of placing a fillet by the three different Truncate option methods.

Invoke the Construct Circular Fillet (no truncation) command from:

Modify tool box	Select the Construct Circular Fillet tool, key-in the Radius in MU:SU:PU in the Tool Settings window, and select None from the Truncate option menu located in the Tool Settings window (see Figure 3–17).
Key-in window	**Fillet Nomodify** (or **fill nmo**) [ENTER]

MicroStation prompts:

Circular Fillet (no truncation) > Select first segment *(Identify the first element or segment.)*
Circular Fillet (no truncation) > Select second segment *(Identify the second element or segment.)*
Circular Fillet (no truncation) > Accept-Initiate construction *(Click the Accept button to accept the placement of the fillet, or click the Reject button to reject the placement of the fillet.)*

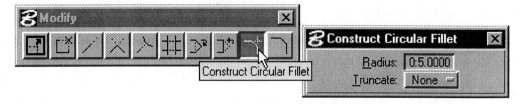

FIGURE 3–17 Invoking the Construct Circular Fillet (no truncation) command from the Modify tool box.

Invoke the Construct Circular Fillet (Truncate Both) command from:

Modify tool box	Select the Construct Circular Fillet tool, key-in the Radius in MU:SU:PU in the Tool Settings window, and select Both from the Truncate option menu located in the Tool Settings window.
Key-in window	**Fillet modify** (or **fill mo**) ⏎

MicroStation prompts:

    Circular Fillet and Trucate Both > Select first segment *(Identify the first element or segment.)*
    Circular Fillet and Truncate Both > Select second segment *(Identify the second element or segment.)*
    Circular Fillet and Truncate Both > Accept-Initiate construction *(Click the Accept button to accept the placement of the fillet, or click the Reject button to reject the placement of the fillet.)*

Invoke the Construct Circular Fillet (Truncate Single) command from:

Modify tool box	Select the Construct Circular Fillet tool, key-in the Radius in MU:SU:PU in the Tool Settings window, and select Single from the Truncate option menu located in the Tool Settings window.
Key-in window	**Fillet Single** (or **fill sin**) ⏎

MicroStation prompts:

> Circular Fillet and Truncate Single > Select first segment *(Identify the first element or segment.)*
> Circular Fillet and Truncate Single > Select second segment *(Identify the second element or segment.)*
> Circular Fillet and Truncate Single > Accept-Initiate construction *(Click the Accept button to accept the placement of the fillet, or click the Reject button to reject the placement of the fillet).*

Construct Chamfer

The Construct Chamfer tool is very similar to the Construct Fillet tool, but it allows you to draw an angled corner instead of an arc. The size of the chamfer is determined by its distance from the corner. If it is to be a 45-degree chamfer, the two distances have to be the same. The Construct Chamfer tool can help you to construct a chamfer between two lines or between adjacent segments of a line string or shape.

Invoke the Construct Chamfer command from:

Modify tool box	Select the Construct Chamfer tool, and key-in the appropriate Distance 1 and Distance 2 in MU:SU:PU in the Tool Settings window (see Figure 3–18).
Key-in window	**Chamfer** (or **ch**) [ENTER]

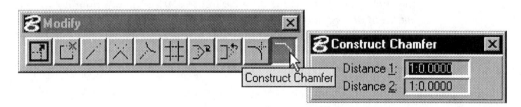

FIGURE 3–18 Invoking the Construct Chamfer command from the Modify tool box.

MicroStation prompts:

> Construct Chamfer > Select first chamfer segment *(Identify the first element or segment, as shown in Figure 3–19.)*
> Construct Chamfer > Select second chamfer segment *(Identify the second element or segment, as shown in Figure 3–19.)*
> Construct Chamfer > Accept-Initiate construction *(Click the Accept button to accept the placement of the chamfer, or click the Reject button to reject the placement of the chamfer.)*

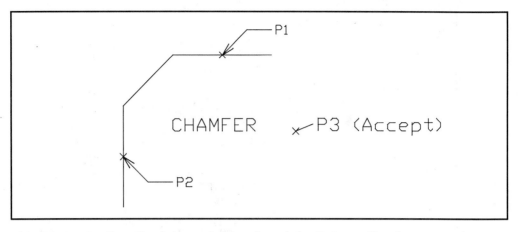

FIGURE 3-19 Example of placing the chamfer with the Construct Chamfer command.

Trim Elements

The Trim Elements tool changes the end point(s) of lines, line strings, arcs, curves, shapes, complex chains, or complex shapes. It removes the portion of the object(s) that extends past the cutting element. Any line, line segment, circle, or arc can be selected as a cutting element.

Invoke the Trim Elements command from:

Modify tool box	Select the Trim Elements tool (see Figure 3–20).
Key-in window	**Trim** (or **tri**) ⏎

MicroStation prompts:

> Trim Element > Select Cutting Element *(Identify the element to define as the cutting element.)*
> Trim Element > Accept, Identify Trim Element/Reject *(Identify the element to trim.)*
> Trim Element > Accept, Identify Trim Element/Reject *(Identify additional elements to trim, or click the Reject button.)*

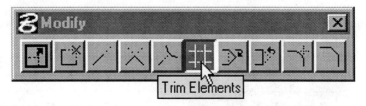

FIGURE 3-20 Invoking the Trim Elements command from the Modify tool box.

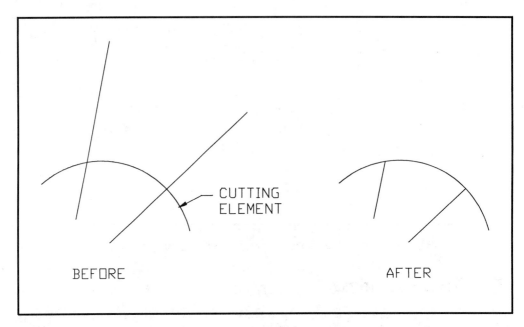

FIGURE 3–21 Example of trimming two lines via the Trim Elements command.

For example, the following command sequence shows how to use the Trim Elements tool to trim the two lines in Figure 3–21.

> Trim Element > Select Cutting Element *(Identify the cutting element.)*
> Trim Element > Accept, Identify Trim Element/Reject *(Identify the line to trim.)*
> Trim Element > Accept, Identify Trim Element/Reject *(Identify the second line to trim.)*
> Trim Element > Accept, Identify Trim Element/Reject *(Click the Reject button to terminate the command sequence.)*

Partial Delete

The Partial Delete tool allows you to delete part of an element. In the case of a line, line string, multi-line, curve, or arc, the Partial Delete tool removes part of the element, and the element is divided into two elements of the same type. Thus, a partially deleted ellipse or circle becomes an arc and a shape becomes a line string.

Invoke the Partial Delete command from:

Modify tool box	Select the Partial Delete tool (see Figure 3–22.)
Key-in window	**Delete Partial** (or **del p**) ⏎

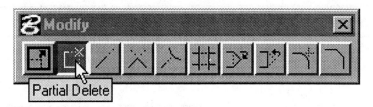

FIGURE 3-22 Invoking the Partial Delete command from the Modify tool box.

MicroStation prompts:

> Delete Part of Element > Select start point for partial delete *(Identify the element where you want to start deleting partially.)*
> Delete Part of Element > Select end point for partial delete *(Place a data point or key-in coordinates for the end point for partial delete.)*

If you identify a closed element (circle, shape, or ellipse) for the first data point, MicroStation prompts you for the direction of the partial delete before it prompts for an end point. The direction can be either counterclockwise or clockwise. See Figure 3–23 for examples of the Partial Delete command.

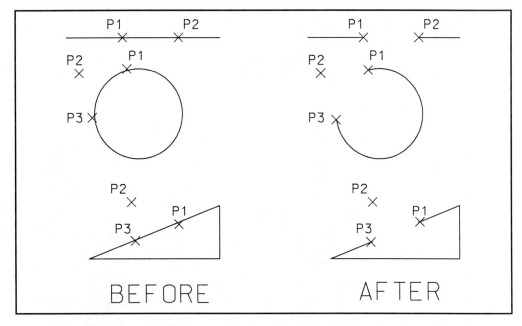

FIGURE 3-23 Examples of deleting part of an element by the Partial Delete command.

DRAWING EXERCISES 3–1 THROUGH 3–5

Use the following table to set up the design files for Exercises 3–1 through 3–3.

SETTING	VALUE
Seed File	SEED2D.DGN
Working Units	MU = IN, SU = 10 TH, PU = 1000
Grid	Master = .25, Reference = 4, Grid Lock ON
Object Elements	Color = 0, Level = 1, Style = 0, Weight = 1
Hidden Lines	Color = 0, Level = 1, Style = 3, Weight = 1
Centerlines	Color = 3, Level = 2, Style = 6, Weight = 0

Exercise 3–1 Machine part.

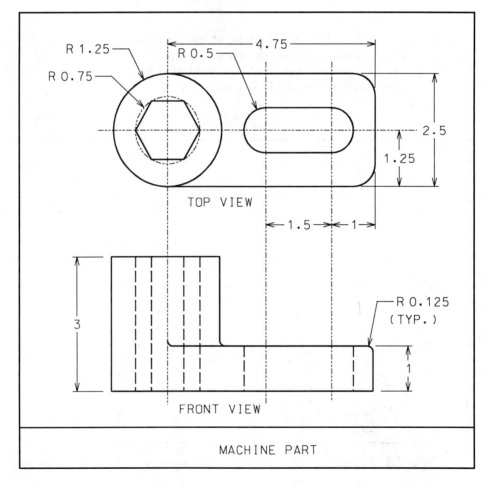

Exercise 3-2 Machine part.

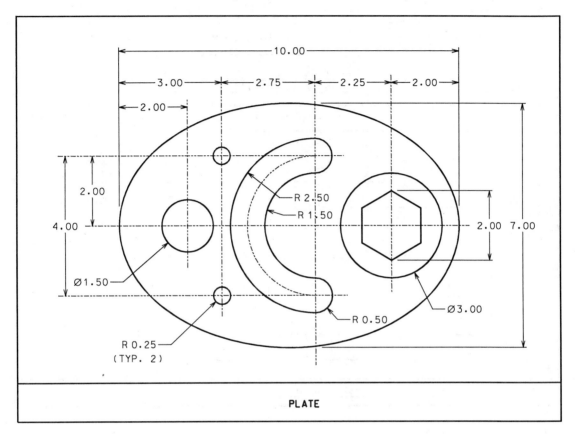

PLATE

Exercise 3–3 Beam clamp.

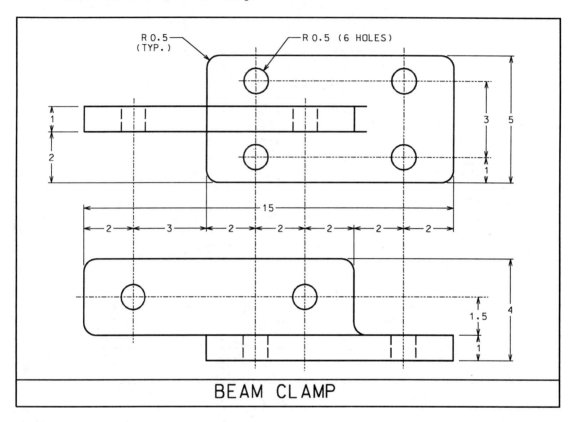

BEAM CLAMP

Use the following table to set up the design files for Exercises 3–4 and 3–5.

SETTING	VALUE
Seed File	SEED2D.DGN
Working Units	MU = ', SU = 12 ", PU = 8000
Grid	Master = .25, Reference = 4, Grid Lock OFF
Object Elements	Color = 0, Level = 1, Style = 0, Weight = 1
Grid Lines	Color = 3, Level = 2, Style = 6, Weight = 0

Exercise 3–4   Topography map.

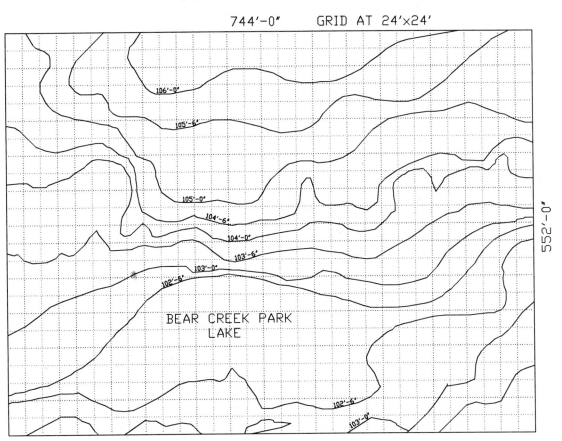

Exercise 3–5 Front elevation.

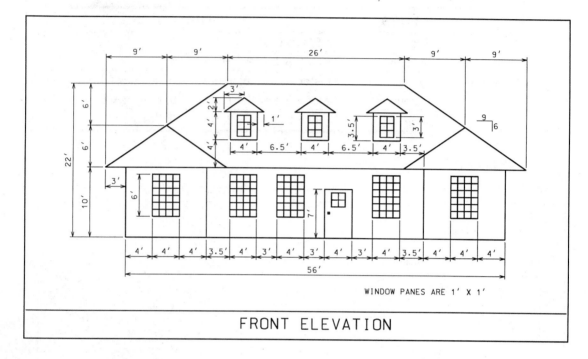

WINDOW PANES ARE 1' X 1'

FRONT ELEVATION

ELEMENT MANIPULATION

MicroStation not only allows you to draw entities easily, but also allows easy manipulation and modification of the objects you have drawn. To manipulate or modify an element is to make a change to one of its existing characteristics.

MicroStation offers two main categories of manipulation commands: single-element manipulation and multi-element manipulations. Single-element manipulation commands allow you to manipulate one element at a time, and multi-element manipulation commands manipulate groups of elements. This is done with Element Selection commands and Fence manipulation commands. This section discusses single-element manipulation commands. Multi-element manipulation commands are described in Chapter 5.

After mastering the element manipulation commands and learning when and how to apply them, you will really appreciate the power and capability of MicroStation. You can draw one element, then use the element manipulation commands to make copies quickly, saving you from having to draw each one separately. You will soon begin to plan ahead to utilize these powerful commands.

All the manipulation commands described here require you to identify the element to be manipulated, then to accept it. To identify an element, position the cursor until it touches the element and click the Data button. At this time the element highlights by changing color. If the highlighted element is the one you wanted to select, continue following the command prompts shown in the prompt field. If the element that is highlighted is *not* the one you wanted to manipulate, click the Reject button to reject the element and try again.

> **NOTE:** Be sure to check the status of your lock settings before you begin to modify your drawing. A good rule to follow is to turn OFF all of the locks that are not being used with the exception of the Snap Lock. It is very frustrating to try to select an element that does not lie on the grid when the Grid Lock is turned ON. The cursor bounces around from grid dot to grid dot, and it may be impossible to identify an element if it is not on the grid. It is simple to toggle the grid lock OFF quickly, identify the object, and then toggle the grid lock back ON again, if needed.

Move Element

The Move Element command allows you to move an element from one location to a new location without changing its orientation or size. The data point you enter to identify the element you want to move also becomes the (base) point on the element to which the cursor is attached. Select this point with care, and use the tentative snap if you need to snap to the element at a precise location (with the appropriate snap

FIGURE 3–24   Invoking the Move Element command from the Manipulate tool box.

mode selected). Once you have moved the element to an appropriate location, click the Reset button to terminate the command sequence. After clicking the Reset button, you can select another element to move, or you can invoke another command to continue working on your design file.

Invoke the Move Element command from:

Manipulate tool box	Select the Move tool (see Figure 3–24).
Key-in window	**Move Element** (or **mov e**) ENTER

MicroStation prompts:

Move Element > Identify element *(Identify an element to move.)*
Move Element > Accept/Reject (Select next input) *(Reposition the element to its new location by providing a data point or keying-in coordinates.)*
Move Element > Accept/Reject (Select next input) *(If necessary, move the element to another location by providing a data point or keying-in coordinates, and/or click the Reset button to terminate the command sequence.)*

For example, the following command sequence shows how to move a line to the center of a circle using the Move Element command (see Figure 3–25).

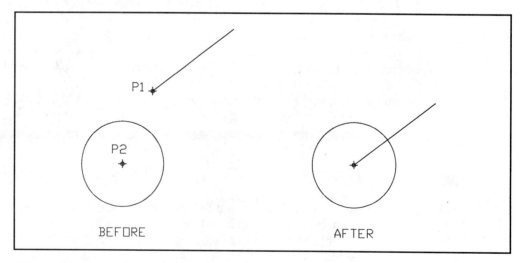

FIGURE 3–25   Example of moving an element with the Move Element command.

Move Element > Identify element *(Identify the line by snapping to the end point of the line.)*
Move Element > Accept/Reject (Select next input) *(Snap to the center of the circle.)*
Move Element > Accept/Reject (Select next input) *(Click the Reset button.)*

Copy Element

The Copy Element command is similar to the Move command, but it places a copy of the element at the specified displacement, leaving the original element intact. The copy is oriented and scaled the same as the original. You can make as many copies of the original as needed. Each resulting copy is completely independent of the original and can be manipulated and modified like any other element. The data point you enter to identify the element you want to copy also becomes the (base) point on the element to which the cursor is attached. Select this point with care, and use the tentative snap if you need to snap to the element at a precise location (with the appropriate snap mode selected).

You can place any number of copies in your design file. Once you are through placing copies, click the Reset button to terminate the command sequence. If necessary, you can select another element to copy, or you can invoke another command to continue working on your design file.

Invoke the Copy Element command from:

Manipulate tool box	Select the Copy tool (see Figure 3–26).
Key-in window	**Copy Element** (or **cop e**) [ENTER]

MicroStation prompts:

Copy Element > Identify element *(Identify an element to copy.)*
Copy Element > Accept/Reject (Select next input) *(Provide the location of the copy by a data point or by keying-in coordinates.)*
Copy Element > Accept/Reject (Select next input) *(If necessary, copy to another location by providing a data point or by keying-in coordinates, and/or click the Reset button to terminate the command sequence.)*

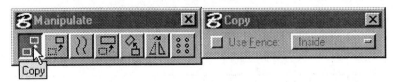

FIGURE 3–26   Invoking the Copy Element command from the Manipulate tool box.

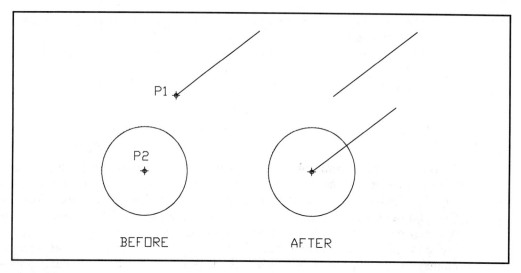

FIGURE 3–27   Example of copying an element by means of the Copy Element command.

For example, the following command sequence shows how to copy a line to the center of a circle using the Copy Element command (see Figure 3–27).

Copy Element > Identify element *(Identify the line by snapping to the end point of the line.)*

Copy Element > Accept/Reject (Select next input) *(Snap to the center of the circle.)*

Copy Element > Accept/Reject (Select next input) *(Click the Reset button.)*

Move Parallel

The Move Parallel command lets you move an element (such as a line, line string, multi-line, circles, curve, arc, ellipse, shape, complex chain, or complex shape) parallel to the original location of the element. The distance may be keyed in or defined by a data point.

Invoke the Move Parallel command from:

Manipulate tool box	Select the Move Parallel tool (see Figure 3–28).
Key-in window	**Move Parallel** (or **mov p**) (ENTER)

FIGURE 3-28   Invoking the Move Parallel by Distance command from the Manipulate tool box.

MicroStation prompts:

> Move Parallel by Distance > Identify element *(Identify an element to move parallel.)*
> Move Parallel by Distance > Accept/Reject (Select next input) *(Reposition the element to its new location by a data point or by keying-in coordinates.)*
> Move Parallel by Distance > Accept/Reject (Select next input) *(If necessary, move it to another location by providing a data point or by keying-in coordinates, and/or click the Reset button to terminate the command sequence.)*

For example, the following command sequence shows how to move a line to another location parallel to the original location using the Move Parallel command (see Figure 3–29).

> Move Parallel by Distance > Identify element *(Identify the line.)*
> Move Parallel by Distance > Accept/Reject (Select next input) *(Place a data point to move the element parallel to the original location.)*
> Move Parallel by Distance > Accept/Reject (Select next input) *(Click the Reset button.)*

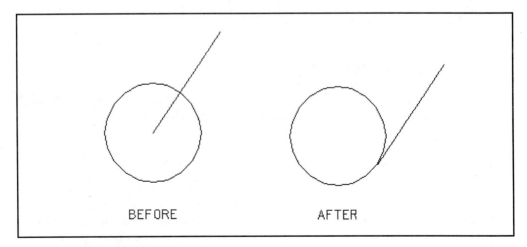

BEFORE   AFTER

FIGURE 3-29   Example of moving an element parallel via the Move Parallel by Distance command.

FIGURE 3–30 Invoking the Move Parallel Key-in command from the Manipulate tool box.

You can also move an element parallel by specifying a distance. To do so, invoke the Move Parallel command from:

Manipulate tool box	Select the Move Parallel tool, key-in the Distance in MU:SU:PU in the Distance edit field, and turn ON the toggle button in the Tool Settings window (see Figure 3–30).
Key-in window	**Move Parallel Keyin** (or **mov p k**)

MicroStation prompts:

Move Parallel by Key-in > Identify element *(Identify an element to move parallel.)*
Move Parallel by Key-in > Accept/Reject (Select next input) *(Reposition the element to its new location by a data point.)*
Move Parallel by Key-in > Accept/Reject (Select next input) *(If necessary, move it to another location by providing a data point and/or click the Reset button to terminate the command sequence.)*

Copy Parallel

Instead of moving the original element parallel, you can make a copy and then move the copy parallel to the original location of the element.

Invoke the Copy Parallel command from:

Manipulate tool box	Select the Move Parallel tool and turn ON the toggle button for Copy in the Tool Settings window (see Figure 3–31).
Key-in window	**Copy Parallel** (or **cop p**)

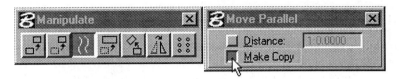

FIGURE 3–31   Invoking the Copy Parallel by Distance command from the Manipulate tool box.

MicroStation prompts:

> Copy Parallel by Distance > Identify element *(Identify an element to copy parallel.)*
> Copy Parallel by Distance > Accept/Reject (Select next input) *(Copy the element to its new location by a data point or by keying-in coordinates.)*
> Copy Parallel by Distance > Accept/Reject > (Select next input) *(If necessary, copy it to another location by providing a data point or by keying-in coordinates, and/or click the Reset button to terminate the command sequence.)*

You can also copy an element parallel by specifying a distance. To do so, invoke the Copy Parallel command from:

Manipulate tool box	Select the Move Parallel tool, key-in the Distance in MU:SU:PU in the Distance edit field, and turn ON the toggle button for Distance and Copy in the Tool Settings window (see Figure 3–32).
Key-in window	**Copy Parallel Keyin** (or **cop p k)** ⌨ENTER

MicroStation prompts:

> Copy Parallel by Key-in > Identify element *(Identify an element to copy parallel.)*
> Copy Parallel by Key-in > Accept/Reject (Select next input) *(Copy the element to its new location by a data point.)*
> Copy Parallel by Key-in > Accept/Reject (Select next input) *(If necessary, copy it to another location by providing a data point, and/or click the Reset button to terminate the command sequence.)*

FIGURE 3–32   Invoking the Copy Parallel by Key-in command from the Manipulate tool box.

Scale Element Original

The Scale command lets you increase or decrease the size of an existing element. If necessary, you can have a different scale factor for the X and Y axes. To enlarge an element, enter a scale factor greater than 1. For instance, a scale factor of 3 makes the selected element three times larger. To shrink an element, use a scale factor between 0 and 1. (Never give a negative scale factor.) For instance, a scale factor of 0.75 shrinks the selected element to three-quarters of its current size.

MicroStation provides two methods by which you can scale an element: setting an appropriate scale factor by key-in, and specifying the scale factor graphically.

Scaling by Key-in To scale an element by keying-in the scale factor, invoke the Scale Element command from:

Manipulate tool box	Select the Scale tool and Active Scale from the Method option menu, then key-in the appropriate scale factor in the edit fields (see Figure 3–33).
Key-in window	**Scale Element** (or **sca e**) ⏎

MicroStation prompts:

> Scale Element > Identify element *(Identify an element to scale.)*
> Scale Element > Enter origin point (point to scale about) *(Reposition the scaled element to its new location by a data point or by keying-in coordinates.)*
> Scale Element > Enter origin point (point to scale about) *(If necessary, scale it again by providing a data point or keying-in coordinates, and/or click the Reset button to terminate the command sequence.)*

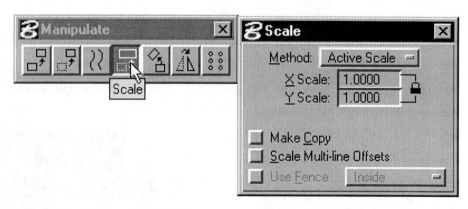

FIGURE 3–33 Invoking the Scale Element command from the Manipulate tool box.

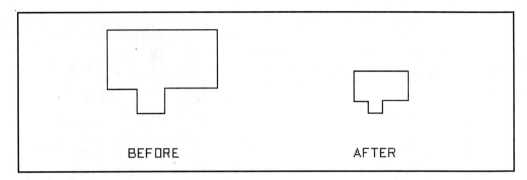

FIGURE 3–34 Example of scaling an element by means of the Scale Element command.

If you want the scale factor for the X and Y axes to be equal, then close the small lock located next to the scale factor in the Tool Settings window. When the lock is closed you can key-in a value in either of the edit fields and the other field is automatically set equal to what you key-in. If the lock is open, you can separately set the scale factors for the X and Y axes.

For example, the following command sequence shows how to scale an element to half its present size using the Scale Element command (see Figure 3–34).

> Scale Element > Identify element *(Identify the element to scale.)*
> Scale Element > Enter origin point (point to scale about) *(Reposition the scaled element to its new location by a data point.)*
> Scale Element > Enter origin point (point to scale about) *(Click the Reset button.)*

Scaling Graphically Scaling graphically involves providing three data points or keying-in their coordinates. The scale factors are computed by dividing the distance between the first and third points by the distance between the first and second points.

To scale an element graphically, invoke the Scale Element command from:

Manipulate tool box	Select the Scale tool and 3 points from the Method option menu (see Figure 3–35).
Key-in window	**Scale Points** (or **sca p**) ⏎

MicroStation prompts:

> Scale Element by 3 Points > Identify element *(Identify an element to scale.)*
> Scale Element by 3 Points > Enter origin point (point to scale about) *(Place a data point or key-in coordinates to define the origin point.)*

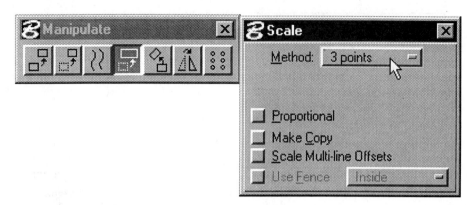

FIGURE 3–35 Invoking the Scale Element by 3 Points command from the Manipulate tool box.

Scale Element by 3 Points > Enter reference point *(Place a data point or key-in coordinates to define the reference point.)*

Scale Element by 3 Points > Enter point to define amount *(Place a data point or key-in coordinates to define the amount of scale.)*

Scale Element by 3 Points > Enter point to define amount *(If necessary, scale it again by providing a data point or keying-in coordinates, and/or click the Reset button to terminate the command sequence.)*

If necessary, to maintain the proportionality of the selected element you can turn on the toggle button for Proportional in the Tool Settings window.

Scale Element Copy

Instead of scaling the original element, you can make a copy and then scale the copy. Similar to the Scale Element command, MicroStation offers two methods by which to scale the copy: setting an appropriate scale factor by key-in, or specifying the scale factor graphically.

Invoke the Scale Element Copy command from:

Manipulate tool box	Select the Scale tool and Active Scale or 3 Points from the Method option menu, then turn ON the Copy toggle button (see Figure 3–36).
Key-in window	**Scale Element** (or **sca e**) [ENTER]

If the Active Scale method is selected, make sure to key-in appropriate scale factors for the X and Y scale edit fields. MicroStation prompts for Scale Element Copy are identical to the ones explained earlier for the Scale Element command.

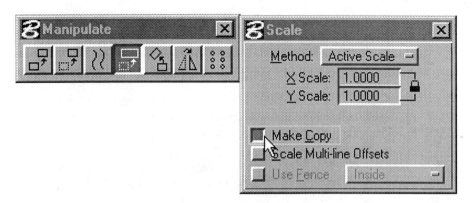

FIGURE 3–36   Invoking the Scale Element Copy command from the Manipulate tool box.

Rotate Element Original

The Rotate Element command changes the orientation of an existing element by rotating it graphically about a specified pivot point. MicroStation provides three methods by which you can rotate an element: rotation to the active angle setting, rotation defined by two data points, and rotation defined by three data points.

Rotation to the Active Angle Setting   To rotate an element by the current active angle setting, invoke the Rotate Element command from:

Manipulate tool box	Select the Rotate tool and Active Angle from the Method option menu, then key-in the appropriate active angle in the edit field (see Figure 3–37).
Key-in window	**Rotate Original** (or **ro or**) ⏎

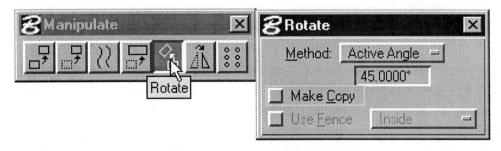

FIGURE 3–37   Invoking the Rotate Element command from the Manipulate tool box.

MicroStation prompts:

> Rotate Element > Identify element *(Identify an element to rotate.)*
> Scale Element > Enter pivot point (point to rotate about) *(Reposition the rotated element to its new location by a data point or by keying-in coordinates.)*
> Scale Element > Enter pivot point (point to rotate about) *(If necessary, rotate it again by providing a data point or keying-in coordinates, and/or click the Reset button to terminate the command sequence.)*

For example, the following command sequence shows how to rotate an element by 45 degrees from its present location using the Rotate Element command (see Figure 3–38).

> Rotate Element > Identify element *(Identify the element to rotate.)*
> Scale Element > Enter pivot point (point to rotate about) *(Reposition the rotated element to its new location by a data point.)*
> Scale Element > Enter pivot point (point to rotate about) *(Click the Reset button.)*

Rotating by 2 Points   Rotating by 2 Points is defined by entering two data points or by keying-in coordinates. The angle of rotation is computed from the two data points.

To rotate an element by 2 points, invoke the Rotate Element command from:

Manipulate tool box	Select the Rotate tool and 2 points from the Method option menu (see Figure 3–39).
Key-in window	**Spin Element** (or **sp el**) [ENTER]

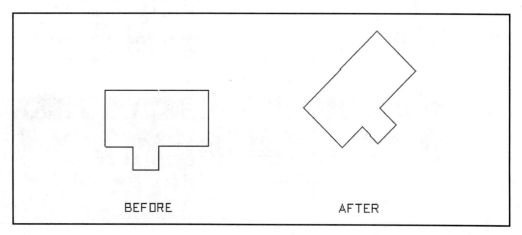

FIGURE 3–38   Example of rotating an element by means of the Rotate Element command.

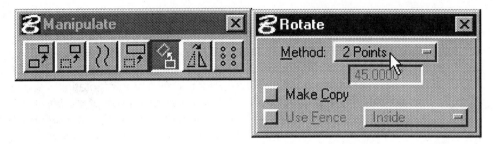

FIGURE 3–39   Invoking the Rotate Element by 2 Points command from the Manipulate tool box.

MicroStation prompts:

> Spin Element > Identify element *(Identify an element to rotate.)*
> Spin Element > Enter pivot point (point to rotate about) *(Place a data point or key-in coordinates to define the pivot point.)*
> Spin Element > Enter point to define amount of rotation *(Place a data point or key-in coordinates to define the amount of rotation.)*
> Spin Element > Enter point to define amount of rotation *(If necessary, rotate it again by providing a data point or keying-in coordinates, and/or click the Reset button to terminate the command sequence.)*

Rotating by 3 Points   Rotating by 3 Points is defined by entering three data points or keying-in their coordinates. The angle of rotation is computed from the three data points.

To rotate an element by 3 points, invoke the Rotate Element command from:

Manipulate tool box	Select the Rotate tool and 3 points from the Method option menu (see Figure 3–40).
Key-in window	**rotate points** (or **ro p**) ⏎

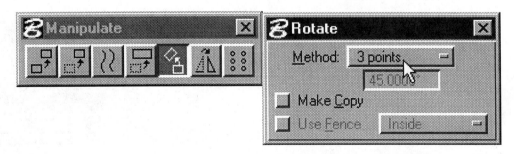

FIGURE 3–40   Invoking the Rotate Element by 3 Points command from the Manipulate tool box.

MicroStation prompts:

Rotate Element by 3 Points > Identify element *(Identify an element to rotate.)*
Rotate Element by 3 Points > Enter pivot point (point to rotate about) *(Place a data point or key-in coordinates to define the pivot point.)*
Rotate Element by 3 Points > Enter point to define start of rotation *(Place a data point or key-in coordinates to define the starting point of rotation.)*
Rotate Element by 3 Points > Enter point to define amount of rotation *(Place a data point or key-in coordinates to define the amount of rotation.)*
Rotate Element by 3 Points > Enter point to define amount of rotation *(If necessary, rotate it again by providing a data point or keying-in coordinates, and/or click the Reset button to terminate the command sequence.)*

Rotate Element Copy

Instead of rotating the original element, you can make a copy and then rotate the copy. Similar to the Rotate Element command, MicroStation offers three methods by which to scale the copy: rotating to the active angle, rotation defined by two data points, and rotation defined by three data points.

Invoke the Rotate Element Copy command from:

Manipulate tool box	Select the Rotate tool and Active Scale, 2 Points or 3 Points from the Method option menu, then turn ON the Copy toggle button (see Figure 3–41).
Key-in window	**Rotate Copy** (or **ro c**)

If the Active Angle method is selected, make sure to key-in the appropriate active angle in the edit field located in the Tool Settings window. The MicroStation prompts for the Rotate Element Copy are identical to the ones just presented for the Rotate Element command.

See Figure 3–42 for an example of rotating a copied element.

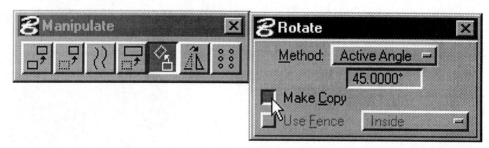

FIGURE 3–41 Invoking the Rotate Element Copy command from the Manipulate tool box.

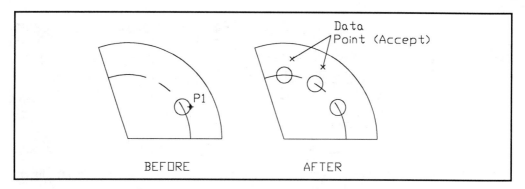

FIGURE 3–42   Example of rotating a copied element.

Mirror Element Original

The Mirror Element command creates a mirror (backward) image of an element. MicroStation provides three different methods by which you can mirror an element. Two of the methods are along the X and Y axes, and the third method is along a defined line (see Figure 3–43).

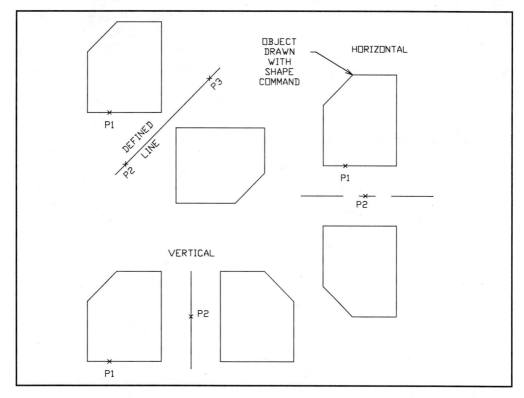

FIGURE 3–43   Examples of mirroring an element by three different methods.

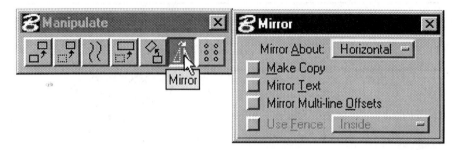

FIGURE 3-44 Invoking the Mirror Element command from the Manipulate tool box.

Mirror of an Element Along the *X* (Horizontal) Axis To place a mirror image of an element along the horizontal axis, invoke the Mirror Element command from:

Manipulate tool box	Select the Mirror tool and Horizontal from the Mirror About option menu (see Figure 3–44).
Key-in window	**Mirror Original Horizontal** (or **mi or h**) ⏎

MicroStation prompts:

> Mirror Element About Horizontal (Original) > Identify element *(Identify an element to mirror.)*
> Mirror Element About Horizontal (Original) > Accept/Reject (Select next input) *(Place a data point or key-in coordinates to place a mirror image of the element.)*
> Mirror Element About Horizontal (Original) > Accept/Reject (Select next input) *(If necessary, mirror it again by providing a data point or keying-in coordinates, or click the Reset button to terminate the command sequence.)*

Mirror of an Element Along the *Y* (Vertical) Axis To place a mirror image of an element along the vertical axis, invoke the Mirror Element command from:

Manipulate tool box	Select the Mirror tool and Vertical from the Mirror About option menu.
Key-in window	**Mirror Original Vertical** (or **mi or v**) ⏎

The prompts are similar to those just presented for mirroring an element along the X axis.

Mirror of an Element Along a Line To place a mirror image of an element along a line (defining two data points), invoke the Mirror Element command from:

Manipulate tool box	Select the Mirror tool and Line from the Mirror About option menu.
Key-in window	**Mirror Original Line** (or **mi or l**) ⏎

MicroStation prompts:

> Mirror Element About Line (Original) > Identify element *(Identify an element to mirror.)*
> Mirror Element About Line (Original) > Enter first point on mirror line *(Place a data point or key-in coordinates to place first point for mirror line.)*
> Mirror Element About Line (Original) > Enter second point on mirror line *(Place a data point or key-in coordinates to place second point for mirror line.)*
> Mirror Element About Line (Original) > Enter second point on mirror line *(If necessary, mirror it again by providing a data point or keying-in coordinates, or click the Reset button to terminate the command sequence.)*

Mirror Element Copy

Instead of mirroring the original element, you can make a copy and then mirror the copy. Similar to the Mirror Element command, MicroStation offers three methods by which to mirror the copy: along the X (horizontal) axis, along the Y (vertical) axis, and along a line defined by two data points.

Invoke the Mirror Element Copy command from:

Manipulate tool box	Select the Mirror tool and Horizontal, Vertical, or Line from the Method option menu, then turn ON the Copy toggle button (see Figure 3–45).
Key-in window	**Mirror Copy** (or **mi co**) ⏎

FIGURE 3-45   Invoking the Mirror Element Copy command from the Manipulate tool box.

The MicroStation prompts for Mirror Element Copy are identical to those just presented for the Mirror Element command.

See Figure 3–46 for an example of mirroring a copied element along a line.

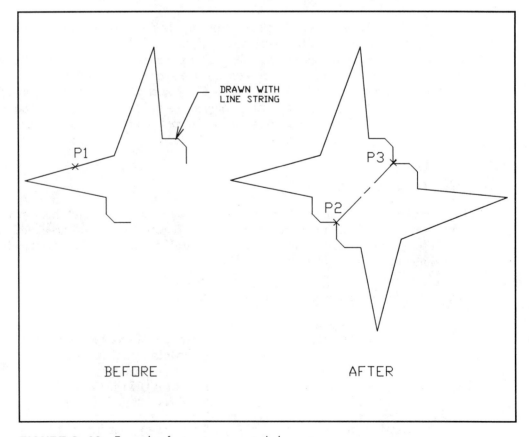

FIGURE 3-46   Example of mirroring a copied element.

Construct Array

The Construct Array command makes multiple copies of a selected element in either rectangular or polar arrays. In a rectangular array, you place copies in rows and columns by specifying the number of rows, the number of columns, and the spacing between rows and columns (row spacing and column spacing may differ). The whole rectangular array can be rotated to a selected angle. In the polar array, you place copies in a circular fashion by specifying the number of copies, the angle between two adjacent copies (delta angle), and whether or not the element will be rotated as it is copied.

Rectangular Array To place multiple copies of an element by rows and columns, invoke the Construct Array (Rectangular) command from:

Manipulate tool box	Select the Construct Array tool and Rectangular from the Array Type option menu (see Figure 3–47).
Key-in window	**Array Rectangular** (or **ar r**) ⏎

In the Tool Settings window, key-in: Active Angle in the Active Angle edit field; the number of rows and columns in the Rows and Columns edit fields, respectively; and the distance between rows and the distance between columns in the Row Spacing and Column Spacing edit fields, respectively.

MicroStation prompts:

> Rectangular Array > Identify element *(Identify an element to array.)*
> Rectangular Array > Accept/Reject (Select the next input) *(Click the Accept button to place copies, or click the Reject button to disregard the selection.)*

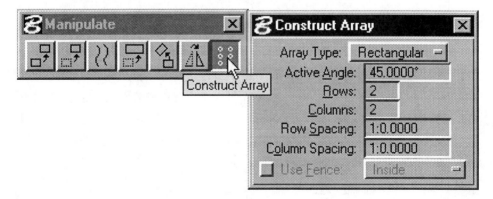

FIGURE 3–47 Invoking the Construct Array (Rectangular) command from the Manipulate tool box.

> **NOTE:** Any combination of a whole number of rows and a whole number of columns may be entered (except both 1 row and 1 column, which would not create any copies). MicroStation includes the original element in the number you enter. A positive distance for the column and row spacing causes the elements to array toward the right and upward. A negative distance for the column and row spacing causes the elements to array toward the left and downward.

The following command sequence exemplifies how to use the Construct Array command to place a rectangular array when the number of rows and the number of columns are set to 6 and 8, respectively, the row distance is set to 1.5 Major Units, and the column distance is set to 2.75 Major units (see Figure 3–48).

Rectangular Array > Identify element *(Identify the element.)*
Rectangular Array > Accept/Reject (Select next input) *(Click the Accept button to place the copies.)*

Polar Array To place multiple copies of an element in a circular fashion, invoke the Construct Array (Polar) command from:

Manipulate tool box	Select the Construct Array tool and Polar from the Array Type option menu (see Figure 3–49).
Key-in window	**Array Polar (or ar p)** ⏎

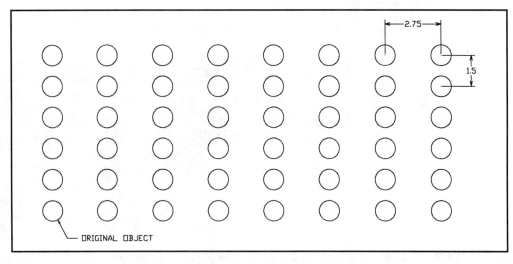

FIGURE 3–48 Example of placing a rectangular array.

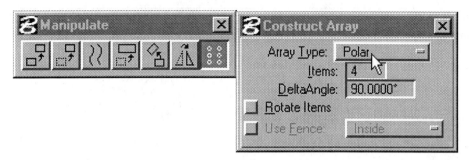

FIGURE 3–49 Invoking the Construct Array (Polar) command from the Manipulate tool box.

In the Tool Settings window, key-in the required number of copies of the selected element in the Items edit field, and specify the angle between adjacent items in the Delta Angle edit field. To rotate the elements as they are copied, toggle the Rotate button to ON. Figure 3–50 shows the difference between rotating and not rotating the elements as they are copied. Once you set all the necessary parameters, Micro-Station prompts:

Polar Array > Identify element *(Identify an element to array.)*
Polar Array > Accept, select center/Reject *(Specify the center point for the array by pressing the Data button or by keying-in coordinates, or click the Reject button to disregard the selection.)*

> **NOTE:** Key-in a whole number for the number of items to be copied, and MicroStation includes the original element in the number of array items. In other words, if you request seven items, your array will consist of the original element and six copies.

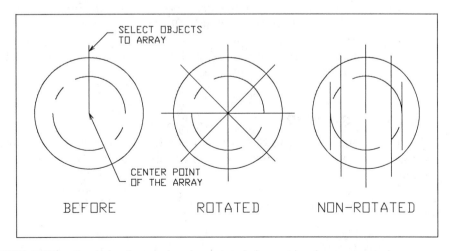

FIGURE 3–50 Example of rotated and unrotated elements as they are copied.

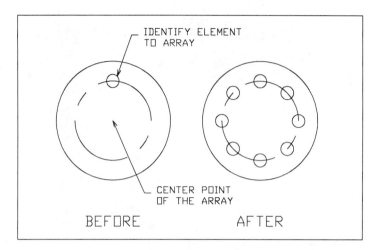

FIGURE 3–51   Example of placing a polar array.

The following command sequence shows an example (see Figure 3–51) of using the Construct Array command to place a polar array when the number of items is set to 8 and the delta angle is set to 45 degrees. MicroStation prompts:

Polar Array > Identify element *(Identify the shape.)*
Polar Array > Accept, select center/Reject *(Place a tentative point at the center of the circle and accept it.)*

UNDO AND REDO

The Undo command undoes the effects of the previous command or group of commands, depending on the option employed. The Redo command is a one-time reversal of the effects of the previous Undo. Commands can be undone because all steps required for each command you use are stored in an Undo buffer in your computer's RAM. The Undo command goes to that buffer to get the information necessary to put things back the way they were before the command was issued. The last command you executed is the first one undone, the next-to-last command is the next one undone, and so on.

Undo Command

The Undo command permits you to select the last command or a marked group of prior commands for undoing. To undo the last operation, invoke the Undo command from:

Standard tool box	Select the Undo tool (see Figure 3–52).
Key-in window	**Undo** (or **und**) ⏎

FIGURE 3–52   Invoking the Undo command from the Standard tool box.

To negate the last drawing operation, you can also select the Undo (action) option in the pull-down menu Edit. MicroStation displays the name of the last command operation that was performed in the pull-down menu Edit in place of (action). When you select the command, MicroStation negates the last drawing operation.

Set Mark and Undo Mark   If you are at a point in the editing session at which you want to experiment but you want to be able to undo the experiment, then you place a mark in the design before you start.

To place a mark, invoke the Set Mark command from:

Pull-down menu	Edit > Set Mark (or ⎇ + **E, M**)
Key-in window	**Mark** (or **mar**) ⏎

To undo all the steps back to when the mark was placed, invoke the Undo Mark command from:

Pull-down menu	Edit > Undo Other > To Mark (or ⎇ + **E, H**)
Key-in window	**Undo Mark** (or **und m**) ⏎

All the commands after the mark was placed are undone.

Undo All   The Undo All command lets you negate all of the drawing operations recorded in the Undo buffer. Think twice before you invoke this command.

To undo all the drawing operations recorded in the Undo buffer, invoke the Undo All command from:

Pull-down menu	Edit > Undo Other > All (or ⎇ + **E, H, A**)
Key-in window	**Undo All** (or **und a**) ⏎

MicroStation displays an alert box warning you that it will undo all of the drawing operations recorded in the Undo buffer. If you are not sure you want that to happen, just cancel the command.

Redo Command

The Redo command permits one reversal of a prior Undo command. It undoes the last undo. To undo the undo, the Redo command should be invoked immediately after the Undo command. You can redo a series of negated operations by repeatedly choosing Redo.

To redo an undo, invoke the Redo command from:

Standard tool box	Select the Redo tool (see Figure 3–53).
Key-in window	**Redo** ⏎

FIGURE 3–53 Invoking the Redo command from the Standard tool box.

Things to Consider Before Undoing

Following are the points to consider before invoking the Undo or Redo commands.

- The Undo buffer resides in your computer's RAM; this buffer is limited in size. If you have issued more commands than the buffer can hold, the oldest commands can no longer be undone. For example, if the buffer can hold only information for 100 commands, you can undo only the last 100 commands. Compressing the design (from the pull-down menu File) clears the Undo buffer. No commands issued before the compress can be undone.
- Exiting from the design clears the Undo buffer. Commands issued in a previous editing session cannot be undone.
- The Undo commands back up through the Undo buffer. They are not always the best way to clean up a problem. For example, if five commands ago you placed a circle you want to get rid of, Undo forces you to undo the four commands issued after the circle placement to get to the circle. In this case, a better way to get rid of the circle is with the Delete Element command.
- When you use one of the Undo commands, you are undoing commands, not elements. If the command manipulated multiple elements, Undo undoes the manipulation of all of those elements. For example, the Fence commands can manipulate hundreds of elements at one time. If you undo a Fence Contents Delete command, you get back all the elements that the fence deleted.

TEXT PLACEMENT

You have learned how to draw the geometric shapes that make up your design. Now it is time to learn how to annotate your design. When you draw by hand on paper, adding descriptions of the design components and the necessary shop and fabrication notes is a time-consuming, tedious process. MicroStation provides several text placement commands and tools that reduce greatly the time and tedium of text placement.

The text placement procedure includes setting up the text parameters (size, line spacing, style, etc.), selecting a placement command, typing your text, and then placing it in the design. Each string of text you place is a single element to which all of the element and fence contents manipulation commands can be applied.

> **NOTE:** If you do not know how to type, you can place text quickly and easily after a period of learning the keyboard and developing typing skills. If you create designs that require a lot of text entry, it may be worth your time to learn to type with all 10 fingers. There are several computer programs that can help you teach yourself to type, and almost all colleges offer typing classes. If you have no time to learn proper typing, there is no need to worry—many "two-finger" typists productively place text in their designs.

Text Parameters

Before you can place text in your design, you have to make sure the text parameters, such as font, text size, line spacing, and justification are set up appropriately.

The Text settings box allows you to set the text parameters. Invoke the Text Settings box from:

Pull-down menu	E<u>l</u>ement > Te<u>x</u>t (or 🖮 + **L, X**) (see Figure 3–54).

MicroStation displays the Text settings box as shown in Figure 3–55.

The parameters that can be changed in the Text settings box are: font; text size (height and width); underlined and vertical text; text slant; line spacing and length; intercharacter spacing; justification; text angle; color, weight, and level; and whether the text attribute is set to ON or OFF. These are discussed next.

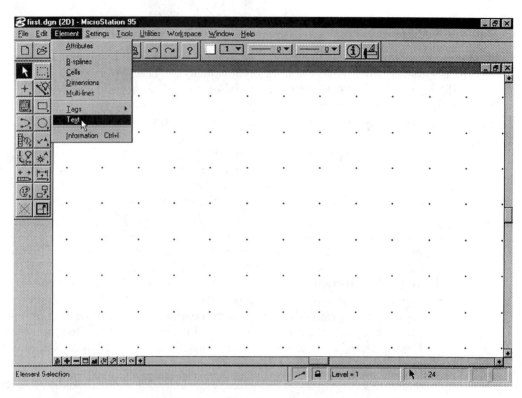

FIGURE 3–54 Invoking the Text settings box from the pull-down menu Element.

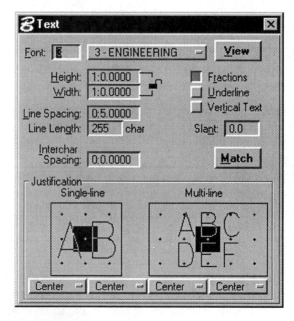

FIGURE 3–55 Text settings box.

Font Before you start placing text, you must decide what style (font) you want to use. Do you want fancy text, italic text, block text, or some other font? Text fonts are identified by numbers, and MicroStation can support up to 255 different fonts. To find out what fonts are loaded in your copy of MicroStation, click the View button in the Text Attributes settings box. MicroStation displays the Fonts settings box listing the available fonts (see Figure 3–56).

The top half of the Fonts settings box lists all the fonts loaded in MicroStation. Each line in the list area describes one font. Use the scroll bar to view all of the available fonts.

To see what a font looks like, click on the font's description line. An example of the font you click on appears in the bottom half of the settings box (see Figure 3–56). Some fonts lack lowercase letters, and some have no single-character fractions. If a font does not include one type of character, that type will *not* show up in the font example. The font description in the upper half of the Fonts settings box also tells you what types of characters the font contains.

Few fonts provide symbols rather than letters and numbers. When you select a symbol font, the letters you type produce symbols rather than the letters. For example, font 102 contains uppercase and lowercase letters that produce different symbols (such as arrowheads) rather than the letters.

To select a font, click on the font's description. MicroStation displays an example in the lower half of the Fonts settings box. Click in the lower half of the window to make the displayed font the active font. You also can select the font by keying-in at the key-in window **FT=<#>** (where <#> is the number of the font) and pressing ⏎. The selected font number becomes the active font.

FIGURE 3–56 Fonts settings box.

After you select a font number, MicroStation displays your selection in the Status bar. The font number you select remains the active font until you select another font number or exit MicroStation. To keep the font number active for the next time you edit the design, select Save Settings from the pull-down menu File.

Text Size After you have selected a text font, you must tell MicroStation what size you want the text to be, both height and width, specified in working units (MU:SU:PU).

If you are drawing an unscaled schematic, or if you are going to plot your design full size, selecting a text size is simple—just enter the size you want your text to be when you plot it.

If you are drawing a design that must be scaled to be plotted, selecting a text size is a little more complicated. As mentioned earlier, you draw objects in MicroStation full size (real-world size), and tell MicroStation what scale to use when it plots the design to paper. MicroStation scales down everything in the design to fit the size of paper you choose for plotting, including the text. Therefore you must scale up your text by the *inverse* of the plot scale so it will be the correct size when you plot.

For example, if you are creating a design that will be plotted at 1″ = 10′, and you want your text size to be .1 in., your text size in the design must be 1 ft (if 1 in. of plotter paper equals 10 ft, then .1 in. of plotter paper equals 1 ft).

Let's put that into a formula:

Text height in design = (design units ÷ plotter units) × plotted text size

Now let's try the formula for providing ⅛-in. text when we plot at ⅛″ = 1′. Our design units are 1 ft, our plotter units are ⅛ in. and we want our plotted text size to be ⅛-in.:

Text height in design = (1′ ÷ ⅛″) × ⅛″ = 1′

Thus, we need to place 1-ft. text size in the design.

To specify the text size, key-in the text height and the text width in the Height and Width edit fields, respectively.

There is a small lock symbol to the right of the text Height and Width fields. If you want your text height and width to be equal, click on the lock symbol to close the lock. When the lock is closed, you can key-in a value in either of the size fields and the other will automatically be set equal to what you type. If the lock is open, you must enter each field separately.

You can also key-in the text size in the key-in window by using one or more of the following key-ins:

TX= <size>   *(to set both the text height and the text width with one command)*
TH= <size>   *(to set only the text height)*
TW= <size>   *(to set only the text width)*

In each key-in command, replace <size> with the text size (in working units) and press ⏎.

Once you set the text size, it remains active until you either change it or exit MicroStation. Select Save Settings from the pull-down menu File to save the settings for the next time you load your design file in MicroStation.

Underline and Vertical Text   To place text with a line below it as shown in Figure 3–57, turn ON the toggle button for Underline in the Text settings box. Similarly, to place text vertical, as shown in Figure 3–57, turn ON the toggle button for Vertical text in the Text settings box.

Slant   To place text at a slant or angle as shown in Figure 3–57, key-in the slant or angle in the Slant edit field in the Text Attributes settings box. The slant or angle can be anywhere from –89 degrees to 89 degrees.

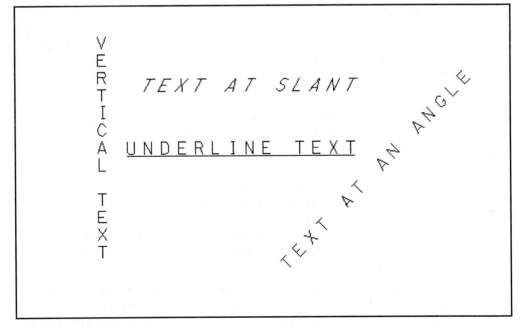

FIGURE 3–57   Examples of placing underlined text, vertical text, slanted text, and text at an angle.

Line Spacing and Line Length When you place text, it becomes one element in your design. While you are typing the text, you can press ⟦ENTER⟧ to create multi-line text that is treated as one element. If you plan to enter multi-line text, you must tell MicroStation how much space to leave between the text lines and the maximum number of characters you want on one line.

There are no firm rules for setting line spacing. But if you set it to a value less than half the text height, the lines may appear too close when plotted.

For the majority of text work, the maximum number of characters per line is not important; just leave it set at the default value of 255 characters (the maximum it can be). If you try to type more characters in one line of text than the maximum allows, the text will wrap to a new line at the maximum number of characters. (It wraps even if you are in the middle of a word.)

To specify the Line Spacing and Line Length, key-in the appropriate values in the Line Spacing edit field (in MU:SU:PU) and the Line Length edit field, respectively.

You can also key-in the Line Spacing and Line Length in the key-in window with the following key-ins:

> **LS=** <space> *(to set space between lines)*
> **LL=** <charc> *(to set the maximum characters per line)*

For <space>, key-in the line spacing in working units; for <charc>, key-in the maximum number of characters per line; then press ⟦ENTER⟧.

Once you set the Line Spacing and Line Length, these settings remain active until either you change them or exit MicroStation. Selecting Save Settings from the pull-down menu File saves the settings for the next time you load your design file in MicroStation.

Intercharacter Spacing When you place text along an element, MicroStation places each character in the text as a separate text element. To specify the spacing between two characters, key-in the value in MU:SU:PU in the Interchar Spacing edit field in the Text settings box. For additional explanation, see the section in Chapter 6 entitled "Place Text Along an Element."

Justification To place the text you typed in, first you have to define a data point in your design. Before you do so, you have to tell MicroStation where to place the text in relation to that data point. That relationship is called the justification. The Text settings box provides an excellent visual aid to setting up the justification (see Figure 3–58).

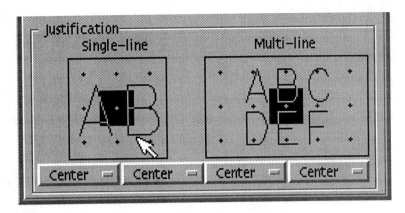

FIGURE 3-58 Text settings box showing the justification options.

In the window are two pictures of large text over a grid of dots. The text is displayed in the currently active font. The dark square in each picture shows the relation of the Data button to the text. The Text String picture on the left defines the justification when you place a single line of text. The Multi-line Text picture defines the justification when you place text that is longer than one line.

To set the justification, click on one of the grid points in the justification pictures, or select the justification from the sets of option menus below the pictures. Once set, the justification remains active until you either change it or exit MicroStation. Select Save Settings from the pull-down menu File to save the active justification for the next editing session.

The Multi-line Text justification also determines which side of the text will be smooth. Additional options available for justification in the Multi-line Text picture are Left Margin and Right Margin. These two justifications employ the Line Length setting that was discussed earlier. When you select a Left Margin justification, the right edge of the multi-string text is placed equivalent to the number of characters of Line Length from the data point. If a Right Margin justification is chosen, the left edge of the multi-string text is placed equivalent to the number of characters of Line Length from the data point.

> **NOTE:** A common mistake of inexperienced MicroStation users (and occasionally of experienced users) is forgetting that the outside settings set the Multi-line Text justification to margin. They click those thinking they are selecting left or right justification. If the line length is set to 255 characters, the results can be startling when the text is placed.

Angle Set the appropriate active angle to place the text string at an angle. This can be set by keying-in **AA**=<angle> in the key-in window. The default Active Angle is 0 degrees. See Figure 3-57.

Color, Weight, and Level Set the appropriate color, weight, and level to place the text. This can be done by invoking the Attributes settings box from the pull-down menu Element or from the Primary toolbar.

Text View Attributes There is one last thing to check before you start placing text in your design file. Make sure the Text view attribute is set to ON. This can be done by invoking the View Attributes from the pull-down menu Settings.

If the Text view attribute is set to ON, all text that is placed in the design will appear in the view; if it is set to OFF, all text disappears from the view. Updates may be completed faster when no text is displayed, but you must be careful not to use the space occupied by the text.

If the Fast Font view attribute is set to ON, all text is displayed in font 127, regardless of the font that was used to place it. Font 127 is a simple font that updates faster than other fonts. Text size is affected by font. So if you turn Fast Font to ON, the text may appear to take up more room than it does with its true font.

If the Text Nodes view attribute is set to ON, you will see a cross and a number placed at the data point of multi-line text strings. For the majority of your work, keep this attribute set to OFF.

Detailed explanation is provided for View Attributes in Chapter 5 and for Text Nodes in Chapter 6.

Place Text Commands

Following are the commands MicroStation provides for placing text.

- The Place Text at Origin command places text at the data point you define.
- The Place Fitted Text command scales the text to fill the space between two data points.
- The Place Text Above Element command places text above a line you have identified.
- The Place Text Below Element command places text below a line you have identified.
- The Place Text on Element command places the text on the identified line and removes the portion of the line where the text is placed.
- The Place Text Along Element command places text along a curved element.
- The Place Note command places text at the end of a line and arrowhead.

When you select one of these seven text placement commands, the Text Editor box is displayed, as shown in Figure 3–59. This box provides a place to type the text and some helpful text editing commands.

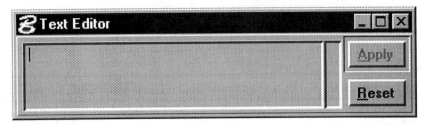

FIGURE 3–59 Text Editor.

If necessary, you can resize the Text Editor box so you can see more of what you are typing. Point to the box border, press the data button, and drag it to the new size.

To type text in the box, place the screen cursor in the box and click the Data button. When you see a text cursor similar to the cursor in a word processor you may start typing.

For multi-line text, press ⏎ at the place where you want the new line to start and continue typing. If you do not press ⏎, the text will wrap to a new line when you reach the right end of the Text Editor box, but all the text will be on one line when you place it in your design. You can place multi-line text only when you press ⏎.

The key-ins described in Table 3–1 position the text cursor within the text in the Text Editor box.

Table 3–1. Positioning the Text Cursor

PRESS:	TO MOVE THE TEXT CURSOR:
←	Left one character
→	Right one character
CTRL + ←	Left one word
CTRL + →	Right one word
HOME	To the beginning of the current text line
END	To the end of the current text line
↑	Up to the previous line of text
↓	Down to the next line of text
PG↑	Straight up into the first text line
PG↓	Straight down into the last text line
CTRL + HOME	Up to the beginning of the first text line
CTRL + END	Down to the end of the last text line

The key-ins described in Table 3–2 delete characters from the text in the Text Editor box.

Table 3–2.   Keys That Delete Text

PRESS:	TO DELETE:
BACKSPACE	The character to the left of the text cursor
DEL	The character to the right of the text cursor
SHIFT + **BACKSPACE**	All characters from the text cursor to the beginning of the word
ALT + **DEL**	All characters from the text cursor to the end of the word
CTRL + **BACKSPACE**	All characters from the text cursor to the beginning of the current line
CTRL + **DEL**	All characters from the text cursor to the end of the current line
Reset button in Text Editor box	All characters in the Text Editor box

The key-ins described in Table 3–3 select or deselect text in the Text Editor box. Selected text is shown with a dark background. Selected text can be moved, copied, or deleted.

Table 3–3.   Selecting Text with Key-Ins

PRESS:	TO SELECT (OR DESELECT IF ALREADY SELECTED):
SHIFT + ←	The character to the left of the text cursor
SHIFT + →	The character to the right of the text cursor
CTRL + **SHIFT** + ←	The characters from the text cursor to the left end of a word
CTRL + **SHIFT** + →	The characters from the text cursor to the right end of a word
CTRL + **A**	To select all text in the Text Editor box
← or →	To deselect all previously selected text

The pointing device actions described in Table 3–4 select or deselect text in the Text Editor box.

Table 3–4. Selecting Text with the Pointing Device

POINTING DEVICE ACTION	RESULT
Press the Data button and drag the screen cursor across the text	Selects all the text you drag across
Double-click the Data button	Selects the word the cursor is in
Hold down [SHIFT] + Data button and drag across the text	Adds more text to the text already selected
Click the Data button in an area where there is no text	Deselects all previously selected text

The actions required to replace, delete, and copy previously selected text are shown in Table 3–5.

Table 3–5. Replacing, Deleting, and Copying Selected Text

ACTION	RESULT
Start typing characters	Replace the selected text with the text you type
Press [BACKSPACE]	Delete all the selected text
Press [DEL]	Delete all the selected text
Press [CTRL] + [INSERT]	Copy the selected text to a buffer
Press [SHIFT] + [INSERT]	Paste the previously copied or deleted text at the text cursor position

In the next section, Place Text By Origin is explained. The remaining text placement commands are explained in Chapter 6.

Place Text By Origin The Place Text command places the text at the data point you define via the active text parameters (font, size, line spacing, line length, and justification), the active color, the active line weight, and the active angle.

You also can place multi-line text by pressing [ENTER] while typing the text in the Text Editor box. Remember that in the Text settings box there are separate justification fields for text strings (all the text in one line) and for multi-line text.

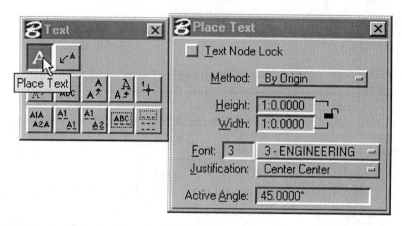

FIGURE 3–60 Invoking the Place Text (By Origin) command from the Text tool box.

To place text by origin, invoke the Place Text command from:

Text tool box	Select the Place Text tool and By Origin from the Method option menu (see Figure 3–60).
Key-in window	**Place Text** (or **pl te**) [ENTER]

Type the appropriate text string in the Text Editor. MicroStation prompts:

Place Text > Enter Text *(Place a data point in the design to indicate the text justification point.)*
Place Text > Enter more chars or position text *(Continue placing copies of the text in the design, change the text in the Text Editor box before continuing, or select another command.)*

Each copy of the text you place becomes a single element that can be manipulated like any other element. The only key point in a text string or multi-line element is the placement point. As you place the text, you can change any of the text or text attributes.

REVIEW QUESTIONS

Write your answers in the spaces provided.

1. The Place Polygon command places polygons that can have a maximum of _____ sides.

2. The Place Point Curve command is used _____ .

3. The Place Stream Curve command is used _____ .

4. The Multi-line command allows you to place up to _____ separate lines of various _____ , _____ , and _____ with a single command.

5. The Place Fillet command joins two lines, adjacent segments of a line string, arcs, or circles with an _____ of a specified radius.

6. Name the three methods by which you can control the removal of extension lines when placing the fillet.

   _____

7. The Chamfer command allows you to draw a _____ instead of an arc.

8. The purpose of the Trim command is _____ .

9. What is the name of the command that will delete part of an element? _____

10. Name the two categories of manipulation commands available in MicroStation.

    _____

11. The Copy command is similar to the Move command, but it _____ .

12. Name at least three element manipulation commands available in MicroStation.

    _____

13. To rotate an element, the key-in command is _____ .

14. The Array command can make multiple copies of a selected element in either _____ or _____ arrays.

15. List the four parameters you have to specify for a rectangular array.

    _____

    _____

16. Explain briefly the functions of the Undo and Redo commands.

_____

_____

17. The Text settings box is invoked from the pull-down menu _____.

18. Name three text parameters that can be changed from the Text settings box.

_____

_____

19. You can change the current font by keying-in _____ .

20. List the two key-ins that can change the text height and text width.

_____

21. Name the text parameter that controls the distance between two lines of text in placing multi-line text.

_____

22. With the current working units set to MU=1 in., SU=4 qt., and PU=1000, how would you set your text size to one-eighth of an inch?

_____

23. If a design is to be plotted at a scale of ½ inch equals 1 foot, what should be the text size in the design to plot at ⅛ inch? (NOTE: Working Units are set to feet, inches, and 1600 positional units per inch.)

_____

PROJECT EXERCISE

This project exercise provides step-by-step instructions for creating the design shown in Figure P3–1. The intent is to guide you in applying the concepts and tools presented in Chapters 1 through 3. (Note that the instructions are not necessarily the most efficient way to draw the objects. Your efficiency will improve as you learn more commands in later chapters.)

This project introduces the use of the following tools:

- Placement: Line String, Arc, Circle
- Manipulation: Mirror, Copy Parallel, Fillet, Array

> **NOTE:** The dimensions are not part of this project. They are included in Figure P3–1 only to show the size of the design.

> **NOTE:** As you complete each step in the project procedures, place a check mark by the step to help you keep up with where you are in the project.

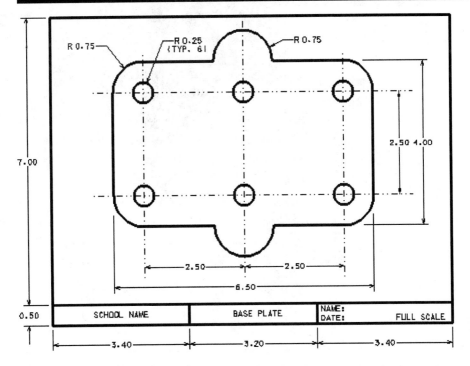

FIGURE P3–1   Completed project design.

Prepare the Design File

This procedure has you start MicroStation, create a design file, and enter the initial settings.

STEP 1: Invoke MicroStation by the normal technique for the operating system on your workstation.

STEP 2: Create a new design file named CH3.DGN using the SEED2D.DGN seed file.

STEP 3: In the Design File dialog box, set the Working Unit ratios to 1:10:1000 (see Figure P3–2).

STEP 4: Set the Grid Unit to .1 and the Grid Reference to 10, and turn OFF the Grid Lock (see Figure P3–3).

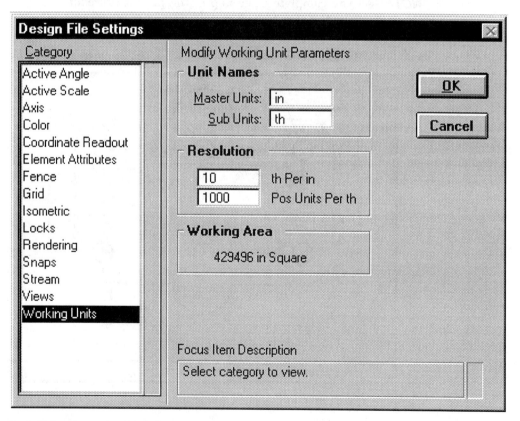

FIGURE P3–2 Set the Working Unit ratios as shown here.

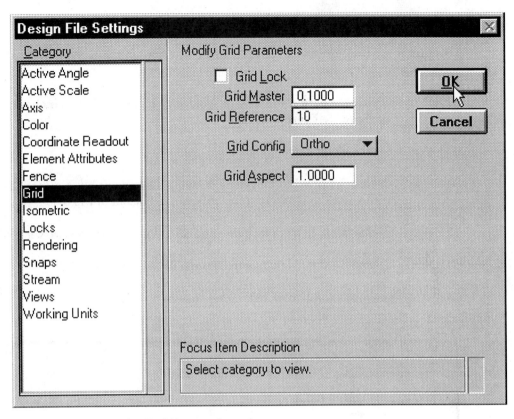

FIGURE P3–3 Set the Grid Units as shown here.

STEP 5: Click the Snaps icon in the Status bar, and select Keypoint mode by pressing [SHIFT].

STEP 6: In the Primary Tools tool box, set the Active Level to 10, the Color to blue, and the Line Weight to 2 (see Figure P3–4).

STEP 7: Invoke the Save settings from the pull-down menu File.

FIGURE P3–4 Set the element attributes as shown here.

Draw the Border and Title Block

This procedure presents the steps for drawing the border and title block, as shown in Figure P3–5.

STEP 1: Create the border by drawing a block 12 inches wide by 9 inches tall, with the lower left corner at **XY=0,0**.

STEP 2: Fit the view.

STEP 3: Create the title block area by drawing a horizontal line across the width of the block and one-half inch above the bottom of the block.

STEP 4: Divide the title block into three equal areas by drawing two vertical lines.

STEP 5: Invoke the Save settings from the pull-down menu File.

Compare your completed border to the one shown in Figure P3–5.

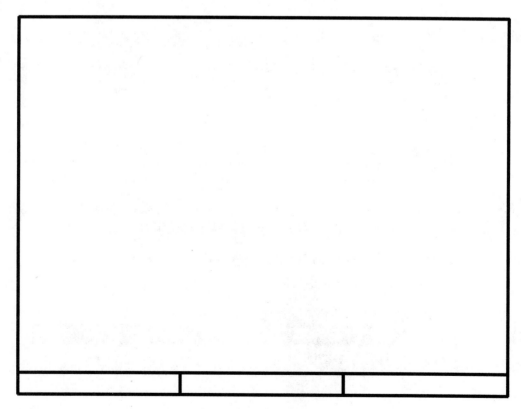

FIGURE P3–5 Border and title block before the title block text is entered.

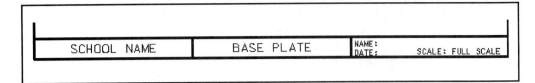

FIGURE P3–6   Filled-in title block.

Fill in the Title Block Text

This procedure has you place text in the title block, as shown in Figure P3–6.

STEP 1:   Change the Line Weight to 0.

STEP 2:   Open the Text settings box from the pull-down menu Element, and set the text parameters as shown in Figure P3–7.

STEP 3:   Invoke the Save settings from the pull-down menu File.

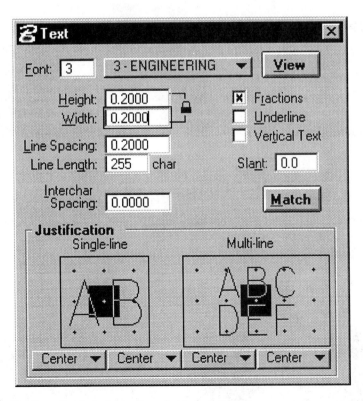

FIGURE P3–7   Enter the text parameters shown here.

STEP 4: Invoke the Place Text command from the Text tool box, and select At Origin from the Tool Settings window.

MicroStation prompts:

> Place Text > Enter Text *(In the Text Editor window type a school or company name, then place the text centered in the left title block area.)*
>
> Place Text > Enter Text *(Click the Text Editor Reset button, type* **BASE PLATE**, *then place the text centered in the center title block area.)*

STEP 5: In the Text settings box, set the Text Height and Width to 0.125, the Line Spacing to 0.1, and both justifications to Left, Top.

STEP 6: In the View Attributes settings box, set the Text Node view attribute to OFF.

STEP 7: Use either the Zoom In or Window Area command to zoom in close to the right title block area.

STEP 8: In the right title block area, place the text strings shown in Figure P3–6. Insert your name to the right of "NAME:" and today's date to the right of "DATE:".

STEP 9: Fit the view, and invoke the Save settings from the pull-down menu File.

Compare your completed title block to the one shown in Figure P3–6.

Draw the Center Lines

This procedure describes the steps required to draw one horizontal centerline and one vertical centerline, then, with the Copy Parallel command, creates the additional centerlines, as shown in Figure P3–8.

STEP 1: Set the Active Level to 2, the Color to green, the Line Weight to 0, and the Line Style to 6. Then invoke the Save settings from the pull-down menu File.

STEP 2: Place the top horizontal centerline 8 inches long starting at **XY= 2.25,6.25**.

STEP 3: Place the left vertical centerline 6.25 inches long starting at **XY=3.5,1.75**.

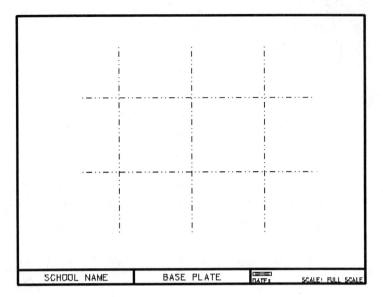

FIGURE P3–8 Completed centerlines.

STEP 4:   Invoke the Move Parallel command from the Manipulate tool box, set the Make Copy and Distance toggle buttons to ON, and key-in **2.5** in the Distance edit field in the Tool Settings window.

MicroStation prompts:

> Copy Parallel by Key-in > Identify element *(Select the horizontal centerline.)*
> Copy Parallel by Key-in > Accept/Reject (select next input) *(Click the Data button below the horizontal line, then click the Reset button to release the line.)*

STEP 5:   Make two parallel copies of the vertical line, each at a distance of 2.5 inches.

Compare your completed centerlines to Figure P3–8.

Draw Part of the Base Plate Outline

This procedure draws the left half of the base plate outline using the Place Line, Fillet, and Arc commands, as shown in Figure P3–9.

STEP 1:   Set the Active Level to 1, the Color to 0, the Line Weight to 2, and the Line Style to 0. Then invoke the Save settings from the pull-down menu File.

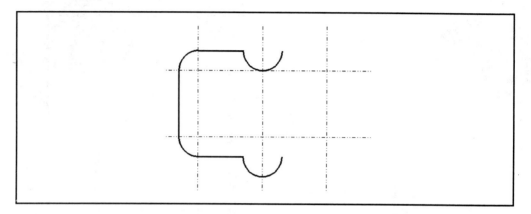

FIGURE P3-9 Result of drawing the left half of the base plate outline.

STEP 2: Place three lines using these precision key-ins (see Figure P3–10):

- **XY=5.25,3**
- **DI=2.5,180**
- **DI=4,90**
- **DI=2.5,0**

STEP 3: Invoke the Construct Circular Fillet command from the Modify tool box, then set the Radius to .75 and the Truncate option to Both in the Tool Settings window.

MicroStation prompts:

Circular Fillet and Truncate Both > Select first segment *(Select the bottom horizontal line that was drawn in Step 2.)*

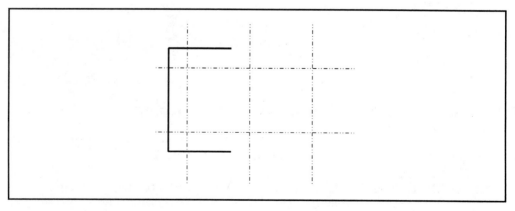

FIGURE P3-10 View after placing three lines in Step 2.

Circular Fillet and Truncate Both > Select second segment *(Select the vertical line.)*
Circular Fillet and Truncate Both > Accept-Initiate construction *(Click the Data button in space to place the fillet.)*

STEP 4: Place a 0.75-inch fillet at the intersection of the vertical line and the top horizontal line.

STEP 5: Invoke Place Arc from the Arcs tool box, select the Edge option from the Method option menu and set the Radius to .75, the Start Angle to 180, and the Sweep Angle to 180 in the Tool Settings window.

MicroStation prompts:

Place Arc By Edge > Identify First Arc Endpoint *(Keypoint Snap to the right end of the bottom horizontal line and place a data point.)*
Place Arc By Edge > Identify First Arc Endpoint *(Keypoint Snap to the right end of the top horizontal line and place a data point. Then click the Reset button.)*

Compare your completed left half to Figure P3–9.

> **NOTE:** The next procedure fixes the rotation of the top arc.

Complete the Base Plate Outline

This procedure uses the Mirror and Copy commands to complete the outline of the base plate, as shown in Figure P3–11.

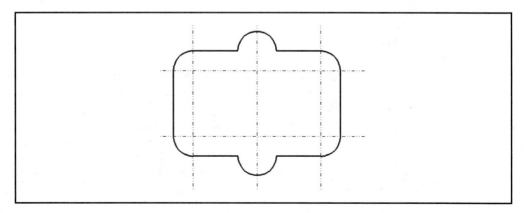

FIGURE P3-11 Completed base plate outline.

STEP 1:   Invoke the Mirror command from the Manipulate tool box, then set Mirror About to Horizontal and set the toggle button for Make Copy to OFF in the Tool Settings window.

MicroStation prompts:

> Mirror Element About Horizontal (Original) > Identify element *(Select the top arc.)*
> Mirror Element About Horizontal (Original) > Accept/Reject (select next input) *(Keypoint snap to the right end of the top horizontal line, place a data point, then click the Reset button to release the arc.)*

STEP 2:   Change the Mirror About option to Vertical, and set the toggle button for Make Copy to ON.

MicroStation prompts:

> Mirror Element About Vertical (Copy) > Identify element *(Select the top fillet.)*
> Mirror Element About Vertical (Copy) > Accept/Reject (select next input) *(Keypoint snap to the center vertical center line, place a data point, then click the Reset button to release the fillet.)*

STEP 3:   Mirror copy the bottom fillet to the right side of the base plate outline.

STEP 4:   Mirror copy the left vertical base plate line to the right side of the outline.

STEP 5:   Invoke the Copy command from the Manipulate tool box.

MicroStation prompts:

> Copy Element > Identify element *(Keypoint Snap to the left end of the top horizontal line in the base plate outline and click the Data button.)*
> Copy Element > Accept/Reject (select next input) *(Keypoint Snap to the right end of the top arc and click the Data button.)*
> Copy Element > Accept/Reject (select next input) *(Keypoint Snap to the right end of the bottom arc, click the Data button, then click the Reset button.)*

Compare your design to Figure P3–11.

Place the Bolt Hole Circles

This procedure uses the Place Circle and Array commands to place the bolt hole circles in the design, as shown in Figure P3–12.

STEP 1:   Click the Snaps icon in the Status bar, and select Intersection mode by pressing SHIFT.

STEP 2:   Invoke the Place Circle command from the Ellipse tool box, select the Radius placement method, and key-in .25 in the Radius edit field in the Tool Settings window.

MicroStation prompts:

Place Circle by Center > Identify Center Point *(Tentative snap at the intersection of the vertical centerline and the lower horizontal centerline, and click the Accept button to place the circle as shown in Figure P3–13. Then click the Reset button.)*

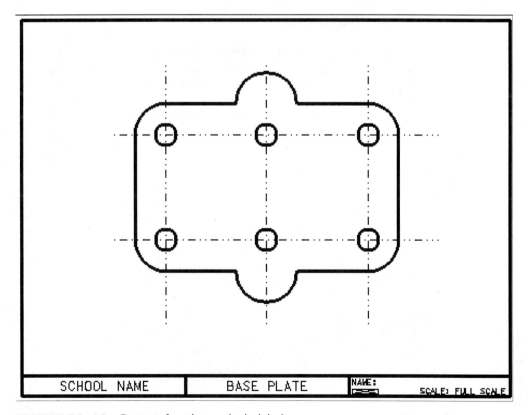

FIGURE P3–12   Design after placing the bolt holes.

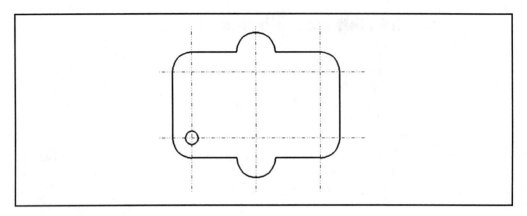

FIGURE P3-13   A circle is placed on the lower left center intersection.

STEP 3:   Invoke the Construct Array command from the Manipulate tool box, then set the Array Type to Rectangular, the Active Angle to 0, Rows to 2, Columns to 3, and the Row and Column Spacing to 2.5 in the Tool Settings window.

MicroStation prompts:

> Rectangular Array > Identify element *(Select the circle.)*
> Rectangular Array > Accept/Reject (select next input) *(Click the Data button in space to initiate construction of the array.)*

STEP 4:   Invoke the Save settings from the pull-down menu File.

Compare your design to Figure P3–12.

DRAWING EXERCISES 3-6 THROUGH 3-10

Use the following table to set up the design files for Exercises 3–6 through 3–9.

SETTING	VALUE
Seed File	SEED2D.DGN
Working Units	MU = IN, SU = 10 TH, PU = 1000
Grid	Master = .1, Reference = 10, Grid Lock ON
Object Elements	Color = 0, Level = 1, Style = 0, Weight = 1
Center Lines	Color = 3, Level = 2, Style = 6, Weight = 0

For Figures 3–6 and 3–7, set the Font to 3 and the Text Height and Width to 0.125″.

Exercise 3–6 Organization chart.

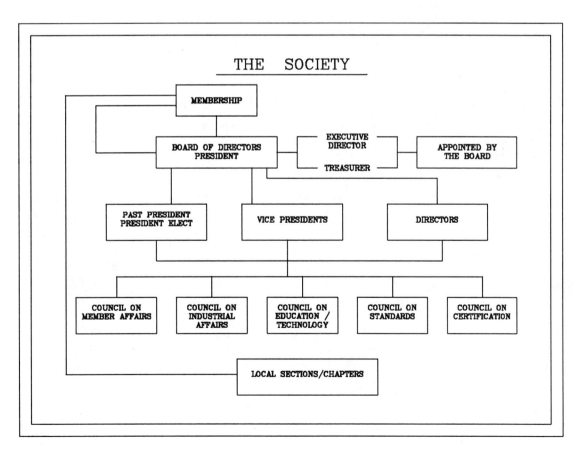

Exercise 3–7 Schematic diagram.

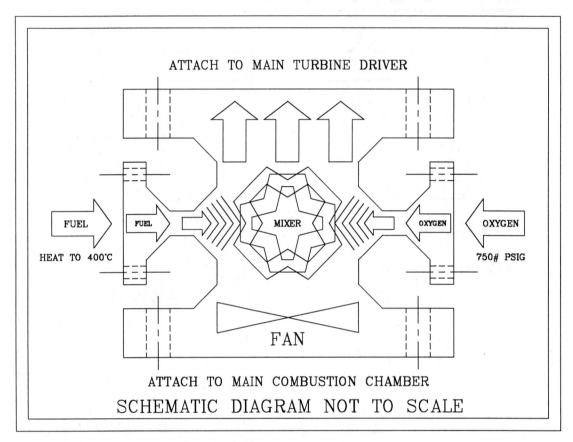

In the following exercises, do not draw the dimensions.

Exercise 3–8   Flange gasket.

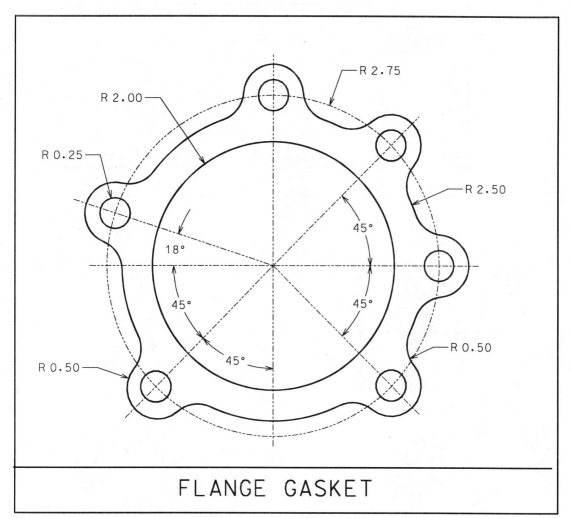

FLANGE GASKET

Exercise 3-9   Machine parts.

SETTING	VALUE
Seed File	SEED2D.DGN
Working Units	MU = mm, SU = 1, PU = 10000
Grid	Master = 1, Reference = 10, Grid Lock OFF
Object Elements	Color = 0, Level = 1, Style = 0, Weight = 1
Hidden Elements	Color = 0, Level = 2, Style = 3, Weight = 1
Center Elements	Color = 1, Level = 3, Style = 6, Weight = 0
Text	Font = 3, Text Height, Width, and Spacing = 3

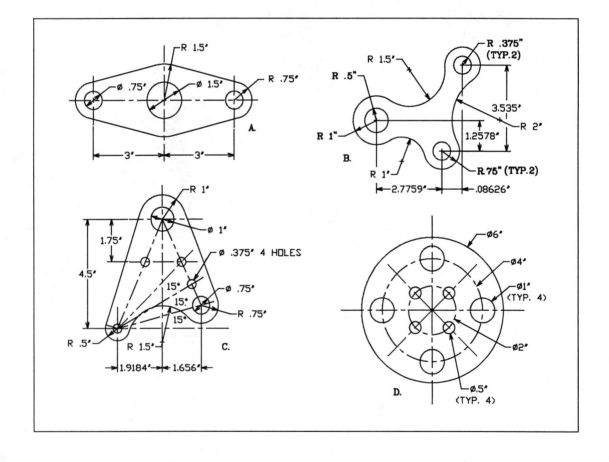

Exercise 3–10 Spring.

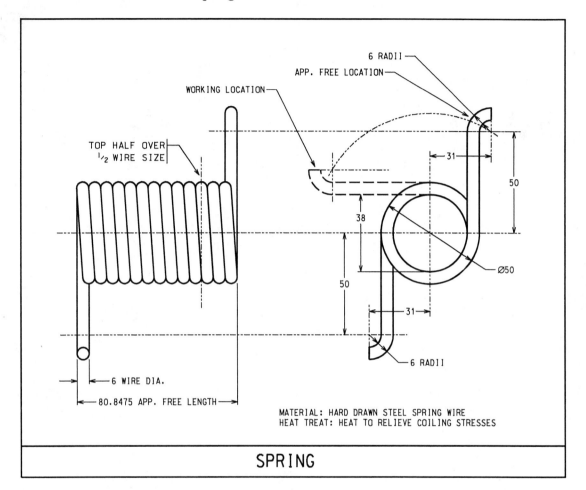

SPRING

ACCUDRAW
AND
SMARTLINE

• • • • • • • • • • • • • • • • • • • •

OBJECTIVES

After completing this chapter, you will be able to:

✓ Set up AccuDraw Settings.

✓ Use AccuDraw to place elements with fewer data points and less typing.

✓ Use the SmartLine command to draw complex models quickly with one command.

GETTING TO KNOW ACCUDRAW

AccuDraw is a powerful new MicroStation feature that increases your drawing productivity by tracking what you did and attempting to anticipate what you will do next. It is a drawing tool similar to grid and snap and it includes a drawing compass, an input window, a settings window with three subwindows, and a set of key-in shortcuts (see Figure 4–1).

Starting AccuDraw

AccuDraw is not active the first time MicroStation is activated, but once you start AccuDraw it opens every time MicroStation is called.

Invoke AccuDraw from:

Primary tool box	Select the Start AccuDraw tool (see Figure 4–2).
Key-in window	**Accudraw Activate** (or **acc a**)

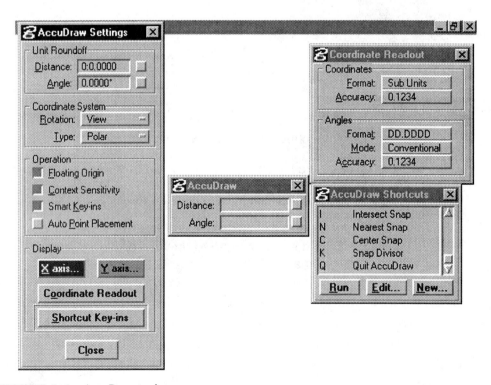

FIGURE 4–1 AccuDraw tools.

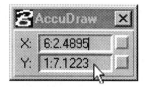

FIGURE 4–2 Invoking the AccuDraw tool from the Primary tool box.

FIGURE 4–3a AccuDraw window shown floating in the View window.

MicroStation displays:

> Start AccuDraw point input tool

The AccuDraw window opens either as a floating window (see Figure 4–3a) or docked at the top of the MicroStation workspace (see Figure 4–3b). After it is activated, it enhances all the available drawing tools.

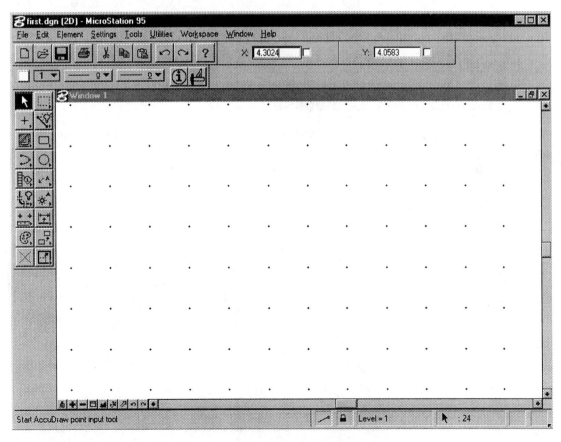

FIGURE 4–3b AccuDraw window docked at the top of the View window.

Closing AccuDraw

If necessary, you can close AccuDraw, but you will probably seldom want to turn it off. It can, though, be closed from:

AccuDraw window control menu	Select Close (or [ALT] + [F4] after clicking on the window)
Key-in window	**Accudraw Quit** (or **acc q**) [ENTER]

The AccuDraw window closes and the next data point does not have a compass around it.

> **NOTE:** Included in the AccuDraw tool set are shortcut key-ins that provide a fast way to request AccuDraw actions and to set constraints on the way AccuDraw acts. The shortcut key-in for closing AccuDraw is the **Q** key. If you key-in **Q** at any time with the focus in the AccuDraw window, then the AccuDraw window closes. All shortcut key-ins are described in Table 4–1 (see later).

The AccuDraw Compass

When AccuDraw is active, the AccuDraw compass appears whenever you place a data point in the design. This compass is the center of the AccuDraw drawing plane and is your main focus for input. The compass consists of three parts (see also Figure 4–4):

- The drawing plane origin point
- The coordinate system indicator
- The orthogonal axis indicators

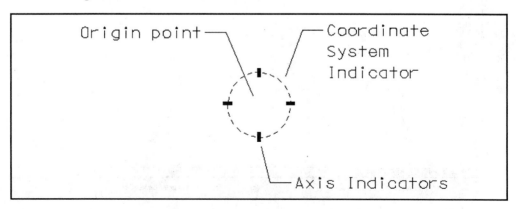

FIGURE 4-4   The parts of the AccuDraw compass.

Drawing Plane AccuDraw provides its own drawing plane and places the plane origin at the center of the compass. Distance and angular values are an offset from the AccuDraw origin, not from the design file origin.

Coordinate System AccuDraw provides polar and rectangular coordinate systems, like the systems provided by the precision key-in commands, except all offsets in the AccuDraw coordinate systems are from the compass origin. The AccuDraw settings window contains a Type option menu in which the desired coordinate system can be selected. Figures 4–5a and 4–5b show the appearance of the compass for both coordinate systems.

Invoke the AccuDraw Settings window from:

Pull-down menu	<u>S</u>ettings > <u>A</u>ccuDraw (or [ALT] + **S, A**)
Key-in window	**Accudraw Dialog Settings** (or **acc d se**) [ENTER]

In the AccuDraw settings window, switch the active coordinate from:

Options menu	Type > Rectangular *(for the Rectangular coordinate system)* or Polar *(for the Polar coordinate system)*
Key-in window	**Accudraw Mode** (or **acc m**) [ENTER] to toggle between the two modes

The coordinate system is switched (there are no MicroStation prompts).

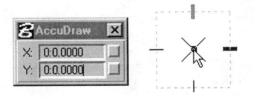

FIGURE 4–5a Compass with the rectangular coordinate system active.

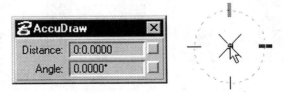

FIGURE 4–5b Compass with the polar coordinate system active.

> *NOTE:* The **Spacebar** key is the shortcut for toggling between the two coordinate systems. If you press the **Spacebar** anytime with the focus in the AccuDraw window, then the compass switches between the two coordinate systems. All shortcut key-ins are described in Table 4–1 (see later).

Orthogonal Axes The compass shows the position of AccuDraw's drawing plane X and Y axes as short tick marks (lines) crossing the compass rectangle or circle.

To aid distinguishing between the two axes, the positive X axis tick mark is a red line and the positive Y axis tick mark is a green line. If necessary, you can change the colors from the AccuDraw Settings window.

In the AccuDraw Settings window, change the axis tick mark colors from:

Display area	Select one of these options: • X axis... (or ⌨ALT + **X**) • Y axis... (or ⌨ALT + **Y**)
Key-in window	N/A

MicroStation opens the Modify Axis Color settings box, as shown in Figure 4–6. To change the color:

1. Select the desired color from the window.
2. Click the OK button to close the settings box.

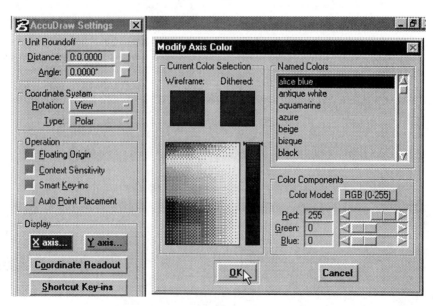

FIGURE 4–6 *Modify Axis Color settings box.*

The location of the AccuDraw compass is controlled by the status of the Floating Origin provided in the AccuDraw Settings box. If it is set to ON, then the AccuDraw compass is displayed whenever you place a data point in the design. If it is set to OFF, then the AccuDraw compass is placed at 0,0.

The AccuDraw Window

AccuDraw window provides a place to type X and Y axis offsets in the Rectangular coordinate system and distance and angle offsets with the Polar coordinate system (see Figures 4–5a and 4–5b). This window almost completely eliminates the need to type precision input codes such as **DL=** and **DI=**.

As you move the screen cursor, the input fields are updated automatically with the cursor's offset from the AccuDraw origin.

Selecting Fields AccuDraw always has the field in focus that you are most likely to type in next, so there is often no need to select the field first. Field focus is indicated by a changing appearance of the field (highlight methods vary among operating systems). If the wrong field is in focus, just click in the correct field to move the focus to it.

When you type in a distance or an angle, it appears in the field that is in focus, and that field is locked until the next data point. Click the Data button to place a data point at the offset shown in the window.

For example: If the compass is in rectangular mode and the dynamic image is snapped to the positive X axis indicator, the Y distance field in the window contains 0 and anything you type appears in, and locks, the X field. The next data point is placed at the X offset from the compass origin and the X input field is unlocked.

Accepting Field Contents When the AccuDraw window fields contain the correct offset from the compass origin, click the Data button to place the data point at the offset values.

Locking Fields Next to each field is a radio button by which you can lock in the present value in the field. A locked field holds its present value until the Data button is clicked. An X appears in the radio button when the field is locked.

Typing a number in a field locks it until the next data point is placed.

> **NOTE:** There are also shortcut key-ins to toggle the coordinate offset locks on and off; **X** and **Y** toggle the rectangular offset locks, **D** toggles the polar distance offset lock, and **A** toggles the polar angle lock. All shortcut key-ins are described in Table 4–1 (see later).

Negative Distances The direction of the screen cursor from the compass origin indicates the direction of your input in the drawing plane, so there is no need to type the negative sign for distances that are to the left of or down from the AccuDraw origin.

Rounding Off Distances and Angles

AccuDraw allows you to set and lock AccuDraw to a distance and angle unit roundoff value. When a unit roundoff lock is set, values are forced to the roundoff value or multiples of it.

Distance Roundoff Lock The Distance Roundoff Lock limits rectangular and polar distances to the roundoff value or multiples of it. The distance is always calculated from the current compass location (not from a grid point).

For example: Set the roundoff value to 5 and lock the value to force all distances (rectangular X and Y, and polar distance) to increase or decrease by increments of 5 (–10, –5, 0, 5, 10, etc.) as you drag the cursor in the design.

Angle Roundoff Lock The Angle Roundoff Lock limits polar angles to the angle roundoff value or multiples of it. Values typed in the AccuDraw window's Angle field override the roundoff value.

For example: Set the Angle roundoff value to 30 degrees to force all angles to increments of 30 degrees (0, 30, 60, 90, etc.) as you drag the cursor in the design.

Unit Roundoff values and locks are set in the top part of the AccuDraw Settings window. The distance and angle roundoffs each have a field for entering the roundoff value in working units (MU:SU:PU) and a radio button for turning the roundoff lock on and off, as shown in Figure 4–7.

> **NOTE:** Values keyed into AccuDraw window fields override the roundoff lock.

In the AccuDraw Settings window, change the roundoff values from:

Unit Roundoff area	Select the Distance field (or [ALT] + **D**) or the Angle field ([ALT] + **A**) and type the value. Select the Lock radio button for each field to be rounded off.

The new settings are applied to the AccuDraw window fields (there are no Micro-Station prompts).

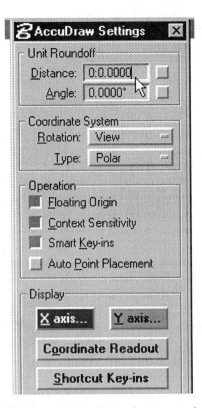

FIGURE 4–7   Unit Roundoff fields in the AccuDraw Settings window.

Recalling the Previous Values

AccuDraw remembers the distance and angle offset values previously used, and it takes the previous distance as a hint for the next distance.

Previous Distance   AccuDraw sets up an invisible circle around the compass origin. The radius of this circle is equal to the length of the previous distance (the distance between the previous two data points). If you move the cursor within the Locate Tolerance of this invisible circle, AccuDraw snaps the cursor to the circle and the offset distance is equal to the previous distance. To turn off the snap, move the cursor outside the Locate Tolerance.

Previous Values   Each time you place a data point, AccuDraw remembers the offsets used to place that point. All distance values are stored in a buffer and all angle values are stored in a separate buffer. Press [PG↑] to load the last value used in the field that is in focus. Press the [PG↑] again and the next-to-last value is loaded. Press the key a third time and the third-from-last value is loaded. And so on.

All distance values are stored in the same buffer, so they can be applied to any coordinate distance field (*X* axis, *Y* axis, or Polar Distance).

Using Smart Lock

The Smart Lock constraints to one of the two axes, X and Y. Depending on where the pointer is located at the time you select Smart Lock, one of two things will occur:

- If the pointer is oriented closer to the X axis of the compass, the pointer will lock to the X axis.
- If the pointer is oriented closer to the Y axis of the compass, the pointer will lock to the Y axis.

To activate the Smart Lock, press [ENTER] when the focus is in the AccuDraw window. Hitting [ENTER] again deactivates Smart Lock and releases the dynamic line back to free motion.

Shortcuts

AccuDraw includes shortcuts for controlling AccuDraw actions (see Table 4–1). The shortcuts are one- or two-character key-ins; some of them have already been mentioned in this chapter. A shortcut is invoked either by typing the shortcut's key-in with the focus in the AccuDraw window or by selecting its description from the AccuDraw Shortcuts window.

To review the listing of the available AccuDraw shortcuts, key-in **?** with the focus in the AccuDraw window. MicroStation opens the AccuDraw Shortcuts window (see Figure 4–8). Select from the list the appropriate shortcut key-in.

If the shortcut is defined by one key, it takes effect as soon as you press the key. If the shortcut requires two keys, pressing the first key opens the AccuDraw Shortcuts window if it is not already open, and all shortcuts with that first letter are highlighted. To invoke the shortcut, either select it from the Shortcuts window or press the second key. After the shortcut is selected, the Shortcuts window closes.

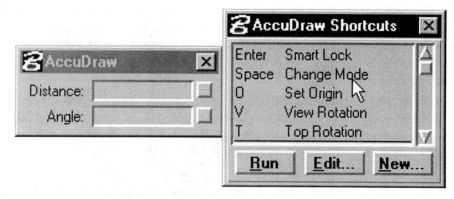

FIGURE 4–8 AccuDraw Shortcuts window.

Table 4–1. AccuDraw Shortcuts

KEY-IN	ACCUDRAW DIRECTIVE
?	Open the AccuDraw Shortcuts window.
Q	Close the AccuDraw command.
Spacebar	Toggle between Rectangular and Polar coordinates.
G, K	Open, or move focus, to the AccuDraw Settings window (same as choosing AccuDraw from the Settings menu).
O	Move the origin point to the current screen cursor location (can also be used to activate AccuDraw before entering a data point).
P	Key-in window appears to key-in single data point.
M	Key-in window appears to key-in multiple data point.
LOCKS	
ENTER	Toggle Smart Lock ON and OFF. When Smart Lock is ON: • In Rectangular mode, it locks the value for the orthogonal axis perpendicular to the axis the compass has snapped to. For example, if the compass is snapped to the X axis, the Y value is zero. • In Polar mode, it locks the Angle to 0, 90, –90, or 180 when the cursor is snapped to an orthogonal axis; or it locks the Distance to the last entered value, if the Angle is not locked.
X	Toggle the Rectangular coordinate X value lock ON and OFF.
Y	Toggle the Rectangular coordinate Y value lock ON and OFF.
D	Toggle the Polar coordinate Distance value lock ON and OFF.
A	Toggle the Polar coordinate Angle value lock ON and OFF.
ROTATE THE DRAWING PLANE	
R, Q	Temporarily rotate the drawing plane about the compass origin point. The lock is turned OFF after the next data point.
R, A	Permanently rotate the drawing plane. It stays active after the current command terminates.
R, Z	Rotate the drawing plane 90 degrees about its Z axis. (In a 2D drawing, the Z axis is perpendicular to the drawing plane.)
T	Rotate the drawing plane to align with the top view.
V	Rotate the drawing plane to align with the view (its normal rotation).
SNAP MODES	
©	Activate Center snap mode
I	Activate Intersect snap mode
N	Activate Nearest snap mode
K	Open the Keypoint Snap divisor window so the snap divisor can be set.

> *NOTE:* There are additional shortcut key-ins for 3D designs that are not listed in Table 4–1.

WORKING WITH ACCUDRAW

You've seen the parts of AccuDraw and how to change the way it functions. Let's look at how we can apply it to various tools available in MicroStation.

Moving the Compass Origin

In almost all uses of AccuDraw, the compass origin is on the previous data point. If necessary, you can move the location of the compass origin. To relocate the compass origin, key-in the shortcut **O** (*not* zero). The compass origin relocation depends on the current location.

- If the compass is currently not visible, it will appear at the last data point location.
- If the compass is currently visible, it will relocate to the current pointer location.
- If there is an active tentative point, then the compass jumps to the tentative point.

Using Tentative Points with AccuDraw

Tentative points can be used with the compass to place elements in precise relationships to other elements, just as was done with precision key-ins. For example: To start a line 2 Master Units to the right of the corner of an existing element:

1. Invoke the Place Line command.
2. Snap to the corner of an existing element from which the offset is to be measured.
3. Key-in the shortcut **O** to release the compass origin and move it to the tentative point.
4. If the Polar coordinate system is not active, press the **Spacebar** to switch to it. (This example uses Polar coordinates, but it can be done in Rectangular coordinates.)
5. In the AccuDraw window, key-in **2** in the Distance field and **0** in the Angle field.
6. Click the Data button, and the first point of the line is placed 2 units to the right of the tentative point, as shown in Figure 4–9.
7. Complete drawing the line.

> *NOTE:* AccuDraw provides shortcut key-ins for selecting some of the tentative snap modes. Table 4–1 lists all shortcut key-ins.

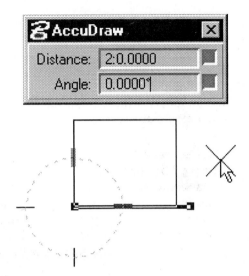

FIGURE 4-9 Example of starting a line at an offset from a tentative point.

Rotating the Drawing Plane

In 2D designs, the AccuDraw drawing plane can be rotated about the Z axis (which is perpendicular to the 2D drawing plane) any time the compass is visible. To rotate the plane, click the first shortcut letter, **R**, and the Shortcuts window appears. Select the type of rotation from the shortcut list of **R** options.

The **RQ** and **RA** shortcuts allow you to define the rotation dynamically by dragging the cursor and clicking the Data button. **RQ** only locks the compass at the selected rotation for the next data point, after which the compass is released. **RA** locks the compass permanently at the selected rotation.

Each time the **RZ** shortcut is selected, the plane is rotated 90 degrees counterclockwise about the Z axis.

> **NOTE:** The compass rotates automatically to the same angle as the previously placed line segment when the context sensitivity toggle button is set to ON. These rotate shortcuts allow you to override that rotation.

Placing Elements with AccuDraw Active

AccuDraw generally enhances placement tools by automating some steps and guiding the user. Here are two examples of using AccuDraw with placement commands.

Ellipse With AccuDraw, the first two data points for the Ellipse still define the primary axis, as before, but the third data point is locked automatically on the secondary axis. You can simply type in the radius or drag the cursor to where it should be.

For example: Place an ellipse with a major axis 8 Master Units long and rotated 30 degrees, and a minor axis 4 units long:

1. Invoke the Place Ellipse command.
2. Place the first data point to define one end of the major axis.
3. If the rectangular compass is active, switch to the polar compass.
4. In the AccuDraw window, set the Distance to 4 and the Angle to 30.
5. Click the Data button to define the major ellipse axis.
6. In the AccuDraw window, set the Distance to 2.
7. Click the Data button to complete the ellipse by defining its minor axis.

Block Fewer steps are required to place a rotated block with specific dimensions when using AccuDraw. Place the first data point, then use Polar coordinates to specify the rotation angle and the length of the block at that angle. Place the data point, and the compass axes rotate to the angle. Switch to Rectangular coordinates and enter the Y axis length to complete the block, then place the final data point.

For example: Place a 3×5 Master Unit block rotated 15 degrees:

1. Invoke the Place Rotated Block command.
2. Place the first data point to define the lower left corner of the rotated block.
3. If the rectangular compass is active, switch to the polar compass.
4. In the AccuDraw window, set the Distance field to 3 and the Angle to 15.
5. Click the Data button to define the bottom edge of the rotated block (the compass switches to rectangular coordinates).
6. In the AccuDraw window, set the X distance to 3 and the Y distance to 5.
7. Click the Data button to complete the rotated block.

Manipulating Elements with AccuDraw Active

AccuDraw also enhances manipulation of elements. Here is an example of placing two copies of the lower left block shown in Figure 4–10.

If AccuDraw is not active, invoke it.

1. Invoke Copy Element from the Manipulate tool box.
2. Open the AccuDraw settings window, set the compass to polar, set and lock the distance roundoff to 2 and the angle roundoff value to 15.

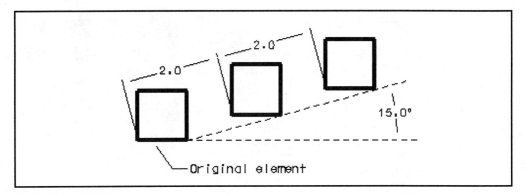

FIGURE 4–10   Example of using AccuDraw with the Copy Element command.

3. Identify the element by snapping with the Tentative point to the lower left corner of the block to be copied, and click the Data button.
4. Drag the cursor until the AccuDraw window shows an angle of 15, then press the **A** key to lock the angle.
5. Drag the cursor until the AccuDraw window shows a distance of 2, then press the **D** key to lock the distance.
6. Click the Data button twice to place the two copies.

Using the AccuDraw tool appropriately you will see a significant increase in productivity.

PLACE SMARTLINE COMMAND

The SmartLine command places a chain of connected line segments and arc segments as individual elements, or as a line string, shape, circle, complex chain, or complex shape. The vertexes between segments can be a sharp point, a tangent arc (rounded), or a chamfer. The command settings (see Table 4–2, later) can be changed on the fly to allow any combination of segments and vertices.

Invoke SmartLine from:

Linear Elements tool bar	Select the Place SmartLine tool (see Figure 4–11) and make the initial tool settings in the Tool settings window (see Table 4–2).
Key-in window	**Place SmartLine** (or **pl sm**) (ENTER)

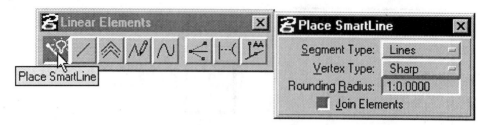

FIGURE 4–11   Place SmartLine tool icon in the Linear Elements tool box.

MicroStation prompts:

> Place SmartLine > Enter first vertex *(Place the first data point to start the SmartLine.)*
>
> Place SmartLine > Enter the next vertex or reset to complete *(Place the remaining data points. Change the Segment and Vertex Type settings as required between points.)*

You can complete the command sequence by clicking the Reset button to create an open element, or you can place a Tentative snap to the first data point and click the Accept button to create a closed element.

> **NOTE:** If the Join Elements check box located in the Tool settings window is turned ON, then the segments between the vertices are joined and the completed SmartLine is one element. If it is set to OFF, then each segment is a separate element.

Placing the Segments

As you are placing a SmartLine, you can switch between placing a line and placing an arc.

- To place a line, define the two segment end points.
- To place an arc, define the arc center and sweep angle.
- To change the direction of an arc, swing the cursor in the desired sweep direction.

Using SmartLine with AccuDraw

The SmartLine command was designed for use with AccuDraw active. When Smart-Line is employed with AccuDraw, the AccuDraw drawing plane automatically:

- Moves to each new data point
- Rotates to align with each newly defined segment, which makes it easier to define new segments tangent or perpendicular to the aligned segment
- Switches to polar coordinates when defining an arc segment

Example of Drawing with SmartLine and AccuDraw This example uses Smart-Line with AccuDraw to draw the object shown in Figure 4–12. The letters in the figure point to the locations of all data points.

1. If AccuDraw is not active, invoke the AccuDraw tool.
2. Open the AccuDraw Settings window.
3. Set and lock the Distance roundoff value to 1.5 and the Angle roundoff value to 90.
4. Set the compass to Polar.
5. Invoke SmartLine from the Lines tool box.
6. Set SmartLine to draw Lines, and place 1.5-inch offset chamfers at the vertices.
7. Define a point to start the object (Point A).
8. Slide the cursor up until the AccuDraw window Distance field displays 3, then click the Data button (Point B).
9. Slide the cursor to the right until the AccuDraw window Distance field displays 3, then click the Data button (Point C).
10. Set SmartLine to place .5 inch rounded vertices.
11. Slide the cursor down until the AccuDraw window Distance field displays 3, then click the Data button (Point D).
12. Slide the cursor to the left until the AccuDraw window Distance field displays 3 and touches the first point. Click the Data button (Point A).

MicroStation creates the object as a complex shape if the Join Elements toggle button is set to ON. If it is set to OFF, the object created consists of five separate lines and three separate arcs.

MicroStation provides various options to draw lines and arcs with the SmartLine tool. See Table 4–2 for details on the various options.

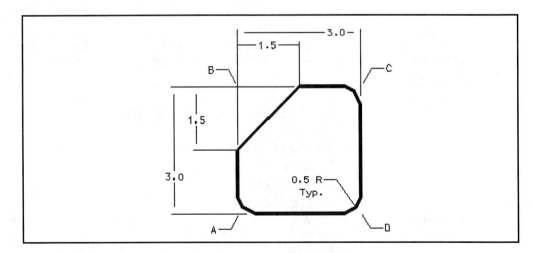

FIGURE 4–12 Example of a drawing made with the SmartLine command.

Table 4–2. The SmartLine Tool Settings

SETTING	EFFECT
Segment Type	Set the element placed with each data point after the first one. Select one of these types: • Line • Arc
Vertex Type	Set the shape of each vertex to one of these types: • Sharp • Rounded (a tangent arc) • Chamfered
Rounding Radius	Enter the rounded vertex radius in working units (MU:SU:PU). **Note:** The "Rounding Radius" prompt appears only when the Vertex Type is "Rounded."
Chamfer Offset	Enter the offset of each end of the chamfer from the vertex point. Each chamfer offset is equal. **Note:** The "Chamfer Offset" prompt appears only when the Vertex Type is "Chamfer."
Join Elements	*Toggle button turned ON:* The segments between the vertices are joined and the completed SmartLine is one element. *Toggle button turned OFF:* Each segment is a separate element.
The following setting appears in the Settings window only if "Join Elements" is checked and you have a tentative point snapped to the first data point of the SmartLine.	
Closed Element	*Set to ON:* Creates a closed element (circle, shape, or complex shape) when the tentative snap is accepted. *Set to OFF:* Accepting the tentative snap does not create a closed element.
The following settings appear in the Settings window only if "Closed Element" is turned ON and you have a tentative point snapped to the first data point of the SmartLine.	
Area	Sets the active area of the closed element to Solid or Hole. (The reason for these settings is discussed in Chapter 11 on Patterning.)
Fill Type	The Fill Type options control the closed element's fill: • None (no fill) • Opaque (filled with active color) • Outlined (filled with fill color)
Fill Color	Sets the fill color for the closed element (unless the Fill Type is set to None): • If Fill Type is Opaque, the active color is selected. • If Fill Type is Outlined, the fill color can be selected here.

REVIEW QUESTIONS

Write your answers in the spaces provided.

1. How do you activate AccuDraw?

    _____

2. Name the two coordinate systems you can use with AccuDraw.

    _____

3. Name three settings you can adjust in the AccuDraw settings box.

    _____

4. What is the purpose of rounding off distances and angles in the AccuDraw settings box?

    _____

5. How do you recall the previous values by using AccuDraw?

    _____

6. What is the shortcut key-in that will move the compass origin from the previous data point?

    _____

7. Explain briefly how you will use the Tentative points with AccuDraw.

    _____

    _____

8. Explain briefly the benefits of manipulating elements with AccuDraw active.

    _____

    _____

9. Explain the difference between the Place Line command and the Place SmartLine command.

    _____

    _____

10. Name the two segment types you can use with the SmartLine command.

    _____

PROJECT EXERCISE

This project exercise provides step-by-step instructions for creating the design shown in Figure P4–1. The intent is to guide you in applying AccuDraw and SmartLine.

> *NOTE:* The dimensions are not part of this project. They are included in Figure P4–1 only to show the size of the design.

Prepare the Design File

In this procedure you start MicroStation, create a design file, and enter the initial settings.

> *NOTE:* As you complete each step in the project procedures, place a check mark by the step to help you keep up with where you are in the project.

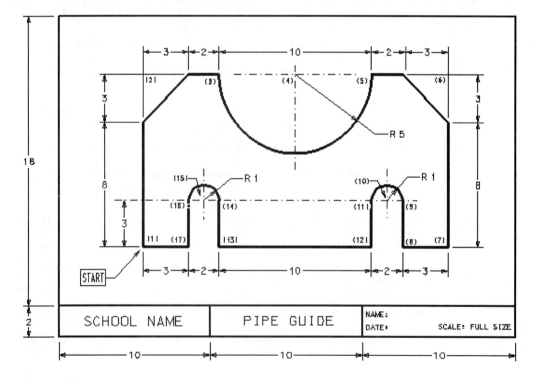

FIGURE P4–1   Completed project design.

FIGURE P4–2   Invoking the AccuDraw tool.

STEP 1:   Invoke MicroStation by the normal technique for the operating system on your workstation.

STEP 2:   Create a new design file named CH4.DGN using the SEED2D.DGN seed file.

STEP 3:   In the Design File dialog box:

- Set the Working Unit ratios to 1:10:1000, the Master Units name to "IN", and the Subunits name to "TH".
- Set the Grid Master to .1 and the Grid Reference to 10, and then turn OFF the Grid lock.

STEP 4:   Invoke the AccuDraw tool from the Primary Tool bar (see Figure P4–2).

STEP 5:   Open the AccuDraw settings box from the pull-down menu Settings, and adjust the settings as follows:

- *Unit Roundoff:* Set the Distance to 1.000 and the toggle button to ON. Then set the Angle to 90.000 degrees and the toggle button ON.
- *Coordinate System:* Set the Rotation to Top and the Type to Rectangular.
- *Operation:* Set the toggle buttons for Floating Origin and Smart Key-ins to ON.
- *Display:* If you have trouble seeing the colors red and green, change the X axis and Y axis colors.

Make sure the settings are properly adjusted by referring to Figure P4–3. Click the Close button to close the settings box.

STEP 6:   Invoke the Save settings from the pull-down menu File.

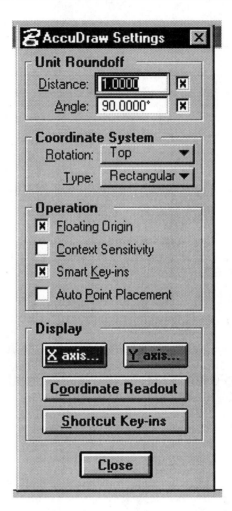

FIGURE P4-3 AccuDraw settings box.

Draw the Border and Title Block

Draw the border and title block as shown in Figure P4–1, employing AccuDraw to aid in element placement.

STEP 1: Invoke the Place Block command from the Polygons tool box.

MicroStation prompts:

Place Block > Enter first point *(Click in the AccuDraw window's "X:" edit field and key-in* **0**. *Click in the "Y:" edit field and key-in* **0**. *Then press* ⏎ENTER.*)*

Place Block > Enter opposite corner *(Key-in* **30** *in the AccuDraw "X:" edit field and* **20** *in the "Y:" edit field. Then click the Data button to place the upper right corner of the block.)*

STEP 2:   Fit the view window.

STEP 3:   Invoke the Place Line command from the Linear Elements tool box.

MicroStation prompts:

Place Line > Enter first point *(Keypoint snap to the lower left corner of the block, type* **O** *to release the AccuDraw origin, and type* **X** *to lock the AccuDraw X axis at 0.0000. Drag the drawing pointer vertically upward until the AccuDraw "Y:" field is equal to 2.0000. Then click the Data button to start the line.)*

Place Line > Enter end point *(Type* **Y** *to lock the AccuDraw Y axis at 0.0000. Then drag the drawing pointer to the right until "X:" equals 30.0000, and click the Data button to complete the line. Click the Reset button.)*

Place Line > Enter first point *(Keypoint snap to the lower left corner of the block, type* **O** *to release the AccuDraw origin, and type* **Y** *to lock the AccuDraw Y axis at 0.0000. Drag the drawing pointer to the right until the AccuDraw "X:" field is equal to 10.0000, then click the Data button to start the line.)*

Place Line > Enter end point *(Type* **X** *to lock the AccuDraw X axis at 0.0000. Then drag the drawing pointer vertically upward until "Y:" equals 2.0000, and click the Data button to complete the line. Click the Reset button.)*

Place Line > Enter first point *(Keypoint snap to the lower left corner of the block, type* **O** *to release the AccuDraw origin, and type* **Y** *to lock the AccuDraw Y axis at 0.0000. Drag the drawing pointer to the right until the AccuDraw "X:" field is equal to 20.0000, then click the Data button to start the line.)*

Place Line > Enter end point *(Type* **X** *to lock the AccuDraw X axis at 0.0000. Then drag the drawing pointer vertically upward until "Y:" equals 2.0000, and click the Data button to complete the line. Click the Reset button.)*

STEP 4:   Place the text in the title block using font 3, 0.6 for the large text size, and 0.3 for the small text size:

- Replace "SCHOOL NAME" with your school or company name, or make up a name.
- Place your name to the right of "NAME."
- Place today's date to the right of "DATE."

Draw the Design

Draw the pipe guide shown in Figure P4–1 using AccuDraw and SmartLine.

STEP 1: Invoke Place SmartLine from the Linear Elements tool box, as shown in Figure P4–4. In the Tool Settings window, set the Vertex Type to Chamfered, and key-in **3** in the Chamfer Offset edit field.

> **NOTE:** Numbers in parentheses have been added to the following MicroStation prompts and to Figure P4–1, to help you keep up with where you are in the procedure of drawing the pipe guide. Those numbers do *not* appear in the MicroStation prompt on the screen.

MicroStation prompts:

(1) Place SmartLine > Enter first vertex *(Place the first data point approximately at the START point shown in Figure P4–1.)*

(2) Place SmartLine > Enter the next vertex or reset to complete *(Type X to lock the AccuDraw X axis at 0.0000, and drag the drawing pointer straight up until the AccuDraw rectangular coordinate "Y:" field equals 11.0000, as shown in Figure P4–5. Then click the Data button.)*

(3) Place SmartLine > Enter the next vertex or reset to complete *(Type Y to lock the AccuDraw Y axis at 0.0000, drag the screen pointer straight to the right until the AccuDraw rectangular coordinates "X:" field equals 5.0000, then click the Data button.)*

(4) Place SmartLine > Enter the next vertex or reset to complete *(Change the SmartLine Segment Type to Arcs, as shown in Figure P4–6.)*

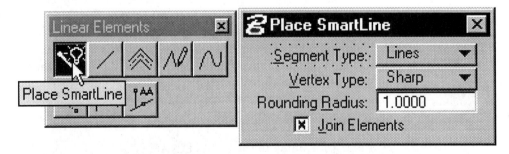

FIGURE P4–4 Invoke Place SmartLine and set the Chamfer Offset to 3.

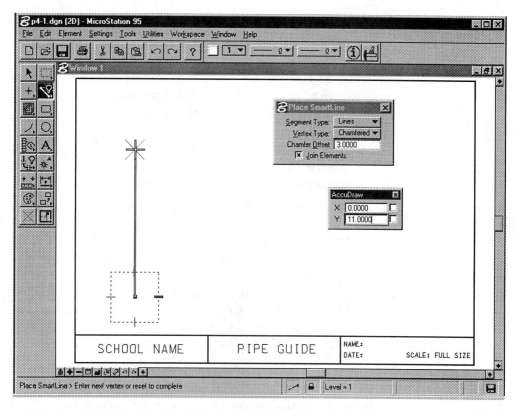

FIGURE P4–5   AccuDraw rectangular coordinate values for data point (2).

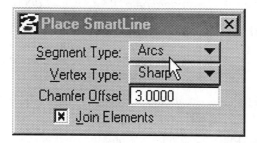

FIGURE P4–6   Place SmartLine Tool Settings window showing the change made to Arcs.

Place SmartLine > Enter arc center *(Type* **Y** *to lock the AccuDraw Y axis at 0.0000, drag the drawing pointer straight to the right until the AccuDraw coordinate "X:" field equals 5.0000, then click the Data button to place the arc center.)*

(5) Place SmartLine > Define the sweep angle *(Type* **Y** *to lock the AccuDraw Y axis at 0.0000, drag the drawing pointer straight to the right until the AccuDraw coordinate "X:" field equals 5.0000, and click the Data button to complete the arc.)*

(6) Place SmartLine > Enter arc center *(Change the SmartLine Segment Type to Lines.)*

Place SmartLine > Enter the next vertex or reset to complete *(Type **Y** to lock the AccuDraw Y axis at 0.0000, drag the drawing pointer to the right until the AccuDraw coordinate "X:" field equals 5.0000, and click the Data button.)*

(7) Place SmartLine > Enter the next vertex or reset to complete *(Type **X** to lock the AccuDraw X axis at 0.0000, drag the drawing pointer down vertically until the AccuDraw coordinate "Y:" field equals –11.0000, and click the Data button.)*

(8) Place SmartLine > Enter the next vertex or reset to complete *(Change the SmartLine Vertex Type to Sharp. Type **Y** to lock the AccuDraw Y axis at 0.0000, drag the drawing pointer to the left until the AccuDraw coordinate "X:" field equals –3.0000, and click the Data button.)*

(9) Place SmartLine > Enter the next vertex or reset to complete *(Type **X** to lock the AccuDraw X axis at 0.0000, drag the drawing pointer vertically up until the AccuDraw coordinate "Y:" field equals 3.0000, and click the Data button.)*

(10) Place SmartLine > Enter the next vertex or reset to complete *(Change the SmartLine Segment Type to Arcs.)*

Place SmartLine > Enter arc center *(Type **Y** to lock the AccuDraw Y axis at 0.0000, drag the drawing pointer to left until the AccuDraw coordinate "X:" equals –1.0000, and click the Data button.)*

(11) Place SmartLine > Define sweep angle *(Type **Y** to lock the AccuDraw Y axis at 0.0000, drag the drawing pointer to left until the AccuDraw coordinate "X:" equals –1.0000, and click the Data button to complete the arc.)*

(12) Place SmartLine > Enter arc center *(Change the SmartLine Segment Type to Lines.)*

Place SmartLine > Enter the next vertex or reset to complete *(Complete the remainder of the pipe guide as shown in Figure P4–1.)*

STEP 2: Invoke the Save settings from the pull-down menu File.

DRAWING EXERCISES 4–1 THROUGH 4–5

Use the following table to set up the design files for Exercises 4–1 through 4–3.

SETTING	VALUE
Seed File	SEED2D.DGN
Working Units	MU = IN, SU = 10 TH, PU = 1000
Grid	Master = .25, Reference = 4, Grid Lock ON

Exercise 4–1   Input-output card.

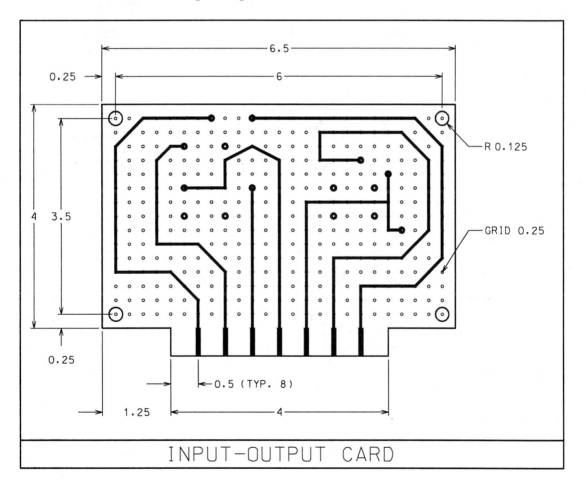

INPUT–OUTPUT CARD

Exercise 4–2   Machine part.

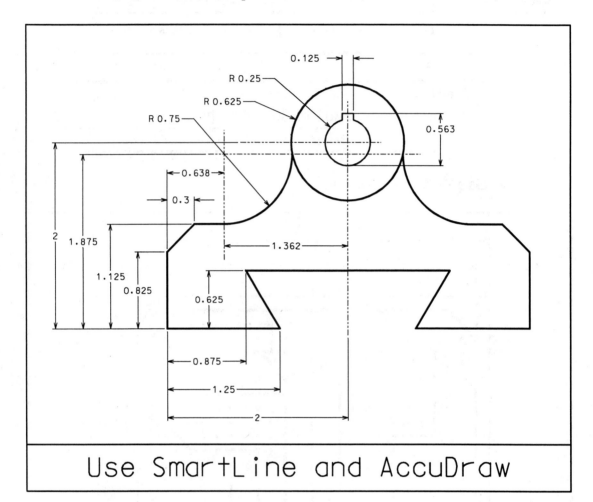

Use SmartLine and AccuDraw

Exercise 4–3 Machine part.

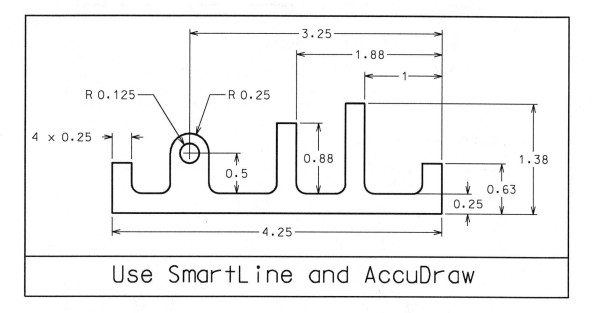

Use SmartLine and AccuDraw

Use the following table to set up the design files for Exercises 4–4 and 4–5.

SETTING	VALUE
Seed File	SEED2D.DGN
Working Units	MU = ', SU = 12", PU = 8000
Grid	Master = .25, Reference = 4, Grid Lock ON

Exercise 4–4 Plot plan.

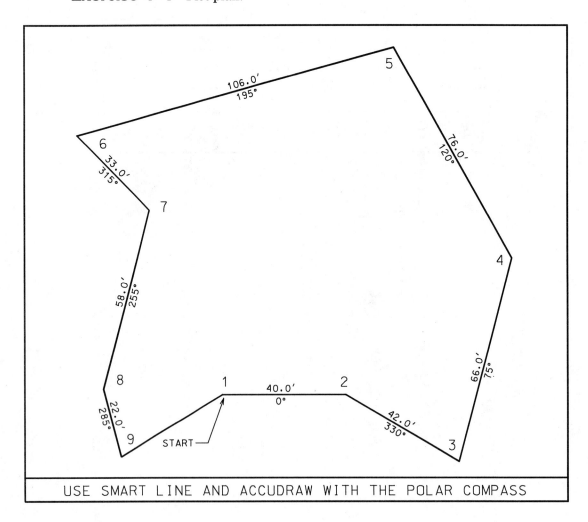

USE SMART LINE AND ACCUDRAW WITH THE POLAR COMPASS

Exercise 4–5   Master bath floor plan.

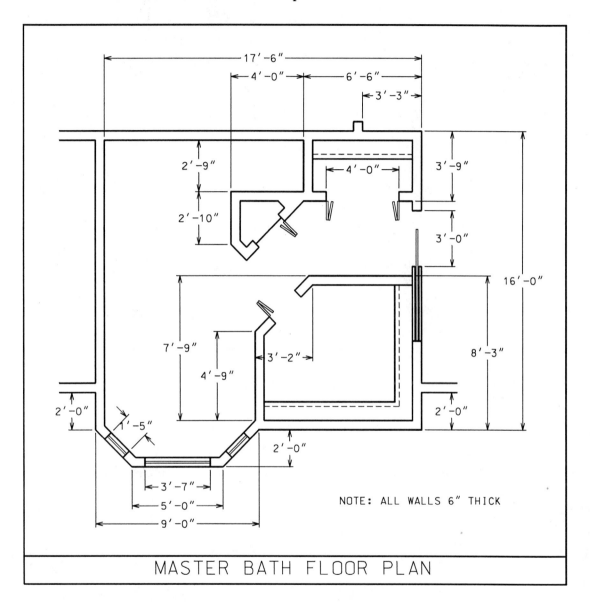

MASTER BATH FLOOR PLAN

CHAPTER

5

MENU PLACING GROUPS OF ELEMENTS

OBJECTIVES

After completing this chapter, you will be able to:

✓ Select elements with the Element Selection command and manipulate them.

✓ Place fences and manipulate fence contents.

✓ Manipulate views of your design.

ELEMENT SELECTION

While you were practicing the element manipulation commands described in the preceding chapters, did little squares occasionally appear on the corners of one of your elements? Did they make the commands act differently from the way the book said they would? This chapter turns those "handles" from a nuisance into a useful feature by showing you how the Element Selection tool provides a powerful new way to manipulate elements.

Selecting Elements with the Element Selection Command

In the previous chapters you first invoked an element manipulation command and then identified the element you wanted to manipulate. With the Element Selection command, you identify an element or group of elements first, then select a manipulation command.

Selected elements are easily spotted because of the square "handles" that appear around the elements. See Figure 5–1 for examples of the handles on different element types.

Invoke the element selection tool from:

Main tool frame	Select the Element Selection tool (see Figure 5–2).
Key-in window	**Choose Element** (or **ch e**) [ENTER]

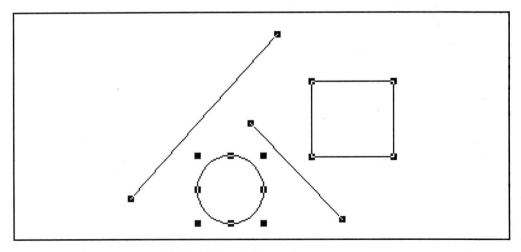

FIGURE 5–1   Examples of the handles on different element types.

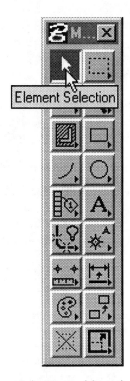

FIGURE 5–2   Invoking the Element Selection tool from the Main tool frame.

The screen pointer changes to an arrow with a circle, similar to the one shown in Figure 5–3, and MicroStation prompts:

> Element Selection *(Use one or more of the selection deselection methods listed next.)*

The following list presents ways to select elements while in Element Selection mode.

- *Select a single element* by clicking the Data button on the element.
- *Add a single element* to the current selection by holding down ⌨ and clicking the Data button on the element to be added.
- *Select a group of elements* by holding down the Data button while you drag a dynamic rectangle around the elements. Release the Data button to select the elements inside the dynamic rectangle.

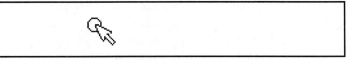

FIGURE 5–3   Screen pointer shape when Element Selection mode is ON.

- *Add a group of elements* to the current selection by holding down **CTRL** and the Data button while you drag a dynamic rectangle around the elements. Release the Data button to add the elements inside the dynamic rectangle to the selection.
- *Select all elements* in the design by choosing the Select All command from:

Pull-down menu	Edit > Select All (or **ALT** + **E, A**)
Key-in window	**Choose All** (or **ch a**) **ENTER**

The following list presents ways to deselect elements that were previously selected.

- *Deselect a single element* by holding down **CTRL** and clicking the Data button on the element.
- *Deselect a group of elements* by holding down **CTRL** and the Data button while you drag a dynamic rectangle around the elements to be deselected. Release the Data button to deselect the elements.
- *Deselect all selected elements* by clicking the Data button anywhere in the design plane.

> **NOTE:** The dragging method can select and deselect elements at the same time. When you release the Data button, elements without handles that are in the rectangle are selected and all elements with handles that are in the rectangle are deselected.

Consolidating Elements into a Group

MicroStation's Group command consolidates selected elements into a group that can be manipulated as a single element. The group has handles on its boundary, as shown in Figure 5–4.

To create a group, select the elements with the Element Selection command, then invoke the Group command from:

Pull-down menu	Edit > Group (or **ALT** + **E, G** or **CTRL** + **G**)
Key-in window	**Group Selection** (or **gr s**) **ENTER**

The selected elements are immediately consolidated into a group with one set of handles on the group boundary (there are no MicroStation prompts).

> **NOTE:** The Group command is dimmed in the pull-down menu Edit if no elements are selected.

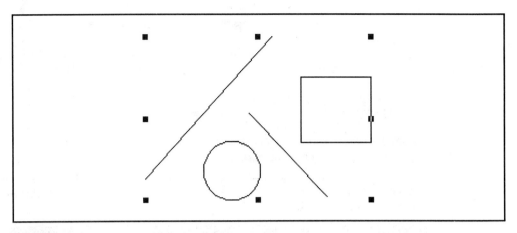

FIGURE 5–4   Example of a selected element group.

Ungrouping Consolidated Elements

MicroStation's Ungroup command returns a group of consolidated elements to individual elements that can be manipulated separately. When consolidated elements are ungrouped, the group boundary handles are replaced by sets of handles on each element.

To ungroup a group, select the group (or groups) via the Element Selection command, then invoke the Ungroup command from:

Pull-down menu	<u>E</u>dit > U<u>n</u>group (or 🄰 + **E**, **N** or 🄲 + **U**)
Key-in window	**Ungroup** (or **un**) 🄴

The selected group (or groups) immediately return into separate elements (there are no MicroStation prompts).

> **NOTE:** The Ungroup command is dimmed in the pull-down menu Edit if no elements are selected.

Locking Selected Elements

MicroStation's Lock command locks selected elements to prevent them from being manipulated. If you attempt to select a locked element for manipulation, Micro-Station ignores the element and displays the message "Element not found" in the Status bar. Locking is an easy way to protect completed parts of a design from accidental changes.

To lock elements, select the elements with the Element Selection command, then invoke the Lock command from:

Pull-down menu	E̲dit > Loc̲k (or ⌨ + **E, K** or ⌨ + **L**)
Key-in window	**Change Lock** (or **cha lo**) ⏎

The selected elements are immediately locked and protected from manipulation (there are no MicroStation prompts).

> **NOTE:** The Lock command is dimmed in the pull-down menu Edit if no elements are selected.

Unlocking Selected Elements

Locked elements can be unlocked with MicroStation's Unlock command. After unlocking, the elements can be manipulated.

To unlock elements, select the elements by means of the Element Selection command, then invoke the Unlock command from:

Pull-down menu	E̲dit > Unl̲ock (or ⌨ + **E, O** or ⌨ + **M**)
Key-in window	**Change Unlock** (or **cha un**) ⏎

The selected elements are immediately unlocked (there are no MicroStation prompts).

> **NOTE:** The Unlock command is dimmed in the pull-down menu Edit if no elements are selected.

Dragging Selected Elements to a New Position

Selected elements can be dragged (moved) to a new location in the design plane.

1. Use the Element Selection command to select the element or elements to be moved.
2. Press and hold the Data button anywhere on one of the selected element outlines (but *not* on a handle).
3. Drag the elements to the new location.
4. Release the Data button to place the elements at the new location.

The elements are placed at the new location and removed from the original location, as shown in Figure 5–5 (there are no MicroStation prompts).

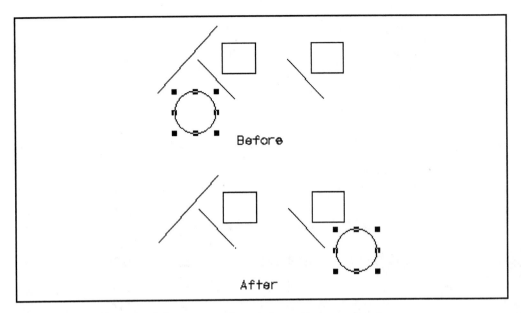

FIGURE 5-5   Example of dragging a selected element to a new location.

Dragging an Element Handle to Change Its Shape

The geometric shape of a selected element can be modified by dragging one of the element's handles to a new location in the design plane:

1. Use the Element Selection command to select the element to be modified.
2. Press and hold the Data button on the element handle to be modified.
3. Drag the handle to the new shape.
4. Release the Data button to complete the modification.

The element's shape is changed to the new geometric shape (there are no Micro-Station prompts).

See Figure 5–6 for an example of modifying an element's shape.

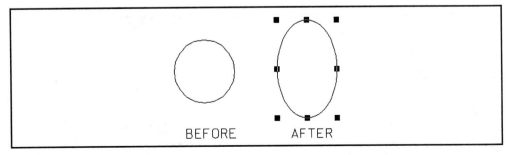

FIGURE 5-6   Example of modifying an element's shape.

Deleting Selected Elements

All selected elements can quickly be deleted by clicking [DEL] on the computer keyboard or by selecting the Delete tool located in the Main tool frame. To delete elements with [DEL]:

1. Use the Element Selection command to select the elements to be deleted.
2. Click [DEL].

All selected elements are deleted (there are no MicroStation prompts).

> **NOTE:** On some systems, the BACKSPACE key will also delete selected elements.

Manipulation of the Selected Elements

Several MicroStation manipulation commands work with elements that were selected with the Element Selection command, including Array, Copy, Delete, Mirror, Move, Rotate, Scale, Spin, and the Change Element Attributes commands.

These manipulation commands affect all selected elements as if they were one element, and the commands exit after completing the requested change.

To manipulate the elements, first select the elements by means of the Element Selection command, then invoke the appropriate manipulation command. The prompts are slightly different from the prompts that you see when you manipulate individual elements. Always read MicroStation's command prompts in the Status bar. For example: the Move and Copy commands still require two data points, but they define the relative distance to move or copy the selected elements. In other words, the new location of the elements has the same relationship to the second data point as the original elements had to the first data point (See Figure 5–7).

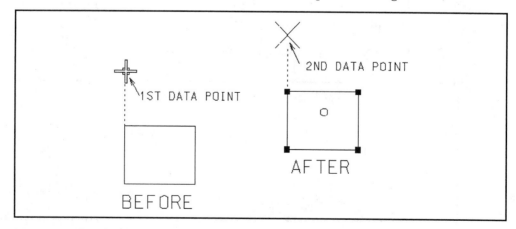

FIGURE 5–7   Example of using the Move command with a selected element.

> **NOTE:** If a command cannot work with selected elements, the element handles disappear when the command is selected.

FENCE MANIPULATION

The fence manipulation commands provide another way to manipulate groups of elements. A fence is placed around the elements to be manipulated, then the fence contents commands can manipulate all elements contained within the fence. Only one fence at a time can be placed in the design plane, and it remains active until either a new fence is placed or the design file is closed.

The Fence tool box is opened from the Main tool frame, as shown in Figure 5–8.

Placing a Fence

Six types of fences can be placed in the design plane (see Figure 5–9 for examples of each shape):

- A block defined by diagonally opposite data points
- A shape defined by a series of vertex data points
- A circle defined by center and an edge data points
- An existing linear shape
- A fence defined by the contents of the selected View
- A fence defined by the contents of the active design file

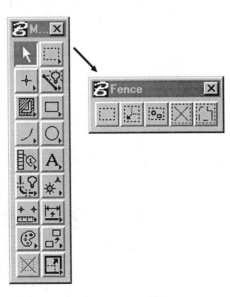

FIGURE 5–8   Fence tool box position in the Main tool frame.

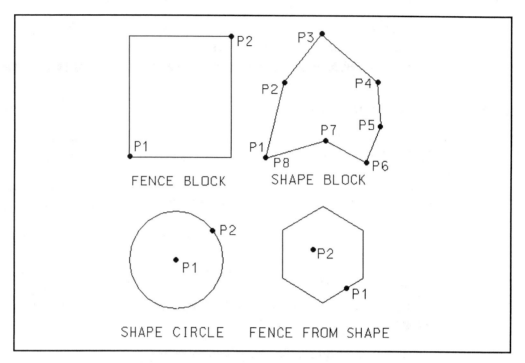

FENCE BLOCK   SHAPE BLOCK

SHAPE CIRCLE   FENCE FROM SHAPE

FIGURE 5–9 Examples of four fence shapes.

Fence Block Invoke the Place Fence Block command from:

Fence tool bar	Select the Place Fence tool and Block from the Fence Type option menu (see Figure 5–10).
Key-in window	**Place Fence Block** (or **pl f b**)

MicroStation prompts:

> Place Fence Block > Enter first point *(Define one corner of the block in the design plane.)*
>
> Place Fence Block > Enter opposite corner *(Define the diagonally opposite corner of the block in the design plane.)*

FIGURE 5–10 Invoking the Place Fence tool from the Fence tool bar.

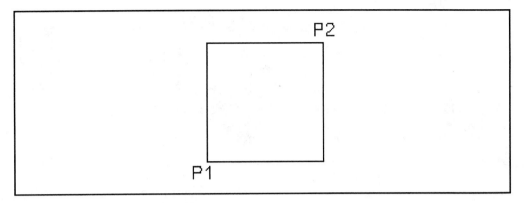

FIGURE 5–11   Example of placing a fence block by precision key-in.

For example, the following command sequence shows how to place a fence block via precision key-in commands (see Figure 5–11):

Place Fence Block > Enter first point **XY=2,2** [ENTER]
Place Fence Block > Enter opposite corner **XY=6,4** [ENTER]

Shape Fence   Invoke the Place Fence Shape command from:

Fence tool bar	Select the Place Fence tool and Shape from the Fence Type option menu (see Figure 5–12)
Key-in window	**Place Fence Shape** (or **pl f s**) [ENTER]

MicroStation prompts:

Place Fence Shape > Enter Fence Points *(Define the location of each fence vertex in the design plane.)*

To complete the fence shape, either place the last vertex data point on top of the first one or click on the Close Shape button in the Tool Settings box, as shown in Figure 5–12.

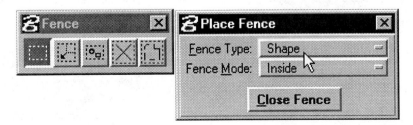

FIGURE 5–12   Invoking the Place Fence Shape command from the Fence tool bar.

FIGURE 5–13   Invoking the Place Fence Circle command from the Fence tool box.

Fence Circle Invoke the Place Fence Circle command from:

Fence tool bar	Select the Place Fence tool and Circle from the Fence Type option menu (see Figure 5–13)
Key-in window	**Place Fence Circle** (or **pl f c**) ⏎

MicroStation prompts:

> Place Fence Circle > Enter circle center *(Define the location of the fence center in the design plane.)*
> Place Fence Circle > Enter edge point *(Define a data point on the edge of the fence circle.)*

Fence from Shape Invoke the Place Fence From Shape Element command from:

Fence tool bar	Select the Place Fence tool and Element from the Fence Type option menu (see Figure 5–14).
Key-in window	**Place Fence From Shape** (or **pl f f**) ⏎

MicroStation prompts:

> Place Fence Shape > Identify element *(Select the linear shape whose outline will define the fence.)*
> Place Fence Shape > (Accept/Reject) Shape Element *(Click anywhere in the design plane to accept the element.)*

FIGURE 5–14   Invoking the Place Fence From Element command from the Fence tool box.

NOTE: The only types of 2D elements that can place a fence from a shape are the Block, Shape, Orthogonal Shape, and Regular Polygon. The selected element is *not* manipulated by the fence contents commands.

Fence View   Invoke the Place Fence From View command from:

Fence tool bar	Select the Place Fence tool and From View from the Fence Type option menu (see Figure 5–15)
Key-in window	**Place Fence View (or pl f vi)** ⏎

MicroStation prompts:

> Create Fence From View > Select View *(Place a data point anywhere on the view to place a fence.)*

MicroStation places a fence that includes all the elements (depending on the Fence Selection mode selected) in the selected view. (See the later section on Views Windows and View Attributes for creating new or modifying existing views.)

To place a fence to include all the elements in the active design file, invoke the Place Fence From Design File command from:

Fence tool bar	Select the Place Fence tool and From Design File from the Fence Type option menu (see Figure 5–16).
Key-in window	**Place Fence Active (or pl f ac)** ⏎

FIGURE 5–15   Invoking the Place Fence From View command from the Fence tool box.

FIGURE 5-16   Invoking the Place Fence From Design File command from the Fence tool box.

MicroStation prompts:

> Create Fence Design File > Select View *(Select the view where you want to place the fence.)*

MicroStation places the fence in the selected view that includes all the elements drawn in the active design file.

Fence Selection Mode

Before you manipulate the contents of a fence, you must set which fence selection mode to use. The active mode determines which elements are actually contained by the fence. For example, you can elect to manipulate all elements completely outside of the fence.

Six Fence Selection Mode options are available from the Tool Settings box when a Fence command is active (see Figure 5–17). The Fence Selection Mode options are also available in the Full Locks settings box.

Fence Mode Types   Following are descriptions of each of the six fence modes.

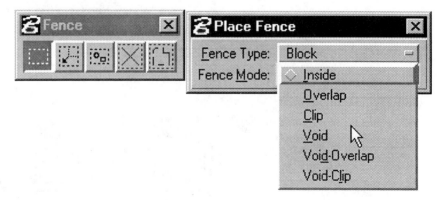

FIGURE 5–17   Fence Mode option menu in the Tool Settings box.

Inside Mode Only the elements completely inside the fence are manipulated when the fence mode Inside is selected. For example, the Delete Fence Contents command deletes circles A, B, and D in Figure 5–18a.

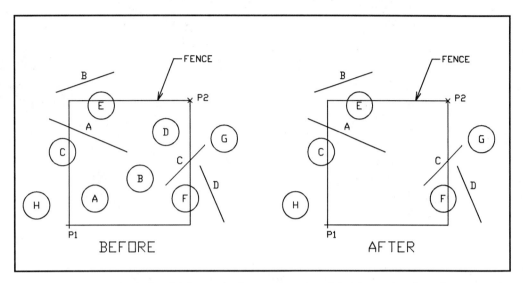

FIGURE 5–18a Example of deleting the fence contents with Inside mode selected.

Overlap Mode Elements inside and overlapping the fence are manipulated when the fence mode Overlap is selected. For example, the Delete Fence Contents command deletes circles A, B, C, D, E, and F and lines A and C in Figure 5–18b.

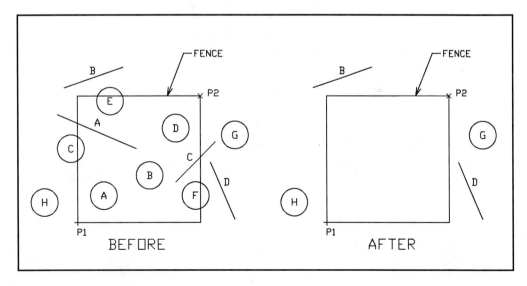

FIGURE 5–18b Example of deleting the fence contents with Overlap mode selected.

Clip Mode The parts of elements inside the fence are manipulated when the fence mode Clip is selected. Elements are clipped at the fence boundary. For example, the Delete Fence Contents command deletes circles A, B, and D, part of circles C, E, and F, and parts of lines A and C in Figure 5–18c.

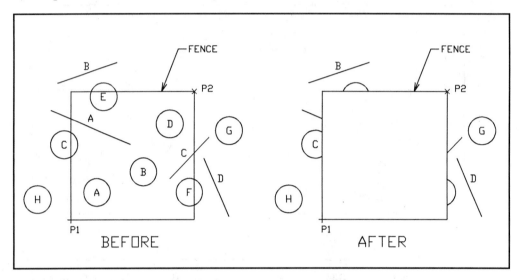

FIGURE 5–18c   Example of deleting the fence contents with Clip mode selected.

Void Mode Elements completely outside the fence are manipulated when the fence mode Void is selected. For example, the Delete Fence Contents command deletes circles G and H and lines B and D in Figure 5–18d.

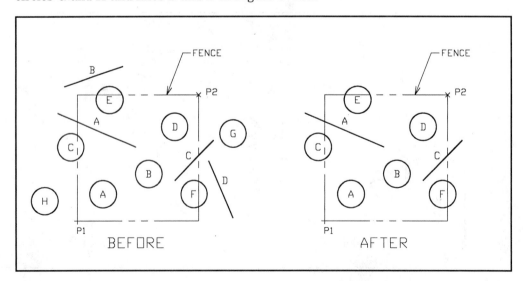

FIGURE 5–18d   Example of deleting the fence contents with Void mode selected.

Void-Overlap Mode All elements outside and overlapping the fence are manipulated when the fence mode Void-Overlap is selected. For example, the Delete Fence Contents command deletes circles C, E, F, G, and H and lines A, B, C, and D in Figure 5–18e.

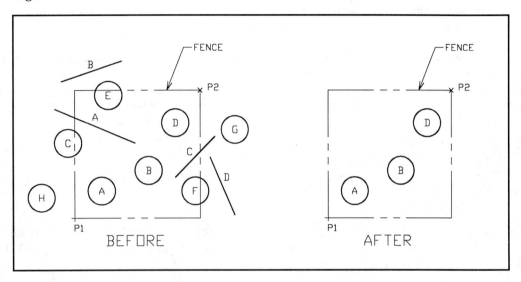

FIGURE 5–18e   Example of deleting the fence contents with Void-Overlap mode selected.

Void-Clip Mode The parts of all elements outside the fence are manipulated when the fence mode Void-Clip is selected. Elements are clipped at the fence boundary. For example, the Delete Fence Contents command deletes circles G and H, and lines B and D, parts of circles C, E, and F, and parts of lines A and C in Figure 5–18f.

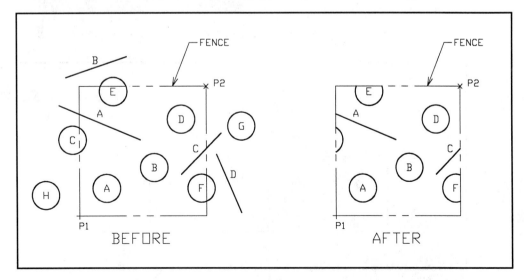

FIGURE 5–18f   Example of deleting the fence contents with Void-Clip mode selected.

Modifying a Fence's Shape or Location

You just finished placing a complicated fence shape and there, sitting outside the fence, is an element that should be inside the fence. There is no need to place the fence again; the Modify Fence tool can modify a fence vertex or move the fence to a new location.

Modifying Fence Shape To modify a fence, invoke the Modify Fence Vertex command from:

Fence tool bar	Select the Modify Fence tool and Vertex from the Modify Mode option menu (see Figure 5–19).
Key-in window	**Modify Fence** (or **mod f**) [ENTER]

MicroStation prompts:

> Modify Fence Vertex > Identify vertex *(Click the Data button on the fence outline near the vertex to be modified, drag the vertex to the new position, and click the Data button again.)*

See Figure 5–20 for an example of modifying a fence.

FIGURE 5–19 Invoking the Modify Fence Vertex command from the Fence tool bar.

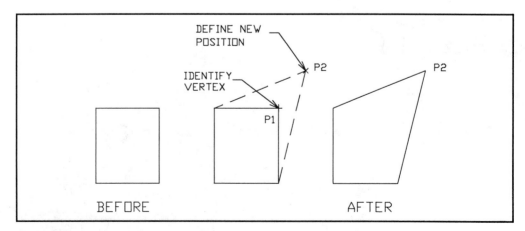

FIGURE 5–20 Example of modifying a fence vertex.

> **NOTE:** After the first data point is placed, a dynamic image of the fence drags with the screen pointer.

Moving a Fence To move a fence to a new location in the design plane, invoke the Move Fence command from:

Fence tool bar	Select the Modify Fence tool and Position from the Modify Mode option menu (see Figure 5–21).
Key-in window	**Move Fence** (or **mov f**) ⏎

MicroStation prompts:

> Modify Fence Block/Shape > Define origin *(Click the Data button in the design plane to identify the relative starting position of the move.)*
> Modify Fence Block/Shape > Define distance *(Click the Data button in the design plane to identify the relative position to which the fence is to be moved.)*

The fence is moved a distance equal to the distance between the two data points, and the relationship of the final fence position to data point 2 is the same as the original fence position was to data point 1.

> **NOTE:** The Modify Fence tool modifies only the shape or position of the fence outline, not the contents of the fence. The Modify Fence Contents tools are used to modify the elements contained by the fence.

Manipulating Fence Contents

After you place a fence and select the appropriate fence selection mode, you are ready to manipulate the contents of the fence. There is a fence contents manipulation equivalent for each of the element manipulation commands discussed in the previous chapters. The only difference is that you do not have to select the elements to manipulate—the fence does that for you.

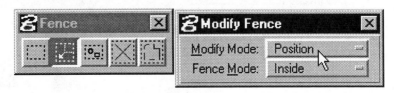

FIGURE 5–21 Invoking the Move Fence command from the Fence tool bar.

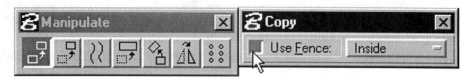

FIGURE 5-22 Invoking the Copy tool from the Manipulate tool bar with the Use Fence toggle button set to ON.

The Copy, Move, Scale Rotate, Mirror, and Array commands in the Manipulate tool bar can be switched between element manipulation and fence contents manipulation. The Use Fence toggle button in the Tool Settings window determines which type of manipulation is done. If the button is set to ON, the fence contents are manipulated; if it is set to OFF, individual elements are manipulated. Similarly, when you invoke the Change Element Attributes tool from the Change Attributes tool bar, a toggle button in the Tool Settings window can switch between element and fence manipulation. Figure 5–22 shows the Manipulate tool bar with the Copy tool selected and the Use Fence toggle button set to ON in the Tool Settings window.

In addition, MicroStation provides three fence contents manipulation tools:

- The Manipulate Fence Contents tool, invoked from the Fence tool box, has an Operations option menu in the Tool Settings window from which you can select the type of manipulation you need (see Figure 5–23).
- The Delete Fence Contents tool, invoked from the Fence tool box, deletes all elements within the contents of the fence.
- The Drop Fence Contents tool, invoked from the Fence tool box, drops all complex elements within the contents of the fence.

For example, to move the contents of the fence to a new location in the design plane, select the Manipulate Fence Contents command from:

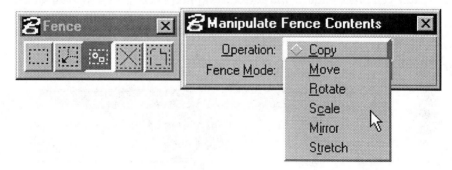

FIGURE 5-23 Manipulate Fence Contents Operations option menu.

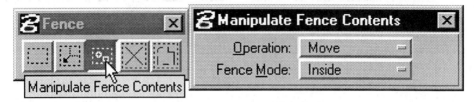

FIGURE 5–24   Invoking the Fence Move command from the Fence tool bar.

Fence tool bar	Select the Manipulate Fence Contents tool and Move from the Operations option menu (See Figure 5–24).
Key-in window	**Fence Move** (or **f m**)

MicroStation prompts:

> Move Fence Contents > Define origin *(Locate the starting position of the move in the design plane.)*
> Move Fence Contents > Define distance *(Locate the final destination in the design plane.)*

Fence Stretch

The Fence Stretch command allows you to stretch the contents of a fence. There is no equivalent element manipulation command.

Fence Stretch ignores fence selection modes. The way it manipulates elements depends on the element's type and location in the contents of the fence:

- Line, Line String, Multi-line, Curve String, Shape, Polygon, Arc, and Cell (see Chapter 10) elements that overlap the fence border are stretched.
- Elements completely inside the fence are moved.
- Circle and Ellipse elements that overlap the fence are ignored.

See Figure 5–25 for an example of stretching the contents of a fence.

To stretch a group of elements, place a fence that overlaps the elements you want to stretch, then select the Fence Stretch command from:

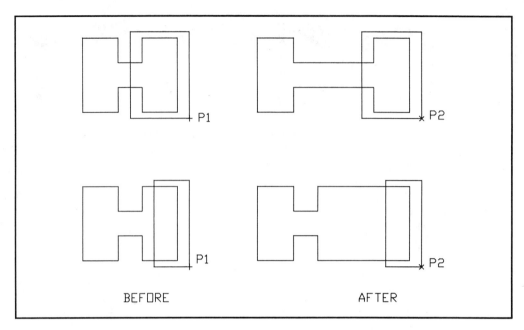

FIGURE 5–25   Example of stretching the contents of a fence.

Fence tool bar	Select the Manipulate Fence Contents tool and Stretch from the Operations option menu (see Figure 5–26).
Key-in window	**Fence Stretch** (or **f s**) ⏎

MicroStation prompts:

> Fence Stretch > Define origin *(Locate a relative point in the design plane to start the stretch.)*
>
> Fence Stretch > Define distance *(Locate a relative point in the design plane to end the stretch.)*

FIGURE 5–26   Invoking the Fence Stretch command from the Fence tool bar.

The new fence location has the same relationship to the second data point as the original fence location did to the first data point.

Removing a Fence

To remove a fence, invoke the Place Fence command and the existing fence will be removed. If you do not want to place another fence, select another command and continue working. There is no separate command to remove a fence.

> **NOTE:** Always remove a fence after you are finished with it to protect from accidental fence contents manipulations. For example, if a fence is defined and you accidentally select the command to delete the fence contents while thinking you selected the delete element command, you are about to delete the contents of the fence.

VIEW WINDOWS AND VIEW ATTRIBUTES

Thus far, you have been working in only one view window. That may have forced you to spend a lot of time using the view commands to set up the view for the areas you needed to draw in. MicroStation actually provides eight separate view windows (or cameras) that let you work in different parts of your design at the same time.

Each view window is identified by its view number (1–8). The view windows are similar to having eight zoom lens cameras that can be pointed at different parts of your design. For instance, in one view you might display the entire drawing; in two other views you might be zoomed in close to widely separated design areas to show great detail (Figure 5–27). All eight views can be opened at the same time on your monitor or on either monitor of a two-monitor workstation.

The view control commands you have already been introduced to (Zoom, Fit, Area, Center, and Update) work on any open view window. Let's look now at the View commands that help you position and size the eight view windows.

Opening and Closing View Windows

View windows are opened and closed either from the Open/Close submenu in the pull-down menu Windows, from the Open/Close dialog box, or by key-in commands.

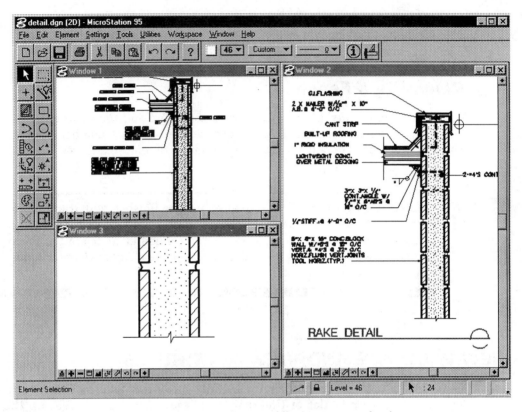

FIGURE 5-27   Example of three views showing different portions of a design.

To open or close one view window, select:

Pull-down menu	Window > Open/Close > View # (or ALT + W, O, #, where # is the number of the view) (see Figure 5–28).
Key-in window	**View Off** (or **vi of**) or **View On** (or **vi on**) ENTER

To open or close several view windows quickly, select:

Pull-down menu	Window Open/Close, Dialog (or ALT + W, O, D, #, where # is the number of the view) (see Figure 5–29).
Key-in window	**View Off** (or **vi of**) or **View On** (or **vi on**) ENTER

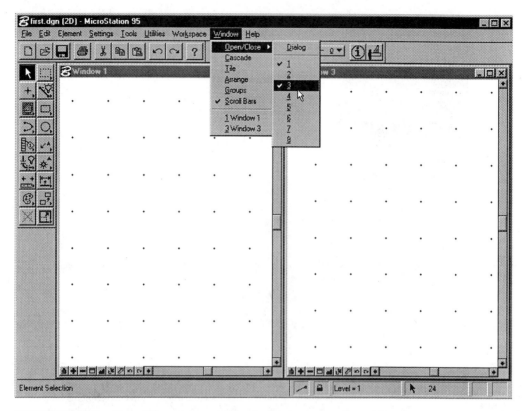

FIGURE 5–28   Open/Close submenu showing view windows 1 and 3 open.

In addition to the Open/Close options just discussed, most operating systems provide a command for closing a window in the window's "Control" menu. Figure 5–30 shows an example of such a window.

> **NOTE:** The view windows you open and close apply only to the current editing session. If you want the current arrangement of the view windows to be the same the next time you open the design file in MicroStation, select the Save Settings option from the pull-down menu File.

FIGURE 5–29   View Open/Close dialog box showing view windows 1 and 3 open.

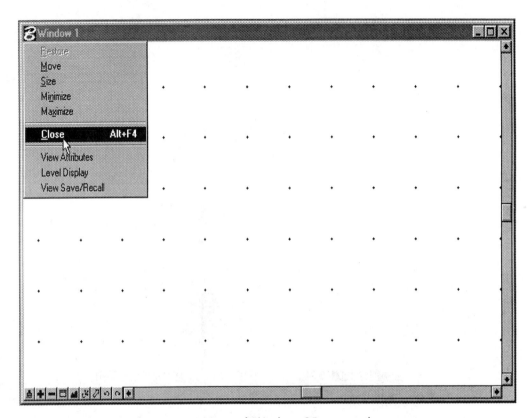

FIGURE 5–30 Window menu in Microsoft Windows 95 view window.

Arranging Open View Windows

The working area can become a little cluttered when several view windows are open, and MicroStation provides three housekeeping commands for cleaning up the clutter: Cascade, Tile, and Arrange. The commands are provided in the pull-down menu Window, as shown in Figure 5–31.

Cascade The Cascade command stacks all open view windows in numerical order, with the lowest-numbered view window on top and the other view window title bars visible behind it, as shown in Figure 5–32.

> **NOTE:** The view arrangement commands do not place any part of the views behind tool boxes that are attached to the side of the MicroStation workspace, as shown in Figures 5–32 and 5–33.

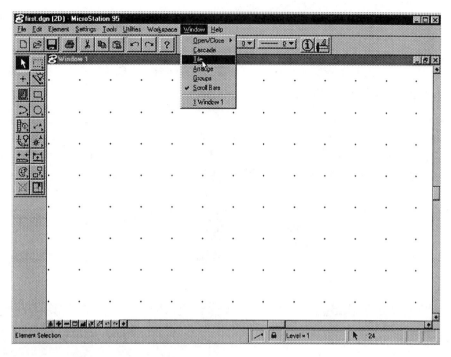

FIGURE 5-31   Window pull-down menu.

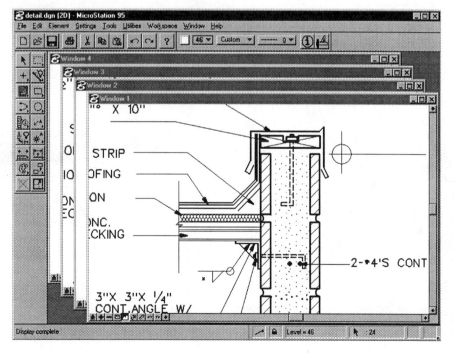

FIGURE 5-32   Example of cascaded view windows.

To cascade the open view windows, select the Cascade command from:

Pull-down menu	<u>W</u>indow > <u>C</u>ascade (or ⌨ + **W, C**)
Key-in window	**Window Cascade** (or **w c**) ⏎

The open view windows are cascaded (there are no MicroStation prompts). To work on a specific view, just click on the Title bar and it will pop up to the top.

Tile The Tile command arranges all open view windows side by side in a tiled fashion, with the lowest-numbered view window in the upper left, as shown in Figure 5–33.

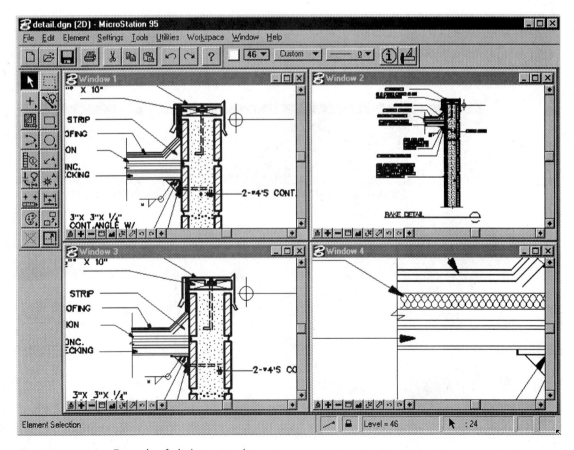

FIGURE 5–33 Example of tiled view windows.

To tile the open view windows, select the Tile command from:

Pull-down menu	<u>W</u>indow > <u>T</u>ile (or [ALT] + **W, T**)
Key-in window	**Window Tile** (or **w t**) [ENTER]

The open view windows are tiled (there are no MicroStation prompts).

Arrange The Arrange command sizes and moves all open view windows as necessary to fill the MicroStation workspace. The command attempts to keep each view window as close to its original size and position as possible.

To arrange the open view windows, select the Arrange command from:

Pull-down menu	<u>W</u>indow > <u>A</u>rrange (or [ALT] + **W, A**)
Key-in window	**Window Arrange** (or **w arr**) [ENTER]

The open view windows are arranged to fill the workspace (there are no MicroStation prompts).

Arranging Individual View Windows

In addition to the commands to open and close windows, MicroStation provides a group of commands for controlling the size and position of individual view windows. You can move a view window to a new location in the workspace, resize it, minimize and maximize it, and pop it to the top when it is buried under a stack of other view windows.

Moving a View Window To move a window to a new location in the MicroStation workspace:

1. Point to the window's title bar.
2. Press and hold the Data button.
3. Drag the window to the new location.
4. Release the Data button.

When you point to the title bar, the screen pointer changes to a different shape. As you drag the window, a dynamic of the window (or its outline) follows the screen pointer.

Resizing a View Window To change the size of a window:

1. Point to the window border.
2. Press and hold the Data button.
3. Drag the border to a new position.
4. Release the Data button.

When you point to a window border, the screen pointer changes to a different shape. As you drag the window border, a dynamic of the window (or its outline) follows the screen pointer.

If you grab the border on a side, you can change the position of only that one border. If you grab the border on a corner, you can change the position of the two adjacent borders at the same time.

Minimizing and Maximizing a View Window View windows contain a "minimize" button and a "maximize" button on the title bar (see Figure 5–34).

- Click the minimize button to reduce the view window to its minimum possible size.
- Click the maximize button to expand the view window to fill the MicroStation workspace and cover all other view windows.

To return a view to the size it was before you clicked one of these buttons, click the button again. For example, if you maximized a view window, click its maximize button to return it to the size it was before being maximized.

> **NOTE:** The appearance of the title bar buttons and of the window move and resize pointers varies among operating systems. For example, the resize pointer in Microsoft Windows 95 has a two-headed arrow pointing in the directions the window border can be dragged.

Finding a View Window The commands to change the size and position of a view window can cause it to cover all or part of other view windows, thus creating a "stack" of windows. There are two ways to bring a buried window to the top of the view window stack:

- If you can see any part of the buried view window's title border or title bar, click on it.
- Open the Window pull-down menu, then click on the view name at the bottom of the pull-down menu. The names of all open view windows are displayed there.

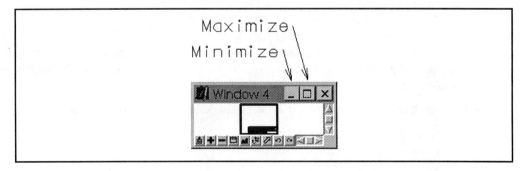

FIGURE 5–34 Minimize and Maximize buttons in Microsoft Windows 95.

Turning the View Window Slider Bar ON and OFF

Each view window contains a horizontal and vertical slider bar that can be used to position the view anywhere within the design plane. These bars can be turned OFF to obtain a little more design plane area display in each view window.

To turn view window slider bars ON and OFF, select:

Pull-down menu	Window > Scroll Bars (or **ALT** + **W, S**)

The command is a toggle switch that switches the state of the slider bars in all open views every time you select it. The slider bars are turned ON or OFF immediately (there are no MicroStation prompts).

> **NOTE:** The view control commands in the bottom left corner of the view windows also disappear when the slider bars are turned OFF. To access them, open the View Control tool bar from the pull-down menu Tools.

Creating and Using View Window Groups

MicroStation provides commands for creating and using named groups of windows in a design file. The groups can be opened and the view window control commands applied only to a selected group.

To active the Window Groups dialog box, select Groups from:

Pull-down menu	Window > Groups (or **ALT** + **W, G**)

The Window Groups dialog box opens and the Groups commands are available. Figure 5–35 presents an example of a Window Groups dialog box with two named groups; Table 5–1 describes the group commands.

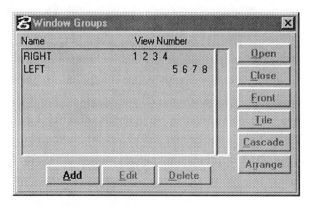

FIGURE 5–35   Window Groups dialog box.

Table 5–1. Window Groups Dialog Box Parts

PART	DESCRIPTION
Names	Contains the group names and view window numbers in each group. Click on the group to select it for use.
Open	Opens the selected group's view windows. The views open at the same size and position as the last time they were opened, or, if this is the first opening in the editing session, with the same size and position as the they were when settings were last saved.
Close	Closes all view windows assigned to the selected group.
Front	Brings the selected group's view windows to the front of other view windows.
Tile	Tiles only the selected group's view windows. Other open view windows are not tiled.
Cascade	Cascades only the selected group's view windows. Other open view windows are not cascaded.
Arrange	Arranges only the selected group's view windows to fill the Micro-Station workspace. Other open view windows are not arranged.
Add	Opens the Edit Window Groups dialog box, where you can create a new group name and assign view window numbers to it (see Figure 5–36).
Edit	Opens the Edit Window Groups dialog box for the selected group, so you can edit the group name and assigned view window numbers.
Delete	Deletes the selected group.

> **NOTE:** New groups and changes to existing groups are saved automatically to the design file. It is not necessary to save settings to retain them.

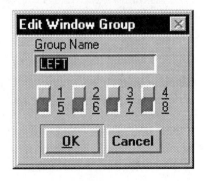

FIGURE 5–36 Edit Window Groups dialog box.

Setting View Attributes

MicroStation allows a set of view attributes to be assigned to each of the open view windows. View attributes control the way elements and drawing aids appear in the views. Attributes are usually turned off to speed up view updating and to reduce clutter in a view. For example, if a view contains a large amount of patterning, turning off the display of patterns can greatly reduce update time.

To open the View Attributes dialog box, select:

Pull-down menu	<u>S</u>ettings > <u>V</u>iew Attributes (or <u>ALT</u> + **S**, **V** or <u>CTRL</u> + **B**)

MicroStation displays View Attributes settings box as shown in Figure 5–37; each view attribute is explained briefly in Table 5–2.

Follow these steps to use the settings box to change view attributes:

1. Click the appropriate attribute toggle button ON or OFF as required.
2. If you want to set the attributes for all view windows, click the All button.
3. If you want to set the attributes for one view window, select its view window number in the View Number option menu and then click the Apply button.

FIGURE 5–37   View Attributes settings box.

Table 5–2.   View Attributes

ATTRIBUTE	TURNS ON AND OFF THE DISPLAY OF . . .
ASC Triad	The Auxiliary Coordinate System (ACS)
Background	The background image loaded with the Active Background command
Camera	The 3D view camera
Constructions	Elements placed with Construction Class mode active
Dimensions	Dimension elements
Dynamics	Dynamic updating of elements as they are placed in the design
Data Fields	Data Field placeholder characters
Fast Cells	The actual cells or a box indicating the area of the design occupied by cells
Fast Curves	The actual curve string or straight line segments indicating the vertices
Fast Font	The actual text font for each text element or MicroStation's fast font
Fast Ref Clipping	The display of the largest block enclosing the reference file clipping boundaries
Fill	The fill color in filled elements
Grid	The grid (if the view is zoomed out far enough, the grid will be turned off even if this attribute is on)
Level Symbology	Elements according to the symbology table rather than the actual element symbology
Line Styles	Elements with their actual line weights (if off, all lines are displayed with style 0, solid)
Line Weights	Elements with their actual line weights (if off, all lines are displayed at line weight 0)
Patterns	Pattern elements
Ref Boundaries	The display of reference file clipping boundaries as dashed polygons
Tags	The tag information for tagged elements
Text	The display of text elements (if off, no text elements are displayed)
Text Nodes	Text nodes as small crosses with numeric identifiers

NOTE: The view attributes setting changes remain in effect until either they are changed again or the design file is closed. To keep them in effect for future editing sessions, select Save Settings from the pull-down menu File.

Saving Views

If you regularly work in several specific areas of a design, MicroStation provides a way for you to return to those areas quickly by saving the view setup and attributes under a user-defined name. To return to one of those areas, you provide the saved view name, then click in the view you want set to have the saved view's setup.

Saving a View To save a view setup, first align a view to display the area of the design you want to save, then set the view attributes you want to have in effect when you use the view.

Invoke the Saved Views settings from:

Pull-down menu	Utilities > Saved Views (or [ALT] + **U, V**)
Key-in window	**SU** <name of view> [ENTER]

MicroStation displays the Saved Views settings box as shown in Figure 5–38.

To save a view, first make sure the number of the view that contains the view setup is displayed in the View options menu in the Saved Views settings box. Then key-in a name and description in the Name edit field and Description edit field, respectively. Saved view names can be from one to six characters long and can consist of any

FIGURE 5-38 Saved Views settings box.

combination of letters, numbers, dashes (-), periods (.), and underscores (_). Try to make your view name descriptive (to the extent that six characters allow). Descriptions are optional and can be up to 27 characters long. Make it a habit always to use the description to explain what the saved view is set to. Your description will help other people who use your design file, and it will help you if you have not used the design file for a few weeks. Once you have provided a name and an optional description, click on the Save button. The view is saved, and the name and description appear in the Saved Views area of the Saved Views settings box. The saved view is now a permanent part of your design file.

You also can save a view by keying in at the key-in window **sv=<name>,<description>** and pressing [ENTER]. Replace <name> with the name you select for the saved view and <description> with a description of the saved view. MicroStation prompts:

> Select view *(Click the Data button in the view that contains the setup you want to save.)*

Attaching a Saved View   To restore a saved view, invoke the Saved Views settings box. Select the name of the view you want to restore from the list. Make sure the Dest View option menu (located at the bottom of the settings box) is displaying the number of the view to which you want to set the saved view. Click the Attach button.

You also can restore a view by keying in at the key-in window field **vi=<name>**, and pressing [ENTER]. Replace <name> with the name of the view to be restored. MicroStation prompts:

> Select view *(Click the Data button in the view where you want to restore the view.)*

Deleting a Saved View   To delete a saved view you no longer need, invoke the Saved Views settings box. Select the name of the view you want to delete from the list. Click on the Delete button, and the selected saved view is deleted.

You also can delete a view by keying-in at the key-in window **dv=<name>** and pressing [ENTER]. Replace <name> with the name of the saved view to be deleted. The saved view is immediately deleted.

> **NOTE:** If you have the Saved Views settings box displayed and you key-in **dv=<name>** to delete a saved view, the name and description of the deleted saved view may remain in the settings box Saved Views list, even though it has been deleted. To update the settings box, close and reopen it.

REVIEW QUESTIONS

Write your answers in the spaces provided.

1. To select several elements by means of the Element Selection command, hold the _____ button and _____ around the elements.

2. To deselect one element from a group of selected elements, hold down the _____ key and click on the element.

3. Briefly explain the purpose of locking individual elements.

_____

_____

4. List the six fence selection modes available in MicroStation.

_____

_____

5. Explain briefly the difference between the Overlap and Void-Overlap mode.

_____

_____

6. How many views are available in MicroStation? _____

7. When MicroStation prompts you to Select View, which cursor button will you choose?

_____

8. List the three most basic steps for operating a Fence.

_____

_____

9. Explain briefly the difference between the Bottom to Top, Cascade, and Tile view commands.

_____

_____

10. List five view attribute options available in the View Attributes Settings box, and describe each one's purpose.

_____

_____

11. Explain briefly the benefits of saving views.

_____

_____

PROJECT EXERCISE

This project exercise provides step-by-step instructions for creating the design shown in Figure P5–1. The intent is to guide you in applying Element Selection, Fence manipulations, and Views.

> **NOTE:** The text and dimensions placed on the structure and members are not part of this project. They are included in Figure P5–1 as an aid to drawing the design.

Prepare the Design File

This procedure starts MicroStation, creates a design file, and enters the initial settings.

> **NOTE:** As you complete each step in the project procedures, place a check mark by the step to help you keep up with where you are in the project.

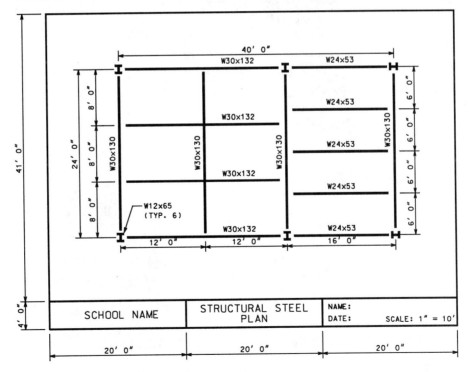

FIGURE P5-1   Completed project design.

STEP 1:   Invoke MicroStation by the normal technique for the operating system on your workstation.

STEP 2:   Create a new design file named CH5.DGN using the SEED2D.DGN seed file.

STEP 3:   In the Design File dialog box

- Set the Working Unit ratios to 1:12:8000, the Master Units as feet ('), and the Subunits as inches (").
- Set the Grid Master to 0.5, the Grid Reference to 2, and the Grid lock to ON.

STEP 4:   Invoke the AccuDraw from the Primary Tool bar.

STEP 5:   Open the AccuDraw settings box from the pull-down menu Settings, and adjust the settings values as follows:

- *Unit Roundoff Distance:* Set at 0.5 and set the toggle button to ON.
- *Unit Roundoff Angle:* Set at 90.000 and set the toggle button to ON.
- *Coordinate System:* Set the Rotation to Top and the Type to Rectangular.
- *Operation:* Set the toggle buttons for Floating Origin and Smart Key-ins to ON.

STEP 6:   With Figure P5–1 as a guide, draw the boarder and title block on level 10.

- Replace "SCHOOL NAME" with your school or company name, or make up a name.
- Place your name to the right of "NAME."
- Place today's date to the right of "DATE."

Draw the First I-beam

This procedure describes the steps required to draw the I-beam shown in Figure P5–2.

STEP 1:   If View Window 2 is not open, select the open/close submenu from the pull-down menu Window, and turn on View Window 2.

STEP 2:   Click in the View Window 1 Title bar to focus on the view.

STEP 3:   Set the Active Level to 1, the Line Weight to 2, and the Color to green.

STEP 4:   Invoke the Save settings from the pull-down menu File.

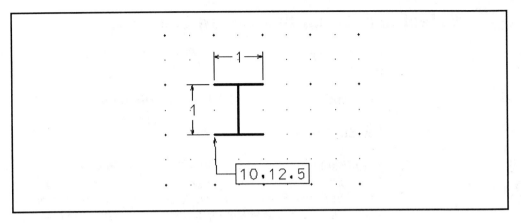

FIGURE P5-2 Draw the first column.

STEP 5: Invoke the Place Line command from the Linear Elements tool box.

MicroStation prompts:

> Place Line > Enter first point *(Keypoint snap to the lower left corner of the border block, type* **O** *to release the AccuDraw origin, and drag the cursor so X axis is set to 10.0000 and Y axis is set to 12.5. Then click the Data button to locate the start of the bottom I-beam line.)*
> Place Line > Enter end point *(Drag the cursor so inset X axis is set to 1.0000 and Y axis is set to 0.0000.)*
> Place Line > Enter end point *(Click the Reset button.)*

STEP 6: In View Window 1, invoke the Window Area command, then, in the Tool Settings window, set the Apply to Window option to 2.

MicroStation prompts:

> Window Area > Define first corner point *(Place a data point about 2 feet above and to the left of the I-beam line that was just completed.)*
> Window Area > Define opposite corner point *(Drag the dynamic rectangle below and to the right of the line, then place a data point to place the view area in View Window 2.)*

STEP 7: Invoke the Save settings from the pull-down menu File.

STEP 8: In View Window 2, use Center Snap to place the vertical 1′ long line centered above the line you just drew and the 1′ long top horizontal line centered above the vertical line, as shown in Figure P5-2.

Select and Group the I-beam Lines

This procedure groups the three lines forming the I-beam so they can be manipulated as one element.

STEP 1:   Invoke the Element Selection tool from the Main tool frame.

MicroStation prompts:

Element Selection *(Position the cursor above and to the left of the I-beam, then press and hold down the Data button while you drag the Selection rectangle around the I-beam. Release the Data button to select the three lines, as shown in Figure P5–3.)*

STEP 2:   Invoke the Group command from the pull-down menu Edit. MicroStation creates a group of the three selected lines. Place a Data point anywhere in the view to remove the handles.

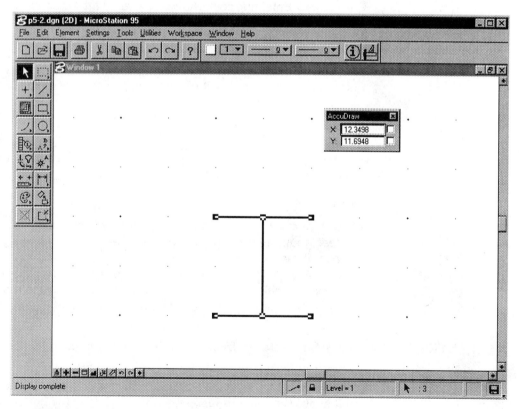

FIGURE P5–3   I-beam handles after element selection.

Create the Two Rows of Columns

This procedure uses the Copy Element, Rotate Copy, Place Fence Block, and Copy Fence Contents commands with AccuDraw to create the two rows of three I-beams each, as shown in Figure P5–4.

STEP 1:   Click the title bar of View Window 1 to return focus to it.

STEP 2:   Invoke the Copy Element command from the Manipulate tool box.

MicroStation prompts:

> Copy Element > Identify element *(Select the I-beam, type* **Y** *to lock AccuDraw's Y axis at 0.0000, then drag the manipulation pointer right to AccuDraw coordinate X = 24. Click the Data button to make the first copy in the bottom row.)*
> Copy Element > Accept/Reject (select next input) *(Type* **Y** *to lock AccuDraw's Y axis at 0.0000, then drag the manipulation pointer to the right to X = 16. Click the Data button to complete the bottom row, as shown in Figure P5–5.)*
> Copy Element > Accept/Reject (select next input) *(Click the Reset button to terminate the command sequence.)*

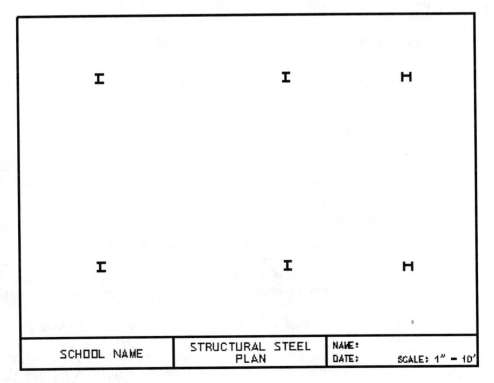

FIGURE P5–4   Two rows of I-beams.

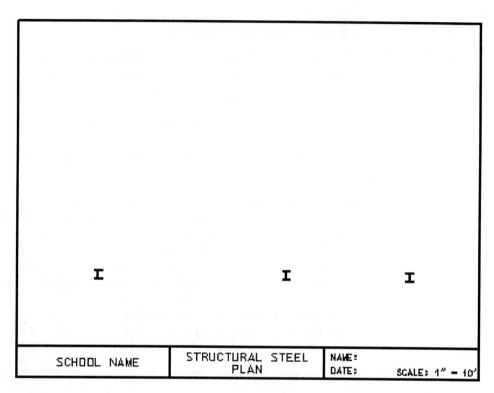

FIGURE P5–5   Bottom row after two copies are made of the I-beam.

STEP 3:   In View Window 1, define a small Window Area, to be placed in View Window 2, around the right-most I-beam.

STEP 4:   Click the title bar of View Window 2 to return focus to it.

STEP 5:   Invoke the Rotate command from the Manipulate tool box. Then, in the Tool Settings window, set the Method to Active Angle, set the Active Angle to 90, and set the toggle button for Make Copy to OFF.

MicroStation prompts:

> Rotate Element > Identify element *(Identify the I-beam.)*
> Rotate Element > Enter pivot point (point to rotate about) *(Click the Data button in the center of the I-beam's vertical line to pivot the I-beam about its center point, then click the Reset button.)*

STEP 6:   Click the title bar of View Window 1 to return focus to it.

STEP 7:   Invoke the Place Fence command from the Fence tool box, then, in the Tool Settings window, set the Fence Type to Block and the Fence Mode to Inside.

MicroStation prompts:

> Place a Fence Block > Enter first point *(Place a data point above and to the left of the left-most I-beam.)*
>
> Place a Fence Block > Enter opposite corner *(Drag the dynamic fence image around the three I-beams, then place a data point to complete the fence.)*

STEP 8: Invoke the Copy command from the Manipulate tool box, then, in the Tool Settings window, set the toggle button for Use Fence to ON.

MicroStation prompts:

> Copy Fence Contents > Define origin *(Place a data point somewhere near the bottom of the view.)*
>
> Copy Fence Contents > Define Distance *(Type* X *to lock AccuDraw's X axis at 0.0000, then drag the manipulation pointer up to Y = 24. Click the Data button to create the top I-beam row, as shown in Figure P5–6.)*
>
> Copy Fence Contents > Define Distance *(Click the Reset button to terminate the command sequence.)*

STEP 9: Invoke the Place Fence command again to remove the fence.

STEP 10: Invoke the Save settings from the pull-down menu File.

Draw the Outside Structural Members

This procedure places a Block element for the outside structural members, then uses the Delete part of the Element command to cut away the parts of the Block that overlap the I-beams, as shown in Figure P5–6.

STEP 1: Set the Active Level to 2, the Line Weight to 2, and the Color to blue.

STEP 2: Place a Block element with its lower left corner in the center of the lower left I-beam and its upper right corner in the center of the upper right I-beam, as shown in Figure P5–7.

STEP 3: Focus on View Window 1, then define a small Window Area, to be placed in View Window 2, around the lower right I-beam.

STEP 4: Focus on View Window 2, then invoke the Delete part of the Element command from the Modify tool box.

MicroStation prompts:

> Delete Part of Element > Select start point for partial delete *(Select the block one Grid point to the left of the I-beam in View Window 2.)*

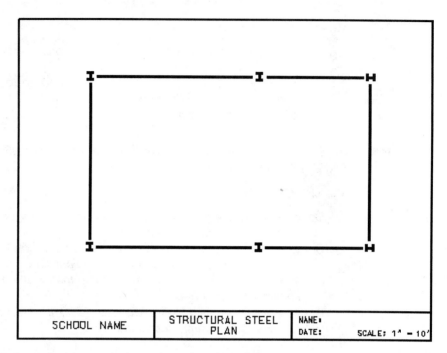

FIGURE P5–6 I-beams and outside structural members.

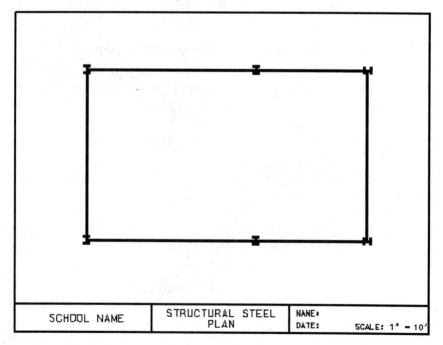

FIGURE P5–7 Result of placing a block for the outside structural members.

Delete Part of Element > Select direction of partial delete *(Drag the manipulation pointer a short distance toward the I-beam, and click the Data button.)*

Delete Part of Element > Select end point of partial delete *(Drag the manipulation point to one Grid point above the I-beam, and place a data point to complete the partial delete, as shown in Figure P5–8.)*

STEP 5:   Focus on View Window 1, then define a small Window Area, to be placed in View Window 2, around the upper right I-beam.

STEP 6:   Focus on View Window 2, then invoke the Delete part of the Element command from the Modify tool box.

MicroStation prompts:

Delete Part of Element > Select start point for partial delete *(Select the line one Grid point below the I-beam.)*

Delete Part of Element > Select end point of partial delete *(Drag the manipulation pointer to one Grid point to the left of the I-beam, and place a data point to complete the partial delete.)*

STEP 7:   Repeat Steps 5 and 6 for the other four I-beams.

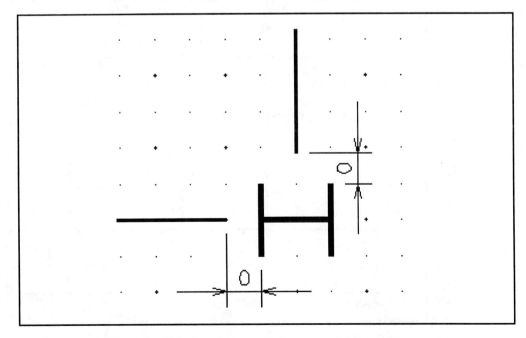

FIGURE P5–8   Amount of block to delete partially over each I-beam.

Draw the Interior Structural Members

This procedure uses the Move Parallel and Extend Element to Intersection commands to draw the interior structural Members as shown in Figure P5–9.

STEP 1: Focus on View Window 1.

STEP 2: Invoke the Move Parallel command from the Manipulate tool box, then, in the Tool Settings window, set the toggle buttons for Distance and Make Copy to ON, and key-in **12** in the Distance edit field.

MicroStation prompts:

> Copy Parallel by Key-in > Identify element *(Select the left vertical line.)*
> Copy Parallel by Key-in > Accept/Reject (select next input) *(Move the manipulation pointer to the right of the element, and click the Data button two times to place two parallel copies of the line, as shown in Figure P5–10. Click the Reset button.)*

STEP 3: Make two parallel copies of the top left horizontal line, each 8′ apart below the line, as shown in Figure P5–11.

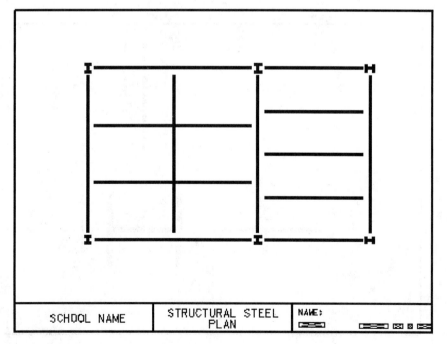

FIGURE P5-9 Completed interior structure members.

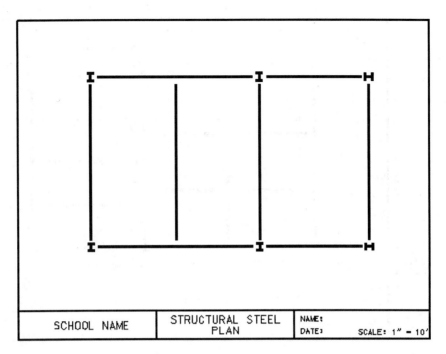

FIGURE P5-10   Place two parallel copies of the left vertical line, 12' apart.

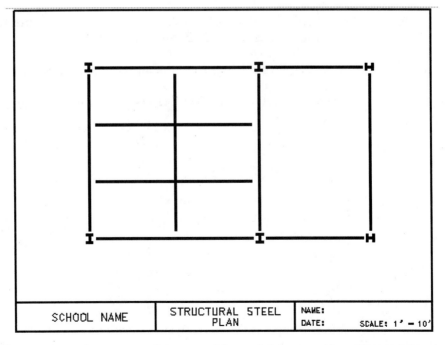

FIGURE P5-11   Place two parallel copies of the top left horizontal line, 8' apart below the line.

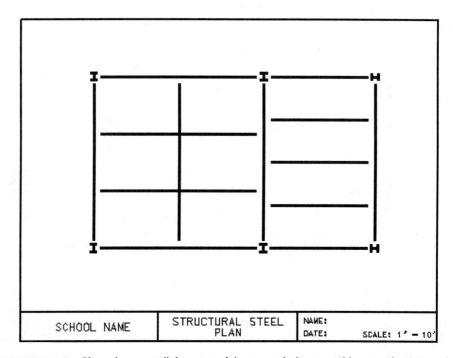

FIGURE P5-12 Place three parallel copies of the top right horizontal line, each 6' apart below the line.

STEP 4: Make three parallel copies of the top right horizontal line, each 6' apart below the line, as shown in Figure P5–12.

STEP 5: Invoke the Save settings from the pull-down menu File.

STEP 6: Refer to the Chapter 8 Project Exercise for placing text and dimensioning.

DRAWING EXERCISES 5-1 THROUGH 5-5

Use the following table to set up the design files for Exercises 5–1 through 5–3.

SETTING	VALUE
Seed File	SEED2D.DGN
Working Units	MU = IN, SU = 10 TH, PU = 1000
Grid	Master = .1, Reference = 10, GRID lock ON

Exercise 5-1   Flange gasket.

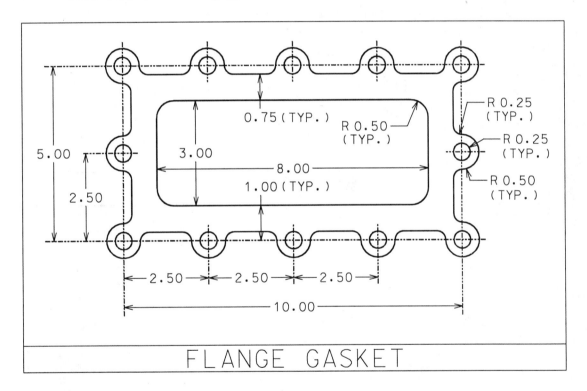

FLANGE GASKET

Exercise 5–2   Machine part.

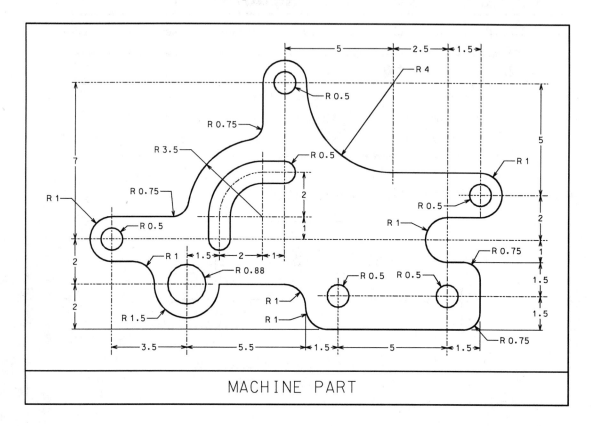

MACHINE PART

Exercise 5–3 Rotary pressure joint.

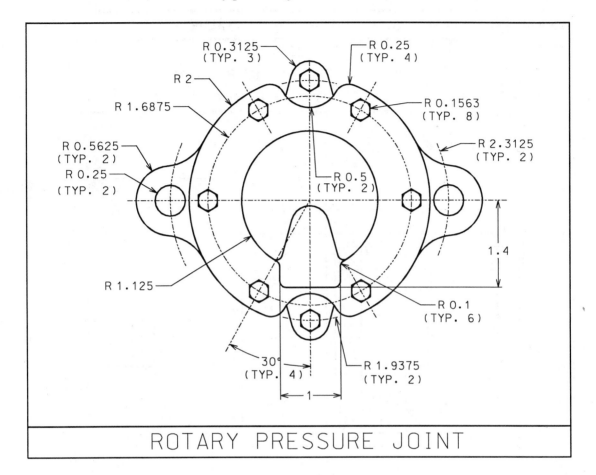

ROTARY PRESSURE JOINT

Use the following table to set up the design files for Exercises 5–4 and 5–5.

SETTING	VALUE
Seed File	SEED2D.DGN
Working Units	MU = ', SU = 12", PU = 1200
Grid	Master = :.5, Reference = 24, GRID lock ON

Exercise 5–4   Leaded glass design.

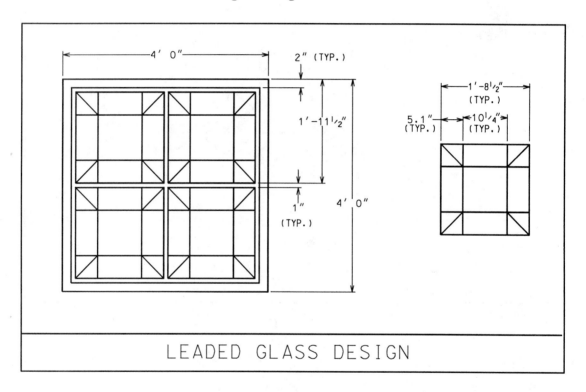

LEADED GLASS DESIGN

Exercise 5–5 Desk.

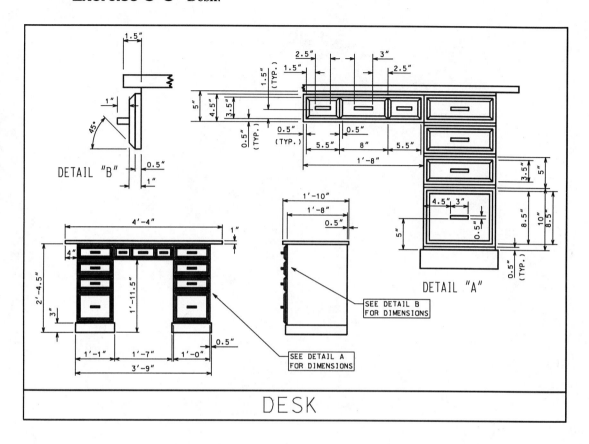

DESK

PLACING TEXT,
DATA FIELDS, AND TAGS

· · · · · · · · · · · · · · · ·

OBJECTIVES

After completing this chapter, you will be able to:

✓ Place single-character fractions.

✓ Use several commands to place text elements.

✓ Import text from other computer applications.

✓ Edit the content of existing text elements.

✓ Manipulate the attributes of existing text.

✓ Place annotations in the drawing.

✓ Create and use "fill-in-the-blanks" Text Node and Data Field elements.

✓ Place and manage Tags.

PLACING TEXT

Chapter 3 discussed setting Text Attributes and placing Text by Origin. In this section we discuss additional text placement tools available in MicroStation.

Placing Natural Fractions in One-Character Positions

Natural fractions are several characters long, which can take up a lot of space in the design. To reduce the space required for such fractions, MicroStation adds one-character natural fractions to several fonts and provides a switch in the Text settings window for turning on these one-character fonts.

Figure 6–1 shows an example of natural fractions placed both as separate characters and as one-character fractions.

Invoke one-character natural fractions placement mode from:

Pull-down menu	Element > Text (or ⌨ + **L, X**)

MicroStation displays the Text settings box. Set the Fractions toggle button to ON, as shown in Figure 6–2.

Natural fractions placed in text strings *after* the button is turned ON are placed as one-character fractions. Existing multicharacter natural fractions are not changed. Invoke the Save Settings command to make the setting permanent.

Multi-Character	One-Character
1/2	$^{1}/_{2}$
1/4	$^{1}/_{4}$
1/8	$^{1}/_{8}$
1/16	$^{1}/_{16}$
1/32	$^{1}/_{32}$
1/64	$^{1}/_{64}$

FIGURE 6–1 *Examples of natural fractions.*

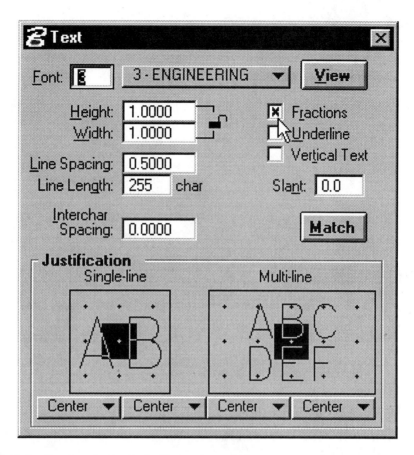

FIGURE 6-2 Fractions button in the Text settings window.

Things to Keep in Mind About Natural Fractions

- If a font does not include natural fractions, or does not contain the particular fractions you enter, those fractions are placed as separate characters even when the Fraction button is ON.
- To find out which fonts support one-character natural fractions, open the View Fonts window from the Text Attributes settings box. If the word "Fractions" is in the Content column, the font supports one-character fractions.
- If you include a natural fraction in a string of text, there must be a space character before and after the fraction in order for MicroStation to recognize it as a natural fraction.
- One-character fractions take up more space than single characters, so you may need to insert extra space characters to keep the fraction from running into the characters before and after it.

Placing Fitted Text

The Place Fitted Text command scales and rotates the text you type in the Text Editor between two data points, as shown in Figure 6–3.

Invoke the Place Fitted Text command from:

Text tool box	Select the Place Text tool and Fitted Text from the Method option menu located in the settings window (see Figure 6–4).
Key-in window	**Place Text Fitted (or pla tex fi)** ⌨ENTER

MicroStation prompts:

> Place Fitted Text > Enter text *(Type the text in the Text Editor window, then define the starting point for placing the text.)*
> Place Fitted Text > Define endpoint of text *(Define the end point of the text.)*
> Place Fitted Text > Enter more chars or position text *(Either place more fitted copies of the text string, enter a new text string, or select another command.)*

Things to Keep in Mind About Fitted Text

- The only Text settings used by the command are the active font and text justification.
- Top, Center, and Bottom text justification determine where the text lines up in relation to an imaginary line between the two data points. The text in Figure 6–3 was placed with Bottom justification.

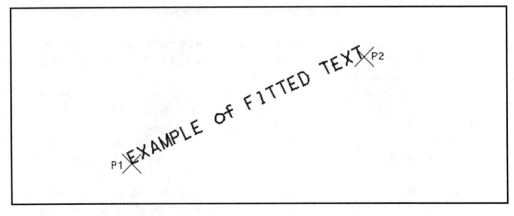

FIGURE 6–3   Example of placing fitted text.

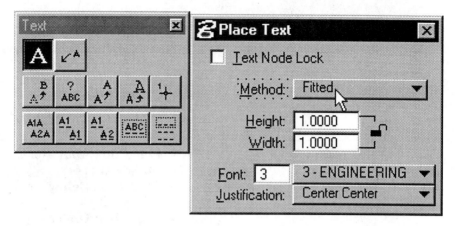

FIGURE 6–4   Invoking the Place Text (Fitted Text) command from the Text tool box.

- If you attempt to insert a line break in the Fitted Text string, MicroStation removes it and keeps the text on one line.
- Fitted Text strings are normal text elements and can be manipulated like any other element.

Placing Text Above, Below, or On an Element

MicroStation provides commands for placing a text string above, below, or on a line or a segment of a linear element, as shown in Figure 6–5.

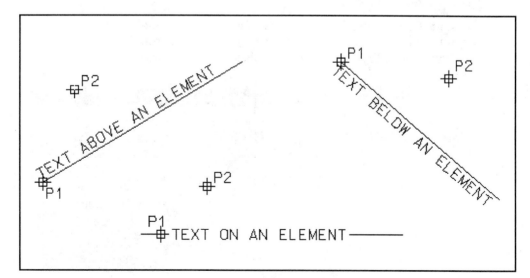

FIGURE 6–5   Examples of text placed above, below, and on a line.

Invoke the commands from:

Text tool box	Select the Place Text tool and Above Element, Below Element, or On Element from the Method option menu located in the settings window (see Figure 6–6).
Key-in window	• **Place Text Above** (or **pla tex ab**) ⏎ • **Place Text Below** (or **pla tex b**) ⏎ • **Place Text On** (or **pla tex o**) ⏎

MicroStation prompts are identical for all of the three Method option menu selections. Following are the MicroStation prompts when the Above option is selected from the Method option menu.

Place Text Above Element > Enter text *(Type the text in the Text Editor window.)*
Place Text Above Element > Identify element *(Identify the element where the text is to be placed. A dynamic image of the text appears above the element.)*
Place Text Above Element > Accept/Reject (Select next input) *(Click the Data button to accept the placement, or click the Reset button to reject it.)*

Things to Keep in Mind About Placing Text Above, Below, or On a Linear Element

■ Left, Center, and Right text justification determine where the text lines up in relation to the point on the line or segment where the element was identified. The examples in Figure 6–5 were all placed with Left text justification.

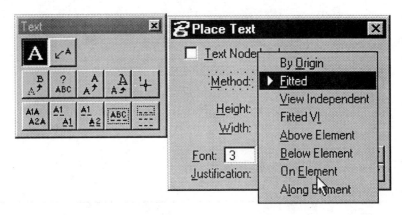

FIGURE 6–6 Above, Below, and On options in the Place Text settings window.

- If you insert a line break in the text string, MicroStation accepts it but places only the first line of the multi-line text string. For example, if you type **Pump** ⏎**ENTER** **3B**, only "Pump" will be placed.
- The space between the element and the text string for the Above and Below commands is equal to the text Line Spacing attribute. Open the Text settings window to change the Line Spacing.
- When text is placed on an element, a hole is cut in the element and the text is placed in the hole. If the element is a line or line string, two separate, unrelated line or line string elements result from the insertion. If the element is a closed shape, it changes to a line string after the insertion.
- Once placed, the text string has no relation to the element it was placed above, below, or on. For example, if the text string placed on an element is deleted, the two element pieces do not rejoin.
- Text strings placed in this way are normal text elements that can be manipulated like any other element.
- If the Text Editor window contains text when you invoke one of these commands, MicroStation skips the first prompt and asks you to select the element.
- If you attempt to select an element when the Text Editor window is empty, MicroStation prompts:

      Enter characters first

  and the element is not selected.

Placing Text Along an Element

The Place Text Along Element command places text above or below an element. The text follows the contour of an arc, a circle, or a curve, and can bend around the vertex of a linear multisegment element. See Figure 6–7 for examples of placing text along elements.

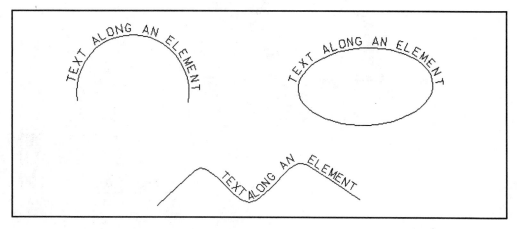

FIGURE 6–7   Examples of text placed along elements.

Text elements are linear, so to make text follow the contour of a curving element, the command places each character as a separate text element. To compensate for tight curves, settings are provided to allow entering the space between each character (Intercharacter Spacing) and the space between the text and the element (Line Spacing) in working units (MU:SU:PU).

Invoke the Place Text Along Element command from:

Text tool box	Select the Place Text tool and Along Element from the Method option menu located in the settings window (see Figure 6–8).
Key-in window	**Place Text Along** (or **pla tex al**) (ENTER)

MicroStation prompts:

Place Text Along Element > Enter text *(Type the text in the Text Editor window.)*
Place Text Along Element > Identify element, text location *(Define the point on the element where the text is to be placed. Dynamic images of the text appear both above and below the element, as shown in Figure 6–9, and you must select the one to place.)*
Place Text Along Element > Accept, select text above/below *(Click the Data button on the side of the element where you want the text placed, or click the Reset button to reject it.)*

The text on the side of the element you selected is placed, and the dynamic image on the other side disappears.

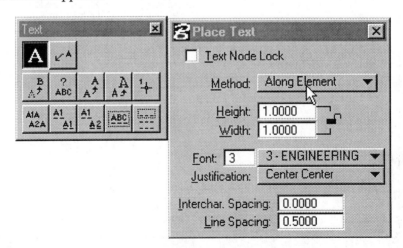

FIGURE 6-8   Invoking the Place Text (Along Element) command from the Text tool box.

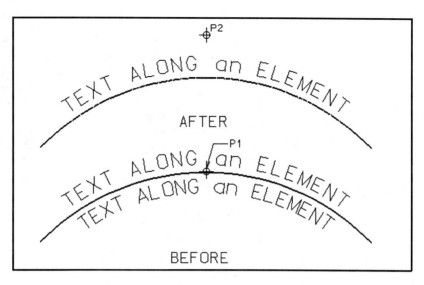

FIGURE 6–9   Example of the dynamic image of text along an element before acceptance.

Things to Keep in Mind About Placing Text Along an Element

- Left, Center, and Right text justification determine where the text lines up in relation to the point where the element was identified. The examples in Figure 6–7 were placed with Center justification.
- If you insert a line break in the text string, MicroStation accepts it but only places the first line of the multi-line text string.
- Once placed, the text string has no relation to the element it was placed along. For example, if you move the element the text was placed along, the text does not move.
- Text strings placed in this way are normal text elements and can be manipulated like any other element.
- If the Text Editor window contains text when you invoke the command, Micro-Station skips the first prompt and asks you to select the element.
- If you attempt to select an element when the Text Editor window is empty, MicroStation prompts:

      Enter characters first

   and the element is not selected.

Placing Notes

The Place Note command allows you to place multi-line as well as single-line notes in the design. In addition, for multi-line notes MicroStation provides an option to draw a box around the notes.

Invoke the Place Note command from:

Text tool box	Select the Place Note tool and Single-line or Multi-line from the Type option menu located in the settings window (see Figure 6–10).
Key-in window	**Place Note** (or **pl not**) ⏎

Single-line Note The Single-line Note command places a single-line note at the end of a leader.

MicroStation prompts:

> Place Note > Define start point *(Define the starting point where the leader arrowhead is to be placed.)*
> Place Note > Define next point or <Reset> to abort *(Define the point where the single-line note text is to be placed.)*

The text is placed with the active font and active text size settings. MicroStation provides three different methods by which to place text at the end of the leader line: In-Line, Above, and Horizontal. You can select one of the available methods from the Dimension Settings window.

Invoke the Dimension Settings window from:

Pull-down menu	Element > Dimensions (or ⎇ + **L, D**).

MicroStation displays the Dimension Settings box, as shown in Figure 6–11. Select the Text settings box from the available settings boxes, and MicroStation displays the available options, as shown in Figure 6–11. Select one of the three available methods to place text at the end of the leader line from the Orientation option menu. The orientation options are described in Table 6–1, and examples of notes placed with each orientation are shown in Figure 6–12.

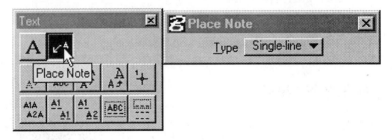

FIGURE 6–10 Invoking the Place Note command from the Text tool box.

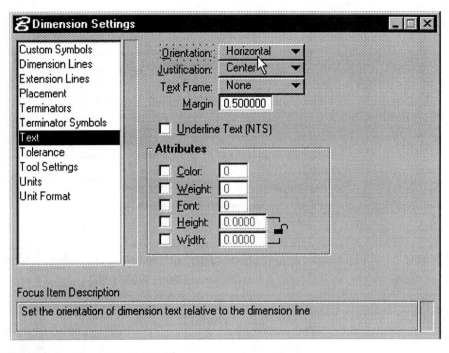

FIGURE 6–11   Dimension Settings box.

Table 6–1.   The Dimension Text Orientation Options

SETTING	PLACES THE NOTE TEXT AT . . .
In-Line	The end of the dimension line and at the same rotation as the line
Above	Above the dimension line and at the same rotation as the line
Horizontal	The end of a horizontal piece of leader line that is attached to the dimension line

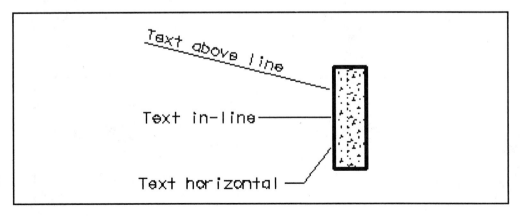

FIGURE 6–12 Examples of Dimension Text Orientation on Single-line Note placement orientation.

Multi-line Note   The Multi-line Note command places a multi-line note at the end of a leader line. To place a multi-line note, invoke the Place Note tool and select Multi-line option from the Type option menu located in the Tool settings window. Note text is placed with the active Text Size settings. In addition, MicroStation provides several tool settings to control the configuration of multi-line notes. If necessary, you can change the settings located in the Tool settings window. Table 6–2 explains the tool settings that control the configurations, and Figure 6–13 shows examples of the configurations.

Table 6–2.   Multi-line Note Tool Settings

SETTING	EFFECT
Font	Selects one of the available fonts
Text Frame	Provides options to frame the note text: • None—no frame is placed • Box—draws a box around the text • Line—places a line next to the smooth margin of the text
Justification	Controls the alignment of the note text: • Left—left margin of text is smooth • Right—right margin of text is smooth • Dynamic—which margin is smooth switches sides so the smooth margin is always next to the end of the dimension line
Generate Leader	If ON, a short horizontal leader line is added to the end of the dimension line next to the note text
Associate Lock	If ON, a tentative snap to an element before placing the first placement point causes the note to be associated with the element If an element with an associated note is moved or scaled, the note's dimension line remains attached to the same place on the element after the moving or scaling is completed, but the note text does not move

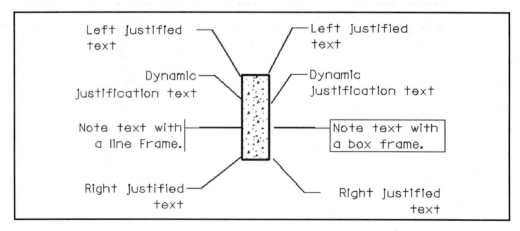

FIGURE 6–13   Examples of multi-line notes.

Importing Text from Another Program

The Import Text command allows you to import text from a file created by another computer application.

The file to be imported must contain only unformatted (ASCII) text from the other application. Thus, the other application's text formatting cannot be imported. For example, Microsoft's Word for Windows word processing application has an export option in its Save As command that creates a text file with line breaks.

The way the command imports the text depends on the number of characters and lines in the text file. The break point is 128 lines, or 2048 characters. If the number of lines or characters in the file is:

- *Less than the break point*, the text is imported as one multi-line text element (a Text Node). All text settings apply to the element, and a dynamic image of the text follows the cursor until you define the placement point. The relationship of the text to the placement point is determined by the active text justification.
- *Greater than the break point*, the text is placed in a "Graphic Group," with each line of text placed as a separate text element. All text settings apply except Text Justification, and there is no dynamic image of the text before you define the placement point. The placement point is *always* the upper left-hand corner of the top line of text.

Invoke the Import Text command from:

Pull-down menu	File > Import > Text (see Figure 6–14)
Key-in window	**Include** (or **in**) ⏎

MicroStation displays the Include Text File dialog box, as shown in Figure 6–15. Select the appropriate file that contains the text to be imported, then click the OK button.

If the text is being placed as a Text Node, MicroStation prompts:

> Import Text File > Enter text node origin *(Define the point in the drawing plane where the text is to be placed.)*

If the text is being placed as a graphic group, MicroStation prompts:

> Import Text File > Identify upper left of text block *(Define the point in the drawing plane where the upper left corner of the text is to be placed.)*

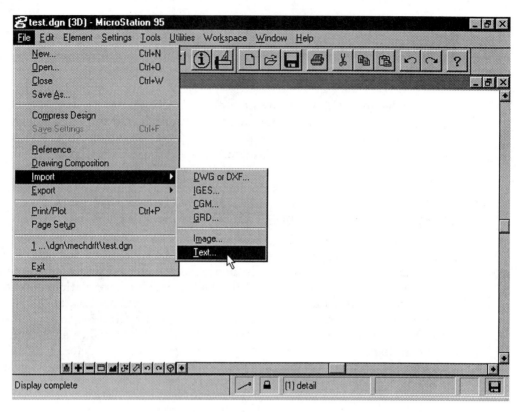

FIGURE 6–14 Invoking the Import Text command from the pull-down menu File.

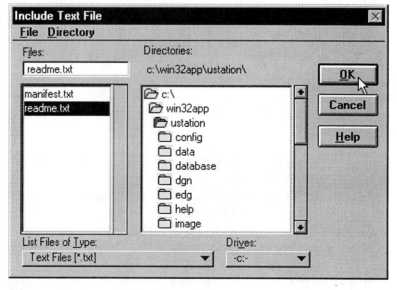

FIGURE 6–15 Include Text File dialog box.

Handling Imported Tabs By default, each tab character in the imported text is replaced with eight space characters. But MicroStation allows you to change the number of spaces before the text is imported. Set the number of tab replacement spaces from:

Key-in window	**TB=<#>** [ENTER] *(Replace <#> with the number of space characters to use—for example: TB=3.)*

MicroStation responds with a message in the right side of the Status bar:

Tab interval = <#>

where <#> is replaced with the number you entered.

Text Attribute Settings The text file can also contain a MicroStation element and text attribute setting key-ins to control the way the text appears when placed.

Rules for Adding Attribute Setting Commands to a Text File

- Standard MicroStation attribute key-ins are used.
- Each key-in must be preceded by a period.
- The key-in must be the only thing on the line.
- The settings act on the text that follows them in the file.
- The key-ins are not placed in the text string.
- If an attribute setting is not included in the file, the drawing's current active setting applies.
- The settings in the imported file become the drawing's active settings after the text is imported.

Table 6–3 lists useful setting key-ins, Table 6–4 lists two additional text control settings that are not element settings, and Figure 6–16 shows an example of using key-ins in an imported text file.

> **NOTE:** An imported file that contains text attribute setting key-ins is always placed as a series of one-line text strings, and the placement point is the upper left corner of the top line of text. Each text element is part of a graphic group.

Table 6–3.   Element Attribute Key-ins

KEY-IN	SETS THE ACTIVE ...
.AA=	Angle degrees
.CO=	Color number
.FT=	Font number
.LS=	Line Spacing in working units (MU:SU:PU)
.LV=	Level number
.TH=	Text Height in working units (MU:SU:PU)
.TW=	Text Width in working units (MU:SU:PU)
.TX=	Text Size (height and width) in working units (MU:SU:PU)
.WT=	Weight number

Table 6–4.   Imported Text Control Settings

SETTING	EFFECT ON THE IMPORTED TEXT
.Indent #	Indents each following line of text with "#" number of spaces
.Newgg	Ends the current graphic group and starts a new one for the following text strings

```
.FT=7
.CO=3
.TH=1:5
.TW=1
This text is placed using font number 7 and color number 3. It is
1:5 working units high and 1 working unit wide.
.FT=0
.CO=0
.WT=2
.TX=:8
This text is placed using font number 0, color number 0, and weight of 2.
It is :8 working units high and wide.
```

FIGURE 6–16   Example of using Element Attributes in an imported text file.

TEXT MANIPULATION COMMANDS

The manipulation commands (such as Move, Copy, and Rotate, among others) manipulate the text element but not the text itself. Changes to the text itself are handled by a set of text manipulation commands that include editing the text, setting the active text settings to match an existing text element, changing a text element's settings to match the current active text settings, copying and incrementing numbers in text elements, and displaying the text settings used to place a text element.

Edit Text Command

The Edit Text command provides a way to change the text in an existing text element.

Invoke the Edit Text command from:

Text tool box	Select the Edit Text tool (see Figure 6–17).
Key-in window	**Edit Text** (or **edi te**) ⏎

MicroStation prompts:

> Edit Text > Identify element *(Select the text element to be edited.)*
> Edit Text > Accept/Reject (Select next input) *(Click the Data button again to accept the text, or click the Reset button to reject it.)*

MicroStation displays the text string in the Text Editor window. After making the required changes and additions to the text, click the Text Editor window's Accept button to place the edited text in the design. Refer to the discussion of "Place Text Commands" in Chapter 3 for notes on using the Text Editor window.

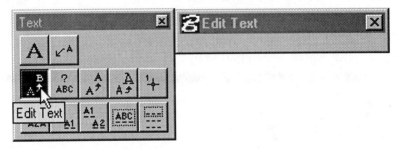

FIGURE 6–17   Invoking the Edit Text command from the Text tool box.

Match Text Attributes Command

The Match Text Attributes command sets the active text attributes to match the attributes that were used to place an existing text element. The command changes the active font, text size, line spacing, and text justification to the settings of the selected text element, and all text placed afterwards uses the new active settings.

Invoke the Match Text Attributes command from:

Text tool box	Select the Match Text Attributes tool (see Figure 6–18).
Key-in window	**Match Text** (or **matc te**) ⏎

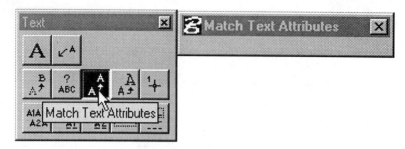

FIGURE 6-18 Invoking the Match Text Attributes command from the Text tool box.

MicroStation prompts:

> Match Text Attributes > Identify text element *(Identify the text element to match.)*
> Match Text Attributes > Accept/Reject (Select next input) *(Click the Data button to set the active settings to selected text element, or click the Reset button to reject it.)*

MicroStation sets the new active text attributes and displays them in the right-hand side of the Status bar. To make these changes permanent, invoke the Save Settings command from the pull-down menu File.

> **NOTE:** The Match Text Attributes command can also be invoked by clicking the Match button in the Text settings box.

Change Text Attributes Command

The Change Text Attributes command changes the attributes of an existing text element from the settings used to place it to the current active settings. For example, if the selected text element's text height is 1:5 Working Units and the active text height is 3:0 Working Units, then with the Change Text Attributes command you can change the text element's text height to 3:0 Working Units.

Invoke the Change Text Attributes command from:

Text tool box	Select the Change Text Attributes tool (see Figure 6–19), and, in the Tool settings window, set the attributes to be changed.
Key-in window	**Modify Text** (or **modi te**) ENTER

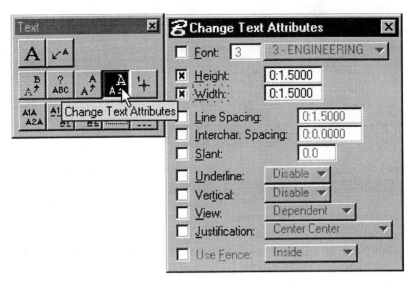

FIGURE 6-19   Invoking the Change Text Attributes command from the Text tool box.

MicroStation prompts:

> Change Text Attributes > Identify text *(Select text element.)*
> Change Text Attributes > Accept/Reject (Select next input) *(Click the Data button to change the attributes of the selected text element, or click the Reset button to reject it. This data point can also select another text element.)*

Display Text Attributes Command

Display Text Attributes is an information-only command that displays the attributes that were used to place an existing text element.

Invoke the Display Text Attributes command from:

Text tool box	Select the Display Text Attributes tool (see Figure 6–20).
Key-in window	**Identify Text** (or **id t**) ⏎

MicroStation prompts:

> Display Text Attributes > Identify text *(Identify the text element.)*

MicroStation displays the attributes in the Status bar. If desired, you can select another text element. The text attributes displayed in the Status bar are different for one-line text elements and multi-line text elements (Text Nodes):

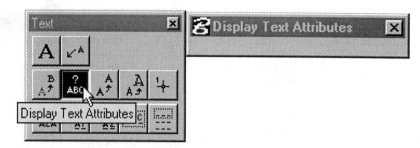

FIGURE 6–20 Invoking the Display Text Attributes command from the Text tool box.

- *For one-line text elements*, the displayed attributes include the text height and width, the level the element is on, and the font number.
- *For multi-line text elements*, the displayed attributes include the Text Node number, the maximum characters per line, the line spacing, the level the element is on, and the font number.

Copy/Increment Text Command

Annotating a series of objects with an incremented identification (such as P100, P101, P102) would be a tedious job without the Copy/Increment Text command. This command copies and increments numbers in text strings. To make incremented copies, just select the element to be copied and incremented, then place data points at each location where an incremented copy is to be placed.

A Tag Increment setting in the Tool settings window allows you to set a positive or negative increment value. For example, an increment value of 10 causes each copy to be 10 greater than the previous one. A value of –10 causes each new copy to be 10 less than the previous one.

Only the numeric portion of a text string is incremented, and, if the string contains more than one numeric portion separated by nonnumeric characters, only the right-most numeric portion is incremented. For example, only the 30 in the string P100-30 will be incremented (P100-31, P100-32, P100-33, and so on).

To place a series of incremented text strings, first place the starting text string, then invoke Copy/Increment Text from:

Text tool box	Select the Copy/Increment Text tool, then, optionally, set the Tag Increment value in the settings window (see Figure 6–21).
Key-in window	**Increment Text** (or **incr t**) [ENTER]

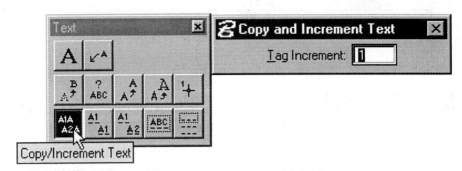

FIGURE 6–21   Invoking the Copy/Increment Text command from the Text tool box.

MicroStation prompts:

> Copy and Increment Text > Identify element *(Identify the text string to be copied and incremented.)*
> Copy and Increment Text > Accept/Reject (Select next input) *(Define the location of each incremented copy, or press the Reset button to reject the copy.)*

TEXT NODES

The Text Node command provides a way to reserve space in a design where text is to be placed later. Once a Text Node is placed, it takes on the active element and text attribute settings. When text is added to the node at a later time, the text takes on those settings.

Nodes are most often used in "fill-in-the-blank" forms that can be inserted in a design and filled in with information specific to the design. A common example is a title block form that has all the required fields held with Text Nodes. Use of the form provides a standard title block layout for all designs.

Viewing Text Nodes

The visual indication of a text node is a unique identification number and a cross indicating the node origin point. Figure 6–22 shows examples of the way empty and filled-in Text Nodes appear in a design.

The Text Node view attribute controls the display and plotting of Text Node indicators for selected views. You can change the Text Node view attribute from the View Attributes settings box (invoked from the pull-down menu Settings). The Text Node toggle button is at the bottom of the right column in the View Attributes window, as shown in Figure 6–23.

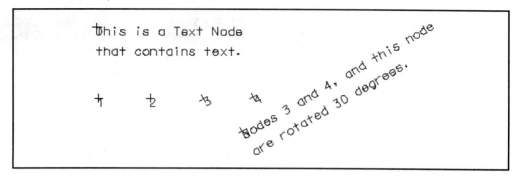

FIGURE 6–22   Examples of Text Node indicators.

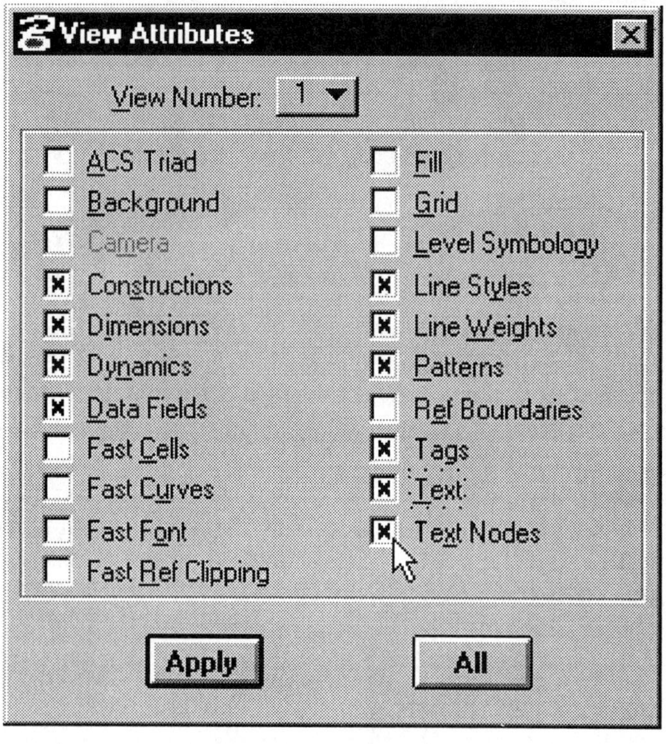

FIGURE 6–23   View Attributes settings box.

Text Node Attributes

The Text Node attributes, such as text size, font, and spacing, are set in the Text settings box and are similar to those for the Place Text command, except for text justification. The text justification is set in the Multi-line Text Justification area of the Text settings box.

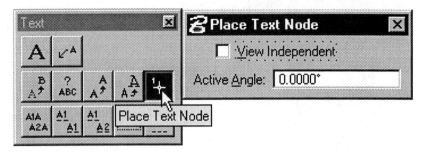

FIGURE 6-24   Invoking the Place Text Node command from the Text tool box.

Placing Text Nodes

To place text nodes, invoke the Place Text Node command from:

Text tool box	Select the Place Text Node tool, then, optionally, set the Active Angle in the settings window (see Figure 6–24).
Key-in window	**Place Node** (or **pla nod**) ⏎

MicroStation prompts:

> Place Text Node > Enter text node origin *(Define the origin point for each node that is to be placed.)*

> **NOTE:** If Text Node view is turned OFF, nothing appears to happen when the Place Text Node command is invoked to place empty nodes. Turn ON Text Node view to see the results of placing empty nodes. The Place Text Node settings include a View Independent option that applies only to 3D designs. If the toggle button is set to ON, Micro-Station prompts:
>
> > Place View Independent Text Node
>
> but there is no difference in the way nodes are placed in a 2D design.

Filling In Text Nodes

To place text on a text node, first turn the Text Node Lock toggle button to ON. You can turn ON the text node lock from the Locks settings box or from the Tool settings window when you invoke the Place Text By Origin command.

Invoke the Place Text command from:

Text tool box	Select the Place Text tool and By Origin from the Method option menu. Then set the toggle button to ON for Text Node Lock in the settings window (see Figure 6–25).

MicroStation prompts:

> Place Text > Enter text *(Enter the text in the Text Editor window, then select and accept the node the text is to be placed on. If the same text is to be placed on another node, select it with the acceptance data point.)*
> Place Text > Select text node or enter more text *(Select another node to place the same text on, or enter more text in the Text Editor window.)*

The text appears on the node after the node is accepted. (There is no dynamic image of the text before acceptance.) The text is placed using the element and text attributes in effect when the node was created.

> **NOTE:** If the selection or acceptance points are placed in an empty space or on a node that already contains text, MicroStation displays
>
> Text node not found
>
> in the Status bar. When the Text Node Lock is set to ON, you cannot place text at any other location except on a Text Node.

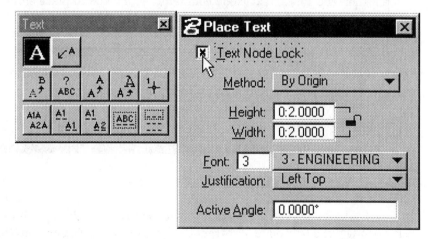

FIGURE 6–25 Invoking the Place Text By Origin command with the Text Node Lock set to ON.

DATA FIELDS

Data Fields or Enter Data Fields are similar to Text Nodes in that they create place holders for text that will be filled in later. Data Fields, though, are more powerful than Text Nodes because there are tools available to automate filling in the fields.

A common use for Data Fields is to provide place holders for descriptive text in cells (symbols). For example, a control valve cell might contain Data Fields for the valve type, size, and identification code. Cells are discussed in Chapter 10.

Data Field Character

Data Fields are created by typing a contiguous string of underscores in ordinary single-line and multi-line text strings. Any of the text placement commands can create the fields (At Origin, Fitted, Above, Below, On, and Along). For example, "_____" is a five-character Enter Data field. When you fill in text, you can have one text character per underscore, so when creating the field you must anticipate the number of text characters that are to be placed in the field when creating the field. If necessary, the Edit Text command can be used to add or remove underscores in existing Data Fields.

> **NOTE:** The underscore is the reserved character used to create fields for Data Field character. If necessary, you can change the reserved character from the MicroStation Preference settings box (explained in detail in Chapter 15 on Customizing MicroStation).

Data Field View Attributes

The View Attributes settings box includes a Data Field toggle button for turning ON and OFF the display of the Data Field underscores for a selected view, as shown in Figure 6–26.

When the Data Field View Attributes toggle button is set:

- OFF—the underscores disappear from the selected view. If a field has been filled in, the fill-in text is still visible.
- ON—the underscores are visible in the selected view. The underscores plot. And, if they have been filled in, the underscores appear at the bottom of each fill-in character.

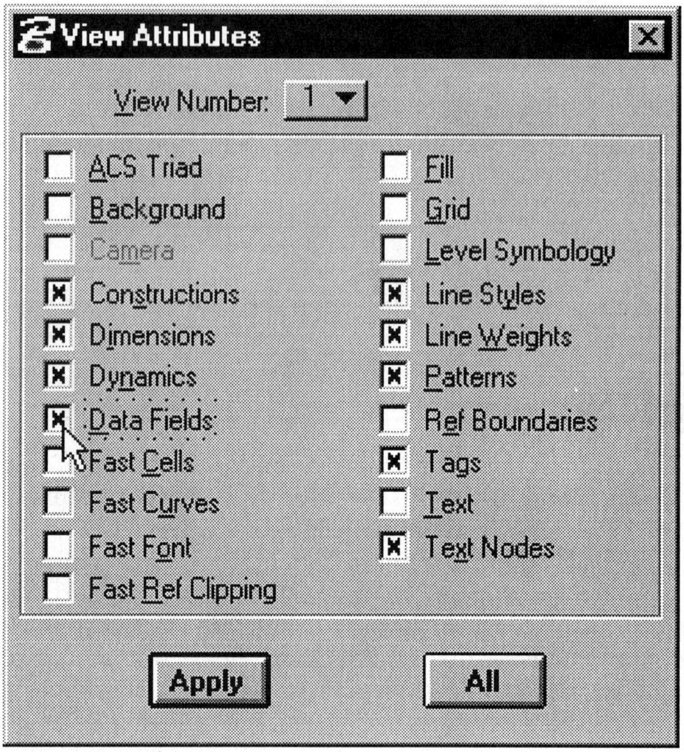

FIGURE 6–26 View Attributes settings box.

Setting Justification for Data Field Contents

The Data Field contents can be justified Left, Right, or Center within the field when there are fewer fill-in characters than underscores. Data Field content justification is different than text string justification, and it is applied to the Data Field only *after* the text string is placed.

Invoke the Data Field justification command from:

Key-in window	Key in one of these justification commands:
	• **Justify Left** (or **ju l**) [ENTER]
	• **Justify Center** (or **ju c**) [ENTER]
	• **Justify Right** (or **ju r**) [ENTER]

MicroStation prompts (prompts are for Center justification):

Center Justify Enter_Data Field > Identify element *(Click on the Data Field to be justified.)*

No acceptance is required for this command. The field is justified as soon as it is selected.

> **NOTE:** If the justified Data Field contains text, the position of that text does not change. If you replace the existing text after changing the justification, the new text takes on the new justification.

Filling In Data Fields

MicroStation provides two tools to fill in text in Data Fields. The Fill In Single Enter-Data Field tool allows you to place text by identifying a specific Data Field. The Auto Fill In Enter-Data Fields tool prompts you to select a specific view, and MicroStation selects the empty Data Fields in the order they were created.

Fill In Single Enter-Data Field Command   Invoke the Fill In Single Enter-Data Field command from:

Text tool box	Select the Fill In Single Enter-Data Field tool (see Figure 6–27).
Key-in window	**Edit Single** (or **edi s**) ⏎

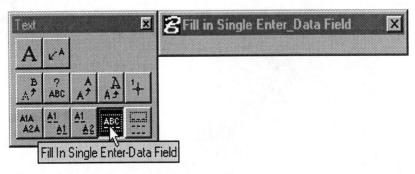

FIGURE 6–27   Invoking the Fill In Single Enter-Data Field command from the Text tool box.

MicroStation prompts:

> Fill in Single Enter_Data Field > Identify element *(Identify the Data Field.)*

The Text Editor window opens. Type the text in the Text Editor window and press
[ENTER]. MicroStation places the text in the selected Data Field. You can continue by
identifying additional Data Fields.

Auto Fill In Enter-Data Fields Command Invoke the Auto Fill In Enter-Data
Fields command from:

Text tool box	Select the Auto Fill In Enter-Data Fields tool (see Figure 6–28).
Key-in window	**Edit Auto** (or **edi au**) [ENTER]

MicroStation prompts:

> Auto Fill in Enter_Data Fields > Select view *(Select the view containing the fields to be filled in.)*
>
> Auto Fill in Enter_Data Fields > <CR> to fill in or DATA for next field *(Type the text in the Text Editor window and press [ENTER], or click the Data button to skip the field.)*

The command continues through the view selecting empty Data Fields in the order
they were created. It skips Data Fields that already contain text.

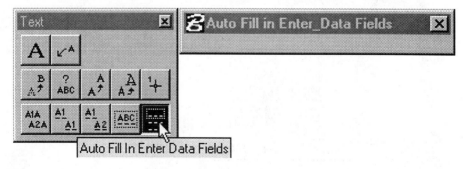

FIGURE 6–28   Invoking the Auto Fill In Enter-Data Fields command from the Text tool box.

Copying Data Fields

To copy the contents of one Data Field to another Data Field, invoke the Copy Enter-Data Field command from:

Text tool box	Select the Copy Enter-Data Field tool (see Figure 6–29).
Key-in window	**Copy ED** (or **cop e**) ⏎

MicroStation prompts:

> Copy Enter_Data Field > Select enter data field to copy *(Select the Data Field containing the text to be copied, then click in each Data Field to which the text is to be copied.)*

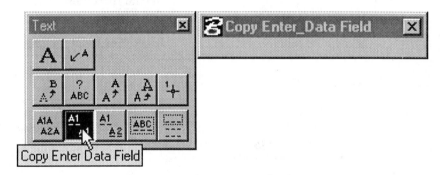

FIGURE 6–29   Invoking the Copy Enter-Data Field command from the Text tool box.

Copying and Incrementing Data Fields

The Copy and Increment Enter-Data Field command copies the text from a filled-in Data Field, then increments the numeric portion of the text and places it in the empty Data Field you select.

A Tag Increment setting in the Tool settings box allows setting a positive or negative increment value. For example, an increment value of 10 causes each copy to be 10 greater than the previous one; a value of –10 causes each new copy to be 10 less than the previous one.

To copy the contents of one Data Field to another Data Field and increment the numeric portion of the copy, invoke the Copy and Increment Enter-Data Field command from:

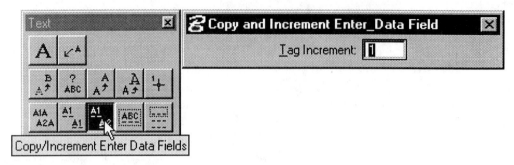

FIGURE 6–30 Invoking the Copy and Increment Enter-Data Field command from the Text tool box.

Text tool box	Select the Copy and Increment Enter-Data Field tool (see Figure 6–30), and, optionally, set the Increment value in the Tool settings window.
Key-in window	**Increment ED** (or **incr e**) [ENTER]

MicroStation prompts:

> Copy and Increment Enter_Data Field > Select enter data field to copy *(Select the Data Field containing the text to be copied, then click in each Data Field to which the text is to be copied and incremented.)*

Editing Text in a Data Field

The number of underscore characters in an existing Data Field can be changed by editing the text string in the Text Editor window.

In the Text Editor window the underscores are represented by spaces enclosed in pairs of angle brackets. For example, "Pump << >>-<< >>" is the way a text string containing two Data Fields appears in the Text Editor window.

- To *shorten a Data Field*, remove spaces from between the angle brackets.
- To *lengthen a Data Field*, insert spaces (or underscores) between the angle brackets.
- To *delete a Data Field* completely, delete the angle brackets and the spaces between them.
- To *insert a new Data Field:*
  1. Position the cursor at the insertion point in the text string.
  2. Type a pair of left angle brackets (<<).
  3. Type the spaces (or underscores) to define the length of the Data Field.

TAGS

Engineering drawings have long served to convey more than just how a model looks. Drawings must tell builders and fabricators how actually to construct the model. This nongraphical information includes such things as material of construction, how many to make, colors, where to obtain materials, and what finishes to apply to surfaces. When models were created on paper, painstaking work was required to extract lists of this information from the drawings. A major innovation of CAD models is the ability to automate the creation of such lists.

MicroStation provides this automation by attaching "Tags" to objects. Any element, or element group, can be tagged with descriptive information, and tag reports can be requested. For example: Each electrical fixture in an architectural floor plan can be tagged with its rating, order number, price, and project name. An estimator could extract a fixture tag report from the design and insert the resulting data in a spreadsheet to obtain the total project cost for electrical fixtures. A purchasing agent could use the tag reports from several projects to order fixtures and take advantage of quantity discounts. Receiving clerks could employ the order numbers and project names to route the received fixtures to the correct projects.

MicroStation's Tag commands are helpful when the tagging requirements are fairly simple and when the project must import or export drawings from other CAD packages that store nongraphical data inside their design files. For more complicated tagging, MicroStation also supports connections to databases (which is beyond the scope of this textbook).

Tags can be placed on any element in a design file. Figure 6–31 shows an example of tags in design files. The tags are assigned to a small point (actually a short line) in

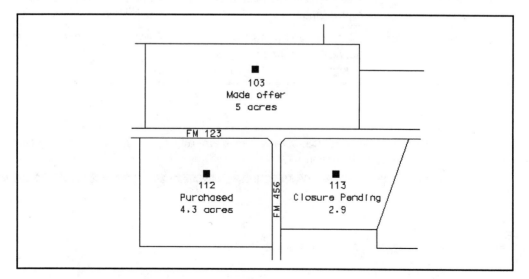

FIGURE 6-31   Tags displayed in a plot plan.

each tract of land in a plot plan. The points are given just to provide an element to hook the tag to. Each "Tract" tag set includes the tract identification number, the purchase status, and the tract size.

Tagging Terms

Adding tags to a design requires an understanding of tag terminology. Table 6–5 defines the important tagging terms.

Table 6–5.   Tagging Terms

TERM	DEFINITION	EXAMPLES
Tag set	A set of associated tags. For each tag, it provides the tag name, display attributes, data type, and default value.	Separate tag sets for doors, windows, and electrical fixtures
Tag	Nongraphical attributes that may be attached to graphical elements.	Part number, size, material of construction, vendor, price
Tag report template	A file that specifies the tag set and the set's member tags to include on each line of the report. One tag set per template.	For the fixtures set, report the part number, rating, price, and project name of each tagged element.
Tag report	A list of all tags based on a tag report template.	F300-2, 220V, $300, New ABC, Inc. building
Tag set library	Files containing tag set definitions for use in multiple design files.	A library of architectural tag sets

> **NOTE:** If you delete or move an element with attached tags, the tags are deleted or moved as well.

Creating a Tag Set and Tags

The first step in creating nongraphical tags in a design is to create the tag set and define the tags in the set.

To create a tag set and to define the tags in a set, open the Tag Sets settings box from:

Pull-down menu	Element > Tags > Define (or 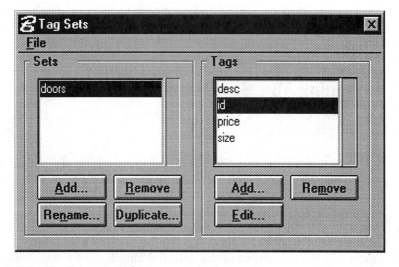 + **L, T, D**).
Key-in window	**MDL load Tags Define (or md l tags define)**

MicroStation displays the Tag Sets settings box as shown in Figure 6–32. All defined tag sets are displayed on the left side of the window, and the tag names for the selected tag set are displayed on the right side of the window. In the pictured example, the design has one tag set (doors) with four tags (desc, id, price, and size). Under the tag set and tag names areas of the settings box are buttons for creating and maintaining the sets and tags.

To create a new tag set name, click the Add... button in the Tag Sets area of the settings box; MicroStation displays the Tag Set Name dialog box, as shown in Figure 6–33. Key-in the Tag Set name in the Name field of the Tag Set Name dialog box, and click the OK button to create the new Tag Set.

To create a new tag under a specific tag set, first highlight the Tag Set from the available Tag Sets list, and click the Add... button from the right side of the settings box under the Tags names. MicroStation displays the Define Tag dialog box, as shown in Figure 6–34.

FIGURE 6–32   Tag Sets settings box.

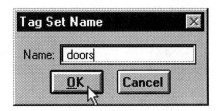

FIGURE 6-33 Tag Set Name dialog box.

FIGURE 6-34 Define Tag dialog box.

Key-in the appropriate information in the fields provided in the Define Tag dialog box. Refer to Table 6–6 for a detailed explanation of the available fields in the Define Tag dialog box.

Maintaining Tag Set Definitions

The Tag Sets settings box provides options for maintaining existing tag set definitions. The options include:

- *Remove*—remove (delete) the selected Tag Set (with all its tags) or Tag. A confirmation window opens, and you initiate the removal by clicking the OK button.
- *Rename*—change a tag set's name. It opens the Tag Set Name window, in which you type the new Tag Set name.
- *Duplicate*—create a duplicate copy of a Tag set. It opens the Tag Set Name window, in which you type the name to use for the duplicate Tag Set.
- *Edit*—edit the attributes of the selected Tag. It opens the Define Tag window for you to edit the tag attributes.

Table 6–6.   Tag Attributes

ATTRIBUTE	DESCRIPTION
Tag Name	The name of the tag
Tag Prompt	A 32-character-maximum text string that will serve to tell the user what the tag is for when it is assigned to an element.
Tag Data Type	Tags are one of three types: • Character—a text string • Integer—a whole number • Real—a number with a fractional part
Variable	A toggle switch that, when OFF, prevents the tag value from being changed with the Edit Tags tool (discussed later). If ON, the value cannot be edited.
Default	A toggle switch that, when OFF, uses the default tag value and prevents the tag value from being changed with the Edit Tags tool. If ON, the toggle switch uses the default but allows editing of the value.
Tag Default Value	A default tag value that is initially assigned to a tag when the tag set is assigned to an element. It can be overridden.
Display Tag	Controls how the tags are displayed in the views and what can be done to them.

Attaching Tags to Elements

To assign a tag to an element, invoke the Attach Tags command from:

Tags tool box	Select the Attach Tags tool and a Tag Set name from the settings window (see Figure 6–35).

FIGURE 6–35   Invoking the Attach Tags command from the Tags tool box.

MicroStation prompts:

> Attach Tags > Identify element *(Identify the element to which tags are to be attached.)*
>
> Attach Tags > Accept/Reject (Select next input) *(Click the Accept button to accept the selected element, and, if required, select the next element to which tags will be attached after the current one is completed.)*

When the element is accepted, the Attach Tags window opens. Figure 6–36 provides an example of the window displaying the tag names for a "doors" tag set; Table 6–7 describes each field.

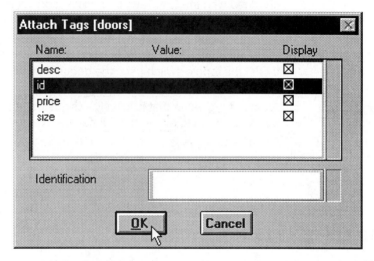

FIGURE 6–36 Typical Attach Tags window.

Table 6–7.   The Fields in the Attach Tags Window

FIELD	DESCRIPTION
Name	The name of each tag in the set
Value	The default value, if any, of each tag in the set
Display	A toggle switch that can be used to turn ON or OFF the display of each tag
Prompt	The input prompt for the selected tag (in Figure 6–36, the prompt for the "id" tag is "Identification")
Value Field	Next to the prompt is an input field where values are entered for the tags. If a tag has a default value, the value appears here when the tag is selected

Filling In Tag Values To fill in the tag values:

1. Optionally, turn the Display button ON or OFF for each of the tags.
2. Select a tag from the window by clicking on its name.
3. Type its value in the entry field, unless the tag has an acceptable default value.
4. Repeat steps 2 and 3 for each tag.
5. Click the OK button to close the window and to place the tag values, or Cancel to discard the changes.

If one or more of the tags are to be displayed, MicroStation prompts:

Attach Tags > Place Tag *(Select the location for placing the tags in the design.)*

The tag values are placed using the active element and text attribute settings. If no tags are to be displayed, there is no prompt for placing the tags.

Editing Attached Tags

To make changes to the tag values attached to an element, invoke the Edit Tags command from:

Tags tool box	Select the Edit Tags tool (see Figure 6–37).
Key-in window	**Edit Tags (or edi ta)** ⏎

MicroStation prompts:

Edit Tags > Identify element *(Select the element containing tags to be edited.)*
Edit Tags > Accept/Reject (Select next input) *(Click the Accept button to accept the selected element, and, if required, select the next element containing tags to be edited.)*

The Edit Tags window opens. Figure 6–38 provides an example of the window displaying the tag names for a "doors" tag set.

FIGURE 6–37 Invoking the Edit Tags command from the Tags tool box.

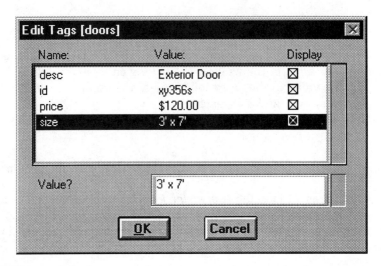

FIGURE 6–38 Typical Edit Tags window.

Editing Tag Values To edit a tag value:

1. Select the tag.
2. Optionally, turn the Display button ON or OFF for the tag.
3. Edit its value in the entry field.
4. Repeat steps 1 through 3 for each tag that must be changed (edited).
5. Click the OK button to close the window and to place the edited tag values, or Cancel to discard the changes and leave the tag values unchanged.

> **NOTE:** Tags that were created with the Variable option OFF cannot be edited.

Reviewing Attached Tags

The Review Tags command allows you to select an element and view the tags attached to it. No changes can be made to the tags with this command.

Invoke the Review Tags command from:

Tags tool box	Select the Review Tags tool (see Figure 6–39).
Key-in window	**Review Tags** (or **rev t**) ⏎

FIGURE 6–39   Invoking the Review Tags command from the Tags tool box.

MicroStation prompts:

> Review Tags > Identify element *(Identify the element containing tags to be reviewed.)*
>
> Review Tags > Accept/Reject (Select next input) *(Click the Accept button to accept the selected element, and, if required, select the next element containing tags to be reviewed.)*
>
> Review Tags > Select Tag to review *(Select the Tag to review.)*

If the selected element has more than one tag set attached:

1. A Review Tags window opens showing the names of the attached tag sets, as in Figure 6–40.
2. Select the tag set to review, and click the OK button.
3. Another Review Tags window opens showing the tags for the selected tag set, as in Figure 6–41.

If the selected element has only one tag set attached, a Review Tags window opens showing the tags for the attached tag set.

FIGURE 6–40   Review Tags window showing attached tag sets.

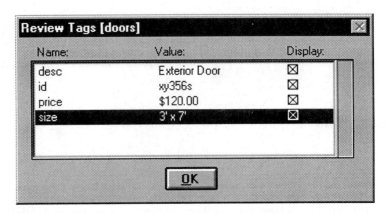

FIGURE 6–41 Review Tags window showing tags in the attached tag set.

Reporting Tags

As mentioned earlier, MicroStation creates a tag report that lists the nongraphical information required to fabricate the model created in the project's design files.

Creating reports is a two-step process. First, a tags template is created to control what is in included in each type of report. Second, a report is generated based on the tag template.

Generating a Tags Template A tag template defines the data columns in a tag report. Each column is either a tag from one tag set or an element attribute. To create a tag templete, open the Generate Template settings box from:

Pull-down menu	Element > Tags > Generate Templates (or 【ALT】 + L, T, T)
Key-in window	**MDL load Tags Template** (or **md l tags template**) 【ENTER】

MicroStation displays the General Templates settings box, as shown in Figure 6–42; Table 6–8 describes the fields in the settings box.

Following are the steps to create a new template in the Generate Templates settings box.

1. Key-in the file name for the report in the Report File Name: edit.
2. For each Tag or element attribute to include in the report, select the name in the Tags column and click the Add button.
3. If you added a name by mistake, select it in the Report Columns list and click the Remove button.
4. When all report columns have been created, select the Save option from the File menu to save the new template using the name currently in the Report File Name field.

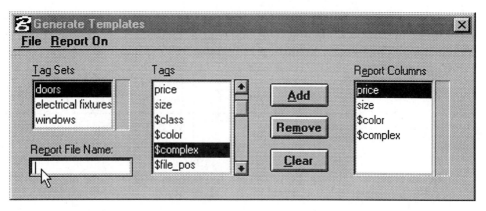

FIGURE 6–42   Typical Generate Templates settings box.

Table 6–8.   Generate Templates Window Fields

FIELD	DESCRIPTION
Tag Sets	Lists the tag sets attached to the design file. Select the one for which the template is to be created.
Tags	Lists all tags in the selected tag set and all element attributes that can be included in the report. The names in the list that start with a dollar sign ($) are element attributes.
Report Columns	Lists the tags and element attributes that have been selected for inclusion in the report. Each name will be the name of a column in the report, and the order in the window determines the column order in the report.
Report File Name	Key-in an eight-character-maximum report file name, and, optionally, a three-character-maximum file extension. This name will be used for the report files generated from this template.
Report On Menu	Select the type of elements to include in the report: • *Tagged elements*—Include only tagged elements in the report. • *All elements*—Include all elements, both tagged and untagged. If all elements are included but no element attribute columns are included, the untagged elements will show up in the report as empty rows.
File Menu	• *Open*—Opens the Open Template dialog box, from which you can select an existing template file to open. • *Save*—Saves the template information to the same file that was previously opened or saved as. • *Save As*—Opens the Save Template As dialog box, from which you can save the template information to any directory path with a file name that you supply in the window. Use this command to save new templates. Both the Open and Save Template As windows display the default template files directory path the first time they are opened.

Generating a Tags Report Tag reports list tags and element data information based on Tags Templates. To generate a tag report, open the Generate Reports settings box from:

Pull-down menu	Element > Tags > Generate Reports... (or [ALT] + **L, T, R**).
Key-in window	**MDL load Tags Report** (or **md l tags report**) [ENTER]

MicroStation displays the Generate Reports settings box, as shown in Figure 6–43; Table 6–9 describes the fields in the settings box.

Following are the steps to generate a report from the Generate Templates settings box:

1. If required, change the directory path and file type to display the required templates.

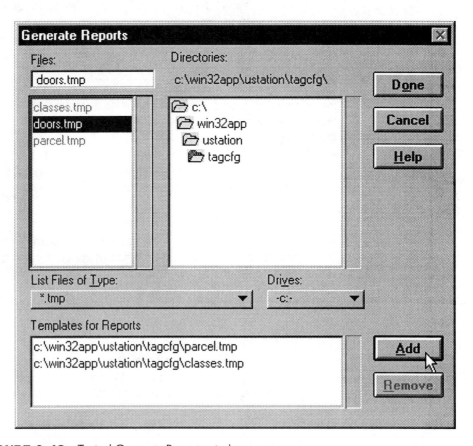

FIGURE 6–43 Typical Generate Reports window.

Table 6–9.   Generate Reports Window Fields

FIELD	DESCRIPTION
Files	Lists the existing tag template files in the directory path shown in Directories.
Directories	Lists the directory path to the templates, and is used to change the path. It opens initially displaying the MicroStation default templates path.
List Files of Type	Provides an option menu for selecting the type of template files to display. It has two options: • *.tmp—List files with the extension "tmp" (the default templates file extension). • All files [*.*]—List all files in the directory path.
Drives	Provides a menu for selecting the letter of the disk drive containing the template files.
Templates for Reports	Displays the templates that have been selected for the report. Separate report files are generated for each template in this list.

2. For each report to be generated, click on the required template file name in the Files list, then click the Add button. The file specification for each selected template appears in the Templates for Reports list.
3. If a mistake was made in selecting a template, select it in the Templates for Reports list, then click the Remove button to remove it. The Remove button is then dimmed, unless a template has been selected.
4. After all required templates have been selected, click the Done button to generate the reports.

Tag reports are created using the template's file name and the "rpt" extension. The reports are stored in MicroStation's default reports path: \USTATION\OUT\TAG\. The folder under which this path is found varies, depending on how MicroStation was installed and the computer's operating system. The complete path is defined in the MS_TAGREPORTS configuration variable.

Accessing the Reports   Tag reports are in ASCII files (also called "flat files") that can be accessed in several ways. For example:

■ View and print a report with one of the operating system's text viewers, such as NotePad in Microsoft Windows.
■ Import a report into another application, such as Excel, the Microsoft Windows spreadsheet application.

Tag Set Libraries

MicroStation provides a tool to export the tag sets created in a design file for insertion in any design file. To export the tag sets from the current design file, open the Define Tags window. The commands to create and use tag set libraries are all in the Define Tags window. Open the Tag Sets settings box from:

Pull-down menu	Element > Tags > Define (or [ALT] + L, T, D).
Key-in window	**MDL load Tags Define** (or **md l tags define**) [ENTER]

MicroStation displays the Tag Sets settings box.

Creating a Tag Set Library   Following are the steps to create a tag set library.

1. Select the tag set from the Sets list box.
2. Invoke the Create... option from Export submenu located in the pull-down menu File, as shown in Figure 6–44. MicroStation displays the Export Tag Library dialog box.
3. Key-in the library file name in the Export Tag Library dialog box, and click the OK button. MicroStation creates a tag set library file with the default file extention "tlb" and stores it in the default reports path \USTATION\OUT\TAG\.

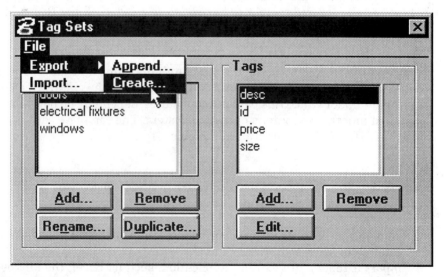

FIGURE 6–44   Invoking the Create option to open the Export Tag Library dialog box.

Appending a Tag Set to an Existing Library In addition to being able to create a new tag set library, MicroStation also provides a tool to append a tag set to an existing library. Following are the steps to append a tag set to an existing library.

1. From the Sets list box located in the Tag Sets settings box, select the tag set to append to an existing library.
2. Invoke the Append... option from the Export submenu located in the pull-down menu File. MicroStation displays the Export Tag Library dialog box.
3. Select the library file name to which the tag set is to be appended, and click the OK button. MicroStation appends the selected tag set to the library.
4. Repeat steps 2 and 3 for each tag set to be appended to a library.

Copying a Tag Set from a Selected Library Following are the steps to copy tag sets from a selected library into the current design.

1. Invoke the Import... option from the pull-down menu File located in the Tag Sets settings box, and MicroStation displays the Open Tag Library.
2. Select the library file, and MicroStation displays the Import Sets dialog box, as shown in Figure 6–45. Select the tag sets to copy into the current design, and click the OK button. MicroStation copies the selected tag sets into the current Tag Sets lists.
3. If more tag sets need to be copied for another library, go back to step 1.

FIGURE 6–45 Typical Import Sets dialog box.

REVIEW QUESTIONS

Write your answers in the spaces provided.

1. To place natural fractions in the one-character position, turn ON the _____ toggle button.

2. The Place Fitted Text command fits the text between two _____.

3. When you place a text string above a line with the Place Text Above command, the distance between the line and the text is controlled by _____ .

4. Explain briefly when you will use Intercharacter Spacing attribute in placing text.

    _____

5. Under what circumstance will you use the Match Text Attributes command?

    _____

6. What would you key-in to set the Tag Increment to 5? _____

7. To determine the text attributes of an existing text in a design file, invoke the _____ command.

8. Explain briefly the purpose of placing nodes in a design file.

    _____

9. Explain briefly the purpose of defining tags.

    _____

10. List the steps involved in generating a template and report files.

    _____

    _____

PROJECT EXERCISE

This project exercise provides step-by-step instructions for creating the circuit board drilling diagram and the hole locations table shown in Figure P6–1. The intent is to guide you in applying text placement and manipulation commands.

> **NOTE:** The dimensions are not part of this project. They are included in Figure P6–1 as an aid to drawing the design.

Prepare the Design File

This procedure starts MicroStation, creates a design file, and enters the initial settings.

> **NOTE:** As you complete each step in the project procedures, place a check mark by the step to help you keep up with where you are in the project.

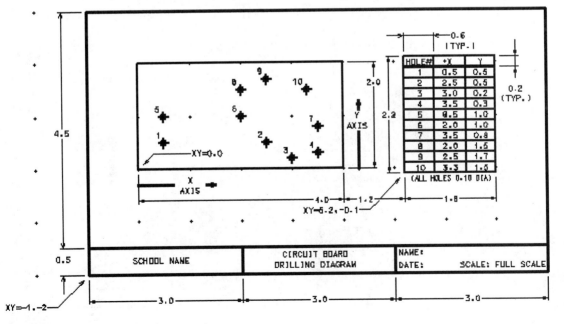

FIGURE P6-1 Completed project design.

STEP 1:   Invoke MicroStation, and create a new design file named CH6.DGN using the SEED2D.DGN seed file.

STEP 2:   In the Design File dialog box set the following:

- Working Unit ratios to 1:10:10000
- Grid Master to 0.1, Grid Reference to 10, and Grid lock ON

STEP 3:   Invoke the Text settings box from the pull-down menu Element, and set the settings shown in Figure P6–2.

STEP 4:   Using Figure P6–1 as a guide, draw the border and title block on level 10, with the lower left corner at XY=–1,–2.

- Replace "SCHOOL NAME" with your school or company name, or make up a name.
- Place your name to the right of "NAME."
- Place today's date to the right of "DATE."

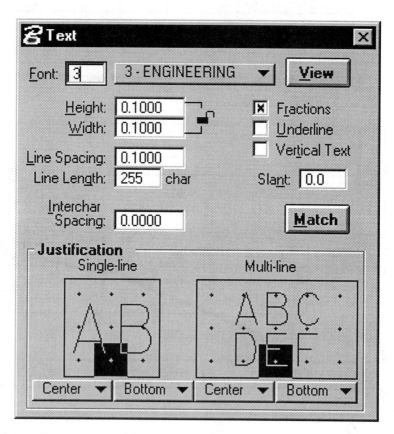

FIGURE P6–2   Text settings used for all text in this project.

Draw the Circuit Board Diagram

This procedure draws the circuit board diagram, as shown in Figure P6–3.

STEP 1: Set the Active Level to 1, the Line Weight to 1, and the Color to blue. Then invoke the Save settings from the pull-down menu File to save the design settings.

STEP 2: Draw the 4 × 2 circuit board outline block with the lower left corner at XY=0,0.

STEP 3: If view window 2 is not open, open it and focus on it.

STEP 4: In view window 2, turn off the display of level 10, then fit the view.

STEP 5: Place a circle of radius 0.1 at XY=0.5,0.5 (Hole #1).

STEP 6: Complete the circuit hole symbol by drawing two lines (each 0.3 Working Units, and long end of 0 line weight) through the circle's center, as shown in Figure P6–4.

STEP 7: Place a Fence Block around the circuit hole symbol (the circle and two lines).

STEP 8: Copy the fence contents to XY=2.5,0.5 (Hole #2).

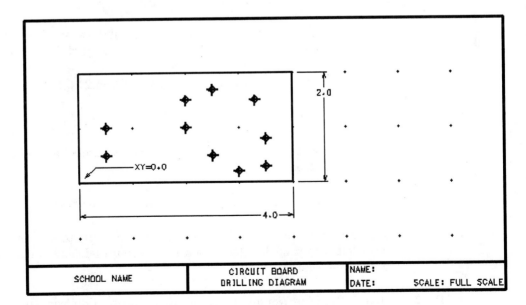

FIGURE P6–3 Circuit board diagram.

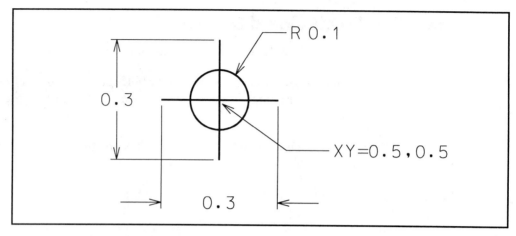

FIGURE P6–4 Circuit hole symbol.

STEP 9: Copy the fence contents to place holes 3–10 on the circuit board. Refer to the table in Figure P6–1 for the X,Y offsets from the lower left corner of the circuit board block (the design origin).

Draw the Hole Locations Table

This procedure draws the hole locations table to the right of the circuit diagram, as shown in Figure P6–5.

STEP 1: In view window 2, pan the view to the right until the area where the table is to be drawn is in the view, along with the right edge of the circuit board.

STEP 2: Place a 1.8 × 2.2 block with its left corner at XY=5.2,–0.1.

STEP 3: Fit the view window 2.

STEP 4: Draw a horizontal line 1.8 units long starting 0.2 units below the top left corner of the block.

STEP 5: Place nine parallel copies of the line, each 0.2 units apart.

STEP 6: Draw a vertical line 2.2 units long starting 0.6 units to the right of the lower left corner of the block, then make a parallel copy of the line 0.6 units to the right.

STEP 7: Change the Line Weight of the second horizontal line from the top to 2, to visually separate the table heading row from the data rows.

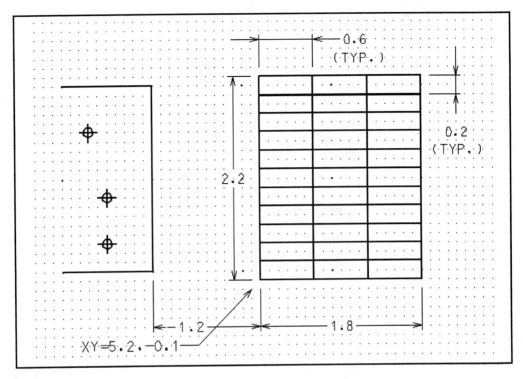

FIGURE P6–5   Hole locations table.

Place Sequential Numbers by the Hole Symbols

This procedure places the number 1 by the first hole symbol, then uses the Copy and Increment Text command to place numbers by the rest of the hole symbols, as shown in Figure P6–6.

STEP 1:   Set the Active Level to 2, the Line Weight to 0, Color to green, and Grid Lock to OFF.

STEP 2:   Invoke the Place Text command from the Text tool box, then, in the Tool Settings window, set the Method to By Origin.

MicroStation prompts:

> Place Text > Enter text *(Key-in 1 in the Text Editor window, then place a data point above and to the left of the first (lower left) hole symbol, as shown in Figure P6–6.)*

STEP 3:   Invoke the Copy and Increment Text command from the Text tool box, then set the Tag Increment to 1.

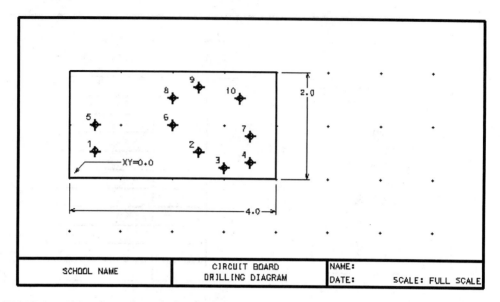

FIGURE P6-6 Circuit board after the holes have been numbered.

MicroStation prompts:

> Copy and Increment Text > Identify element *(Select the number 1 that was placed in the previous step.)*
> Copy and Increment Text > Accept/Reject (Select next input) *(Drag the dynamic image to above and to the left of hole 2 and place a data point.)*

> **NOTE:** The number is not incremented until it is placed, so the dynamic image shows the last number.

> Copy and Increment Text > Accept/Reject (Select next input) *(Continue placing numbers by the hole symbols until all have numbers. Use Figure P6–6 as a guide to placement.)*

Fill in the Hole Locations Table

This procedure uses the Place Text command to fill in the three table columns, as shown in Figure P6–7.

STEP 1: Pan view window 2 to the right until the table is completely within the view.

HOLE#	· · X · ·	· · Y · ·
· 1 · ·	· 0.5 ·	· 0.5 ·
· 2 · ·	· 2.5 ·	· 0.5 ·
· 3 · ·	· 3.0 ·	· 0.2 ·
· 4 · ·	· 3.5 ·	· 0.3 ·
· 5 · ·	· 0.5 ·	· 1.0 ·
· 6 · ·	· 2.0 ·	· 1.0 ·
· 7 · ·	· 3.5 ·	· 0.8 ·
· 8 · ·	· 2.0 ·	· 1.5 ·
· 9 · ·	· 2.5 ·	· 1.7 ·
· 10 ·	· 3.3 ·	· 1.5 ·

(ALL HOLES 0.10 DIA)

FIGURE P6-7   Filled-in hole locations table.

STEP 2:   Invoke the Place Text by Origin command and key-in all text for the left table column in the Text Editor, as shown in Figure P6–8.

NOTE: To see all rows in the Text Editor window (as shown in Figure P6–8), drag down the lower window border.

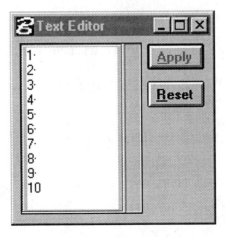

FIGURE P6-8   Text Editor window after all text in table column 1 has been keyed in.

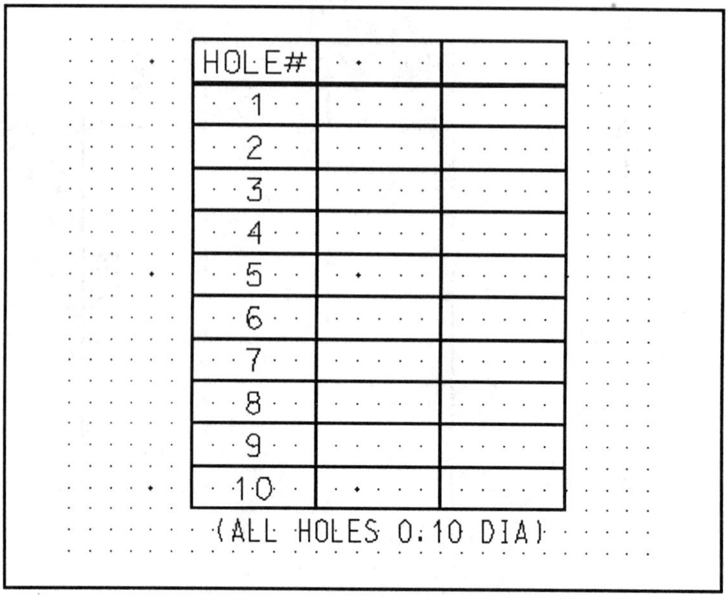

FIGURE P6–9 Table with the Hole # row filled in.

STEP 3: Drag the text rows into the left table column, align them with the table, and place a data point, as shown in Figure P6–9. Click the Reset button to clear the Text Editor window.

STEP 4: Place the text in the X and Y table rows using the same method as in steps 2 and 3.

STEP 5: In the Tool Settings window, set the Text Width to 0.09.

STEP 6: Place the text string (ALL HOLES 0.10 DIA) below the table.

STEP 7: Turn on the level 10. Focus on view window 1 and fit the view.

STEP 8: Invoke the Save Settings from the pull-down menu File to save the settings.

DRAWING EXERCISES 6–1 THROUGH 6–5

Use the following table to set up the design files for Exercises 6–1 and 6–2.

SETTING	VALUE
Seed File	SEED2D.DGN
Working Units	MU = IN, SU = 10 TH, PU = 1000
Grid	Master = .1, Reference = 10, GRID lock ON

Exercise 6–1   Textbook logo.

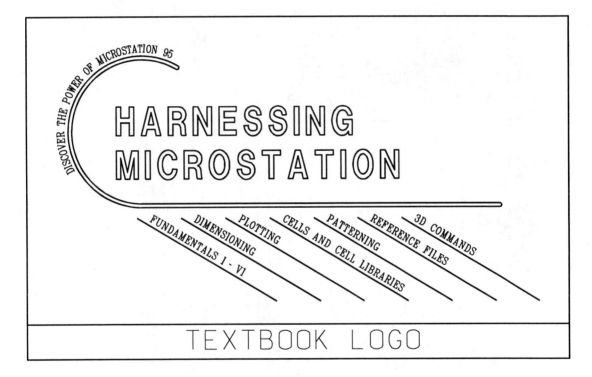

TEXTBOOK LOGO

Exercise 6–2 Terminal strip.

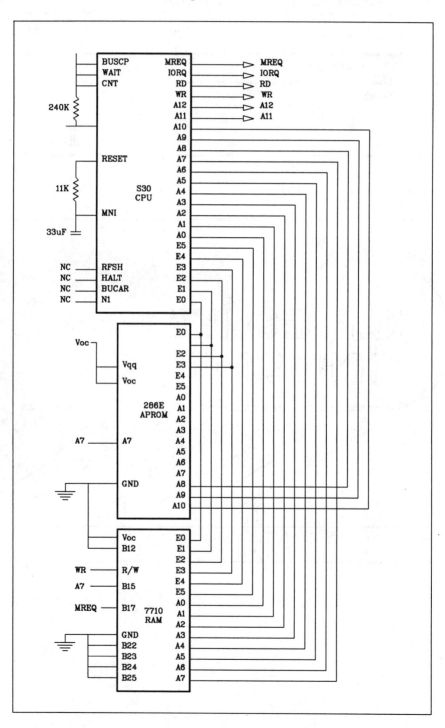

Use the following table to set up the design files for Exercises 6–3 through 6–5.

SETTING	VALUE
Seed File	SEED2D.DGN
Working Units	MU = ', SU = 12", PU = 12000
Grid	Master = :.5, Reference = 24, GRID lock ON

In Exercise 6–3, make your best estimate to determine the dimensions of the building section.

Exercise 6–3   Building section.

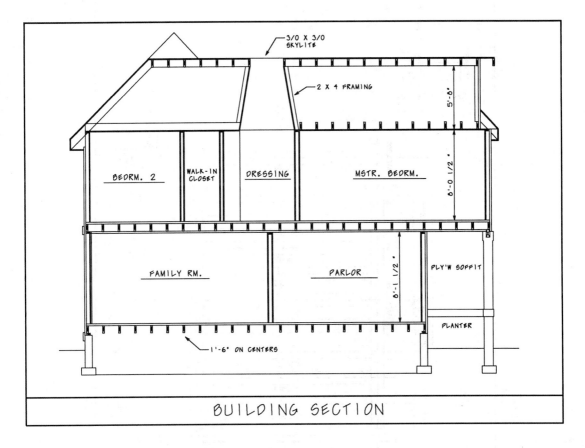

For Exercise 6–4, draw the structural plan and place the descriptive text. Do *not* draw the dimensions.

Exercise 6–4 Structural steel plan.

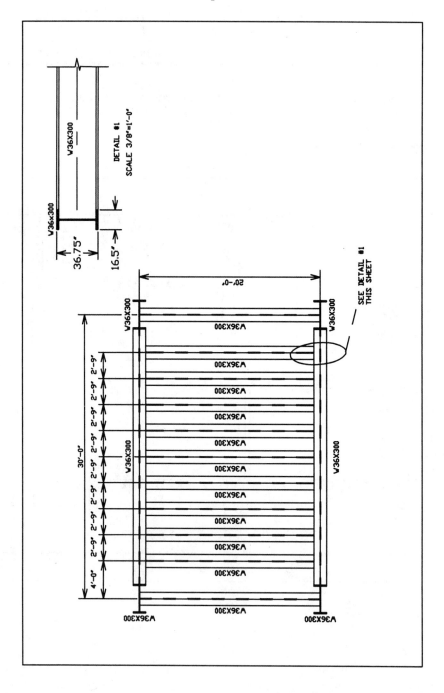

Exercise 6–5   Site plan.

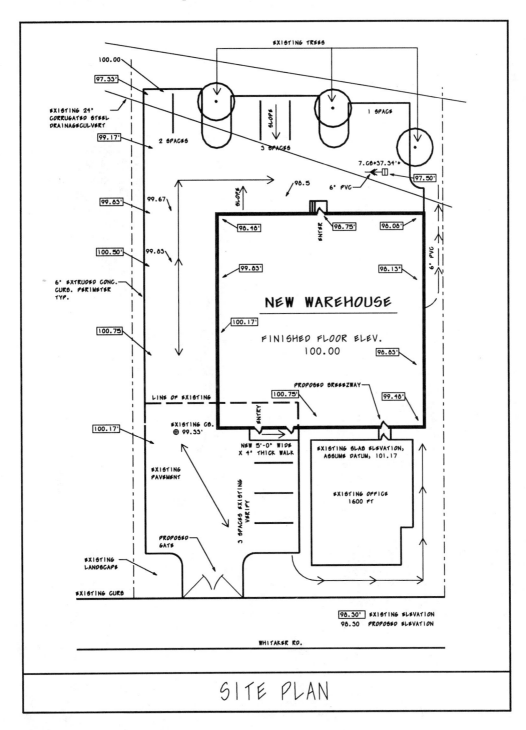

SITE PLAN

OBJECTIVES

After completing this chapter, you will be able to:

✓ Extend Elements.

✓ Modify vertices and arcs.

✓ Modify elements with AccuDraw.

✓ Create complex shapes and chains.

✓ Modify multi-line joints.

ELEMENT MODIFICATION—EXTENDING LINES

MicroStation allows you not only to place elements easily, but also to modify them as needed. Three commands helpful for cleaning up and for modifying elements are available in MicroStation. The commands include Extend Element, Extend Elements to Intersection, and Extend Element to Intersection available from the Modify Element tool box.

Extend Element

The Extend Element command functions to extend or shorten a line, line string, or multi-line via a graphically defined length (with a data point) or via a keyed-in distance.

To extend an element graphically, invoke the Extend Element command from:

Modify tool box	Select the Extend Element tool (see Figure 7–1).
Key-in window	**Extend Line** (or **ext l**) ⏎

MicroStation prompts:

> Extend Line > Identify element *(Identify the element near the end to be extended or shortened.)*
> Extend Line > Accept or Reject (Select next input) *(Drag the element to the new length and click the Data button to accept, or click the Reject button to disregard the modification.)*

The following command sequence shows an example (see Figure 7–2) of using the Extend Element tool to extend a line:

> Extend Line > Identify element *(Identify the line.)*
> Extend Line > Accept/Reject (Select next input) *(Click the Data button to extend the line.)*

FIGURE 7–1   Invoking the Extend Element command from the Modify Element tool box.

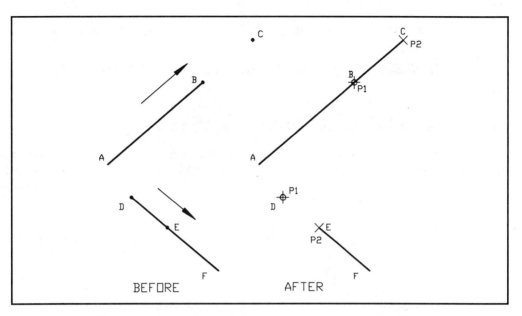

FIGURE 7–2 Examples of extending and shortening an element graphically.

To extend an element by keying-in the distance, invoke the Extend Element command from:

Modify tool box	Select the Extend Element tool, turn on the Toggle button for Distance, and key-in the distance in the Tool Settings window (see Figure 7–3).
Key-in window	**Extend Line Keyin** (or **ext l k**) ⌨ENTER

MicroStation prompts:

> Extend Line by Key-in > Identify element *(Identify the element near the end to be extended or shortened.)*
> Extend Line by Key-in > Accept/Reject (Select next input) *(Click the Data button again anywhere in the design plane to accept the extension.)*

FIGURE 7–3 Invoking the Extend Element tool via key-in from the Modify Element tool box.

> **NOTE:** To shorten the element, key-in a negative distance in the Distance edit field.

Extend Elements to Intersection

Two elements can be extended or shortened to create a clean intersection between the two. Elements that can be extended to a common intersection with each other are lines, line strings, arcs, half ellipses, and quarter ellipses. Figure 7–4 shows several examples of possible extensions to intersection.

To extend two elements to their common intersection, invoke the Extend 2 Elements to Intersection command from:

Modify tool box	Select the Extend Elements to Intersection tool (see Figure 7–5).
Key-in window	**Extend Line 2** (or **ext l 2**)

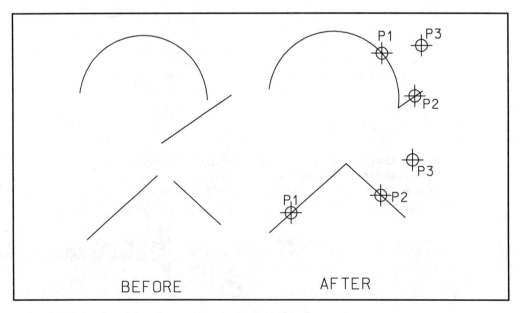

FIGURE 7–4 Examples of extending elements to a common intersection.

FIGURE 7–5 Invoking the Extend Elements to Intersection tool from the Modify Element tool box.

MicroStation prompts:

> Extend 2 Elements to Intersection > Select first element to extension *(Identify one of the two elements.)*
> Extend 2 Elements to Intersection > Select element for intersection *(Identify the second element.)*
> Extend 2 Elements to Intersection > Accept/Initiate Intersection *(Place a data point anywhere in the view to initiate the intersection.)*

Dynamic update shows the intersection as soon as you select the second element, but the intersection is not actually created until you accept it by clicking the Data button a third time.

> **NOTE:** If an element overlaps the intersection, select it on the part you want to keep. The part of the element beyond the intersection is deleted. If dynamic update shows the wrong part of the element deleted, click the Reset button to back up and try again.

Extend Element to Intersection

The Extend Element to Intersection command serves to change the end point of the selected line to extend to a selected line, line string, shape, circle, or arc. Elements that can be extended are lines, line strings, arcs, half ellipses, and quarter ellipses. Figure 7–6 shows several examples of possible extensions to intersection.

To extend an element to its intersection with another element, invoke the Extend Element to Intersection command from:

Modify tool box	Select the Extend Element to Intersection tool (see Figure 7–7).
Key-in window	**Extend Line Intersection** (or **ext l in**) ⏎

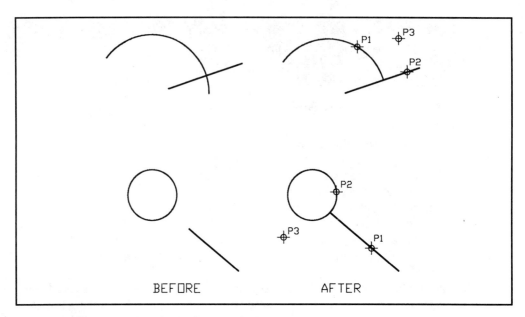

FIGURE 7–6   Examples of extending an element to an intersection.

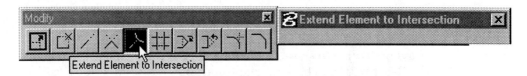

FIGURE 7–7   Invoking the Extend Element to Intersection tool from the Modify Element tool box.

MicroStation prompts:

> Extend Element to Intersection > Select first element for extension *(Identify the element to extend.)*
> Extend Element to Intersection > Select element for intersection *(Identify the element to which the first element will be extended.)*
> Extend Element to Intersection > Accept/Initiate Intersection *(Place a data point anywhere in the view to initiate the intersection.)*

Dynamic update shows the intersection as soon as you select the second element, but the intersection is not actually created until you accept it by clicking the Data button a third time.

> **NOTE:** If the element to be extended overlaps the intersection, select it on the part you want to keep. The part of the element beyond the intersection is deleted. If dynamic update shows the wrong part of the element deleted, click the Reset button to back up and try again.

ELEMENT MODIFICATION—MODIFYING VERTICES

Several commands are available to modify the geometric shape of elements by moving, deleting, or inserting vertices. For example, you can change the size of a block by grabbing and moving one of the vertices of the block, or you can turn the block into a triangle by deleting one of the vertices.

Modify Element

The Modify Element command can modify the geometric shape of any type of element except text elements. Here are the types of modifications it can make:

- Move a vertex or segment of a line, line string, multi-line, curve, B-spline control polygon, shape, complex chain, or complex shape
- Scale a block about the opposite vertex
- Modify rounded segments of complex chains and complex shapes created with the Place SmartLine tool while preserving their tangency
- Change rounded segments of complex chains and complex shapes to sharp, and vice versa
- Scale a circular arc while maintaining its sweep angle (Use the Modify Arc Angle command to change the sweep angle of an arc.)
- Change a circle's radius or the length of one axis of an ellipse (If the ellipse axes are made equal, the ellipse becomes a circle and only the radius can be modified after that.)
- Move dimension text or modify the extension line length of a dimension element

Typical element modifications are shown in Figure 7–8.

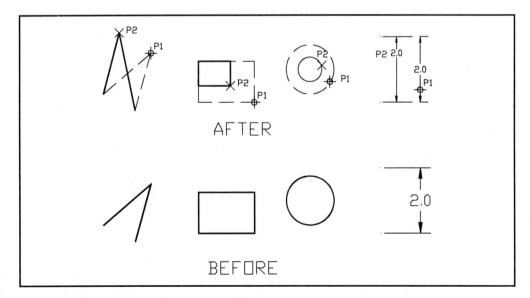

FIGURE 7–8   Examples of element modifications.

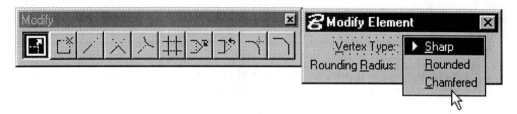

FIGURE 7–9 Modify Element Tool Settings window.

When a vertex is selected for modification, the Tool Settings window presents options for modifying the shape of the vertex. Figure 7–9 shows a typical Modify Element Tool Settings window; the settings are described in Table 7–1.

Table 7–1. Modify Element Tool Settings for Vertices

SETTING	EFFECT OF SETTING
Vertex Type	Set the shape of each vertex to one of these types: • Sharp • Rounded (a Fillet) • Chamfered
Round Radius	Enter the rounded vertex radius in working units (MU:SU:PU). *Note:* The "Rounding Radius" prompt appears only when the Vertex Type is "Rounded."
Chamfer Offset	Enter the offset of each end of the chamfer from the vertex point. Each offset is equal. *Note:* The "Chamfer Offset" prompt appears only when the Vertex Type is "Chamfer."
Orthogonal	If an orthogonal vertex is identified, turn this ON to maintain the orthogonal shape of the vertex.

Invoke the Modify Element command from:

Modify tool box	Select the Modify Element tool (see Figure 7–10).
Key-in window	**Modify Element** [ENTER]

MicroStation prompts:

Modify Element > Identify element *(Identify the element to be modified.)*
Modify Element > Accept/Reject (Select next input) *(Move the selection point to the desired new location and place a data point to complete the modification, or click the Reset button to deselect the element.)*

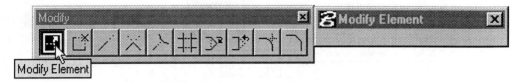

FIGURE 7-10   Invoking the Modify Element command from Modify tool box.

> **NOTE:** If you select a segment near its center, the segment is moved. If you select it near an end, that vertex is moved.

Using Modify Element and AccuDraw Together   Turn on AccuDraw before invoking the Modify Element command to benefit from the extra drawing aids AccuDraw provides. Those aids make Modify Element a more efficient command. For example, the angle can be locked for a line to make it easy to adjust only the line length, or the length can be locked to make it easy to change only the rotation angle.

Delete Vertex

The Delete Vertex command removes a vertex from a shape, line string, or curve string. Figure 7–11 shows an example of deleting a vertex from a line string.

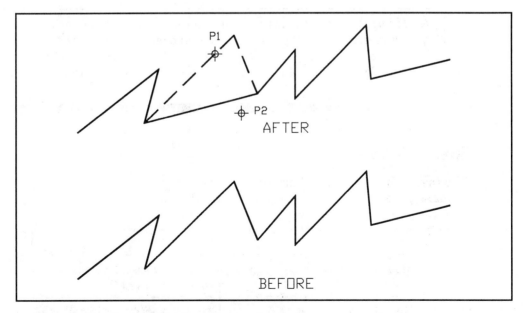

FIGURE 7-11   Example of deleting a vertex from a line string.

FIGURE 7-12 Invoking the Delete Vertex command from the Modify Element tool box.

To delete a vertex from an element, invoke the Delete Vertex command from:

Modify tool box	Select the Delete Vertex tool (see Figure 7–12).
Key-in window	**Delete Vertex** (or **del v**) ⏎

MicroStation prompts:

Delete Vertex > Identify element *(Identify the element near the vertex you want to delete.)*
Delete Vertex > Accept/Reject (Select next input) *(Click the Data button to accept the deleted vertex, or click the Reject button to disregard the modification.)*

When you select the vertex to delete, dynamic update shows the element without the vertex, but it is not actually removed until you click the Data button again. The second data point can also select another vertex to delete.

> **NOTE:** If the element has only the minimum number of vertices re-
> quired to define that type of element, you cannot delete a vertex from
> it. The command indicates it is deleting the vertex, but nothing is
> deleted. For example, a minimum of three vertices is required to define
> a shape.

Insert Vertex

The Insert Vertex command inserts a new vertex into a shape, line string, or curve string. Figure 7–13 shows an example of inserting a vertex for a line string.

To insert a vertex from an element, invoke the Insert Vertex command from:

Modify tool box	Select the Insert Vertex tool (see Figure 7–14).
Key-in window	**Insert Vertex** (or **ins v**) ⏎

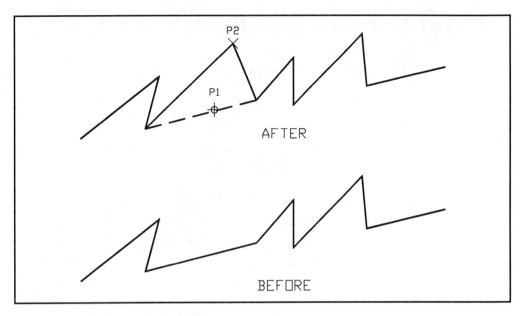

FIGURE 7-13   Example of inserting a vertex.

MicroStation prompts:

> Insert Vertex > Identify element *(Identify the element at the point where you want the vertex inserted.)*
> Insert Vertex > Accept/Reject (Select next input) *(Drag the new vertex to where you want it in the design plane and click the Data button to insert it, or click the Reject button to reject your selection.)*

When you select the element at the point where you want the new vertex inserted, a dynamic image of the new vertex follows the screen pointer until you place the second data point where you want the vertex located. The second data point causes the new vertex to be inserted, and dynamic update continues dragging the new vertices. Click the Reset button or select another MicroStation command once you are through with the modification.

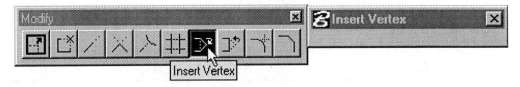

FIGURE 7-14   Invoking the Insert Vertex command from the Modify Element tool box.

ELEMENT MODIFICATION—MODIFYING ARCS

After you place an arc, you can modify its radius, sweep angle, and axis. The commands are available in the Arcs tool box, or you can key-in the commands at the key-in window.

Modify Arc Radius

The Modify Arc Radius command changes the length of the radius of the selected arc. Figure 7–15 shows examples of modifying an arc radius.

To modify the radius of an arc, invoke the Modify Arc Radius command from:

Arcs tool box	Select the Modify Arc Radius tool (see Figure 7–16).
Key-in window	**Modify Arc Radius** (or **modi a r**) [ENTER]

MicroStation prompts:

Modify Arc Radius > Identify element *(Identify the arc to modify.)*
Modify Arc Radius > Accept/Reject (Select next input) *(Reposition the arc and click the Data button to place it, or click the Reject button to reject the modification.)*

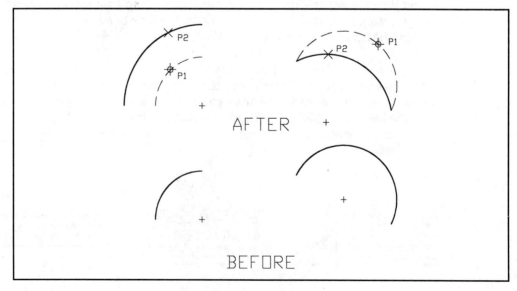

FIGURE 7–15   Examples of modifying an arc radius.

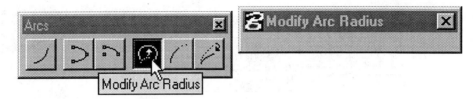

FIGURE 7-16   Invoking the Modify Arc Radius command from the Arcs tool tox.

Dynamic update shows the arc following the screen pointer after you select the arc. The arc is actually modified once you place the second data point, after which dynamic update continues to drag the arc. Click the Reset button or select another MicroStation command once you are through modification.

Modify Arc Angle

The Modify Arc Angle command increases or decreases the sweep angle of the selected arc. Figure 7–17 shows examples of modifying an arc angle.

To modify the sweep angle of an arc, invoke the Modify Arc Angle command from:

Arcs tool box	Select the Modify Arc Angle tool (see Figure 7–18).
Key-in window	**Modify Arc Angle** (or **modi a an**) ⏎

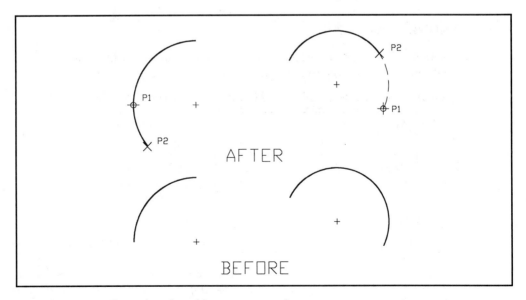

FIGURE 7-17   Examples of modifying an arc angle.

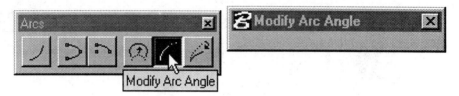

FIGURE 7-18 Invoking the Modify Arc Angle command from the Arcs tool box.

MicroStation prompts:

> Modify Arc Angle > Identify element *(Identify the arc near the end whose sweep angle you want to modify.)*
> Modify Arc Angle > Accept/Reject (Select next input) *(Reposition the end of the arc and click the Data button to place it, or click the Reject button to reject the modification.)*

Dynamic update shows the arc following the screen pointer after you select the arc. The arc sweep angle is actually modified once you place the second data point, after which dynamic update continues to drag the arc. Click the Reset button or select another MicroStation command once you are through with the modification.

> **NOTE:** If you drag the sweep angle around until the arc appears to be a circle, it is still an arc. Arcs that look like circles can be confusing later when using commands like patterning. If the arc should have been a circle, place a circle and delete the arc.

Modify Arc Axis

The Modify Arc Axis command changes the major or minor axis radius of the selected arc. Figure 7–19 shows an example of modifying an arc axis.

To modify an arc axis, invoke the Modify Arc Axis command from:

Arcs tool box	Select the Modify Arc Axis tool (see Figure 7–20).
Key-in window	**Modify Arc Axis** (or **modi a ax**) ENTER

MicroStation prompts:

> Modify Arc Axis > Identify element *(Identify the arc whose axis has to be modified.)*
> Modify Arc Axis > Accept/Reject (Select next input) *(Reposition the axis of the arc and click the Data button to place it, or click the Reject button to reject the modification.)*

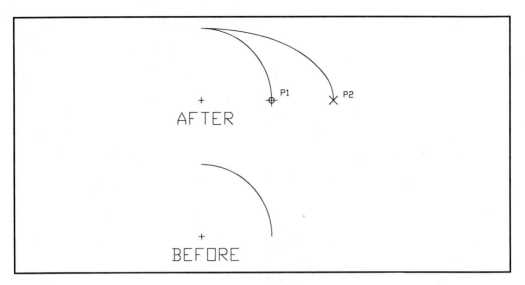

FIGURE 7-19   Example of modifying an arc axis.

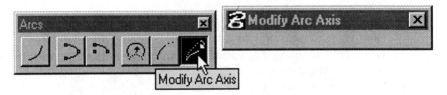

FIGURE 7-20   Invoking the Modify Arc Axis command from the Arcs tool box.

Dynamic update shows the arc following the screen pointer after you select the arc. The arc is actually modified once you place the second data point, after which dynamic update continues to drag the arc. Click the Reset button or select another MicroStation command once you are through with the modification.

CREATING COMPLEX CHAINS AND SHAPES

The Create Complex Chain and Create Complex Shape commands turn groups of connected elements into one complex element. A complex shape is a closed element (you could say it holds water), and a complex chain is an open element (the water can flow out between the two ends of the chain). The element manipulation commands treat the elements in a complex groupings as one element.

When you create a complex chain or shape from separate elements, the elements take on the current active element attributes (all the available settings in the Element Attributes settings box), and any gaps between the elements are closed. You can key-in Maximum allowable gap in the Max Gap edit field. Figure 7–21 shows a group of individual elements before and after being turned into a complex shape.

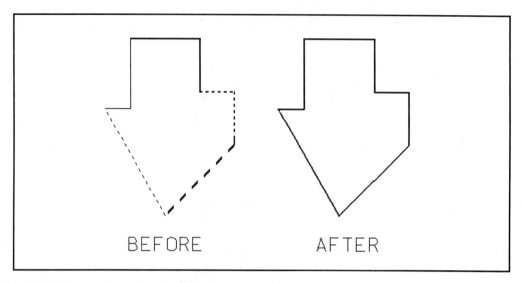

BEFORE   AFTER

FIGURE 7–21 Example of a shape being turned into a complex shape.

You can create a complex chain or shape manually by selecting each element to be included, or automatically by letting MicroStation find each element. If you want the elements that make up the complex chain or shape to be individual elements again, you can drop them with the Drop Complex command (the dropped elements keep the parameters of the complex shape).

A quick way to check to see if you really created a complex group from the elements is to apply one of the element manipulation commands to it. If the elements are complex, dynamic update shows an image of all elements following the screen pointer, and the element type in the Status bar tells you it is either a Complex Chain or a Complex Shape.

> **NOTE:** It is easy to make a mistake in creating complex chains and shapes, and only experience will make you competent. If you goof while creating a complex chain or shape, undo it and try again. Do not give up—you will get the hang of it!

Creating a Complex Chain Manually

When you create a complex chain manually, you must select and accept, in order, each of the elements to be included in the chain. Any gaps between the elements are closed, and the complex chain takes on the current active element attributes.

FIGURE 7-22   Invoking the Create Complex Chain command from the Groups tool box.

To create a complex chain manually, invoke the Create Complex Chain command from:

Groups tool box	Select the Create Complex Chain tool and Manual from the Method option menu in the Tool settings window (see Figure 7–22).
Key-in window	**Create Chain** (or **cre ch**) ⏎

MicroStation prompts:

> Create Complex Chain > Identify element *(Identify the first element to include in the complex chain.)*
> Create Complex Chain > Accept/Reject (Select next input) *(Identify the next element to include in the complex chain and continue selecting elements in order until all elements are selected. When all elements are selected, click the Reset button to create the complex chain.)*

Figure 7–23 provides an example of creating a complex chain manually.

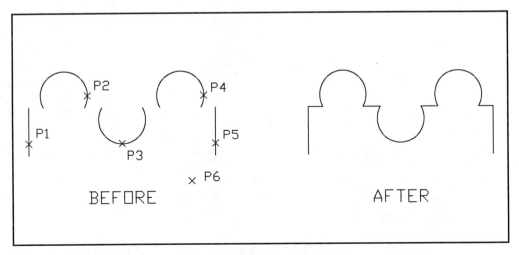

FIGURE 7-23   Example of creating a complex chain manually.

> **NOTE:** Sometimes when you update a view, the lines closing the gaps between elements in the complex chain may disappear. They are still there—update the view again, and they should reappear.

Creating a Complex Chain Automatically

To create a complex chain automatically, start by selecting and accepting the first element in the chain. After that, MicroStation finds and highlights more elements, in series, and you must accept or reject each one.

The automatic version of the command also allows you to specify a search tolerance that tells MicroStation how far away, in working units, from the end of the previous element it can search for another element. If the tolerance is set to zero, the next element must touch the last selected one before MicroStation finds it.

If there are two or more possible elements at a junction, MicroStation tells you that there is a fork in the path and selects one of the possible elements. You can either accept or reject the element and have MicroStation highlight another possible element in the fork.

> **NOTE:** If the complex chain contains many elements, and there are not very many forks, the automatic method is probably faster than the manual method. If there are many fork points, creating the chain manually may go faster.

To create a complex chain automatically, invoke the Create Complex Chain command from:

Groups tool box	Select the Create Complex Chain tool and Automatic from the Method option menu in the Tool settings window (see Figure 7–24).
Key-in window	**Create Chain Automatic** (or **cre ch a**) [ENTER]

MicroStation prompts:

Automatic Create Complex Chain > Identify element *(Identify the first element to include in the complex chain.)*

FIGURE 7-24 Invoking the Create Complex Chain Automatic command from the Groups tool box.

> Automatic Create Complex Chain > Accept/Reject (Select next input) *(Move the screen pointer in the direction you want the search to go and click the Data button to accept the first element, or click the Reject button to reject it and start over.)*

If there are no forks in the path from the previous element, MicroStation prompts:

> Automatic Create Complex Chain > Accept Chain Element *(Click the Data button to accept the element and continue the search, or click the Reset button to complete the chain with the previous element.)*

If there is a fork in the path from the previous element, MicroStation prompts:

> Automatic Create Complex Chain > Fork—Accept/Reject path *(To accept the fork element MicroStation selected, click the Data button; click the Reject button to disregard the current selection and select another fork element.)*

The process continues until MicroStation cannot find another element to add or until you reject a selection when there is no fork in the path. You *cannot* end a search at a fork point. Figure 7–25 shows an example of creating a complex chain automatically.

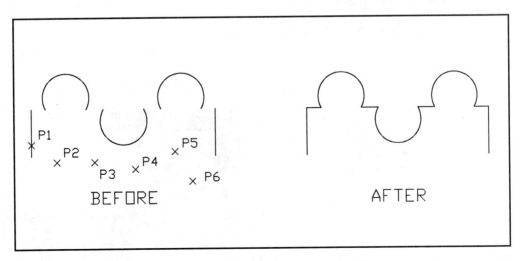

FIGURE 7-25 Example of creating a complex chain automatically.

Creating a Complex Shape Manually

To create a complex shape manually, you must select and accept, in order, each of the elements to be included in the shape. Any gaps between the elements are closed, and the complex chain takes on the current active element attributes.

To create a complex shape manually, invoke the Create Complex Shape command from:

Groups tool box	Select the Create Complex Shape tool and Manual from the Method option menu; if necessary, key-in the gap distance in the Max Gap edit field in the Tool settings window (see Figure 7–26).
Key-in window	**Create Shape (or cre s)**

MicroStation prompts:

> Create Complex Shape > Identify element *(Identify the first element to include in the complex shape.)*
> Create Complex Shape > Accept/Reject (Select next input) *(Identify the next element to include in the complex shape and continue selecting elements in order until all elements are selected. When all elements are selected, click the Reset button to create the complex shape.)*

Figure 7–27 provides an example of how to create a complex chain manually.

If the end of the last element is touching the start of the first element, you can click the Data button back on top of the first element to close the shape without clicking the Reset button.

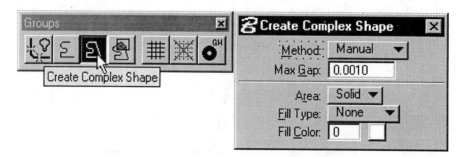

FIGURE 7–26   Invoking the Create Complex Shape command from the Groups tool box.

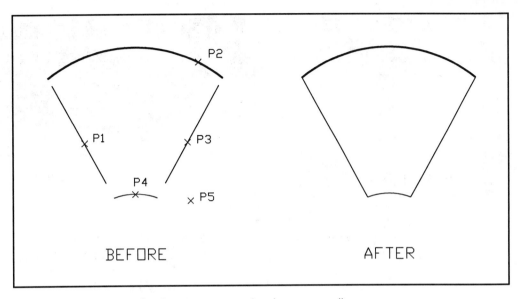

FIGURE 7-27   Example of creating a complex shape manually.

Creating a Complex Shape Automatically

To create a complex shape automatically, start by selecting and accepting the first element in the shape. After that, MicroStation finds and highlights more elements, in series, and you must accept or reject each one.

If there are two or more possible elements at a junction, MicroStation tells you there is a fork in the path and picks one of the possible elements. You can either accept or reject the element and have MicroStation highlight another possible element.

The automatic version of the command also allows you to specify a search tolerance that tells MicroStation how far away, in working units, from the end of the previous element it can search for another element. If the tolerance is set to zero, the next element must touch the last selected one before MicroStation finds it.

> **NOTE:** If the complex shape contains many elements, and there are not very many forks, the automatic method is probably faster than the manual method. If there are many fork points, creating the shape manually may go faster.

To create a complex shape automatically, invoke the Create Complex Shape command from:

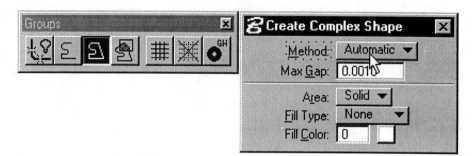

FIGURE 7–28 Invoking the Create Complex Shape Automatic command from the Groups tool box.

Groups tool box	Select the Create Complex Shape tool and Automatic from the Method option menu; if necessary, key-in the gap distance in the Max Gap edit field in the Tool settings window (see Figure 7–28).
Key-in window	**Create Shape Automatic** (or **cre s a**) [ENTER]

MicroStation prompts:

> Automatic Create Complex Shape > Identify element *(Identify the first element to include in the complex shape.)*
> Automatic Create Complex Shape > Accept/Reject (Select next input) *(Move the screen pointer in the direction you want the search to go and click the Data button to accept the first element, or click the Reject button to reject it and start over.)*

If there are no forks in the path from the previous element, MicroStation prompts:

> Automatic Create Complex Shape > Accept Shape Element *(Click the Data button to accept the element and continue the search, or click the Reset button to complete the chain with the previous element.)*

If there is a fork in the path from the previous element, MicroStation prompts:

> Automatic Create Complex Chain > Fork—Accept/Reject path *(To accept the fork element MicroStation selected, click the Data button; click the Reject button to disregard the current selection and select another fork element.)*

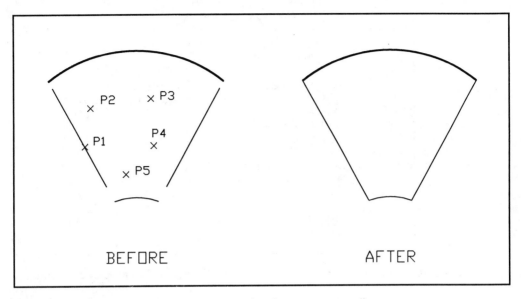

FIGURE 7-29 Example of creating a complex shape automatically.

The process continues until MicroStation cannot find another element to add or until you reject a selection when there is no fork in the path. You *cannot* end a search at a fork point. If you press the Reset button when another element is highlighted, that element is not used in the shape. Figure 7–29 shows an example of creating a complex shape automatically.

Create Region

The Create Region command creates a complex shape, similar to Complex Shape commands. You can create a complex shape from either of the following:

- The union, intersection, or difference between two or more closed elements
- A region bounded by elements that have end points that are closed together by the Maximum Gap

Creating a Complex Shape From Element Intersection The Intersection option allows you to create a complex shape from a composite area formed from the area that is common to two closed elements.

To create a complex shape from the intersection of two overlapping circles as shown in Figure 7–30, invoke the Create Region command from:

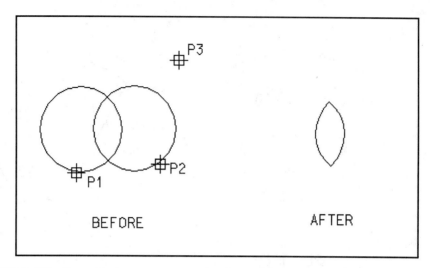

FIGURE 7–30   Example of creating a complex shape with the Intersection option.

FIGURE 7–31   Invoking the Create Region From Element Intersection command from the Create Region tool box.

Groups tool box	Select the Create Region tool and Intersection from the Method option menu; if necessary, turn ON the toggle button to keep the original element in the Tool settings window (see Figure 7–31).
Key-in window	**Create region intersection** (or **cre r i**) [ENTER]

MicroStation prompts:

Create Region From Element Intersection > Identify element *(Identify one of the two circles.)*

Create Region From Element Intersection > Accept/Reject (Select next input)
  (Identify the second circle.)
Create Region From Element Intersection > Accept/Reject (Select next input)
  (Click the Data button again to accept the selection of the second circle.)
Create Region From Element Intersection > Identify additional/Reset to complete
  (Click the Reset button to create the complex shape.)

Creating a Complex Shape From Element Union The Union option allows you to create a complex shape from a composite area formed in such a way that there is no duplication between two closed elements. The total resulting area can be equal to or less than the sum of the areas in the original closed elements.

To create a complex shape from the union of two overlapping circles as shown in Figure 7–32, invoke the Create Region command from:

Groups tool box	Select the Create Region tool and Union from the Method option menu; if necessary, turn ON the toggle button to keep the original element in the Tool settings window (see Figure 7–33).
Key-in window	**Create region union** (or **cre r u**) ⏎

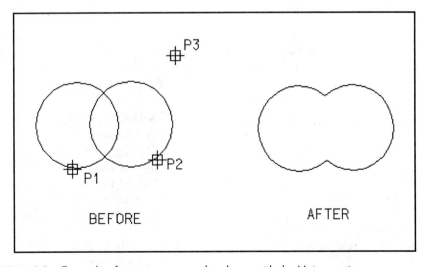

FIGURE 7–32 Example of creating a complex shape with the Union option.

FIGURE 7-33   Invoking the Create Region From Element Union command from the Create Region tool box.

MicroStation prompts:

> Create Region From Element Union > Identify element *(Identify one of the two circles.)*
>
> Create Region From Element Union > Accept/Reject (Select next input) *(Identify the second circle.)*
>
> Create Region From Element Union > Accept/Reject (Select next input) *(Click the Data button again to accept the selection of the second circle.)*
>
> Create Region From Element Union > Identify additional/Reset to complete *(Click the Reset button to create the complex shape.)*

Creating a Complex Shape From Element Difference   The Difference option allows you to create a complex shape from a closed element after removing from it any area it has in common with a second element.

To create a complex shape from the difference of two overlapping circles as shown in Figure 7–34, invoke the Create Region command from:

Groups tool box	Select the Create Region tool and Difference from the Method option menu; if necessary, turn ON the toggle button to keep the original element in the Tool settings window (see Figure 7–35).
Key-in window	**Create region difference** (or **cre r d**) [ENTER]

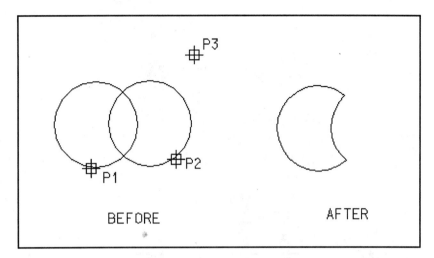

FIGURE 7–34 Example of creating a complex shape with the Difference option.

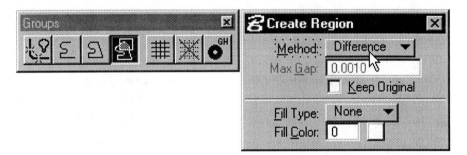

FIGURE 7–35 Invoking the Create Region From Element Difference command from the Create Region tool box.

MicroStation prompts:

Create Region From Element Difference > Identify element *(Identify the circle on the left.)*
Create Region From Element Difference > Accept/Reject (Select next input) *(Identify the circle on the right.)*
Create Region From Element Difference > Accept/Reject (Select next input) *(Click the Data button again to accept the selection of the second circle.)*
Create Region From Element Difference > Identify additional/Reset to complete *(Click the Reset button to create the complex shape.)*

Creating a Complex Shape From An Enclosed Area The Flood option allows you to create a complex shape made up of one or more elements. MicroStation prompts you to pick a point inside the closed area. When you place the first data point inside the area, MicroStation searches for the elements that enclose the area, highlights pieces of the elements as it finds them, and then creates the complex shape.

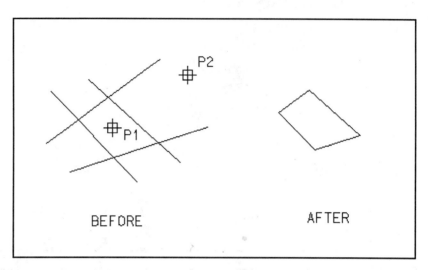

FIGURE 7–36 Example of creating a complex shape with the Flood option.

To create a complex shape from an enclosed area as shown in Figure 7–36, invoke the Create Region command from:

Groups tool box	Select the Create Region tool and Flood from the Method option menu; if necessary, turn ON the toggle button to keep the original element in the Tool settings window (see Figure 7–37).
Key-in window	**Create region flood** (or **cre r f**) (ENTER)

FIGURE 7–37 Invoking the Create Region From Area Enclosing Point command from the Create Region tool box.

MicroStation prompts:

> Create Region From Area Enclosing Point > Enter data point *(Place a data point inside the enclosed area.)*
> Create Region From Area Enclosing Point > Accept-Create a complex shape *(Click the Accept button to accept the complex shape.)*

DROPPING COMPLEX CHAINS AND SHAPES

If you want to return the elements in a complex chain or shape to individual elements, you can drop their complex status. The Drop Complex Status command drops an individual complex group. The Fence Drop Complex Status drops all complex groups within the boundary of a fence.

Dropped complex elements return to being individual elements, but they keep the element parameters (color, weight, etc.).

Dropping a Complex Chain or Shape

To drop a complex chain or shape, invoke the Drop Complex Status command from:

Drop tool box	Select the Drop Complex Status tool (see Figure 7–38).
Key-in window	**Drop Complex** (or **dr c**) [ENTER]

MicroStation prompts:

> Drop Complex Status > Identify element *(Identify the complex chain or shape to drop into individual elements.)*
> Drop Complex Status > Accept/Reject (select next input) *(Click the Accept button to accept the change in status from complex element into individual elements, or click the Reject button to disregard the change in the status.)*

FIGURE 7–38 Invoking the Drop Complex Status command from the Drop tool box.

Dropping Several Complex Chains or Shapes

The Drop Complex Status of Fence Contents command breaks all the complex elements enclosed in a fence into separate elements. Before you invoke the command, place a fence that encloses all the complex elements you want to drop and select the fence lock you want to use.

Invoke the Drop Fence Contents command from:

Fence tool box	Select the Drop Fence Contents tool (see Figure 7–39).
Key-in window	**Fence drop** (or **fe dr**) ⏎

MicroStation prompts:

Drop Complex Status of Fence Contents > Accept/Reject *(Click the Accept button to accept the change in status from complex element into individual elements, or click the Reject button to disregard the change in the status.)*

FIGURE 7–39 Invoking the Drop Fence Contents command from the Fence tool box.

MODIFYING MULTI-LINES

Chapter 3 introduced placing multi-line elements. The multi-line joint commands help you modify the intersections of two multi-lines or cut holes in the lines of one multi-line. The commands are available in the Multi-line Joints tool box that is opened from the pull-down menu Tools.

Construct Closed Cross Joint

The Construct Closed Cross Joint command cuts all lines that make up the first multi-line selected at the point where it crosses the second multi-line, as shown in Figure 7–40.

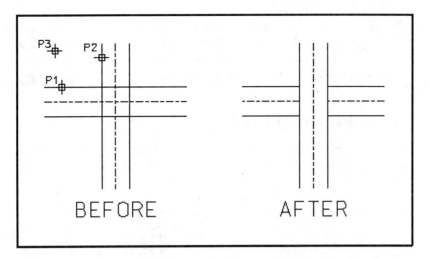

FIGURE 7-40   Example of using a Construct Closed Cross Joint command.

Invoke the Construct Closed Cross Joint command from:

Multi-line Joints tool box	Select the Construct Closed Cross Joint tool (see Figure 7–41).
Key-in window	**Join Cross Closed** (or **jo cr c**) ⏎

MicroStation prompts:

Construct Closed Cross Joint > Identify element *(Identify the multi-line P1 as shown in Figure 7–40.)*
Construct Closed Cross Joint > Identify element *(Identify the multi-line P2 as shown in Figure 7–40.)*
Construct Closed Cross Joint > Identify element *(Click the Data button anywhere in the view to initiate cleaning up of the intersection, or click the Reject button to disregard the changes.)*

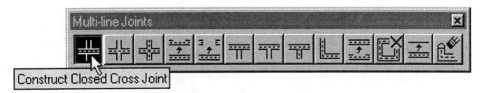

FIGURE 7-41   Invoking the Construct Closed Cross Joint command from the Multi-line Joints tool box.

> **NOTE:** For each Multi-Line Joint command, dynamic update shows the intersection cleaned up after the second data point, but it does not become permanent until you provide the third data point.

Construct Open Cross Joint

The Construct Open Cross Joint command cuts all lines that make up the first multi-line you select and cuts only the outside line of the second multi-line, as shown in Figure 7–42.

Invoke the Construct Open Cross Joint command from:

Multi-line Joints tool box	Select the Construct Open Cross Joint tool (see Figure 7–43).
Key-in window	**Join Cross Open** (or **jo cr o**) (ENTER)

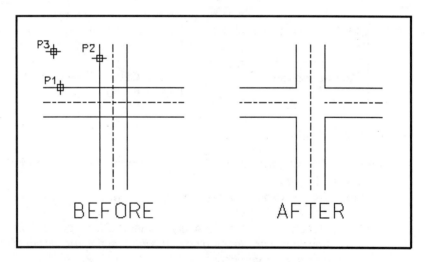

FIGURE 7–42   Example of using a Construct Open Cross Joint command.

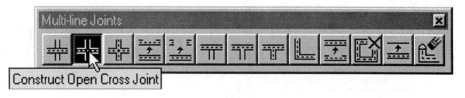

FIGURE 7–43   Invoking the Construct Open Cross Joint command from the Multi-line Joints tool box.

MicroStation prompts:

> Construct Open Cross Joint > Identify element *(Identify the multi-line P1 as shown in Figure 7–42.)*
> Construct Open Cross Joint > Identify element *(Identify the multi-line P2 as shown in Figure 7–42.)*
> Construct Open Cross Joint > Identify element *(Click the Data button anywhere in the view to initiate cleaning up of the intersection, or click the Reject button to disregard the changes.)*

Construct Merged Cross Joint

The Construct Merged Cross Joint command cuts all lines that make up each of the intersecting multi-line you select, except the center lines, as shown in Figure 7–44. If there are no center lines, all lines in each multi-line are cut.

Invoke the Construct Merged Cross Joint command from:

Multi-line Joints tool box	Select the Construct Merged Cross Joint tool (see Figure 7–45).
Key-in window	**Join Cross Merge** (or **jo cr m**) ⏎

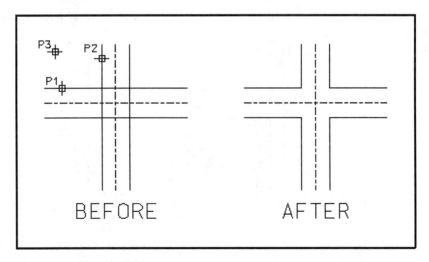

FIGURE 7–44 Example of using a Construct Merged Cross Joint command.

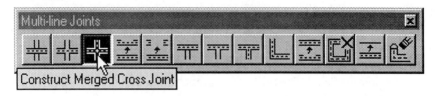

FIGURE 7-45   Invoking the Construct Merged Cross Joint command from the Multi-line Joints tool box.

MicroStation prompts:

> Construct Merged Cross Joint > Identify element *(Identify the multi-line P1 as shown in Figure 7–44.)*
> Construct Merged Cross Joint > Identify element *(Identify the multi-line P2 as shown in Figure 7–44.)*
> Construct Merged Cross Joint > Identify element *(Click the Data button anywhere in the view to initiate cleaning up of the intersection, or click the Reject button to disregard the changes.)*

Construct Closed Tee Joint

The Construct Closed Tee Joint command extends or shortens the first multi-line you identify to its intersection with the second multi-line. The first multi-line ends at the near side of the intersecting multi-line, which is left intact, as shown in Figure 7–46.

Invoke the Construct Closed Tee Joint command from:

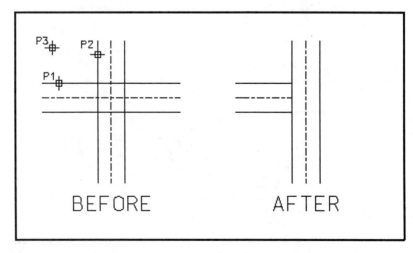

FIGURE 7-46   Example of using a Construct Closed Tee Joint command.

FIGURE 7–47   Invoking the Construct Closed Tee Joint command from the Multi-line Joints tool box.

Multi-line Joints tool box	Select the Construct Closed Tee Joint tool (see Figure 7–47).
Key-in window	**Join Tee Closed** (or **jo t c**)

MicroStation prompts:

> Construct Closed Tee Joint > Identify element *(Identify the multi-line P1 as shown in Figure 7–46.)*
> Construct Closed Tee Joint > Identify element *(Identify the multi-line P2 as shown in Figure 7–46.)*
> Construct Closed Tee Joint > Identify element *(Click the Data button anywhere in the view to initiate cleaning up of the intersection, or click the Reject button to disregard the changes.)*

Construct Open Tee Joint

The Construct Open Tee Joint command is similar to the Closed Tee Joint command, except it leaves an open end at the intersecting mutli-line, as shown in Figure 7–48.

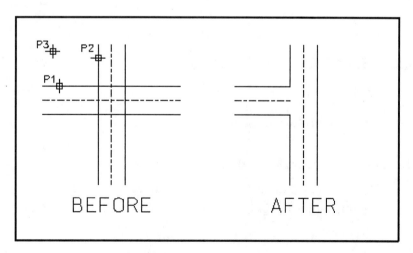

FIGURE 7–48   Example of using a Construct Open Tee Cross Joint command.

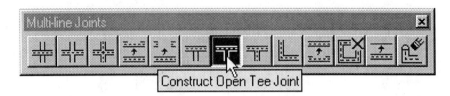

FIGURE 7–49 Invoking the Construct Open Tee Joint command from the Multi-line Joints tool box.

Invoke the Construct Open Tee Joint command from:

Multi-line Joints tool box	Select the Construct Open Tee Joint tool (see Figure 7–49).
Key-in window	**Join Tee Open** (or **jo t o**) ⏎

MicroStation prompts:

Construct Open Tee Joint > Identify element *(Identify the multi-line P1 as shown in Figure 7–48.)*
Construct Open Tee Joint > Identify element *(Identify the multi-line P2 as shown in Figure 7–48.)*
Construct Open Tee Joint > Identify element *(Click the Data button anywhere in the view to initiate cleaning up of the intersection, or click the Reject button to disregard the changes.)*

Construct Merged Tee Joint

The Construct Merged Tee Joint command is similar to the Open Tee Joint command, except the center line of the first multi-line is extended to the center line of the intersecting multi-line, as shown in Figure 7–50.

Invoke the Construct Merged Tee Joint command from:

Multi-line Joints tool box	Select the Construct Merged Tee Joint tool (see Figure 7–51).
Key-in window	**Join Tee Merge** (or **jo t m**) ⏎

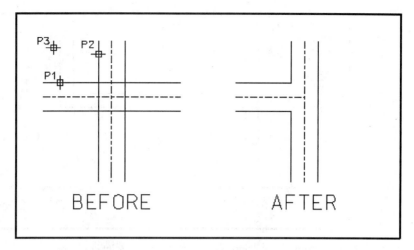

FIGURE 7-50   Example of using a Construct Merged Tee Joint command.

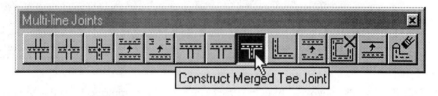

FIGURE 7-51   Invoking the Construct Merged Tee Joint command from the Multi-line Joints tool box.

MicroStation prompts:

> Construct Merged Tee Joint > Identify element *(Identify the multi-line P1 as shown in Figure 7–50.)*
> Construct Merged Tee Joint > Identify element *(Identify the multi-line P2 as shown in Figure 7–50.)*
> Construct Merged Tee Joint > Identify element *(Click the Data button anywhere in the view to initiate cleaning up of the intersection, or click the Reject button to disregard the changes.)*

Construct Corner Joint

The Construct Corner Joint command lengthens or shortens each of the two multi-lines you select as necessary to create a clean intersection, as shown in Figure 7–52.

Invoke the Construct Corner Joint command from:

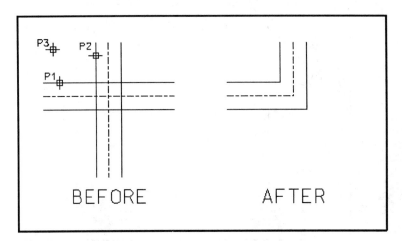

FIGURE 7–52 Example of using a Construct Corner Joint command.

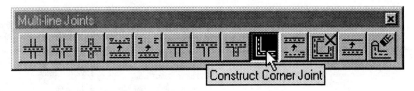

FIGURE 7–53 Invoking the Construct Corner Joint command from the Multi-line Joints tool box.

Multi-line Joints tool box	Select the Construct Corner Joint tool (see Figure 7–53).
Key-in window	**Join Corner** (or **jo c**) ⏎

MicroStation prompts:

> Construct Joint > Identify element *(Identify the multi-line P1 as shown in Figure 7–52.)*
> Construct Joint > Identify element *(Identify the multi-line P2 as shown in Figure 7–52.)*
> Construct Joint > Identify element *(Click the Data button anywhere in the view to initiate cleaning up of the intersection, or click the Reject button to disregard the changes.)*

Cut Single Component Line

The Cut Single Component Line command cuts a hole in the line you select in a multi-line from the first data point to the second data point, as shown in Figure 7–54.

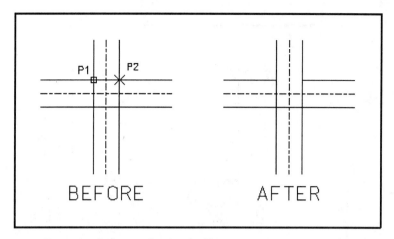

FIGURE 7-54   Example of using a Cut Single Component Line command.

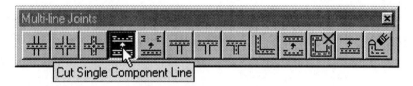

FIGURE 7-55   Invoking the Cut Single Component Line command from the Multi-line Joints tool box.

Invoke the Cut Single Component Line command from:

Multi-line Joints tool box	Select the Cut Single Component Line tool (see Figure 7–55.)
Key-in window	**Cut Single** (or **cu s**) ⏎

MicroStation prompts:

> Cut Single Component Line > Identify element *(Identify the multi-line at P1 as shown in Figure 7–54.)*
> Cut Single Component Line *(Identify the multi-line at P2 as shown in Figure 7–54 to remove the portion of the line.)*

Cut All Component Lines

The Cut All Component Lines command cuts a hole in the multi-line you select from the first data point to the second data point, as shown in Figure 7–56.

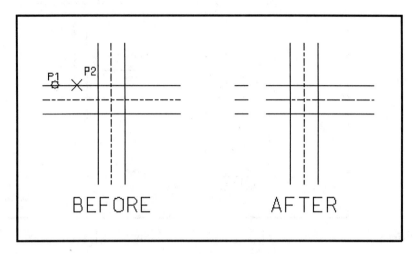

FIGURE 7-56 Example of using a Cut All Component Lines command.

Invoke the Cut All Component Lines command from:

Multi-line Joints tool box	Select the Cut All Component Lines tool (see Figure 7–57.)
Key-in window	**Cut All** (or **cu a**) ⏎

MicroStation prompts:

> Cut All Component Lines > Identify element *(Identify the multi-line at P1 as shown in Figure 7–56.)*
> Cut All Component Lines *(Identify the multi-line at P2 as shown in Figure 7–56 to remove the portion of the multi-line.)*

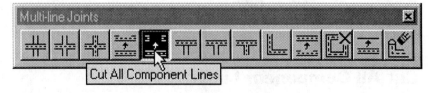

FIGURE 7-57 Invoking the Cut All Component Lines command from the Multi-line Joints tool box.

Uncut Component Lines

The Uncut Component Lines command provides a special undo command for multi-lines. With it you can undo a cut in one line of a multi-line. Identify one end of the cut with a data point, then accept it with a second data point, as shown in Figure 7–58.

Invoke the Uncut Component Lines command from:

Multi-line Joints tool box	Select the Uncut Component Lines tool (see Figure 7–59).
Key-in window	**Uncut** (or **un**) 🄴

MicroStation prompts:

> Uncut Component Lines > Identify element *(Identify the multi-line at P1 as shown in Figure 7–58.)*
> Uncut Component Lines *(Place a data point to accept the change.)*

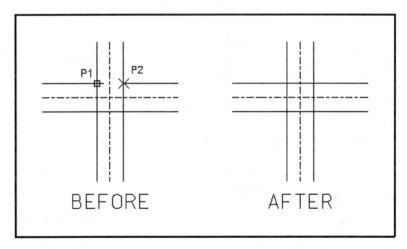

FIGURE 7–58   Example of using a Uncut Component Lines command.

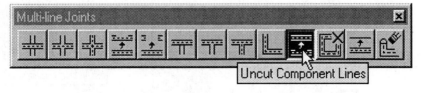

FIGURE 7–59   Invoking the Uncut Component Lines command from the Multi-line Joints tool box.

> **NOTE:** Place the first data point right at one end of the cut you want to close. If you get a message in the Status bar saying the element was not found, try another data point. It often fails to find the cut on the first attempt.

Multi-line Partial Delete

The Multi-line Partial Delete command enables you to delete a multi-line partially without losing any previously created breaks. MicroStation provides four options under the Cap Mode option menu:

- None: No caps are created, similar to Cut All Component Lines tool.
- Current: Uses the start cap and end cap definitions of the identified multi-line.
- Active: Uses the active multi-line start cap and end cap definitions.
- Joint: Uses the identified multi-line's joint definition instead of the end cap definition; ensures the end cap will always be 90 degrees.

Detailed explanation is provided in Chapter 15 for creating or modifying multi-line definitions.

Invoke the Multi-line Partial Delete command from:

Multi-line Joints tool box	Select the Multi-line Partial Delete tool and select one of the four options from the Mode option menu (see Figure 7–60).
Key-in window	**Mline Partial Delete** (or **ml p d**) ⏎

MicroStation prompts:

> Multi-line Partial Delete > Identify multi-line at start of delete *(Identify the multi-line at one end of the part to delete.)*
> Multi-line Partial Delete > Define length of delete *(Place a data point to define the length of the delete.)*

FIGURE 7–60 Invoking the Multi-line Partial Delete command from the Multi-line Joints tool box.

FIGURE 7–61   Invoking the Move Multi-line Profile command from the Multi-line Joints tool box.

Move Multi-line Profile

The Move Multi-line Profile command will move an individual component line of a multi-line or reposition the workline of a multi-line without moving its component lines. MicroStation allows you to change Component or Workline from the Move option menu available in the Tool Settings window.

Invoke the Move Multi-line Profile from:

Multi-line Joints tool box	Select the Move Multi-line Profile tool and select one of the two options from the Move option menu (see Figure 7–61.)
Key-in window	**Uncut** (or **un**) 🄴🄽🅃🄴🅁

MicroStation prompts:

> Move Multi-line Profile > Identify multi-line component to move *(Identify the component to move.)*
> Move Multi-line Profile > Define component position *(Place a Data point to reposition the component.)*

Edit Multi-line Cap

The Edit Multi-line Cap command changes the end cap of a multi-line. MicroStation provides four options under the Cap Mode option menu:

- None: Removes any end caps. The effect is the same as with the Cut All Component Lines tool.
- Current: Does not change the end cap; enabled only when Adjust Angle is turned ON.
- Active: Uses the active multi-line definitions for the end cap.
- Joint: Uses the identified multi-line's joint definition instead of the end cap definition; ensures the end cap will always be 90 degrees.

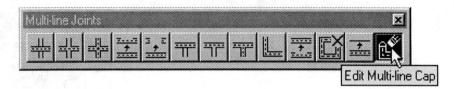

FIGURE 7–62 Invoking the Edit Multi-line Cap command from the Multi-line Joints tool box.

Invoke the Edit Multi-line Cap command from:

Multi-line Joints tool box	Select the Edit Multi-line Cap tool and select one of the four options from the Cap Mode option menu (see Figure 7–62).
Key-in window	**Mline Edit Cap** (or **ml e c**) ⏎

MicroStation prompts:

Edit Multi-line Cap > Identify multi-line near the end cap to modify *(Identify the multi-line near the end cap.)*

Edit Multi-line Cap > Data to change the end cap (reset to reject) *(Place a data point to change the end cap, or click the Reject button to disregard the change.)*

REVIEW QUESTIONS

Write your answers in the spaces provided.

1. Explain briefly the different options available with the Extend Line command.

   _____

   _____

2. List the element types that can be modified by means of the Modify Element command.

   _____

   _____

3. List the commands available to modify an arc.

   _____

   _____

4. Explain the difference between creating a chain manually and creating one automatically.

   _____

   _____

5. To drop a complex chain, invoke the _____ command.

6. Explain the difference between the Construct Closed Cross Joint command and the Construct Merged Cross Joint command.

   _____

   _____

7. Explain the difference between the Construct Closed Tee Joint command and the Construct Merged Tee Joint command.

   _____

   _____

8. Give the steps involved in moving the Multi-line profile.

   _____

   _____

PROJECT EXERCISE

This project exercise provides step-by-step instructions for creating the Utility – Storage Floor Plan shown in Figure P7–1. The intent is to guide you in applying the Multi-line setting, placement, and joints commands.

> **NOTE:** The dimensions are not part of this project. They are included in Figure P7–1 as an aid to drawing the design.

Prepare the Design File

This procedure starts MicroStation, creates a design file, and enters the initial settings.

> **NOTE:** As you complete each step in the project procedures, place a check mark by the step to help you keep up with where you are in the project.

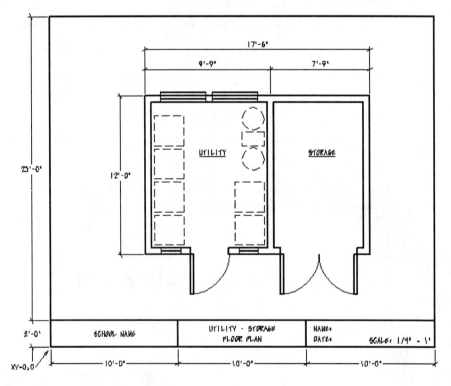

FIGURE P7–1 Completed project design.

STEP 1: Invoke MicroStation, and create a new design file named CH7.DGN using the SEED2D.DGN seed file.

STEP 2: In the Design File dialog box set the:

- Working Unit ratios to 1:12:8000, the Master Unit name to feet ('), and the Sub Unit name to inches (").
- Grid Master to 0.5, Grid Reference to 2, and Grid lock ON.

STEP 3: Invoke the Text settings box from the pull-down menu Element, and adjust the settings as follows:

- Font = 41 - Architecture
- Text Height = 0.4
- Text Width = 0.3
- Line Spacing = 0.4
- Both justifications = Center, Center

STEP 4: Using Figure P7–1 as a guide, draw the 30′ × 25′ border and title block on level 10, with the lower left corner at XY=0,0.

- Replace "SCHOOL NAME" with your school or company name, or make up a name.
- Place your name to the right of "NAME."
- Place today's date to the right of "DATE."

STEP 5: Fit the view, compress the design, and save the design settings.

Enter the Multi-line Settings

This procedure sets up the multi-line element to be used to draw the walls of the utility – storage floor plan.

STEP 1: Open the Multi-lines settings box by selecting Multi-lines from the pull-down menu Element.

STEP 2: If the multi-line list box contains more than two lines, delete the extra lines. To delete each extra line:

- Select a line in the Components area of the Multi-lines settings box.
- Invoke the Delete command from the pull-down menu Edit (Multi-lines settings box).

STEP 3: Select the first line in the Component list box, set the Attributes, and set the offset to 0.0000 (Work line), as shown in Figure P7–2.

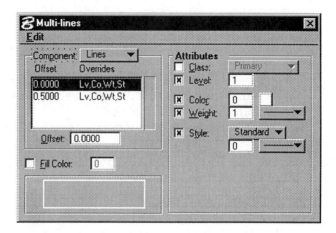

FIGURE P7–2 Settings for the Work line in the walls Multi-line element.

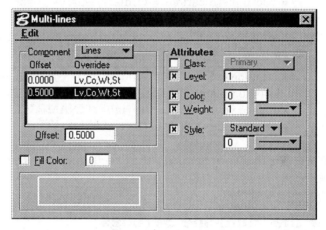

FIGURE P7–3 Setting the Attributes for the second line in the Component list box.

STEP 4: Select the second line in the Component list box and set the Attributes as shown in Figure P7–3.

STEP 5: Select Start Cap from the Component option menu and set the Attributes as shown in Figure P7–4.

STEP 6: Select End Cap from the Component option menu, and set the Attributes as shown in Figure P7–5.

STEP 7: Close the Multi-lines settings box.

> **NOTE:** For a detailed explanation about creating customized multi-lines, refer to Chapter 15, Customizing MicroStation.

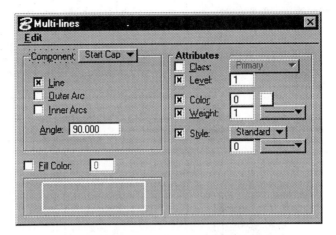

FIGURE P7–4   Start Cap settings for the walls Multi-line element.

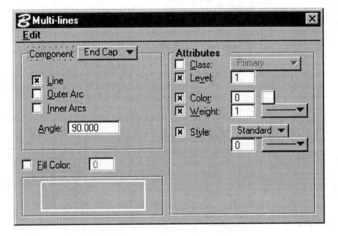

FIGURE P7–5   End Cap settings for the walls Multi-line element.

Draw the Walls

This procedure uses the Multi-line command to draw the utility – storage floor plan walls, as shown in Figure P7–6.

STEP 1:   Set the Active Level to 1, Line Weight to 2, and Color to green. Invoke the Save Settings from the pull-down menu File to save the settings.

STEP 2:   Invoke the Place Multi-line command from the Linear Elements tool box, set Place By to Work line, as shown in Figure P7–7.

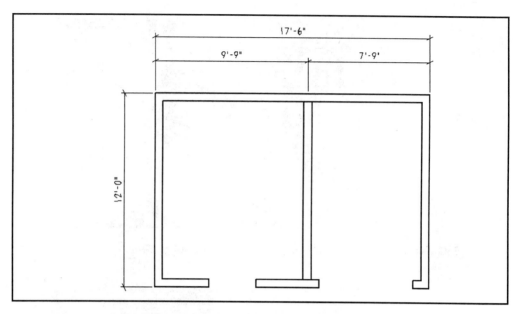

FIGURE P7–6 The walls before holes are cut for the windows.

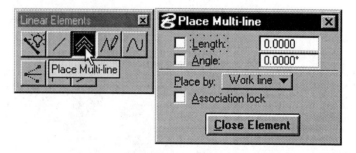

FIGURE P7–7 Invoking the Place Multi-line command and the Tool Settings window.

MicroStation prompts:

Place Multi-line > Enter first point *(Key-in* **xy=24,7** *in the key-in window and press* ⏎*.)*

Place Multi-line > Enter vertex or Reset to complete *(Key-in* **DI=1,0** *in the key-in window and press* ⏎*.)*

Place Multi-line > Enter vertex or Reset to complete *(Key-in* **DI=12,90** *in the key-in window and press* ⏎*.)*

Place Multi-line > Enter vertex or Reset to complete *(Key-in* **DI=17.5,180** *in the key-in window and press* ⏎*.)*

Place Multi-line > Enter vertex or Reset to complete *(Key-in* **DI=12,270** *in the key-in window and press* ⏎*.)*

Place Multi-line > Enter vertex or Reset to complete *(Key-in* **DI=3.5,0** *in the key-in window and press* ⏎*.)*

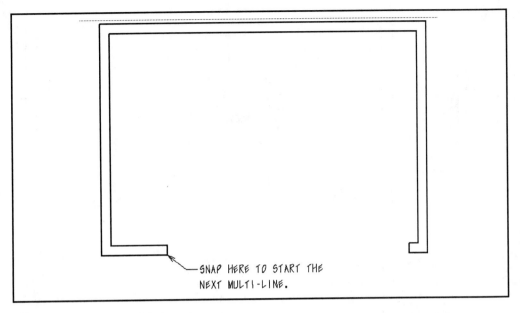

FIGURE P7–8   First Multi-line element.

> Place Multi-line > Enter vertex or Reset to complete *(Click the Reset button.)*

The completed Multi-line element is shown in Figure P7–8.

STEP 3:   With the Multi-line command still active, start the next short piece of multi-line outer wall by Keypoint snapping to the lower right corner of the bottom left horizontal wall, as shown by the note in Figure P7–8.

In the key-in window, key in the following two values:

- **DL=3,0** [ENTER]
- **DL=4,0** [ENTER]

Click the Reset button to complete the placement. The completed Multi-line element is shown in Figure P7–9.

STEP 4:   Draw the interior wall by Keypoint snapping to the inside of the top left corner of the outer wall, as shown by the note in Figure P7–9.

In the key-in window, key in the following two values:

- **DL=9,0** [ENTER]
- **DL=0,–11** [ENTER]

Click the Reset button to complete the placement. The completed Multi-line element is shown in Figure P7–6.

FIGURE P7–9   Completed outer wall Multi-line elements.

Cut Holes for Placing Windows in the Outer Wall

This procedure uses the Multi-line Joints commands to clean up the inner and outer wall intersections and to cut four holes in the utility room wall for windows, as shown in Figure P7–10.

STEP 1:   Open the Multi-line Joints tool box by selecting Multi-line Joints from the pull-down menu Tools.

STEP 2:   To create the joint at the top of the interior wall, invoke the Construct Open Tee Joint command from the Multi-line Joints tool box.

MicroStation prompts:

Construct Open Tee Joint > Identify element *(Select the interior Multi-line element near its top, select the exterior Multi-line element, then click the Data button in space to complete the joint.)*

STEP 3:   Repeat step 2 for the joint at the bottom of the interior wall.

STEP 4:   To create the window openings next to the utility room door, invoke the Cut All Component Lines command from the Multi-line Joints tool box.

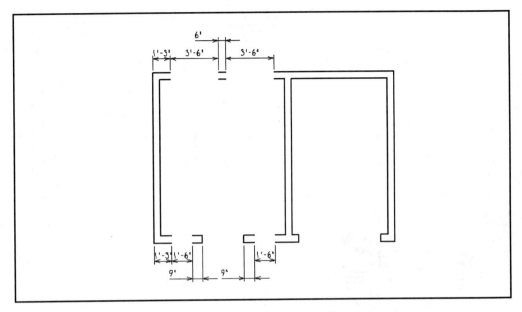

FIGURE P7–10   The walls after cutting holes for windows and wall unions.

MicroStation prompts:

> Cut All Component Lines > Identify element *(Keypoint snap to the lower left outside corner of the outer wall. In the key-in window, key-in* **DL=1.25,0** *and press* ⌷ENTER⌷*.)*
>
> Cut All Component Lines *(In the key-in window, key-in* **DL=1.5,0** *and press* ⌷ENTER⌷*.)*
>
> Cut All Component Lines > Identify element *(Keypoint snap to the lower left corner of the wall on the right side of the utility room door. In the key-in window, key-in* **DL=.75,0** *and press* ⌷ENTER⌷*.)*
>
> Cut All Component Lines *(In the key-in window, key-in* **dl=1.5,0** *and press* ⌷ENTER⌷*.)*

STEP 5:   Use the Cut All Component Lines command to cut two 3.5'-wide window holes in the top wall of the utility room. Use the dimensions in Figure P7–10 as a guide.

Draw the Windows with the Place Multi-line Command

This procedure changes the Multi-line settings, then uses the Place Multi-line command to place windows in the opening created in the utility room exterior walls, as shown in Figure P7–11.

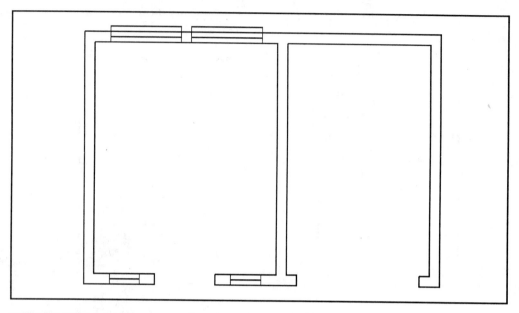

FIGURE P7-11 Utility room walls with windows inserted.

STEP 1: Open the Multi-lines settings box by selecting Multi-lines from the pull-down menu Element.

STEP 2: In the Multi-lines settings box, invoke the Insert command from the pull-down menu Edit. Set the Offset of the inserted line to 0.25 and its Attributes to the same values as the other two lines.

STEP 3: Invoke the Place Multi-line command from the Linear Element tool box, and place Multi-line elements in the spaces on each side of the utility room door.

STEP 4: In the Multi-lines settings box, insert a fourth line, with an offset of 0.75 and the same attribute values as the other three lines.

STEP 5: Place Multi-line elements in the spaces cut into the top utility room wall.

Complete the Floor Plan

This procedure places the equipment in the utility room and the room names in each room, as shown in Figure P7–12.

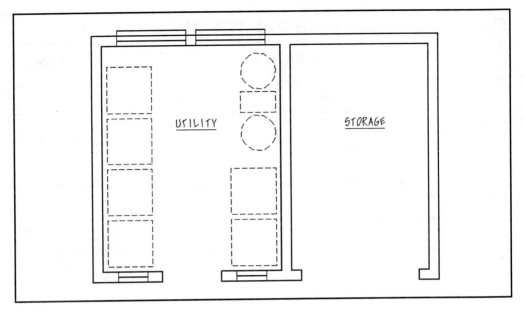

FIGURE P7–12 Completed floor plan.

STEP 1: Place the equipment symbols in the utility room with the following dimensions:

- 6 each, 2.25′ × 2.25′ blocks
- 1 each, 1.0′ × 1.75′ block
- 2 each, 0.875-radius circles

STEP 2: Place the room names with the same text font and size as the title block text.

STEP 3: Invoke the Fit View command to fit the view in the window view.

STEP 4: Compress the design and save the design settings.

DRAWING EXERCISES 7–1 THROUGH 7–5

Use the following table to set up the design files for Exercises 7–1 through 7–3.

SETTING	VALUE
Seed File	SEED2D.DGN
Working Units	MU = IN, SU = 10 TH, PU = 1000
Grid	Master = .1, Reference = 10

Exercise 7–1 Machine part.

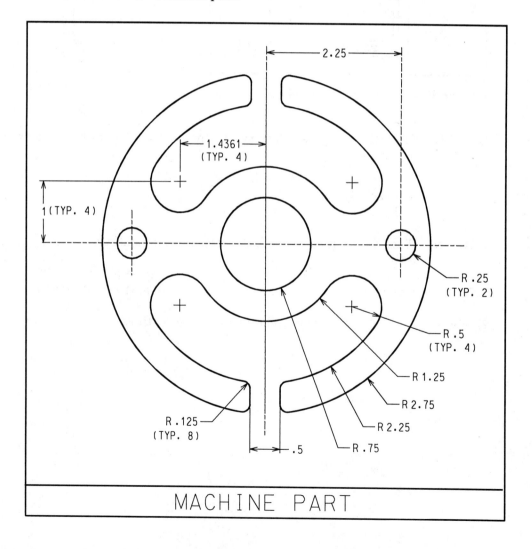

MACHINE PART

Exercise 7–2 Bracket set.

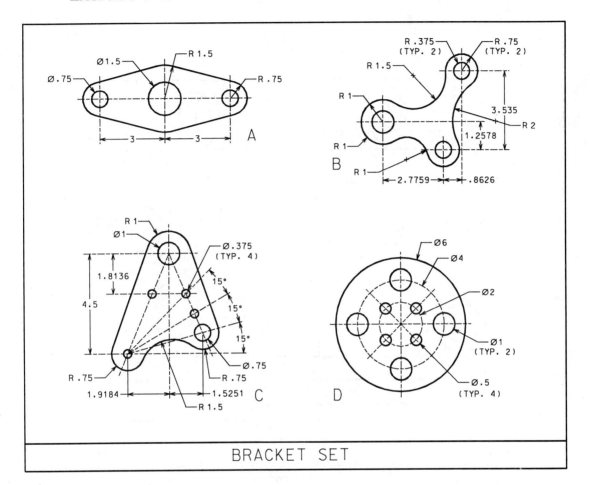

BRACKET SET

Exercise 7–3 Mounting bracket.

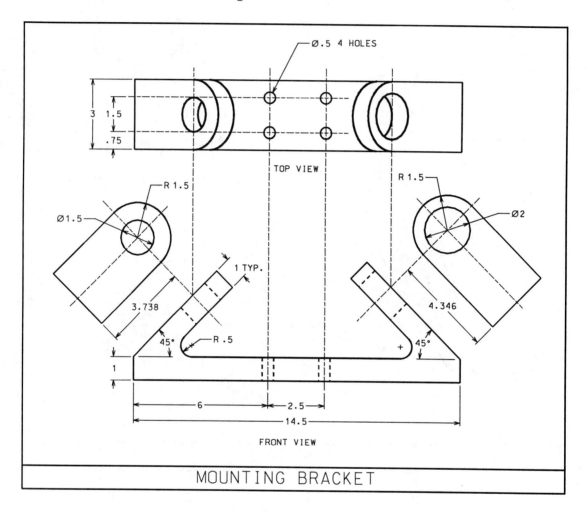

MOUNTING BRACKET

Use the following table to set up the design files for Exercises 7–4 and 7–5.

SETTING	VALUE
Seed File	SEED2D.DGN
Working Units	MU = ', SU = 12", PU = 12000
Grid	Master = :.5, Reference = 24

Exercise 7–4 Small business park plan.

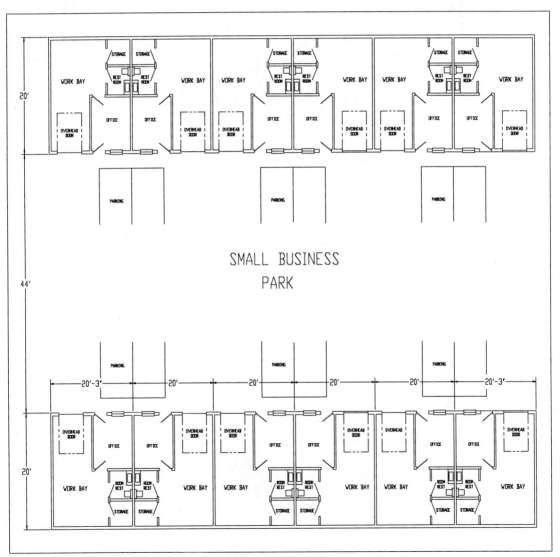

Exercise 7–5 Self-storage warehouse plan.

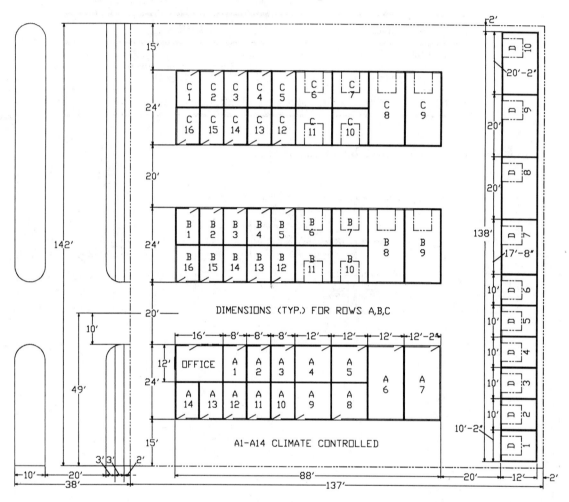

MEASUREMENT AND DIMENSIONING

· · · · · · · · · · · · · · ·

OBJECTIVES

After completing this chapter, you will be able to:

✓ Use the measurement commands, such as Measure Distance, Measure Radius, Measure Angle, Measure Length, and Measure Area.

✓ Use the dimensioning commands for linear, angular, and radial measurement.

✓ Adjust the dimension settings.

MEASUREMENT COMMANDS

"Is that line really 12 feet long?" "What's the radius of that circle?" "What is the surface area of that foundation?" MicroStation can answer these questions with the measurement commands.

The measurement commands do nothing to your design. They just display distances, areas, and angles in the Status bar.

All measurement commands are available from the Measure tool box, shown in Figure 8–1.

Measure Distance

MicroStation provides four distance measurement options. Distance options include measuring the distance between points you define, the distance along an element between points you define, the perpendicular distance from an element, and the minimum distance between two elements.

Measure Distance Between Points This command measures the cumulative straight-line distance from the first data point, through successive data points, to the last data point you define.

Invoke the Measure Distance Between Points command from:

Measure tool box	Select the Measure Distance tool and Between Points from the Distance option menu located in the Tool Settings window (see Figure 8–2).
Key-in window	**Measure Distance Points** (or **meas dis po**) ⏎

FIGURE 8–1 Measure tool box.

FIGURE 8–2 Invoking the Measure Distance Between Points command from the Measure tool box.

MicroStation prompts:

> Measure Distance Between Points > Enter start point *(Place a data point to start the measurement.)*
>
> Measure Distance Between Points > Define distance to measure *(Place a data point to define the distance to measure and continue placing data points to define additional measurement segments. Click the Reset button to terminate the command sequence.)*

As you place each data point, the cumulative linear distance between points is displayed in the Status bar.

Measure Distance Along Element This command measures the cumulative distance along an element, from the data point that selects it through successive data points on the element to the last data point you define.

Invoke the Measure Distance Along Element command from:

Measure tool box	Select the Measure Distance tool and Along Element from the Distance option menu located in the Tool Settings window (see Figure 8–3).
Key-in window	**Measure Distance Along** (or **meas dis a**) [ENTER]

MicroStation prompts:

> Measure Distance Along Element > Identify element first point *(Place a data point on the element to start the measurement.)*
>
> Measure Distance Along Element > Enter end point *(Place a data point on the element to end the measurement.)*
>
> Measure Distance Along Element > Measure more points/Reset to select *(Continue placing data points on the element to obtain the cumulative measurement from the first data point through the succeeding points, or click the Reset button to terminate the measurement.)*

As you place each data point after the first one, the cumulative distance along the element is displayed in the Status bar.

FIGURE 8–3 Invoking the Measure Distance Along Element command from the Measure tool box.

Measure Distance Perpendicular From Element This command measures the perpendicular distance from a point to an element.

Invoke the Measure Distance Perpendicular From Element command from:

Measure tool box	Select the Measure Distance tool and Perpendicular from the Distance option menu located in the Tool Settings window (see Figure 8–4).
Key-in window	**Measure Distance Perpendicular** (or **meas dis p**) ⏎

MicroStation prompts:

> Measure Distance Perpendicular From Element > Enter start point *(Identify the element from which to measure the perpendicular distance.)*
> Measure Distance Perpendicular From Element > Enter end point *(Place a data point to measure the perpendicular distance to the element.)*
> Measure Distance Perpendicular From Element > Measure more points/Reset to select *(Continue placing data points to obtain additional perpendicular measurements from the element, or click the Reset button to terminate the measurement.)*

As you place each data point after identifying the element, a dashed line indicating the perpendicular distance appears in the design, and the perpendicular distance is displayed in the Status bar. The dashed line is a temporary image that disappears when you update the view or select another command.

FIGURE 8–4 Invoking the Measure Distance Perpendicular From Element command from the Measure tool box.

> **NOTE:** If you place the measurement end point beyond the end of a linear element (such as a line or a box), the perpendicular is calculated from an imaginary extension of the measured element.

Measure Minimum Distance Between Elements This command measures the minimum distance between two elements.

Invoke the Measure Minimum Distance Between Elements command from:

Measure tool box	Select the Measure Distance tool and Minimum Between from the Distance option menu located in the Tool Settings window (see Figure 8–5).
Key-in window	**Measure Distance Minimum** (or **meas dis m**) ⏎

MicroStation prompts:

> Measure Minimum Distance Between Elements > Identify first element *(Identify the first element.)*
> Measure Minimum Distance Between Elements > Accept, Identify second element/Reject *(Identify the second element, or click the Reject button to start all over again.)*
> Measure Minimum Distance Between Elements > Accept, Initiate min dist calculation *(Click the Data button to initiate the minimum distance calculation.)*

After you place the third data point, a dashed line appears in the design to indicate where the minimum distance is, and the minimum distance is displayed in the Status bar. The dashed line is a temporary image that disappears when you update the view or select another command.

FIGURE 8–5 Invoking the Measure Minimum Distance Between Elements command from the Measure tool box.

FIGURE 8-6 Invoking the Measure Radius command from the Measure tool box.

Measure Radius

The Measure Radius command displays in the Status bar the radius of arcs, circles, partial ellipses, and ellipses.

Invoke the Measure Radius command from:

Measure tool box	Select the Measure Radius tool (see Figure 8–6).
Key-in window	**Measure Radius** (or **meas r**) [ENTER]

MicroStation prompts:

Measure Radius > Identify element *(Identify the element to measure the radius.)*
Measure Radius > Accept, Initiate Measurement *(Click the Data button to accept the element and initiate the measurement.)*

After the second data point is placed, the element's radius is displayed, in the current Working Units, in the Status bar. If the element you are measuring is an ellipse or a partial ellipse, the major axis and minor axis radii are displayed.

Measure Angle

The Measure Angle Between Lines command measures the minimum angle formed by two elements.

Invoke the Measure Angle Between Lines command from:

Measure tool box	Select the Measure Angle tool (see Figure 8–7).
Key-in window	**Measure Angle** (or **meas a**) [ENTER]

FIGURE 8–7   Invoking the Measure Angle command from the Measure tool box.

MicroStation prompts:

> Measure Angle Between Lines > Identify first element *(Identify the first element.)*
> Measure Angle Between Lines > Accept, Identify second element *(Identify the second element to measure the angle.)*
> Measure Angle Between Lines > Accept, Initiate Measurement *(Click the Data button to accept the element and initiate the measurement.)*

After you accept the elements, the angle between the two elements is displayed in the Status bar.

Measure Length

The Measure Length command measures the total length of an open element or the length of the perimeter of a closed shape.

When you invoke the Measure Length command, a Tolerance (%) field appears in the Tool Settings window. Tolerance sets the maximum allowable percentage of the distance between the true curve and the approximation for measurement purposes. A low value produces a very accurate measurement but may take a long time to calculate. The default value is sufficient in most cases.

Invoke the Measure Length command from:

Measure tool box	Select the Measure Length tool (see Figure 8–8).
Key-in window	**Measure Length** (or **meas l)** [ENTER]

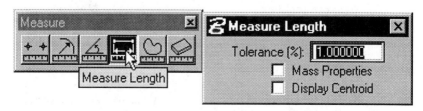

FIGURE 8–8   Invoking the Measure Length command from the Measure tool box.

MicroStation prompts:

> Measure Length > Identify element *(Identify the element to measure.)*
> Measure Length > Accept, Initiate Measurement *(Click the Data button to accept the element and initiate the measurement.)*

After the second data point is placed, the total length of the element, or element perimeter, is displayed in the Status bar.

You can use this command to measure the cumulative length of several elements by first employing the Element Selection command to select all the elements you want to include in the measurement. After selecting the elements, select Measure Length from the Measure tool box, and the cumulative length of all selected elements appears in the Status bar. In addition, you can turn the toggle switch to ON for Mass Properties in the Tool settings window, and MicroStation displays in a window the Mass Properties of the selected elements.

Measure Area

MicroStation provides seven different ways to measure areas, which can be selected from the Method option menu when you invoke the Area command from the Measure tool box. Area options include measuring the area of a closed element; a fence; the intersection, union, or difference of two overlapping closed elements; a group of intersecting elements; or a group of points.

When you select the Measure Area command, a Tolerance (%) field appears in the Tool Settings window. Tolerance sets the maximum allowable percentage of the distance between the true curve and the approximation for area calculation purposes. A low value produces a very accurate area but may take a long time to calculate. The default value is sufficient in most cases.

Measure Area   The Measure Area command measures the area of a closed element, such as a circle, ellipse, shape, or block.

Invoke the Measure Area command from:

Measure tool box	Select the Measure Area tool and Element from the Method option menu in the Tool Settings window (see Figure 8–9).
Key-in window	**Measure Area Element** (or **meas ar e**) ⏎

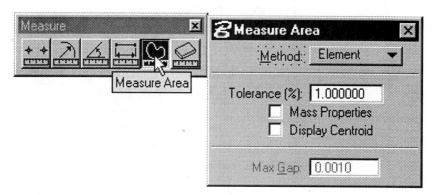

FIGURE 8–9   Invoking the Measure Area command from the Measure tool box.

MicroStation prompts:

> Measure Area > Identify element *(Identify the closed element to measure the area.)*
> Measure Area > Accept, Initiate Measurement *(Click the Data button to accept the element and initiate the measurement.)*

After the second data point is selected, the element's area and perimeter length are displayed in the Status bar.

You can use this command to measure the cumulative area of several closed elements by first employing the Element Selection command to select all the elements you want to include in the area measurement. After selecting the elements, select Measure Area from the Measure tool box, and the cumulative area of all selected elements then appears in the Status bar.

Measure Area Fence   This command measures the area enclosed by a fence block or fence shape.

Place a fence and then invoke the Measure Fence Area command from:

Measure tool box	Select the Measure Area tool and Fence from the Method option menu in the Tool Settings window (see Figure 8–10).
Key-in window	**Measure Area Fence (or meas ar f)** ⌨

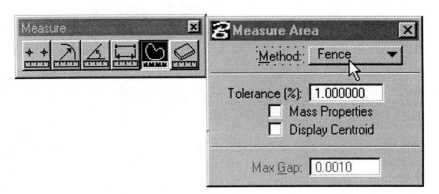

FIGURE 8-10 Invoking the Measure Fence Area command from the Measure tool box.

MicroStation prompts:

> Measure Fence Area > Accept/Reject Fence Contents *(Click the Data button to accept the fence contents to measure the area, or click the Reject button to disregard the measurement.)*

MicroStation displays the area of the fence in the Status bar.

Measure Area Intersection, Union, or Difference   These options measure areas formed by two intersecting closed elements. The intersection option allows you to determine the area that is common to two closed elements. The union option allows you to determine the area in such a way that there is no duplication between two closed elements. The difference option allows you to determine the area that is formed from a closed element after removing from it any area that it has in common with a second element.

Invoke the Measure Element Union (or Difference, or Intersection) Area commands from:

Measure tool box	Select the Measure Area tool and Union, Difference, or Intersection from the Method option menu in the Tool Settings window (see Figure 8–11).
Key-in window	**Measure Area Union | Difference | Intersection** (or **meas ar u | d | i**) ⏎

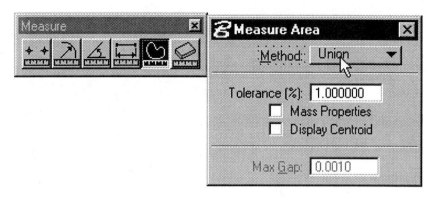

FIGURE 8-11   Invoking the Measure Element Union Area command from Measure tool box.

MicroStation prompts:

> Measure Element Union Area > Identify the element *(Identify the first element.)*
> Measure Element Union Area > Accept/Reject (Select next input) *(Identify the second element.)*
> Measure Element Union Area > Accept/Reject (Select next input) *(Click the Data button to accept the element, or identify another element.)*
> Measure Element Union Area > Identify Additional/Reset to terminate *(Identify additional elements, or click the Reset button to terminate and initiate the measurement.)*

After you select the second element, MicroStation displays an image of only the part of the two elements that is included in the type of area you select. After the third data point is placed, the elements reappear in their entirety, and MicroStation displays the area and perimeter length in the Status bar.

Measure Area Flood   This measures the area enclosed by a group of elements. The elements must either touch or overlap, and they must enclose the area to be measured completely.

Invoke the Measure Area Enclosing Point command from:

Measure tool box	Select the Measure Area tool and Flood from the Method option menu in the Tool Settings window (see Figure 8–12).
Key-in window	**Measure Area Flood** (or **meas ar f)** ⏎

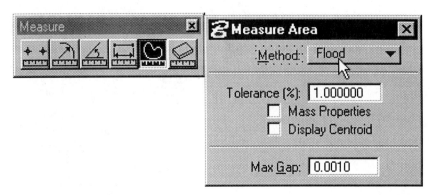

FIGURE 8–12 Invoking the Measure Area Enclosing Point command from the Measure tool box.

MicroStation prompts:

> Measure Area Enclosing Point > Enter data point inside area *(Click the Data button inside the area enclosed by the elements.)*
> Measure Area Enclosing Point > Accept, Initiate Measurement *(Click the Data button to accept and initiate measurement.)*

After you click the Data button, a small spinner will appear in the Status bar. The spinner spins to indicate that MicroStation is determining the area enclosed by the elements. As MicroStation traces the area, it highlights the elements. When the area has been determined, the spinner stops spinning and the area and perimeter length appear in the Status bar.

> **NOTE:** Make sure the area you click inside is completely enclosed by connected elements. If it is not, MicroStation may spend a very long time trying to find an enclosed area using adjacent elements before it gives up and displays an error message in the Status bar.

Measure Area Points This command measures the area formed by a set of data points you enter. It assumes the perimeter of the area is formed by straight lines between the data points. An image of the area is displayed as you enter the data points. The image is temporary and disappears when you update the screen or select another command.

Invoke the Measure Area Defined By Points command from:

FIGURE 8–13   Invoking the Measure Area Defined By Points command from the Measure tool box.

Measure tool box	Select the Measure Area tool and Points from the Method option menu in the Tool Settings window (see Figure 8–13).
Key-in window	**Measure Area Points** (or **meas ar p**) [ENTER]

MicroStation prompts:

> Measure Area Defined By Points > Enter shape vertex *(Place data points to define the vertices of the area to be measured. When the area is completely defined, click the Reset button to initiate area measurement.)*

As you are entering data points, a closed dynamic image of the area appears on the screen. When you press the Reset button, the area and the perimeter length appear in the Status bar.

DIMENSIONING

MicroStation's dimensioning features provide an excellent way to add dimensional information to your design, such as lengths, widths, angles, tolerances, and clearances.

Dimensioning of any drawing is generally one of the last steps in manual drawing; however, it does not need to be the last step in your MicroStation drawing. If you place the dimensions and find out later they must be changed because the size of the objects

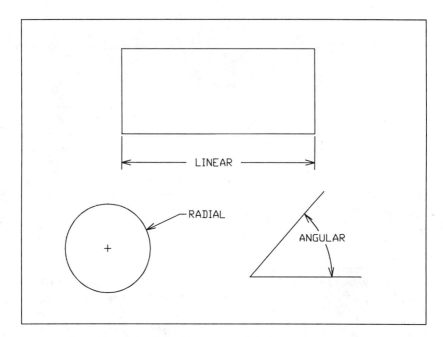

FIGURE 8–14 Examples of the three basic types of dimensions.

FIGURE 8–15 Dimension tool box.

they are related to have changed, MicroStation allows you to stretch or extend the objects and have the dimensions change automatically to the new size. MicroStation provides three basic types of dimensions: linear, angular, and radial dimensioning. Figure 8–14 shows examples of these three basic types of dimensions.

All the available dimensioning tools in MicroStation are found in the Dimension tool box, as shown in Figure 8–15.

Dimensioning Terminology

The following terms occur commonly in the MicroStation dimensioning procedures.

Dimension Line This is a line with markers at each end (arrows, dots, tick marks, etc.). The dimensioning text is located along this line; you may place it above the line or in a break in the dimension line. Usually, the dimension line is inside the measured area. If there is insufficient space, MicroStation places the dimensions and draws two short lines outside the measured area with arrows pointing inward.

Extension Lines The extension lines (also called *witness lines*) are the lines that extend from the object to the dimension line. Extension lines normally are drawn perpendicular to the dimension line. (Several options that are associated with this element will be reviewed later in this chapter.) Also, you can suppress one or both of the extension lines.

Arrows or Terminators The arrows are placed at one or both ends, depending on the type of dimension line placed. MicroStation allows you to place arrows, tick marks, or arbitrary symbols of your own choosing. You can also adjust the size of any of these three symbols.

Dimension Text This is a text string that usually indicates the actual measurement. You can accept the default measurement computed automatically by Micro-Station, or change it by supplying your own text.

Figure 8–16 shows the different components of a typical dimension.

Leader The leader line is a line from text to an object on the design, as shown in Figure 8–17. For some dimensioning, the text may not fit next to the object it describes; hence, it is customary to place the text nearby and draw a leader from it to the object.

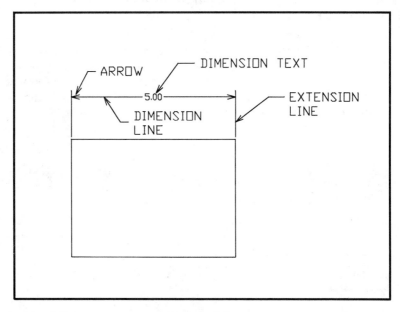

FIGURE 8–16 Different components of a typical dimension.

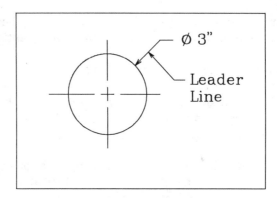

FIGURE 8-17 Example of placing a leader line.

Associative Dimensioning

Dimensions can be placed as either associative dimensions or normal (nonassociative) dimensions. Associative dimensioning links dimension elements to the objects dimensioned. An association point does not have its own coordinates, but is positioned by the coordinates of the point with which it is associated. When you invoke manipulation commands (such as Stretch) to modify an object, MicroStation modifies the dimension text automatically to reflect the change. It also draws the dimension entity at its new location, size, and rotation. If you want to edit individual components of a dimension, you can drop the dimension via the Drop dimension command to separate an associative dimension into its individual simpler objects.

To place associative dimensions, the Association Lock must be set to ON. This can be done from the Tool Settings window when you invoke one of the dimensioning tools, as shown in Figure 8-18. If you place a dimension when the Association Lock is OFF, then the dimension will not associate with the object dimensioned; and if the object is modified, the dimension is not changed.

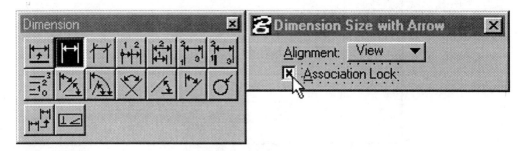

FIGURE 8-18 Displaying a toggle for the Association Lock in the Tool Settings window.

Placing associative dimensions can significantly reduce the size of a design file that has many dimensions, since a dimension element is usually smaller than its corresponding individual elements.

Alignment Controls

The alignment controls the orientation of linear dimensions. View, Drawing, True, and Arbitrary are the options available. The options are selected from the Alignment option menu in the Tool Settings window when you invoke one of the linear dimensioning tools.

- The View option aligns linear dimensions parallel to the view X or Y axis. This is useful when dimensioning 3D reference files with dimensions parallel to the viewing plane.
- The Drawing option aligns linear dimensions parallel to the design plane X or Y axis.
- The True option aligns linear dimensions parallel to the element being dimensioned. The extension lines are constrained to be at right angles to the dimension line.
- The Arbitrary (2D only) option places linear dimensions parallel to the element being dimensioned. The extension lines are not constrained to be at right angles to the dimension line. This is useful when dimensioning elements in 2D isometric drawings. The Iso Lock toggle button must be set to ON.

Figure 8–19 shows examples of placing linear dimensions with different alignment controls.

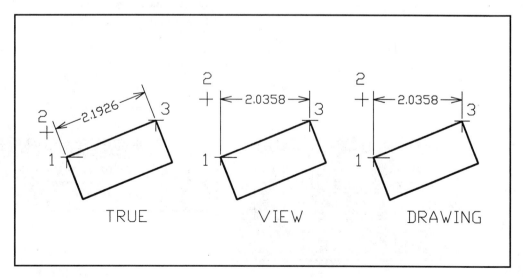

FIGURE 8-19   Examples of placing linear dimensions with different alignment controls.

Linear Dimensioning

Linear dimensioning tools allow you to dimension such linear elements as line and line string. Following are the tools available to dimension the linear elements.

- Dimension Size with Arrows: This tool allows you to dimension the linear distance between two points (length).
- Dimension Size with Stroke: This is similar to the Dimension Size with Arrow tool, except the terminators are set to strokes instead of arrows.
- Dimension Location: With this tool you can dimension linear distances from an origin (datum), with the dimensions placed in line (chained).
- Dimension Location (Stacked): This tool also allows you to dimension linear distances from an origin (datum), but with the dimensions stacked.
- Dimension Size Perpendicular to Points: With this tool you can dimension the linear distance between two points. The first two data points entered define the dimension's *Y* axis.
- Dimension Size Perpendicular to Line: This tool dimensions the linear distance perpendicular from an element to another element or point. The dimension's *Y* axis is defined by the element identified.

Dimension Size with Arrows   To place linear dimension with arrows, invoke the Dimension Size with Arrows command from:

Dimension tool box	Select the Dimension Size with Arrows tool. If necessary, turn ON the Toggle button for the Association Lock and select one of the available options for Alignment from the Tool Settings window (see Figure 8–20).
Key-in window	**Dimension Size Arrow** (or **dim si a**) ⏎

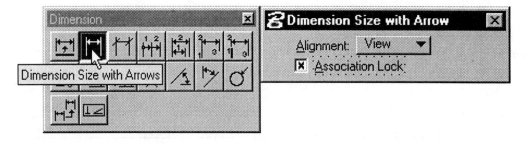

FIGURE 8–20   Invoking the Dimension Size with Arrow command from the Dimension tool box.

MicroStation prompts:

> Dimension Size with Arrow > Select start of dimension *(Place a data point as shown in Figure 8–21 (point 1) to define the starting point of the dimension.)*
> Dimension Size with Arrow > Define length of extension line *(Place a data point as shown in Figure 8–21 (point 2) to define the length of the extension line.)*
> Dimension Size with Arrow > Select dimension endpoint *(Place a data point as shown in Figure 8–21 (point 3) to define the end point of the dimension.)*
> Dimension Size with Arrow > Select dimension endpoint *(Continue placing data points as shown in Figure 8–21 (points 4 and 5) to continue linear dimensioning in the same direction, or click the Reset button to change the direction, or click the Reset button twice to start all over again.)*

> **NOTE:** Make sure to use the appropriate Snap Lock when placing the data points for the starting point and end point of the dimension line.

After placing the first end point of the linear dimension, MicroStation displays in the Status bar the message *Press Return to edit dimension text.* To edit the dimension text, press ENTER. MicroStation will then display the Dimension Text dialog box similar to the one shown in Figure 8–22. The asterisk (*) in the Primary Text edit field indicates the current default dimension text string. If you need to change the default dimension string, delete the the asterisk (*) and key-in the new dimension text string. If you need to add any prefix and/or suffix text string to the default dimension text string, keep the asterisk (*) and type in the appropriate text string in the Text edit field. Click the OK button to keep the changes, or click the Cancel button to disregard the changes, and MicroStation closes the Dimension Text dialog box.

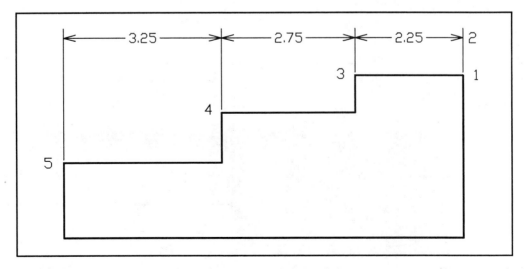

FIGURE 8–21   Example of placing linear dimensioning with the Dimension Size with Arrows tool.

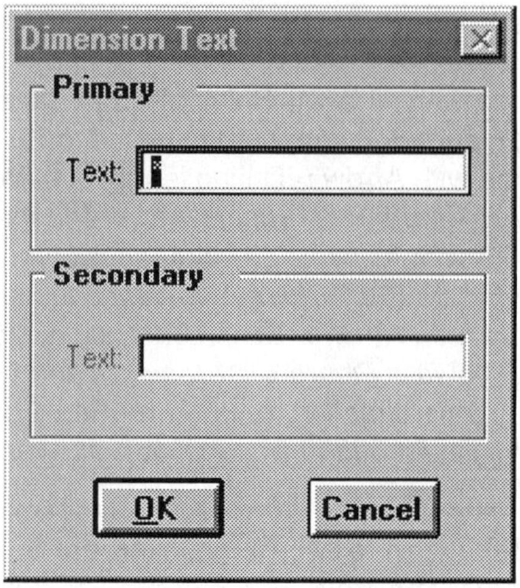

FIGURE 8–22 Dimension Text dialog box.

NOTE: Before you press ⏎ to edit the dimension text, make sure your focus (blinking cursor) is in the Key-in window.

Dimension Size with Stroke To place linear dimensions with strokes, invoke the Dimension Size Stroke command from:

Dimension tool box	Select the Dimension Size Stroke tool. If necessary, turn ON the Toggle button for the Association Lock and select one of the available options for Alignment from the Tool Settings window (see Figure 8–23).
Key-in window	**Dimension Size Stroke** (or **dim si s**) ⏎

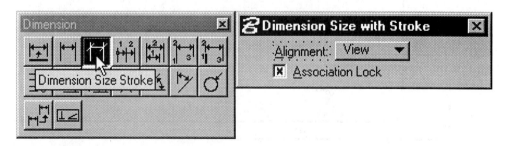

FIGURE 8–23 Invoking the Dimension Size Stroke command from the Dimension tool box.

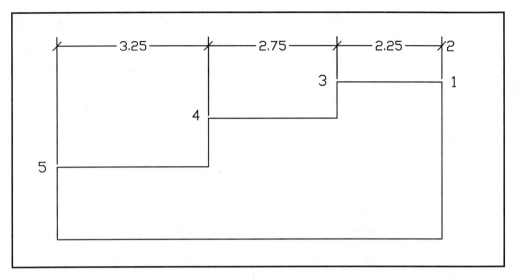

FIGURE 8–24   Example of placing linear dimensioning with the Dimension Size Stroke tool.

MicroStation prompts are similar to those for the Dimension Size with Arrows command, except instead of placing arrows at the end of the dimension line, Micro-Station places strokes, as shown in Figure 8–24.

Dimension Location   The Dimension Location command enables you to dimension linear distances from an origin (datum), as shown in Figure 8–25. The dimensions are placed in line (chain). All dimensions are measured on an element originating

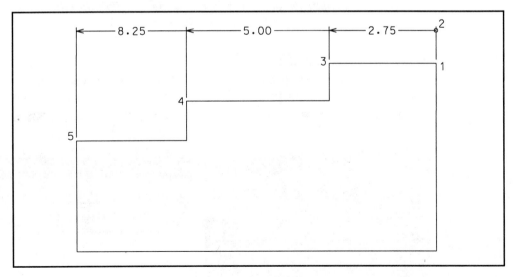

FIGURE 8–25   Example of placing linear dimensioning from an origin (datum) with the Dimension Location command.

from a common surface, centerline, or center plane. The Dimension Location command is commonly used in mechanical drafting.

To place linear dimensions in a chain, invoke the Dimension Location command from:

Dimension tool box	Select the Dimension Location tool. If necessary, turn ON the Toggle button for the Association Lock and select one of the available options for Alignment from the Tool Settings window (see Figure 8–26).
Key-in window	**Dimension Location Single** (or **dim lo si**) ⏎

MicroStation prompts:

Dimension Location > Select start of dimension *(Place a data point to define the origin.)*

Dimension Location > Define length of extension line *(Place a data point to define the length of the extension line.)*

Dimension Location > Select dimension endpoint *(Place a data point to define the end point of the dimension. If necessary, press ⏎ to edit the dimension text.)*

Dimension Location > Select dimension endpoint *(Continue placing data points to continue linear dimensioning in the same direction, or click the Reset button to change the direction, or click the Reset button twice to start all over again.)*

NOTE: Make sure to use the appropriate Snap Lock when placing the data points for the starting point and end point of the dimension line.

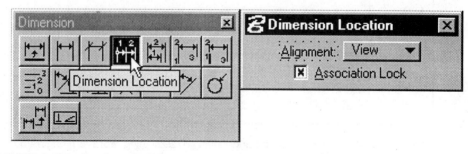

FIGURE 8–26 Invoking the Dimension Location command from the Dimension tool box.

Dimension Location (Stacked) With the Dimension Location (Stacked) command you can dimension linear distances from an origin (datum), as shown in Figure 8–27. The dimensions are stacked. All dimensions are measured on an element originating from a common surface, centerline, or center plane. The Dimension Location (Stacked) command is commonly used in mechanical drafting because all dimensions are independent, even though they are taken from a common datum. If necessary, you can change the stack offset distance; see the later section on Dimension Settings.

To place linear dimensions in a stack, invoke the Dimension Location (Stacked) command from:

Dimension tool box	Select the Dimension Location (Stacked) tool. If necessary, turn ON the Toggle button for the Association Lock and select one of the available options for Alignment from the Tool Settings window (see Figure 8–28).
Key-in window	**Dimension Location Stacked (or dim lo st)**

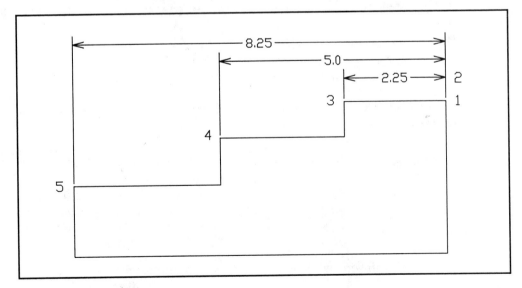

FIGURE 8–27 Example of placing linear dimensioning (stacked) from an origin (datum) via the Dimension Location (Stacked) command.

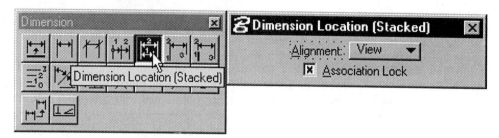

FIGURE 8–28 Invoking the Dimension Location (Stacked) command from the Dimension tool box.

MicroStation prompts:

> Dimension Location (Stacked) > Select start of dimension *(Place a data point to define the origin.)*
>
> Dimension Location (Stacked) > Define length of extension line *(Place a data point to define the length of the extension line.)*
>
> Dimension Location (Stacked) > Select dimension endpoint *(Place a data point to define the end point of the dimension line. If necessary, press [ENTER] to edit the dimension text.)*
>
> Dimension Location (Stacked) > Select dimension endpoint *(Continue placing data points to continue linear dimensioning in the same direction, or click the Reset button to change the direction, or click the Reset button twice to start all over again.)*

> **NOTE:** Make sure to use the appropriate Snap Lock when placing the data points for the starting point and end point of the dimension line.

Dimension Size Perpendicular to Points The Dimension Size Perpendicular to Points command can dimension the linear distance between two points. The first two data points entered define the dimension's Y axis, as shown in Figure 8–29.

To place linear dimensions between two points, invoke the Dimension Size Perpendicular to Points command from:

Dimension tool box	Select the Dimension Size Perpendicular to Points tool. If necessary, turn ON the Toggle button for the Association Lock from the Tool Settings window (see Figure 8–30).
Key-in window	**Dimension Size Perpendicular to Points** (or **dim si p p**) [ENTER]

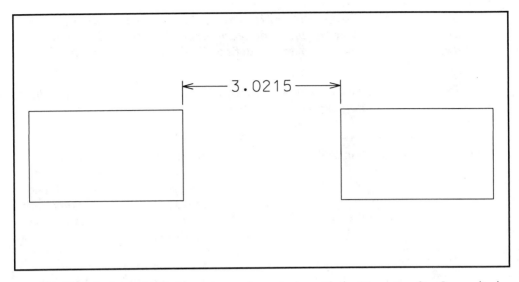

FIGURE 8–29 Example of placing linear dimensioning with the Dimension Size Perpendicular to Points command.

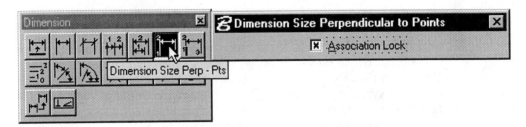

FIGURE 8–30 Invoking the Dimension Size Perpendicular to Points command from the Dimension tool box.

MicroStation prompts:

> Dimension Size Perpendicular to Points > Select base of first dimension line *(Place a data point to define the base point of the first dimension line.)*
> Dimension Size Perpendicular to Points > Select end of extension line *(Place a data point to define the length of the extension line.)*
> Dimension Size Perpendicular to Points > Select dimension endpoint *(Place a data point to define the end point of the dimension line.)*

> **NOTE:** Make sure to use the appropriate Snap Lock when placing the data points for the starting point and end point of the dimension line.

Dimension Size Perpendicular to Line   The Dimension Size Perpendicular to Line command dimensions the linear distance perpendicular from an element to another element. The dimension's Y axis is defined by the element identified.

To place a linear dimension perpendicular from one element to another, invoke the Dimension Size Perpendicular to Line command from:

Dimension tool box	Select the Dimension Size Perpendicular to Line tool. If necessary, turn ON the Toggle button for the Association Lock from the Tool Settings window (see Figure 8–31).
Key-in window	**Dimension Size Perpendicular to Line (or dim si p l)** ENTER

MicroStation prompts:

> Dimension Size Perpendicular to Line > Select base of first dimension line *(Place a data point to define the base point of the first dimension line.)*
> Dimension Size Perpendicular to Line > Select end of extension line *(Place a data point to define the length of the extension line.)*
> Dimension Size Perpendicular to Line > Select dimension endpoint *(Place a data point to define the end point of the dimension line.)*

> **NOTE:** Make sure to use the appropriate Snap Lock when placing the data points for the starting point and end point of the dimension line.

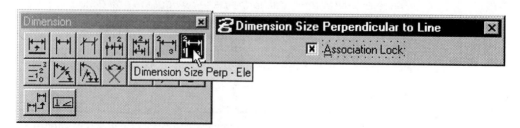

FIGURE 8–31   Invoking the Dimension Size Perpendicular to Line command from the Dimension tool box.

Dimension Ordinates

Ordinate dimensioning is common in mechanical designs. It labels distances along an axis from a point of origin on the axis along which the distances are measured. See Figure 8–32 for an example of ordinate dimensioning.

To place ordinate dimensions, invoke the Dimension Ordinates command from:

Dimension tool box	Select the Dimension Ordinates tool. If necessary, turn ON the Toggle button for the Association Lock and select one of the available options in the Alignment option menu from the Tool Settings window (see Figure 8–33).
Key-in window	**Dimension Ordinate (or dim o)** ⏎

MicroStation prompts:

Dimension Ordinates > Select ordinate origin *(Place a data point from which all ordinate labels are to be measured.)*

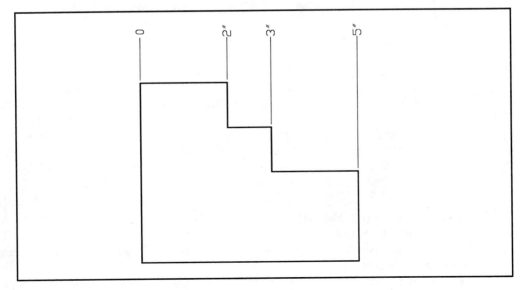

FIGURE 8–32   *Example of ordinate dimensioning.*

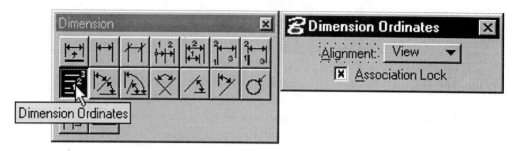

FIGURE 8–33   Invoking the Dimension Ordinates command from the Dimension tool box.

Dimension Ordinates > Select ordinate direction *(Place a data point to indicate the rotation of the ordinate axis.)*

Dimension Ordinates > Select dimension endpoint *(Place a data point to define the end point of the dimension line. If necessary, press* **ENTER** *to edit the dimension text.)*

Dimension Ordinates > Select start of dimension *(Place data points at each place where you want an ordinate dimension placed. These points define the base of the extension line. After placing all the points, click the Reset button to terminate the command sequence.)*

> **NOTE:** To prevent the text for a higher ordinate from overlapping the text for a lower ordinate, turn ON the toggle button for Stack Dimensions (from the Dimension Settings box—Tool Settings category).

Angular Dimensioning

The angular dimensioning tools create dimensions for the angle between two non-parallel lines, using the conventions that conform to the current dimension variable settings. "Angle" is defined by *Webster's Ninth New Collegiate Dictionary* as "a measure of an angle or of the amount of turning necessary to bring one line or plane into coincidence with or parallel to another." Following are the five different tools available to create angular dimensions.

- Dimension Angle Size: To dimension angles. Each dimension (except the first) is computed from the end point of the previous dimension.
- Dimension Angle Location: To dimension angles. Each dimension is computed from the dimension origin (datum).
- Dimension Angle Between Lines: To dimension the angle between two lines, two segments of a line string, or two sides of a shape.

- Dimension Angle from X axis: To dimension the angle between a line, a side of a shape, or a segment of a line string and the view X axis.
- Dimension Angle from Y axis: To dimension the angle between a line, a side of a shape, or a segment of a line string and the view Y axis.

Dimension Angle Size To place angular dimensioning with the Dimension Angle Size command, invoke the tool from:

Dimension tool box	Select the Dimension Angle Size tool. If necessary, turn ON the Toggle button for Association Lock from the Tool Settings window (see Figure 8–34).
Key-in window	**Dimension Angle Size (or dim a s)** ⏎

MicroStation prompts:

> Dimension Angle Size > Select start of dimension *(Place a data point as shown in Figure 8–35 (point P1) to define the start of the dimension, which is measured counterclockwise from this point.)*
> Dimension Angle Size > Define length of extension line *(Place a data point as shown in Figure 8–35 (point P2) to define the length of the extension line.)*
> Dimension Angle Size > Enter point on axis *(Place a data point as shown in Figure 8–35 (point P3) to define the vertex of the angle.)*
> Dimension Angle Size > Select dimension endpoint *(Place a data point as shown in Figure 8–35 (point P4) to define the end point of the dimension line. If necessary, press ⏎ to edit the dimension text.)*
> Dimension Angle Size > Select dimension endpoint *(Continue placing data points for angular dimensioning, and click the Reset button to complete the command sequence.)*

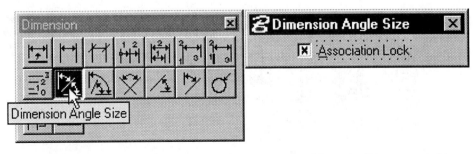

FIGURE 8–34 Invoking the Dimension Angle Size command from the Dimension tool box.

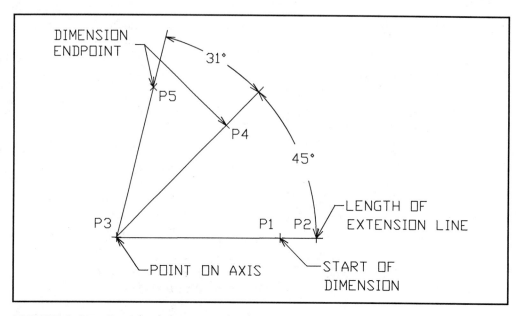

FIGURE 8–35 Example of placing angular dimensioning via the Dimension Angle Size command.

Dimension Angle Location To place angular dimensioning with the Dimension Angle Location command, invoke the tool from:

Dimension tool box	Select the Dimension Angle Location tool. If necessary, turn ON the Toggle button for Association Lock from the Tool Settings window (see Figure 8–36).
Key-in window	**Dimension Angle Location** (or **dim a lo**) [ENTER]

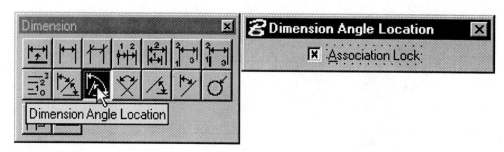

FIGURE 8–36 Invoking the Dimension Angle Location command from the Dimension tool box.

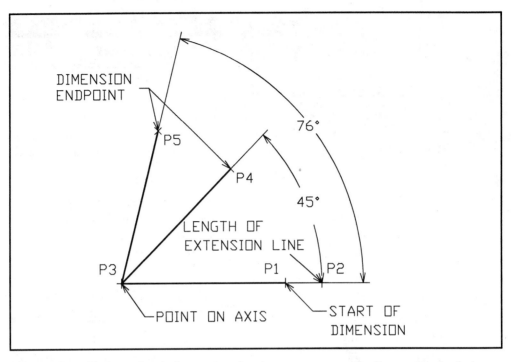

FIGURE 8–37 Example of placing angular dimensioning via the Dimension Angle Location command.

MicroStation prompts:

> Dimension Angle Location > Select start of dimension *(Place a data point as shown in Figure 8–37 (point P1) to define the start of the dimension, which is measured counterclockwise from this point.)*
>
> Dimension Angle Location > Define length of extension line *(Place a data point as shown in Figure 8–37 (point P2) to define the length of the extension line.)*
>
> Dimension Angle Location > Enter point on axis *(Place a data point as shown in Figure 8–37 (point P3) to define the vertex of the angle.)*
>
> Dimension Angle Location > Select dimension endpoint *(Place a data point as shown in Figure 8–37 (point P4) to define the end point of the dimension. Press ⏎ to edit the dimension text.)*
>
> Dimension Angle Location > Select dimension endpoint *(Continue placing data points for angular dimensioning, and click the Reset button to complete the command sequence.)*

Dimension Angle Between Lines To place angular dimensioning with the Dimension Angle Between Lines command, invoke the tool from:

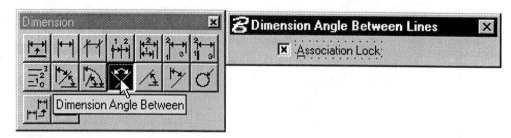

FIGURE 8–38 Invoking the Dimension Angle Between Lines command from the Dimension tool box.

Dimension tool box	Select the Dimension Angle Between Lines tool. If necessary, turn ON the Toggle button for Association Lock from the Tool Settings window (see Figure 8–38).
Key-in window	**Dimension Angle Lines** (or **dim a l**) [ENTER]

MicroStation prompts:

Dimension Angle Between Lines > Select first line *(Identify the first line or segment, as shown in Figure 8–39 (point P1).)*

Dimension Angle Between Lines > Select second line *(Identify the second line or segment, as shown in Figure 8–39 (point P2).)*

Dimension Angle Between Lines *(Place a data point to define the location of the dimension line, as shown in Figure 8–39 (point P3).)*

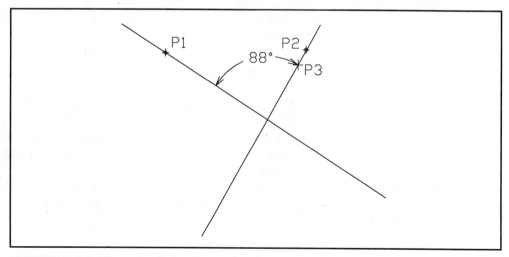

FIGURE 8–39 Example of placing angular dimensioning with the Dimension Angle Between Lines command.

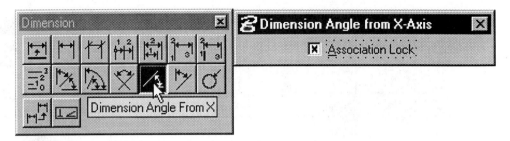

FIGURE 8–40   Invoking the Dimension Angle from X-Axis command from the Dimension tool box.

Dimension Angle from X-Axis   To place angular dimensioning with the Dimension Angle from X-axis command, invoke the tool from:

Dimension tool box	Select the Dimension Angle from X-axis tool. If necessary, turn ON the Toggle button for Association Lock from the Tool Settings window (see Figure 8–40).
Key-in window	**Dimension Angle X** (or **dim a x**) [ENTER]

MicroStation prompts:

> Dimension Angle from X-Axis > Identify element *(Identify the element, as shown in Figure 8–41 (point P1).)*
> Dimension Angle from X-Axis > Accept, define dimension axis *(Place a data point, as shown in Figure 8–41 (point P2), to specify the location and direction of the dimension.)*

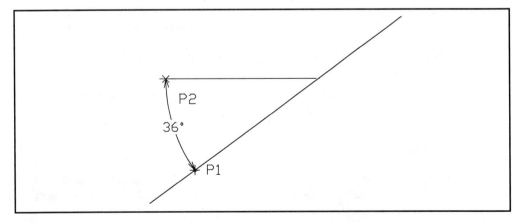

FIGURE 8–41   Example of placing angular dimensioning with the Dimension Angle from X-Axis command.

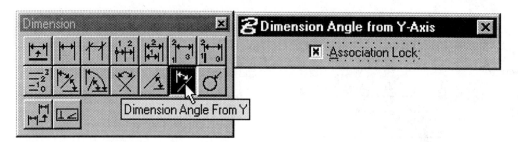

FIGURE 8-42   Invoking the Dimension Angle from Y-Axis command from the Dimension tool box.

Dimension Angle from Y-Axis   To place angular dimensioning with the Dimension Angle from Y-axis command, invoke the tool from:

Dimension tool box	Select the Dimension Angle from Y-axis tool. If necessary, turn ON the Toggle button for Association Lock from the Tool Settings window (see Figure 8–42).
Key-in window	**Dimension Angle Y** (or **dim a y**) ⏎

MicroStation prompts:

> Dimension Angle from Y-Axis > Identify element *(Identify the element.)*
> Dimension Angle from Y-Axis > Accept, define dimension axis *(Place a data point to specify the location and direction of the dimension.)*

Dimension Arc Size   The Dimension Arc Size command lets you dimension a circle or circular arc. Each dimension is computed from the end point of the previous dimension, except the first one, similar to the Dimension Angle Size command.

To dimension arcs with the Dimension Arc Size command, invoke the tool from:

Key-in window	**Dimension Arc Size** (or **dim ar s**) ⏎

MicroStation prompts:

> Dimension Arc Size > Select start of dimension *(Place a data point, as shown in Figure 8–43 (point P1), to define the origin point. The dimension is measured counterclockwise from this point.)*
> Dimension Arc Size > Define length of extension line *(Place a data point, as shown in Figure 8–43 (point P2), to define the length of the extension line.)*

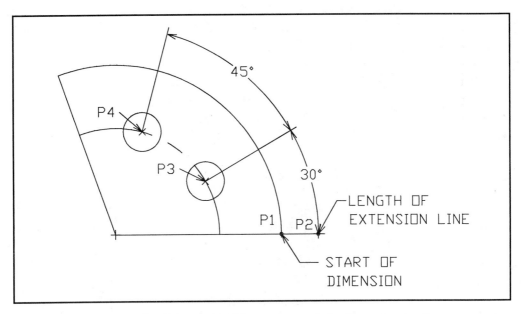

FIGURE 8-43   Example of placing arc dimensioning with the Dimension Arc Size command.

Dimension Arc Size > Select dimension endpoint *(Place a data point, as shown in Figure 8–43 (point P3), to define the dimension end point. If necessary, press* ⟦ENTER⟧ *to edit the dimension text.)*

Dimension Arc Size > Select dimension endpoint *(Continue placing data points to continue angular dimensioning, and click the Reset button to terminate the command sequence.)*

Dimension Arc Location   The Dimension Arc Location command enables you to dimension a circle or circular arc. Each dimension is computed from the dimension origin (datum), as shown in Figure 8–44.

To dimension arcs with the Dimension Arc Location command, invoke the tool from:

Key-in window	**Dimension Arc Location** (or **dim ar l**) ⟦ENTER⟧

MicroStation prompts:

Dimension Arc Location > Select start of dimension *(Place a data point to define the origin point. The dimension is measured counterclockwise from this point.)*

Dimension Arc Location > Define length of extension line *(Place a data point to define the length of the extension line.)*

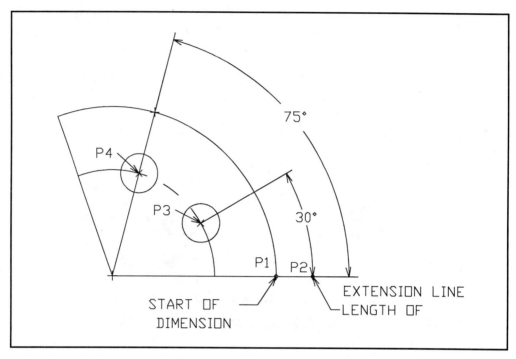

FIGURE 8–44 Example of placing arc dimensioning via the Dimension Arc Location command.

Dimension Arc Size > Select dimension endpoint *(Place a data point to define the dimension end point. If necessary, press* ENTER *to edit the dimension text.)*
Dimension Arc Size > Select dimension endpoint *(Continue placing data points to continue angular dimensioning, and click the Reset button to terminate the command sequence.)*

Dimension Radial

The Dimension Radial feature provides tools to create dimensions for the radius or diameter of a circle or arc and to place a center mark. Following are the tools available for radial dimensioning:

- Radius: To dimension the radius of a circle or a circular arc.
- Radius Extended: Identical to the Radius tool, except the leader line continues across the center of the circle, with terminators that point outward.
- Diameter: To dimension the diameter of a circle or a circular arc.
- Diameter Extended: Identical to the Diameter tool, except the leader line continues across the center of the circle, with terminators that point outward.
- Center Mark: To place a center mark at the center of a circle or circular arc.

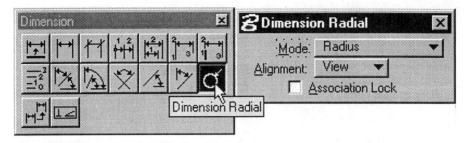

FIGURE 8–45 Invoking the Dimension Radius command from the Dimension tool box.

Dimension Radius To place a radial dimension with the Dimension Radius command, invoke the tool from:

Dimension tool box	Select the Dimension Radial tool and select Radius from the Mode option menu. If necessary, turn ON the Toggle button for Association Lock and select one of the available options for Alignment from the Tool Settings window (see Figure 8–45).
Key-in window	**Dimension Radius** (or **dim radiu**) [ENTER]

MicroStation prompts:

> Dimension Radius > Identify element *(Identify a circle or arc, as shown in Figure 8–46.)*
> Dimension Radius > Select dimension endpoint *(Place a data point inside or outside the circle or arc to place the dimension line, as shown in Figure 8–46.)*

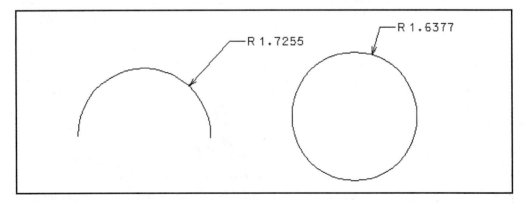

FIGURE 8–46 Examples of placing radial dimensions with the Dimension Radius tool.

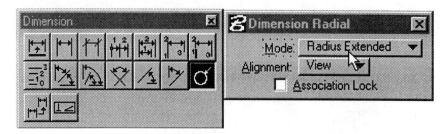

FIGURE 8–47 Invoking the Dimension Radius (Extended Leader) command from the Dimension tool box.

Dimension Radius (Extended Leader) To place radial dimensioning with the Dimension Radius (Extended Leader) command, invoke the tool from:

Dimension tool box	Select the Dimension Radial tool and select Radius Extended from the Mode option menu. If necessary, turn ON the Toggle button for Association Lock and select one of the available options for Alignment from the Tool Settings window (see Figure 8–47).
Key-in window	**Dimension Radius Extended** (or **dim radiu e**) (ENTER)

MicroStation prompts:

Dimension Radius (Extended Leader) > Identify element *(Identify a circle or arc, as shown in Figure 8–48.)*

Dimension Radius (Extended Leader) > Select dimension endpoint *(Place a data point inside or outside the circle or arc to place the dimension line as shown in Figure 8–48.)*

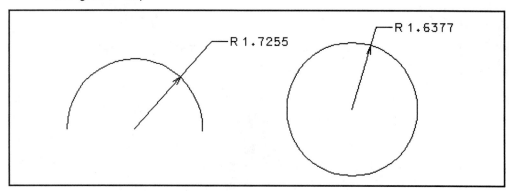

FIGURE 8–48 Examples of placing radial dimensions with the Dimension Radius (Extended Leader) tool.

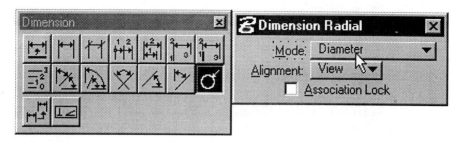

FIGURE 8–49   Invoking the Dimension Diameter command from the Dimension tool box.

Dimension Diameter   To place diameter dimensioning with the Dimension Diameter command, invoke the tool from:

Dimension tool box	Select the Dimension Radial tool and select Diameter from the Mode option menu. If necessary, turn ON the Toggle button for Association Lock and select one of the available options for Alignment from the Tool Settings window (see Figure 8–49).
Key-in window	**Dimension Diameter (or dim d)** ⏎

MicroStation prompts:

Dimension Diameter > Identify element *(Identify a circle or arc, as shown in Figure 8–50.)*
Dimension Diameter > Select dimension endpoint *(Place a data point inside or outside the circle or arc to place the dimension line, as shown in Figure 8–50.)*

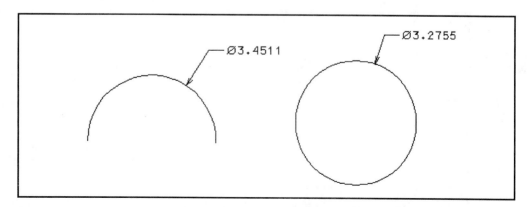

FIGURE 8–50   Examples of placing diameter dimensions with the Dimension Diameter tool.

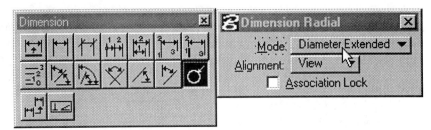

FIGURE 8–51 Invoking the Dimension Diameter Extended command from the Dimension tool box.

Dimension Diameter (Extended Leader) To place diameter dimensioning with the Dimension Diameter (Extended Leader) command, invoke the tool from:

Dimension tool box	Select the Dimension Radial tool and select Diameter Extended from the Mode option menu. If necessary, turn ON the Toggle button for Association Lock and select one of the available options for Alignment from the Tool Settings window (see Figure 8–51).
Key-in window	**Dimension Diameter Extended** (or **dim d e**) [ENTER]

MicroStation prompts:

Dimension Diameter (Extended Leader) > Identify element *(Identify a circle or arc, as shown in Figure 8–52.)*
Dimension Diameter (Extended Leader) > Select dimension endpoint *(Place a data point inside or outside the circle or arc to place the dimension line, as shown in Figure 8–52.)*

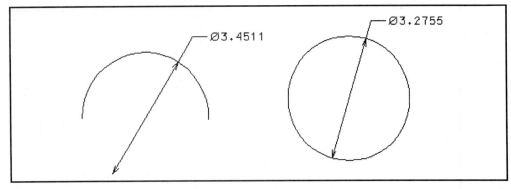

FIGURE 8–52 Examples of placing diameter dimensions via the Dimension Diameter Extended tool.

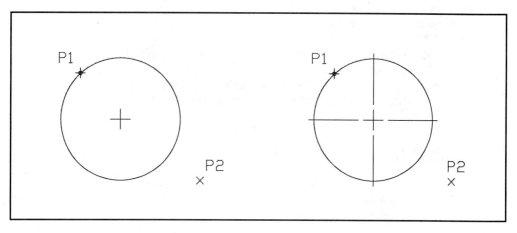

FIGURE 8–53   Examples of placing center marks by the Place Center Mark tool with different line types.

Place Center Mark   The Place Center Mark command can place a center mark at the center of a circle or circular arc, as shown in Figure 8–53.

To place a center mark with the Place Center Mark command, invoke the tool from:

Dimension tool box	Select the Dimension Radial tool and select Center Mark from the Mode option menu. If necessary, turn ON the Toggle button for Association Lock, select one of the available options for Alignment, and key-in the appropriate size of the center mark in the Center Size edit field in the Tool Settings window (see Figure 8–54).
Key-in window	**Dimension Center Mark** (or **dim c m)** ENTER

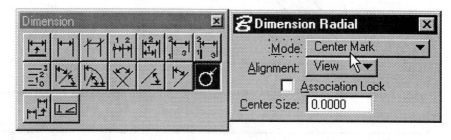

FIGURE 8–54   Invoking the Dimension Center Mark command from the Dimension tool box.

MicroStation prompts:

> Place Center Mark > Identify element *(Identify a circle or arc to place a center mark on.)*
> Place Center Mark > Accept (next input) *(Click the Accept button, or identify another circle or arc to place the center mark.)*

Label Line

The Label Line command places the line length above the line you select and the line rotation angle below the line. You can place a label on a line, line string, block, closed shape, or multi-line.

MicroStation determines which side of the element is the top; what the angle of rotation is depends on how you drew it. The angle of the line or line segment, for example, is measured as a counterclockwise rotation from the first data point to the second. Exercise care in deciding how to draw elements you plan to label with the Label Line command, or you may not get the angle of rotation you expected. See Figure 8–55 for examples of line labels.

Invoke the Label Line command from:

Key-in window	**Label Line (or l l)** 

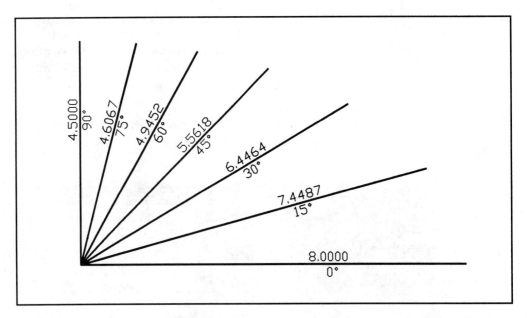

FIGURE 8-55   Examples of line labels.

MicroStation prompts:

Label Line > Identify element *(Identify the element on which you want to place the label.)*

Label Line > Accept/Reject (Select next input) *(Click the Data button to accept, or click Reset to disregard the dimensioning.)*

Dimension Element

The Dimension Element provides a fast way to dimension an element. Simply identify the element and MicroStation selects the type of dimensioning command it thinks is best. For linear elements it selects one of the linear dimensioning commands; for circles, arcs, and ellipses it selects one of the radial dimensioning commands.

When you invoke the Dimension Element command, the command name Dimension Element appears in the Status bar. As soon as you select an element, the name of the dimensioning command MicroStation intends to use appears in the Status bar. If you don't want that selected dimension command, press ENTER and MicroStation switches to another dimensioning command. Keep pressing ENTER until you find the command you want to use.

Invoke the Dimension Element command from:

Dimension tool box	Select the Dimension Element tool. If necessary, turn ON the Toggle button for Association Lock and select one of the available options for Alignment in the Tool Settings window (see Figure 8–56).
Key-in window	**Dimension Element** (or **dim e)** ENTER

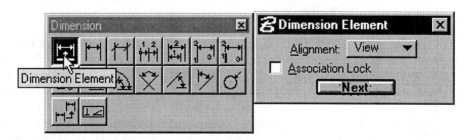

FIGURE 8–56 Invoking the Dimension Element command from the Dimension tool box.

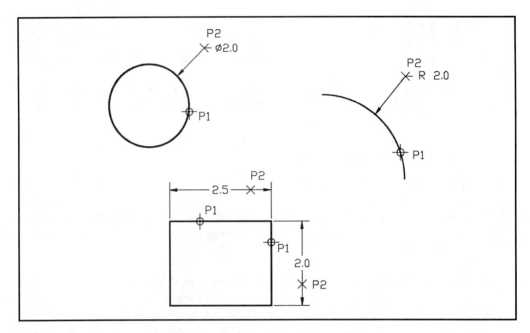

FIGURE 8–57 Examples of placing dimensioning with the Dimension Element command.

MicroStation prompts:

> Dimension Element > Select element to dimension *(Identify the element or segment of the block or line string element.)*
> Dimension Element > Accept (Press Return to switch command) *(Place a data point to indicate where you want the dimension placed, or press* ENTER *as many times as necessary to find the dimensioning command you want to use and place a data point for the location of the dimension element.)*

For most dimension commands, the second data point indicates the length and direction of the extension line. See Figure 8–57 for examples of placing dimensions with the Dimension Element command.

Geometric Tolerance

The Geometric Tolerance settings box (see Figure 8–58) helps you to build feature control frames with geometric tolerance symbols. The feature control frames are used with the Place Note command and Place Text command. The pull-down menu Fonts available in the settings box allows you to select one of the two fonts, 100—Ansi symbols and 101—Feature Control Symbols. When a specific font is chosen, the buttons in the settings box reflect the availability of the symbols in the selected font. Whenever you want to add the symbols, click on the buttons as part of placing the text to the Place Note command and Place Text command.

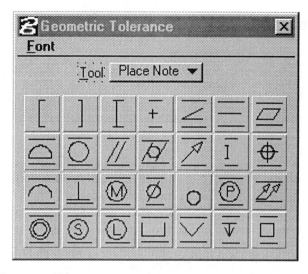

FIGURE 8–58   *Geometric Tolerance settings box.*

The left bracket ([) and right bracket (]) form the ends of compartments; the vertical line (|) separates compartments.

Invoke the Geometric Tolerance settings box from:

Dimension tool box	Select the Geometric Tolerance tool (see Figure 8–59).
Key-in window	**MDL LOAD GEOMTOL** ⏎

Select one of the two tools from the Geometric Tolerance settings box, Place Note or Place Text. MicroStation sets up the appropriate tool settings in the Tool Settings window. Follow the prompts to place text.

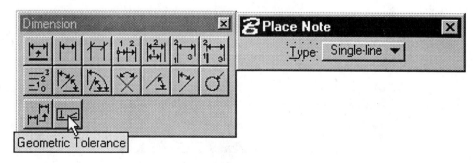

FIGURE 8–59   *Invoking the Geometric Tolerance command from the Dimension tool box.*

Dimension Settings

Each time a dimension is drawn, it conforms to the dimension settings in effect at the time. If necessary, you can change the dimension settings at any time. Designers and drafters in particular disciplines usually need to change a few settings relating to dimensions. However, each discipline seems to use a different group of settings frequently.

MicroStation's dimensioning tools are flexible enough to accommodate users in all disciplines. The entire set of dimensioning settings can be saved in their respective states as a dimension style with a name, by which it can be recalled for application to a dimension later in the design session.

To make changes to the existing dimension settings, invoke the Dimension Settings box from:

Pull-down menu	Element > Dimensions (or [ALT] + **L, D**).
Key-in window	**Dialog Dimsettings**

MicroStation displays the Dimension Settings box, as shown in Figure 8–60, which serves to control the settings for dimensioning.

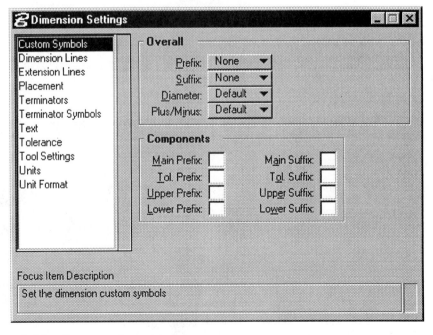

FIGURE 8–60 Dimension Settings box.

MicroStation lists the available categories in alphabetical order on the left side of the settings box in which dimension settings are grouped. Selecting a specific category causes the appropriate controls to be displayed to the right of the category list.

Following are the categories and associated controls available in the Dimension Settings box.

Custom Symbols The Custom Symbols category provides controls for specifying symbols (characters from symbol fonts or cells) for prefixes and suffixes, and for overriding the diameter and plus-or-minus symbol, as shown in Figure 8–61. Table 8–1 explains briefly all the options available under the Custom Symbols category.

In addition you can also specify additional single characters as dimension text prefixes and suffixes in the settings box.

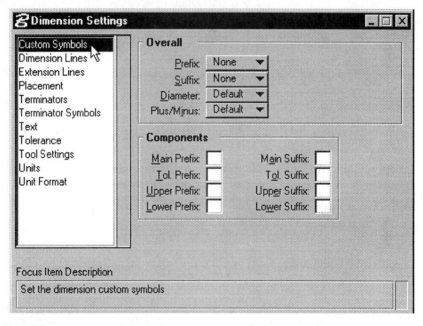

FIGURE 8–61 Dimension Settings box, Custom Symbols category.

Table 8–1. Custom Symbols Category Controls

CATEGORY	CONTROLS
Prefix	Controls the specification of a custom prefix symbol, and is placed preceding the dimension text.
	None No prefix is added to the dimension.
	Symbol Select a specific character from a selected font.
	Cell Key-in a name of a cell, and it is placed as a shared cell (refer to Chapter 10 for a detailed explanation of Cells).
	(continued on next page)

Table 8–1. Custom Symbols Category Controls *(continued)*

CATEGORY	CONTROLS
Suffix	Controls the specification of a custom suffix symbol, and is placed following the dimension text. None — No suffix is added to the dimension. Symbol — Select a specific character from a selected font. Cell — Key-in a name of a cell, and it is placed as a shared cell (refer to Chapter 10 for a detailed explanation of Cells).
Diameter	Controls the specification of an alternate diameter symbol, and allows you to select a specific character from a selected font.
Plus/Minus	Controls the specification of an alternate plus/minus symbol, and allows you to select a specific character from a selected font.

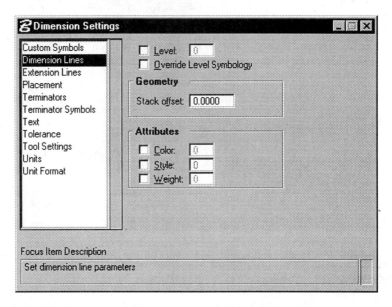

FIGURE 8–62 Dimension Settings box, Dimension Lines category.

Dimension Lines The Dimension Lines category provides controls for characteristics of dimension lines, as shown in Figure 8–62. Table 8–2 explains briefly all the options available under the Dimension Lines category.

Extension Lines The Extension Lines category provides controls for characteristics of extension lines, as shown in Figure 8–63. Table 8–3 explains briefly all the options available under the Extension Lines category.

Table 8–2. Dimension Lines Category Controls

CATEGORY	CONTROLS
Attributes	Controls to override the active element attributes of Dimension Lines: Color, Style, Weight, and Level. To override the Level Symbology, set the toggle button to ON to Override Level Symbology (see Chapter 13 for a detailed discussion about setting up a level symbology table).
Geometry	The Stack Offset controls the distance between dimension lines in stacked dimensions. Key-in the value in MU:SU:PU.

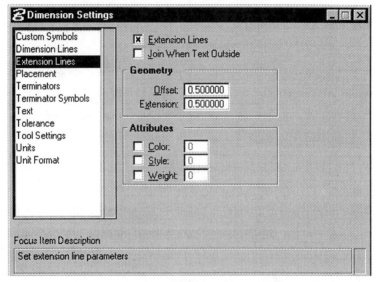

FIGURE 8–63   Dimension Settings box, Extension Lines category.

Table 8–3. Extension Lines Category Controls

CATEGORY	CONTROLS
Attributes	Controls to override the active element attributes of Extension Lines: Color, Style, and Weight.
Geometry	The Offset edit field controls the distance (MU:SU:PU) between the start of the extension line and the object line. The Extension edit field controls the distance (MU:SU:PU) that the extension line extends beyond the dimension line.
Extension Lines	Controls the effect of the placement and appearance of extension lines. The toggle button is set to ON when you need to place the extension lines.
Join When Text Outside	Controls the placement of a connecting line between extension lines and text placed outside extension lines. The toggle button is set to ON to place the connecting line.

Placement The Placement category provides controls for dimension alignment, dimension text location, and placement of dimensions in general, as shown in Figure 8–64. Table 8–4 explains briefly all the options available under the Placement category.

Table 8–4.   Placement Category Controls

CATEGORY	CONTROLS	
Alignment	Controls the orientation of linear dimensions.	
	View	Aligns linear dimensions parallel to the view X or Y axis.
	Drawing	Align linear dimensions parallel to the design plane X or Y axis.
	True	Aligns linear dimensions parallel to the element being dimensioned.
	Arbitrary	Aligns linear dimensions parallel to the element being dimensioned. The extension lines are not constrained to be at right angles to the dimension line.
	Figure 8–65 shows examples of placing linear dimensions via different alignment controls.	
Location	Controls the location of dimension text.	
	Automatic	Places the dimension according to the justification.
	Semi-Auto	Places the dimension according to the justification setting if the text fits between the extension lines. If not, you can position the text anywhere in the design.
	Manual	Place the text anywhere in the design without regard to the justification settings.
Adjust Dimension Line	If it is set to ON, the dimension line and text are dynamically moved and the extension lines are dynamically extended if there is insufficient space to fit the dimension text without overlaying the existing dimension text.	
Reference File Units	Controls the dimensioning of the Reference file.	
	ON	Computed in the units of the reference file.
	OFF	Computed in the units of the current design file.
Relative Dimension Line	Used when modifying dimension elements.	
	ON	Length of extension lines remains the same.
	OFF	Length of extension lines is allowed to vary.
Center Size	Sets the size of the center mark.	

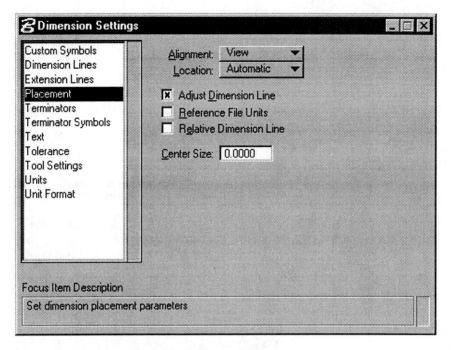

FIGURE 8–64   Dimension Settings box, Placement category.

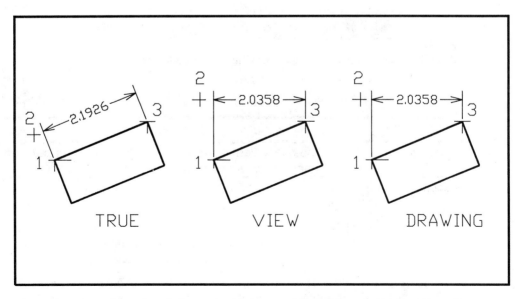

FIGURE 8–65   Examples of placing linear dimensions via different alignment controls.

Terminators The Terminators category provides controls for Orientation, Geometry, and Attributes, as shown in Figure 8–66. Table 8–5 explains briefly all the options available under the Terminators category.

Terminator Symbols The Terminator Symbols category provides controls to specify alternate symbols (characters from symbol fonts or cells) for each of the four default dimension terminators, as shown in Figure 8–67. Table 8–6 explains briefly all the options available under the Terminator Symbols category.

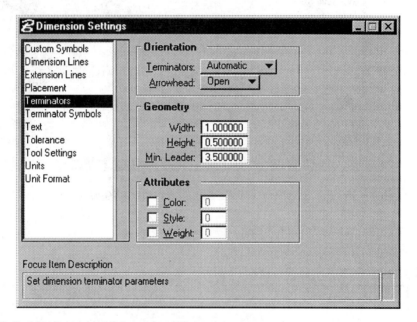

FIGURE 8–66 Dimension Settings box, Terminators category.

Table 8–5. Terminators Category Controls

CATEGORY	CONTROLS
Orientation	Controls the orientation of terminators (auto, inside, outside, and reversed) and arrowheads (open, closed, filled).
Geometry	Controls the width and height of the terminators.
	Width Sets the default terminator width, in text height units.
	Height Sets the default terminator height, in text height units.
	Min. Leader Sets the space, in text height units, between extension lines and dimension text.
Attributes	Controls to override the active element attributes of Terminators: Color, Style, and Weight.

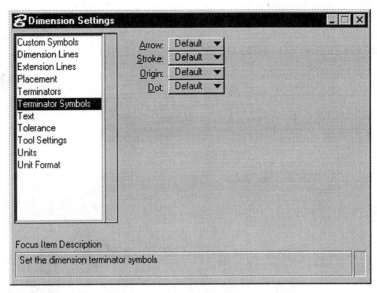

FIGURE 8–67 Dimension Settings box, Terminator Symbols category.

Table 8–6. Terminator Symbols Category Controls

CATEGORY	CONTROLS
Arrow	Controls the specification of an alternate to MicroStation's default arrowhead.
	Default Places the default arrowhead.
	Symbol Selects a specific character from a selected font.
	Cell Key-in a name of a cell, and it is placed as a shared cell (refer to Chapter 10 for a detailed discussion of Cells).
Stroke	Controls the specification of an alternate to MicroStation's default stroke.
	Default Places the default stroke.
	Symbol Selects a specific character from a selected font.
	Cell Key-in a name of a cell, and it is placed as a shared cell.
Origin	Controls the specification of an alternate to MicroStation's default origin.
	Default Places the default origin.
	Symbol Selects a specific character from a selected font.
	Cell Key-in a name of a cell, and it is placed as a shared cell.
Dot	Controls the specification of an alternate to MicroStation's default dot.
	Default Places the default dot.
	Symbol Selects a specific character from a selected font.
	Cell Key-in a name of a cell, and it is placed as a shared cell.

Text The Text category provides controls, as shown in Figure 8–68, for the placement and appearance of dimension text. Table 8–7 explains briefly all the options available under the Text category.

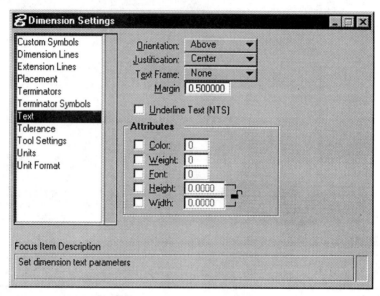

FIGURE 8–68   Dimension Settings box, Text category.

Table 8–7.   Text Category Controls

CATEGORY	CONTROLS
Orientation	Sets the orientation of dimension text relative to the dimension line.
	In Line Places text on the dimension line.
	Above Places text above the dimension line.
	Horizontal Places text horizontal to the dimension line.
	Figure 8–69 shows examples of placing linear dimension with different orientation modes.
Justification	Sets the justification of dimension text.
	Left Left justification.
	Center Center justification.
	Right Right justification.
	Figure 8–70 shows examples of placing linear dimension with different justification modes.
Text Frame	Sets the framing of dimension text.
	None No frame.
	Box Boxed frame.
	Capsule Capsule frame.
	Figure 8–71 shows examples of placing linear dimension with different Text frame modes.

Table 8–7.   Text Category Controls *(continued)*

CATEGORY	CONTROLS
Margin	Sets the space, in text height units, between the leader line and the dimension text.
Underline Text	Sets the underlining of the dimension text. ON Dimension text is underlined. OFF Dimension text is not underlined.
Attributes	Controls to override the active element attributes of Dimension text: Color and Weight. In addition, you can also set the Font and text size for dimension text to override the regular text settings.

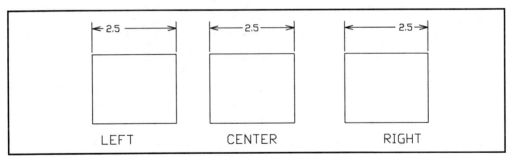

FIGURE 8–69   Examples of placing linear dimensioning in different Orientation modes.

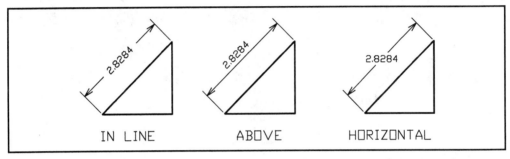

FIGURE 8–70   Examples of placing linear dimensioning in different Justification modes.

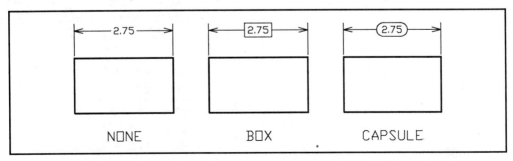

FIGURE 8–71   Examples of placing linear dimensioning in different Text Frame modes.

Tolerance The Tolerance category provides controls, as shown in Figure 8–72, for the generation of toleranced dimensions. Table 8–8 explains briefly all the options available under the Tolerance category.

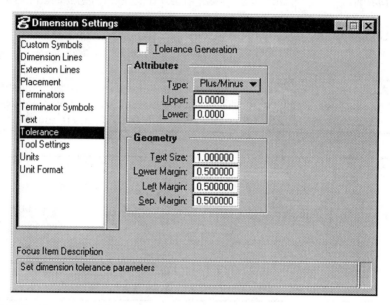

FIGURE 8–72 Dimension Settings box, Tolerance category.

Table 8–8.   Tolerance Category Controls

CATEGORY	CONTROLS	
Tolerance Generation	Controls the generation of the Tolerances.	
	ON	Tolerances are generated when either Upper or Lower is set to a nonzero value.
	OFF	Tolerances are not generated.
Attributes	Contains controls to set the tolerance type and the upper and lower tolerance limits.	
	Type	Options menu sets the tolerance type. Plus/Minus option expresses the dimension in the upper and lower limits. Limit option is expressed as Plus and Minus limits.
	Upper	Sets the upper tolerance limits, in MU:SU:PU.
	Lower	Sets the lower tolerance limits, in MU:SU:PU.
Geometry	Contains controls for the size and position of the tolerance text relative to the dimension text.	
	Text Size	Sets the tolerance text size, specified as a multiple of the dimension text Height and Width.

Table 8–8.   Tolerance Category Controls *(continued)*

CATEGORY	CONTROLS	
Geometry *(continued)*	Lower Margin	Sets the space, in text height units, between the dimension line and the bottom of the dimension text.
	Left Margin	Sets the horizontal space, in text height units, between tolerance text and dimension text.
	Sep. Margin	Sets the vertical space, in text height units, between tolerance values.

Tool Settings The Tool Settings category, as shown in Figure 8–73, controls the settings associated with individual dimensioning tools. Table 8–9 explains briefly all the options available under the Tool Settings category.

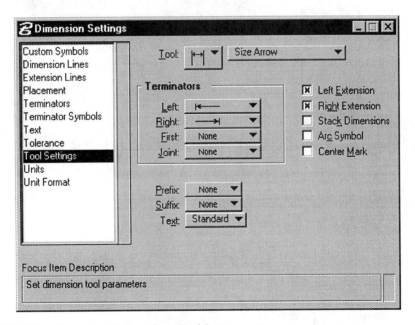

FIGURE 8-73 Dimension Settings box, Tool Settings category.

Table 8–9.   Tool Settings Category Controls

CATEGORY	CONTROLS
Tool	Sets the tool whose associated settings are displayed—select a tool from either the graphical or textual option menu. The controls show only the settings for the chosen tool. Set the appropriate settings for the selected tool. This method allows you to customize an individual dimensioning tool.

Units The Units category, as shown in Figure 8–74, controls settings that affect the type of units used in dimension text. Table 8–10 explains briefly all the options available under the Units category.

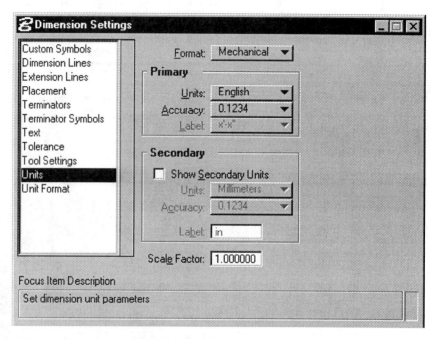

FIGURE 8–74 Dimension Settings box, Units category.

Table 8–10. Units Category Controls

CATEGORY	CONTROLS
Format	Control provides two options: AEC — Places dimensions in units of feet and inches (English) and millimeters (metric). Mechanical — Places dimensions in units of inches (English) and millimeters (metric). If necessary, set the toggle button for Show Secondary Units to ON and set the appropriate settings. See Table 8–11 for details on the Primary and Secondary Unit options.
Scale Factor	Sets the scale factor to dimension length.

Table 8–11.   Primary and Secondary Unit Options

FORMAT	PRIMARY UNITS	ACCURACY	SECONDARY UNITS	ACCURACY
AEC	Feet	1 to 8 decimal places and ½ to ¹⁄₆₄	Millimeters, centimeters, and meters	1 to 8 decimal places
	Meters	1 to 8 decimal places	Inches, feet	1 to 8 decimal places and ½ to ¹⁄₆₄
MECHANICAL	Inches	1 to 8 decimal places and ½ to ¹⁄₆₄	Millimeters, centimeters, and meters	1 to 8 decimal places
	Millimeters	1 to 8 decimal places	Feet, inches	1 to 8 decimal places and ½ to ¹⁄₆₄

Unit Format The Unit Format category, as shown in Figure 8–75, controls settings that affect the unit display format in dimension text. Table 8–12 explains briefly all the options available under the Unit Format category.

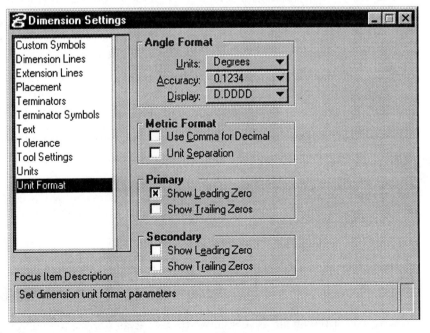

FIGURE 8–75   Dimension Settings box, Unit Format category.

Table 8–12.   Unit Format Category Controls

CATEGORY	CONTROLS
Angle Format	Controls that specify the format for angular dimension text.
	Units — Two options available. Degrees option allows you to dimension arcs in degrees, with an option to display in decimal form or degrees, minutes, and seconds (DD^MM'SS") from one to four decimal places. Length option allows you to dimension arcs in current working units.
Metric Format	Controls to adjust settings that affect the display of dimension values in Metric format.
Primary	Controls to set the settings for primary dimension text.
	Show Leading Zero — If it is set to ON, primary dimension text for a dimension of less than 1.0 is preceded by a leading zero.
	Show Trailing Zero — If it is set to ON, primary dimension text is filled with zeros, if necessary, to the number of decimal places specified by the Accuracy.
Secondary	Controls to set the settings for secondary dimension text.
	Show Leading Zero — If it is set to ON, secondary dimension text for a dimension of less than 1.0 is preceded by a leading zero.
	Show Trailing Zero — If it is set to ON, secondary dimension text is filled with zeros, if necessary, to the number of decimal places specified by the Accuracy.

After making the necessary settings in the Dimension Settings box, save the settings as a dimension style. Refer to Chapter 15 for details on saving the current dimension settings as a style.

Match Dimension Settings

The steps required to set up dimension settings involve several settings from various categories and are rather time consuming. After setting everything up, it is all too easy to forget to save it as a Style or to save it as part of the current design file by using the Save Settings command. If you lose the dimension settings but have placed

FIGURE 8-76   Invoking the Match Dimension command from the Match tool box.

dimension elements with appropriate settings in your design, the Match Dimension command can set the current settings by matching them to the settings in effect when the dimensions were placed.

Invoke the Match Dimension command from:

Match tool box	Select the Match Dimension tool (see Figure 8–76).
Key-in window	**Match Dimension** (or **mat d**) ENTER

MicroStation prompts:

> Match Dimension Settings > Identify element *(Identify the dimension element whose dimension settings you want to match.)*
> Match Dimension Settings > Accept/Reject (Select next input) *(Click the Data button to set the selected dimension element settings as the current dimension settings, or click the Reject button to reject the settings.)*

Update Dimension

The Update Dimension command can change a dimension element to the active dimension attributes.

Invoke the Update Dimension command from:

Dimension tool box	Select the Update Dimension tool (see Figure 8–77).
Key-in window	**Change Dimension** (or **chan d**) ENTER

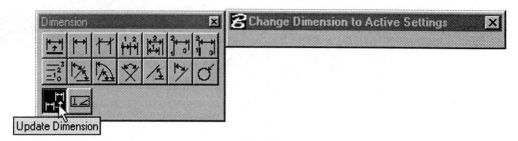

FIGURE 8–77 Invoking the Update Dimension command from the Dimension tool box.

MicroStation prompts:

Change Dimension to Active Settings > Identify element *(Identify the dimension element to set it to the active dimension attributes.)*

Match Dimension Settings > Accept/Reject (Select next input) *(Click the Data button to update the dimension attributes to the selected element, or click the Reject button to disregard the selection of the element.)*

REVIEW QUESTIONS

Write your answers in the spaces provided.

1. The dimension line is a _____ .

2. The extension lines are _____ .

3. The leader line is a _____ .

4. Associative dimensioning links _____ .

5. To place associative dimensions, the Association Lock must be _____ .

6. What are the three options available for orientation of dimension text relative to the dimension line?

   _____

7. The justification field setting for dimension text applies only when the _____ mode is selected.

8. Name the two options that are available with dimension text length format.

   _____

9. What are the three types of linear dimensioning available in MicroStation?

   _____

10. The linear dimensioning commands are provided in the _____ tool box.

11. Name the two types of dimensioning included in circular dimensioning.

    _____

12. The Dimension Angle Size command is used to _____ .

13. The Place Center Mark command serves to _____ .

14. List the four options available with the Measure Distance command.

    _____

15. The Measure Radius command provides information on such elements as:

    _____

16. List the seven area options available with the Measure Area command.

    _____

    _____

17. The Measure Area Flood option measures the area enclosed _____
    _____ .

18. The Geometric Tolerance settings box is used to build _____
    _____ .

19. Ordinate dimensions are used to label _____ .

20. The Label Line command places the _____ and _____ .

PROJECT EXERCISE

This project exercise provides step-by-step instructions for placing dimensions on the Chapter 3 project design, as shown in Figure P8–1. The intent of this project is to guide you in applying the Dimension settings and dimension placement tools.

> **NOTE:** If you have not drawn this design, refer to the instructions at the end of Chapters 3.

Set Up Dimensioning for the Chapter 3 Project

This procedure loads the Chapter 3 project design file in MicroStation, then enters the Dimension settings.

> **NOTE:** As you complete each step in the project procedures, place a check mark by the step to help you keep up with where you are in the project.

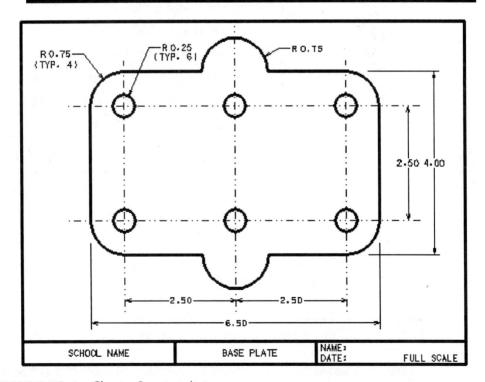

FIGURE P8–1   Chapter 3 project design.

STEP 1: Invoke MicroStation using the normal technique for the operating system on your workstation, and open the Chapter 3 project design file named CH3.DGN.

STEP 2: If necessary, invoke the Fit View command to fit the view.

STEP 3: Open the Dimension Settings box by selecting Dimensions from the pull-down menu Element. MicroStation displays the dimension settings similar to Figure P8–2.

STEP 4: Set the dimension settings as follows in the Dimension Settings box.

Placement	Set the Alignment option menu to View. Set the Location option menu to Automatic. Set the Adjust Dimension Line toggle button to ON.
Text	Set the Orientation option menu to Horizontal. Set the Justification option menu to Center. Set the Text Frame to None. Set the Margin to 0.50000. Set the Text Height and Width to 0.1250.
Units	Set the Format option menu to Mechanical. Set the Primary Units option menu to English. Set the Primary Accuracy to 2 decimal places.
Units Format	Set the Angle Units option menu to Degrees. Set the Angle Accuracy to 2 decimal places. Set the Angle Display option menu to D.DDDD Set the Show Trailing Zero toggle button to ON.

STEP 5: Invoke the Save Settings command from the pull-down menu File to save the settings.

NOTE: No dimension tolerance settings are required, because tolerance dimensioning is not used on this design.

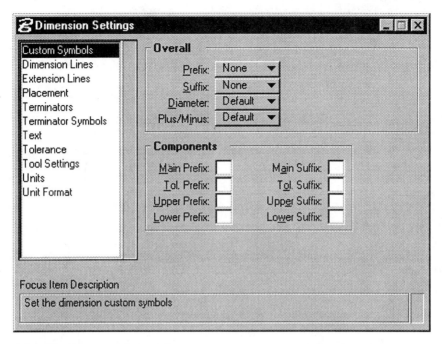

FIGURE P8–2   Dimension Settings box.

Place the Radial Dimensions

This procedure places the radial dimensions and adds text below the dimension on the circle, as shown in Figure P8–3.

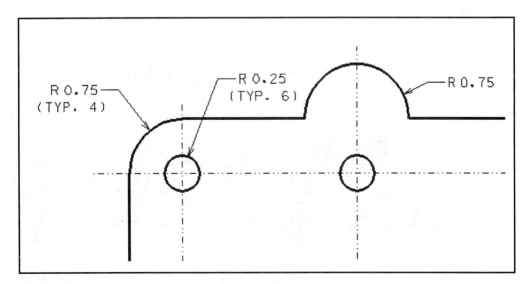

FIGURE P8–3   Completed radial dimensions.

STEP 1:   Invoke the Dimension Radial command from the Dimension tool box. Then, in the Tool Settings window, set the Mode to Radius and the Alignment to View, and turn ON the Association Lock (see Figure P8–4).

MicroStation prompts:

> Dimension Radius > Identify element *(Select the top, left fillet.)*
> Dimension Radius > Select dimension endpoint *(Drag the image of the dimension text to the location where you want to place it, then place a data point to complete the dimension.)*

STEP 2:   Place a radial dimension on the top-left circle.

STEP 3:   Place a radial dimension on the top arc.

STEP 4:   Invoke the Place Text at Origin command from the Text tool box, then, in the Tool Settings window, set the text Height and Width to 0.125.

MicroStation prompts:

> Place Text > Enter text *(In the Text Editor window, type the string (TYP. 4). Place the text centered under the fillet's dimension text, as shown in Figure P8–3.)*

STEP 5:   Repeat the procedure of step 4 to place (TYP. 6) below the circle's dimension text.

STEP 6:   Invoke the Save Settings from the pull-down menu File and save the settings.

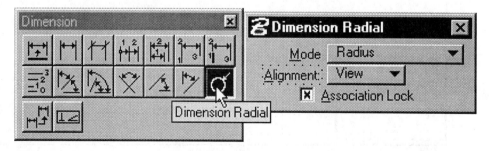

FIGURE P8–4   Invoking the Dimension Radial tool from the Dimension tool box.

Place Outer Linear Dimensions

This procedure places the linear overall length and width dimensions, as shown in Figure P8–5.

STEP 1:   To place the height dimension, invoke the Dimension Size with Arrow command from the Dimension tool box. Then, in the Tool Settings window, set the Alignment to View and turn ON the Association Lock (see Figure P8–6).

MicroStation prompts:

> Dimension Size with Arrow > Select start of dimension *(Keypoint snap at the joining point between the horizontal line and the top fillet, and place a data point to define the starting point of the dimension.)*
>
> Dimension Size with Arrow > Define length of extension line *(Drag the placement pointer about 1.5 Master Units straight to the right, then place a data point to define the length of the extension line.)*
>
> Dimension Size with Arrow > Select dimension endpoint *(Keypoint snap at the joining point between the horizontal line and the bottom fillet, and place a data point to complete the height dimension.)*

STEP 2:   Click the Reset button twice, then dimension the 6.5 horizontal length of the base plate.

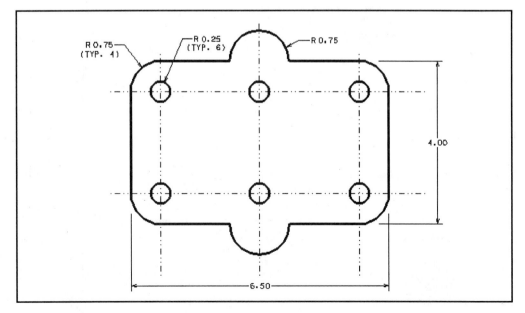

FIGURE P8–5   Completed length and width dimensions.

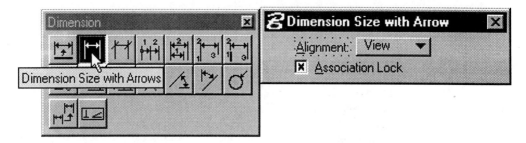

FIGURE P8-6 Invoking the Dimension Size with Arrow command from the Dimension tool box.

Place Centerline Dimensions

This procedure turns off placement of extension lines, then dimensions the center-lines, as shown in Figure P8–7.

STEP 1: If the centerlines are not long enough to hold the dimensions, extend them with the Extend Line command.

STEP 2: Open the Dimension settings box by selecting Dimensions from the pull-down menu Element. MicroStation displays the dimensions settings.

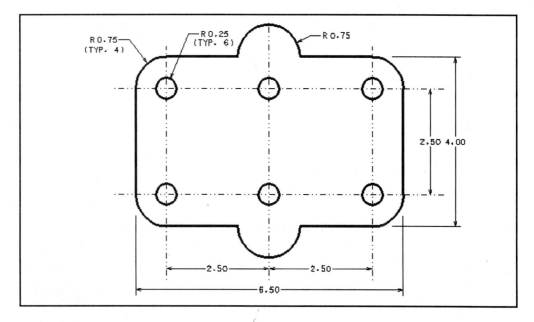

FIGURE P8-7 Completed overall length and width dimensions.

STEP 3:   In the Dimension Settings box, select the Extension Lines option, then set the toggle button to OFF for the Extension Lines. The settings box should now match the settings shown in Figure P8–8.

STEP 4:   To place the vertical dimension, invoke the Dimension Size with Arrow command from the Dimension tool box.

MicroStation prompts:

> Dimension Size with Arrow > Select start of dimension *(Keypoint snap to the right end of the top centerline, then place a data point.)*
> Dimension Size with Arrow > Define length of extension line *(Drag the placement pointer about .25 Master Units to the right, then place a data point.)*
> Define Size with Arrow > Select dimension endpoint (Keypoint snap to the right end of the lower horizontal centerline.)

STEP 5:   Click the Reset button twice, then place the horizontal centerline dimensions.

STEP 6:   Invoke the Save Settings command from the pull-down menu File to save the settings.

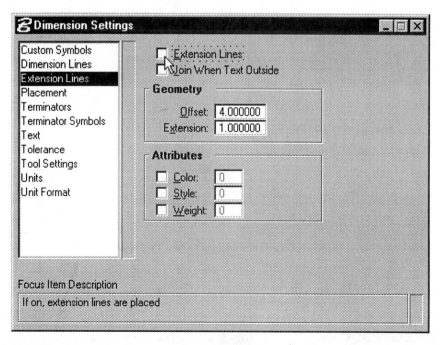

FIGURE P8–8   Dimension Settings box with both extension lines set to OFF.

DRAWING EXERCISES 8–1 THROUGH 8–5

Exercise 8–1 Use Mechanical dimensioning to place dimensions on the flange gasket created in Exercise 3–8 on page 3–77.

Exercise 8–2 Use Mechanical dimensioning to place dimensions on the machine part created in Exercise 4–2 on page 4–28.

Exercise 8–3 Tolerance dimensioning.

Use the following table to set up the design file for Exercise 8–3, then draw and dimension the object shown in the figure.

SETTING	VALUE
Seed File	SEED2D.DGN
Working Units	MU = IN, SU = 10 TH, PU = 1000
Grid	Master = .1, Reference = 10

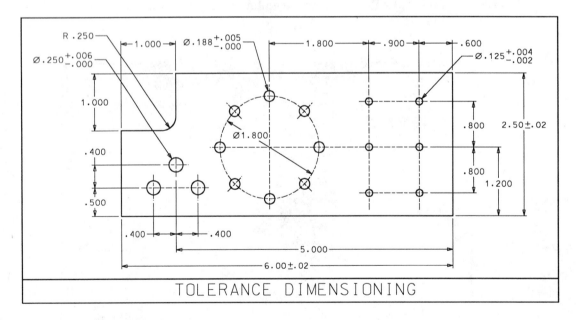

TOLERANCE DIMENSIONING

Exercise 8–4 Use AEC dimensioning to place dimensions on the master bedroom floor plan created in Exercise 4–5 on page 4–31.

Exercise 8–5 Use AEC dimensioning to place dimensions on the desk created in Exercise 5–5 on page 5–55.

CHAPTER

9

PLOTTING

One task has not changed much in the transition from board draft-ing to CAD, and that is obtaining a hard copy. The term *hard copy* describes a tangible reproduction of a screen image. The hard copy is usually a reproducible medium from which prints are made, and it can take many forms, including slides, videotape, prints, and plots. This chapter describes the most common process for getting a hard copy: plotting.

OBJECTIVES

After completing this chapter, you will know:

✓ How the plotting process works.

✓ What components are involved in the process.

✓ How to create a plot file.

✓ How to create a hard copy.

OVERVIEW OF THE PLOTTING PROCESS

In manual drafting, if you need your design to be done in two different scales, you physically have to draw the design for different scales. In CAD, on the other hand, with minor modifications you can plot the same design in different scale factors on different-size paper.

To plot a design with MicroStation you carry out a three-step process:

1. Set up the view to be plotted or place a fence around the part of the design to be plotted.
2. Use the Plot settings box to preview the plot and create a plot file.
3. Send the plot file to the plotter.

MicroStation lets you get a hard copy of your design file by creating a "plot file" and sending the file to a plotting device to create a hard copy.

The plot file describes all the elements in the plot area in a language the plotting device can understand, and provides commands to control the plotting device. It is separate from your design file, and contains the design as it existed when the plot file was created. If you make changes to the design after creating the plot file and want to plot the new design, you must create a new plot file.

MicroStation stores plot files in the directory path contained in the MS_PLTFILES configuration variable. By default, that path is <disk>:\USTATION\OUT\PLOT. Replace <disk> with the letter of the disk that contains the MicroStation program. (See Chapter 15 for a detailed explanation of configuration variables.)

Plotting devices (printers and plotters) put the information contained in the plot file on the hard copy page. MicroStation supports many types and models of plotting devices. There are electrostatic plotters that provide only shades of gray and more expensive models that plot in color. Pen plotters use ink pens contained in a movable rack. A mechanical control mechanism selects pens and moves them across the page under program control.

MicroStation provides a **plotter driver file** for each supported plotting device. The information contained in this file (combined with the information you supply through the Plot settings box) tells MicroStation how to create the plot file and send it to the plotting device.

The path and name of the default plotter driver file is contained in the MS_PLTR configuration variable. The default path is <device>:\USTATION\PLOTDRV\. Replace <device> with the letter of the disk containing the MicroStation program.

The plotter driver file name usually consists of the device model number plus .PLT as the extension. MicroStation provides two plotter driver files for most plotting devices, one for English measurement units and one for metric units. See Table 9–1 for the list of the supported plotters and corresponding sample plotter driver files supplied with MicroStation 95.

The plotter driver file specifies the following:

- Plotter model
- Number of pens the plotter can use
- Resolution and units of distance on the plotter
- Pen change criteria
- Name, size, offset, and number for all paper sizes
- Stroking tolerance for arcs and circles
- Border around the plot and information about the border comment
- Pen speeds, accelerations, and force where applicable
- Pen to element color or weight mapping
- Spacing between multiple strokes on a weighted line
- Number of strokes generated for each line weight
- Definitions for user-defined line styles (for plotting only)
- Method by which plots are generated
- Actions to be taken at plot's start and end and on pen changes

Table 9–1. Supported Plotters and Corresponding Sample Plotter Driver Configuration Files

SUPPORTED PLOTTER	PLOTTER DRIVER FILE
Calcomp 906	cal906.plt
Calcomp 907	cal104x.plt, cal524xx.plt, cal906.plt, cal907.plt, ver8536.plt, ver8524.plt
Calcomp 960	cal960.plt
DMPL (Houston Instrument)	hidmp40.plt, hidmp56.plt, hidmp52.plt, ioline.plt
EPSP	epson8.plt, epson8h.plt, epson24.plt
HP-GL	drftpro.plt, mutoh500.plt, drftmstr.plt, hp7470a.plt, hp7550a.plt, hp7580b.plt, hp7585b.plt, hp7475a.plt, hp7440a.plt
HP-GL/2	hpgl2.plt, hpljet3.plt, hpljet4.plt, hpljet4v.plt, hpdjet.plt, hpxl300.plt, hp650c.plt, drftprop.plt, novajet2.plt
PCL	hpljet.plt, hlp200c.plt, hppc.plt
PostScript	pscript.plt, pscriptc.plt

Plotter driver files can be edited with any text editor. For more information on the contents of these files, and changes you can make to them, consult the *MicroStation User Guide*.

> **NOTE:** If you modify a sample plotter driver file, it is a good idea to retain the original file and to save the modified file as a new file with a different name.

CREATING PLOT FILES

To create a plot file, invoke the Plot/Print command from:

Pull-down menu	File > Plot/Print (or [CTRL] + **P**)
Key-in window	**Plot** (or **plo**) [ENTER]

MicroStation displays the Plot settings box, as shown in Figure 9–1.

MicroStation displays the name of the selected plotter driver file name on the right side of the Plot settings box.

If necessary, you can change the plotter driver file by selecting from:

Plot settings box tool bar	Plotter Driver (see Figure 9–2)
Pull-down menu (Plot settings box)	Setup > Driver... (or [ALT] + **S, D**)

MicroStation displays the Select Plotter Driver File dialog box, as shown in Figure 9–3. Select the appropriate driver file and click the OK button.

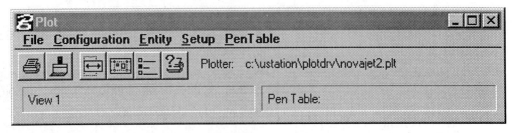

FIGURE 9-1 Plot settings box.

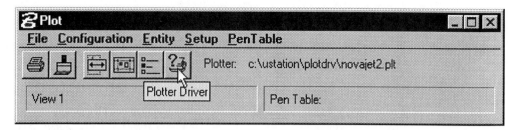

FIGURE 9-2   Invoking the Plotter Driver from the Plot settings box tool bar.

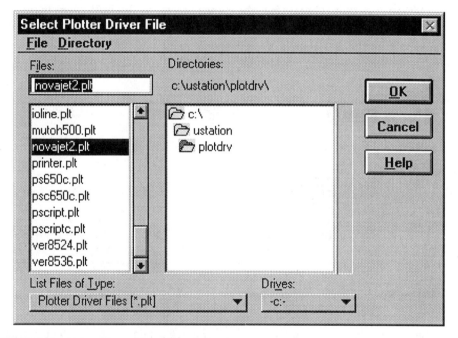

FIGURE 9-3   Select Plotter Driver File dialog box.

If you are using Microsoft Windows and select printer.plt as the plotter driver file, MicroStation plots with the default printer selected in the Windows Printer Manager.

> **NOTE:** The initial default plotter driver file is specified by the MS_PLTR configuration variable. If you change the plotter driver file, MicroStation automatically updates the MS_PLTR configuration variable with the new device name.

Selecting the Area of the Design to Plot

By default, MicroStation selects View 1 as the view to plot. If necessary, you can change the view to plot by invoking the command from:

Pull-down menu (Plot settings box)	<u>E</u>ntity > <u>V</u>iew > 1 to 8 (or **ALT** + **E, V**)

MicroStation displays the selected view number in the left corner of the settings box. To plot from the view containing the fence, first place the fence to include the elements to plot. Then select the Fence option in the pull-down menu Entity in the Plot settings box. MicroStation displays the view number with the word "Fence" in the left corner of the settings box.

Page Setup

To set the page for plotting, invoke the Page Setup command from:

Plot settings box tool bar	Select the Page Setup tool (see Figure 9–4).
Pull-down menu (Plot settings box)	<u>S</u>etup > <u>P</u>age... (or **ALT** + **S, P**)

MicroStation displays the Page Setup dialog box, as shown in Figure 9–5.

Select the desired page size from the Page Size option menu. The Rotate 90° toggle button determines whether or not the plot is rotated 90 degrees on the page. Click the OK button to close the Page Setup dialog box.

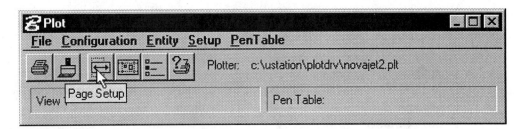

FIGURE 9–4 Invoking the Page Setup command from the Plot settings box tool bar.

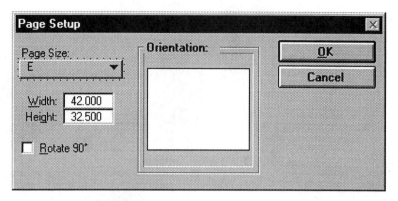

FIGURE 9–5   Page Setup dialog box.

Plot Layout

The Plot Layout settings box allows you to adjust the margins and scale of the plot. To set the plot layout, invoke the Plot Layout command from:

Plot settings box tool bar	Select the Plot Layout tool (see Figure 9–6).
Pull-down menu (Plot settings box)	Setup > Layout... (or [ALT] + **S, L**)

MicroStation displays the Plot Layout dialog box, as shown in Figure 9–7.

The black rectangle in the Page Layout area represents the selected page for the selected plotter. The blue rectangle inside it represents the plot area. If Fence is chosen, the blue rectangle represents the smallest rectangular area that encloses the fenced area.

The Left Margin and Bottom Margin edit fields set the left and bottom edges of the printable area of the paper to the origin of the plot. To center the plot area, turn ON the toggle button for Center to Page, and automatically MicroStation displays the new offset settings for Left Margin and Bottom Margin.

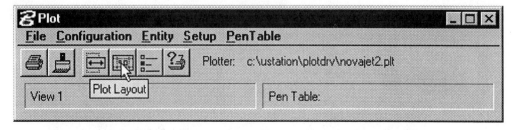

FIGURE 9–6   Invoking the Plot Layout command from the Plot settings box tool bar.

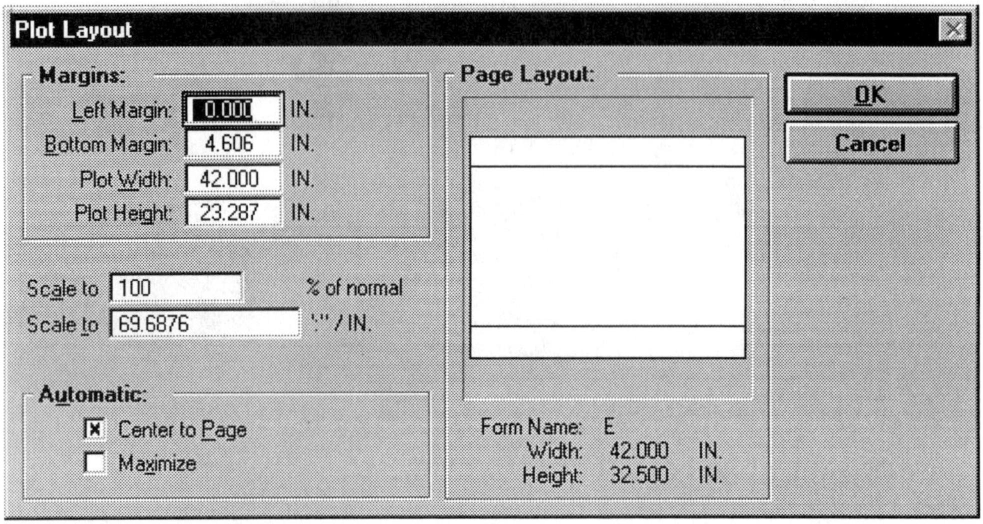

FIGURE 9–7 Plot Layout dialog box.

The Plot Width and Plot Height edit fields display the size of the plot for the selected page. The "Scale to" edit fields display the percentage of normal size and the ratio of Master Units to plotter units. If you make changes in one of the four fields, Micro-Station reflects the corresponding changes in the remaining three edit fields. For example, if you set the design to be plotted to 50% of normal, then automatically MicroStation displays the scale in terms of the ratio of Master Units to plotter units and the appropriate Plot Width and Plot Height.

Turn ON the toggle button for Maximize to fit the selected view or fenced area into as much of the printable area as possible. The plot is centered either horizontally or vertically if it does not fit the printable area exactly.

Click the OK button to save the changes and close the Plot Layout dialog box.

Plot Options

The Plot Options settings box allows you to adjust the appearance of the plot. Invoke the Plot Options settings from:

Plot settings box tool bar	Select the Plot Options tool (see Figure 9–8).
Pull-down menu (Plot settings box)	Setup > Options... (or ALT + S, O)

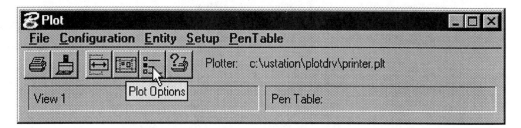

FIGURE 9–8 Invoking the Plot Options command from the Plot settings box tool bar.

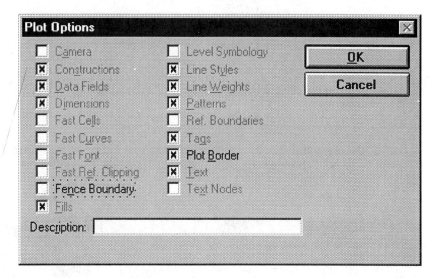

FIGURE 9–9 Plot Options dialog box.

MicroStation displays the Plot Options dialog box, as shown in Figure 9–9.

Toggle the check boxes to turn ON or OFF the appearance options. If the element to plot is a view or a fence, the View Attributes settings box determines most aspects of the plot's appearance, and the corresponding options in the Plot Options settings box are dimmed (disabled). If necessary, make the changes in the View Attributes settings box.

If necessary, you can add a comment to the plot by typing the appropriate information in the Description edit field. Click the OK button to save the changes and close the Plot Options dialog box.

Previewing the Plot

To display a plot preview image, invoke the Preview command from:

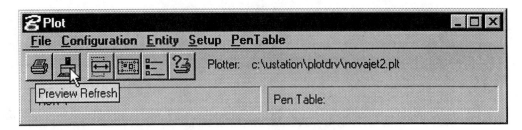

FIGURE 9–10 Invoking the Preview Refresh command from the Plot settings box tool bar.

Plot settings box tool bar	Select the Preview Refresh tool (see Figure 9–10).
Pull-down menu (Plot settings box)	File > Preview (or [ALT] + F, V)

MicroStation expands the Plot settings box to reveal the preview image, as shown in Figure 9–11, and changes the title of the settings box from "Plot" to "Plot Preview."

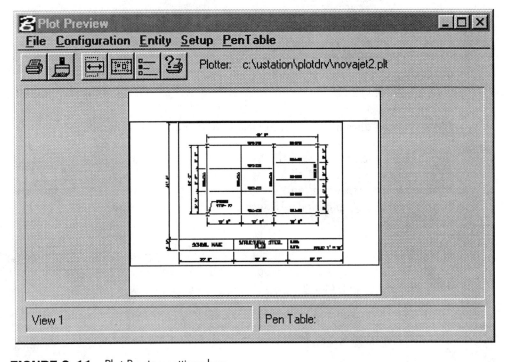

FIGURE 9–11 Plot Preview settings box.

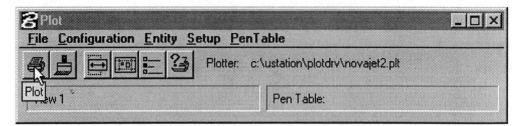

FIGURE 9–12   Invoking the Plot command from the Plot settings box tool bar.

Creating a Plot File

To create a plot file, invoke the Plot command from:

Plot settings box tool bar	Select the Plot tool (see Figure 9–12).
Pull-down menu (Plot settings box)	File > Plot (or [ALT] + **F**, **P**)

MicroStation displays the Save Plot As dialog box, as shown in Figure 9–13.

The default plot file name is the same as the design file name, and the .000 extension is added to the file name. If necessary, change the plot file name, then click the OK button to create the plot file.

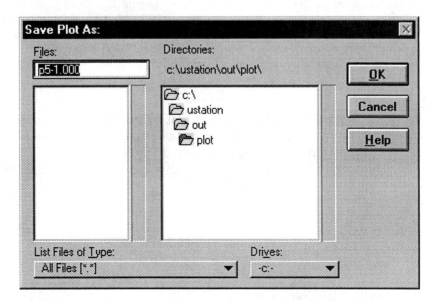

FIGURE 9–13   Save Plot As dialog box

By default, the plot file is saved in the <disk>:USTATION/OUT/PLOT/ directory. Replace <disk>: with the letter of the disk that contains the MicroStation program.

If the selected file name already exists, an Alert window opens. Click the OK button to overwrite the file, or click the Cancel button to return to the Save File As dialog box and enter a new file name.

> **NOTE:** If the plotter is connected to a parallel port, then instead of providing a file name, you can key-in **LPT1** or **LPT2** (depending on which parallel port the plotter is connected to). The plotter will generate a hard copy without creating a plot file.

GENERATING THE PLOT FROM THE PLOT FILE

The PLOTUTIL utility program sends a plot file to a plotter. You can run the utility on another PC without MicroStation. Make sure to copy the PLOTUTIL utility and the configured plotter driver file to the PC from which you want to plot the design files.

At the DOS prompt, type **PLOTUTIL** and press ⏎. MicroStation prompts for the file name to plot. Type the name of the plot file name and press ⏎, and the design file is plotted.

You can also use PLOTFILE.BAT batch file to plot from the plot file. The batch file sets the environment variables used by PLOTUTIL to locate the plotter driver file (MS_PLTR) and the plot files (MS_PLTFILES). If necessary, you can change the settings of the environment variables.

PLOT CONFIGURATION FILES

Plot configuration files let you save the plot information specific to a design file. Plot configuration files are a way to streamline repetitive plotting tasks. Information saved in a plot configuration file includes:

- Plotting area
- Plot option settings
- Fence location
- Displayed levels
- Page size, margin, and scale
- Pen table if attached

Before you create a plot configuration file, set the controls in the Plot settings box. To create a plot configuration file, invoke the Plot Configuration File dialog box from:

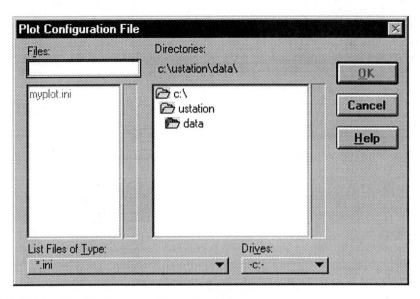

FIGURE 9–14   Plot Configuration File dialog box.

| Pull-down menu (Plot settings box) | Configuration > New... (or ⌨ **ALT** + **C, N**) |

MicroStation displays the Plot Configuration File dialog box, as shown in Figure 9–14.

Key-in the name of the configuration file in the Files edit field and click the OK button. MicroStation saves the configuration to the given file name with the .INI extension, and by default it is saved in the <disk>:USTATION/DATA/ directory.

To open an existing configuration file, invoke the Open command from the pull-down menu Configuration in the Plot settings box. MicroStation displays the Plot Configuration File dialog box. Select the appropriate configuration file and click the OK button. MicroStation makes the necessary changes to the plot settings.

PEN TABLES

The pen table is a data structure that allows you to modify the appearance of a plot without modifying the design file, by performing one or more of the following at plot-creating time:

- Changing the appearance of elements
- Determining the plotting order of the active design file and its attached reference files
- Specifying text string substitutions

A pen table is stored in a pen table file. The pen table consists of sections that are tested against each element in the design. When a match is found, the output options are applied to the element. The modified element is then converted into plot data, which in turn is written to the plot file. At no time are the elements of the design file or its reference files modified.

Creating a Pen Table

To create a pen table, invoke the New command from:

Pull-down menu (Plot settings box)	PenTable > New... (or ⌨ᴬᴸᵀ + **P, N**)

MicroStation displays the Create New Pen Table file dialog box. Key-in the pen table file name and click the OK button. MicroStation displays the Modify Pen Table settings box, as shown in Figure 9–15.

By default, MicroStation adds the section called NEW in the Sections list box. You can either rename the section or insert a new one and delete the NEW section.

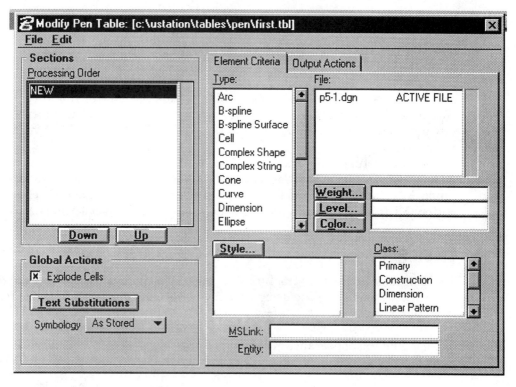

FIGURE 9–15   Modify Pen Table settings box.

Renaming a Pen Table Section

To rename a section, first select the name of the section in the list box, then invoke the Rename command from:

Pull-down menu (Modify Pen Table settings box)	Edit > Rename Section... (or [ALT] + E, R)

MicroStation displays the Rename Section dialog box. Key-in the new name and click the OK button to rename the section.

Inserting a New Pen Table Section

Above an Existing Section To insert a new section above an existing section, first select the name of the section in the list box, then invoke the Insert New Section Above command from:

Pull-down menu (Modify Pen Table settings box)	Edit > Insert New Section Above... (or [ALT] + E, A)

MicroStation displays the Insert Section dialog box. Key-in the new name and click the OK button to insert the new section.

Below an Existing Section To insert a new section below an existing section, first select the name of the section in the list box, then invoke the Insert New Section Below command from:

Pull-down menu (Modify Pen Table settings box)	Edit > Insert New Section Below... (or [ALT] + E, B)

MicroStation displays the Insert Section dialog box. Key-in the new name and click the OK button to insert the new section.

Deleting a Pen Table Section

To delete a section, first select the name of the section in the list box, then invoke the Delete Section command from:

Pull-down menu (Modify Pen Table settings box)	Edit > Delete Section (or [ALT] + E, D)

MicroStation deletes the selected section from the list box.

If necessary, you can change the section's position in the processing order. First select the section in the list box, then click ⬇ or ⬆ to change the processing order.

Modifying a Pen Table Section

To modify a pen table section, follow these numbered steps.

STEP 1: Highlight the name of the section to modify from the Sections list box.

STEP 2: *Optional:* Set the toggle button for Explode Cells.

ON Each cell component element is evaluated independently against the element criteria; the defined output action applies to each element of the cell.

OFF Each cell header is evaluated against the element criteria; the defined output action applies to each element of the cell.

STEP 3: *Optional:* To substitute text in the design with alternate text for plotting, click the Text Substitutions button. MicroStation displays the Text Substitutions settings box, as shown in Figure 9–16.

To insert a text substitution entry, invoke the Insert New command from:

Pull-down menu (Text Substitutions settings box)	Edit > Insert New (or [ALT] + **E, I**)

An entry labeled "Original" appears in the list box and in the Actual edit field. Replace "Original" with the string in the design to be replaced for plotting purposes. Type the replacement text string in the Replacement edit field and press [ENTER].

> **NOTE:** The defined text string substitutions apply universally to all text elements in the plot and only to exact matches of the specified strings.

In addition, you can also replace a text string in a design with a file name, current date, or time.

To replace a text string in a design with a file name, date, or time, select options from the pull-down menu Edit (Text Substitutions settings box) as shown in Table 9–2.

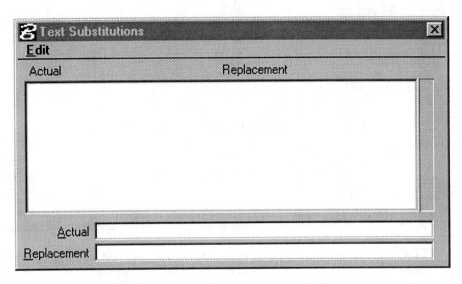

FIGURE 9-16 Text Substitutions settings box.

Table 9-2. Replacing a Text String with a File Name, Date, or Time

EDIT MENU ITEM	ACTUAL STRING IN THE DESIGN*	REPLACEMENT STRING FOR PLOTTING	EFFECT
Insert Abbreviated Filename	$FILENAME$	_FILEA_	Replaces the actual text string with the file name of the active design file. The replacement file name is truncated to the size of the actual string.
Insert Filename	$FILE$	_FILE_	Replaces the actual text string with the file name of the active design file. No truncation.
Insert Date	$DATE$	_DATE_	Replaces the actual text string with the current date.
Insert Time	$TIME$	_TIME_	Replaces the actual text string with the current time.

* The actual text string is shown with the dollar sign character ($) as the delimiter character just to differentiate it from normal text. It is *not* necessary to have the delimiter character as part of the text string in the design file. You can replace any text string in the design with the file name, date, or time.

To delete a text substitution entry, first highlight the text string substitution, then invoke the Delete command from:

Pull-down menu (Text Substitutions settings box)	Edit > Delete (or ALT + E, D)

The selected text string substitution is deleted from the settings box.

> **NOTE:** You can see the substitutions to the text string by clicking the Preview Refresh icon in the Plot Preview settings box.

STEP 4: To set the element criteria, first select the Element Criteria tab (as shown in Figure 9–17), located in the top right side of the Modify Pen settings box.

Then select element types from the Type list box, a file name from the File list box, and the class or classes of elements to include in the

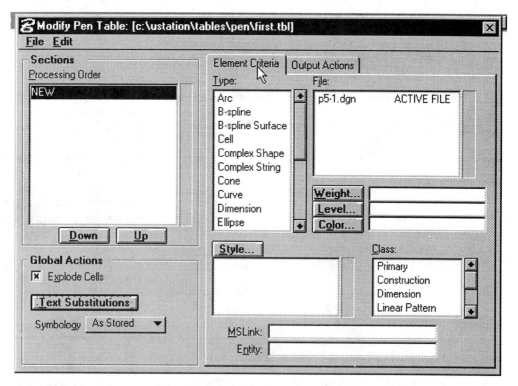

FIGURE 9–17 Selecting the Element Criteria tab in the Modify Pen settings box.

selection criteria. To select multiple items from the list box, hold down
[CTRL] and then select the items.

> **NOTE:** The File list box lists the name of the active design
> file and all the reference files attached to the active design
> file.

You can also select or deselect all the element types, files, and classes by
selecting the appropriate command from the pull-down menu Edit in the
Pen settings box.

In addition, you can set the selection criteria based on weight, level, color,
or style by keying-in the appropriate values in the edit fields or by
clicking the appropriate button in the Modify Pen settings box. Micro-
Station displays the appropriate dialog boxes, as shown in Figure 9–18.

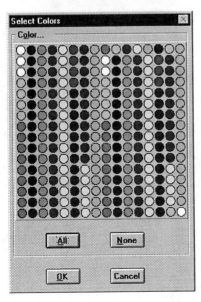

FIGURE 9–18   Select Weights, Select Levels, Select Colors, and Select Line Style dialog boxes.

Use the controls in the dialog box to make the selections, and click the OK button to close the dialog box.

STEP 5: To set the output actions, first select the Output Actions tab (as shown in Figure 9–19), located in the top right side of the Modify Pen settings box.

Select one of the available options from the Master Control option menu. Table 9–3 explains the available Master Control options.

Optional: Turn ON the toggle button for Priority to set the priority. Key-in the desired priority value (range: –2147483648 to 2147483647) in the Priority edit field. Elements with a lower priority value are plotted before elements with a higher priority value. Unprioritized elements are always plotted before all prioritized elements.

> **NOTE:** Do not prioritize elements unless it is significant to the plot, since prioritized elements require additional processing time and memory.

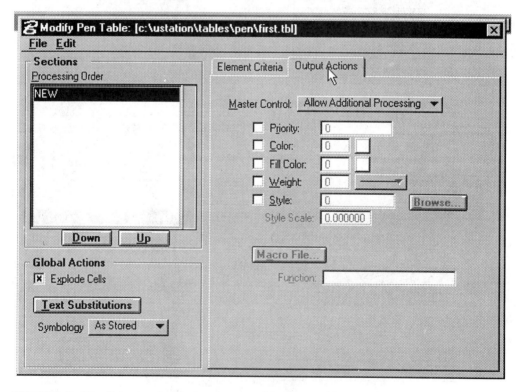

FIGURE 9–19 Selecting the Output Actions tab in the Modify Pen settings box.

Table 9–3.   Master Control Menu Options

MASTER CONTROL OPTION	EFFECT
Allow Additional Processing (default)	The output actions are applied to the selection criteria, and any loaded MDL applications that you desire to process the element are invoked.
No Additional Processing	The output actions are applied to the selection criteria, and no MDL applications that you desire to process the element are invoked.
Don't Display Element	The elements that satisfy the selection criteria are not plotted, and no MDL applications that you desire to process the element are invoked.
Call BASIC Macro Function	The output actions are applied to the selection criteria, and additional processing is performed by the designated function in the designated BASIC macro.

Optional: Turn ON the toggle buttons to override the Color, Weight, Level, and Style appropriately for the elements that satisfy the selection criteria. Key-in the values in the edit fields or choose the desired attributes from the pop-up palette. If the element is to be plotted with a custom line style, key-in the desired line style scale factor in the Style Scale field.

STEP 6:   Before you plot, click the Preview Refresh icon in the Plot Preview settings box. MicroStation displays in the Preview box all the elements that are set to plot, with appropriate changes as per the settings of the Output Actions. Once you are satisfied with the changes, create the plot file.

STEP 7:   To save the pen table, invoke the Save command from:

Pull-down menu (Modify Pen Table settings box)	File > Save (or [ALT] + **F**, **S**)

MicroStation saves the modifications made to the existing pen table.

To save the modifications to a different pen table file, invoke the Save As command from:

Pull-down menu (Modify Pen Table settings box)	File > Save As (or [ALT] + **F, A**)

MicroStation displays the Create Pen Table File dialog box. Key-in the name of the file to save the settings, and click the OK button.

STEP 8:   To disable pen table processing, unload the pen table. To unload the pen table, invoke the Unload command from:

Pull-down menu (Modify Pen Table settings box)	File > Exit/Unload (or [ALT] + **F, X**)

MicroStation unloads the pen table.

You can also unload the pen table from the pull-down menu Pen Table located in the Plot settings box.

PROJECT EXERCISE

This project exercise provides step-by-step instructions for plotting the Chapter 5 Project Exercise design, shown in Figure P9–1.

> **NOTE:** As you complete each step in the project procedures, place a check mark by the step to help you keep up with where you are in the project.

Set Up the Design for Plotting

This procedure prepares the structural steel plan design for plotting.

STEP 1: Start MicroStation and open the design file named CH5.DGN.

> **NOTE:** If you did not do the Chapter 5 project, refer to Chapter 5 for instructions.

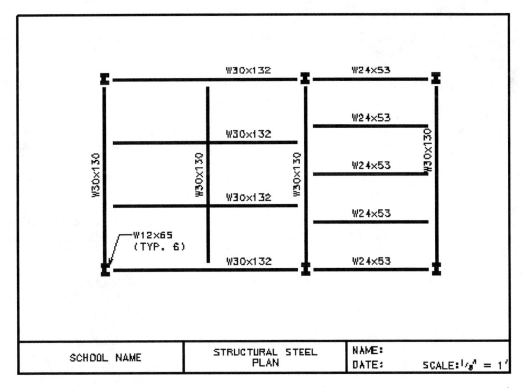

FIGURE P9–1 Completed project design.

STEP 2: Invoke the Fit View command to fit the view window.

STEP 3: Set the default Snap mode to Keypoint.

STEP 4: Invoke the Place Fence command from the Fence tool box, and, in the Tool Settings window, select the Block option.

MicroStation prompts:

Place Fence Block > Enter first point *(Keypoint snap to one corner of the border block, then place a data point.)*
Place Fence Block > Enter opposite corner *(Keypoint snap to the diagonally opposite corner, then place a data point to complete placing the Fence Block.)*

> **NOTE:** A successful Keypoint snap is indicated by the tentative cross appearing on the corner and the entire border block's switching to the highlight color.

Set Up the Plotting Parameters

This procedure opens the Plot settings box, sets the required plotting parameters, and plots the fence contents.

STEP 1: Invoke the Print/Plot command from the pull-down menu File. MicroStation displays the Plot settings box.

STEP 2: Select the appropriate plotter driver by clicking the Plotter Driver tool in the Plot settings box. (For this exercise we have selected hp7585b.plt).

STEP 3: Select the Fence option from the pull-down menu Entity in the Plot settings box.

STEP 4: Invoke the Page Setup tool from the Plot settings tool box, and set the Page Size as shown in Figure P9–2. Click the OK button to close the dialog box.

STEP 5: Invoke the Plot Layout tool from the Plot settings tool box, and set the Plot Layout settings as shown in Figure P9–3. Click the OK button to close the dialog box.

> **NOTE:** The plotting scale is set to plot at $\frac{1}{4}'' = 1'\text{-}0''$ on a Size-D paper.

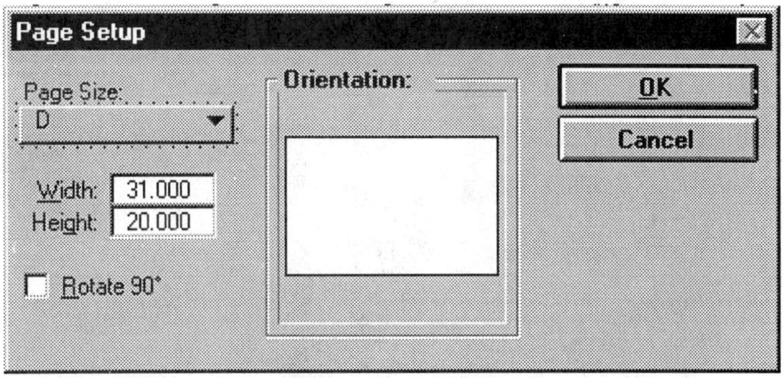

FIGURE P9–2 Page Setup dialog box.

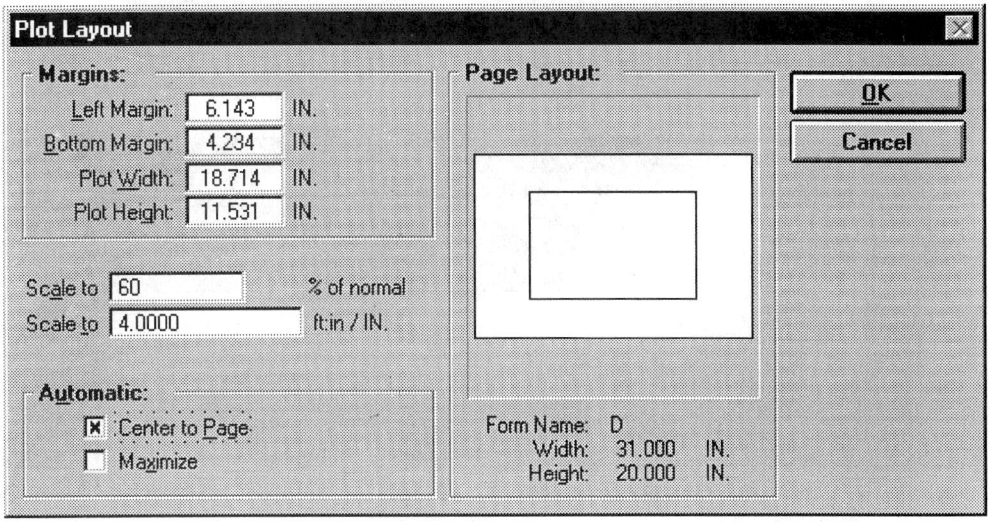

FIGURE P9–3 Plot Layout dialog box.

STEP 6: Invoke the Plot Options tool from the Plot settings tool box and set the toggle button for Plot Border to OFF as shown in Figure P9–4. Click the OK button to close the dialog box.

STEP 7: Invoke the Preview Refresh command from the Plot settings box tool bar to preview the way the design will look on the page (see Figure P9–5).

STEP 8: Submit the plot to the printer/plotter by invoking the Plot command from the Plot settings box tool bar.

NOTE: Leave the Plot settings box open for the next procedure.

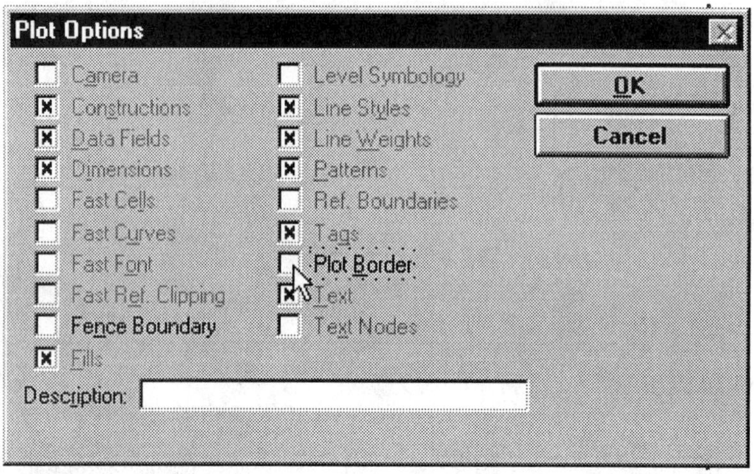

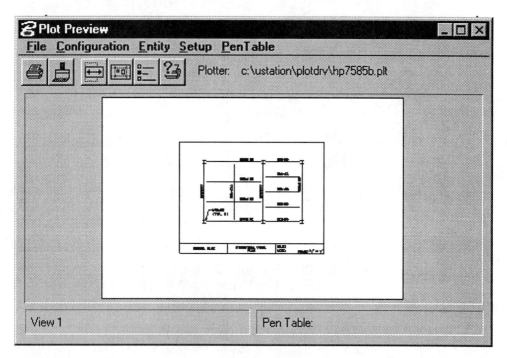

FIGURE P9–4   Plot Options dialog box.

FIGURE P9–5   The Plot settings box with Plot Preview turned on.

Plot the Design Again With All Elements at Weight 0

This procedure uses the Pen Table option to plot the same design with all elements at weight 0.

STEP 1: Invoke the New... command from the pull-down menu PenTable in the Plot settings box.

STEP 2: In the Create Pen Table File window, key in **CH9.TBL** in the Files edit field, then click the OK button. MciroStation displays the Modify Pen Table settings box similar to Figure P9–6.

STEP 3: Click the Output Actions tab. Set the toggle button for Weight to ON and set the Line Weight to 0.

STEP 4: Invoke the Save command from the pull-down menu File in the Modify Pen Table settings box.

STEP 5: Invoke the Preview Refresh command from the Plot settings box tool bar to preview the way the design will look after the modification in the Pen Table settings box.

> **NOTE:** This weight setting is for plotting only. The weight of the elements in the design is unchanged.

STEP 6: Invoke the Plot command from the Plot settings box tool bar to plot the design with all elements at weight 0.

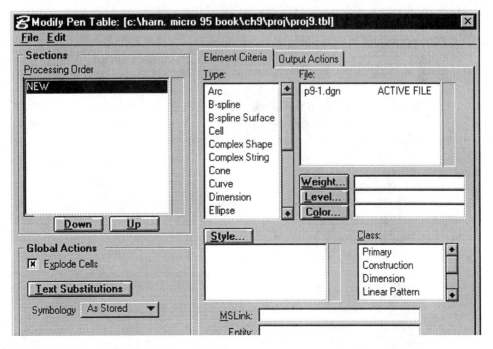

FIGURE P9–6 Modify Pen Table settings box.

DRAWING EXERCISES 9–1 THROUGH 9–5

The following exercises have you create plots of the exercises that were dimensioned in Chapter 8. The requested plot scales are intended to create plots on letter-size (8.5″ × 11″) paper.

- If the printer/plotter you have access to can handle larger sheet sizes, plot at larger scales.
- If the printer/plotter you have access to cannot plot at the recommended scales, reduce the scale by half. For example, if it cannot create a full-scale plot, create a half-scale plot.

Exercise 9–1 Load the design created in Exercise 3–8 (p. 3–77), fit the view, size the view window to minimize the space outside the design area, then plot the view at full scale (1.0000 IN:TH/IN).

Exercise 9–2 Load the design created in Exercise 4–2 (p. 4–28), place a fence by snapping to diagonally opposite corners of the design border, then plot the contents of the fence at full scale (1.0000 IN:TH/IN).

Exercise 9–3 Load the design created in Exercise 8–3 (p. 8–72), place a fence by snapping to diagonally opposite corners of the design border, then plot the contents of the fence at full scale (1.0000 IN:TH/IN).

Exercise 9–4 Load the design created in Exercise 4–5 (p. 4–31), place a fence by snapping to diagonally opposite corners of the design border, then plot the contents of the fence at ¼″ = 1′ (4.0000 ′.″/IN).

Exercise 9–5 Load the design created in Exercise 5–5 (p. 5–55), place a fence by snapping to diagonally opposite corners of the design border, then plot the contents of the fence at ½″ = 1′ (2.0000 ′.″/IN).

10

CELLS AND CELL LIBRARIES

OBJECTIVES

After completing this chapter, you will be able to:

- ✓ Create cell libraries.
- ✓ Attach cell libraries.
- ✓ Create cells.
- ✓ Select active cells.
- ✓ Place cells.
- ✓ Place line terminators.
- ✓ Place point elements, characters, and cells.
- ✓ Maintain cells and cell libraries.
- ✓ Place and maintain shared cells.
- ✓ Use and modify cells from cell selector.

CELLS

Cells are like the variously shaped cutouts in a manual drafting template. You draw standard symbols on paper by tracing the outline of the symbol's cutout in the template. In MicroStation you do the same thing by placing a copy of a cell in your design file. Figure 10–1 shows some common uses of cells in various engineering disciplines.

Even though a cell contains separate elements, the copy you place in a design file acts like a single element when manipulated with commands such as Delete, Rotate, Array, and Mirror. When placing cells, you can change the scale and/or rotation angle of the original object(s). Cells save time by eliminating the need to draw the same thing more than once, and they also promote standardization.

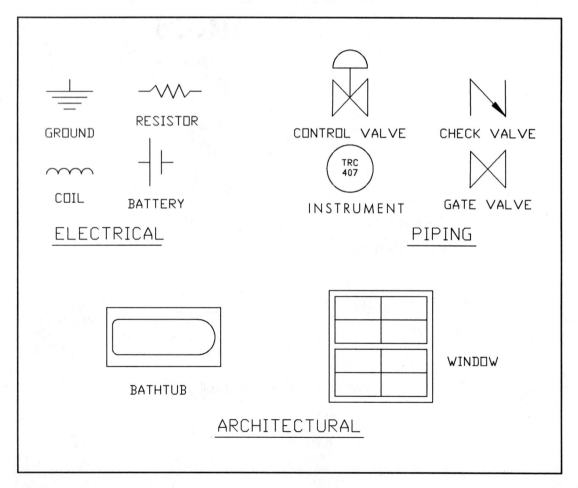

FIGURE 10–1 Common uses of cells in various engineering disciplines.

CELL LIBRARIES

If cells are like the holes in a plastic template, cell libraries are the template. A cell library is a DOS file that holds cells. Most engineering companies that use Micro-Station have several cell libraries to provide standard symbols for all of their design files. Some companies also create sets of cells stored in libraries that they offer for sale.

You can access any of the cells from the cell library and place copies of them in your current design file. If you create a new cell, it is automatically placed in the library that is currently attached to your design file.

You can also place a cell that is not in the attached cell library by keying-in the name of the cell. MicroStation searches for the cell in the cell library list specified by the Cell Library List configuration variable (MS_CELLIST). (Refer to Chapter 15 for how to set up the configuration variables.) Cell libraries are searched in their order in the list. If wild-card characters are involved, cell libraries are searched in alphabetical order.

Although there is no limit to the number of cells you can store in a library, you don't want to end up with a very large, hard-to-manage library. It is advisable to create separate cell libraries for specific disciplines, such as electrical fixtures, plumbing, HVAC, and so on.

Creating a New Cell Library

To start the process of creating a new cell library, invoke the Cell Library settings box from:

Pull-down menu	Element > Cells (or **⌨ALT** + **L, C** [see Figure 10–2]).
Key-in window	**Dialog Cell maintenance** (or **di ce**) **ENTER**

A settings box appears similar to the one shown in Figure 10–3.

To create a new cell library file, open the Create Cell Library dialog box from:

Pull-down menu in the Cell Library settings box	File > New

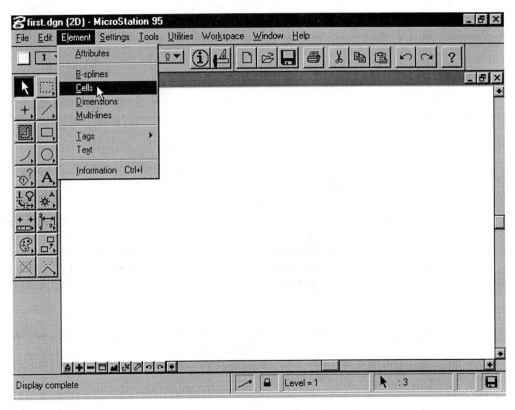

FIGURE 10-2 Invoking the Cell Library settings box from the pull-down menu Element.

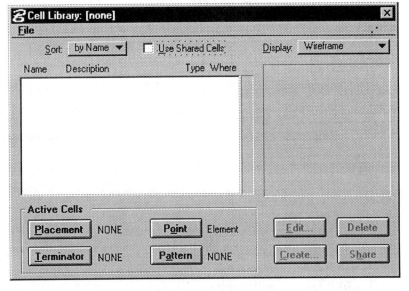

FIGURE 10-3 Cell Library settings box.

MicroStation displays the Create Cell Library dialog box, as shown in Figure 10–4.

Following are the steps to create a new cell library file.

1. Check the Seed File specification at the bottom of the dialog box. It should be:
    - SEED2D.CEL for a 2-dimensional design.
    - SEED3D.CEL for a 3-dimensional design.
2. If necessary, you can change the seed file. Click the Select button to open the dialog box for selecting a seed file, and select the appropriate seed file.
3. Key-in the name of the file (from one to eight characters) for the new library in the Name edit field. Do *not* type a period or extension. MicroStation appends the ".CEL" extension to the file name.
4. Click the OK button to create the new cell library and to close the Create Cell Library dialog box.

> **NOTE:** Before you close the dialog box, make sure the cell library file is created in the appropriate directory. If it isn't, find and select the appropriate directory from the Directories list before you key-in the file name.

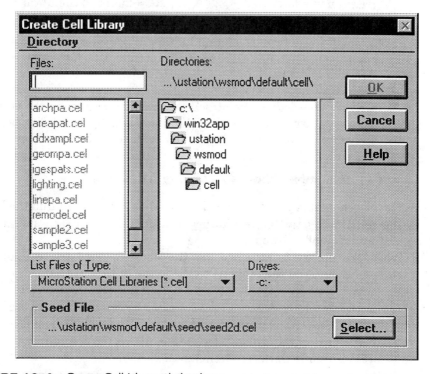

FIGURE 10–4 Create Cell Library dialog box.

When you create a new cell library, MicroStation automatically attaches it to your current design file and acknowledges the attachment with a message in the Status bar.

Your cell library is now available for use. You can start creating cells to store in your new library.

Attaching an Existing Cell Library

To start the process of attaching an existing cell library file to the active design file, first invoke the Cell Library settings box from:

| Pull-down menu | Element > Cells (or [ALT] + L, C) |

To attach the cell library file, open the Attach Cell Library dialog box from:

| Pull-down menu in the Cell Library settings window | File > Attach |
| Key-in window | RC=<name of the library> [ENTER] |

MicroStation displays the Attach Cell Library dialog box. Select the appropriate cell library from the file list, and click the OK button to attach the library and close the Attach Cell Library dialog box.

MicroStation acknowledges the attachment with a message in the status bar. Once the cell library is attached, the Cell List in the Cell Library settings box displays the names and descriptions of the cells, similar to the one shown in Figure 10–5.

Things to Remember About Cell Library Attachment

- The attachment is permanent as long as MicroStation can find the library file.
- You can attach only one cell library at a time. If you attach another library, the first attachment is dropped.
- When the library is attached, all the library's cells are available to you for placement, and you can store new cells in the library as well.

> **NOTE:** The new cells you create are stored only in the cell library that is attached to the current design file, not in the cell libraries that are attached through the environmental variable.

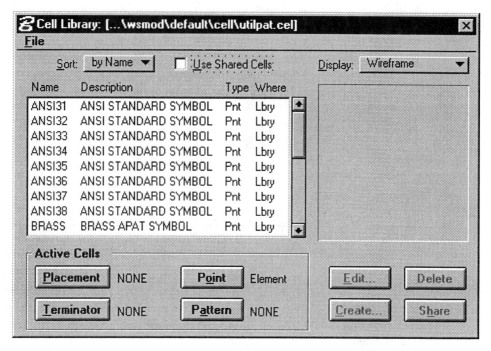

FIGURE 10–5   Listing of the cell names and descriptions in the Cell Library settings box.

CREATING YOUR OWN CELLS

When you need to place copies of a symbol for which no cell currently exists, you can create your own cell (symbol), store it in the library, then use it in any design file.

Before You Start

Here are a few things to consider before starting to draw the elements that will make up your cell.

Working Units   The Working Units in the design file you use to create the cell should be the same as the Working Units of the design files in which you plan to place copies of the cell. If the Working Units are different, you may have to scale the cell every time you place it.

Cell Elements   There are no restrictions on the elements that make up the cell. All element types can be placed in a cell; they can be drawn on any level; and they can be any color, weight, or style. The elements you draw do not become a cell. The cell is made by copying your elements into the attached cell library. After you create your cell, you may delete the original elements from the design file.

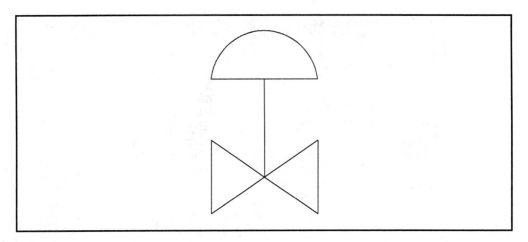

FIGURE 10-6 *Example of a symbol drawn upright and facing to the right.*

Cell Rotation Always draw the object you are going to make into a cell with 0 degrees of rotation. That means it should be upright and facing to the right (see Figure 10–6). Sticking with 0 rotation for cells makes it easier to understand what happens to the cell when it is rotated.

Cell Origin Cells are placed by defining the cell's origin point in the design. This origin point is created during the process of creating the cell. Care must be given to selecting exactly where in the cell elements to create the origin. If the cell is to be placed connected to other elements, place the origin point at the connection point. For instance, if the cell is a control valve, place the origin where the valve is to be attached to the pipeline, as shown in Figure 10–7.

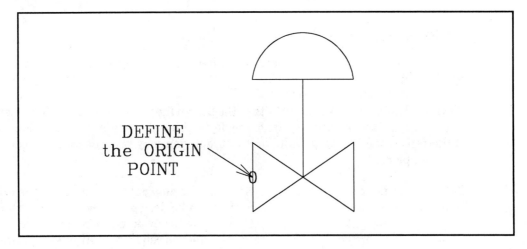

FIGURE 10-7 *Example of defining a cell origin.*

Steps for Creating a Cell

Following are the steps to create a new cell.

STEP 1:   Draw the elements.

STEP 2:   Group the elements by one of these two methods:

- Invoke the Element Selection tool and drag and select the elements.
- Place a fence around the elements and set the fence mode to Inside.

STEP 3:   Define the cell's origin point by invoking the Define Cell Origin command from:

Cells tool box	Select the Define Cell Origin tool (see Figure 10–8).
Key-in window	**Define Cell Origin (or de c o)** ⏎

MicroStation prompts:

Define Cell Origin *(Place a data point where the origin is to be located. Snap, if necessary, to place the point precisely.)*

> **NOTE:** If you accidentally set the origin point in the wrong place, just place another one. The cell will be created using the last point. The letter "O" appears at each origin placement point. The "O" is not an element; it only indicates that an origin has been placed.

STEP 4:   Click the Create button located in the bottom right corner of the Cell Library settings box. MicroStation displays the Create New Cell dialog box, similar to the one shown in Figure 10–9.

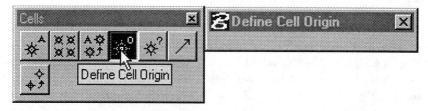

FIGURE 10–8   Invoking the Define Cell Origin command from the Cells tool box.

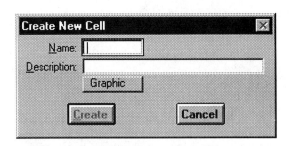

FIGURE 10–9 Create New Cell dialog box.

STEP 5: Click in the Name field in the Create New Cell dialog box, and enter a name for your cell (don't press ⟦ENTER⟧). You must provide a one- to six-character alphanumeric name for your cell. In addition to letters and numbers, the name can contain dashes (-) and underscores (_) but not spaces. Help out other people who will have to use your cells by creating descriptive cell names (as best as you can in six characters).

Good Examples: PNP is a good name for a cell that provides a PNP transistor. If the cell provides a globe valve symbol, a good name might be GLBVAL.

Bad Examples: CELL-1 is a legal cell name but does not provide any information about the intended use of the cell. GLOBE-VALVE is an unacceptable cell name because it contains too many characters.

STEP 6: Click on the Description field, an optional field, and enter a 1- to 27-character description for your cell. It describes the cell's purpose. Take the time to provide a description for every cell you create. If your cell libraries contain lots of cells, the descriptions will help other users figure out the purpose you intended for the cell. It will also help you when you go back to the cell library after being away from it for a few weeks.

STEP 7: Select the appropriate cell type from the option menu. Cells that can be placed in a design come in two types—Graphic and Point. The default cell type is Graphic. In the next section we will discuss the difference between the two types and how to specify which type to create.

STEP 8: Click the Create button.

When you complete the procedure, the fenced elements are copied to the attached cell library, and your new cell appears in the cells list area of the Cell Library settings box (see Figure 10–10). In addition to the cell name, the cells list displays the cell description, type, and location. The cell is available for placement in the current design file and in any other design files to which your cell library is attached.

Refer to Figure 10–11 to review the steps for the creation of a cell.

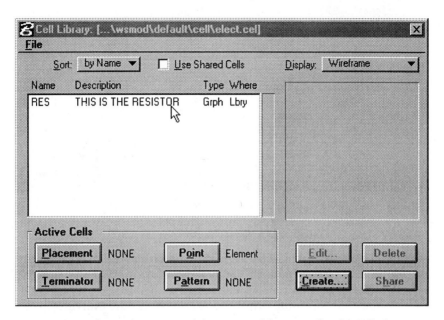

FIGURE 10–10   Displaying the name and description of the new cell in the Cell Library settings box.

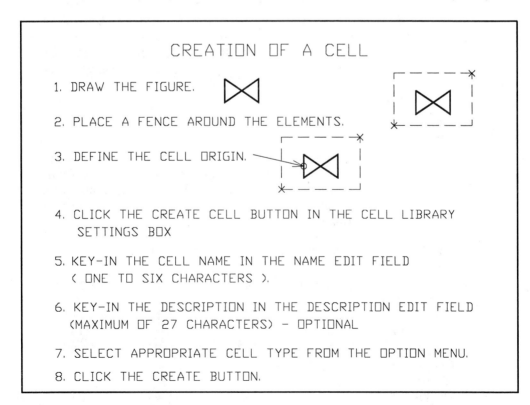

CREATION OF A CELL

1. DRAW THE FIGURE.

2. PLACE A FENCE AROUND THE ELEMENTS.

3. DEFINE THE CELL ORIGIN.

4. CLICK THE CREATE CELL BUTTON IN THE CELL LIBRARY
   SETTINGS BOX

5. KEY-IN THE CELL NAME IN THE NAME EDIT FIELD
   (ONE TO SIX CHARACTERS).

6. KEY-IN THE DESCRIPTION IN THE DESCRIPTION EDIT FIELD
   (MAXIMUM OF 27 CHARACTERS) - OPTIONAL

7. SELECT APPROPRIATE CELL TYPE FROM THE OPTION MENU.

8. CLICK THE CREATE BUTTON.

FIGURE 10–11   Review of the steps for creating a cell.

Graphic and Point Cell Types

As just mentioned, two cell types, Graphic and Point, can be placed in your design. The default cell type is Graphic (also called Normal). Here are the differences between Graphic and Point cells.

A Graphic cell, when placed in a design file:

- Keeps the symbology (color, weight, and style) of its elements.
- Remembers the levels on which its elements were drawn. (MicroStation provides two methods for placing the cells—Absolute and Relative modes, discussed in detail later in the chapter.)
- Retains the keypoints of each cell element.

A Point cell, when placed in a design file:

- Takes on the current active symbology settings (color, weight, and style).
- Places all cell elements on the current active level, regardless of what level they were drawn on.
- Has only one keypoint—the cell's origin point. The individual cell elements do not have keypoints.

Selecting the Cell Type You can select either Graphic or Point cell type from the Create New Cell dialog box option menu when you provide the cell's name and description. The option menu has four cell types. The other two, Menu and Tutorial, do not create cells that can be placed in your design file. They are for customizing the way you use MicroStation and are beyond the scope of this book.

ACTIVE CELLS

To place a copy of a cell in your current design file, you must first make the cell the active placement cell. This is done by clicking on the cell name from the cell list provided in the Cell Library settings box and clicking one of the four buttons provided under Active Cell. The four types of active cells give you the freedom to place the cell under varying conditions in your design file.

- The active placement cell is used with a group of commands that place cells at a data point.
- The active line terminator cell is used with a tool that places a cell on the end of an element.
- The active point cell is used with a group of commands that place cells in geometric relation to other elements.
- The active pattern cell is used with a group of commands that create patterns in a closed shape.

Active placement, active terminator, and active point cells are explained in detail in this chapter. Active pattern cells are explained in Chapter 11.

Alternate Methods You also can use key-in to select an active cell for each type of cell placement. At the key-in window, type:

AC=<name> *and press* ⏎ *to select the active placement cell.*
LT=<name> *and press* ⏎ *to select the active terminator cell.*
PT=<name> *and press* ⏎ *to select the active point cell.*
AP=<name> *and press* ⏎ *to select the active pattern cell.*

In each command, replace <name> with the name of the cell you want to use.

Example: **AC=COIL** ⏎

Several cell placement commands provide a cell name field in the Tool Settings window. You can also select the active cell by keying-in its name in this field.

Active Placement Cell

Four commands are provided to place the active placement cell at data points in your design file. The commands are as follows:

- Place Active Cell—Places copies of the active placement cell at data points you specify. The cell is placed at the active angle and active scale.
- Place Active Cell (Interactive)—Places copies of the active placement cell interactively and allows you graphically to specify the cell rotation and scale.
- Select and Place Active Cell—Lets you select a cell already placed in your design file to be the active placement cell, then places copies at the data points you specify.
- Place Active Cell Matrix—Places a rectangular matrix (rectangular array) of the active placement cell, with the lower left corner of the matrix at the data point you specify.

Invoke the Place Active Cell command from:

Cells tool box	Select the Place Active Cell tool (see Figure 10–12).
Key-in window	**Place Cell Icon** (or **pla ce ic**) ⏎

MicroStation prompts:

Place Active Cell > Enter cell origin *(Define the origin point at each location where a copy of the cell is to be placed.)*

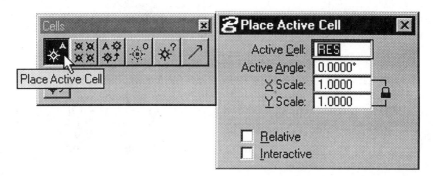

FIGURE 10–12 Invoking the Place Active Cell command from the Cells tool box.

Each time you place a data point, a copy of the cell is placed such that its origin is at your data point. While this command is active, the screen cursor drags a dynamic image of the cell enclosed in a box. The cell's origin point is at the screen cursor position.

> **NOTE:** If you do not have an active cell and invoke the Place Active Cell command, MicroStation displays the message *No Active Cell* in the Status bar. You must declare an active cell before you can use this command (discussed earlier in this section).

The Place Active Cell command places the active cell at the current active angle and active scale. Change the angle and scale any time while you are using the command, and the next cell copy you place will use your new angle and scale settings. This feature allows you to place the active cell rotated and scaled all in one operation.

Change the angle and scale by keying-in the values in the Tool Settings box. In addition to the edit boxes provided in the Tool Settings window when you invoke the Place Active Cell tool, two toggle buttons are provided. One is for relative placement of the cell, the other for interactive placement of the cell.

Placing Graphic Cell in Absolute or Relative Mode MicroStation allows you to place graphic cells in Absolute or Relative mode when you use the Place Active Cell or Select and Place Active Cell commands. (The Select and Place Active Cell command is explained later in this chapter.) The default placement mode for each command is Absolute. To place cells in Relative mode, turn ON the toggle button Relative in the Tool Settings window.

In **Absolute** placement mode, the graphic cell's elements are placed on the levels on which they were drawn originally, regardless of the active level setting. For example, if a graphic cell contains elements on levels 1 and 3, they are placed in the design file on levels 1 and 3 (see Figure 10–13a).

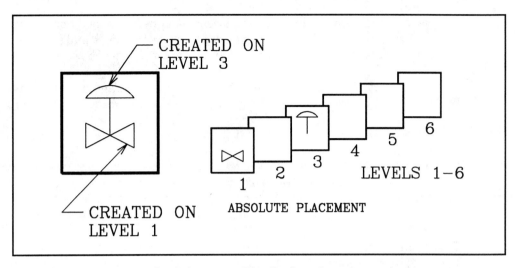

FIGURE 10–13a Example of placing a cell by Absolute placement mode.

In **Relative** placement mode, the graphic cell element on the lowest level is placed on the active level and all other cell levels are shifted by the same amount as the lowest level. For example, if the graphic cell with elements on levels 1 and 3 is placed in Relative mode, and the active level is 4, the cell elements on level 1 are moved to level 4 and the cell elements on level 3 are moved to level 6 (4 + 2 = 6) (see Figure 10–13b).

If you want to place a graphic cell by Relative mode, make sure the toggle button is turned ON for Relative mode.

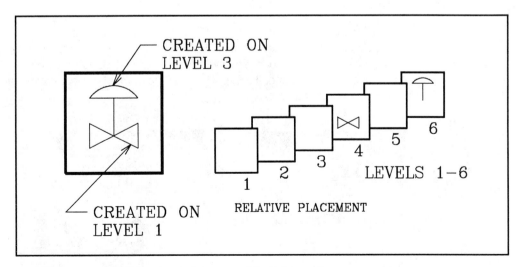

FIGURE 10–13b Example of placing a cell by Relative placement mode.

Interactive Placement Interactive placement is helpful when you need to align your cell with existing elements but you don't know what angle and scale to make it. You define the angle and scale graphically as you place the cell.

To place the active cell interactively, turn ON the toggle button for Interactive in the Tool Settings window. When a cell is placed interactively, MicroStation prompts:

> Place Active Cell (Interactive) > Enter cell origin *(Define the origin point of the cell.)*
> Place Active Cell (Interactive) > Enter scale or corner point *(Either place a data point to scale the cell or key-in the scale factor in the key-in window.)*
> Place Active Cell (Interactive) > Enter rotation angle or point *(Either place a data point to rotate the cell or key-in the rotation angle in the key-in window.)*

Select and Place Cell Often, when working in an existing design, you will need to place additional copies of a cell that was placed earlier but is no longer your active placement cell. The Select and Place Cell command allows you to select that cell for placement simply by clicking on a copy of the cell in the design plane. The cell you click becomes the active placement cell, and dynamic update shows it at the screen pointer position. Additional data points place copies of the cell.

Invoke the Select and Place Cell command from:

Cells tool box	Select the Select and Place Cell tool (see Figure 10–14).
Key-in window	**Select Cell Icon (or sele c i)** ⏎

MicroStation prompts:

> Select and Place Cell > Identify element *(Select the cell to be copied.)*
> Select and Place Cell > Accept/Reject (Select next input) *(Accept the cell by placing a data point at the location where the first copy is to be placed.)*
> Select and Place Cell > Enter cell origin *(Place a data point at the location of each additional copy of the cell.)*

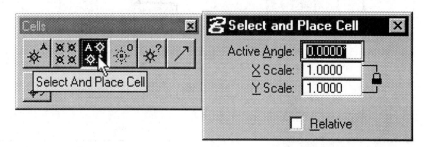

FIGURE 10–14 Invoking the Select and Place Cell command from the Cells tool box.

The Select and Place Cell command places the active cell at the active angle and scale, just as the Place Active Cell command did. Set the angle and scale in the Tool Settings window.

> ***NOTE:*** Similar to the Place Active Cell command, you can place the cell in Relative mode by toggling the Relative button to ON.

When you click on a cell in your design file, MicroStation checks to make sure it is actually a cell. When you click the second time to indicate where you want to place a copy of the cell, MicroStation checks to see if the cell is in the currently attached cell library. If the cell is not in the currently attached library, MicroStation displays the message *Cell not found* in the Status bar and waits for you to select another cell.

Place Active Cell Matrix Do you need to place two rectangular rows of electronic components in a circuit diagram? The Place Active Cell Matrix command can do it for you. With this command, you can place the active cell quickly in a rectangular matrix whose parameters you define (see Figure 10–15).

The Place Active Cell Matrix command requires five parameters:

- Active Cell: The active cell name
- Rows: The number of rows in the matrix
- Columns: The number of columns in the matrix
- Row Spacing: The space, in Working Units, between the rows
- Column Spacing: The space, in Working Units, between the columns

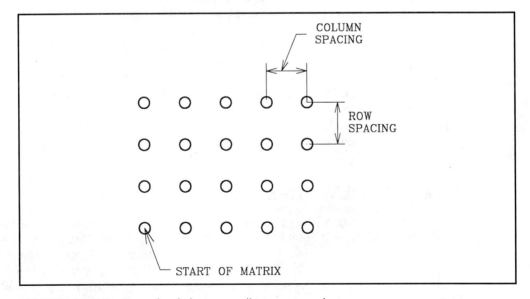

FIGURE 10–15 Example of placing a cell in a rectangular array.

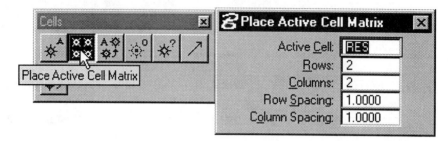

FIGURE 10–16 Invoking the Place Active Cell Matrix command from the Cells tool box.

The row and column spacing is from origin point to origin point. It is not the distance between the cells.

Invoke the Place Active Cell Matrix command from:

Cells tool box	Select the Place Active Cell Matrix tool (see Figure 10–16), then set the matrix parameters in the Tool Settings window.
Key-in window	**Matrix Cell** (or **matr c**)

MicroStation prompts:

Place Active Cell Matrix > Enter lower left corner of matrix *(Place a data point to define the origin location of the cell in the lower left corner.)*

The data point you place to start the matrix designates the position of the origin of the lower left cell in the matrix (see Figure 10–15).

The Place Active Cell Matrix command places each cell in the matrix at the active angle and active scale. The edit fields available in the Tool Settings window for this command do not include angle and scale fields. You have to use the settings boxes available from the pull-down menu Settings or key-in the active angle and active scale.

Place Active Line Terminator

There will be occasions when you want to place a cell (such as an arrowhead) at the end of a line and have it rotated to match the line's rotation. This can be done by invoking the Place Active Line Terminator command. It places the active terminator cell at the end of the element you select and automatically rotates it to match the rotation of the element at the point of connection. See Figure 10–17 for examples of placing line terminators.

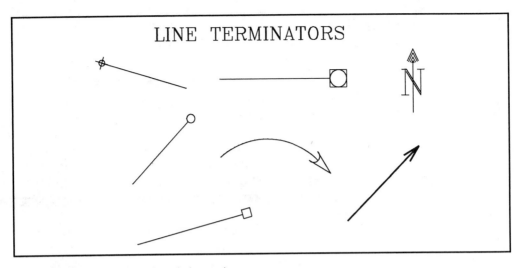

FIGURE 10–17   Examples of placing line terminators.

Invoke the Place Active Line Terminator command from:

Cells tool box	Select the Place Active Line Terminator tool (see Figure 10–18), and, optionally, enter the terminator cell name in the Tool Settings window.
Key-in window	**Place Terminator** (or **pla ter**) (ENTER)

MicroStation prompts:

> Place Active Line Terminator > Identify element *(Select the element near the end where the terminator is to be placed.)*
> Place Active Line Terminator > Accept/Reject (Select next input) *(Click the Data button again to place the terminator, and, optionally, select another element to place a terminator.)*

If your second data point does not identify another element, MicroStation displays the message *Element not found* in the Status bar. Ignore the message.

FIGURE 10–18   Invoking the Place Active Line Terminator command from the Cells tool box.

> **NOTE:** If you do not have an active cell and invoke the Place Active Line Terminator command, MicroStation displays the message *No Active Cell* in the Status bar.

> **NOTE:** Beginning users of MicroStation often select the element to place a terminator by first snapping to the element with the Tentative button. That is not necessary, because MicroStation finds the end of the element automatically. Just place a data point near the end point on which you want to place the terminator.

Terminator Scale The Place Active Line Terminator command has its own scale factor. If the scale factor is:

- Greater than 1, the cell is scaled up.
- Equal to 1, the cell is placed at its true size.
- Less than 1, the cell is scaled down.

The scale is set in the Tool Settings window. You can change the terminator scale as often as necessary while placing terminator cells. Each time you change it, the next terminator cell you place is scaled to your new factor.

> **NOTE:** The Place Active Line Terminator command does not use the active angle. It rotates the cell as necessary to match the rotation of the element it terminates.

Point Placement

MicroStation provides six point commands that place a dot, character, or cell in your design file. The six commands are

Place Active Point—Places a single point at the data point you specify.

Construct Points Between Data Points—Places a set of equally spaced points between two data points.

Project Point Onto Element—Places a point on an element at the point on the element nearest to a data point.

Construct Point at Intersection—Places a point at the intersection of two elements.

Construct Points Along Element—Places a set of equally spaced points along an element between two data points on the element.

Construct Point at @Dist Along Element—Places one point at a predefined distance along an element from a data point.

Types of Points Before you use any of the point commands, you must set the type of point you want to place. An options menu allows you to select the type of point; two edit fields for providing corresponding information are provided in the Tool Settings window, shown in Figure 10–19. The available point types are as follows.

Element—Places dots (0-length lines). To make these dots more noticeable, increase the active line weight before placing them.

Character—Places a text character in the currently active font. If a symbol font is active, the character point will be a symbol. Font characters are placed at the active angle of rotation. Key-in the appropriate character in the Character edit field located in the Tool Settings window.

Cell—Places the currently active point cell as the point. Point cells are placed at the active angle and active scale. Key-in the appropriate cell name in the Cell edit field located in the Tool Settings window.

You can also select a cell as the active point from the Cell Library settings box. To do so:

1. Open the Cell Library settings box from the pull-down menu Element.
2. Find the cell you want in the Cell List and highlight it by clicking with the Data button.
3. Click on the Point button (located on the bottom left of the settings box).

> **NOTE:** Don't confuse using a cell as the active point with point and graphic cells. You can make either a point or a graphic cell the active point cell. The Point commands place graphic cells in the Absolute mode only.

Place Active Point Invoke the Place Active Point command from:

Points tool box	Select the Place Active Point tool (see Figure 10–19).
Key-in window	**Place Point (or pla po)** ⏎

FIGURE 10–19 Invoking the Place Active Point command from the Points tool box.

MicroStation prompts:

> Place Active Point > Enter point origin *(Place a data point.)*

You can place any number of points in one command sequence. Press the Reset button to terminate the command sequence.

Construct Points Between Data Points The Construct Points Between Data Points command will place a specified number of points (element, character, or cell) between two data points. The number of points placed includes the two placed on your data points.

Invoke the Construct Points Between Data Points command from:

Points tool box	Select the Construct Points Between Data Points tool (see Figure 10–20).
Key-in window	**Construct Points Between** (or **constru po b**) [ENTER]

MicroStation prompts:

> Construct Pnts Between Data Points > Enter first point *(Place a data point to define the location of the first point in the series.)*
> Construct Pnts Between Data Points > Enter end point *(Place a data point to define the location of the last point in the series.)*

After you place the first set of points, you can continue placing additional sets. Each set will use the last data point of the previous set as its starting point. To start over with a first data point again, click the Reset button on your pointing device. See Figure 10–21 for an example of placing 10 points between two data points.

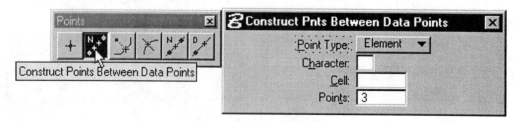

FIGURE 10–20   Invoking the Construct Points Between Data Points command from the Points tool box.

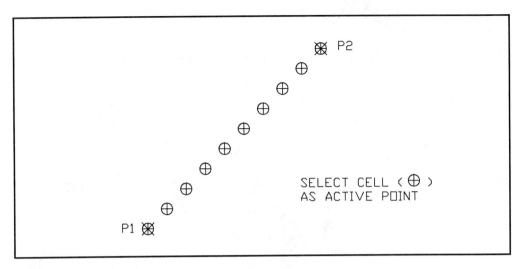

FIGURE 10–21 Example of placing 10 points between two data points.

Project Point Onto Element The Project Point Onto Element command places the active point (element, character, or cell) on the selected element at the point projected from the acceptance data point.

Invoke the Project Point Onto Element command from:

Points tool box	Select the Project Point Onto Element tool (see Figure 10–22).
Key-in window	**Construct Point Project** (or **constru po p**) [ENTER]

MicroStation prompts:

> Construct Active Point Onto Element > Identify element *(Select the element.)*
> Construct Active Point Onto Element > Accept/Reject (Select next input) *(Select the point in the design from which to project the point, and, optionally, select the next element to which a point is to be projected.)*

FIGURE 10–22 Invoking the Project Point Onto Element command from the Points tool box.

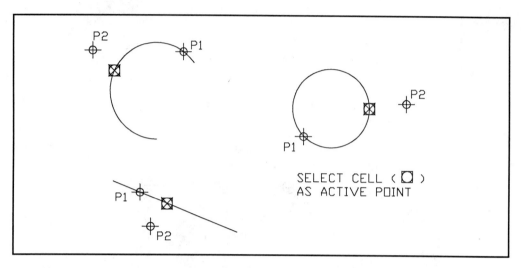

FIGURE 10–23 Example of placing an active point projected onto an element.

If your accept Data button does not identify another element, MicroStation displays the message *Element not found* in the Status bar. Ignore the message. See Figure 10–23 for an example of how to place an active point projected onto an element.

> **NOTE:** The only purpose of the first data point is to identify the element to which the projection will be made. There is no need to use the Tentative button when identifying the element. The second data point is the one that may need precise placement.

Construct Point at Intersection The Construct Point at Intersection command places an active point (element, character, or cell) at the intersection of two elements.

Invoke the Construct Point at Intersection command from:

Points tool box	Select the Construct Point at Intersection tool (see Figure 10–24).
Key-in window	**Construct Point Intersection (or constru po i)** [ENTER]

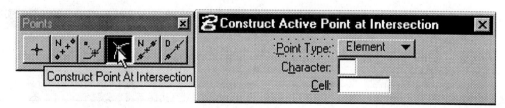

FIGURE 10–24 Invoking the Construct Point at Intersection command from the Points tool box.

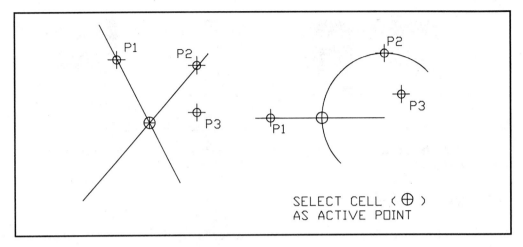

FIGURE 10–25 Example of placing an active point at an intersection of two elements.

MicroStation prompts:

> Construct Active Point at Intersection > Select element for intersection *(Select one of the elements.)*
>
> Construct Active Point at Intersection > Select element for intersection *(Select the other element.)*
>
> Construct Active Point at Intersection > Accept - Initiate intersection *(Place a data point to place the point.)*

The acceptance data point only initiates placement of the point; it does not identify another element. See Figure 10–25 for an example of how to place an active point at an intersection of two elements.

> **NOTE:** If the two elements intersect more than once (such as a line crossing a circle), identify the two elements close to the intersection where you want the point to be placed. There is no need to use the Tentative button. Just place the Data button close to the intersection.

Construct Points Along Element The Construct Points Along Element command places a set of active points (elements, characters, or cells) equally spaced along an element between two data points on the element.

Invoke the Construct Points Along Element command from:

Points tool box	Select the Construct Points Along Element tool (see Figure 10–26).
Key-in window	**Construct Point Along** (or **constru po a)** [ENTER]

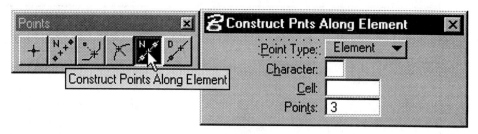

FIGURE 10–26 Invoking the Construct Points Along Element command from the Points tool box.

MicroStation prompts:

> Construct Pnts Along Element > Enter first point *(Select the element at the location where the first point is to be placed.)*
> Construct Pnts Along Element > Enter end point *(Define the location on the element where the last point is to be placed, and the points are placed.)*

You can continue placing points along elements, and, if necesssary, you can also change the active point at any time while placing them. See Figure 10–27 for an example of how to place 10 points along an element between two data points.

Construct Point at @Distance Along Element The Construct Point at @Distance Along Element command places the active point (element, character, or cell) at a keyed-in distance along an element from the data point that identified the element.

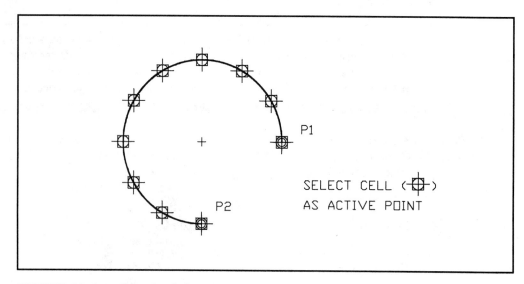

FIGURE 10–27 Example of placing 10 points along an element between two data points.

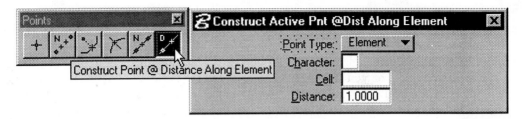

FIGURE 10–28 Invoking the Construct Point at @Distance Along Element command from the Points tool box.

Invoke the Construct Point @Distance Along Element command from:

Points tool box	Select the Construct Point @Distance Along Element tool (see Figure 10–28).
Key-in window	**Construct Point Distance** (or **constru po d)** ⏎

MicroStation prompts:

> Construct Active Pnt @ Dist Along Element > Identify element *(Identify the element.)*
> Construct Active Pnt @ Dist Along Element > Accept/Reject (Select next input)
> *(Place a data point to accept the construction, and, optionally, select the next element for construction.)*

You can continue selecting elements along which you want to place a point, and you can change the distance at any time while using the command. See Figure 10–29 for an example of how to place a point at a specified distance along an element.

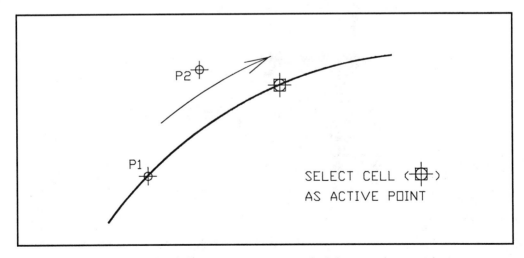

FIGURE 10–29 Example of placing a point at a specified distance along an element.

CELL SELECTOR

As mentioned earlier, MicroStation allows you to place cells by invoking one of the available Place Cell tools and selecting the appropriate cell from the Cell Library settings box, or you can key-in the name of the cell in the Tool Settings window. In addition, you can also place cells by selecting the appropriate cell from the Cell Selector settings box. The Cell Selector settings box shows thumbnail representations of the cells stored in a cell library.

Opening the Cell Selector Settings Box

Open the Cell Selector settings box from:

Pull-down menu	Utilities > Cell Selector (or ⌨ + **U, S**)

MicroStation displays a Cell Selector settings box, as shown in Figure 10–30. If a cell library is already attached to the current design file, MicroStation displays thumbnail representations of the cells stored in the library, as shown in Figure 10–30.

If you have not already attached a cell library to the current design file when you open the Cell Selector settings box, MicroStation opens the Select Cell Library dialog box. Select the cell library file you want to attach to the current design file from the Files list box, and click the OK button to close the dialog box. MicroStation displays thumbnail representations of the cells stored in the attached library.

Clicking a cell thumbnail button in the Cell Selector settings box has the effect of activating the associated cell and selecting the Place Active Cell tool.

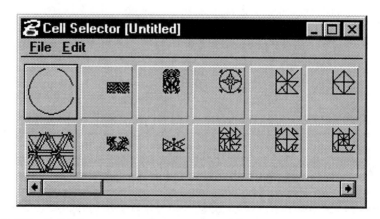

FIGURE 10–30 Cell Selector settings box.

Customizing the Button Configuration

The settings box is resizable and can be customized with buttons for cells from different cell libraries. Each button can be set to display either the associated cell thumbnail representation or the cell name, and it can be associated with a key-in, which is activated when the button is clicked.

MicroStation allows you to save the button configuration to a cell selector file with a file extension of .CSF. The cell selector files contain each button's configuration information and the size and number of buttons in the configuration.

By default, MicroStation loads the button configuration set by the system variable MS_CELLSELECTOR. If the system variable is not defined, then the cells from the attached library are loaded in the Cell Selector settings box. If neither condition is met, then MicroStation displays a dialog box for selecting a cell library when you open the Cell Selector settings box.

Assigning a File Name To assign a file name to the current button configuration, invoke the New command from:

Pull-down menu from Cell Selector settings box	File > New ... (or [ALT] + **F, N**)

MicroStation displays the Define Cell Selector File dialog box. Key-in the name of the file to assign a file name to the current button configuration.

Saving the Current Configuration To save the current button configuration, invoke the Save command from:

Pull-down menu from Cell Selector settings box	File > Save (or [ALT] + **F, S**)

MicroStation saves the current button configuration to the given file name.

Opening the Previously Saved Configuration To open the previously saved button configuration, invoke the Open command from:

Pull-down menu from Cell Selector settings box	File > Open... (or [ALT] + **F, O**)

MicroStation displays the Select Cell Selector File dialog box. Select the appropriate file name from the Files list box to open the previously saved cell selector configuration file.

Saving the Current Configuration to a New Cell Selector File To save the current button configuration to a new cell selector file, invoke the Save As command from:

Pull-down menu from Cell Selector settings box	File > Save As... (or [ALT] + **F, A**)

MicroStation displays the Save Cell Selector File dialog box. Key-in the name of the file to save the current button configuration.

Adding Buttons from Other Cell Libraries As mentioned earlier, Cell Selector settings box displays the thumbnail representations of the cells stored in a cell library. MicroStation allows you to open additional cell libraries from the Cell Selector settings box and load the buttons with additional cells. In other words, MicroStation allows you to display the cells from various cell libraries in the Cell Selector settings box, and you can select any of the cell buttons to place a cell in your current design file. To load additional cell libraries, invoke the Load Cell Library command from:

Pull-down menu from Cell Selector settings box	File > Load Cell Library... (or [ALT] + **F, L**)

MicroStation displays the Select Cell Library to Load dialog box. Select the appropriate file name from the Files list box to load the cell library into the current button configuration.

Editing Button Settings

To edit one of the button settings, click the appropriate button in the Cell Selector settings box, and then invoke the button tool from:

Pull-down menu from Cell Selector settings box	Edit > Button (or [CTRL] + **B**)

MicroStation displays the Configure Cell Selection Button settings box, as shown in Figure 10–31.

> **NOTE:** You can also edit the button configuration by double-clicking the button in the Cell Selector settings box. MicroStation displays the Configure Cell Selection Button settings box.

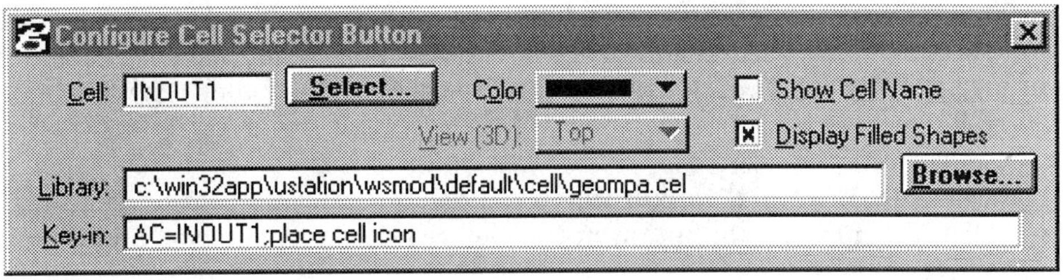

FIGURE 10–31   Configure Cell Selection Button settings box.

- The **Cell** edit field displays the cell name of the selected button. If necessary, you can change the cell name by selecting a different name from the Select Cell settings dialog box displayed when you click the Select... button.
- The **Color** option menu allows you to select a different color for the display of the thumbnail representation of the cell.
- The toggle button for **Show Cell Name** controls the display of the cell name on the button instead of the thumbnail representation.
- The toggle button for **Display Filled Shapes** controls the display of the filled shapes on the button.
- The **Library** edit field displays the name of the cell library associated with the selected button. If necessary, you can change the cell library by selecting a different name from the Select Cell Library dialog box displayed when you click the Select... button.
- The **Key-in** edit field shows the key-in associated with the cell to be inserted. You can key-in multiple key-ins separated by a semi-colon (;). This field can contain up to 511 characters.

Inserting a New Button   To insert a new button after the button that has the focus, invoke the Insert command from:

Pull-down menu from Cell Selector settings box	Edit > Insert... (or [CTRL] + **V**)

MicroStation displays the Define Button settings box, as shown in Figure 10–32.

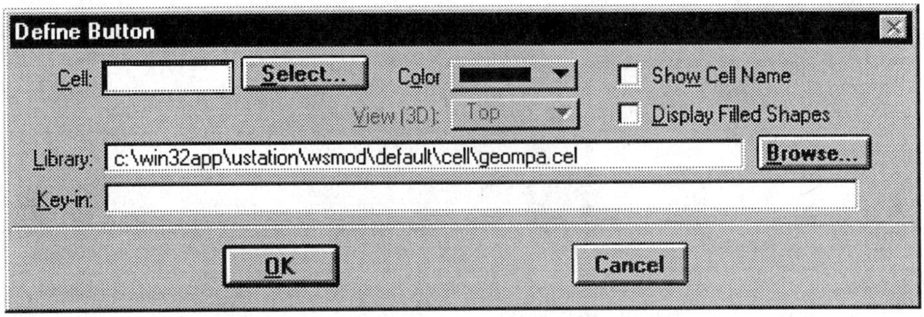

FIGURE 10–32   Define Button settings box.

Key-in or select the appropriate cell library and the cell to define the selected button. Type the associated key-in in the key-in edit field. Click the OK button to configure the new button, or click the Cancel button to close the dialog box without configuring the new button.

Deleting Button Configurations To delete the configuration of a single button, click the appropriate button in the Cell Selector settings box, and then invoke the Delete tool from:

| Pull-down menu from
Cell Selector settings box | Edit > Delete (or **CTRL** + **X**) |

MicroStation deletes the configuration of the selected button.

To clear the configuration for all buttons, invoke the Clear Configuration command from:

| Pull-down menu from
Cell Selector settings box | Edit > Clear Configuration (or
ALT + **E, C**) |

MicroStation clears the configuration for all buttons in the Cell Selector settings box.

Changing Button and Gap Size To change the size of the buttons in pixels, invoke the Button Size command from:

| Pull-down menu from
Cell Selector settings box | Edit > Button Size... (or
ALT + **E, S**) |

MicroStation displays the Define Button Size dialog box, as shown in Figure 10–33.

The Button Size and Gap Size edit fields set the size (in pixels) of the button and of the gap between the buttons, respectively.

FIGURE 10–33 Define Button Size dialog box.

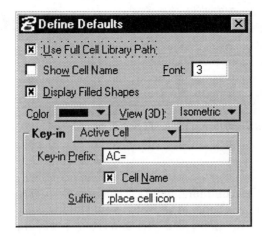

FIGURE 10–34 Defaults settings box.

Standardizing New Button Configurations MicroStation allows you to set the defaults for new button configuration. This allows you to standardize all the new button configurations. To set the defaults for new button configuration, invoke the Defaults command from:

Pull-down menu from Cell Selector settings box	Edit > Defaults (or CTRL + D)

MicroStation displays the Defaults settings box, as shown in Figure 10–34.

Set the appropriate default settings in the Defaults settings box and close the settings box. MicroStation uses all the settings set in the Defaults settings box for new button configuration.

CELL HOUSEKEEPING

You have seen several commands that place copies of cells in your design file. Now let's look at additional commands that affect cells already placed in your design file. The available commands include:

■ Identify Cell displays the name and other related information of the selected cell.
■ Replace Cell replaces a cell in the design file with another cell with the same name from the currently attached cell library.
■ Drop Complex Status breaks up a cell into its individual elements. The elements lose their identity as a cell.
■ Drop Fence Contents breaks up all cells contained in a fence to their individual elements. The elements lose their identities as cells.
■ Fast Cells View speeds up view updates by displaying only a box showing the location of all cells in the view, rather than the cell elements.

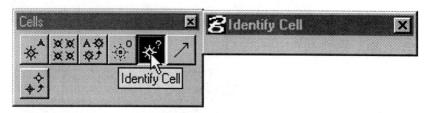

FIGURE 10–35   Invoking the Identify Cell command from the Cells tool box.

Identify Cell

The Identify Cell command displays the name of a selected cell and the levels the cell is on. It is useful when you want to use a cell already placed in your design file as a terminator cell or point cell but don't know the cell's name. The information is displayed in the Status bar.

To determine the name of a cell in the active design, invoke the Identify Cell command from:

Cells tool box	Select the Identify Cell tool (see Figure 10–35).
Key-in window	**Identify Cell** (or **id c**) ⏎

MicroStation prompts:

> Identify Cell > Identify element *(Identify the cell.)*
> Identify Cell > Accept/Reject (Select next input) *(Place a data point to accept the cell, and, optionally, to select the next cell.)*

The name of the cell appears in the Status bar after the second data point.

Replace Cell

The Replace Cell command replaces a cell in your design file with the cell of the same name from the attached cell library. It is useful when the design of a cell is changed and there are copies of the old cell in your design file.

To replace a cell in the active design, invoke the Replace Cell command from:

Cells tool box	Select the Replace Cell tool (see Figure 10–36).
Key-in window	**Replace Cell** (or **rep c**) ⏎

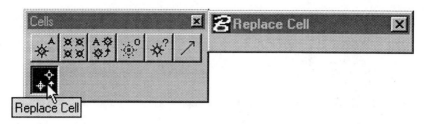

FIGURE 10–36 Invoking the Replace Cell command from the Cells tool box.

MicroStation prompts:

> Replace Cell > Identify element *(Identify the cell.)*
> Replace Cell > Accept/Reject (Select next input) *(Place a data point to initiate the replacement, and, optionally, to select the next cell.)*

The name of the cell appears in the Status bar after the second data point.

The second data point also can identify another cell to be replaced.

If you need to replace a shared cell (more of this later in this chapter), identify one of them and MicroStation will replace all the instances of the shared cell with the same name.

> ***NOTE:*** The replaced cell may shift position in your design file. That happens when the new cell's origin point was not defined in the same relationship to the cell elements as the old cell's origin.

Drop Complex Status

The cells placed in your design file are "complex shapes" that act like one element when manipulated. If you need to change the shape of a cell in your design file, you must first "drop" the cell to break it into separate elements. The Drop Complex Status command does that for you. A dropped cell loses its identity as a cell and becomes separate, unrelated elements.

To drop a cell, first invoke the Drop Complex Status command from:

Drop tool box	Select the Drop Complex Status tool (see Figure 10–37).
Key-in window	**Replace Cell** (or **rep c**) ⏎

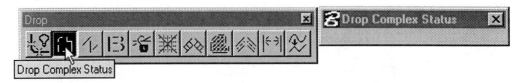

FIGURE 10-37 Invoking the Drop Complex Status command from the Drop tool box.

MicroStation prompts:

> Drop Complex Status > Identify element *(Identify the cell to be dropped.)*
> Drop Complex Status > Accept/Reject (Select next input) *(Place a data point to drop the cell, and, optionally, to select the next cell to be dropped.)*

Drop Fence Contents

The Drop Fence Contents command breaks all the cells enclosed in a fence into separate elements. Before you select this command, place a fence and select the appropriate fence lock that encloses all the cells you want to drop.

Place a fence around the elements to be dropped, and invoke the Drop Fence Contents command from:

Fence tool box	Select the Drop Fence Contents tool (see Figure 10–38).
Key-in window	**Replace Cell** (or **rep c**) ⏎

MicroStation prompts:

> Drop Complex Status of Fence Contents > Accept/Reject fence contents *(Place a data point to drop all cells associated with the fence.)*

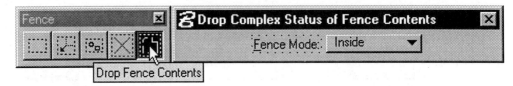

FIGURE 10-38 Invoking the Drop Fence Contents command from the Fence tool box.

> **NOTE:** Whenever you want to create a cell that includes another existing cell, drop the cell before it is included in the creation of the new cell. This prevents accidentally creating a "nested cell." A nested cell is a cell that is within another cell. Cells that contain nested cells only point to the library location of the nested cells. They do not actually store the nested cell elements with their elements. If you delete a cell from the cell library that is nested in other cells, you also delete part of all the cells that refer to it.

Fast Cells View

Numerous cells in a view may cause view updates to be completed too slowly. If you see that happening, you can speed up updating by turning on the Fast Cells View attribute. When that attribute is ON for a view, a box is displayed at each cell location, rather than at the cell elements. The box is the same size as the cell's range.

To turn on the Fast Cells View attribute:

1. Open the View Attributes settings box from the pull-down menu Settings.
2. Turn ON the Fast Cells toggle button.
3. Check the View options menu, and, if necessary, change it to the number of the view where you want the Fast Cells View attribute to be ON.
4. Click the Apply button to turn on the attribute for the selected view.
5. If you no longer need the View Attributes settings box, close it.

The Fast Cells View attribute stays ON for the selected view until you turn it OFF or exit from MicroStation. To make it permanent, select Save Settings from the pull-down menu File.

> **NOTE:** Turn OFF Fast Cells View before you plot, if you want the cells to appear in the plot.

LIBRARY HOUSEKEEPING

You've seen how to place cells in your design file and take care of them. Now let's look at some housekeeping commands that help you take care of the cells in the attached cell library. The discussion includes explanations of how to

- Edit a cell's name and description.
- Delete a cell from the Cell Library.
- Compress the attached Cell Library.
- Create a new version of a cell.

All these tools affect the cells in the attached library, not the cells in your design file.

Editing a Cell's Name and Description

The Edit Cell Information dialog box, which is available from the Cell Library settings box, allows you to change a cell's name and description. If you need to create a new version of a cell, and you want to keep the old one around, rename it before creating the new version. If the person who designed the cell failed to provide a description, you can provide one to help other users of the cell library figure out what is in it. Following is the step-by-step procedure for renaming a cell and/or adding or changing the cell description.

1. If the Cell Library settings box is not already open, select cells from the pull-down menu Element to open it.
2. Select the cell you want to edit from the Cells list.
3. Click the Edit button to open the Edit Cell Information dialog box (see Figure 10–39).
4. Make the necessary changes to the cell name and description.
5. Click the Modify button to make the necessary changes and close the Edit Cell Information dialog box.

> **NOTE:** Changing the cell name and description does not affect the cells already in the design file (or any other design file). They keep their old names.

Alternate Method   To rename a cell: from the key-in window, type **CR=<old>**, <new>, and press ⏎. Replace <old> with the cell's current name and <new> with the new cell name. The key-in only changes the cell names. You cannot use a key-in to change descriptions.

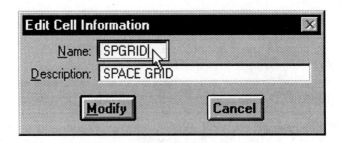

FIGURE 10–39   Edit Cell Information dialog box.

Deleting a Cell from the Library

If a cell becomes obsolete, or if it was not drawn correctly, it can be deleted from the cell library using the Delete button in the Cell Library settings box. When you ask to delete a cell, MicroStation opens an Alert dialog box to ask you if you really want to delete the cell. Following is the step-by-step procedure for deleting a cell from the Cell Library.

1. If the Cell Library settings box is not already open, select Cells from the pull-down menu Element to open it.
2. Select the cell you want to delete from the Cells list.
3. Click the Delete button.
4. The Alert dialog box opens to ask you if you really want to delete the cell.
5. If you really want to delete it, click the OK button. If you selected the wrong cell or change your mind, click the Cancel button.

> **NOTE:** This procedure deletes a cell from the cell library. It does not delete copies of the cell already placed in the design file (or any other design file).

Alternate Method To delete a cell: from the key-in window, type **CD=<name>**, and press [ENTER]. Replace <name> with the cell's name.

When you use the key-in to delete a cell, MicroStation does not open the Alert window to ask you if you really want to delete the cell.

> **NOTE:** The Undo command will not undo the deleting of a cell from the attached library.

Compressing the Attached Cell Library

Deleting a cell from a cell library does not really delete it. The cell is marked as deleted and is no longer available, but its elements still take up space in the cell library file on the disk. To get rid of the no-longer-usable cell elements, you must compress the cell library with the Compress Library option in the Cell Library settings box's pull-down menu File. Following is the step-by-step procedure to compress the Cell Library.

1. If the Cell Library settings box is not already open, select Cells from the pull-down menu Element to open it.
2. From the pull-down menu File in the Cell Library settings box, select Compress.

The attached cell library is compressed, and the Status bar indicates that the Cell Library is compressed.

Creating a New Version of a Cell

Occasionally the need will arise to replace a cell with an updated version of that cell. The geometric layout of the object represented by the cell may have changed, or you may have discovered that a mistake was made when the cell was drawn.

Follow this procedure to create a new version of a cell:

1. Place a copy of the cell in a design file that has the same Working Units as the design file in which the cell was created.
2. Drop the cell.
3. Delete the old cell from the library, or rename it.
4. Make the required changes to the cell elements.
5. If possible, place the cell origin at the same place as in the old cell.
6. Create the new cell from the modified elements.
7. If you deleted the old cell, compress the library.
8. If you had already placed copies of the cell in your design files, invoke the Replace Cell command to replace those copies with the new version of the cell.

SHARED CELLS

Thus far, each time you placed a cell, a separate copy of the cell's elements was placed in the design file. That uses up a lot of disk space in a design file that contains many cells.

Shared cells can help with the disk space problem. Each time you place a shared cell, the placement refers back to the shared copy rather than placing more elements in your design file. No matter how many copies of a shared cell you place, only one copy is actually in your design file.

When you declare a cell to be shared, MicroStation places a copy of it in your design file. You can have the shared cell's elements stored in your design file even though no copies of the cell have ever been placed in the design plane. Later, when you use the cell placement commands, the placements refer to the locally stored cell elements rather than to the copy in the library. Shared cells can be placed even when no cell library is attached.

Let's look how you can:

- Turn on the shared cell feature.
- Determine which cells are shared.
- Declare a cell to be shared.
- Place shared cells.
- Turn a shared cell into an unshared cell.
- Delete the shared cell copy from your design file.

Turning on the Shared Cell Feature

The Use Shared Cells toggle button in the Cell Library settings box (see Figure 10–40) turns the shared cell feature ON or OFF. Each time you click the button, you toggle between using shared cells and not using them.

Determining Which Cells Are Shared

When the shared cells feature is ON, all shared cells in your design file show up in the Cells List in the Cell Library settings box (see Figure 10–40). You can find the shared cells by viewing the Where column in the Cells List area. Shared cells are indicated by "Shrd" in that column.

If the shared cell is also in the currently attached cell library, the list shows the shared copy in your design file—not the one in the library.

Each time you select a shared cell in your design file, the Status bar will tell you it is a shared cell.

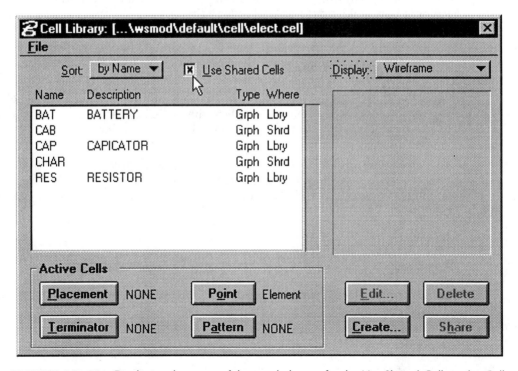

FIGURE 10–40 Displaying the status of the toggle button for the Use Shared Cells in the Cell Library settings box.

Declaring a Cell to Be Shared

Use the Share button located in the bottom right in the Cell Library settings box to place copies of the shared cells in your design file. Following is the step-by-step procedure.

1. If the Cell Library settings box is not already open, select Cells from the pull-down menu Element to open it.
2. If the shared cells feature is not currently active, click on the Use Shared Cells button to turn it ON.
3. Select the cell you want to be shared from the Cells List.
4. Click the Share button.

When you click the Share button, "Shrd" appears in the Where column of the selected cell, and a copy of the cell is placed in your current design file.

You just stored a shared copy of the cell in your design file without actually placing the cell. This is a handy way to create a seed file for a group of design files that will use the same set of cells. The procedure includes creating a new design file, attaching the cell library, and declaring all required cells shared. Then you can create new design files by copying the new seed file. Each copied file contains a copy of the elements that make up the shared cells.

Placing Shared Cells

When the Use Shared Cells button in the Cell Library settings box is set to ON (depressed), all cell placement tools place shared cells. Placing a cell makes the cell shared, even if you have not declared the cell to be shared previously.

The commands that place the active placement, terminator, and point cells all work the same for shared cells as they do for unshared cells. The Replace Cell command automatically replaces all the copies of the shared cell when you identify one of them.

Turning a Shared Cell Into an Unshared Cell

A cell that was placed shared can be turned into an unshared cell (with its own copy of the cell elements).

Invoke the Drop Shared Cell command from:

Key-in window	**Replace Cell** (or **rep c**) ⏎

MicroStation prompts:

> Convert Shared Cell to Unshared Cell > Identify element *(Select the shared cell to be converted.)*
> Convert Shared Cell to Unshared Cell > Accept/Reject (Select next input) *(Place a second data point to convert the selected cell, and, optionally, select the next cell to convert.)*

If no cell is selected with the second data point, the error message *Element not found* appears in the Status bar. Ignore it.

Deleting the Shared Cell Copy from Your Design File

The placements of shared cells can be deleted like any other element, but the actual shared cell copy takes a little more work to delete. It is done in the Cell Library settings box via the Delete button.

Here is the procedure for deleting the shared cell elements from your design file.

1. Either delete all placements of the shared cell or make them into unshared cells (see earlier).
2. If the Cell Library settings box is not already open, select Cells from the pull-down menu Element to open it.
3. If the Use Shared Cells toggle button is OFF, turn it ON.
4. Select the shared cell you want to delete from the Cells List and make sure the cell has "Shrd" in the Where column.
5. Click the Delete button (located in the bottom right of the Cell Library settings box).
6. The Alert dialog box opens to ask you if you really want to delete the cell. If you really want to delete it, click the OK button.

If you selected the wrong cell, click the Cancel button. This procedure deletes only the copy of the shared cell elements in your design file. It does not delete anything from the attached cell library.

> **NOTE:** If there are still any placements of the shared cell in your design file when you try to delete the shared cell, an Alert dialog box appears with a message stating that you cannot delete the cell. In this case the Alert dialog box's Cancel and OK buttons only close the box—click on either one of them.

DIMENSION-DRIVEN CELLS

MicroStation allows you to create a special type of a cell called a dimension-driven cell. When you place the dimension-driven cell, you can dynamically change relationships between the elements that were defined when it was created. For a detailed explanation about creating dimension-driven cells, refer to Chapter 13.

REVIEW QUESTIONS

Write your answers in the spaces provided.

1. Explain briefly the difference between a cell and cell library.

   _____

2. How many cell libraries can you attach at one time to a design file? _____

3. List the steps involved in creating a cell.

   _____

   _____

4. What is the alternate key-in **AC=** used for? _____

5. What is the file that has an extension of .CEL? _____

6. What does it mean to place a cell Absolute?

   _____

7. What does it mean to place a cell Relative?

   _____

8. Explain briefly the differences between a graphic cell and a point cell.

   _____

   _____

9. How many cells can you store in a library? _____

10. What is the purpose of defining an active cell as a terminator?

    _____

11. What is the purpose of turning ON the Fast Cells View attribute?

    _____

12. Explain briefly the benefits of declaring a cell as a shared cell.

    _____

    _____

PROJECT EXERCISE

This project exercise provides step-by-step instructions for creating the design shown in Figure P10–1. The intent is to guide you in creating and using cells.

> **NOTE:** The dimensions included in several figures in this project are presented only as an aid to completing the design. They are *not* to be drawn.

Prepare the Design File

This procedure starts MicroStation, creates a design file, and enters the initial settings.

> **NOTE:** As you complete each step in the project procedures, place a check mark by the step to help you keep up with where you are in the project.

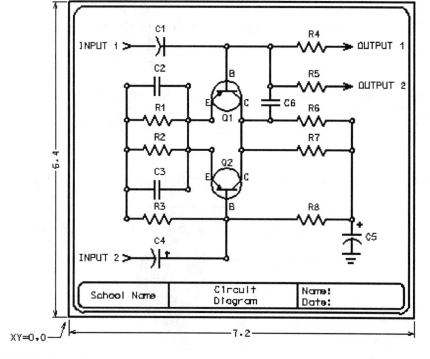

FIGURE P10–1 Completed project design.

STEP 1: Invoke MicroStation using the normal technique for the operating system on your workstation.

STEP 2: Create a new design file named CH10.DGN using the SEED2D.DGN seed file.

In the Design File dialog box set the:

- Working units Master Units name to IN (for inches), the Sub Units name to TH (for tenths of an inch), and the resolution ratio to 10 and 1000.
- Grid Master to 0.1, Grid Reference to 10, and Grid Lock to ON.

STEP 3: Set the Active Level to 1 and Line Weight to 1.

STEP 4: Invoke the Save Settings command from the pull-down menu File and save the settings.

Create the Arrowhead Cell

This procedure creates the arrowhead shown in Figure P10–2, creates a cell library, and creates a cell from a copy of the arrowhead elements.

STEP 1: Align a view window to display an area about 1 inch by 1 inch.

STEP 2: Invoke the Place Line command from the Linear Elements tool box, and, in the Tool Settings window, set the Length to 0.1 inch, the Angle to 160, and the Length and Angle toggle buttons to ON.

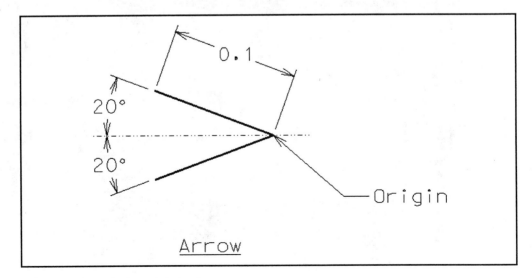

FIGURE P10–2 Arrowhead cell.

MicroStation prompts:

Place Line > Enter first point *(Place a data point to place the 0.1-inch line at 160 degrees rotation.)*

Place Line > Enter first point *(In the Tool Settings window, change the Angle to 200 degrees, then place the line at the right end of the previous line.)*

Place Line > Enter first point *(Click the Reset button, and, in the Tool Settings window, set the toggle buttons for the Length and Angle locks to OFF.)*

STEP 3: Place a Fence Block around the two lines that form the arrowhead.

STEP 4: Invoke the Define Cell Origin command from the Cells tool box.

MicroStation prompts:

Define Cell Origin > Define origin *(Place a data point on the arrow's point, as shown in Figure P10–2.)*

STEP 5: Open the Cells settings box by selecting the Cells from the pull-down menu Element. MicroStation displays the Cells settings box, as shown in Figure P10–3.

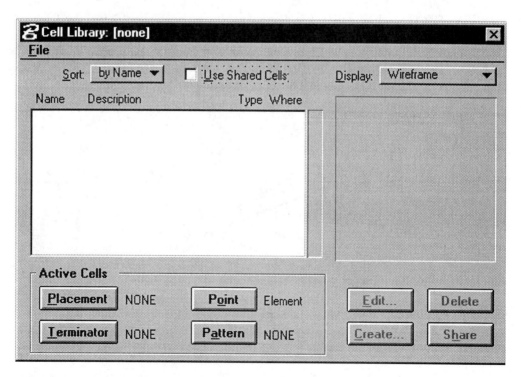

FIGURE P10–3 Cell Library settings box.

STEP 6: Invoke the New command from the pull-down menu File in the Cell Library settings box to create a new Cell Library. MicroStation opens the Create Cell Library dialog box.

STEP 7: In the Create Cell Library dialog box's Files window, key-in the file name **PROJ10.CEL**, then click the OK button to create and attach the cell library.

STEP 8: In the Cell Library settings box, click the Create button to open the Create New Cell dialog box.

STEP 9: In the Create New Cell dialog box, do the following:

- Key-in **arrow** in the Name field.
- Key-in **Arrowhead symbol** in the Description field.
- Select the Point option menu.
- Click the Create button to create the cell.

STEP 10: Delete the two lines and remove the fence.

Create Additional Cells

This procedure draws the objects shown in Figure P10–4 and creates cells from them.

> **NOTE:** Draw only the heavy-line-weight electronic symbols shown in Figure P10–4. Do *not* place the text or dimensions. The grid, text, and dimensions are shown only as an aid to creating the symbols.

STEP 1: Draw the resistor symbol (upper left object).

STEP 2: Create a cell from the resistor elements:

a. Place a Fence Block around the resistor.

b. Define a cell origin at the left end of the resistor, as indicated in Figure P10–4.

c. Create a Point cell named "res" and described as "Resistor Symbol."

STEP 3: Delete the resistor elements from the design file, and update the view.

STEP 4: Draw all elements in the PNP transistor symbol (bottom row, right symbol), except the arrowhead.

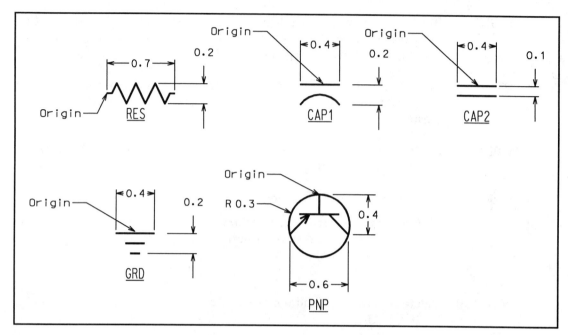

FIGURE P10–4 Electronic symbols.

STEP 5: To place the arrowhead in the PNP transistor symbol, invoke the Place Active Line Terminator command from the Cells tool box, and, in the Tool Settings window, key-in **arrow** in the Terminator field and **1** in the Scale field.

MicroStation prompts:

> Place Active Line Terminator > Identify element *(Identify the line close to the end point of the line where you want to place the arrow.)*
> Place Active Line Terminator > Accept/Reject (Select next input) *(Click the Data button in space to place the arrowhead on the line.)*

STEP 6: Create a point cell from the transistor elements using "PNP" as the cell name and "PNP Transistor symbol" for the description.

STEP 7: Draw and create point cells of the other three electronic symbols shown in Figure P10–4. Place the origin at the location indicated in the figure, and use the underlined text for the cell names. Here are the names and descriptions of each cell:

- CAP1 Capacitor symbol 1
- CAP2 Capacitor symbol 2
- GRD Ground symbol

STEP 8: Delete the symbols from the design file.

Create the Circuit Diagram

This procedure uses the electronic symbol cells to create the diagram shown in Figure P10–1.

STEP 1: With Figure P10–1 as a guide, draw the border and title block on level 10.

- Replace "SCHOOL NAME" with your school or company name, or make up a name.
- Place your name to the right of "NAME."
- Place today's date to the right of "DATE."

STEP 2: Set up the view window:

- Fit the view.
- Set the Active Level to 2.
- Set the Line Weight to 1 and the Color to green.

STEP 3: Invoke the Save Settings command from the pull-down menu File to save the settings.

> **NOTE:** The following steps place a transistor symbol cell, then draw outward from the transistor. There are several equally productive ways to draw the diagram.

STEP 4: Invoke the Place Active Cell command from the Cells tool box, and, in the Tool Settings window, key-in **pnp** in the Active Cell edit field, **0** in the Active Angle edit field, and **1** in the X and Y Scale edit fields. Set the toggle buttons for Relative and Interactive to OFF.

MicroStation prompts:

Place Active Cell > Enter cell origin *(Place a data point to place the cell approximately at the same location as shown for the top PNP transistor symbol in Figure P10–1.)*

Place Active Cell > Enter cell origin *(Click the Reset button to terminate the command sequence.)*

STEP 5: Use the Mirror Element About Horizontal (Copy) command to create a mirror image copy of the just-placed PNP cell below the original, as shown in Figure P10–5.

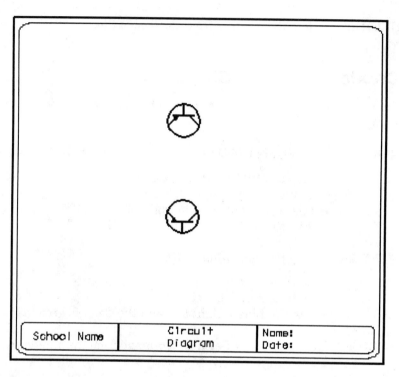

FIGURE P10–5 Two copies of the PNP cell.

STEP 6: Continue drawing lines and placing cells by referring to Figure P10–1.

> **NOTE:** Most of the CAP1 and CAP2 cells must be placed rotated. To rotate them, key-in **270** (or **-90**) in the Tool Setting window's Active Angle field before placing the cell.

STEP 7: Place circles on the line intersections with the Place Circle By Center command, with the Radius field set to 0.05.

STEP 8: Remove the lines from inside the intersection circles with the Trim Element command by using the circles as the Cutting Element.

STEP 9: Invoke the Save Settings command from the pull-down menu File to save the settings.

DRAWING EXERCISES 10–1 THROUGH 10–5

Use the following table to set up the design files for all Chapter 10 exercises.

SETTING	VALUE
Seed File	SEED2D.DGN
Working Units	MU = IN, SU = 10 TH, PU = 1000
Grid	Master = .1, Reference = 10, Grid lock ON

Exercises 10–1 through 10–3

Create the piping flowsheet symbols shown in Figure E10–1, and make each into a cell. Use the cells to create the flow diagrams in Exercises 10–1 through 10–3.

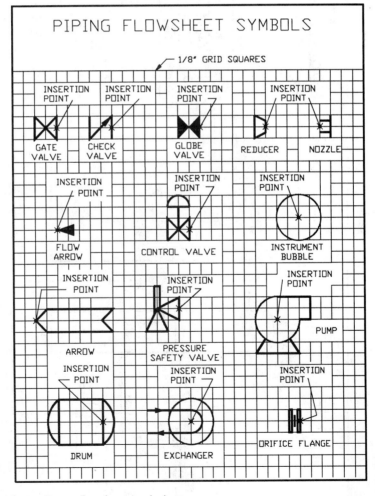

FIGURE E10–1   Piping flowsheet symbols.

Exercise 10-1 Process flow diagram.

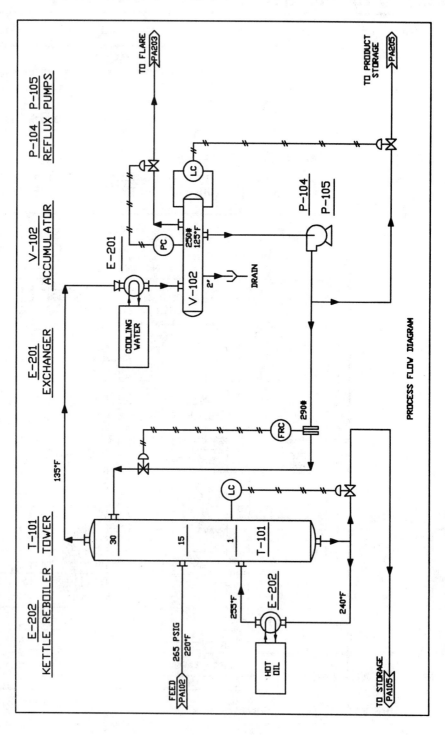

Exercise 10–2 Reactor and exchanger flow diagram.

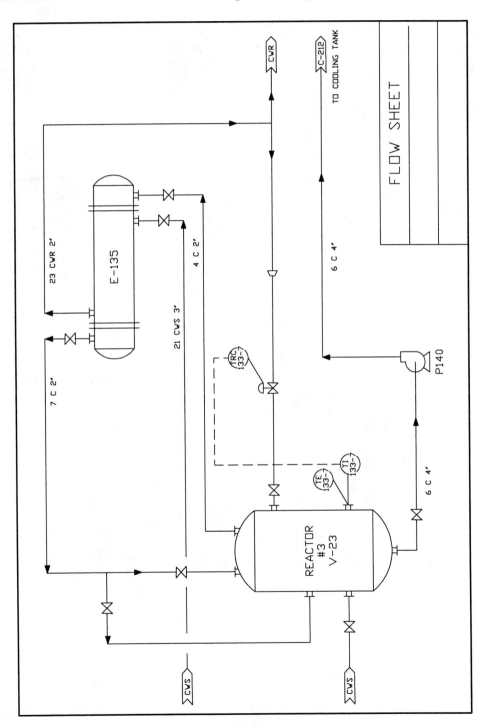

Exercise 10–3 Wastewater control panel.

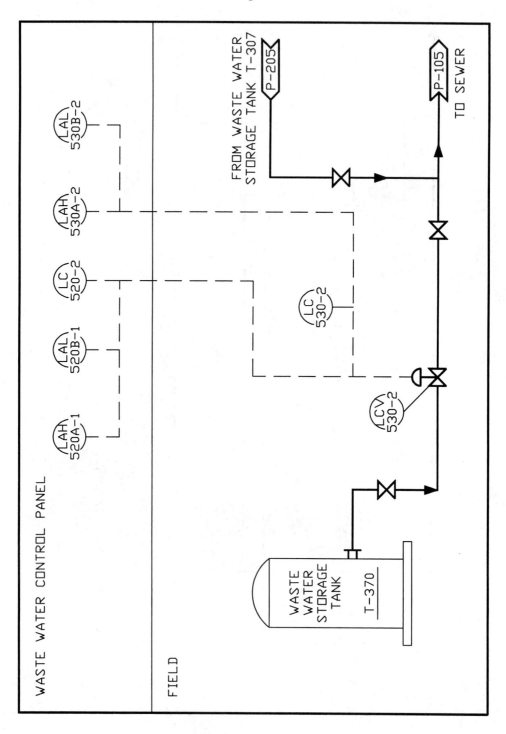

Exercises 10-4 and 10-5

Create the electrical symbols shown in Figure E10–2, and make each into a cell. Use the cells to create the diagrams in Exercises 10–4 and 10–5.

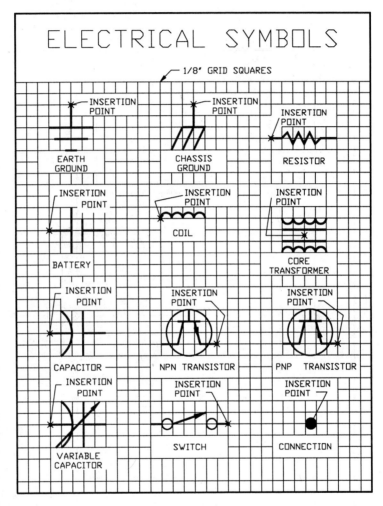

FIGURE E10–2 Electrical symbols.

Exercise 10–4 Electrical diagram.

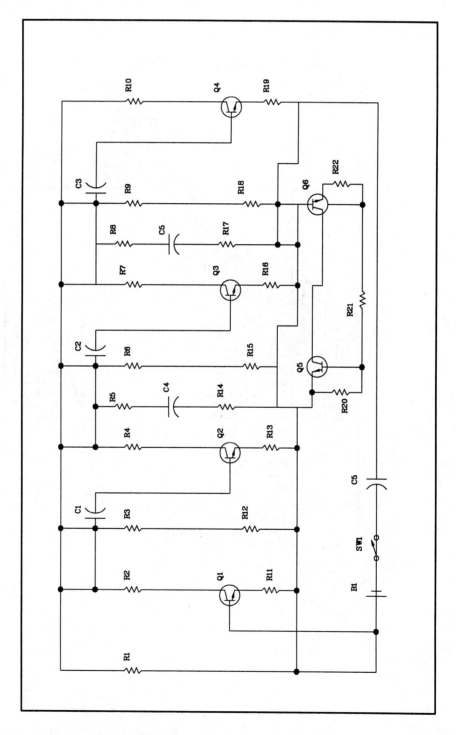

Exercise 10–5 Electrical diagram.

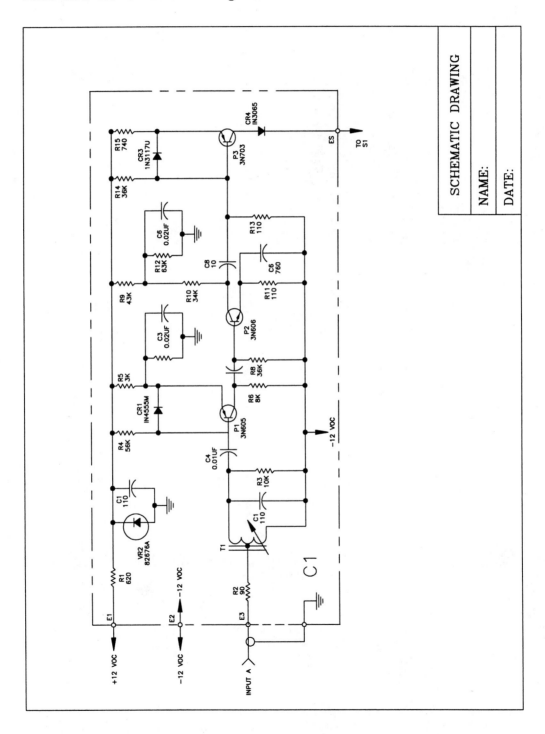

CHAPTER

11

PATTERNING

Patterns are used in drawings for several reasons. Cutaways (cross sections) are hatched to help the viewer differentiate among components of an assembly and indicate what the material is made of. Patterns on surfaces depict material and add to the readability of the drawing. In general, patterns help communicate information about the model in the drawing. Because drawing patterns is a repetitive task, it is an ideal computer-aided drafting application.

OBJECTIVES

After completing this chapter, you will be able to:

✓ Control the display of patterns in view windows.

✓ Place hatching, crosshatching, and area patterns via seven placement methods.

✓ Manipulate patterns.

✓ Fill elements.

CONTROLLING THE VIEW OF PATTERNS

Patterning can place so many elements in a design that view updates may start taking an unacceptable time to complete on slow workstations. To overcome that, MicroStation provides the pattern view attribute to turn the display of pattern elements ON and OFF.

The Patterns view attribute should be ON when placing new patterns so the placement results can be seen. When work with patterns is completed, the Patterns view attribute can be turned OFF to speed up view updates. Figure 11–1 shows a crosshatch pattern with the view attribute ON and with it OFF.

To change the Patterns view status, invoke the View Attributes settings box from:

Settings pull-down menu	Select <u>V</u>iew Attributes tool (or ⌨ + **S, V**)
Key-in window	**Dialog Viewsettings** (or **dia views**) ⏎

MicroStation displays the View Attributes settings box, as shown in Figure 11–2. Set the Patterns view attribute button ON or OFF, then click the Apply button to set the attributes for the view window number shown at the top of the window, or click the All button to set the attributes for all open view windows.

> **NOTE:** If you place patterns in a view where the Patterns view attribute is turned OFF, the patterns are placed but they do not show up on the screen. To avoid the confusion that can cause, remember to make sure the Patterns view is set to ON before placing patterns.

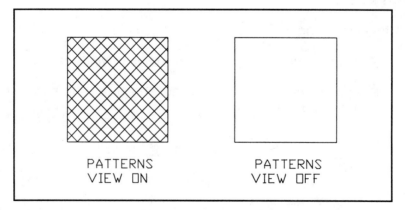

PATTERNS
VIEW ON

PATTERNS
VIEW OFF

FIGURE 11–1   Example of turning the Patterns view attribute ON and OFF.

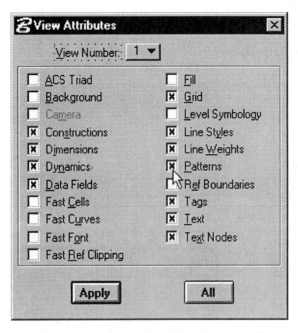

FIGURE 11–2   View Attributes settings box with the Patterns view attribute turned ON.

PATTERNING COMMANDS

MicroStation provides three commands for placing patterns in a design file:

- **Hatch Area** places a set of parallel lines in the pattern area by invoking the Hatch Area command from the Patterns tool box, as shown in Figure 11–3a.
- **Crosshatch Area** places two sets of parallel lines in the pattern area by invoking the Crosshatch Area command from the Patterns tool box, as shown in Figure 11–3b.
- **Pattern Area** fills the pattern area with tiled copies of the active pattern cell by invoking the Pattern Area command from the Patterns tool box, as shown in Figure 11–3c.

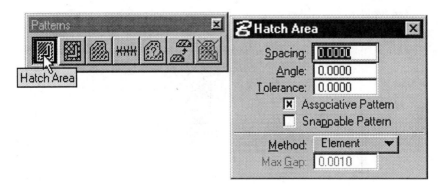

FIGURE 11–3a   Hatch Area icon and settings box.

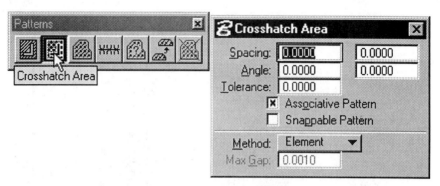

FIGURE 11-3b Crosshatch Area icon and settings box.

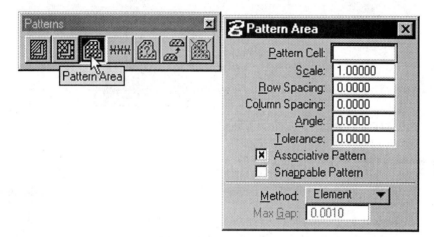

FIGURE 11-3c Pattern Area icon and settings box.

Examples of the patterns placed by each command are shown in Figure 11–4.

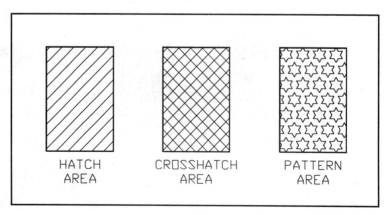

FIGURE 11-4 Examples of hatching, crosshatching, and patterning.

TOOL SETTINGS FOR PATTERNING

The following discussion describes the tool settings for the three patterning commands.

Spacing Spacing sets the space in Working Units (MU:SU:PU) between patterning elements.

- Hatching: One field to set the space between the lines
- Crosshatching: Two fields to set the space between each set of lines
- Pattern Area: Two fields to set the space between cell rows and columns

If the Hatch space or both of the Crosshatch spaces are zero, an error is displayed in the Status bar and no pattern is placed. Zero spaces are okay for the Pattern Area command.

If one of the crosshatch line-set spaces is set to zero, it will be placed equal to the other line-set spacing.

Angle Angle sets the rotation angle (from the positive X axis direction) for the patterning elements.

- Hatching: One field to set the angle of the lines
- Crosshatching: Two fields to set the angle of each set of lines
- Pattern Area: One field to set the angle of the rows of cells

If one of the crosshatch line-set angles is greater than zero and the other is equal to zero, the zero set is placed at complement to the other set. For example, if the first set's angle is 45 degrees and the second is zero degrees, the first set is placed at 45 degrees and the second set at 135 degrees (180 – 45).

Tolerance Tolerance sets the variance between the true section curve and the approximation when a curved element is patterned. The curve is approximated by a series of straight line segments, and a low tolerance number increases the accuracy of the approximation by reducing the length of each segment. The low tolerance number also means a larger design file and slower pattern placement.

Associative Pattern Associative Pattern is a toggle switch that, when ON, associates the pattern elements with the element they pattern when the patterns are placed with the Element method. Changes to an associated element also effect the pattern. For example, if the element is stretched, the pattern expands to fill the new size. Figure 11–5 shows an example of pattern association.

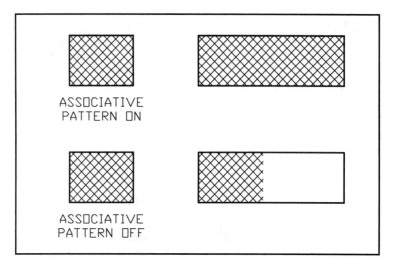

ASSOCIATIVE
PATTERN ON

ASSOCIATIVE
PATTERN OFF

FIGURE 11–5 Example of the associative pattern setting.

Snappable Pattern This is a toggle switch that, when it is set to ON, allows snapping to the pattern elements after they are placed. If it is set to OFF, tentative points cannot snap to the pattern elements. This toggle switch does not affect the patterned element.

Pattern Cell This setting is used only by the Pattern Area command, to provide the name of the cell for filling the pattern area. If no cell name is provided, the Pattern Cell command displays an error message in the Status bar and no pattern is placed.

Scale This setting is used only by the Pattern Area command, to scale the cell placements. A number less than 1 reduces the size of each placement; a number greater than 1 increases the size.

> **NOTE:** If the cell to be used for the pattern area was created with different Working Unit ratios than the design file, the cell may need to be scaled. If you are not sure of the correct scale, make the cell the active placement cell, then select the Place Active Cell command. The dynamic image of the cell shows you what size it is in your design. Adjust the cell placement scale until the dynamic image is the correct size, then set the Pattern Area scale to the same value.

Method This option sets how the patterned area is determined. Methods are discussed later in the chapter.

Max Gap This option sets the maximum space in Working Units (MU:SU:PU) between the enclosing elements in Flood patterning mode (see the next section, on methods).

METHOD TOOL-SETTING MENU

Seven methods are provided in the Tool Settings window for defining the area to be patterned. The methods are selected from the Method pop-up menu in the Patterns tool settings window, as shown in Figure 11–6.

The following list describes the patterning area methods; Figure 11–7 shows examples of each method.

- **Element** patterns a selected closed element, such as a Shape, Ellipse, Closed B-spline Curve, or between components of a multi-line.
- **Fence** patterns the area enclosed by a fence.
- **Intersection** patterns the area common to two or more overlapping elements.
- **Union** patterns two or more selected elements as if they were one element. The elements do not have to overlap.
- **Difference** patterns the part of the first selected closed element that does not overlap the other selected closed elements. If the first element is completely inside the second element, no pattern is placed.
- **Flood** patterns the area enclosed by a set of separate elements surrounding the placement data point. If there is a gap between enclosing elements that is greater than the Max Gap tool setting, the area is not patterned and an error message appears in the Status bar. If the area is complicated, the command may take a long time to decide if the area is truly enclosed.
- **Points** patterns a temporary closed shape created by a set of data points placed after the command is invoked.

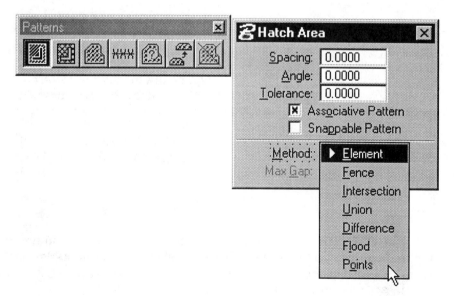

FIGURE 11–6 Patterns Method pop-up menu.

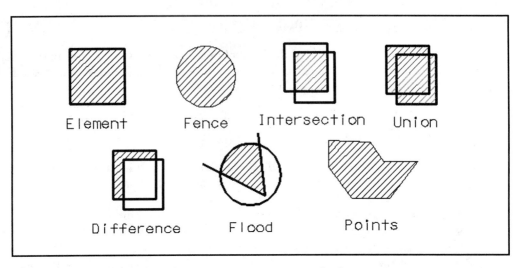

FIGURE 11-7 Examples of the seven area patterning methods.

PLACING PATTERNS

Invoke the patterning placement commands from:

Patterns tool box	Select the required pattern placement command: • Hatch Area (see Figure 11–3a) • Crosshatch Area (see Figure 11–3b) • Pattern Area (see Figure 11–3c) Optionally, modify the pattern settings in the Tool Settings window.
Key-in window	• **Hatch** (or **ha**) ⏎ • **Crosshatch** (or **cro**) ⏎ • **Pattern Area** (or **pat**) ⏎

NOTE: The placement prompts depend on the area definition method selected. The following discussion shows the prompts for each area method and uses the Hatch Area command as an example. The prompts are the same for Crosshatch and Pattern Area.

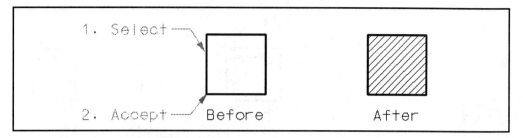

FIGURE 11-8 Example of patterning a closed element.

Element

When the patterning area method is Element, MicroStation prompts:

> Hatch Area > Identify element *(Select the closed element to be patterned as shown in Figure 11–8.)*
> Hatch Area > Accept @pattern intersection point *(Click the Data button again to accept the element and initiate pattern placement.)*

> **NOTE:** For each patterning area method, the acceptance point defines a point through which pattern elements pass—one line for Hatch Area, the intersection of two lines for Cross-hatch Area, and the origin point of one of the pattern cells for Pattern Area. If the acceptance point is not within the patterned area, the intersection will be on the edge of the area at the closest extension of the acceptance point.

Fence

When the patterning area method is Fence, MicroStation prompts:

> Hatch Fence > Accept/Reject fence contents *(Place a data point to define an intersection point for the pattern, as shown in Figure 11–9, and initiate patterning.)*

The example in Figure 11–9 is a circular fence. The fence is not part of the pattern and removing it does not affect the pattern.

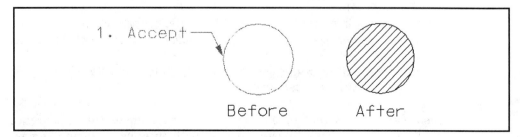

FIGURE 11-9 Example of patterning a fence.

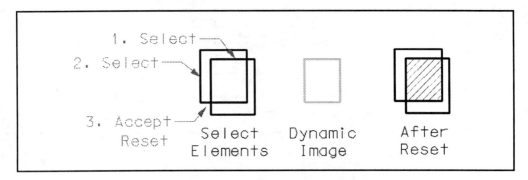

FIGURE 11-10 Example of intersection patterning.

Intersection

When the patterning area method is Intersection, MicroStation prompts:

> Hatch Element Intersection > Identify element *(Select the first element, as shown in Figure 11–10.)*
> Hatch Element Intersection > Accept/Reject (Select next input) *(Select all the other elements that make up the intersection, then click the Data button in space.)*
> Hatch Element Intersection > Identify additional/Reset to complete *(Click the Reset button to initiate the patterning.)*

As each element is accepted, the dynamic image changes the appearance of the selected elements to show only the intersection area. The elements are not affected, and reappear after the command is completed.

Union

When the patterning area method is Union, MicroStation prompts:

> Hatch Element Union > Identify element *(Select the first element, as shown in Figure 11–11.)*
> Hatch Element Intersection > Accept/Reject (Select next input) *(Select all the other elements that make up the intersection, then click the Data button in space.)*
> Hatch Element Union > Identify additional/Reset to complete *(Click the Reset button to initiate the patterning.)*

As each element is accepted, the dynamic image changes the appearance of the selected elements to show the union area with interior segments removed. The elements are not affected, and reappear after the command is completed.

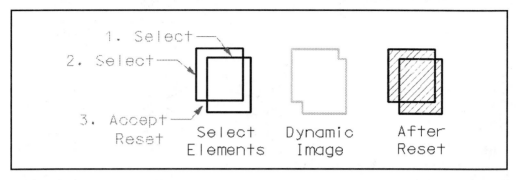

FIGURE 11–11 Example of union patterning.

Difference

When the patterning area method is Difference, MicroStation prompts:

> Hatch Element Difference > Identify element *(Select the first element, as shown in Figure 11–12.)*
> Hatch Element Difference > Accept/Reject (Select next input) *(Select all the other elements that make up the intersection, then click the Data button in space.)*
> Hatch Element Difference > Identify additional/Reset to complete *(Click the Reset button to initiate the patterning.)*

As each element is accepted, the dynamic image changes the appearance of the selected elements to show only the difference area. The elements are not affected, and reappear after the command is completed.

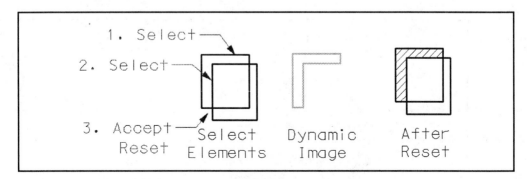

FIGURE 11–12 Example of difference patterning.

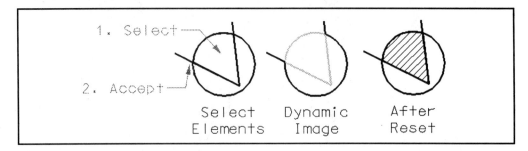

FIGURE 11-13 Example of flood patterning.

Flood

When the patterning area method is Flood, MicroStation prompts:

> Hatch Area Enclosing Point > Enter data point inside area *(Place a data point inside the area to be patterned, as shown in Figure 11–13.)*
> Hatch Area Enclosing Point > Accept @ pattern intersection point *(Click the Data button again to initiate patterning.)*

After the first data point is placed, a dynamic image is drawn around the perimeter of the flood area.

Points

When the patterning area method is Intersection, MicroStation prompts:

> Hatch Area Defined By Points > Enter shape vertex *(Place the first three vertex points of the shape, as shown in Figure 11–14.)*
> Hatch Area Defined By Points > Enter point or Reset to complete *(Continue entering shape vertex points, or click the Reset button to complete the shape and initiate patterning.)*
> Hatch Area Defined By Points > Identify additional/Reset to complete *(Click the Reset button to initiate the patterning.)*

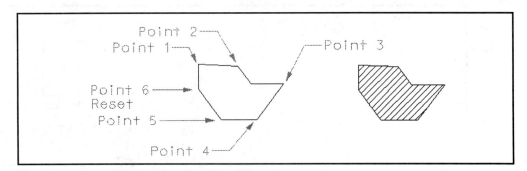

FIGURE 11-14 Example of patterning an area enclosed by points.

After the third point, the dynamic image shows the shape of the pattern area if the Reset button is clicked.

LEAVING HOLES IN PATTERNS

Often the area to be patterned contains elements that should not be patterned. MicroStation provides Solid and Hole area placement modes to handle such situations. Solid elements can be patterned, but Hole elements cannot.

For example: The windows in a wall elevation should not be covered when a brick pattern is placed on the wall. Place the wall with Solid Area mode set to ON, and place the windows with Hole Area mode set to ON. Pattern the wall element using Element mode and the windows will not be covered by the brick pattern, as shown in Figure 11–15.

Text placed with Hole Area mode set to ON also cannot be patterned, as shown in Figure 11–16.

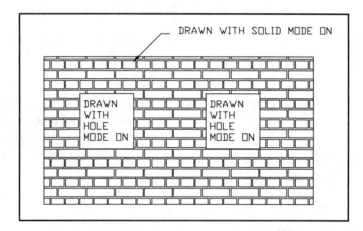

FIGURE 11–15   Example of the effect of Hole elements within a patterned element.

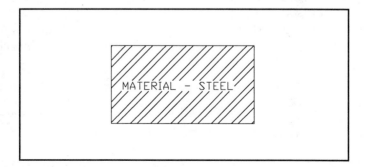

FIGURE 11–16   Example of patterning over a text string placed in Hole Area mode.

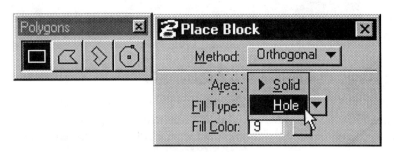

FIGURE 11-17 Example of Area mode tool setting for a closed element placement command.

The Tool Settings window for each command that places closed elements, includes a menu for setting the Area mode. An example is shown in Figure 11–17.

> **NOTE:** Only the Element and Fence patterning methods recognize hole elements. The other patterning methods (Intersection, Union, Difference, Flood, and Points) ignore the Hole Area elements.

Changing an Element's Area If an element was placed via the wrong Area mode, you can change it to the correct area with the Change Element to Active Area command. Invoke the command from:

Change Attributes tool box	Select the Change Element to Active Area tool, and select the required area (Hole or Solid) in the Tool Settings window (see Figure 11–18).
Key-in window	**Change Area (or Chan a)** [ENTER]

MicroStation prompts:

Change Element to Active Area > Identify element *(Identify the element.)*
Change Element to Active Area > Accept/Reject (Select next input) *(Click the Data button to initiate the area change, or click Reset to reject the selected element. Optionally, also select the next element to be changed.)*

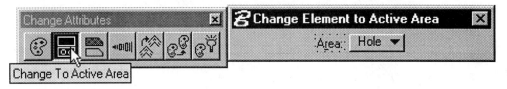

FIGURE 11-18 Invoking the Change Element to Active Area command from the Change Attributes tool box.

DELETING PATTERNS

A special delete command for patterns deletes all pattern elements but not the element that contained the pattern. Invoke the Delete Pattern command from:

Patterns tool box	Select the Delete Pattern tool (see Figure 11–19).
Key-in window	**Delete Pattern** (or **del pat**) ⏎

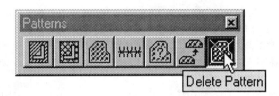

FIGURE 11–19   Invoking the Delete Pattern from the Patterns tool box.

MicroStation prompts:

Delete Pattern > Identify element *(Identify the pattern to be deleted, then click the Data button again to accept and delete the pattern.)*

> **NOTE:** Patterns can contain a large number of elements. After deleting patterns, select the Compress Design command from the pull-down menu File to remove the deleted elements from the design file.

MATCHING PATTERN ATTRIBUTES

If additional patterns need to be placed with the same patterning attribute settings as existing patterns, the Match Active Pattern command provides a fast way to set the attributes. The command sets the active patterning attributes to match those of a selected pattern.

Invoke the Match Active Pattern command from:

Patterns tool box	Select the Match Active Pattern tool (see Figure 11–20).
Key-in window	**Match Pattern** (or **matc pat**) ⏎

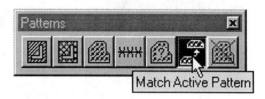

FIGURE 11–20 Invoking the Match Pattern Attributes command from the Patterns tool box.

MicroStation prompts:

> Match Pattern Attributes > Identify element *(Identify the element containing the pattern to be matched.)*
> Match Pattern Attributes > Accept/Reject (Select next input) *(Click the Data button to accept the element or the Reject button to reject it.)*

After the second data point is placed, the active patterning elements match those of the selected pattern, and the active settings appear in the Status bar.

> **NOTE:** The Match Pattern Attributes command is also available in the Match tool box that is opened from the pull-down menu Tools.

FILLING AN ELEMENT

The tool settings for closed-element placement (such as Circle and Shape) include a Fill Type menu that helps you fill the interior of the element with color. The Fill Type menu includes three settings:

- **None** The element is transparent.
- **Opaque** The element is filled with the active (outline) color.
- **Outlined** The fill color of the element is controlled by the Fill Color attribute (which can be different from the element outline color).

In addition to the Fill Type menu, a Fill Color menu is provided for setting the color of the:

- Fill and outline when the Opaque Fill Type is active.
- Fill only when the Outlined Fill Type is active.

Figure 11–21 shows a typical Tool Settings window, with the Fill Type menu open; Figure 11–22 shows examples of opaque and outlined fill types.

To place filled closed elements, just select the desired placement command, then select the desired Fill Type and follow the prompts in placing the elements.

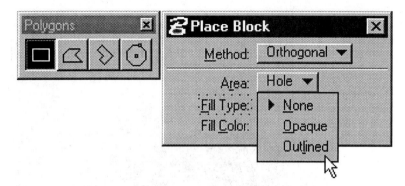

FIGURE 11–21   Fill Type menu in the Tool Settings window.

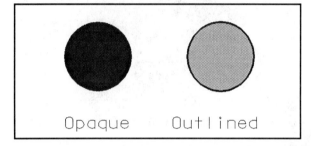

FIGURE 11–22   Example of Opaque and Outlined Fill Types.

Area Fill View Attribute

Before placing filled closed elements, make sure the Fill View attribute is turned ON for the view window being used to place the elements. If the attribute is set to OFF, filled elements appear to be transparent, and they plot that way.

To set the Fill View attribute, invoke the View Attributes window from:

Settings pull-down menu	Select View Attributes (or ⌨ + S, V)
Key-in window	**Dialog viewsettings** (or **dia views**) ⌨

Set the Fill switch ON or OFF as required (see Figure 11–23), then:

- Click the Apply button to apply the view settings to the View Number shown at the top of the window.
- Click the All button to apply the view settings to all open views.

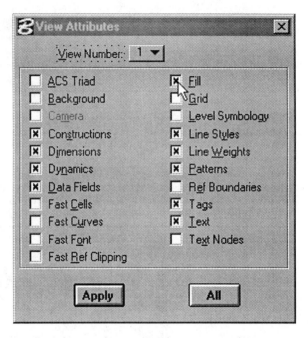

FIGURE 11–23 The Fill attribute in the View Attributes settings box.

The applied view attributes stay in effect until they are changed or the file is closed. To make the settings permanent, select Save Settings from the pull-down menu File.

> **NOTE:** If a plotter does not print the fill area of elements, it may be because of a setting in the plotter's configuration file. Consult the MicroStation technical documentation for information on plotter configuration.

Changing the Fill Type of an Existing Element

The Change Element to Active Fill Type command changes the fill type of existing elements. Invoke the command from:

Change Attributes tool box	Select the Change Element to Active Fill Type tool, and set the desired Fill Type option in the Tool Settings window (see Figure 11–24).
Key-in window	**Dialog Change Fill** (or **chan f)** [ENTER]

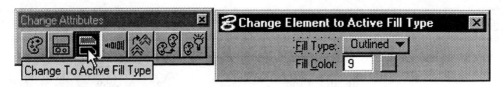

FIGURE 11–24 Invoking the Change Element to Active Fill Type command from the Change Attributes tool box.

MicroStation prompts:

> Change Element to Active Fill Type > Identify element *(Select the element to be changed.)*
> Change Element to Active Fill Type > Accept/Reject (Select next input) *(Click the Data button again to initiate the Fill Type change and, optionally, select the next element to change; or click the Reset button to reject the element.)*

If the second data point is not on an element, the error message "Element not found" appears in the Status bar. Ignore this message.

REVIEW QUESTIONS

Write your answers in the spaces provided.

1. List the three commands MicroStation provides for area patterning.

   _____

2. Explain briefly the difference between the Hatch Area and Crosshatch Area patterning.

   _____

   _____

3. List the methods that are available to set the area patterning.

   _____

4. Explain with illustrations the differences between the Intersection, Union, and Difference options in area patterning.

   _____

   _____

5. Explain the difference between the Element and Points options in area patterning.

   _____

   _____

6. What is the purpose of providing a second data point in hatching a closed element?

   _____

7. The Pattern Area command places copies of the Active Patterning _____ in the area you select.

8. What is the purpose of turning ON the Associative Pattern toggle button?

   _____

9. What is the purpose of placing elements in a Hole Area mode?

   _____

10. Explain briefly the purpose of invoking the Match Pattern Attributes command.

    _____

    _____

11. Explain briefly the three options available for area fill placement.

    _____

    _____

12. Explain the steps involved in switching an existing element between area fill modes.

    _____

    _____

PROJECT EXERCISE

This project exercise provides step-by-step instructions for creating the design shown in Figure P11–1. The intent is to guide you in placing patterns.

Prepare the Design File

This procedure starts MicroStation, creates a design file, and enters the initial settings.

> **NOTE:** As you complete each step in the project procedures, place a check mark by the step to help you keep up with where you are in the project.

STEP 1: Invoke MicroStation by the normal technique for the operating system on your workstation.

STEP 2: Create a new design file named CH11.DGN using the SEED2D.DGN seed file.

In the Design File dialog box:

- Set the Working Units Master Units name to ' (for feet), the Sub Units name to " (for inches), and the resolution ratio to 12 and 8000.
- Set the Grid Master to 0.25, Grid Reference to 4, and Grid lock to ON.

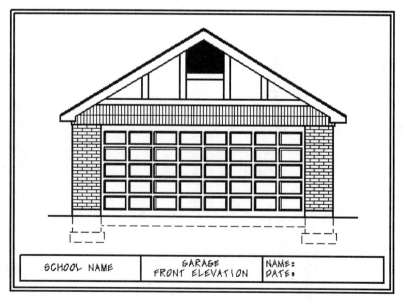

FIGURE P11–1 Completed project design.

STEP 3: Invoke the Save Settings from the pull-down menu File to save the settings.

STEP 4: Draw the border and title block on level 10 (the outer border block is 30′6″ wide by 21′6″ high):

- Replace "SCHOOL NAME" with your school or company name, or make up a name.
- Place your name to the right of "NAME."
- Place today's date to the right of "DATE."

Create Cells

This procedure creates the garage door panel cell shown in Figure P11–2 and the brick patterning cell shown in Figure P11–3.

STEP 1: Align a view window to display an area about 3′ × 3′.

STEP 2: Create a cell library file named CH11.CEL.

STEP 3: Use Figure P11–2 as a guide to draw the two rectangles making up the garage door panel. Do not draw any of the dimensions or text.

STEP 4: Create a cell from the two rectangles named *panel*, with the origin defined at the lower left corner of the outer rectangle.

STEP 5: Delete the two rectangles.

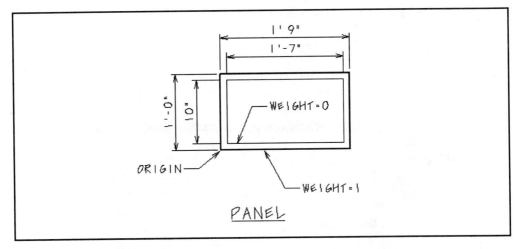

FIGURE P11–2 Garage door panel cell construction.

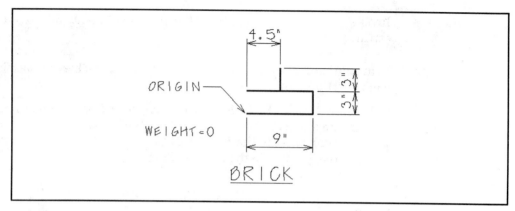

FIGURE P11-3 Brick pattern cell construction.

STEP 6: Use Figure P11-3 as a guide to draw the brick pattern.

> **NOTE:** The brick pattern lines in Figure P11-3 are shown heavy to make them easier to distinguish from the dimensions. Draw them at Line Weight 0.

STEP 7: Create a cell from the brick elements named *brick*, with the origin defined at the lower left corner. Do *not* draw any of the dimensions or text.

STEP 8: Delete the brick elements.

STEP 9: Fit the view and save the design settings.

Draw the Garage

This procedure creates the garage front elevation, as shown in Figure P11-4.

> **NOTE:** If a dimension is missing, estimate the proper placement.

STEP 1: Set the Line Weight to 1, Active Level to 2, Color to Green.

STEP 2: Using Figure P11-5 as a guide, draw the garage wall and door. Use the Place Block command to create the outline of the brick wall on each side of the garage door.

STEP 3: With Figure P11-6 as a guide, draw the garage roof.

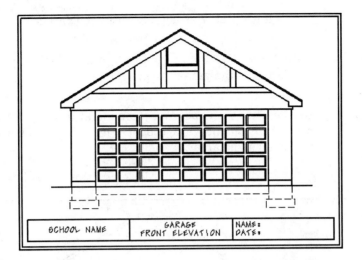

FIGURE P11–4 Garage front elevation.

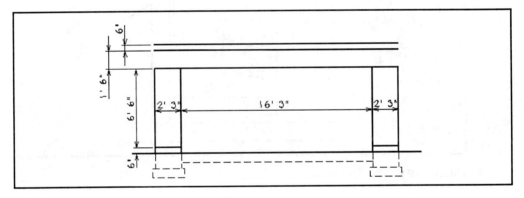

FIGURE P11–5 Garage wall and door detail.

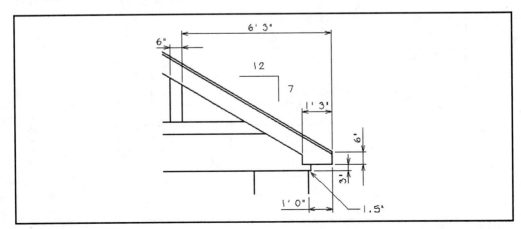

FIGURE P11–6 Garage roof detail.

STEP 4: With Figure P11–7 as a guide, draw the garage attic vent.

STEP 5: With Figure P11–8 as a guide, place a copy of the panel cell in the lower left corner of the garage door.

STEP 6: Invoke the Construct Array command to place a rectangular array of panel cells in the garage door. Figure P11–9 shows the required tool settings for the array.

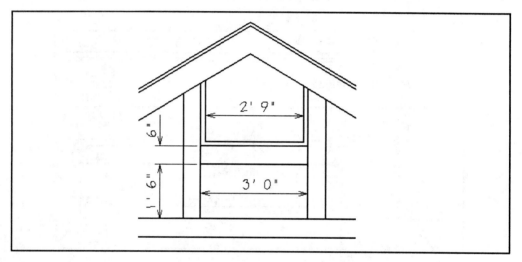

FIGURE P11–7 Garage vent detail.

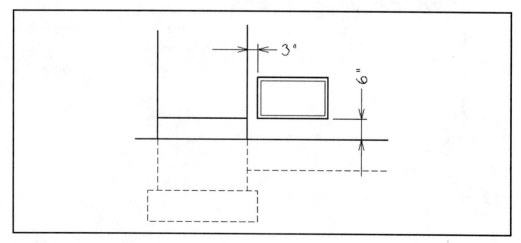

FIGURE P11–8 Garage door detail.

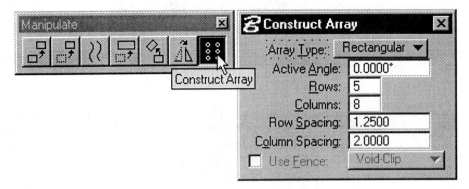

FIGURE P11-9 *Construct Array tool settings.*

Place the Brick Patterns

This procedure uses the Pattern Area command to place the brick pattern on each side of the garage door, the Crosshatch Area command to place the brick pattern above the garage door, and the Hatch Area command to place the louvers in the attic vent.

STEP 1: Set the Active Level to 4.

STEP 2: Use the Window Area command to fill the view with the rectangle on the right side of the garage door.

STEP 3: Invoke the Pattern Area command from the Patterns tool box, and, in the Tool Settings window, adjust the tool settings as shown in Figure P11–10.

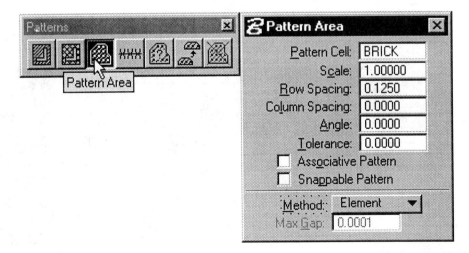

FIGURE P11-10 *Pattern Area tool settings.*

NOTE: If you did not use a closed element for the brick walls, set the patterning Method to Flood.

MicroStation prompts:

> Pattern Area > Identify element *(Select the block element to be patterned on the right side of the garage door.)*
>
> Pattern Area > Accept @pattern intersection point *(Keypoint snap to the lower left corner of the block element to be patterned, then place a data point to initiate patterning.)*

STEP 4: Arrange the view window to display the block element on the left side of the garage door, and use the Pattern Area command to place a brick pattern in it.

STEP 5: Arrange the view window to display all of the area above the garage door that is to be filled with two vertical brick rows.

STEP 6: Invoke the Crosshatch Area command from the Patterns tool box, and, in the Tool Settings window, make the tool settings shown in Figure P11–11.

MicroStation prompts:

> Crosshatch Area > Enter data point inside area *(Click inside the brick area above the garage door.)*
>
> Crosshatch Area > Accept @pattern intersection point *(Keypoint snap to the lower left corner of the area to be crosshatched, as shown in Figure P11–12, then place a data point to initiate crosshatching.)*

STEP 7: Arrange the view window to fill the view with the attic vent area.

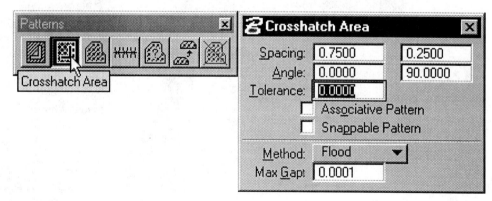

FIGURE P11–11 Required Crosshatch Area tool settings.

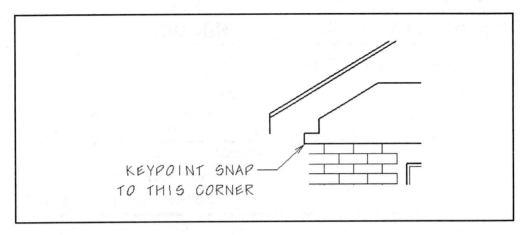

FIGURE P11–12 Acceptance point for crosshatching.

STEP 8: Invoke the Hatch Area command from the Patterns tool box, and, in the Tool Settings window, make the tool settings shown in Figure P11–13.

MicroStation prompts:

> Hatch Area > Enter data point inside area *(Click inside the vent area.)*
> Hatch Area > Accept @pattern intersection point *(Keypoint snap to the lower left corner of the area to be hatched, then place a data point to initiate hatching.)*

STEP 9: Invoke the Fit View command to fit the view.

STEP 10: Invoke the Save Settings command from the pull-down menu File to save the settings.

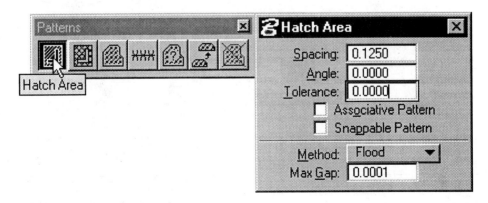

FIGURE P11–13 Required Hatch Area tool settings.

DRAWING EXERCISES 11–1 THROUGH 11–5

Exercises 11–1 through 11–3

Use the following table to set up the design files for Exercises 11–1 through 11–3.

SETTING	VALUE
Seed File	SEED2D.DGN
Working Units	MU = IN, SU = 10 TH, PU = 1000
Grid	Master = .1, Reference = 10, Grid lock to ON

Exercise 11–1   Nozzle.

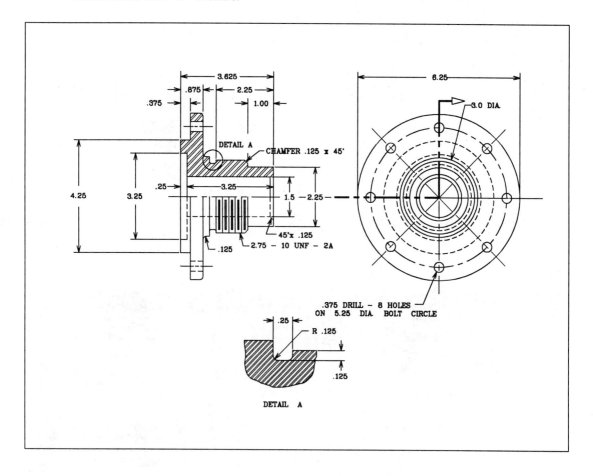

Exercise 11–2 Beam compass pointer.

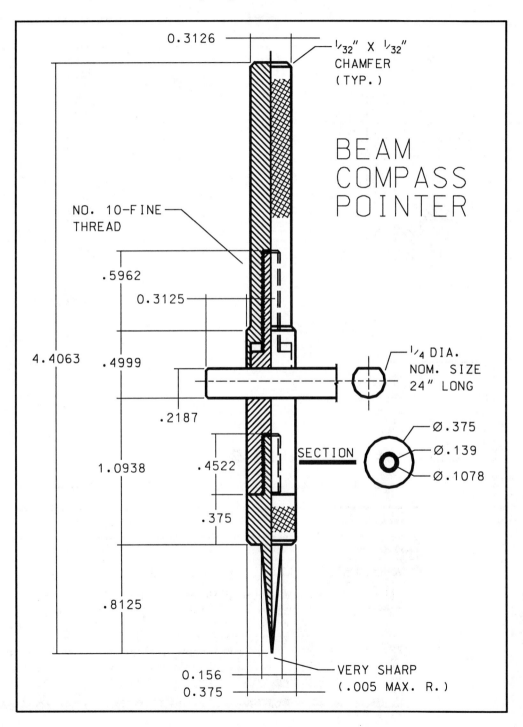

0.3126

1/32" X 1/32" CHAMFER (TYP.)

BEAM COMPASS POINTER

NO. 10-FINE THREAD

.5962

0.3125

4.4063   .4999

1/4 DIA. NOM. SIZE 24" LONG

.2187

Ø.375
Ø.139
Ø.1078

SECTION

1.0938   .4522

.375

.8125

0.156
0.375

VERY SHARP (.005 MAX. R.)

Exercise 11–3 Backplate cast aluminum.

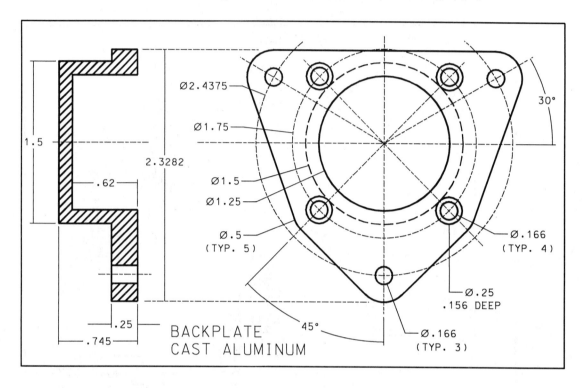

BACKPLATE
CAST ALUMINUM

Exercises 11–4 and 11–5

Use the following table to set up the design files for Exercises 11–4 and 11–5.

SETTING	VALUE
Seed File	SEED2D.DGN
Working Units	MU = ′, SU = 12″, PU = 12000
Grid	Master = :.5, Reference = 24, GRID lock to ON

NOTE: The cells used for area patterning in these two exercises were taken from a cell library furnished with MicroStation. The path to the cell library is: \USTATION\WSMOD\DEFAULT\CELL\ARCHPA.CEL

Exercise 11–4 Parade stand.

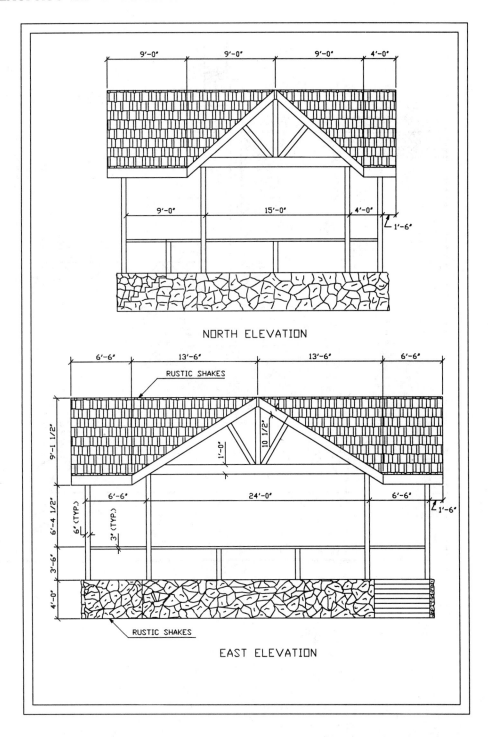

NORTH ELEVATION

EAST ELEVATION

Exercise 11–5 Architectural detail.

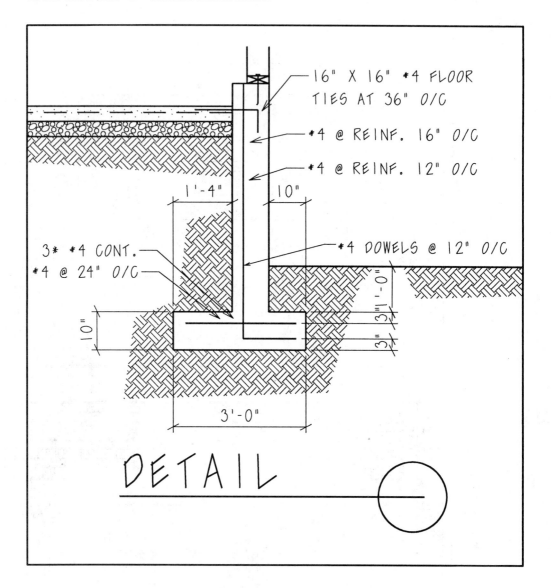

16" X 16" #4 FLOOR TIES AT 36" O/C

#4 @ REINF. 16" O/C

#4 @ REINF. 12" O/C

1'-4"

10"

#4 DOWELS @ 12" O/C

3* #4 CONT.

#4 @ 24" O/C

1'-0"

3"

3"

10"

3'-0"

DETAIL

CHAPTER

12

REFERENCE FILES

One of the most powerful time-saving features of MicroStation is its ability to view other design files while you are working in your design file. MicroStation lets you display the contents of up to 255 other design files (default is set to 32 design files) while working in your current design file. This function is in the form of reference files.

OBJECTIVES

After completing this chapter, you will be able to:

✓ Attach a reference file.

✓ Move a reference file in the design plane.

✓ Scale your view of a reference file.

✓ Rotate your view of a reference file.

✓ Mirror your view of a reference file.

✓ Clip off part of your view of a reference file.

✓ Detach a reference file.

✓ Reload a reference file.

OVERVIEW OF REFERENCE FILES

When a design file is referenced externally in your design file, you can view and tentative point snap to all elements in the reference file, but each drawing's data is still stored and maintained in a separate design file. The only information about the referenced design file that becomes a permanent part of your design file is the name of the referenced design file and its directory path.

If necessary, you can use the regular Copy (or Fence Copy) command to copy selected elements of the reference file into your design file. Once the elements are copied into your current design file, they become part of the current design file. This method is very useful if, for example, a design file that was drawn previously contains information that can be used in your current design file.

Reference files may be scaled, moved, rotated, and viewed by levels via commands that are specifically programmed to work with reference files. The reference file behaves as one element when you manipulate it with reference file manipulation commands. The only exception is the regular Copy command, in which the elements behave as individual elements. All of the manipulations are performed on your view of the referenced file, not the actual file. You cannot edit or modify the contents of a referenced file. If you need to make any changes to it, you actually have to load that file in MicroStation.

When you attach an external reference file, it is permanently attached until you detach it. When you open a design file, MicroStation automatically reloads each reference file; thus, you see the current version of each reference file when you view your design file.

EXAMPLES OF USING REFERENCE FILES

Borders and title blocks are an excellent example of design files that are useful as reference files. The elements that make up the border use considerable space in a file and usually amount to around 40 to 50 KB. If a border and title block is drawn in each design file, it would waste a large amount of space, especially if you multiply 50 KB by 100 design files. If reference files are used correctly, they can save a lot of disk space.

Accuracy and efficient drawing time are other important design features that are enhanced through the use of reference files. As mentioned earlier, when an addition or change is made to a design file that is serving as a reference file, all the design files that use that file will reflect the modifications. For example, let's say the name of the company is changed. Just change the company name in the title block design file, and all the design files that use the title block as a reference file automatically display the new company name the next time they are accessed. (Can you imagine accessing 100 design files to correct one small detail?) Reference files save time and ensure the drawing accuracy required to produce a professional product.

When combined with the networking capability of MicroStation, external references give the project manager powerful new tools for coping with the realities of file management. The project manager can, by combining drawings through the referencing tools, see instantaneously the work of the various departments or designers working on a particular aspect of the project. If necessary, you can overlay a drawing where appropriate, track the progress, and maintain document integrity. At the same time, departments need not lose control over individual designs and details.

Let's look at an example of this function in operation. Let's say that you are a supervisor with three designers reporting to you. All three of them are working on a project; each one is responsible for one-third of the project. As a supervisor you want to know how much progress each designer has made at the end of each day. Instead of calling up each of the three design files to see the progress, you can create a dummy design file and attach the three design files as reference files. Every day you can call up the dummy design file, and MicroStation will display the latest versions of the reference files attached to your design file. This will make your job a lot easier and give you an opportunity to put together all three pieces of the puzzle to see how they fit into the evolving design.

As mentioned earlier, you can attach by default 32 reference files at any time to a design file. If necessary, you can increase this number to 255 reference files. This change is made in the Preference dialog box invoked from the pull-down menu Workspaces. The valid range is 16 to 255. MicroStation allocates approximately 0.5 KB of memory for each allowed reference file, regardless of whether an attachment actually exists. Thus, you should set the maximum no higher than necessary. A change in the Preference dialog box is not effective until the next time you start MicroStation.

In addition to attaching a design file as a reference file, you can attach a raster image file as a reference file. Monochrome, continuous-tone (gray-scale), or color images in a variety of supported image formats can be attached.

ATTACHING A REFERENCE FILE

To attach a reference file, invoke the Attach Reference file command from:

Reference Files tool box	Select the Attach Reference File tool (see Figure 12–1).
Pull-down menu (Reference Files settings box)	<u>T</u>ools > <u>A</u>ttach... (or [ALT] + **T, A**)
Key-in window	**Attach Reference** (or **RF=**) [ENTER]

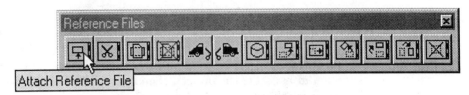

FIGURE 12-1 Invoking the Attach Reference File command from the Reference Files tool box.

MicroStation displays the Attach Reference File dialog box, as shown in Figure 12–2. Select from the list box the design file to attach as a reference file and click the OK button.

MicroStation displays another dialog box, similar to the one shown in Figure 12–3, where you can enter additional, optional information. The top part of the dialog box displays the name and path of the design file being attached as a reference file. To retain the reference file's full path specification in the attachment information, turn ON the toggle button for Save Full Path.

Click in the Logical Name edit field and type in a name. The logical name is a short identifier or nickname you can use later to identify the reference file being attached. The logical name is optional, unless you attach the same design file more than once to the current design file.

The next edit field is for a Description. The Description, which is optional, can serve to describe the purpose of the attachment. If more than two or three reference files

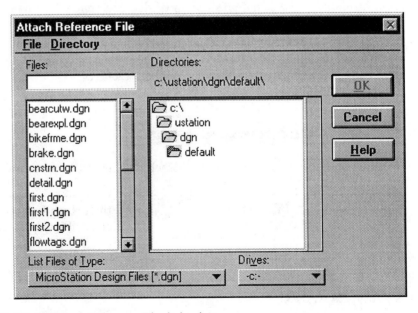

FIGURE 12-2 Attach Reference File dialog box.

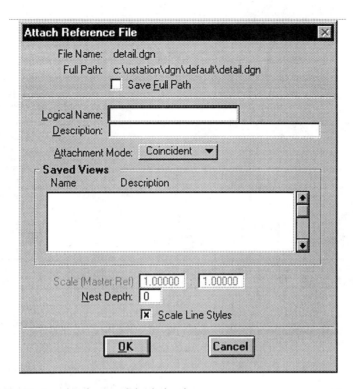

FIGURE 12-3 Optional Reference File dialog box.

are attached, it allows you to identify the purpose of attachment quickly. The Description cannot exceed 40 characters.

Select one of the two options available in the Attachment Mode. By default, Attachment Mode is set to Coincident. In Coincident mode, MicroStation attaches the reference file in such a way that the coordinates of the reference file's design plane are aligned with those of the active design file, without any rotation, scaling, or offset.

If the Attachment Mode is set to Saved View, you can select one of the available Saved Views from the list box. A saved view allows you to display a clipped portion of the design file. You can attach the saved view at a specified scale factor by entering the appropriate scale factor in the dialog box. The Saved View mode is available only when you have saved views in the design file that is being attached as a reference file. (See Chapter 5 for how to save views.)

The Scale edit field allows you to specify the scale factor as a ratio between the Master Units of the active design file and the Master Units of the reference file.

NOTE: You can specify the scale factor only when you attach a saved view of the reference file.

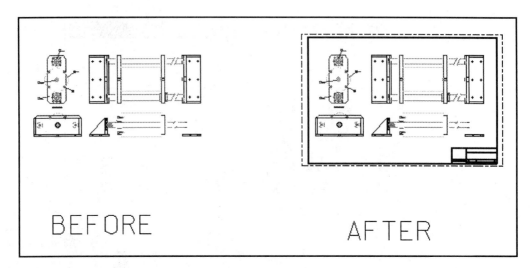

FIGURE 12-4 Design before and after attaching a reference file.

The Scale Line Styles toggle button controls the scaling of the custom line style. If it is set to ON, custom line style components (for example, dashes) are scaled by the Scale (Master:Ref) factors. If it is set to OFF, custom line style components are not scaled.

Click the OK button to attach the selected reference file to the current design file, or click the Cancel button to cancel the reference file attachment.

You can reference the same design file more than one time. The only restriction is that you must provide a unique logical name for each attachment. Though it is not required, it is advisable to use the Description field to explain each attachment. That will save other people time in figuring out why the same file is referenced more than once. For example, the same design file might be referenced more than one time when different parts of the referenced design serve as details in your design file.

Figure 12–4 shows a design before and after attaching a reference file (title block).

Listing of the Attached Reference Files

To list the reference files attached to the current design files, invoke:

Pull-down menu	File > Reference (or ⟨ALT⟩ + **F**, **R**)

MicroStation displays the Reference File settings box, as shown in Figure 12–5. The settings box lists all the reference files attached to the current design file. In addition to the listing of the reference files, the settings box also provides the logical name of the reference file, and the status of the Display, Snap, and Locate options of the reference files.

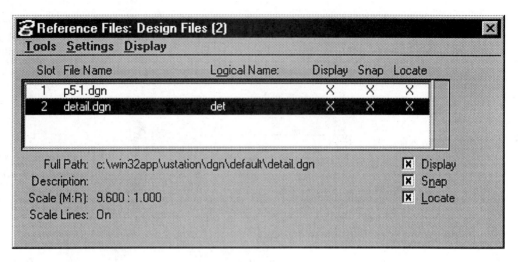

FIGURE 12-5 Reference File settings box.

The Display controls the screen display of the specified reference file. If for some reason you don't want to display the reference file but still want to keep it attached, set the Display toggle button to OFF; MicroStation will not display or plot the specified reference file.

The Snap control gives the ability to tentative point snap to any element visible from the reference file. If you set the Snap to OFF, you can see the elements on the screen display but cannot tentative snap to any element in the specified reference file. If you set the Snap to ON, you can see the elements on the screen display as well as tentative snap to any element in the specified reference file.

The Locate control allows you to locate elements that are displayed on your screen as a reference file and to copy them into your file via the Copy command. If you set Locate to OFF, you can see the elements on the screen display but cannot identify the elements to use with the Copy command. If you set the Locate to ON, you can see the elements on the screen display as well as identify them for use with the Copy command.

The default settings for the Display, Snap, and Locate options are set in the Preferences. If necessary, you can change the status of Display, Snap, and Locate by first selecting the appropriate reference file from the list box and then changing the status of the options located in the bottom right side of the settings box.

If necessary, you can also change the logical name and description of an attached reference file. Double click the name of the reference file in the list box; MicroStation displays the Attachment Settings box as shown in Figure 12–6. Edit the Logical Name and Description. If necessary, you can also change the path of the attached reference file. Click on the Browse button, and select the reference file in the

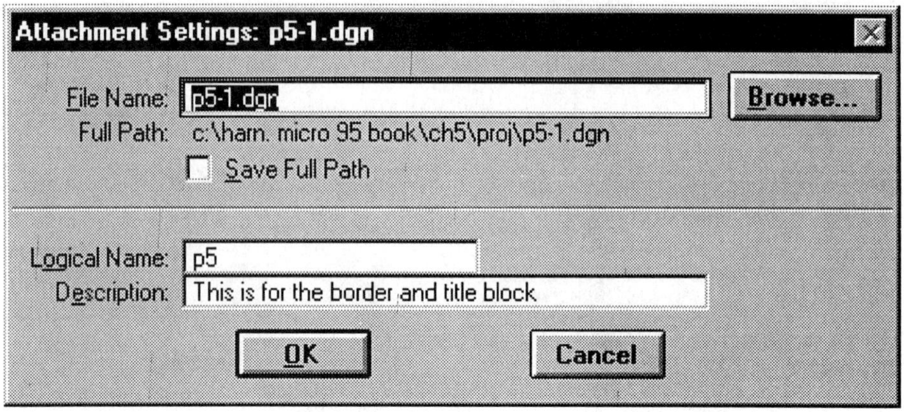

FIGURE 12–6 Attachment Settings box.

Reattach Reference File dialog box. This step is necessary only if you have moved the attached reference file to another directory or drive after initial attachment and MicroStation cannot locate the reference file.

REFERENCE FILE MANIPULATIONS

MicroStation provides a set of manipulation commands specifically designed to manipulate reference files. As mentioned earlier, the reference file behaves as one element, and there is no way to drop it. The reference manipulation commands include Move, Scale, Rotate, Mirror Horizontal, Mirror Vertical, Clip Boundary, Clip Mask, and Clip Mask Delete.

Move Reference File

The Move Reference File command allows you to move a reference file from one location to another. This command is useful whenever you want to reposition the reference file. Before you invoke the command, highlight the reference file by clicking the Data button in the Reference File settings box.

To move a reference file, invoke the Move Reference file command from:

Reference Files tool box	Select the Move Reference File tool (see Figure 12–7).
Pull-down menu (Reference Files settings box)	<u>T</u>ools > <u>M</u>ove (or ⌨ + **T, M**)
Key-in window	**Reference Move** (or **refe mov**) ⏎

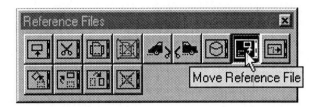

FIGURE 12–7 Invoking the Move Reference File command from the Reference Files tool box.

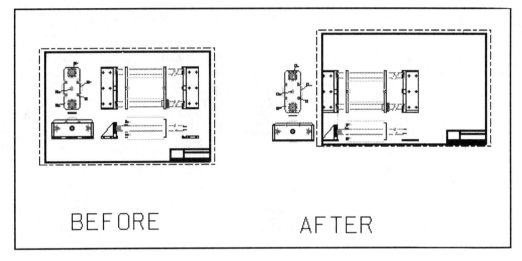

BEFORE   AFTER

FIGURE 12–8 The design view before and after moving a reference file.

MicroStation prompts:

Move Reference File > Enter point to move from *(Place a data point anywhere on the reference file.)*
Move Reference File > Enter point to move to *(Place a data point where you want to move the reference file in reference to the first data point.)*

When the file has completely finished updating, the command is complete. To move another reference file or the same file to another location, start the entire operation again. Figure 12–8 shows a view before and after moving a reference file border.

Scale Reference File

The Scale Reference File command allows you to enlarge or reduce a reference file. Before you invoke the command, highlight the reference file by clicking the Data button in the Reference File settings box.

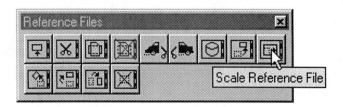

FIGURE 12-9 Invoking the Scale Reference File command from the Reference Files tool box.

To scale a reference file, invoke the Scale Reference file command from:

Reference Files tool box	Select the Scale Reference File tool (see Figure 12–9).
Pull-down menu (Reference Files settings box)	<u>T</u>ools > <u>S</u>cale... (or 🄰ᴸᵀ + **T, S**)
Key-in window	**Reference Scale** (or **refe s**) ⏎ᴱᴺᵀᴱᴿ

In the Tool Settings window specify the scale factor in terms of a ratio of the Master Units of the active design file to the Master Units of the reference file.

MicroStation prompts:

> Scale Reference File > Enter point to scale reference file about *(Place a data point from which the file will scale.)*

For example, a ratio of 3:1 scales a reference file up three times; a ratio of 1:5 scales a reference file down five times. If you make a mistake, you can always invoke the Undo command to undo the last operation.

When the file has completely finished updating, the command is complete. To scale another reference file or the same file with a different scale factor, start the entire operation again.

> **NOTE:** The scale factor ratio between the active design file and the reference file is *not* cumulative. For instance, if you specify a scale of 3:1 followed by 6:1, the final result will be 6:1. Figure 12–10 shows a view before and after scaling the reference file border.

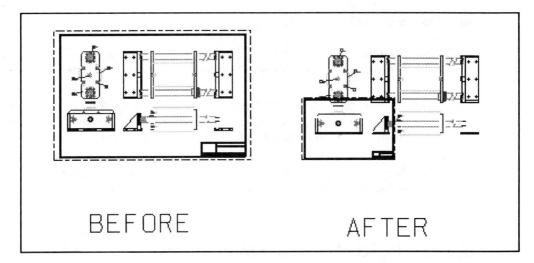

BEFORE   AFTER

FIGURE 12–10   This design shows a view before and after scaling a reference file.

Rotate Reference File

The Rotate Reference File command allows you to rotate a reference file to any angle around a pivot point. Before you invoke the command, highlight the reference file by clicking the Data button in the Reference File settings box.

To rotate a reference file, invoke the Rotate Reference file command from:

Reference Files tool box	Select the Rotate Reference File tool (see Figure 12–11).
Pull-down menu (Reference Files settings box)	<u>T</u>ools > <u>R</u>otate... (or 🄰 + **T, R**)
Key-in window	**Reference Rotate (or refe ro)** ⏎

In the Tool Settings window specify the rotation angle.

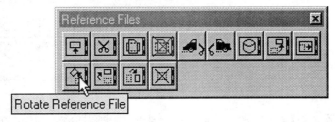

FIGURE 12–11   Invoking the Rotate Reference File command from the Reference Files tool box.

MicroStation prompts:

> Rotate Reference File > Enter point to rotate reference file about *(Place a data point to define a pivot point about which the reference file rotates.)*

For example, an angle of 60 degrees rotates the reference file 60 degrees counter-clockwise from its current position around a pivot point. If you make a mistake, you can always invoke the Undo command to undo the last operation.

When the file has completely finished updating, the command is complete. To rotate another reference file or to reposition the same file, start the entire operation again.

Mirror Horizontal Reference File

The Mirror Horizontal Reference File command allows you to mirror a reference file about the horizontal (or *X*) axis. Before you invoke the command, highlight the reference file by clicking the Data button in the Reference File settings box.

To mirror a reference file about the horizontal, invoke the Mirror Reference file Horizontal command from:

Reference Files tool box	Select the Mirror Reference File Horizontal tool (see Figure 12–12).
Pull-down menu (Reference Files settings box)	Tools > Mirror Horizontal (or [ALT] + **T, H**)
Key-in window	**Reference Mirror Horizontal** (or **refe m h**) [ENTER]

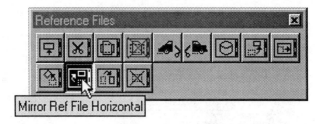

FIGURE 12–12 Invoking the Mirror Reference File Horizontal command from the Reference Files tool box.

MicroStation prompts:

> Mirror Reference File About Horizontal > Enter point to mirror about *(Place a data point to define the mirror axis.)*

When the file has completely finished updating, the command is complete. To mirror horizontally, another reference file or the same file, start the entire operation again.

Mirror Vertical Reference File

The Mirror Vertical Reference File command allows you to mirror a reference file about the vertical (or *Y*) axis. Before you invoke the command, highlight the reference file by clicking the Data button in the Reference Files settings box.

To mirror a reference file about the vertical, invoke the Mirror Reference file Vertical command from:

Reference Files tool box	Select the Mirror Reference File Vertical tool (see Figure 12–13).
Pull-down menu (Reference Files settings box)	<u>T</u>ools > Mirror <u>V</u>ertical (or 🖮 + **T, V**)
Key-in window	**Reference Mirror Vertical** (or **refe m v**) ⏎

MicroStation prompts:

> Mirror Reference File About Vertical > Enter point to mirror about *(Place a data point to define the mirror axis.)*

When the file has completely finished updating, the command is complete. To mirror vertically another reference file, start the entire operation again.

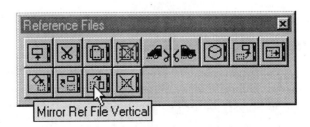

FIGURE 12–13 Invoking the Mirror Reference File Vertical command from the Reference Files tool box.

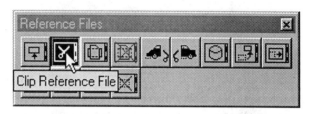

FIGURE 12–14 Invoking the Clip Reference File command from the Reference Files tool box.

Reference Clip Boundary

The Reference Clip Boundary command lets you display only a desired portion of a reference file. Before you invoke the command, highlight the reference file by clicking the Data button in the Reference Files settings box. Then place a Fence on the reference file to draw the clipping boundary. Make sure the fence defines the desired area. The clipping boundary can have up to 60 vertices. You can even place a circular fence. Nonrectangular clipping boundaries are displayed in a view and plotted only if Fast Reference File clipping is set to OFF for the selected view.

To clip a boundary, first place a fence, then invoke the Clip Reference File command from:

Reference Files tool box	Select the Clip Reference File tool (see Figure 12–14).
Pull-down menu (Reference Files settings box)	<u>T</u>ools > Clip <u>B</u>oundary (or [ALT] + **T, B**)
Key-in window	**Reference Clip Boundary** (or **refe c bo**) [ENTER]

MicroStation displays only the part of the reference file enclosed within the fence. If you make a mistake, you can always invoke the Undo command to undo the last operation.

Reference Clip Mask

The Reference Clip Mask command, like the Clip Boundary command, allows you to display only a portion of a reference file. Clip Boundary displays the part inside a fence, whereas the Clip Mask command displays the part outside the fence.

Before you invoke the command, highlight the reference file by clicking the Data button in the Reference Files settings box. Then place a Fence on the reference file

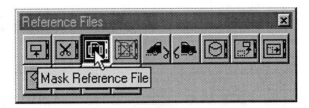

FIGURE 12–15   Invoking the Mask Reference File command from the Reference Files tool box.

to draw the clipping mask. Make sure the fence defines the desired area. The clipping mask can have up to 60 vertices.

To clip a mask, first place a fence, then invoke the Mask Reference File command from:

Reference Files tool box	Select the Mask Reference File tool (see Figure 12–15).
Pull-down menu (Reference Files settings box)	<u>T</u>ools > Clip Mas<u>k</u> (or ⌨ **ALT** + **T, K**)
Key-in window	**Reference Clip Mask** (or **refe c m**) ⌨ **ENTER**

MicroStation displays only the part of the reference file outside the fence. If you make a mistake, you can always invoke the Undo command to undo the last operation.

Deleting Reference File Clipping Mask(s)

The Delete Reference File Clipping Mask(s) command can selectively delete a reference file's clipping mask(s).

To delete a reference file's clipping mask(s), invoke the Delete Reference File Clipping Mask(s) command from:

Reference Files tool box	Select the Delete Clip Mask tool (see Figure 12–16).
Pull-down menu (Reference Files settings box)	<u>T</u>ools > Clip Mask De<u>l</u>ete (or ⌨ **ALT** + **T, L**)
Key-in window	**Reference Clip Mask Delete** (or **refe c m d**) ⌨ **ENTER**

MicroStation deletes the selected clip mask.

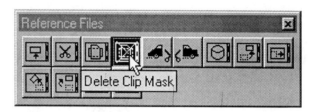

FIGURE 12-16 Invoking the Delete Clip Mask command from the Reference Files tool box.

Detaching the Reference File

Whenever you no longer need the reference file, you can detach it from the current design file. Once the reference file is detached, there is no more link between the reference file and the current design file.

Before you invoke the command, highlight the reference file you want to detach by clicking the Data button on the file name in the Reference Files settings box.

To detach a reference file, invoke the Detach Reference File command from:

Reference Files tool box	Select the Detach Reference File tool (see Figure 12–17).
Pull-down menu (Reference Files settings box)	<u>T</u>ools > <u>D</u>etach (or ⌥ + **T, D**)
Key-in window	**Reference Detach** (or **refe d**) ENTER

MicroStation displays an alert box to confirm that the selected reference file is to be detached. Click the OK button to detach.

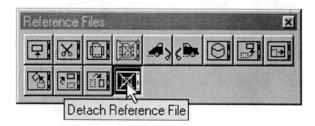

FIGURE 12-17 Invoking the Detach Reference File command from the Reference Files tool box.

To detach all the attached reference files, invoke the Detach All command from:

Pull-down menu (Reference Files settings box)	Tools > Detach All (or [ALT] + **T, T**)
Key-in window	**Reference Detach All** (or **refe d all**) [ENTER]

MicroStation displays an alert box to confirm that all the reference files are to be detached. Click the OK button to detach all the reference files.

Reloading the Reference File

MicroStation reloads automatically all reference files attached to a design file only when you first open the design file. The Reload command has been provided to reread the reference file whenever it is desirable to do so while working in the design file. The Reload command is helpful, especially in a network environment, to access the latest version of the reference design file while you are working in a design to which it has been attached.

Before you invoke the command, highlight the reference file you want to reload by clicking the Data button in the Reference Files settings box.

To reload a reference file, invoke the Reload Reference File command from:

Reference Files tool box	Select the Reload Reference File tool (see Figure 12–18).
Pull-down menu (Reference Files settings box)	Tools > Reload (or [ALT] + **T, E**)
Key-in window	**Reference Reload** (or **refe r**) [ENTER]

MicroStation reloads the selected reference file.

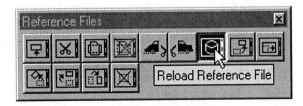

FIGURE 12–18 Invoking the Reload Reference File command from the Reference Files tool box.

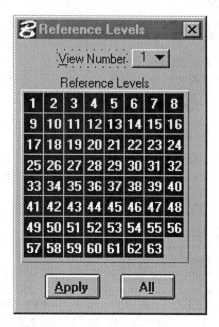

FIGURE 12–19   Reference Levels settings box.

Levels and Level Symbology

In addition to controlling the displays of the reference file, you can manipulate the displays of specific levels in a reference file. To manipulate the levels, first highlight the reference file you want to manipulate by clicking the Data button in the Reference Files settings box, then invoke the Levels settings box from:

Pull-down menu (Reference Files settings box)	Settings > Levels (or [ALT] + **S, L**)

MicroStation displays the Reference Levels settings box, as shown in Figure 12–19. Select the level numbers you want to turn OFF/ON, whichever the case may be. Once the selection is completed, click the Apply button. Before you click the Apply button, make sure you have selected the appropriate view number from the View Number options menu.

Similarly, you can manipulate the Level Symbology (explained in Chapter 13) for a reference file.

REVIEW QUESTIONS

Write your answers in the spaces provided.

1. List at least two benefits of using reference files.

   _____

2. By default, how many reference files can you attach to a design file?

   _____

3. What effect does attaching reference files have on a design file size?

   _____

4. List the commands that are specifically provided to manipulate reference files.

   _____

   _____

5. Give the steps involved in attaching a reference file.

   _____

   _____

6. Explain the difference between the Reference Clip Boundary command and the Reference Clip Mask command.

   _____

   _____

7. List the steps involved in detaching a reference file.

   _____

   _____

PROJECT EXERCISE

This project exercise provides step-by-step instructions for creating the design shown in Figure P12–1. The intent is to guide you in using reference files to complete a design.

This project creates separate design files for:

- Pipe rack plot plan
- Pump foundation plot plan
- Border
- Complete design formed from references to the other three design files

> **NOTE:** As you complete each step in the project procedures, place a check mark by the step to help you keep up with where you are in the project.

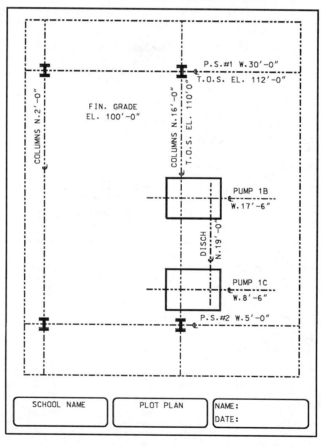

FIGURE P12–1 Completed project design.

Create the Pipe Rack Plot Plan

This procedure creates the design shown in Figure P12–2. The pipe rack is drawn using offsets from the design origin point.

STEP 1: Invoke MicroStation via the normal technique for the operating system on your workstation.

STEP 2: Create a new design file named RACK.DGN using the SEED2D.DGN seed file.

STEP 3: Set the following design parameters:

- Working Units Master Units name to ' (for feet), the Sub Units name to " (for inches), and the resolution ratio to 12 and 8000
- Grid Master to 0.5, Grid Reference to 2, and Grid lock to OFF
- Active Level = 2
- Line Weight = 1
- Line Style = 6
- Color = Yellow

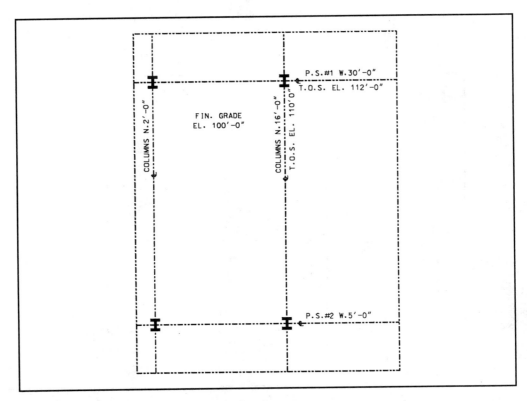

FIGURE P12–2 Completed pipe rack plot plan.

STEP 4: Invoke the Save Settings command from the pull-down menu File to save the design settings.

STEP 5: Draw the following two unconnected lines:

- XY=2,0 to DL=0,35
- XY=0,5 to DL=28,0

STEP 6: Make parallel copies of the two lines:

- Horizontal line: 25 feet above the original line
- Vertical line: 14 feet to the right of the original line

STEP 7: Draw a block from XY=0,0 to XY=28,35, as shown in Figure P12–3.

STEP 8: Set the element attributes to:

- Active Level = 1
- Line Style = 0
- Line Weight = 4
- Color = Black

STEP 9: Draw a 1 foot by 1 foot I-beam centered on the lower left centerline intersection, as shown in Figure P12–4.

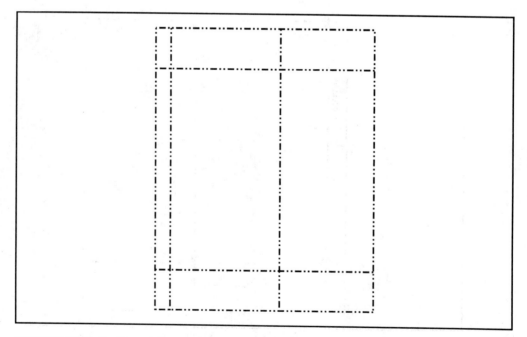

FIGURE P12–3 Pipe rack centerlines and perimeter.

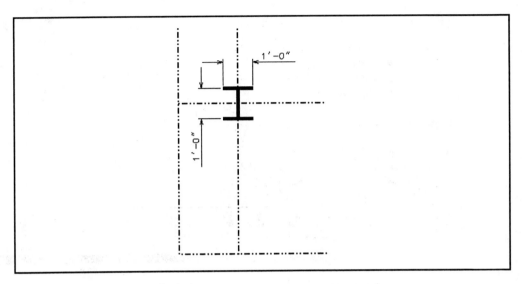

FIGURE P12–4 Lower left I-beam.

STEP 10: Use the Array command to place a rectangular array with the following settings (see Figure P12–5):

- Rows = 2
- Columns = 2
- Row spacing = 25
- Column spacing = 14

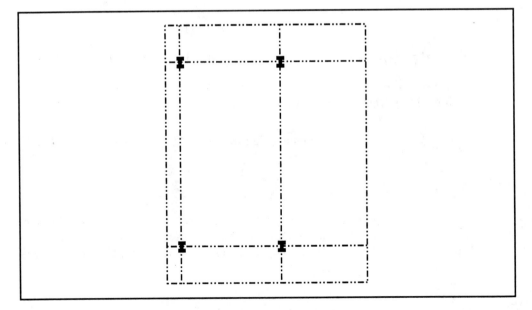

FIGURE P12–5 Results of the Rectangular Array command.

STEP 11: Set the element attributes to:

- Active Level = 3
- Line Style = 0
- Line Weight = 0
- Color = Black

STEP 12: Set the text parameters to:

- Font = 3
- Height and Width = 0.125
- Line Spacing = 0.125

> **NOTE:** The text size is 0.125′, so it will plot 0.125″ (⅛″) high at a plot scale of ¼″ = 1′.

STEP 13: Place all text shown in Figure P12–2.

> **NOTE:** To place the symbol on the centerlines, set the Font to 15 (IGES1001), and place the lowercase letter **q**.

STEP 14: Invoke the Save Settings command from the pull-down menu File to save the design settings.

Create the Pump Foundations Plot Plan

This procedure creates the design shown in Figure P12–6. The foundations are drawn using offsets from the design origin point.

STEP 1: Create a new design file named PUMPS.DGN using the SEED2D.DGN seed file.

STEP 2: Set up the design settings as follows:

- Working Units Master Units name to ′ (for feet), the Sub Units name to ″ (for inches), and the resolution ratio to 12 and 8000
- Grid Master to 0.5, Grid Reference to 2, and Grid lock to OFF
- Active Level = 2
- Line Weight = 1
- Line Style = 6
- Color = Yellow

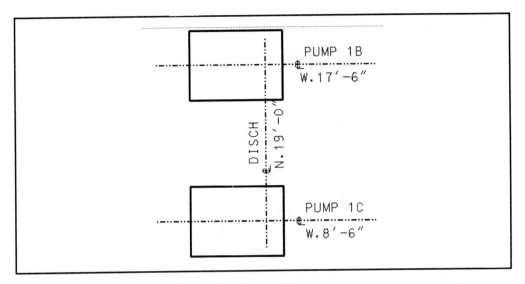

FIGURE P12–6   Pump foundations plot plan.

STEP 3:   Invoke the Save Settings command from the pull-down menu File to save the design settings.

STEP 4:   Draw the following two unconnected lines:

- XY=12.5,8.5 to DL=13,0
- XY=19,7 to DL=0,12

STEP 5:   Make a parallel copy of the horizontal line 9′ above the original.

STEP 6:   Set the element parameters to:

- Active Level = 1
- Line Style = 0
- Line Weight = 2
- Color = Black

STEP 7:   Draw a block from XY=14.5,6.5 to DL=5.5,4, as shown in Figure P12–7.

STEP 8:   Make a copy of the block exactly 8′ above the original.

STEP 9:   Set the element attributes to:

- Active Level = 3
- Line Style = 0
- Line Weight = 0
- Color = Black

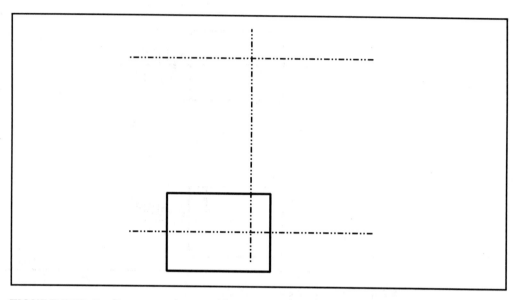

FIGURE P12–7 Pump centerlines and lower pump foundations.

STEP 10: Set the text parameters to:

- Font = 3
- Height and Width = 0.125′
- Line Spacing = 0.125′

STEP 11: Place text as shown in Figure P12–6.

STEP 12: Invoke the Save Settings command from the pull-down menu File to save the design settings.

Create the Border

This procedure creates the design shown in Figure P12–8.

STEP 1: Create a new design file named BORDER.DGN using the SEED2D.DGN seed file.

STEP 2: Adjust the design settings as follows:

- Working Units Master Units name to IN (for inches), the Sub Units name to TH (for tenths of an inch), and the resolution ratio to 10 and 1000
- Grid Master to 0.1, Grid Reference to 10, and Grid lock to ON
- Active Level = 1

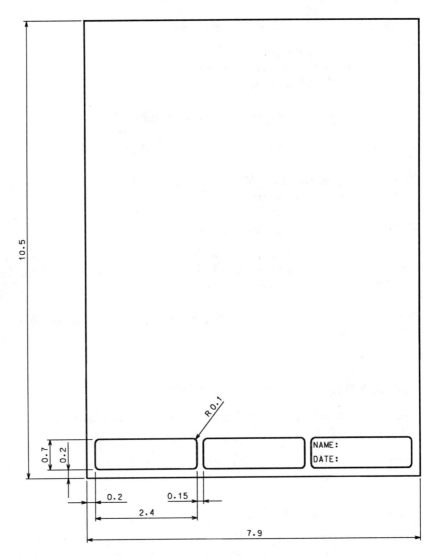

FIGURE P12–8 Letter-size border.

- Line Weight = 1
- Line Style = 0
- Color = Black

STEP 3: Invoke the Save Settings command from the pull-down menu File to save the design settings.

STEP 4: Draw the border and title block using the dimensions shown in Figure P12–8.

STEP 5: Set the following parameters:

- Line Weight = 0
- Text Height and Width = .125″
- Text Font = 3

STEP 6: Place the text as shown in Figure P12–8.

STEP 7: Invoke the Fit View command to fit the view.

STEP 8: Open the Save Views settings box by selecting Saved Views from the pull-down menu Utilities.

STEP 9: In the Saved Views settings box:

- Key-in **border** in the Source Name field.
- Key-in **Letter-size border** in the Source Description field.
- Click the Save button to create a saved view.

STEP 10: Invoke the Save Settings command from the pull-down menu File to save the design settings.

Create the Complete Design

This procedure creates the composite design by referencing the previous design files (see Figure P12–1).

STEP 1: Create a new design file named CH12.DGN using the SEED2D.DGN seed file.

STEP 2: Set up the design settings as follows:

- Working Units Master Units name to ′ (for feet), the Sub Units name to ″ (for inches), and the resolution ratio to 12 and 8000
- Grid Master to 0.5, Grid Reference to 2, and Grid lock to OFF
- Active Level = 1
- Line Weight = 0
- Line Style = 0
- Color = Black

STEP 3: Open the Reference Settings box by selecting Reference from the pull-down menu File.

STEP 4: Invoke the Attach command from the pull-down menu Tools in the Reference Files settings box. MicroStation opens the Attach Reference File dialog box.

STEP 5: Select RACK.DGN from the appropriate directory, and click the OK button to attach the design file as a reference file to the current design file. MicroStation displays the Attach Reference File dialog box.

STEP 6: In the Attach Reference file dialog box, set the following settings:

- Key-in **rack** in the Logical Name field.
- Key-in **Pipe rack plot plan** in the Description field.
- Click the OK button to attach the pipe rack design file as a reference file.

STEP 7: Invoke the Fit View All command to fit the view window.

STEP 8: Similarly, attach the PUMPS.DGN design file as a reference file, keying-in **pumps** for the Logical Name and **Pump foundations** for the Description.

STEP 9: Also attach BORDER.DGN as a reference file. In the Attach Reference File dialog box, set the following settings:

- Key-in **border** in the Logical Name field.
- Key-in **The drawing border** in the Description field.
- Select the border saved view from the Saved Views list box.
- Set the Scale (Master:Ref) ratio to 4 to 1, as shown in Figure P12–9.
- Click the OK button.

> **NOTE:** The Scale (Master:Ref) ratio scales the border for plotting at $\frac{1}{4}'' = 1'$. This works because the border design has inches as its Master Units and the active design has feet as its Master Units. The ratio of 4 to 1 means every four feet of active design displays one inch of border reference, or $1'' = 4'$ (divide both sides of the equation by 4 and you get $\frac{1}{4}'' = 1'$).

STEP 10: Drag the reference file dynamic outline until all of the pipe rack is inside and close to the top of the outline, then click the Data button to place the border.

STEP 11: If the border is not correctly placed, select it in the Reference Files settings box, then invoke the Move command from the pull-down menu Tools in the Reference Files settings box.

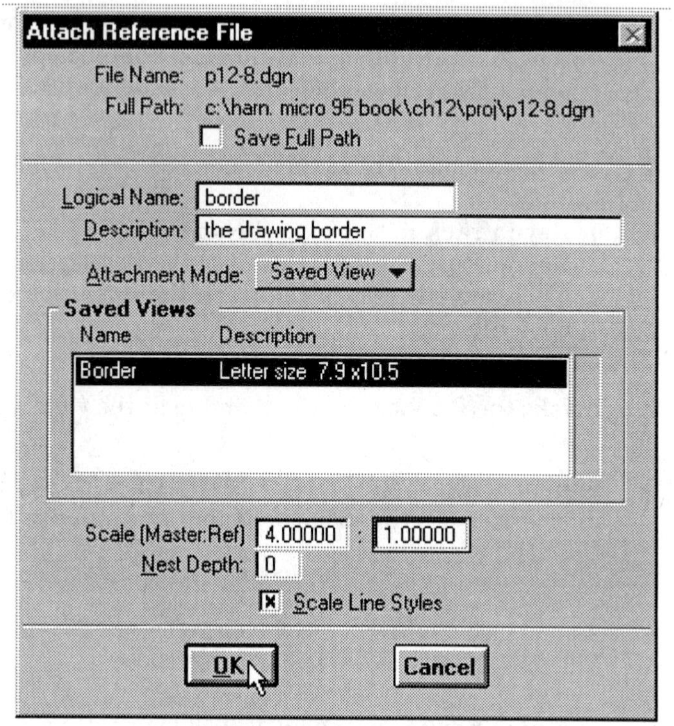

FIGURE P12–9   Settings for attaching the border.

MicroStation prompts:

> Move Reference File > Enter point to move from *(Place a data point somewhere in the design.)*
>
> Move Reference File > Enter point to move to *(Move the drawing pointer the direction and distance the border needs to be moved, then place a second data point to move the reference file.)*

STEP 12:   Set the text parameters to:

- Font = 3
- Text Height and Width = 0.125′

STEP 12:   Fill in the title block text as shown in Figure P12–1.

STEP 13:   Invoke the Fit View command to fit the view.

STEP 14:   Invoke the Save Settings command from the pull-down menu File to save the design settings.

DRAWING EXERCISES 12–1 THROUGH 12–5

Use the following table to set up the design files for Exercises 12–1 through 12–5.

SETTING	VALUE
Seed File	SEED2D.DGN
Working Units	MU = IN, SU = 10th, PU = 1000
Grid	Master = .25, Reference = 4

Exercise 12–1 Border. Draw the border shown in the figure. This border is used in the following exercises.

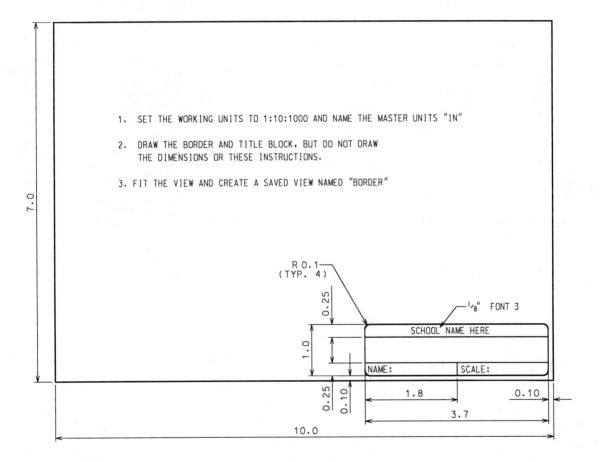

Exercise 12–2 Create a design file. Reference the border in the new file, then reference the machine part drawings created in Exercises 3–1, 4–2,and 11–3. Clip the boundery of each of the machine parts, scale each one to one-half its true size (Master:ref 0.50000:1.00000), then move each one inside the border.

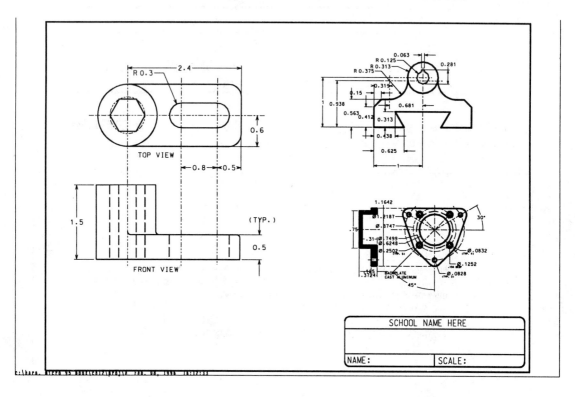

Exercise 12–3 Open the front elevation design drawn in Exercise 6–3. If the design includes a border, delete it. Reference the border design file's "Border" saved view at an attach scale of ⅛″ = 1′ (Master:ref 4.00000:1.00000).

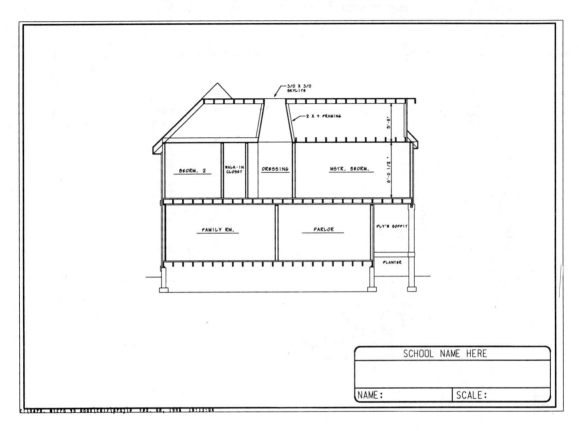

Exercise 12–4 Draw the two parts of a flow diagram shown in Figures E12–4a and E12–4b. Put each part in a separate design file. Place the ends of the off-page lines at the *XY* coordinates shown in each figure. The dimension shown in the first figure is intended only to provide a feel for the size of the diagrams. Do *not* draw the dimension or *XY* coordinates.

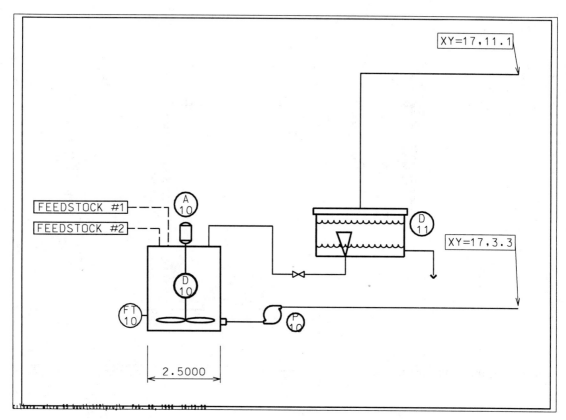

FIGURE E12–4a   Flow diagram A.

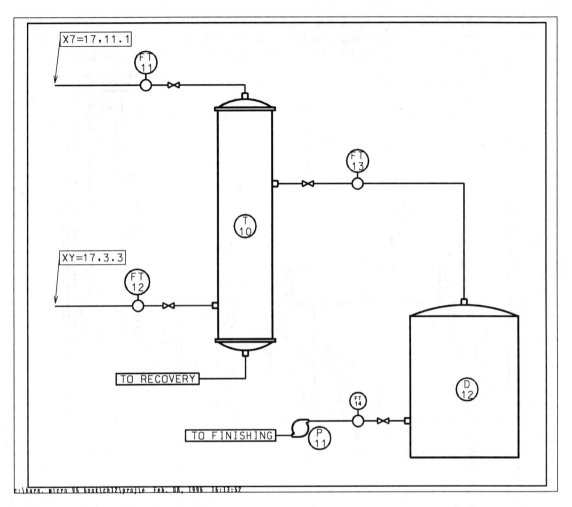

FIGURE E12–4b Flow diagram B.

Exercise 12–5 Completed flow diagram. Create a design file, then reference the two flow diagram parts A and B to create the complete diagram. Reference the border and scale it to encompass the complete flow diagram, as shown in the figure.

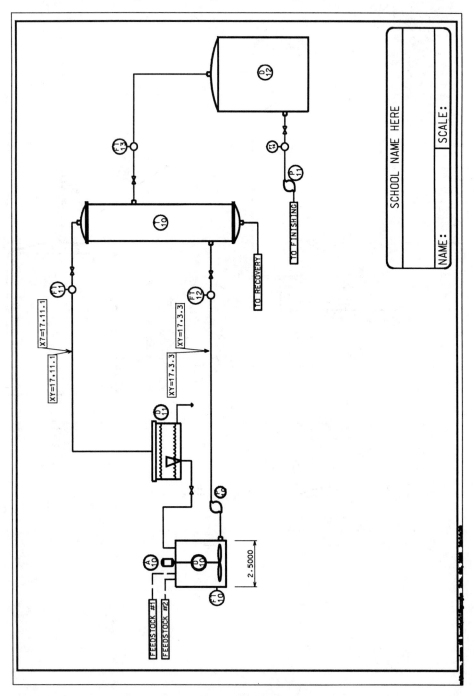

13

SPECIAL FEATURES

• • • • • • • • • • • • • • • •

MicroStation provides some special features that are used less often than the commands described earlier in this book, but provide added power and versatility. This chapter briefly introduces several such features. For more detailed information on each feature, consult the documentation furnished with MicroStation and the online help.

OBJECTIVES

After completing this chapter, you will be able to:

✓ Create and use graphic groups.

✓ Select groups of elements according to various selection criteria.

✓ Define a level symbology to help you determine what level elements are on.

✓ Change the highlight and vector cursor colors.

✓ Open AutoCAD drawings as MicroStation design files.

✓ Save MicroStation design files as AutoCAD drawings.

✓ Import from and export to other CAD graphic formats.

✓ Save and display graphic images.

✓ Place text from a glossary of standard terms and add text to the glossary.

✓ Place flags.

✓ Create dimension-driven designs.

GRAPHIC GROUPS

The Add To Graphic Group command allows you to group elements together so they act as if they were one element when you apply element manipulation commands with the Graphic Group Lock set to ON. The Drop From Graphic Group command allows you to drop elements from a graphic group or drop the entire group.

MicroStation commands create elements that are part of a graphic group, as follows:

- Imported text files of more than 128 lines, or more than 2,048 characters, are placed with all text lines in one graphic group.
- The Place Text Along command makes each character a separate element and places all the characters as one graphic group.
- The elements of a pattern are part of one graphic group, but the element they pattern is not part of the group.

Adding Elements to a Graphic Group

To add elements to a graphic group, invoke the Add To Graphic Group command from:

Groups tool box	Select the Add To Graphic Group tool (see Figure 13–1).
Key-in window	**Group Add** (or **gr a**) ⌨ENTER

MicroStation prompts:

Add to Graphic Group > Identify element *(Identify the element.)*

FIGURE 13-1   Invoking the Add To Graphic Group command from the Groups tool box.

If the selected element is *not* already in a graphic group, a new group is started and MicroStation prompts:

> Add to Graphic Group > Add to new group (Accept/Reject) *(Identify the next element to add to the new group, or click the Reset button to reject the selected element.)*

If the selected element is already in a graphic group, elements will be added to that group and MicroStation prompts:

> Add to Graphic Group > Add to existing group (Accept/Reject) *(Identify the first element to be added to the existing graphic group, or click the Reset button to reject the selected group.)*
> Add to Graphic Group > Accept/Reject (select next input) *(If more elements are to be added to the new or existing group, select each one. When all elements have been selected, click the Data button in space to accept adding the last selected element.)*

Manipulating Elements in a Graphic Group

The Graphic Group Lock controls the effect the element manipulation commands have on elements in a graphic group. If the lock is set to OFF, the commands manipulate only the selected element. If the lock is set to ON, all elements in the graphic group are highlighted and manipulated (even if you cannot see them in the view you are working in). For example, if the graphic group lock is set to OFF and you select one of the elements in a graphic group to be deleted, only that element is deleted. If the lock is set to ON, all elements in the graphic group are deleted.

> **NOTE:** Only the element manipulation commands check the status of the Graphic Group Lock. The Fence contents commands ignore the Graphic Group Lock and manipulate the elements depending on the Fence Lock.

The Graphic Group Lock is toggled ON and OFF in the Full or Lock Toggles settings boxes and in the Locks submenu (see Figure 13–2).

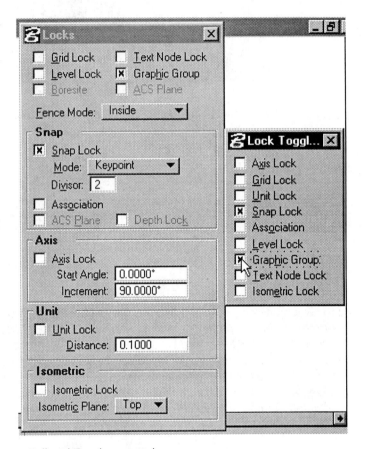

FIGURE 13-2 Full and Toggle settings box.

> **NOTE:** If the Graphic Group Lock is set to ON, you can determine if the element you select for manipulation is in a group by looking at the element type description in the Status bar. If the element is in a graphic group, the message includes "(GG)."

Copying Elements in a Graphic Group

The Graphic Group Lock affects the way the element copy and fence contents copy commands handle elements in a graphic group.

- If the graphic group lock is set to OFF, the copied elements are not part of any graphic group.
- If the lock is set to ON, the element copy command copies the entire graphic group, and the copies form a new graphic group.
- If the lock is set to ON, only the graphic group elements in the fence are copied, and the copies become a new, separate graphic group.

FIGURE 13–3   Invoking the Drop From Graphic Group command from the Groups tool box.

Dropping Elements from a Graphic Group

The Drop From Graphic Group command drops:

- The selected element when the Graphic Group Lock is set to OFF.
- All elements in the group when the Graphic Group Lock is set to ON.

To drop elements from a graphic group, invoke the Drop From Graphic Group command from:

Groups tool box	Select the Drop From Graphic Group tool (see Figure 13–3).
Key-in window	**Group Drop** (or **gr d**) [ENTER]

MicroStation prompts:

> Drop From Graphic Group > Identify element *(Identify the element.)*
> Drop From Graphic Group > Accept/Reject (Select next input) *(If more elements are to be dropped, select each one. When all elements have been selected, click the Data button in space to accept dropping the last selected element.)*

SELECTION BY ATTRIBUTES

The Select By Attributes option from the pull-down menu Edit allows you to limit the selection of elements for manipulation to those that meet certain element attributes. For example, if all red ellipses on level 10 need to be changed to the color green, use the Select By Attributes settings box to select only those elements, then apply the color change to the selected elements. Handles appear on the selected elements, just as they did with the selection command described in Chapter 5. You can delete the selected elements, move them, copy them, change their attributes, and apply several other manipulation commands to them.

Select By Attributes Settings Box

The Select By Attributes settings box contains several fields, selection menus, and options to open other settings boxes (see Figure 13–4).

The settings box is made up of the following parts:

- Selection by levels (upper left of the box)
- Selection by element types (upper right of the box)
- Selection by symbology—color, line style, or line weight (lower left of the box)
- The Mode field, which contains three selection menus that control the way the selection criteria are applied.
- The Properties button, which opens the Select By Properties settings box (see Figure 13–5) where you can choose to select elements by property attributes (such as only filled elements) and classes (such as construction elements)
- The Tags button, which opens the Select By Tags settings box (see Figure 13–6) where you can limit your selection to elements that contain only certain tags or combinations of tags
- The Execute button at the bottom left of the box, which puts into effect the selection criteria currently set in the fields

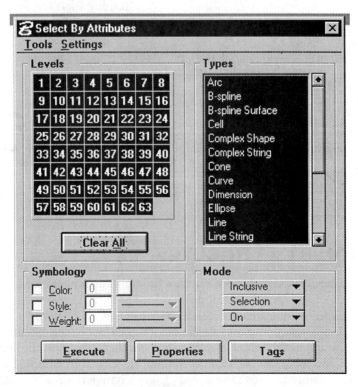

FIGURE 13–4   Select By Attributes settings box.

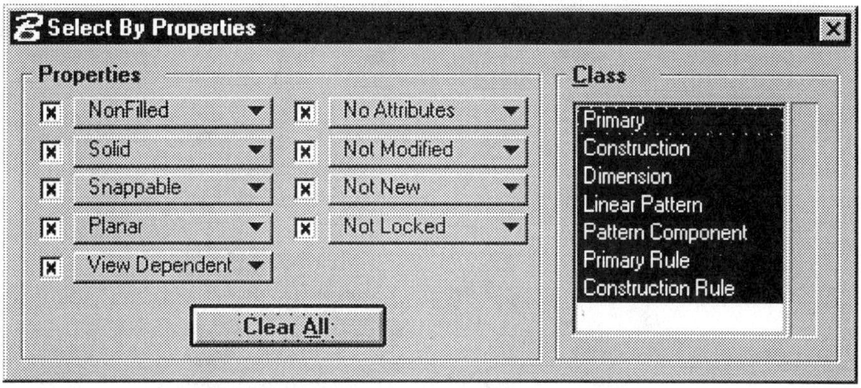

FIGURE 13–5   Select By Properties settings box.

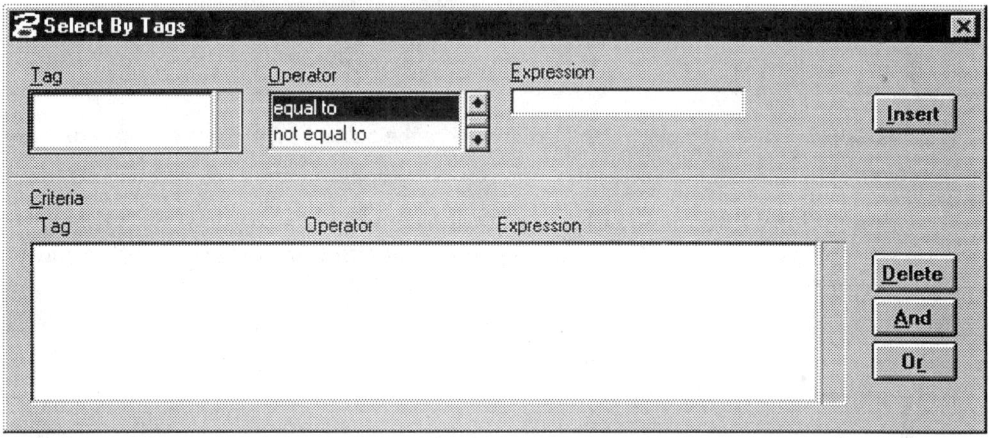

FIGURE 13–6   Select By Tags settings box.

> **NOTE:** Your selection criteria can be based on one item in one of the fields or on a combination of items in one or more fields—for example, all elements on level 10 or only ellipses on level 5 that are filled.

Selection by Level

The Levels field contains a grid of level numbers and a switch button (see Figure 13–7). If a level number is shown with a dark background, it is part of the selection criteria. A light background means the level is not part of the selection criteria.

To switch the state of a single level, click the Data button on it. To change the state of a group of elements, drag the screen pointer across them while holding down the Data button. For example, if you wish to select elements on levels 10 through 15, set those six levels to a dark background and all other levels to a light background.

FIGURE 13-7   Displaying the Levels field of the Select By Attributes settings box.

The option button below the level numbers field is a toggle switch that either clears all levels or selects all levels. The name of the button says what action it is going perform when you click it.

Selection by Type

The Types field contains a list of all element types (see Figure 13–8). Type names shown with a dark background are part of the selection criteria. A light background means that type is not part of the selection criteria.

To select a specific type and turn off all others, click the Data button on the desired type. To select additional types, hold down the [CTRL] key while clicking the Data button on type names. To select a contiguous group of types, drag the screen pointer across them while holding down the Data button. For example, to select only ellipses and line string, click the Data button on the Ellipse type, then [CTRL]-click the Data button on the Line String type.

Selection by Symbology

The Symbology field allows you to include element color, style, and weight in the selection criteria (see Figure 13–9). To add a symbology item to the selection criteria, turn ON the button to the left of the item's name, then select a value in the menu to the right of the item's name. For example, if the color button is set to ON,

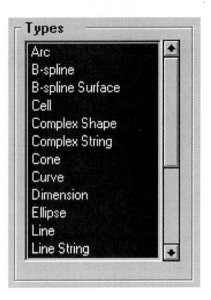

FIGURE 13–8   Displaying the Types field of the Select By Attributes settings box.

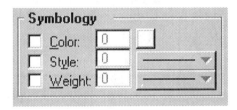

FIGURE 13–9   Displaying the Symbology field of the Select By Attributes settings box.

elements that are the color shown in the color field are the only ones included in the selection criteria.

Controlling the Selection Mode

The Mode field contains three option menus (see Figure 13–10) that control the way the selection criteria are applied when you click the Execute button at the bottom left of the settings box.

The first option menu located in the Mode field has two options: Inclusive and Exclusive:

- Inclusive: Select only elements that meet the selection criteria.
- Exclusive: Select only elements that do not meet the selection criteria.

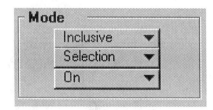

FIGURE 13-10 Displaying the Mode field of the Select By Attributes settings box.

For example, if the selection criterion is set to type Ellipse, Inclusive mode causes all ellipses to be selected, and selection in Exclusive mode causes all elements except ellipses to be selected.

The second option menu located in the Mode field has three options: Selection, Location, and Display:

- Selection: Immediately select (place handles on) all elements that meet the selection criteria when the Execute button is pressed.
- Location: Turn on the selection criteria but do not select any elements when the Execute button is pressed. Use the Element Selection command to select elements that meet the criteria in this mode. Elements that do not meet the criteria cannot be selected.
- Display: Turn on the selection criteria, and make all elements that do not meet the criteria disappear from the view when the Execute button is pressed. No handles are placed on the remaining elements, so the Element Selection command must be used to select from the elements that still appear in the view.

> **NOTE:** If Display mode has caused elements to disappear from the view, you must execute the criteria in Location mode, then update the view to make them reappear.

The third option menu located in the Mode field has two options: OFF and ON:

- OFF—When the Execute button is pressed, turns off the previously set selection criteria so it has no effect on element selection.
- ON—When the Execute button is pressed, turns on the current selection criteria so it can be used.

> **NOTE:** If you close the Select By Attributes settings box with a selection criterion in effect, an Alert window appears prompting you to click OK or Cancel. OK will keep the selection criterion in effect, and Cancel will turn off the criterion.

Select By Properties Settings Box

Use the Select By Properties settings box to include additional element attributes in the selection criteria. Open this box by clicking the Properties button in the Select By Attributes settings box.

On the left side of the box, select element Properties settings (see Figure 13–11). Each property has an options menu from which you can select the property to be included in the selection criteria. To select a property, turn the toggle button to ON and then select a setting from the Properties option menu. For example, the area property options menu allows you to select one of the two available options, Solid or Hole elements.

The button below the Properties area is a toggle switch that turns ON or OFF all the property buttons. The name of the button says what will happen next. If it displays Select All, it turns ON all the options in the Properties area; if it displays Clear All, then it turns OFF all the options in the Properties area.

On the right side of the box is a field in which you select what class or classes of elements to include in the selection criteria (see Figure 13–12). If the class is shown with a dark background, it is included. Each name is a toggle switch. Clicking the Data button on the class name adds it to or removes it from the selection criteria. For example, if you want to select only elements in the construction class, set the word Construction in the menu to have a dark background, and set all the others to have a light background.

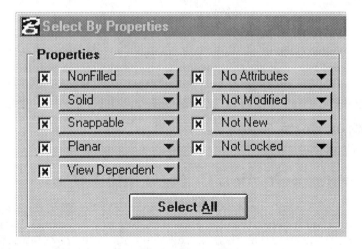

FIGURE 13–11 Displaying the Properties in the Select By Properties settings box.

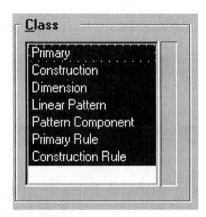

FIGURE 13–12 Displaying the Class listing in the Select By Properties settings box.

Select By Tags Settings Box

The Select By Tags settings box (see Figure 13–13) is used to specify criteria based on tag values. If selection criteria based on tag values are specified, elements that do not have attached tags with the specified tag name(s) will not be selected, located, or displayed.

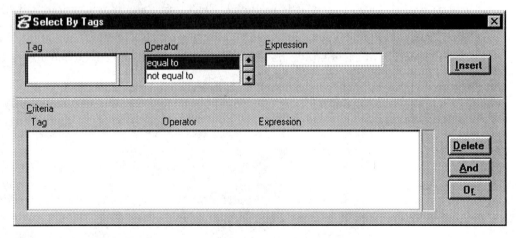

FIGURE 13–13 Select by Tags settings box.

Putting Selection Criteria into Effect

Once you set all the selection criteria, click the Execute button in the Select By settings box to select the elements according to the settings. Handles appear (depending on the settings) on the selected elements. After completing the selection criteria, invoke the appropriate element manipulation command and follow the prompts.

LEVEL SYMBOLOGY

Designers often make extensive use of the 63 available levels to help organize the various parts of a design. For example, a plot plan may have separate levels for roadways, descriptive text, foundations, utilities, the drawing border, and title block information. An architectural plan might have the walls on one level, the dimensions on another level, electrical information on still another level, and so on. Separating parts of the design by level allows designers to turn on only the part they need to work on and allows them to plot parts of the design separately.

Keeping up with what level everything is on can be confusing. MicroStation's level symbology reduces the confusion by setting unique combinations of display color, weight, and style for each level. When level symbology is set to ON, all elements are displayed using the symbology assigned to the level the elements are on, rather than their true symbology. For example, if level 10 symbology is set to display elements red, dashed, and weight 5, all elements on level 10 display with that symbology, no matter what their actual color, weight, and style settings are.

The View Attributes settings box controls the display of level symbology by turning ON and OFF for selected views.

> **NOTE:** If you plot a view in which level symbology is set to ON, the elements are plotted with level symbology rather than their true symbology.

The Level Symbology dialog box provides options for creating and modifying level symbology settings. Invoke the Level Symbology settings window from:

Pull-down menu	Settings > Level > Symbology...
Key-in window	**Dialog Levelsymb** (or **dia le**) [ENTER]

MicroStation displays the Level Symbology dialog box, as shown in Figure 13–14. The Level Symbology dialog box contains the following fields:

- Level, Color, Style, Weight table—The table on the left side of the dialog box shows the current symbology settings for each level.
- Settings—The Settings area on the top right of the box is where you set the symbology for each level number selected in the table.
- Overrides—The Overrides area determines which symbology settings are used. If the button is set to ON (appears depressed, with a dark center), that symbology setting is in use. For example, if the color button is set to ON and the style and weight buttons are set to OFF, elements on each level are displayed using the level symbology color, but each element's true style and weight are displayed.

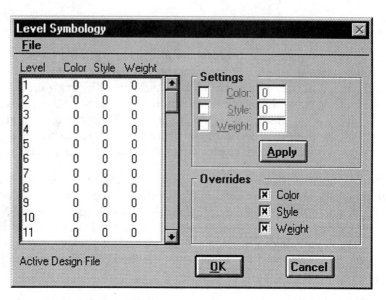

FIGURE 13–14   Level Symbology dialog box.

■ OK and Cancel buttons—To save the level symbology settings click the OK button. To discard any changes you made, click the Cancel button. You must click one of the two buttons to close the Level Symbology dialog box before you can do anything else in MicroStation.

Following is the procedure to set up a level symbology or to modify an existing one.

1. Open the Level Symbology dialog box.
2. Highlight the level by clicking with the Data button in the left side of the box.
3. Select a color, style, and/or weight from the dialog box and click the Apply button.
4. Repeat steps 2 and 3 until all level symbology is set.
5. Turn on the override for each level symbology you want to use.
6. Click the OK button to save the level symbology changes.

> **NOTE:** Changes to the level symbology setup are permanent. You do not have to invoke Save Settings to keep them.

Following is the procedure to display the level symbology attributes.

1. Open the View Attributes settings box.
2. Set the Level Symbology toggle button to ON.
3. If you want to turn on level symbology for only one view, set the View Number to the one you want and click the Apply button.
4. If you want the level symbology display to be ON for all open views, click the All button.

NOTE: Any changes you make to the View Attributes are lost when you exit MicroStation, unless you select Save Settings from the pull-down menu File.

CHANGING THE HIGHLIGHT AND POINTER COLOR

The highlight and drawing pointer colors can be changed from the Design File settings window. These colors are used for:

- Highlighting selected elements.
- The drawing pointer when a data point is placed and when an element is manipulated.
- The locate tolerance circle that appears on the pointer during manipulations.

A common case where different colors may be required is when many elements in the design use the same colors. In that case, there is no visual indication that an element has been selected, and the pointer can be hard to see.

To change the colors, invoke the Design File Settings box from:

Pull-down menu	Settings > Design File..., (or ⌐ALT + **S, D**), then select Color from the Category menu (see Figure 13–15).
Key-in window	**MDL Load Dgnset** (or **md l dgnset**) ⌐ENTER

In the Design File Settings window:

1. Pop up the Element Highlight Color menu and select the desired color for highlighting elements.
2. Pop up the Drawing Pointer Color menu and select the desired color for the drawing pointer.
3. Click the OK button to make the new colors active.
4. To make the changes permanent in this design file, select Save Settings from the pull-down menu File.

NOTE: The color changes apply only to the design file in which they were changed. Each design file has its own highlight and pointer color settings.

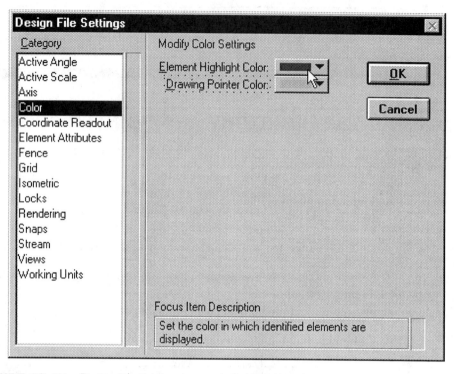

FIGURE 13–15 Design File Settings box, with Color selected.

> **NOTE:** Do not set the colors the same as the view window background color. If the color is the same, highlighted elements and the pointer cannot be seen.

IMPORTING AND EXPORTING DRAWINGS IN OTHER FORMATS

MicroStation can import files containing graphic information in several file exchange formats and can export drawings to those formats.

- Several formats can be imported directly in MicroStation from the MicroStation Manager and File Open windows.
- Design files can be exported to several formats from the File Save As window.
- Export and Import options are also provided in the pull-down menu File.

The support of these other formats allows MicroStation users to share design files with clients and vendors using other CAD and graphic applications.

Supported Formats

Table 13–1 describes file exchange formats that MicroStation can open directly and save and that are also available in the Import and Export submenus from the pull-down menu File. Table 13–2 describes file exchange formats that are available only from the Import and Export submenus.

Table 13–1. File Exchange Formats Available for Opening and Saving Files

FORMAT	IMPORT	EXPORT	DESCRIPTION
DWG	Yes	Yes	Native format AutoCAD drawings
DXF	Yes	Yes	Drawing Interchange Format—developed by Autodesk, Inc., to exchange graphic data among many CAD and graphics applications. DWG and DXF imports are handled identically.
CGM	Yes	Yes	Computer Graphics Metafile Format—an ANSI standard for the exchange of picture data between different graphics applications; device and environment independent
GRD	Yes	Yes	MicroStation Field Format
IGES	Yes	Yes	Initial Graphics Exchange Specification Format—a public domain ANSI standard file format that is intended as an international standard for the exchange of product definition data among different CAD applications

Table 13–2. File Exchange Formats Available in the Import and Export Submenus

FORMAT	IMPORT	EXPORT	DESCRIPTION
Image	Yes	No	Several graphics formats used by text processing and publication graphics packages
Text	Yes	No	ASCII text files (discussed in Chapter 6)
3D	No	Yes	MicroStation's 3-dimensional design file format. If the open design file is 3D, there will be an option to save it as a 2D (2-dimensional) drawing.

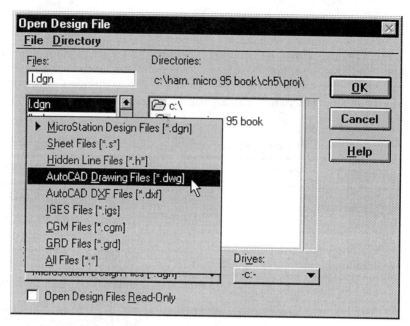

FIGURE 13–16 Selecting the format of a file to be opened.

Opening a File Containing Another File Format

The file formats shown in Table 13–1 can be opened directly in MicroStation. The conversion to design file format is done as the file opens.

To open a drawing created in another format from either of the MicroStation Manager or Open Design File dialog boxes:

1. Pop up the "Open Files of Type" menu (see Figure 13–16).
2. Select the format of the drawing to be opened.
3. Follow the usual procedures for opening a file.

Saving a Design File That Is in Another File Format

The file formats shown in Table 13–1 can be saved from the File Save As dialog box. The conversion to the other file format is done as the file is saved. To save a design file in another format:

1. Open the Save As dialog box from the pull-down menu File.
2. Pop up the "List Files of Type" menu (see Figure 13–17).
3. Select the format to be used.
4. Supply a directory path and file name.
5. Click the OK button to initiate the conversion and close the dialog box.

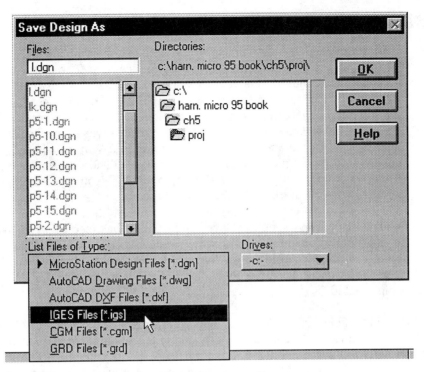

FIGURE 13-17 Selecting the format to save a design file as.

The contents of the design file are converted to the other format, and the design file remains open in MicroStation.

Importing and Exporting Other Formats into an Open Design File

The file formats described in Tables 13–1 and 13–2 are available for import and export from an open design file. The Import and Export options are available from the pull-down menu File.

- The Import command inserts the imported file contents into the open design file. The elements in the imported file are converted to design file elements. Image files remain as images in the design file and are not an element.
- The action of the Export command varies among the formats. In some cases it opens the Save As window, then follows that window with an Export window containing options to control the way the design file is opened. In other cases, the Export window opens directly.

For detailed information on importing and exporting, refer to the technical documentation furnished with MicroStation.

MANIPULATING IMAGES

In MicroStation, the term "image" refers to graphics files that can be inserted in word processing and graphics processing applications. The pictures of MicroStation windows presented in this textbook are examples of such images. MicroStation provides a set of tools for creating, manipulating, and viewing images under the pull-down menu Utilities, as shown in Figure 13–18. For example, a programmer created an automated drawing procedure that involves several custom dialog boxes; a technical writer is creating a training guide in a Windows-based word processing package and needs pictures of the dialog boxes. The programmer uses the Image Capture option to capture the dialog boxes as bit-mapped image files that the technical writer can insert in the manual file.

Save This option opens the Save Image dialog box (see Figure 13–19) from which the contents of one of the eight view windows can be saved as an image file using one of several available image formats. To determine the required image format, refer to the documentation furnished with the application for which the image is being created.

Capture This option opens the Screen Capture settings box (see Figure 13–20) from which you can select several methods of capturing all or part of the image on the workstation screen. Each capture method opens a Capture Output dialog box in which you can specify a file name and directory path for the captured screen image.

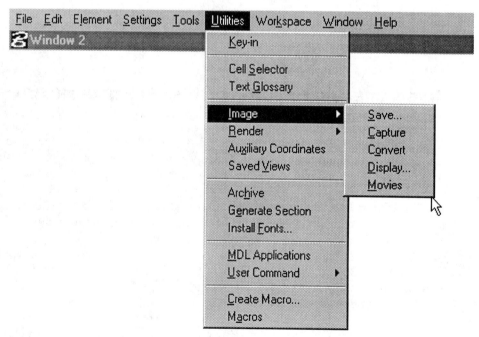

FIGURE 13–18 Image tools submenu in the Utilities menu.

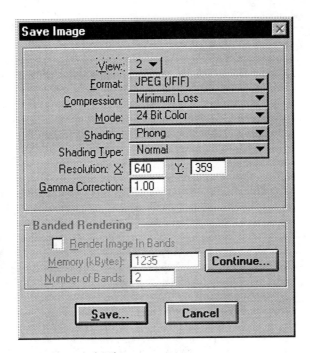

FIGURE 13–19 Save Image dialog box.

The Screen Capture methods include:

- Capture Screen—Capture the entire screen.
- Capture Rectangle—Capture the contents of a rectangle you define within the MicroStation workspace.
- Capture View—Capture the contents of the view you select. Windows on top of the view are also captured.
- Capture View Window—Capture the contents and window border of the view you select. Windows on top of the view are also captured.

FIGURE 13–20 Screen Capture settings box.

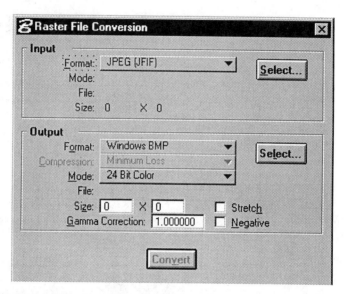

FIGURE 13–21 Raster File Conversion settings box.

Convert This option opens the Raster File Conversion settings box (see Figure 13–21) in which you can select an Input image file and convert it to an Output format file using a file name and path you specify.

Display This option opens the Display Image dialog box (see Figure 13–22) from which you can select an image file to view in a separate window (see Figure 13–23).

Movies This option opens the Movies settings box (see Figure 13–24) from which an animated sequence file can be selected for viewing in a separate window.

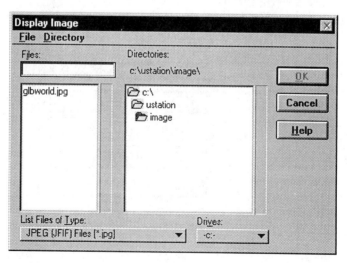

FIGURE 13–22 Display Image dialog box.

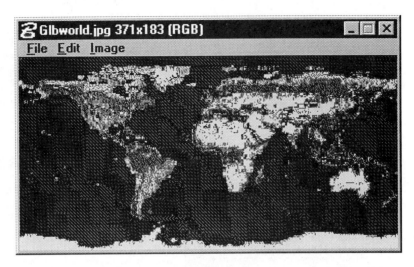

FIGURE 13-23 Example of displaying an image file in the Display Image window.

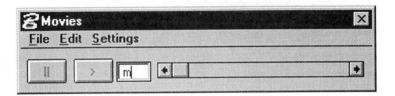

FIGURE 13-24 Movies settings box.

GLOSSARY TEXT

A large part of the textual annotation added to engineering models consists of standard terms and phrases. MicroStation helps speed up placing such text by providing a text glossary tool. Standard terms and phrases can be selected from the glossary for insertion in a design, and new ones can be added to the glossary.

Glossary Settings Box

Glossary text is viewed, selected, and placed from the Glossary settings box. Open the Glossary settings box from:

Pull-down menu	Utilities > Text Glossary (or [ALT] + U, G)
Key-in window	**mdl Load Glossary (or md l glossary)** [ENTER]

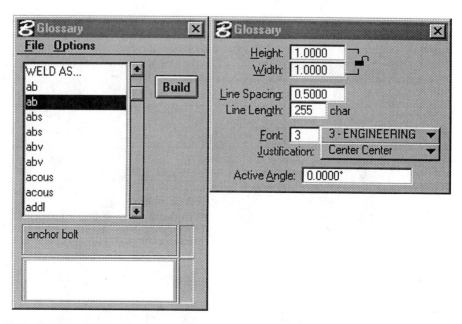

FIGURE 13-25 Glossary settings box.

MicroStation displays a Glossary settings box, as shown in Figure 13–25. Table 13–3 describes the windows fields.

> **NOTE:** When the Build button is pressed the first time, the text attribute settings appear in the Tool Settings window. These settings control the appearance of the glossary text when it is placed in the design and can be changed before placing the text.

Constructing Text Strings from Glossary Text

Follow these steps to create and place a text string from the Glossary settings box.

1. Open the Glossary settings box as described previously.
2. If the required glossary is in a file other than the MicroStation default file, use the Open option in the Glossary settings box's pull-down menu File to open the glossary file.
3. Select the alias for the glossary text you need.
4. Click the Build button to insert the selected text in the Place Text String field.
5. Repeat steps 2 and 3 for each piece of glossary text to be inserted.
6. Edit the text in the Place Text String field, if required, to complete constructing the text string.
7. Optionally, change the text attribute settings in the Tool Settings window.
8. Place a data point in the design to place the text.

Table 13–3. Glossary Settings Box Fields

FIELD	DESCRIPTION
File menu	The pull-down menu File contains the Open option that allows you to select the file containing the glossary text. The window opens, displaying the contents of the default glossary file whose path is contained in the MS_GLOSSARY configuration variable. The default path is: \USTATION\WSMOD\DEFAULT\DATA\EXAMPLE.GLS
Options menu	The pull-down menu Options contains the Case submenu for selecting the case to use when placing the selected glossary text in the design: • Default—Place the text as it appears in the Place Text String field. • Uppercase—Make the entire text string uppercase when it is placed. • Lowercase—Make the entire text string lowercase when it is placed.
Alias list	The field on the left side of the window lists the text aliases. Aliases are short abbreviations that identify the glossary text strings. Click on an alias to select it. In Figure 13–25 the "ab" alias is highlighted.
Associated Text	When an alias is selected, the glossary text associated with the alias appears in the Associated Text field just below the Alias List field. In Figure 13–25 the field contains "anchor bolt," which is the text associated with the "ab" alias highlighted in the Alias list field.
Build button	When the Build button is pressed, the text in the Associated Text field is inserted in the Place Text String field at the bottom of the window. Each time the button is clicked, the text associated with the selected alias is appended to the end of the text already in the Place Text String field (separated by a space).
Place Text String	The text string to be placed in the design is constructed in the field at the bottom of the window. Text strings are constructed here by clicking the Build button and by typing in the field.

When the text string is placed in the design, the Place Text String field in the Glossary settings box is cleared. To clear the Place Text String field without placing the text in it, click the Reset button.

> **NOTE:** When you open the Glossary settings box, insert glossary text *before* typing in the Place Text String field. If you type in it first, the typed text is replaced by the first glossary text you select.

Creating Glossary Text

Glossary text is contained in ASCII files that can be edited from word processing applications, and additional glossary files can be created.

The default glossary, USTATION\WSMOD\DEFAULT\DATA\EXAMPLE.GLS, contains a large number of glossary entries, which makes finding specific entries in the Glossary window rather time consuming. A more effective way to use glossaries is to create separate glossary files for each type of drawing. For example, create CIVIL.GLS to hold civil engineering terms and MECH.GLS to hold mechanical engineering terms.

Here is a procedure for creating custom glossary files.

1. Make a copy EXAMPLE.GLS.
2. Open the copy in a word processing application.
3. Delete all glossary terms not related to the discipline for which the glossary is being created.
4. Add any required terms that were not in EXAMPLE.GLS.
5. Save the new glossary and close the word processing application.
6. Repeat steps 1 through 5 for each glossary to be created.

Instructions for creating new glossary text in a glossary file are provided at the beginning of EXAMPLE.GLS, as shown in Figure 13–26.

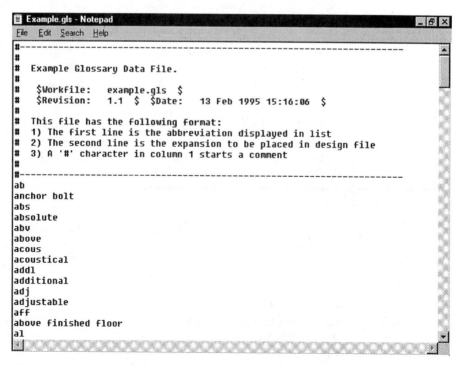

FIGURE 13-26 Top lines of EXAMPLE.GLS, the default glossary file.

PLACING FLAGS

Flags provide a way for the people working on the design file to place reminders and suggestions into the file. A flag appears in the design plane as a symbol that must be opened to view the message it contains.

The following discussion presents the tool settings and placement steps.

Place Flag Command

Several tool settings are available to control the configuration of flags. Table 13–4 explains the tool settings; Figure 13–27 shows examples of typical flag symbols placed in a design.

Table 13–4.   Place Flag Tool Settings

SETTING	EFFECT
Scale	Scales the flag symbol. A number greater than 1 increases the size and a number less than 1 decreases the size.
Level	Controls what level the flag is placed on.
Class	Provides a menu for setting the flag's class to one of: • Primary • Construction (if the Construction view attribute is turned OFF for a view, the flag will not be seen in the view or plotted)
Transparent	If ON, the image's background pixels are set to black to make the image appear to be transparent.
Image	The name of the bit map file containing the symbol to be used for the flag. See Figure 13–27 for examples of symbol images and the names of the files containing the images.
Browse	Click this button to open a Browse window in which another image file can be chosen. The default directory for Browse contains a set of image files supplied with MicroStation. The maximum size of an image is 320 × 320 pixels.

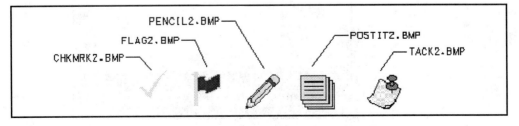

FIGURE 13–27   Typical flag images and their bit map file names.

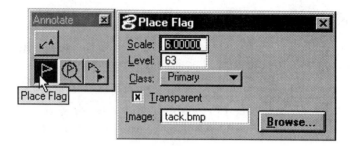

FIGURE 13-28 Invoking the Place Flag command from the Annotate tool box.

Invoke the Place Flag command from:

Annotate tool box	Select the Place Flag tool, and enter the required placement settings in the Tool Settings window (see Figure 13–28).
Key-in window	**Place Flag** (or **pla fl**) ⏎

MicroStation prompts:

> Place Flag > Identify location *(Define the point where the flag is to be placed.)*

After the flag location is defined, the Define Flag Information window opens (see Figure 13–29). Type the flag's message in this window and:

- Click OK—to place the message with the flag and close the window.
- Click Cancel—to close the window without placing text with the flag.

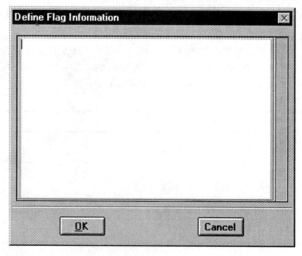

FIGURE 13-29 Define Flag Information window.

FIGURE 13–30   Invoking the Show/Edit Flag command from the Annotate tool box.

Show/Edit Flag Command

The Show/Edit Flag command displays the flag's message and allows editing the message content.

Invoke the Show/Edit Flag command from:

Annotate tool box	Select the Show/Edit Flag tool (see Figure 13–30).
Key-in window	**Show Flag** (or **sho fl**) ⏎

MicroStation prompts:

   Show/Edit Flag > Select flag *(Click the Data button on the flag to be viewed or edited.)*
   Show/Edit Flag > Accept/Reject *(Click the Data button again to accept the selected flag.)*

After the flag is accepted, the Define Flag Information window opens, and the message is ready for viewing or editing. After completing the required action:

■ Click OK—to save any message editing and close the window.
■ Click Cancel—to close the window without saving message editing.

Update Flag Command

The Update Flag command changes the image used for an existing flag's symbol to the image currently set in the Place Flag's tool settings Image field. Before invoking the Update Flag command, invoke the Place Flag command and use the settings box Browse button to find and select the correct image.

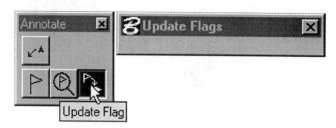

FIGURE 13-31   Invoking the Update Flag command from the Annotate tool box.

Invoke the Update Flag command from:

Annotate tool box	Select the Update Flag tool (see Figure 13–31).
Key-in window	**Flag Update** (or **fla u**) ⏎

MicroStation prompts:

> Update Flag > Select flag *(Select the flag to be updated.)*
> Update Flag > Accept/Reject *(Click the Data button again to update the flag symbol.)*

DIMENSION-DRIVEN DESIGN

Dimension-driven design provides a set of tools to define constraints on the elements that make up a design. These constraints control the size and shape of the design, so the design can be adjusted for changing requirements by simply entering new dimension values.

Dimension-driven cells are cells defined from constrained designs. The dimensions of such cells can be changed as they are placed.

Example of a Constrained Design

We introduce dimension-driven design by describing the steps required to create the model shown in Figure 13–32. Before we start constructing the model, let's look at the constraints on the model and at the effect of changing a constraint.

The Constraints   The design in the figure contains several "construction" elements that graphically represent the constraints:

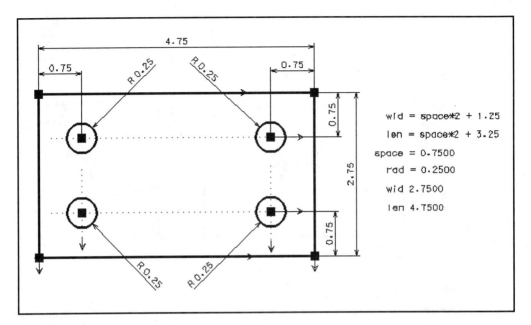

FIGURE 13-32 Example of a constrained design.

■ The dashed lines with arrows on one end are the construction lines to which the design is attached (some of the construction lines are covered by the lines and circles of the design).

■ The equations and variables to the right of the model define the constraints.

■ The Construction View attribute controls the display of construction elements. Figure 13–32 shows the view with Construction lines set to ON.

The following constraints were placed on the design of Figure 13–32:

■ The angle of the construction lines are fixed, as indicated by the arrows.

■ The construction line intersections are constrained to always be connected, as indicated by the small circles.

■ The radius of the circles are set by the "rad = 0.2500" variable.

■ The circles are constrained always to be centered on the intersections of the interconstruction lines.

■ The space between the center of each circle and the adjacent design edges are set by the "space = 0.7500" variable.

■ The overall length of the design is set by the "len = space*2 + 3.25" equation. The equation multiples the circle-center-to-edge space by 2 and adds 3.25 to that total (4.75 = 0.75*2 + 3.25).

■ The overall width of the design is set by the "wid = space*2 + 1.25" equation. The equation multiplies the circle-center-to-edge space by 2 and adds 1.25 to that total (2.75 = 0.75*2 + 1.25).

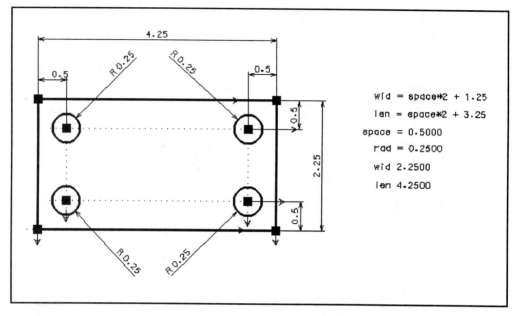

FIGURE 13–33 Effect of changing the space constraint from 0.75 to 0.5.

Effect of Changing a Constraint To illustrate the effect of changing a constraint, we use the Text Edit command to change the space variable to 0.5 Master Units ("space = 0.5"), then we use the Re-solve Constraints command to solve the design for the new value. Figure 13–33 shows that by changing the space constraint:

- We moved the circles closer to the outer edge of the design.
- We decreased the overall length and width of the design.

The overall size was reduced because the space we changed is part of the constraint on the overall length and width.

Dimension-Driven Design Terms

Following are common terms in dimension-driven design.

- **Constraint**—Information that controls how a construction is handled within a model. A constraint can be one of the following types:
  — Location—Fixes the location of a point in the design plane.
  — Geometric—Controls the position or orientation of two or more elements relative to each other.
  — Dimensional—Controlled by a dimension.
  — Algebraic—Controlled by an equation that expresses a relationship among variables.

- **Construction**—An element, such as a line or circle, on which constraints can be placed to control its relation to other constructions in the model.
- **Well-Constrained**—A set of constructions that is completely defined by constraints and has no redundant constraints. It has what is needed to define it and no more.
- **Underconstrained**—A set of constructions that does not have enough constraints to define completely its geometric shape.
- **Redundant**—A constraint applied to a construction that is already well-constrained. It provides no useful information for the construction.
- **Degrees of Freedom**—A number that sums up a dimension driven cell's ambiguity. The cell is underconstrained.
- **Solve**—Constructing the model from the given set of constraints. Each time a constraint is modified or added, the model is solved for the new set of constraints. If the model can be solved for the constraints, the model is updated; if not, an error message is displayed in the Status bar.

Dimension-Driven Design Tools

Dimension-driven tool boxes are available in the DD Design submenu. Invoke the submenu from:

Pull-down menu	Select <u>T</u>ools > DD <u>D</u>esign (or [ALT] + **T, D**).
Key-in window	**Dialog Toolbox DDDtools** (or **dia tools dddt**) [ENTER]

MicroStation displays the Dimension-Driven tool frame, consisting of four tool boxes as shown in Figure 13–34.

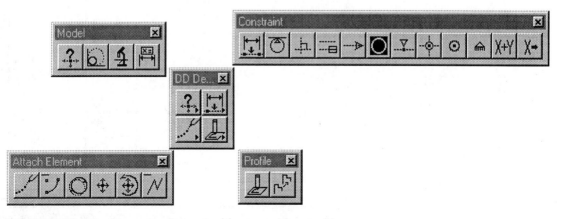

FIGURE 13–34 Dimension-Driven tool frame and four tool boxes.

The tool boxes are:

- **Constraint**—Provides tools for placing constraints on the construction elements that are to define the model.
- **Attach Elements**—Provides tools for attaching elements, such as lines and arcs, to the constrained construction elements.
- **Model**—Provides tools for solving and obtaining information about the construction.
- **Profile**—Provides tools for drawing a construction profile and for converting elements to a construction profile.

Creating a Dimension-Driven Design

A dimension-driven design requires careful planning before creating the design, and numerous tools are available to constrain the design. A good way to be introduced to the method is to walk through the creating of a design. The following discussion creates the model shown earlier in Figure 13–32.

Draw Construction Elements Set the line weight to zero; draw the lines and circles, as shown in Figure 13–35. The elements do not have to be drawn to specific dimensions because the constraints to be added later set the dimensions of the design. Draw the elements in the Primary mode.

Constrain Angle of Line or Ellipse This command enables you to fix the line's orientation or ellipse rotation angle. To constrain the rotation angle of the lines as shown in Figure 13–35, invoke the Constrain Angle command from:

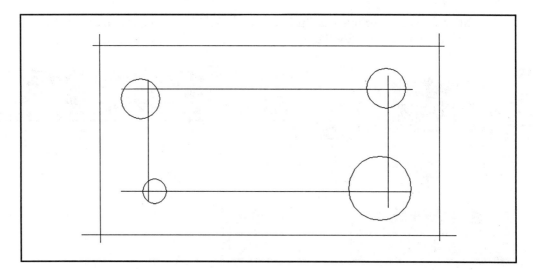

FIGURE 13–35 Design construction lines and circles.

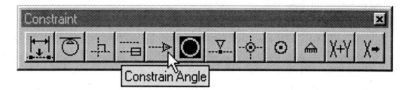

FIGURE 13–36 Invoking the Constrain Angle command from the Constraint tool box.

Constraint tool box	Select the Constrain Angle tool (see Figure 13–36).
Key-in window	**Constrain Angle** (or **constra an**) ENTER

MicroStation prompts:

> Fix Angle of Line or Ellipse > Identify line (or ellipse) *(Identify one of the lines, and click the Data button again to accept it. The second point does not select another element.)*

An arrow appears at one end of the line, its color changes to yellow and line style to dashed, and it is changed to a construction element. This constraint ensures that the lines always remain at their original rotation angle.

Identify the remaining lines in the figure to constrain the rotation angle. Figure 13–37 shows the result of constraining the rotation angle of all the lines.

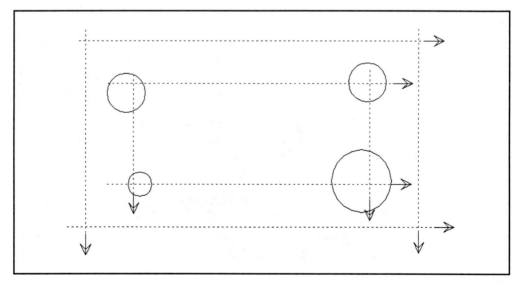

FIGURE 13–37 Result of constraining the angles of the lines.

> **NOTE:** If the Construction view attribute is turned OFF in the view you are working in, the constrained elements disappear from the view.

Constrain Point At Intersection This command either constrains a point to lie at the intersection of two constructions or forces two constructions to pass through a point. The two constructions can be any kind of construction except points. To constrain the line intersections as shown in Figure 13–35, invoke the Constrain Point At command from:

Constraint tool box	Select the Constrain Point At tool (see Figure 13–38).
Key-in window	**Constrain Intersection** (or **constra I**) ⌨

MicroStation prompts:

Constrain Point at Intersection > Identify construction *(Identify one of the inter-secting lines near the point of intersection, then select the other intersecting line.)*
Constrain Point at Intersection > Identify point or Accept+RESET *(Click the Data button in space, then click the Reset button to constrain the point.)*

A small circle appears at the constrained intersection. This constraint ensures that when one line is modified, the constrained lines always pass through the constraining point.

To constrain the remaining intersections, repeat the procedure. Figure 13–39 shows the result of constraining the intersections.

Constrain Two Points to Be Coincident This command lets you constrain two points to the same location (coincident), two circles to be concentric (have the same center), or a point to lie at the center of a circle. To constrain the circles to be centered at the intersection points as shown in Figure 13–35, invoke the Constrain Points Coincident command from:

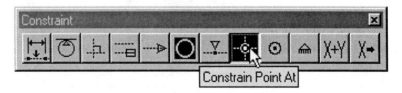

FIGURE 13–38 Invoking the Constrain Point At command from the Constraint tool box.

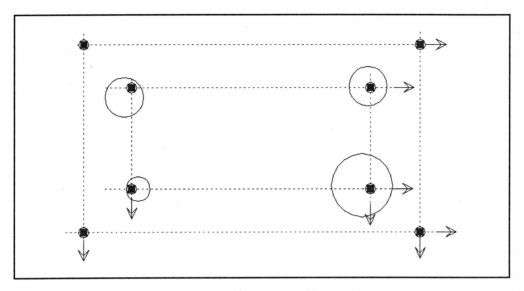

FIGURE 13–39   Result of constraining the construction line intersections.

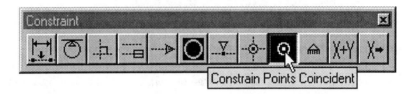

FIGURE 13–40   Invoking the Constrain Two Points to Be Coincident command from the Constraint tool box.

Constraint tool box	Select Constrain the Points Coincident tool (see Figure 13–40).
Key-in window	**Constrain Concentric (or constra conc)** ⏎

MicroStation prompts:

> Constrain Two Points to Be Coincident > Identify point (or ellipse) *(Identify the intersection point the circle is to be centered about, then select the circle.)*
> Constrain Two Points to Be Coincident > Accept *(Click the Data button in space to complete the constraint.)*

This constraint causes the circles to change to construction elements that are yellow and dashed. The circles are constrained to stay centered over the intersections when the positions of the intersecting lines are modified.

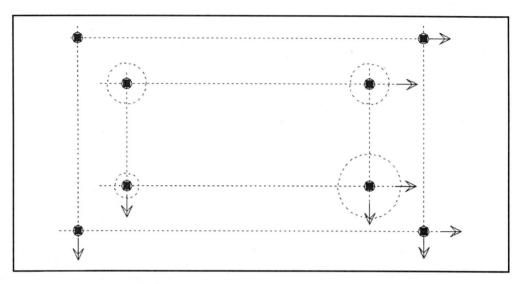

FIGURE 13–41 Result of constraining the circles.

Repeat the procedure to constrain the remaining circles to the intersection points. Figure 13–41 shows the result of constraining the circles to the intersection points.

Fix Point at Location This command enables you to fix the location of a point (or the center of a circle or ellipse) in the design. To attach the design as shown in Figure 13–35 to a specific location in the design plane, invoke the Fix Point command from:

Constraint tool box	Select the Fix Point tool (see Figure 13–42).
Key-in window	**Constrain Location** (or **constra l**) [ENTER]

MicroStation prompts:

> Fix Point at Location > Identify point (or ellipse) *(Select the lower left intersection point, then click the Data button a second time to accept the point.)*

This command fixes the design to a location in the design plane, and this point remains fixed when changes are made to the size of the constrained design.

FIGURE 13–42 Invoking the Fix Point command from the Constraint tool box.

FIGURE 13–43   Invoking the Construct Attached Line-String or Shape command from the Attach Element tool box.

Construct Attached Line-String or Shape   With this command you can create a line-string or shape with its vertices attached to construction points, circles, or constraints. It is recommended to set a higher value for active line weight so that you can easily distinguish it from the construction elements. To connect the shape as shown in Figure 13–35, invoke the Attach Line-String or Shape command from:

Attach Element tool box	Select the Attach Line-String Or Shape tool (see Figure 13–43).
Key-in window	**Attach Lstring** (or **at ls**) ⏎

MicroStation prompts:

> Construct Attached Line String or Shape > Identify point or constraint *(Select one of the constraint points on an intersection of a pair of the outer lines, then select the constraint point at the other end of one of the lines.)*
> Construct Attached Line String or Shape > Identify point, or RESET to finish *(Select the other two constraint points on the outer lines, then select the first constraint point again to complete the shape.)*

When the first constraint point is selected again, a closed shape is placed attached to the four points, as shown in Figure 13–44. Changes to the position of the constraint points will change the shape of the attached shape element.

Construct Attached Ellipse or Circle   This command enables you to create and attach a circle to a construction circle or an ellipse to a construction ellipse. To attach the design circles to the construction circles as shown in Figure 13–35, invoke the Construct Attached Ellipse or Circle command from:

Attach Element tool box	Select the Attach Ellipse tool (see Figure 13–45).
Key-in window	**Attach Circle** (or **at ci**) ⏎

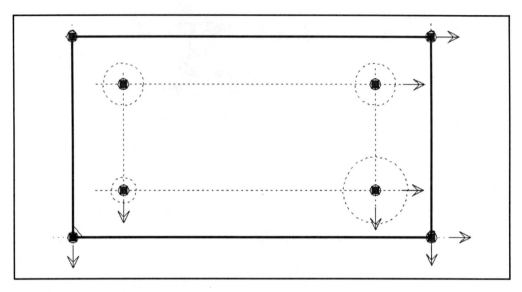

FIGURE 13–44 Result of drawing the design's outline shape.

FIGURE 13–45 Invoking the Construct Attached Ellipse or Circle command from the Attach Element tool box.

MicroStation prompts:

> Construct Attached Ellipse or Circle > Identify ellipse *(Select one of the construction circles, then click the Data button in space to accept the circle.)*

This attachment causes the design circle always to stay centered on the inner construction line intersections. Repeat the procedure for the remaining circles. The result of attaching design circles to each of the construction circles is shown in Figure 13–46.

Add dimensions on the design as shown in Figure 13–47. Set the Association lock to ON before placing the dimensions. Associating the dimensions with the design elements allows the dimensions to be used as constraints.

> **NOTE:** Ignore the dimension values now. The dimensions will be constrained and their values set later.

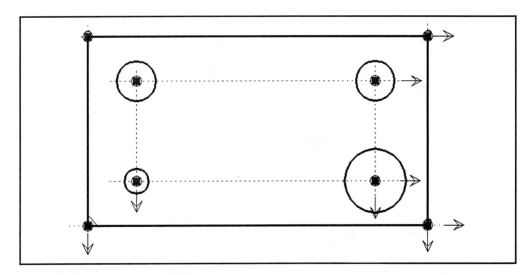

FIGURE 13–46 Result of drawing the design's circles.

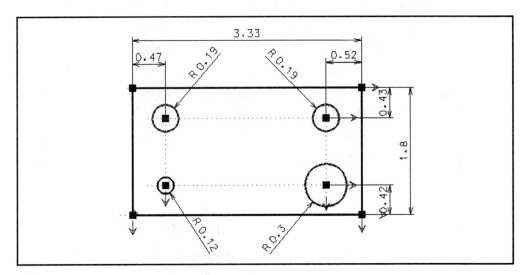

FIGURE 13–47 Result of dimensioning the design.

Place the following text strings for the equations and variables by using the Place Text at Origin command, and place each line of text in separate, one-line text elements. Place the text to the right of the design.

```
wid = space*2 + 1.25
len = space*2 + 3.25
space = 0.75
rad = 0.25
wid
len
```

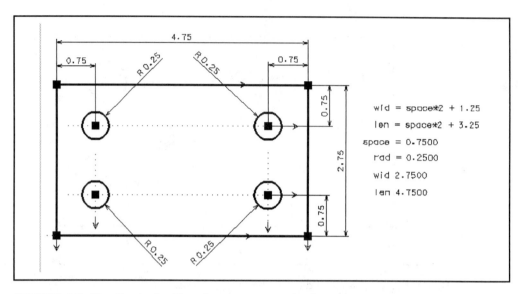

FIGURE 13–48 Result of adding the text strings to the design.

Figure 13–48 shows the design after adding the text.

Assign Variable to Dimensional Constraint With this command you can assign a constant or variable to a dimensional constraint. The constant or variable then represents the dimension's value in equations. Assign the "rad" variable as the radius of each and every circle, as shown in Figure 13–35. Invoke the Assign Variable to Dimensional Constraint command from:

Constraint tool box	Select the Assign variable tool (see Figure 13–49).
Key-in window	**Constrain Variable** (or **constra v**) [ENTER]

FIGURE 13–49 Invoking the Assign Variable to Dimensional Contraint command from the Constraint tool box.

MicroStation prompts:

> Assign Variable to Dimensional Constraint > Identify variable *(Select the "rad = 0.25" text string.)*
> Assign Variable to Dimensional Constraint > Identify constraint *(Select the radial dimension of one of the circles.)*
> Assign Variable to Dimensional Constraint > Accept *(Click the Data button in space to assign the "rad" variable to the circle's dimension.)*

Repeat the procedure for each of the four circles, and the circles are made equal to the "rad" value (0.25) and the radius dimensions are all updated.

Similarly, constrain the space between each circle center and the adjacent design edges with the Assign Variable command to Dimensional Constraint to assign the "Space" variable to each of the four circle-center-to-edge dimensions.

Assign Equation This command assigns an algebraic constraint—an equation that expresses a constraint relationship between variables, numerical constants, and built-in functions and constants—to a model. Create the "wid" and "len" equations by invoking the Assign Equation command from:

Constraint tool box	Select the Assign Equation tool (see Figure 13–50).
Key-in window	**Constrain Equation** (or **constra e**) [ENTER]

MicroStation prompts:

> Assign equation > Identify equation *(Select the "wid = space*2 + 1.25" text string.)*
> Assign equation > Identify variable, or RESET to finish *(Select the "space = 0.75" text string, select the "wid" text string, then click the Data button in space to complete defining the "wid" equation.)*

Similarly, invoke the Assign equation command again to create the "len" equation by selecting "len = space*2 + 3.25", "space = 0.75", and "len."

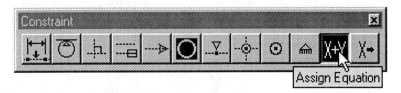

FIGURE 13–50 Invoking the Assign equation command from the Constraint tool box.

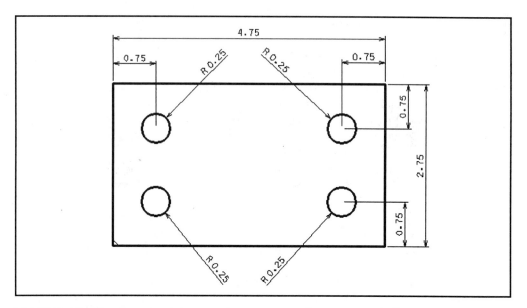

FIGURE 13–51 Completed design with construction elements turned off.

Constrain the design's outline dimensions by invoking the Assign Variable command to assign "len" to the overall horizontal dimension and "wid" to the overall vertical dimension.

Figure 13–51 shows the completed design with the Construction view attribute turned OFF so only the actual design is displayed.

> **NOTE:** After the design is completed, it may be necessary to invoke the Modify Element command to adjust the position of some dimension elements and move the text strings.

Modifying a Dimension-Driven Design

Dimension-driven designs are modified by changing one of the variable values and then re-solving the design. Constraint equations and variables can be changed by editing the text strings or by invoking the Modify Value command. For example, the design we just constructed contains four variables:

■ The "wid" and "len" variables are set equal to equations that contain constants (1.25 and 3.25). The constants can be changed by editing the equations with the Edit Text command. These two constants control the horizontal and vertical space between the circles.

- The "space" variable is set equal to a constant (0.75) that can be changed either by editing the text string via the Edit Text command or with the Modify Value command. Changing this variable changes the position of the circles and, because it appears in the two equations, the overall width and length of the design.
- The "len" variable is set equal to a constant (0.25) that can be changed to control the size of the circles.

Modify Value of Dimension or Variable This tool can edit the value of a dimensional constraint. To change the variable, invoke the Modify Value of Dimension or Variable command from:

Model tool box	Select the Modify Value tool (see Figure 13–52).
Key-in window	**Model Edit_dimension** (or **mode e**) [ENTER]

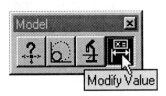

FIGURE 13–52 Invoking the Modify Value of Dimension or Variable command in the Model tool box.

MicroStation prompts:

> Modify Value of Dimension or Variable > Identify element *(Select the dimension or variable to be changed.)*
> Modify Value of Dimension or Variable > Accept *(Click the Data button in space to accept the selected element.)*
> Modify Value of Dimension or Variable > Enter a value *(Enter the new value in the Settings window Text field, and press* [ENTER] *to re-solve the design for the new value.)*

Re-solve Constraints If the Edit Text tool is used to change a variable's value, then the design must be "re-solved" to apply the new constraint value. To re-solve the design, invoke the Re-solve Constraint command from:

Model tool box	Select the Re-solve Constraints tool (see Figure 13–53).
Key-in window	**Update Model** (or **up m**) [ENTER]

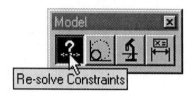

FIGURE 13–53 Invoking the Re-solve Constraints command from the Model tool box.

MicroStation prompts:

> Re-solve Constraints > Identify element *(Select the variable that has been changed or the text of a dimension that is constrained to the variable, then click the Data button in space to initiate re-solving of the design.)*

Creating a Dimension-Driven Cell

Dimension-driven cells are created from dimension-driven designs when the Construction view attribute is set to ON and all of the construction elements of the design are included in the design. When a dimension-driven cell is placed in a design file, its constraints can be changed.

> **NOTE:** If the Construction view attribute is set to OFF when a cell is created from a dimension-driven design, the cell is *not* a dimension-driven cell.

REVIEW QUESTIONS

Write your answers in the spaces provided.

1. Explain briefly the purpose of creating a graphic group.

   _____

   _____

2. List the steps in creating a graphic group.

   _____

   _____

3. Explain the purpose of the Graphic Group Lock setting.

   _____

   _____

4. Explain briefly the purpose of element selection by element type.

   _____

   _____

5. Explain briefly the benefits of setting up a level symbology table.

   _____

   _____

6. List the steps involved in setting up a level symbology table.

   _____

   _____

7. List the steps involved in converting a MicroStation design file to an AutoCAD drawing file.

   _____

   _____

8. Explain briefly the benefits of dimension-driven design.

   _____

   _____

14

MICROSTATION AND MICROSOFT WINDOWS

• • • • • • • • • • • • • • •

MicroStation 95 is a true 32-bit application that runs in Windows 3.1, the Windows 95 operating system, and the Windows NT operating system. This is made possible by utilizing the Win32 application programming interface (API) supported natively by Windows 95 and Windows NT. For Windows 3.1, Win32 is supported by installing the Win32s extension. The user interface is the same regardless of which Windows version is run.

When MicroStation 95 is run under Windows, several new and useful features become available within MicroStation and for sharing data between MicroStation and other applications.

OBJECTIVES

After completing this chapter, you will be able to:

✓ Run MicroStation 95 with Windows 95.

✓ Run other applications with MicroStation 95.

✓ Use the system clipboard.

✓ Use two screens.

✓ Create DDE links.

RUNNING MICROSTATION 95 WITH WINDOWS 95

MicroStation 95 is a true 32-bit application based on Micro- Station's Win32 API. When installed in the Windows 95 operating system, the MicroStation program group is added to the Start menu, and, if necessary, shortcuts can be created on the desktop and Start menu.

Creating a MicroStation 95 Shortcut on the Desktop

As mentioned in Chapter 1, you can start the MicroStation program in the Windows 95 operating system from the MicroStation 95 group in the Start menu. To make it easier to start the program, create a shortcut by placing the MicroStation icon on the desktop (see Figure 14–1). Then, just by double-clicking the icon, you will be able to start the program.

There are several ways of creating shortcuts. The following procedure is one of them.

1. Open the "My Computer" window by double-clicking on its desktop icon.
2. Open the disk drive containing the MicroStation software by double-clicking on the disk's icon in the "My Computer" window.
3. Display the contents of the MicroStation directory (ex: \USTATION).
4. Select USTATION.EXE with the right mouse button, drag it onto the Windows 95 desktop, then release the mouse button.
5. A pop-up menu appears; select the "Create ShortCut(s) Here" option.
6. Optionally, edit the shortcut title below the shortcut icon by clicking one time in the title, then clicking again to open the name for editing.

To start the MicroStation 95 program from the shortcut, just double-click on the shortcut icon.

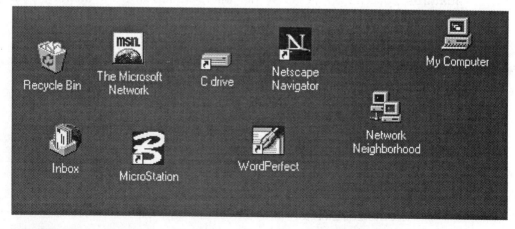

FIGURE 14–1 A shortcut to MicroStation 95 on the Windows 95 desktop.

Creating a MicroStation 95 Shortcut in the Start Menu

If necessary, you can also add a shortcut to MicroStation 95 in the Windows 95 Start menu (see Figure 14–2). There are several ways of creating shortcuts. Here is one way.

1. Open the "My Computer" window by double-clicking on its desktop icon.
2. Open the disk drive containing the MicroStation software by double-clicking on the disk's icon in the "My Computer" window.
3. Display the contents of the MicroStation directory (ex: \USTATION).
4. Select USTATION.EXE with the right mouse button, drag it over the Windows 95 Start menu name in the Taskbar. When you see the name of the file above the Start name, release the right mouse button.
5. Optionally, edit the shortcut title by moving the pointer on the Start menu and click the right mouse button. Select the menu item Open from the pop-up menu; the Start menu window appears. Locate the MicroStation icon, click one time in the title, then click again to open the name for editing. Make the necessary changes to the title and close the Start menu window.

To start MicroStation 95 from its shortcut in the Start menu, just open the Start menu, then click on the MicroStation program line near the top of the menu.

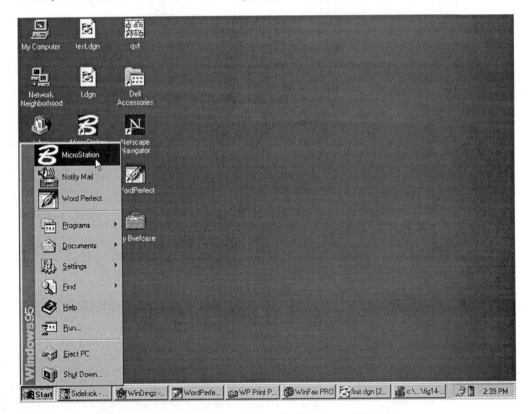

FIGURE 14–2   A shortcut to MicroStation 95 in the Windows 95 Start menu.

FIGURE 14–3 A design file shortcut on the Windows 95 desktop.

Creating Shortcuts to Design Files

Shortcuts for regularly used design files can be created on the desktop (see Figure 14–3) and in the Start menu. To create them, follow the procedures just described, except drag the design file's icon rather than the program icon.

When a design file is opened in MicroStation, Windows 95 creates a shortcut to the file in the Start>Documents submenu (see Figure 14–4). Select the design file from that menu to open it again in MicroStation.

RUNNING OTHER APPLICATIONS WITH MICROSTATION 95

Other applications can run in Windows 95 at the same time MicroStation 95 is running. Here are some ways to open other applications and to switch to other applications that are already open.

- Start another application while MicroStation 95 is running by selecting it from the Start menu.
- If there is a shortcut to the other application, double-click on the shortcut to open the other application.
- Press [ALT] + [TAB] to pop up another application that is already open.
- Switch to another open application by clicking on its icon in the Taskbar.
- Click the MicroStation application window Minimize button to reduce the window to an icon and expose the other open application windows. Then click in an application window to make it active.
- Reduce the MicroStation application window to less than full screen, so part of the other open application windows can be seen, then click in an application's window to bring it to the front of the stack.

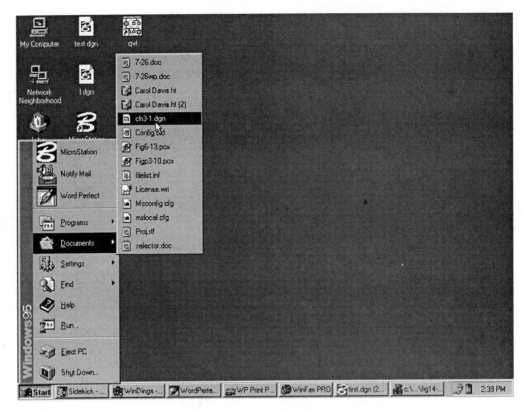

FIGURE 14-4 Documents submenu in the Windows 95 Start menu.

USING TWO SCREENS

Microsoft Windows 95 supports only one video screen, but hardware can be obtained to allow the Windows desktop to be split across two screens. Because Windows 95 thinks the two screens are actually one desktop, application windows can end up split across the two screens.

Two Application Windows Option

MicroStation provides a Two Application Windows option in the Preferences dialog box to overcome the limits imposed by Windows 95 on a two-video-screen configuration.

Open the Preferences dialog box from:

Pull-down menu	Workspace > Preferences (or [ALT] + E, P or [CTRL] + V)
Key-in window	**MDL LOAD USERPREF** (or **md l userpref)** [ENTER]

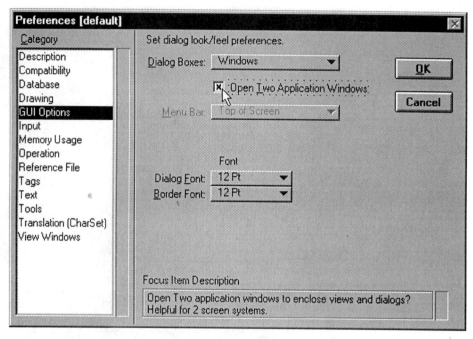

FIGURE 14–5   Preferences dialog box.

MicroStation opens the Preferences dialog box, similar to Figure 14–5.

In the Preferences dialog box:

1. Select the category GUI Options.
2. Set the toggle to ON for the Open Two Application Windows option (see Figure 14–5).
3. Click the OK button to close the Preferences dialog box.
4. Exit MicroStation program and restart the MicroStation program to apply the new settings.

To turn OFF the Two Application Windows option, repeat this above procedure, but set the toggle button to OFF for the Open Two Application Windows option in step 2.

When the toggle button for Open Two Application Windows is set to ON, MicroStation starts by opening both application windows on the primary video screen. One of the windows is always the primary window and has a "(1)" in the title bar; the other window is the secondary window and has a "(2)" in the title bar (see Figure 14–6). If necessary, drag the secondary application window to the other video screen.

MicroStation treats the two application windows as one single application, and both are always active. This allows moving back and forth between the two screens interactively without having first to select a screen.

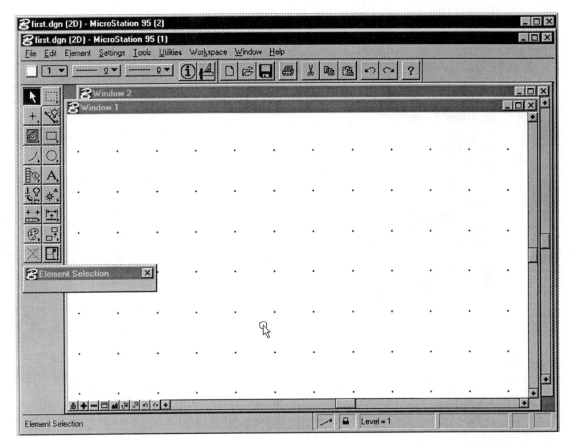

FIGURE 14-6   Example of two MicroStation application windows on one video screen.

Moving Boxes and Windows Between Application Windows

All MicroStation boxes and view windows open in the primary application window, but most can be moved to the secondary application window.

Settings Boxes   Settings boxes are moved from one application window to the other by selecting the Change Screen option from the box's Control menu, as shown in Figure 14-7. Open the Control menu by clicking on the white-on-blue B on the left corner of the box's title bar.

View Windows   View windows 1-4 open in the primary application window, and view windows 5-8 open in the secondary application window. All view windows can be moved between application windows by selecting the Change Screen option from their Control menu.

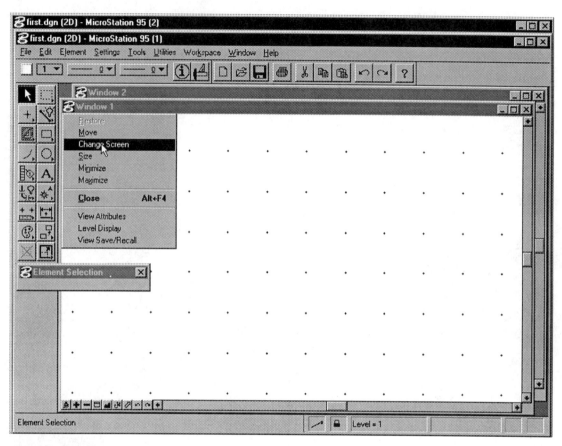

FIGURE 14-7 Change Screen option in a Control menu.

Tool Boxes and Tool Frames Tool boxes and tool frames are moved between application windows by dragging them to the other window.

Dialog Boxes Dialog boxes cannot be moved to the secondary application window.

Main Pull-Down Menu The Main pull-down menu (also called Menu bar) cannot be moved to the secondary application window.

> **NOTE:** The Two Application Windows option can also be used when the workstation has only one video screen. Both the primary and the secondary application windows appear on the screen. To switch from one application window to the other, just click in the desired window.

USING THE SYSTEM CLIPBOARD

MicroStation's pull-down menu Edit contains the Copy, Cut, and Paste commands (see Figure 14–8) that move elements to and from the Window's "clipboard." The contents of the clipboard can be pasted into the current design file, into other design files, and even into other computer applications that support the clipboard operations. Elements placed on the clipboard remain there even after MicroStation is exited. If necessary, you can even see the contents of the clipboard in the clipboard viewer.

Copying Elements to the Clipboard

To copy elements to the clipboard, select the elements to be copied via the Element Selection tool, then select the Copy command from:

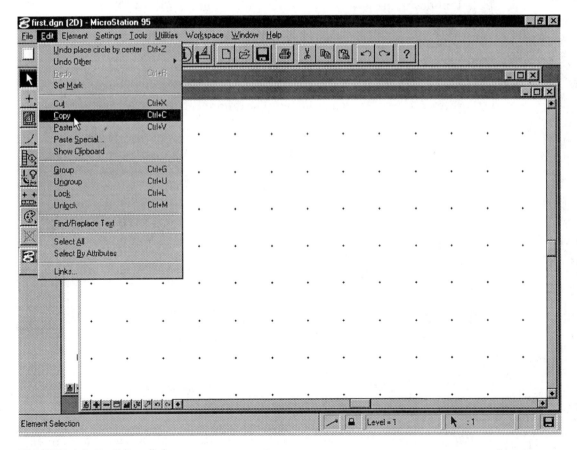

FIGURE 14–8 Edit pull-down menu.

Pull-down menu	Edit > Copy (or ⌥ + E, C or ⌃ + C)
Key-in window	**Clipboard Copy** (or **cli co**) ⏎

A copy of the selected elements is immediately placed on the clipboard and the command exits (there are no MicroStation prompts). The original elements remain in the design file.

Moving Elements to the Clipboard

To move elements to the clipboard, first select the element or elements to be cut using the Element Selection tool, then select the Cut command from:

Pull-down menu	Edit > Cut (or ⌥ + E, X or ⌃ + X)
Key-in window	**Clipboard Cut** (or **cli cu**) ⏎

The selected elements are immediately placed to the clipboard and the command exits (there are no MicroStation prompts). The original elements are deleted from the design file.

Pasting Elements from the Clipboard

To paste elements from the clipboard onto the design plane, select the Paste command from:

Pull-down menu	Edit > Paste (or ⌥ + E, P or ⌃ + V)
Key-in window	**Clipboard Paste** (or **cli p**) ⏎

MicroStation prompts:

> Paste from Clipboard > Enter point to paste *(Identify the location where the elements are to be placed.)*

The contents of the clipboard are placed onto the design plane and the command exits.

If you need to paste another copy of the elements from the clipboard, you must invoke the command again.

Similarly, you can also cut, copy, and paste elements such as audio notes, text, or graphics from another application to MicroStation.

> **NOTE:** The Copy and Cut commands are dimmed in the pull-down menu Edit if no elements are selected, and the Paste command is dimmed if the clipboard is empty.

Viewing the Contents of the Clipboard

To view the contents of the clipboard, select the Show Clipboard command from:

Pull-down menu	Edit > Show Clipboard (or ALT + E, P or CTRL + V)
Key-in window	**Clipboard Show** (or **cli s**) ENTER

MicroStation displays the Show Clipboard window, with contents of the clipboard similar to Figure 14–9.

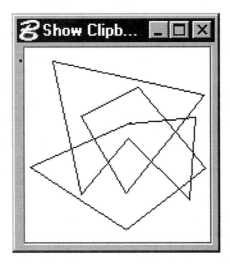

FIGURE 14–9 Show Clipboard window displaying the contents of the clipboard.

CREATING DYNAMIC DATA EXCHANGE (DDE) LINKS

In Microsoft Windows 95, MicroStation 95 supports DDE (dynamic data exchange). DDE allows the creating of "live" links to MicroStation from other applications and the sending of key-in commands to MicroStation from other applications.

For detailed information on DDE, refer to the technical manuals furnished with MicroStation and the documentation for the application you want to link to Micro-Station.

· · · · · · · · · · · · · · · · · · · ·

CHAPTER

15

CUSTOMIZING MICROSTATION

· · · · · · · · · · · · · · · · · · · ·

MicroStation is an extremely powerful program off the shelf. But, like many popular engineering and business software programs, it does not automatically do all things for all users. It does, however, permit users to make changes and additions to the core program to suit individual needs and applications. Word processors offer a feature by which you can save a combination of many keystrokes and invoke them at any time with just a few keystrokes. This is known as a *macro*. Database management programs have their own library of user functions that can also be combined and saved as a user-named, custom-designed command. These programs also allow you to create and save standard blank forms for use later to be filled out as needed. Utilizing these features to make your own copy of a generic program unique and more powerful for your particular application is known as *customizing*.

OBJECTIVES

Customizing MicroStation can include several facets. After completing this chapter, you will be able to:

✓ Create settings groups and edit existing groups.

✓ Provide names for levels and group them into user-defined group names.

✓ Create multi-line definitions and save them to a file.

✓ Create custom line styles.

✓ Create and modify workspace components: the project configuration, the user configuration, and the user interface.

✓ Customize the function keys.

✓ Install fonts.

✓ Archive design files and their associated resources.

SETTINGS GROUPS

MicroStation allows you to define a settings group with a user-specified name in three categories: Drawing (default), Scale, and Working Units. Under each settings group of the Drawing category, you can define individual group components. You can set element attributes such as color, weight, line style, level, and class, associating with a primitive command (such as Place Line, Place Text) as a part of the group component. As a group component you can also save the current multi-line definition and active dimension settings. You can define any number of group components for each settings group.

MicroStation provides an option to save the settings groups and group components to an external file, and by default the file will have an extension .STG. This file follows the same concept as the cell library. Once created, the settings file may be attached to any of your design files and activate one of the settings groups and corresponding group component. Selecting a component does the following:

- All element attributes associated with the component are set as specified in the component definition.
- If a key-in is defined for the component, the corresponding command is selected, letting you place an element or elements without invoking the command from a tool box.

Selecting a Settings Group and Corresponding Component

The Select Settings box allows you to select a settings group and corresponding group component from the currently attached settings group file. The settings box also provides an option to attach another settings group file and invoke a settings group and corresponding group component.

To open the Select Settings box, invoke the Manage command from:

Pull-down menu	Settings > Manage (or [ALT] + S, M)
Key-in window	**Setmgr Select Settings** (or **setm s s**)

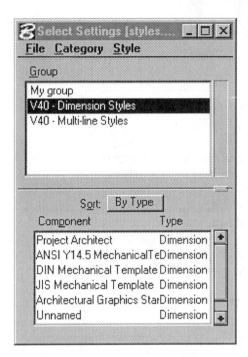

FIGURE 15–1 Select Settings box.

MicroStation displays the Select Settings box, as shown in Figure 15–1. MicroStation displays the name of the currently opened settings group file as part of the title of the settings box. The settings box is divided into two parts. By default, the top part lists the names of the available drawing settings groups. The bottom part of the settings box lists the name and type of each component from the selected settings group. To invoke one of the components, select the name of the component, and settings associated with the component are set as specified in the definition. If a key-in is defined for the component, the corresponding tool is selected, letting you place an element(s) without using a tool box.

Attaching a Settings Group File

To attach a settings group file to a design file, invoke the Open... command from:

Pull-down menu (Select Settings box)	File > Open... (or [ALT] + **F**, **O**)

MicroStation displays the Open Existing Settings File dialog box. Select the settings group file (extension .STG) from the Files list box, and click the OK button or press [ENTER] to attach it to the design file. MicroStation lists the available groups and corresponding components.

Modifying a Settings Group

The Edit Settings box allows you to define, modify, and delete settings groups and group components. To open the Edit Settings box, invoke the Edit command from:

Pull-down menu (Select Settings box)	<u>F</u>ile > <u>E</u>dit (or  + **F**, **E**)

MicroStation displays the Edit Settings box, as shown in Figure 15–2. MicroStation displays the name of the currently opened settings group file as part of the title of the settings box. The settings box is divided into two parts. By default, the top part lists the names of the available drawing settings groups. The bottom part of the settings box lists the name and type of each component from the selected settings group. The Category options menu sets the category for the listing of groups in the Group list box. The Sort options menu sets the manner in which components are sorted in the Component list box By Name or By Type.

Creating a Settings Group File To create a new settings group file, invoke the New... command from:

Pull-down menu (Edit Settings box)	<u>F</u>ile > <u>N</u>ew... (or  + **F**, **N**)

FIGURE 15–2 Edit Settings box.

MicroStation displays the Create New Settings File dialog box. Key-in the name of the file in the Files edit field, and click the OK button to create a new settings file.

Creating a Settings Group To create a new settings group, invoke the Create Group command from:

Pull-down menu (Edit Settings box)	Edit > Create > Group (or [ALT] + **E, C, G**)

MicroStation adds a new group, called "Unnamed," to the Group list box. You can change the name from "Unnamed" to any appropriate name in the name edit field located just below the listing of the Group names list box. The maximum number of characters for the group name is 31.

Deleting a Settings Group To delete a settings group, first select the group to be deleted from the Group list box and invoke the Delete command from:

Pull-down menu (Edit Settings box)	Edit > Delete... (or [ALT] + **E, D**)

MicroStation opens an alert box for confirming the deletion. Click the OK button to delete the group. MicroStation deletes the group and all its components.

Creating a New Component To create a new component, first select the settings group under which you want to create a new component. Select one of the seven component types available from:

Pull-down menu (Edit Settings box)	Edit > Create > <component types> (or [ALT] + **E, C**)

MicroStation adds a new component type "Unnamed," with the listing of the component type, to the Components list box . You can change the name from "Unnamed" to any appropriate name in the name edit field box located just below the listing of the Component names list box. The maximum number of characters for the group name is 31.

Table 15–1 lists the component types and corresponding tools that can be used with each component type.

Table 15–1.   Component Types and Corresponding Tools

COMPONENT TYPE	TOOL
Active Point	Points tool box
Area Pattern	Pattern tool box
Cell	Cells tool box
Dimension	Dimension tool box
Linear	Linear Elements tool box
	Polygons tool box
	Arcs tool box
	Ellipses tool box
	Curves tool box
Multi-line	The key-in **PLACE MLINE CONSTRAINED** corresponds to the Place Multi-line tool
Text	Text tool box

Modify a Component   To modify a component, first select the component from the Component list box, and invoke the Modify command from:

Pull-down menu (Edit Settings box)	<u>E</u>dit > <u>M</u>odify (or ⌨ + **E, M**)

MicroStation displays the appropriate component settings box.

Make the necessary changes in the settings box. Or, instead, click the Match button, and MicroStation matches the settings in the settings box to the selected element. Click the Save button to save the settings and close the settings box. To disregard the changes, click the Close button.

The **Modify Point Component settings box** (see Figure 15–3) allows you to modify the options available related to Construct Point commands. To set the key-in that will be activated automatically when the component is selected, set the key-in toggle button to ON and type the appropriate key-in for the Construct Points command. Set the appropriate element attributes (level, color, weight, and line style) that will be activated automatically when the component is selected. Select one of the three point types, Zero-Length Line, Cell, or Character from the Type options menu. If you select the Cell option, set the appropriate settings in the Cell section of the Modify settings box. If you select the Character option, set the appropriate settings in the Character section of the Modify settings box.

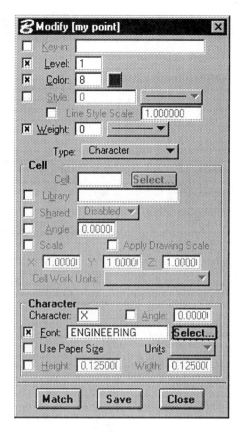

FIGURE 15–3 Modify Point Component settings box.

The **Modify Area Pattern Component settings box** (see Figure 15–4) allows you to modify the options available related to hatching and patterning commands. To set the key-in that will be activated automatically when the component is selected, set the key-in toggle button to ON and type the appropriate key-in for the hatching or patterning command. Set the appropriate element attributes (level, color, weight, and line style) that will be activated automatically when the component is selected. Select one of the two pattern types, Pattern or Hatch. If you select the Pattern option, set the appropriate settings in the Pattern section of the Modify settings box. If you select the Hatch option, set the appropriate settings in the Hatch section of the Modify settings box.

The **Modify Cell Component settings box** (see Figure 15–5) allows you to modify the options available related to cell placement commands. To set the key-in that will be activated automatically when the component is selected, set the key-in toggle button to ON and type the appropriate key-in for the cell placement command. Set the appropriate element attributes (level, color, weight, and line style) that will be activated automatically when the component is selected. Key-in the name of the cell library, the cell name, and the appropriate scale factors that will be automatically

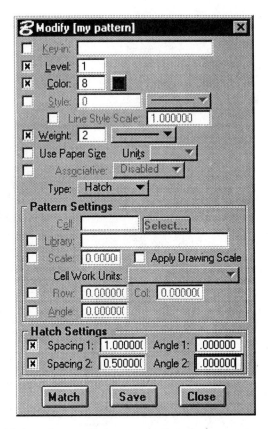

FIGURE 15-4 Modify Area Pattern Component settings box.

activated when the component is selected. Select one of the two cell types, Placement or Terminator, from the Type options menu. If the Placement option is selected, then the Cell selection will become the Active Cell when the component is selected in the Select Settings window. If the Terminator option is selected, then the Cell selection will become the Active Line Terminator.

> **NOTE:** The Level, Color, Style, and Weight controls can affect placement of a cell using the component only if the specified cell was created as a point cell.

The **Modify Dimension Component settings box** (see Figure 15–6) allows you to modify the options available related to the Dimension component definition. To set the key-in that will be activated automatically when the component is selected, set the key-in toggle button to ON and type the appropriate key-in for the dimension placement command. Set the appropriate element attributes (level, color, weight, and line style) that will be activated automatically when the component is selected.

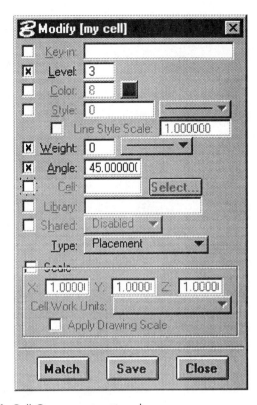

FIGURE 15–5 Modify Cell Component settings box.

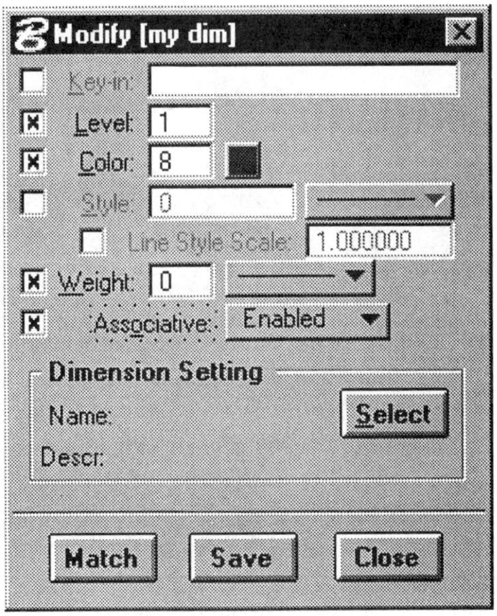

FIGURE 15–6 Modify Dimension Component settings box.

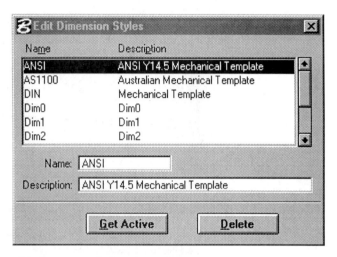

FIGURE 15–7 Edit Dimension Styles settings box.

As part of the Component definition, select the dimension style that will set the appropriate dimension settings. Click the Select button to select one of the available dimension styles. MicroStation displays the Select Dimension Definition dialog box listing the available dimension styles. Select the dimension style from the list box and click the OK button. Or, if you want to use the current dimension settings, then first save the dimension settings on a given style name. Invoke the Dimension tool from:

Pull-down menu (Edit Settings box)	Style > Dimension (or [ALT] + S, D)

MicroStation displays the Edit Dimension Styles settings box, as shown in Figure 15–7.

Click the Get Active button and MicroStation adds a new dimension style "Dim0." You can change the name from "Dim0" to any appropriate name in the Name edit field, and close the settings box.

Click the Select button from the Modify settings box to select the newly created dimension style from the Select Dimension Definition dialog box.

The **Modify Linear Component settings box** (see Figure 15–8) allows you to modify the options available related to placement of lines, polygons, arcs, circles, ellipses, and curves. To set the key-in that will be activated automatically when the component is selected, set the key-in toggle button to ON and type the appropriate key-in for the Linear command. Set the appropriate element attributes (level, color, weight, line style, area, and fill) that will be activated automatically when the component is selected.

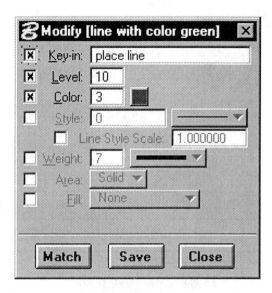

FIGURE 15–8 Modify Linear Component settings box.

The **Modify Multi-line Component settings box** (see Figure 15–9) allows you to modify the options available related to multi-line component definition. To set the key-in that will be activated automatically when the component is selected, set the key-in toggle button to ON and type the appropriate key-in for the multi-line placement command. Set the appropriate element attributes (level, color, weight, and line style) that will be activated automatically when the component is selected.

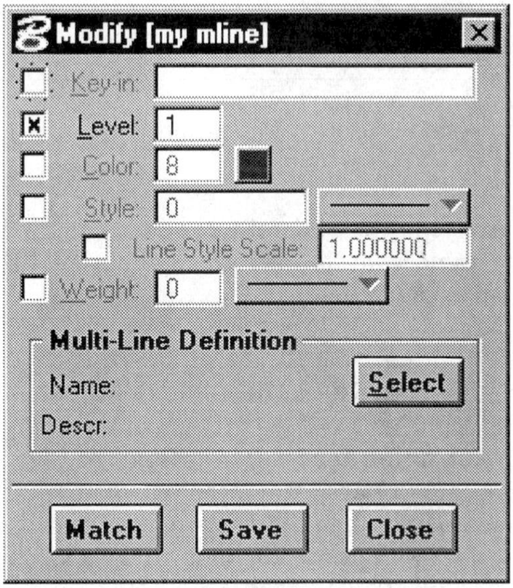

FIGURE 15–9 Modify Multi-line Component settings box.

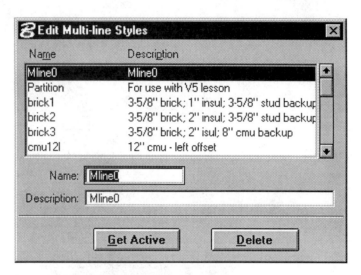

FIGURE 15–10 Edit Multi-line Styles settings box.

As part of the component definition, select the multi-line definition that will be set when you invoke the component. Click the Select button to select one of the available multi-line definitions. MicroStation displays the Select Multi-line Definition dialog box listing the available multi-line definitions. Select the multi-line definitions from the list box and click the OK button. Or, if you want to use the current multi-line definition, then first save the definition on a given style name. Invoke the Multi-Line tool from:

Pull-down menu (Edit Settings box)	Style > Multi-Line (or [ALT] + S, M)

MicroStation displays the Edit Multi-line Styles settings box, as shown in Figure 15–10.

Click the Get Active button. MicroStation adds a new multi-line style "Mline0." You can change the name from "Mline0" to any appropriate name in the Name edit field and close the settings box.

Click the Select button from the Modify settings box to select the newly created multi-line style from the Select Multi-line Definition dialog box.

The **Modify Text Component settings box** (see Figure 15–11) allows you to modify the options available related to placement of text. To set the key-in that will be activated automatically when the component is selected, set the key-in toggle button to ON and type the appropriate key-in for the place text command. Set the appropriate element attributes (level, color, weight, line style, area, and fill) and text attributes (slant angle, line length, line spacing, fraction, vertical, underline, justification,

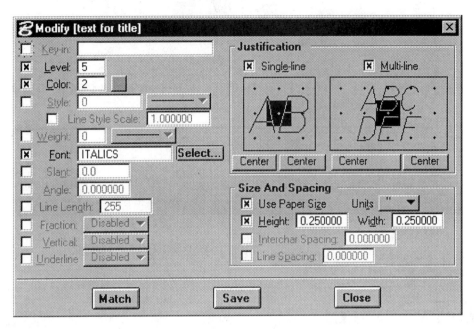

FIGURE 15–11   Modify Text Component settings box.

font, size, and intercharacter spacing) that will be activated automatically when the component is selected.

In addition, you can also specify the relationship between plotting units and design Master Units by selecting one of the available scale settings. To list the available scale settings, select Scale... from:

Pull-down menu (Select Settings box)	<u>C</u>ategory > <u>S</u>cale (or [ALT] + **C, S**)

MicroStation displays the Select Scale dialog box. To set the scale, double-click the scale settings in the list box and close the dialog box.

You can also set the current Working Units by selecting one of the available Working Units settings. To list the available Working Units settings group, select Working Units... from:

Pull-down menu (Select Settings box)	<u>C</u>ategory > <u>W</u>orking Units... (or [ALT] + **C, W**)

MicroStation displays the Select Working Units dialog box. The dialog box lists the available Working Units settings. To change the Working Units to one of the listed Working Units for the current design, double-click the Working Units setting to make its settings active and close the dialog box. An alert box opens for confirming the adjustment of the Working Units settings.

Importing Dimension and Multi-line Styles from Version 4

To import dimension and multi-line styles created with MicroStation Version 4 as a group, invoke the Import... tool from:

Pull-down menu (Edit Settings box)	Style > Import > V4 Styles (w/Names)... (or [ALT] + S, I, N)

MicroStation displays the Select V4 Style File dialog box. Each style that is selected is converted to a component of the new group and assigned a name identical to its style name.

NAMING LEVELS

In Chapter 2 you were introduced to placing elements on individual levels. Each design file is provided with 63 levels and each level is assigned a number between 1 and 63, inclusive. To make a level active, key-in **LV=<number>** and press [ENTER]. You can turn ON and OFF levels by keying **ON=<number>** and **OF=<number>**, respectively. Instead of keying a level number, you can assign an alphanumeric "name" that represents a level number and then substitute the "name" for the "number" when using the key-ins. By assigning a name to a level, it is easier to remember what type of elements will be placed on a specific level. Let's say you want to place dimensioning on level 10. Instead of remembering level 10 for dimensioning, assign a name "dim" for level 10. Whenever you want to place dimensioning, make sure you are in the dim level by making it the active level by keying-in **LV=dim** and pressing [ENTER]. It may also be helpful to assign level names if you have a need to "translate" a drawing into or out of MicroStation from or to another CAD system.

In addition to assigning a level name, MicroStation allows you to provide a group name. Under a group name you can assign a set of level names or numbers, and MicroStation allows you to control the display of levels by keying-in a group name for ON and OFF key-in commands. Level names and group names are analogous to the files and directories in DOS.

MicroStation provides an option to save to an external file the level name assignments and level group definitions composing the level structure. You can store any number of definitions to a single file, and by default the file will have an extension .LVL. This file follows the same concept as the cell library. Once created, the level structure file may be attached to any of your design files and activate one of the definitions stored in the file.

Assigning Level Names and Group Names

The View Levels settings box allows you to assign level names and group names in addition to setting an active level and turning the level display ON and OFF. To assign level names and group names in addition to controlling the display of levels, open the View Levels settings box from:

Pull-down menu	Settings > <u>L</u>evel > <u>D</u>isplay (or [ALT] + **S, L, D** or [CTRL] + **E**)

MicroStation displays the View Levels settings box, as shown in Figure 15–12.

Display MicroStation displays three different layouts (by level numbers, level names, or level groups), depending on the option selected from the pull-down menu Display of the View Levels settings box. By default, MicroStation displays the level numbers layout; see Figure 15–12. See Chapter 2 for a detailed explanation for the level numbers layout.

The level names layout displays the names of the levels similar to the one shown in Figure 15–13. The active level name is displayed in red. To turn ON or OFF a set of level(s), select all the level name(s) to be included (dragging or [CTRL]-clicking selects multiple levels) from the level operations layout display and click the ON or the OFF button. To make a level active, select a level name and click the Active button.

FIGURE 15–12   View Levels settings box.

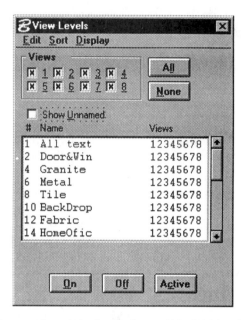

FIGURE 15–13 Level names layout displaying the names of the levels.

The level group layout lists the group names and corresponding levels similar to the one shown in Figure 15–14. The active level name is displayed in red. To turn ON or OFF a specific group, select the group name from the group operations layout display and click the ON or the OFF button. To turn ON or OFF a set of level(s), select all the

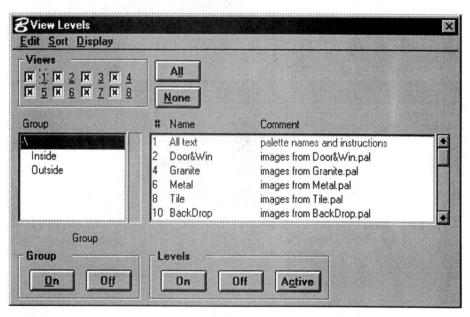

FIGURE 15–14 Level group layout lists the group names and their corresponding levels.

level name(s) to be included (dragging or 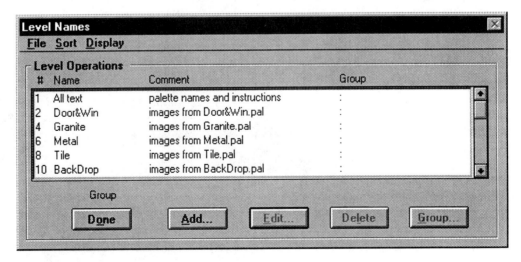-clicking selects multiple levels) from a specific group name and click the ON or the OFF button. To make a level active, select a level name and click the Active button.

Defining Names To assign level names and group names, open the Level Names dialog box from:

Pull-down menu (View Levels settings box)	Edit > Define Names... (or [ALT] + **E, D**)
Pull-down menu	Settings > Level > Names... (or [ALT] + **S, L, N**)

MicroStation displays the Level Names dialog box, as shown in Figure 15–15.

The Level Names dialog box has two alternate layouts, chosen from the Display menu, as shown in Figure 15–16. The Level Operations layout displays all the level names assigned in the current level structure file. The Level Group operations layout displays all the group names assigned in the current level structure file.

The **Level Operations** layout lists the level name, comment, and group affiliation (with path) for each named level, as shown in Figure 15–16. The list is sorted by the criteria specified in the Sort Criteria dialog box (invoked from the pull-down menu Sort...). If a level is a member of multiple level groups, it is listed multiple times— once for each group of which it is a member. To operate on a level, you must first select it. Dragging or [CTRL]-clicking selects multiple levels.

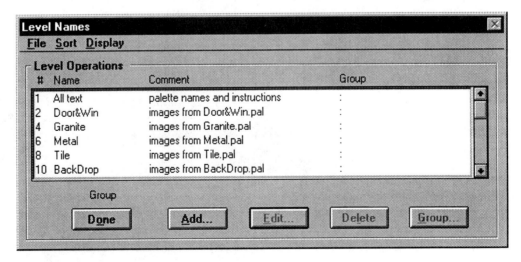

FIGURE 15–15 Level Names dialog box.

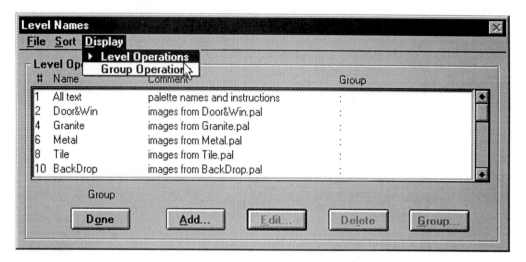

FIGURE 15-16 The Level Names dialog box has two alternate layouts chosen from the Display menu.

To assign a level name, invoke the Level Name dialog box by clicking the Add... button. MicroStation displays the Level Name dialog box, similar to the one shown in Figure 15–17. Key-in the level number in the Number edit field, the level name in the Name edit field (maximum valid number of characters is 16), and any comment in the Comment edit field (maximum valid number of characters is 32).

To change the level name, the assigned level number, or the comment, first select the level to be changed in the list box, then click the Edit button. MicroStation displays the Level Name dialog box. Make the necessary changes and click the OK button.

To remove a level name from the list box, first select the level to be removed in the list box, then click the Delete button. MicroStation removes the selected level name assignment from the list box.

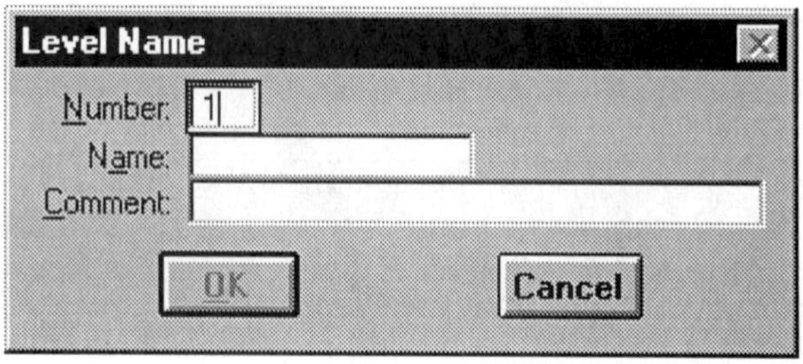

FIGURE 15-17 Level Name dialog box.

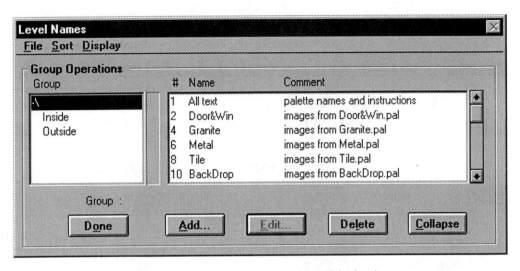

FIGURE 15–18 The Group operations layout lists names of the level groups in a tree structure.

The **Group Operations** layout lists the names of the level groups in a tree structure under the group listing, as shown in Figure 15–18. To list the levels assigned to a group, click the group name. MicroStation lists the level numbers, with corresponding level names, including the comments. The list is sorted by criteria specified in the Sort Criteria dialog box. The full path to the selected group is shown below the list box.

The backslash symbol (\) indicates the "root" of the structure. Each group that has subgroups is indicated with a symbol. The minus sign (–) indicates that the group's subgroups are listed below. The plus sign (+) indicates the group's subgroups are not listed. Double-clicking a group name indicated with a minus or plus sign toggles the listing of its subgroups.

To assign a group or subgroup name, invoke the Level Group dialog box by clicking the Add... button. MicroStation displays the Level Group dialog box, similar to the one shown in Figure 15–19. Key-in the level group name in the Name edit field (maximum valid number of characters is 16).

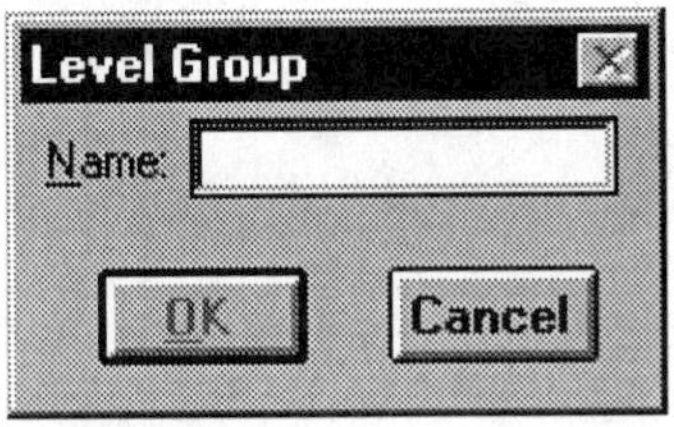

FIGURE 15–19 Level Group dialog box.

To change the group name, first select the group to be changed in the list box, then click the Edit button. MicroStation displays the Level Group dialog box. Make the necessary changes and click the OK button.

To remove a group name from the list box, first select the group to be removed in the list box, then click the Delete button. MicroStation removes the selected group name assignment and its subgroups, if any, and discontinues component level name assignment.

To list the selected group's subgroups, click the Collapse button. The Collapse button is disabled (dimmed) if the selected group does not have any subgroups.

Assigning Levels to a Group To assign a set of level(s) to a group name, first select all the level name(s) to be included (dragging or <kbd>CTRL</kbd>-clicking selects multiple levels) from the Level Operations layout display. Open the Select Target Group dialog box from:

| Level Names settings box (Level operations display) | Select the <u>G</u>roup... button (or <kbd>ALT</kbd> + **G**) |

MicroStation displays the Select Target Group dialog box, as shown in Figure 15–20. The Select Target Group dialog box enables you to copy or move the selected level(s) to a group.

The dialog box lists the names of level groups in a tree structure, indicated by the indenting of successive levels. The backslash symbol (\) indicates the "root" of the structure. To specify a group as the destination for the selected level(s), first click the group name. To add the level to the selected group without deleting it from its present group, click the Copy to Group button. If you want to delete from the present group, if any, then click the Move to Group button. The Collapse button toggles the listing of the selected group's subgroups. The Cancel button closes the dialog box without copying or moving the selected level(s).

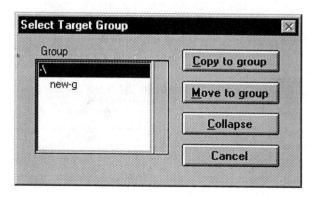

FIGURE 15–20 Select Target Group dialog box.

Saving the Level Structure

To save the current level structure, invoke the Save command from:

Pull-down menu (Level Names settings box)	File > Save... (or **ALT** + **F, S**)

MicroStation displays the Save Level Structure dialog box. Key-in the file name in the File edit field and click the OK button to save the level structure. The default extension for the file name is .LVL.

> **NOTE:** You can save the level structure for the active design file by invoking the Save Settings command from the pull-down menu File.

Attaching the Level Structure to the Current Design File

To attach an existing level structure file to the current design file, invoke the Open command from:

Pull-down menu (Level Names settings box)	File > Open... (or **ALT** + **F, O**)

MicroStation displays the Open Level Structure dialog box. Select the level structure file from the file list box and click the OK button, or press **ENTER**, to attach the level structure to the current design file.

Removing the Level and Group Assignment Names

To remove the level and group assignment names from the list box, invoke the Remove command from:

Pull-down menu (Level Names settings box)	File > Remove... (or **ALT** + **F, R**)

MicroStation displays an alert box to confirm the request. Click the OK button to remove all the level name assignments from the design file.

To close the Level Names settings box, click the Done button.

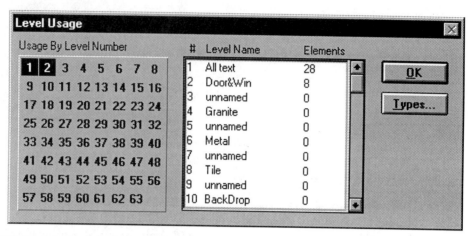

FIGURE 15–21 Level Usage dialog box.

LEVEL USAGE IN THE ACTIVE DESIGN

MicroStation lists the level usage by name and number in addition to providing information on the number of elements placed on each level. Open the Level Usage dialog box from:

Pull-down menu	Settings > Level > Usage... (or <kbd>ALT</kbd> + S, L, U)

MicroStation displays the Level Usage dialog box, as shown in Figure 15–21.

The level numbers with a dark background are the ones that have elements. Click the Types... button to get the listing of element types in the design file.

MULTI-LINE DEFINITION

A *multi-line* is a special element type made up of a series of parallel lines. Depending on how it is defined, one multi-line can have up to 16 line components. Each of the components can be defined at varying distances (offsets) and have its own level, color, weight, and line style.

Since a multi-line is a customized element, its components can be assigned a "style" name and can be saved and stored as part of a settings group. The Style Library concept is similar to that of the Cell Library in that it can be "attached" to any design file. The individual styles can then be made active and used as needed.

Once a multi-line is defined and made active, a multi-line can be placed in your design by invoking the Place Multi-line command (see Chapter 3).

Multi-lines Settings Box

The Multi-lines settings box controls the active multi-line definition. A sample of the multi-line that is currently defined is displayed in the lower left corner.

To create or modify a multi-line definition, invoke the Multi-Lines settings box from:

Pull-down menu	<u>E</u>lement > <u>M</u>ulti-lines (or (ALT) + **E, M**)
Key-in window	**Dialog multiline** (or **di mu**) (ENTER)

MicroStation displays the Multi-lines settings box as shown in Figure 15–22.

The Component option menu located in the top left-hand corner of the settings box allows you to set the component type—Lines, Start Cap, End Cap, and Joints—whose attributes can be modified. The menu options in the Multi-lines settings box depends on the type of the component option selected.

Lines Option The Lines option provides the controls for selecting the attributes for line components and setting offset distances, as shown in Figure 15–22. The list box lists the component lines and corresponding attribute settings in the active multi-

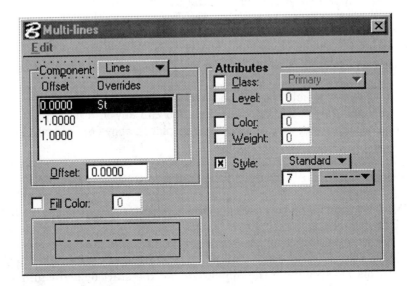

FIGURE 15–22 Multi-lines settings box.

line definition. To delete a component line from the active multi-line definition, first select the component line from the list box, then invoke the Delete command from:

Pull-down menu (Multi-lines settings box)	Edit > Delete (or **[ALT]** + **E, D**)

MicroStation deletes the selected component line from the multi-line definition.

To add a component line to the active multi-line definition, invoke the Insert command from:

Pull-down menu (Multi-lines settings box)	Edit > Insert (or **[ALT]** + **E, I**)

MicroStation adds a new component line before the selected line in the list box.

To add a component line with the same attributes as the selected line to the active multi-line definition, invoke the Duplicate command from:

Pull-down menu (Multi-lines settings box)	Edit > Duplicate (or **[ALT]** + **E, U**)

MicroStation adds a component line with the same attributes as the selected line.

To set the attributes for an individual component line, select the component line and set the appropriate controls for the attributes located in the top right side of the Multi-lines settings box. If the toggle button to the left of a control is ON, the corresponding setting is effective for the selected component. If the toggle button is set to OFF, the active attribute setting is effective and the control is dimmed. The controls are analogous to those in the Element Attributes settings box.

The Offset edit field sets the distance in Working Units (MU:SU:PU) from the work line to the selected component line. You can key-in a positive or negative distance, depending on whether the line is to be placed above or below the work line.

When the Fill Color toggle button is set to ON, the entire area between the outermost component lines of the multi-line is filled with the chosen color.

MicroStation displays a sample of the multi-line definition on the lower left corner of the settings box.

Start Cap or End Cap Option The Start Cap or End Cap option provides the controls for specifying the appearance of the start or end cap, as shown in Figure 15–23. The Line toggle button controls the display of the cap as a line. The Angle

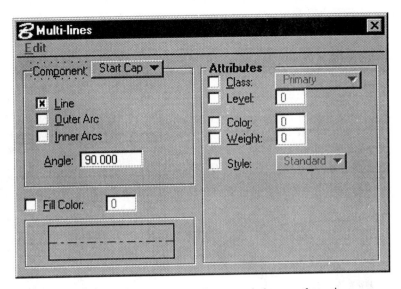

FIGURE 15-23 Start Cap selection displaying the controls for specifying the appearance of the start cap.

edit field sets the cap's line angle in degrees. The Outer Arc toggle button controls the display of the cap as an arc connecting the outermost component lines. The Inner Arcs toggle button controls the display of the cap, with arcs connecting pairs of inside component lines. If there is an even number of inside component lines, all are connected; if there is an odd number of inside component lines (three or more), the middle line is not connected. Controls for the attributes for the caps are located in the top right side of the Multi-lines settings box. If the toggle button to the left of a control is set to ON, the corresponding setting is effective for the caps. If the toggle button is set to OFF, the active attribute setting is effective and the control is dimmed. The controls are analogous to those in the Element Attributes settings box.

Joints Option The Joints option provides the only control available for specifying the appearance of the Joints, as shown in Figure 15-24. If it is set to ON, the joint lines are displayed at vertices. Similar to caps, controls for the attributes for the joints are located on the top right side of the Multi-lines settings box. If the toggle button to the left of a control is set to ON, the corresponding setting is effective for the joints. If the toggle button is set to OFF, the active attribute setting is effective and the control is dimmed. The controls are analogous to those in the Element Attributes settings box. When the Fill Color toggle button is set to ON, the entire area between the outermost component lines of the multi-line is filled with the chosen color.

You can save the Multi-line definition as a group component. For a detailed explanation, see the section on Settings Groups earlier in this chapter.

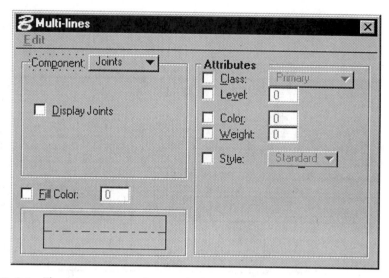

FIGURE 15–24 The Joints option selection displaying the only control available for specifying the appearance of the Joints.

CUSTOM LINE STYLES

In addition to standard line styles (LC = 0 . . . LC = 7), MicroStation allows you to create custom line styles. Custom line styles are created and stored in a style library file (extension .RSC). The style library file delivered with MicroStation is called LSTYLE.RSC. As with the cell library, line styles are created, stored, then recalled as needed. Once a library is created, it is attached to a design file, and all the line styles stored in the library are available. Only one style library can be attached at any time. If no style library is attached, MicroStation's standard line styles (LC = 0 . . . LC = 7) will still be available.

> **NOTE:** If you copy or move your MicroStation design file from one PC to another, be sure to copy the style library as well. Your custom line styles will not appear in your design if the style library is not present.

Activating a Custom Line Style

To browse, activate line styles, and set line style modifiers, open the Line Styles settings box from:

Primary tool box	Line Style option menu > Custom (see Figure 15–25)
Key-in window	**Linestyle Settings** (or **lines s**) `ENTER`

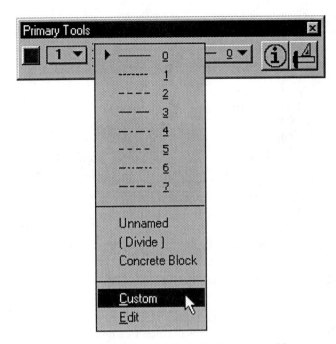

FIGURE 15–25   Selecting Custom line styles from the Primary tool box.

MicroStation displays the Line Styles settings box, similar to Figure 15–26.

The settings box lists the names of line styles from the default line style library LSTYLE.RSC unless it is set for a different line style library. Double-clicking a line style name makes the line style the active line style for element placement. To display all the attributes associated with line styles, turn ON the Show Details toggle button. MicroStation displays a Line Styles settings box similar to Figure 15–27.

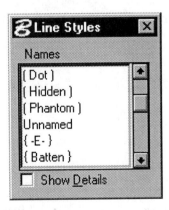

FIGURE 15–26   Line Styles settings box.

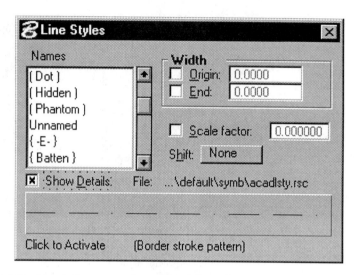

FIGURE 15–27   Line Styles settings box with additional options displayed.

At the bottom of the settings box, MicroStation shows the line style and description of the line style selected in the Names list box with active modifiers applied. Click anywhere on the sample to make the line style the active line style for element placement. If necessary, you can modify the starting and ending width for the strokes as defined in the line style definition. To change the starting width, turn ON the Origin toggle button and key-in the Width in Master Units in the Origin edit field. To change the ending width, turn ON the End toggle button and key-in the Width in Master Units in the End edit field.

The Scale factor sets the scale to all displayable characteristics (dash length and width, point symbol size) of the active line style. To change the scale factor, turn ON the Scale factor toggle button and key-in the scale factor in the Scale factor edit field.

The Shift option menu sets the distance or fraction by which each stroke pattern in the active line style is shifted or adjusted.

Defining and Modifying Line Styles

To define and modify existing custom line styles, open the Line Style Editor settings box from:

Primary tool box	Line Style option menu > Edit (see Figure 15–28)
Key-in window	**Linestyle Edit (or lines e)** ⏎

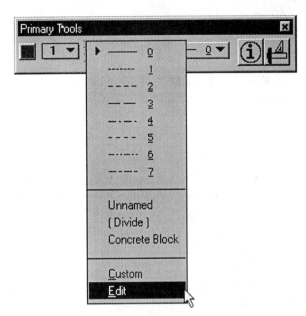

FIGURE 15–28 Invoking the Linestyle Edit command from the Primary tool box.

MicroStation displays the Line Style Editor settings box, similar to Figure 15–29.

Line style definitions are stored in line style libraries. The settings box lets you open and define or modify line styles. If a line style library is open, its file specification is displayed in the title bar.

MicroStation lists the names of all the available line styles in the Styles list box. Selecting a name causes a sample of the line style to be displayed. In the Components list box, MicroStation lists the types and descriptions of all line styles components. If >> is displayed left of its Type, the component is linked directly to the line style

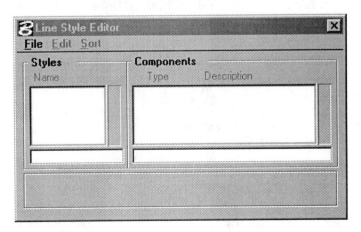

FIGURE 15–29 Line Style Editor settings box.

whose name is selected in the Styles list box. Selecting a component causes a sample line with the component to be displayed. To modify a component, you must first select the component and make the necessary changes.

Attaching an Existing Line Style Library To attach an existing line style library, invoke the Open command from:

Pull-down menu (Line Style Editor settings box)	File > Open... (or 🖮 + **F, O**)

MicroStation displays the Open Line Style Library dialog box. Select the line style library file from the Files list box and either click the OK button or press ⏎ to attach the library to the current design file.

Creating a New Line Style Library To create a new line style library, invoke the New command from:

Pull-down menu (Line Style Editor settings box)	File > New (or 🖮 + **F, N**)

MicroStation displays the Create Line Style Library dialog box. Key-in the name of the new style library file in the Files edit field and either click the OK button or press ⏎ to create and attach the library to the current design file.

Creating a New Line Style To create a new line style, invoke the Create Name command from:

Pull-down menu (Line Style Editor settings box)	Edit > Create > Name (or 🖮 + **E, C, N**)

MicroStation adds a new line style, named "Unnamed," in the Styles list box. Unnamed is automatically selected and is linked to the component selected in the Components list box. If necessary, you can change the name from "Unnamed" to an appropriate line style.

MicroStation provides three tools—Stroke Pattern, Point, and Compound—to customize the line style; they are available in the Create submenu of the pull-down menu Edit.

The **Stroke Pattern** setting provide controls for creating, modifying, and deleting stroke pattern line style components. Open the Stroke Pattern settings from:

Pull-down menu (Line Style Editor settings box)	Edit > Create > Stroke Pattern (or 🖮 + **E, C, S**)

MicroStation displays the settings to set the Stroke Pattern Attributes and Stroke Pattern, as shown in Figure 15–30.

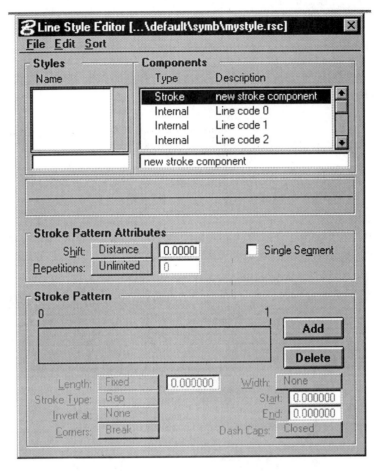

FIGURE 15–30 Line Style Editor with Stroke Pattern settings.

- The Shift options menu sets the distance or fraction by which the stroke pattern is shifted or adjusted.
- The Repetitions options menu sets the number of times the stroke pattern is repeated throughout the length of an element or element segment. The number of repetitions needs to be fixed.
- The Single Segment toggle button controls the truncation of the stroke pattern at the end of each element segment.
- The Add button adds a new gap stroke at the end of the stroke pattern. The maximum number of strokes is 32. Each dash stroke is represented by a filled bar. Each gap stroke is represented by an unfilled bar. Click anywhere on the stroke for modification. The stroke is highlighted. Dragging a stroke's handle changes the stroke's length.
- The Length edit field sets the selected stroke length in Master Units.
- The Stroke Type options menu allows you to switch a highlighted stroke from gap to dash or vice versa.

- The Corners options menu controls the behavior of the selected stroke when it extends farther than an element vertex.
- The Width options menu controls the effect of width settings on the selected dash stroke.
- The Dash Caps options menu sets the type of end cap on the selected dash stroke when displayed with width.

The **Point** settings provides controls for creating, modifying, and deleting point line style components. Open the Point settings from:

Pull-down menu (Line Style Editor settings box)	Edit > Create > Point (or [ALT] + **E, C, P**)

MicroStation displays the settings to set the Point settings, as shown in Figure 15–31.

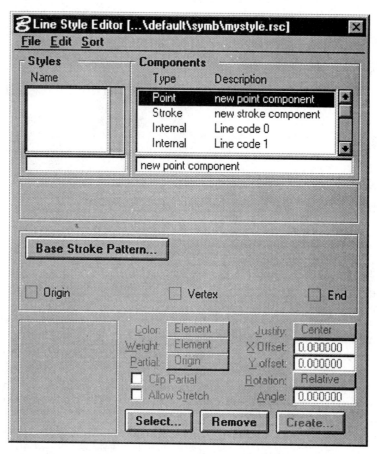

FIGURE 15–31 Line Style Editor with Point settings.

- The Base Stroke Pattern... button opens the Base Stroke Pattern dialog box, from which you can select the stroke pattern component on which the selected point symbol component is based.
- The Origin toggle button selects the origin (first vertex of an element) with which a symbol can be associated.
- The Vertex toggle button selects the internal vertices (of an element) with which a single symbol can be associated.
- The End toggle button selects the end (last vertex of an element) with which a symbol can be associated.

> **NOTE:** If a symbol is associated with either the origin, the vertex, or the last vertex of an element, the symbol is displayed (below and left of the settings box), and the controls for adjusting the related settings (below and right of the settings box) are enabled.

The **Compound** settings provide controls for creating, modifying, and deleting compound line style components. Open the Compound settings from:

Pull-down menu (Line Style Editor settings box)	Edit > Create > Compound (or ALT + **E, C, C**)

MicroStation displays the settings to set the Compound settings, as shown in Figure 15–32.

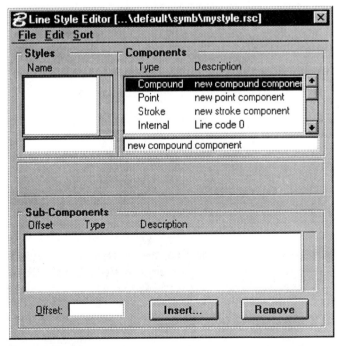

FIGURE 15–32 Line Style Editor with Compound settings.

- The Sub-Components list box lists the offsets, types, and descriptions of all subcomponents of the compound component selected in the Components list box.
- The Offset edit field sets the distance, in Master Units measured perpendicular from the work line, by which the selected component is displayed parallel to the work line. If the Offset is set to zero, the selected component is displayed on the work line.
- The Insert... button opens the Select Component dialog box, from which you can select a subcomponent to insert in the compound component selected in the Components list box.
- The Remove button removes the subcomponent selected in the Sub-Components list box from the compound component selected in the Components list box.

Deleting a Line Style To delete a line style from the list box, invoke the Delete command from:

| Pull-down menu (Line Style Editor settings box) | Edit > Delete (or **ALT** + **E, D**) |

MicroStation deletes the selected line style from the list box.

Linking the Component To link the selected component from the Components list to the selected line style from the Styles list box, invoke the Link command from:

| Pull-down menu (Line Style Editor settings box) | Edit > Link (or **ALT** + **E, L**) |

MicroStation links the selected component to the line style selected in the Styles list box.

Saving the Line Style Library To save the line styles library, invoke the Save command from:

| Pull-down menu (Line Style Editor settings box) | File > Save (or **ALT** + **F, S**) |

MicroStation saves the currently open line style library.

Step-by-Step Procedure for Creating a New Line Style Following is the step-by-step procedure to a create a line style called FLOWARR, consisting of a 1.5-inch-long line segment followed by a filled arrowhead (0.1 inch wide, 0.125 inch long).

STEP 1: Open the Line Style Editor settings box.

STEP 2: Create a new line style library called HARNESS.RSC

STEP 3: Invoke the Name tool under the submenu Create from the pull-down menu Edit. MicroStation adds a new line style, named "Unnamed," in the Styles list box. Change the "Unnamed" to "FLOWARR" in the edit field located under the Name list.

STEP 4: Select the Stroke Pattern option from the submenu Create from the pull-down menu Edit. The description "new stroke component" will be added to the list. Change the description to read "LINE CODE FOR FLOW ARROW" in the edit field located under the Description list.

STEP 5: Select the Link option from the pull-down menu Edit. This establishes a relationship between the new line style name and the new component.

STEP 6: In the Stroke Pattern Attributes section of the settings box, set the Shift Distance to 0.0 and the Repetitions value to Unlimited.

STEP 7: Click the Add button to add a new gap stroke.

STEP 8: Select Fixed in the Length option menu and key-in 1.5 in the Length edit field. Set the Stroke Type option menu to Dash, the Invert at option menu to None, and the Corners option menu to Break. The characteristics of the stroke pattern will change to reflect these settings.

STEP 9: Click the Add button to add a new gap stroke at the end of the stroke pattern.

STEP 10: Place a data point anywhere in the new stroke pattern. The stroke is highlighted.

STEP 11: Select Fixed in the Length option menu and key-in 0.125 in the Length edit field. Set the Stroke Type option menu to Dash, the Invert at option menu to None, the Corners option menu to Break, the Width option menu to Full, the Start Width value to .1, the End Width value to 0.0, and the Dash Caps option menu to Closed. The characteristics of the stroke pattern will change to reflect these settings (see Figure 15–33).

STEP 12: Save the newly created line style by invoking the Save command under the pull-down menu File in the Line Style Editor settings box.

STEP 13: Close the Line Style Editor settings box.

STEP 14: Test the newly created line style by setting the active line style to FLOWARR.

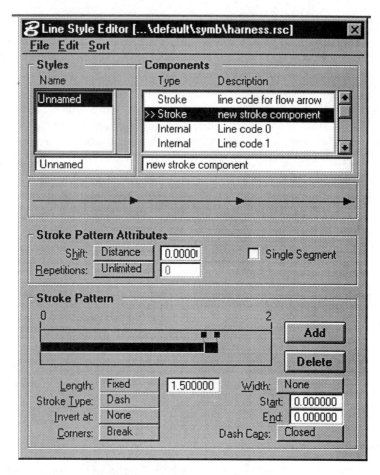

FIGURE 15–33 Displaying the new line type in the settings box.

WORKSPACE

A *workspace* is a customized drafting environment that permits the user to set up MicroStation for specific purposes. You can set up as many workspaces as you need. A workspace consists of "components" and "configuration files" for both the user and the project.

MicroStation comes with a set of workspaces for various disciplines. For example, MicroStation is delivered with a sample "civil" workspace. When the civil workspace is active, the files and tools you need to perform civil engineering design and drafting are available by default.

When the civil workspace is active, tools and tool boxes that are unrelated to that discipline are removed from the interface so that they do not get in your way.

Setting Up the Active Workspace

You can select the default workspace from the MicroStation Manager. At the bottom of the MicroStation Manager dialog box (see Figure 15–34), four option menus are provided that allow you to change the major components of the workspace before opening a design file.

Workspace Option Menu The Workspace option menu allows you to select the default workspace from the available workspaces. Selecting a workspace from the list reconfigures MicroStation to use that workspace's components. Selecting a workspace also resets the search path to a corresponding subdirectory for loading design files. In addition, MicroStation sets the associated project and user interface. Table 15–2 lists the sample workspaces provided and the components included in each workspace.

When MicroStation is started with any workspace as the default workspace, a preference file is created for that workspace, unless one already exists. The settings in the preferences are set either to default settings or to AutoCAD Transition settings, depending on the active user interface component.

To create a new workspace, invoke the New... option from the Workspace option menu. MicroStation displays the Create Workspace dialog box, similar to Figure 15–35.

FIGURE 15–34 MicroStation Manager.

Table 15–2.   Sample Workspaces and Components

SAMPLE WORKSPACE	USER INTERFACE	PROJECT	PREFERENCES
Default	Default	Default	Default
Architecture	Arch	Architecture	Default
Civil Engineering	Civil	Civil Engineering	Default
Mechanical Engineering	Mech	Mechanical	Default
AutoCAD Transition	AutoCAD	Default	AutoCAD

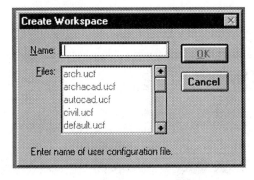

FIGURE 15–35   Create Workspace dialog box.

Key-in the name of the new workspace in the Name edit field and click the OK button. MicroStation displays another dialog box, similar to Figure 15–36. Key-in the description (optional) in the Description edit field. If necessary, change the components by clicking the appropriate Select... button for Project, User Interface, or Preferences. Click the OK button to close the dialog box. MicroStation sets the newly created workspace as the default workspace.

Project Option Menu   The selection of the project sets the location and names of data files associated with a specific design project. If necessary, you can change the selection of the project from the Project option menu.

User Interface Option Menu   The selection of the user interface sets a specific look and feel of MicroStation's tools and general on-screen operation. If necessary, you can change the selection of the interface from the User Interface option menu. Micro-Station comes with discipline-specific interfaces: civil, architecture, mechanical engineering, drafting, and mapping, and in addition it has interfaces for previous versions (V. 4 and V. 5) and AutoCAD users.

To create a new interface, invoke the New... option from the Interface option menu. MicroStation displays the Create User Interface dialog box, similar to Figure 15–37.

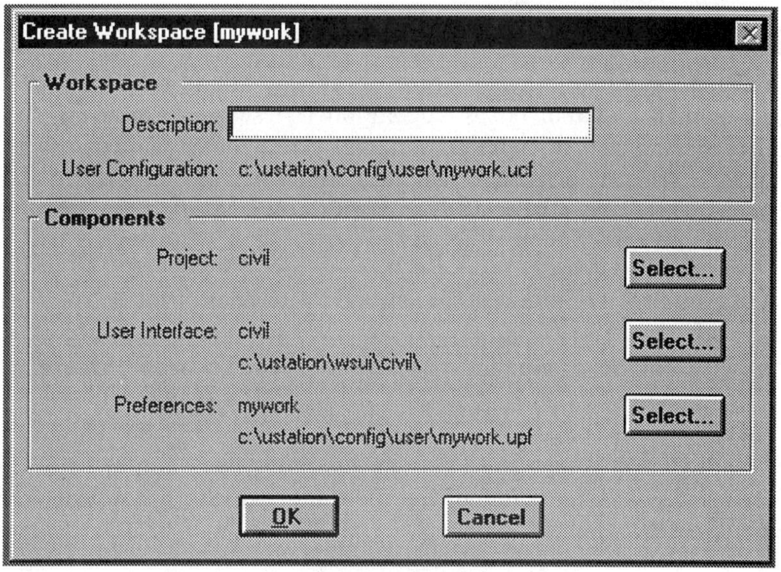

FIGURE 15-36 Create Workspace (name) dialog box.

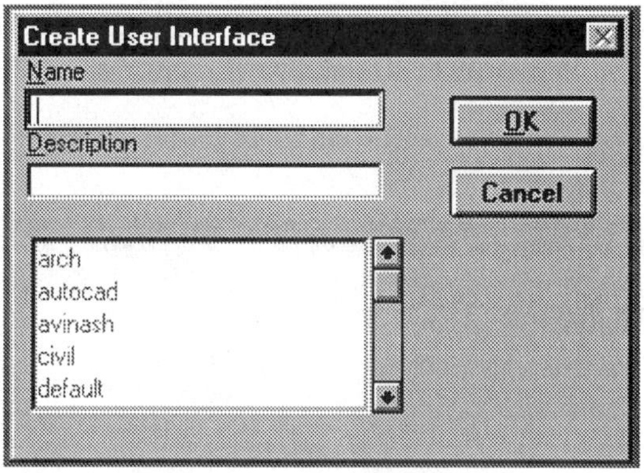

FIGURE 15-37 Create User Interface dialog box.

Key-in the name of the new user interface in the Name edit field and a description in the Description edit field (optional). Click the OK button to close the dialog box. MicroStation creates an interface directory under the USTATION/WSUI subdirectory and sets the newly created user interface as the default user interface. The new interface takes the default interface as its starting point. Any changes you make while using this new interface is written only to the new interface.

Style Option Menu The Style option menu allows you to select whether to use the older Command Window (V. 4 and V. 5) method of communicating with MicroStation or the new Status bar. The default selection is the Status bar. Whichever style you select, MicroStation will remember it from session to session.

Setting User Preferences

Preferences are settings that control the way MicroStation operates and the way its tool frames and tool boxes appear on the screen. For example, they affect how MicroStation uses memory on a user's system, how windows are displayed, and how reference files are attached by default. You can change the settings to suit your needs. The user preferences are saved under the same name as the workspace, with the file extension .UCF.

To set the user preferences, invoke the Preferences from:

Pull-down menu	Workspace > Preferences... (or [ALT] + **K, P**)

MicroStation displays the Preferences dialog box, similar to Figure 15–38. MicroStation displays the name of the file under which preference settings are saved as part of the title bar.

User Preferences are divided into categories. The Category list box lists all the available categories. Selecting a category causes the appropriate controls to be displayed to the right of the category list. Each category controls a specific aspect of MicroStation's appearance or operation. Table 15–3 describes briefly all the settings available in the Preferences dialog box.

Click the OK button to save the settings and close the Preferences dialog box.

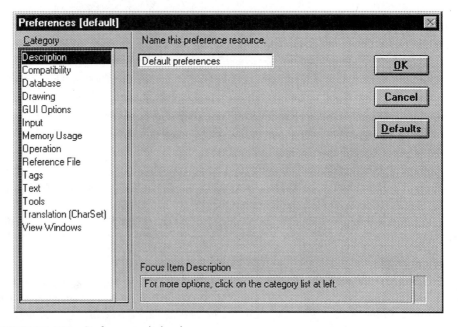

FIGURE 15–38 Preferences dialog box.

Table 15-3.   Preferences Settings

CATEGORY	PREFERENCE SETTING	DESCRIPTION	DEFAULT
Compatibility	Compatibility Option menu	Sets the MicroStation version number	5.0+
	Dimensions toggle button	Set to ON to place dimensions elements	ON
	Multi-lines toggle button	Set to ON to place multi-lines	ON
	Shared Cells toggle button	Set to ON to place shared cells	ON
	Associative Patterning toggle button	Set to ON to enable associative patterning	ON
Database	Block Database Undeletes toggle button	Set to ON, it is impossible to undo the deletion of an element that has a database linkage	OFF
	Use Single AE/MSFORMS Tables toggle button	Set to ON, single AE and MSFORMS tables are maintained	OFF
	Use Database Msline Cache toggle button	Set to ON, a cache of database linkages is maintained	OFF
Drawing	Exact Colors edit field	Sets the number of colors that can be displayed exactly as they are defined	Depends on hardware configuration
	Max. Grid Pts/View edit field	Sets the maximum number of displayable grid points in a view, counted horizontally	90
	Max. Grid Refs/View edit field	Sets the maximum number of displayable grid references (crosses) in a view, counted horizontally	40
	Line Weights...	Sets the display width (in pixels) for each of the 32 line weights	1:1 (2:1 in DOS version)

Table 15–3. Preferences Settings (continued)

CATEGORY	PREFERENCE SETTING	DESCRIPTION	DEFAULT
GUI Options	Dialog Boxes option menu	Sets the graphical user interface standard that MicroStation emulates or adheres to	Window
	Open Two Application Windows (Windows only) toggle button	Set to ON, MicroStation application windows are opened for use on a two-screen system	OFF
	Dialog (Font) option menu	Sets the text size, in points, in dialog and settings boxes	10 pt (DOS); 12 pt (Windows)
	Border (Font) option menu	Sets the text size, in points, in window borders	10 pt (DOS); 12 pt (Windows)
Input	Start in Parse All Mode toggle button	Set to ON, the parsing function is enabled as MicroStation starts	ON
	Disable Drag Operations	Set to ON, MicroStation disregards Data button-up operation when the pointer is in views	OFF
	[CTRL] + **Z** to Exit	Set to ON, pressing [CTRL] + **Z** exits MicroStation	OFF
Memory Usage	Max Element Cache edit field	Sets the maximum amount of memory, in KB, reserved to store elements	8000
	Resource Cache edit field	Sets the amount of memory, in KB, reserved for resources read from MicroStation resources files and application resource files	24
	Undo Buffer edit field	Sets the amount of memory, in KB, reserved for recording the possible negation using Undo	256

Table 15–3. Preferences Settings *(continued)*

CATEGORY	PREFERENCE SETTING	DESCRIPTION	DEFAULT
Memory Usage *(continued)*	Font Cache edit field	Sets the maximum size, in KB, of the section of memory reserved for data used to display text elements	30
	Conserve Memory toggle button	Set to ON, MicroStation sacrifices speed in some functions in order to use less memory	OFF
	Disable OLE Automation (Windows only) toggle button	Set to ON, OLE Automation Server capability is disabled unless MicroStation is started by an OLE Automation request	OFF
Operation	Locate Tolerance edit field	Sets the size of the searched area around the pointer for selecting an element	10
	Point Size option menu	Sets the size of the crosshair pointer	Normal
	Pointer Type option menu	Controls the alignment of the pointer's crosshairs	Orthogonal
	Display Levels option menu	Controls whether level Names or Numbers are shown in screen controls	Names
	Immediately Save Design toggle button	Set to ON, MicroStation does not maintain a backup file and does not have a Save item on the menu File	ON
	Save Settings on Exit toggle button	Set to ON, the File menu's Save Settings item is disabled	OFF
	Compress Design on Exit toggle button	Set to ON, deleted elements are automatically removed from the active design file upon closing	OFF

Table 15–3.   Preferences Settings *(continued)*

CATEGORY	PREFERENCE SETTING	DESCRIPTION	DEFAULT
Operation *(continued)*	Enter into Untitled Design toggle button	Set to ON, when you start MicroStation it automatically creates and opens a design file named "untitled.dgn"	OFF
	Reset Aborts Fence Operations toggle button	Set to ON, resetting during a fence manipulation halts the operation	ON
	Level Lock Applies for Fence Operations toggle button	Set to OFF, fence contents manipulations ignore the Level Lock setting	ON
	Use Semaphore File for Locking toggle button	Set to ON, enables users to specify that a "semaphore" file be used to control write access to files	OFF
Reference File	Locate On When Attached toggle button	Set to ON, the capability to identify elements in a particular reference file is turned on when the reference file is attached	ON
	Snap On When Attached toggle button	Set to ON, the capability to snap to elements in a particular reference file is turned on when the reference file is attached	ON
	Use Color Table toggle button	Set to OFF, MicroStation ignores any color table attached to a reference file for display purposes	ON
	Use Level Names toggle button	Set to ON, reference file level names are displayed as part of the level information	ON
	Cache When Display Off toggle button	Set to OFF, memory caching of reference files that are not displayed is disabled	OFF

Table 15–3. **Preferences Settings** *(continued)*

CATEGORY	PREFERENCE SETTING	DESCRIPTION	DEFAULT
Reference File *(continued)*	Reload When Changing Files toggle button	Set to OFF, cached reference files are kept in memory when one design file is closed and another is opened	OFF
	Save Settings to Save Changes toggle button	Set to OFF, the results of reference file manipulations are immediately permanent	OFF
	Ignore Update Sequence toggle button	Set to ON, the Update Sequence menu item is disabled	OFF
	Store Full Path When Attached toggle button	Set to ON, the Save Full Path check box is ON by default	OFF
	Update Self Attachments toggle button	Set to ON, you can modify self-attached reference file elements, and the changes to the master file will be updated in the self-attached reference files	ON
	Max Reference Files edit field	Sets the maximum number of reference files that can be attached to the active design file	32
	Nest Depth edit field	Sets the number of levels of nested attachments	0
Tags	Prompt on Duplicate Tag Sets toggle button	Set to ON, MicroStation displays an alert box for duplication	ON
	Use Design File Tag Sets By Default toggle button	Set to ON, tag sets in the design file cannot be replaced by tag sets of the same names in cell libraries from which cells are placed	OFF

Table 15–3. Preferences Settings *(continued)*

CATEGORY	PREFERENCE SETTING	DESCRIPTION	DEFAULT
Tags *(continued)*	Place Tags in Some Graphic Group toggle button	Set to ON, when a tag set is attached to an element all tags in the set become members of the same graphic group	ON
Text	Display Text with Lines Styles toggle button	Set to OFF, displayed with standard solid line style	OFF
	Fit Text by Inserting Space toggle button	Set to OFF, places fitted text by enlarging or shrinking the characters of text	OFF
	Fixed-width Character Spacing toggle button	Set to OFF, spacing between characters is measured from the end of one character to the beginning of the next character	OFF
	Preserve Text Nodes toggle button	Set to ON, text placed as a text node will remain a text node, even if edited down to one line	OFF
	Justify Enter Data Fields Like IGDS toggle button	Set to OFF, the odd space in a center-justified enter data field containing an odd number of extra blank spaces is positioned at the beginning of the enter data field	OFF
	Edit Character edit field	Sets the text character that denotes each character in an enter data field	—
	Smallest Text edit field	Sets the size, in pixels, above which text is drawn	4

Table 15–3. Preferences Settings *(continued)*

CATEGORY	PREFERENCE SETTING	DESCRIPTION	DEFAULT
Text *(continued)*	Underline Spacing (%) edit field	Sets the distance, as a percentage of the text height, between the baseline and underlining	20
	Degree Display Character edit field	Sets the ASCII character used to display the degree symbol	176
	Text Editor Style option menu	Sets the type of text editing interface	Traditional
Tools	Single Click option menu	Controls how tools are selected with a single click of the Data button	Locked
	Default Tool option menu	Sets the tool that is automatically selected upon completion of a one-time function	Element selection
	Highlight option menu	Sets the color with which tools are highlighted to indicate locked selection	Color
	Layout option menu	Affects the size of tool boxes	Regular
	Tool Size option menu	Sets the size of tool icons	Small
	View Pop-ups option menu	Sets the method used to open the pop-up menu	[SHIFT]-Reset
	Auto-Focus Tool Settings Window toggle button	Set to ON, the input focus automatically moves to the Tool Settings window when a tool with settings is selected	ON
	All Pop-Downs in Tool Setting Window toggle button	Set to ON, Version 5 palettes do not have pop-downs	ON
	Auto-Open Tool Settings Window toggle button	Set to ON, the Tool Settings window opens automatically when MicroStation starts	ON

Table 15–3. Preferences Settings *(concluded)*

CATEGORY	PREFERENCE SETTING	DESCRIPTION	DEFAULT
Translation (CharSet)	Character Translation Table	Sets the character translation table, which converts external ASCII characters to the form of ASCII used internally by MicroStation	Default
View Windows	Scroll Bars on View Windows toggle button	Set to ON, view windows are displayed with borders, including scroll bars and view control bars	ON
	Black Background → White toggle button	Set to ON, the view background color, if set to black, is displayed in white	OFF
	Tile Like IGDS toggle button	Set to OFF, four views are tiled in the same manner as in IGDS	OFF
	Use Backing Store toggle button	Set to ON, maintains an off-screen copy of each view window so obscured areas can be refreshed instantly when windows are rearranged	ON
	Gamma Correction edit field	Affects the brightness of rendered images	1.0
	Direct Drawing (Windows only) option menu	Affects the techniques used to display bitmap in view windows	OFF

Working with Configuration Variables

MicroStation allows you to make necessary changes to the user configuration variables and their respective directory path from the Configuration Variables dialog box. Invoke the Configuration Variables dialog box from:

Pull-down menu	<u>W</u>orkspace > <u>C</u>onfiguration... (or [ALT] + **W, C**)

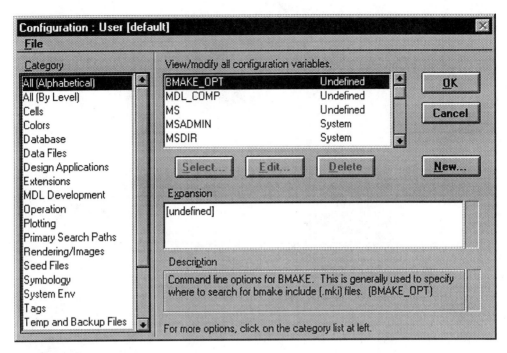

FIGURE 15-39 Configuration dialog box.

MicroStation displays the Configuration dialog box similar to the Figure 15-39.

The Category list box lists all the available categories. When you select a category, MicroStation lists the controls for settings of that category on the right side of the dialog box. In the Expansion field, the expansion of the variable is shown. In the Description field, a description of the variable and its name are shown.

Use the controls to modify the definition. The procedure varies for the different types of configuration variables.

If a configuration variable needs a path specification, then MicroStation displays a Select Path dialog box similar to Figure 15-40. Select the appropriate directory and click the Add button. MicroStation adds the path for the selected directory in the Directory List box. You can add multiple directories to the list. Click the Done button to close the dialog box.

If a configuration variable needs a directory specification, then MicroStation displays a Select Directory dialog box similar to Figure 15-41. Select the appropriate directory and click the OK button to close the dialog box.

If a configuration variable needs a file name specification, then MicroStation displays a Select File dialog box similar to Figure 15-42. Select the desired file from the appropriate directory and click the OK button to close the dialog box.

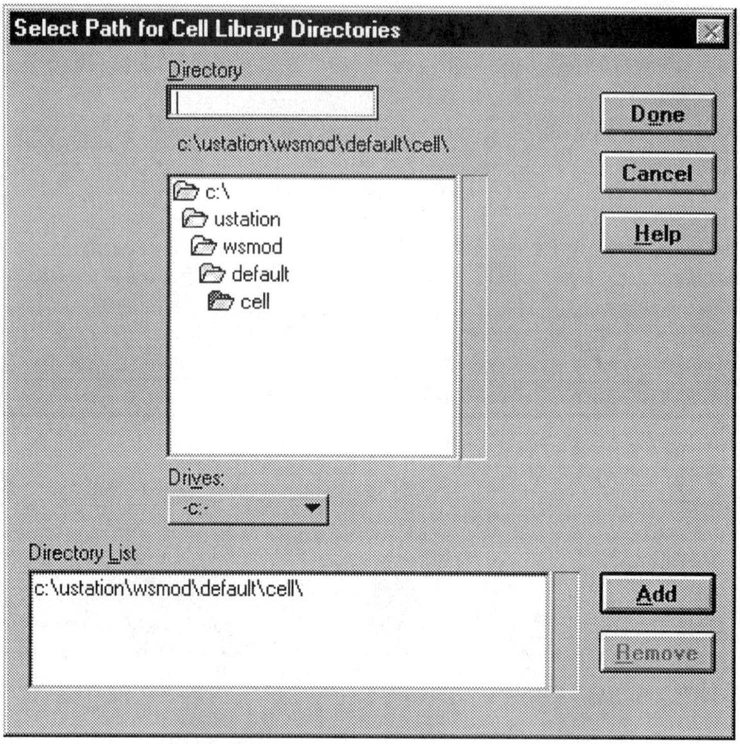

FIGURE 15–40   Select Path dialog box.

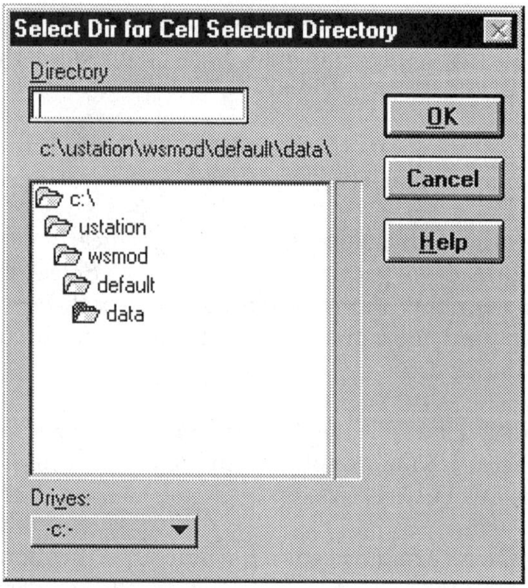

FIGURE 15–41   Select Directory dialog box.

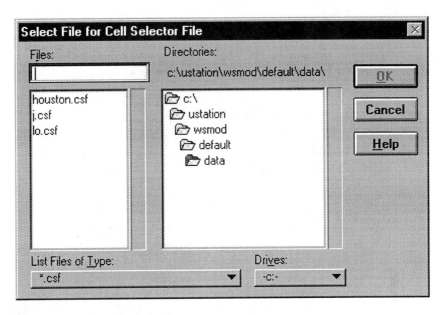

FIGURE 15–42 Select File dialog box.

If a configuration variable needs a keyword configuration variable, then Micro-Station displays an Edit Configuration Variable dialog box similar to Figure 15–43. Key-in the desired variable in the New Value edit field. The keyword is also shown in the Expansion field. Click the OK button to close the dialog box.

Table 15–4 lists all the available configuration variables by category.

Click the OK button to save the configuration variable settings and close the dialog box.

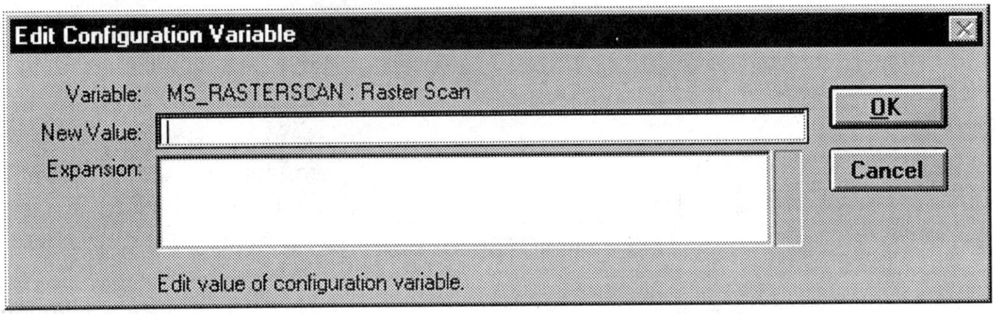

FIGURE 15–43 Edit Configuration Variable dialog box.

Table 15–4.   Available Configuration Variables

CATEGORY	VARIABLE	DESCRIPTION
B/RAS	BRAS	Directory containing the "bras.rsc" resource file
	BRAS_RASTER	Default directory for the Load and Preview dialog boxes when no other raster file is loaded
	BRAS_FILTER	Filter Default filter (e.g., "*.*") for Load and Preview dialog boxes
	BRAS_MAX_SCAN	The maximum number of scan lines a raster file can have
	BRAS_MAX_X	Maximum scan line length (pixels) a raster file can have
	BRAS_MAX_FG_ RUNS	Maximum number of foreground run lengths per scan line in a raster file
	BRAS_BKLOAD_ TICKS	Background Load Ticks Time (in MicroStation timer ticks) between background loading time slices
	BRAS_BKLOAD_ SCANS	Number of raster scan lines loaded for each time slice of BRAS fast loading
Cells	MS_CELL	Director Search path(s) for cell libraries
	MS_CELLLIST	List of cell libraries to be searched for cells not found in the current library
	MS_MENU	Cell library file containing menu cells
	MS_TUTLIB	Library Cell library containing tutorial cells
Colors	MS_DEFCTBL	Default Color Table Default color table if design file has none
	MS_RMENCTBL	Right Menu Color Table Default menu colors (dialog boxes, borders, etc.) for right screen—specifies a color table (.tbl) file
	MS_LMENCTBL	Color Table Default menu colors (dialog boxes, borders, etc.) for left screen—specifies a color table (.tbl) file

Table 15–4. Available Configuration Variables *(continued)*

CATEGORY	VARIABLE	DESCRIPTION
Database	MS_DBASE	Search path(s) for database files
	MS_SERVER	MDL application to load the database interface software
	MS_DBEXT	The database interface "server" application
	MS_LINKTYPE	User data linkage types recognized by the database interface software (see MS_LINKTYPE)
	MS_TAGREPORTS	Output directory for tag reports
	MS_TAGTEMPLATES	Directory containing tag report templates
Data Files	MS_SETTINGS	Open settings file
	MS_SETTINGSDIR	Directory containing settings files
	MS_LEVELNAMES	Directory containing level structure files
	MS_GLOSSARY	List of files for use with the Glossary settings box (see Utilities > Glossary)
Design Applications	MS_DGNAPPS	List of MDL applications to load automatically when a design file is opened
MDL Development	MS_DBGSOURCE	Location of source code for MDL applications (used by MDL debugger)
	MS_MDLTRACE	Additional debugging print statements when debugging MDL applications
	MS_DBGOUT	Output of MDL debugger
	MS_DEBUGFAULT	If set, automatically invokes the debugger when a fault is detected while an MDL application is active
	MS_DEBUG	If set to an integer with bit 1 on, do not time out

Table 15–4.   Available Configuration Variables *(continued)*

CATEGORY	VARIABLE	DESCRIPTION
Operation	MS_FKEYMNU	Open function key menu file
	MS_SYSTEM	If set, MicroStation allows the user to escape to the operating system
	MS_APPMEN	Location of application and sidebar menus
	MS_TRAP	Set to "NONE," "MDL," or "ALL" (default)
Plotting	MS_PLTFILES	Directory for plotting output files
	MS_PLTR	Name of plotter configuration file
Primary Search	MS_DEF	Search path(s) for design files
	MS_DESIGNFILTER	File filter for opening and creating design files
	MS_RFDIR	Search path(s) for reference files
	MS_MDLAPPS	Search path(s) for MDL applications displayed in the MDL dialog box
	MS_MDL	Search path(s) for MDL applications or external programs loaded by MDL applications
	MS_RSRCPATH	Search path(s) for resource files loaded by MDL applications
Rendering	MS_MATERIAL	Search path(s) for material palettes
	MS_PATTERN	Search path(s) for pattern maps
	MS_BUMP	Search path(s) for bump maps
	MS_IMAGE	Search path(s) for images
	MS_IMAGEOUT	Directory in which created image files are stored
	MS_SHADOWMAP	Directory where shadow maps will be read from and written to
Seed Files	MS_SEEDFILES	Search path(s) for all seed files
	MS_DESIGNSEED	Default seed file

Table 15–4. Available Configuration Variables *(continued)*

CATEGORY	VARIABLE	DESCRIPTION
Seed Files *(continued)*	MS_CELLSEED	Default seed cell library
	MS_SHEETSEED	Seed sheet file drawing composition, DWG import, and IGES import
	MS_TRANSEED	Default seed file for DWG, CGM, and IGES translations
Symbology	MS_SYMBRSRC	List of symbology resource files—last one in list has highest priority
System Environment	MS	The MicroStation root installation directory used by MDL sample "make" files
	MS_CONFIG	Main MicroStation configuration file—sets up all configuration variables
	MS_EDG	Directories used by EDG (not MicroStation)
	MDL_COMP	Command text string to be inserted at the beginning of the command line by the MDL compiler (used to specify where to search for included files)
	RSC_COMP	Text string to be inserted at the beginning of the command line by the resource compiler (used to specify where to search for included files)
	BMAKE_OPT	Command line options for BMAKE (used to search for bmake include (.mki) files)
	MS_ DEBUGMDLHEAP	If set (to the base name of an MDL application or "ALL"), use extended malloc for debugging
Temp and Backup Files	MS_BACKUP	Default directory for backup files
	MS_TMP	Directory for temporary files created and deleted by MicroStation
	MS_SCR	Directory for scratch files created by MicroStation

Table 15–4. Available Configuration Variables *(continued)*

CATEGORY	VARIABLE	DESCRIPTION
Translation	MS_CGMIN	CGM Input Directory for CGM translations
	MS_CGMOUT	Output directory for CGM translations
	MS_CGMLOG	Output directory for CGM log files
	MS_CGMTABLES	Directory containing the CGM translation tables
	MS_CGMINSET	Settings file for the CGMIN application
	MS_CGMOUTSET	Settings file for the CGMOUT application
	MS_DWGIN	Input directory for DWG translations
	MS_DWGOUT	Output directory for DWG translations
	MS_DWGLOG	Output directory for DWG log files
	MS_DWGTABLES	Directory containing the DWG translation tables
	MS_DWGINSET	Settings file for the DWGIN application
	MS_DWGOUTSET	Settings file for the DWGOUT application
	MS_IGESIN	Input directory for IGES translations
	MS_IGESOUT	Output directory for IGES translations
	MS_IGESLOG	Output directory for IGES log files
	MS_IGESINSET	Settings file for IGES import
	MS_IGESOUTSET	Settings file for IGES export
User Commands	MS_UCM	Search path(s) for user commands
	MS_INIT	Name of user command to be executed at startup
	MS_EXITUC	Name of user command to be executed at exit

Table 15–4.   Available Configuration Variables *(continued)*

CATEGORY	VARIABLE	DESCRIPTION
User Commands *(continued)*	MS_NEWFILE	Name of user command to be executed when a new file is opened
	MS_APP	Apps from "TSK" state—search path(s) of applications started from "TSK" statements in user commands
Uncategorized	MS_BANNER	Text file to be displayed in MicroStation's startup banner dialog
	MS_CMDWINDRSC	Command Window resource file—default is used if undefined
	MS_CODESET	AMDL application for handling multi-byte character sets
	MS_DATA	Directory for data files created or used by MicroStation
	MS_DEFCHARTRAN	Default character translation table
	MS_DEMOONLY	If set, MicroStation runs in demonstration mode only
	MS_DGNOUT	Directory containing design files created as a result of "on-the-fly" translation from other file formats
	MS_EXE	Directory containing the Micro-Station executable program
	MS_GUIHAND	Identifies auxiliary handlers
	MS_HELPPATH	Path to help files
	MS_INITAPPS	List of initial startup MDL applications
	MS_RIGHTLOGICKB	Right to Left Character—if set, type from right to left (used for foreign language support)
	MS_RSRC	Main MicroStation resource file; typically set to "ustation.rsc"
	MS_RSRVCLRS	Number of colors MicroStation does not use
	MS_TUT_UCMS	Directory containing user commands that drive tutorials

Table 15–4. Available Configuration Variables *(concluded)*

CATEGORY	VARIABLE	DESCRIPTION
Uncategorized *(continued)*	MS_UNDO	If set, overrides the user preference Undo Buffer
	MS_USERLICENSE	File containing MicroStation license information
	MS_WINDOWMGR	Tells MicroStation which window manager is in use ("MOTIF" or "OPENLOOK"); MicroStation can usually infer this
	WRK_DD_IGDS	Directory for IGDS user commands

Customizing the User Interface

MicroStation allows you to customize any or all of the parts of the active workspace user interface:

- Tool frames and tool boxes
- View border tools
- Pull-down menu

Customization of MicroStation's user interface are stored in user interface modification files. Whenever you create a new user interface, MicroStation creates a subdirectory under the WSUI directory with the given name of the new user interface. By default, MicroStation places the default user interface file (ustn.r01) in the subdirectory. If part of the interface is modified, then the file name of the user interface modification file is "ustn" with the file name extension "m" followed by a number from 01 to 99. Each time an interface modification file is saved with the same file name, the number in its suffix is incremented. Therefore, the files might be named "ustn.m01," "ustn.m02," and so on. If the tool box or dialog box modified is provided by an MDL (MicroStation Development Language) application, the file name of the user interface modification file is the file name of the MDL application.

Customizing Tool Frames The Customize settings box enables you to customize tool frames. Open the Customize settings box from:

Pull-down menu	Workspace Customi*z*e (or [ALT] + **K, Z**)

MicroStation displays a Customize settings box similar to Figure 15–44.

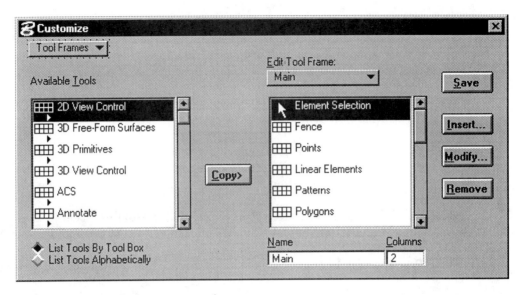

FIGURE 15–44 Customize settings box.

Follow these steps to modify or create a new tool frame:

STEP 1:   Select Tool Frames from the option menu near the setting box's upper left corner. By default, MicroStation lists the available tool boxes in the Available Tools list box (left side of the settings box) and lists the tool boxes from the Main tool frame in the Edit Tool Frame list box (right side of the settings box).

STEP 2:   Select one of the three available tool frames to customize (3D tools, DD Design, or Main) from the Edit Tool Frame option menu.

or

Select the Create Tool Frame from the Edit Tool Frame option menu to create a new tool frame. MicroStation displays the Create Tool Frame dialog box, as shown in Figure 15–45. Key-in the name of the new tool frame and click the OK button. MicroStation adds the new tool frame to the Edit Tool Frame option menu.

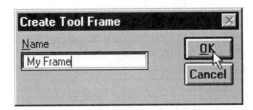

FIGURE 15–45 Create Tool Frame dialog box.

STEP 3: From the available tool boxes listed on the Available Tools list box (left side of the settings box), select the tool box you want to insert in the Tool Frame, and drag and drop it at the appropriate location in the Edit Tool Frame list box.

STEP 4: If necessary, you can rearrange the tool boxes by dragging and dropping in the Edit Tool Frame list box.

STEP 5: If necessary, you can remove the tool box from the Tool Frame list box. First select the tool box to remove from the list box, then click the Remove button. MicroStation removes the selected tool box from the tool frame.

STEP 6: Click the Save button to save the Modification/Addition to Tool Frames. MicroStation displays the customized version of the Tool Frame(s).

STEP 7: If no further changes have to be made, close the Customize settings box.

Customizing Tool Boxes The Customize settings box can also customize tool boxes. Open the Customize settings box from:

Pull-down menu	Workspace > Customize (or [ALT] + **K, Z**)

MicroStation displays a Customize settings box similar to Figure 15–44.

Follow these steps to modify or create a new tool box:

STEP 1: Select Tool Box from the option menu near the setting box's upper left corner. By default, MicroStation lists the available tool boxes in the Available Tools list box (left side of the settings box) and lists the available tools from the Standard Tool Box in the Edit Tool Box list box (right side of the settings box).

STEP 2: Select one of the available tool boxes to customize from the Edit Tool Box option menu.

or

Select Create Tool Box from the Edit Tool Box option menu to create a new tool box. MicroStation displays Create Tool Box dialog box, as shown in Figure 15–46. Key-in the name of the new tool box and click the OK button. MicroStation adds the new tool box to the Edit Tool Box option menu.

STEP 3: From the available tool boxes listed on the Available Tools list box (left side of the settings box), double-click the Tool Box name, MicroStation

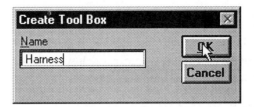

FIGURE 15–46   Create Tool Box dialog box.

lists the available tools. Select the tool you want to insert in the Tool Box, and drag and drop it at the appropriate location in the Edit Tool Box list box.

STEP 4:   If necessary, you can rearrange the tools by dragging and dropping in the Edit Tool Box list box.

STEP 5:   If necessary, you can remove the tool from the Tool list box. First select the tool to remove from the list box, then click the Remove button. MicroStation removes the selected tool from the tool box.

STEP 6:   To insert a new tool, click the Insert... button. MicroStation displays a dialog box, as shown in Figure 15–47.

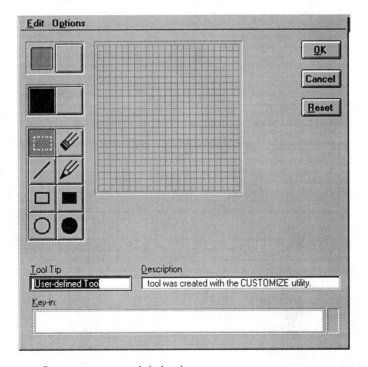

FIGURE 15–47   Creating a new tool dialog box.

Use the drawing tools to create the icon for the new tool. Key-in the tool tip text and description for the new tool in the Tool Tip and Description edit fields. Key-in the action string to be associated with the tool in the Key-in edit field. If a multiple key-in action string is specified, the key-ins must be separated by semi-colons (;). For example, the following key-in sets the color to red, the line weight to 3, the active level to 3, and invokes the Place Line command:

CO=RED;WT=3;LV=3;PLACE LINE

Click the OK button to close the dialog box.

STEP 7: To modify a tool, first select the tool to modify from the list box, then click the Modify button. MicroStation displays a dialog box, as shown in Figure 15–48.

If necessary, use the drawing tools to modify the icon. Make the necessary modifications to the tool tip text, description, and key-ins. Click the OK button to close the dialog box.

STEP 8: Click the Save button to save the Modification/Addition to Tool Boxes. MicroStation displays the customized version of the Tool Box(es).

STEP 9: If no further changes have to be made, close the Customize settings box.

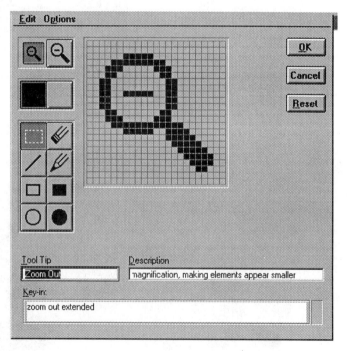

FIGURE 15–48 Modify tool dialog box.

Customizing View Border Tools The Customize settings box can also customize view border tools. Open the Customize settings box from:

Pull-down menu	Wor<u>k</u>space > Customi<u>z</u>e (or [ALT] + **K, Z**)

MicroStation displays a Customize settings box similar to Figure 15–44.

Follow these steps to modify view border tools:

STEP 1: Select View Border from the option menu near the setting box's upper left corner. By default, MicroStation lists the available tools in the Available Tools list box (left side of the settings box) and lists the Tools from the 2D View Border in the Edit Tools list box (right side of the settings box).

STEP 2: Select one of the two available view borders to customize (2D View Border or 3D View Border) from the Edit View Border option menu.

STEP 3: From the available tools listed on the Available Tools list box (left side of the settings box), select the tool you want to insert in the View Border, and drag and drop it at the appropriate location in the Edit View Border list box.

STEP 4: If necessary, you can rearrange the tools by dragging and dropping in the Edit View Border list box.

STEP 5: If necessary, you can remove a tool from the View Border list box. First select the tool to remove from the list box, then click the Remove button. MicroStation removes the selected tool from the View Border.

STEP 6: Click the Save button to save the Modification/Addition to View Border. MicroStation displays the customized version of the View Border.

STEP 7: If no further changes have to be made, close the Customize settings box.

Customizing the Pull-down Menu The Customize settings box can also customize the pull-down menu. Open the Customize settings box from:

Pull-down menu	Wor<u>k</u>space > Customi<u>z</u>e (or [ALT] + **K, Z**)

MicroStation displays a Customize settings box similar to Figure 15–44.

Follow these steps to modify the pull-down menu:

STEP 1: Select Menu Bar from the option menu near the setting box's upper left corner. By default, MicroStation lists the available menus in the Available list box (left side of the settings box) and lists the menus from the Main menu bar in the Edit Menu Bar list box (right side of the list box). The Available list box is used only for inserting menus and menu items.

STEP 2: To modify a menu name, first select the Menu name in the Edit Menu Bar list box, then click the Modify... button. MicroStation displays a Modify Menu dialog box similar to Figure 15–49. Make the modifiction in the Label edit field and click the OK button.

To modify a menu item, first double-click the menu name. MicroStation expands the menu. Select the menu item to modify, then click the Modify... button. MicroStation displays a Modify Menu Item dialog box similar to Figure 15–50.

To modify the menu item name, type the new name in the Label edit field.

> **NOTE:** Make sure to insert at the appropriate place the tilde (~) character immediately before the character that will be the mnemonic access character—for example E~dit for E_dit.

To enable or disable the item in the menu, turn Enabled ON or OFF.

If necessary, make the modifications for any action string associated with the item.

To attach a submenu to the item, turn on SubMenu attached, and click the Attach Tool Box... button. MicroStation displays the Select Tool Box dialog box. Select the appropriate tool box from the list box, and click the OK button to attach the Tool Box to the item.

FIGURE 15–49 Modify Menu dialog box.

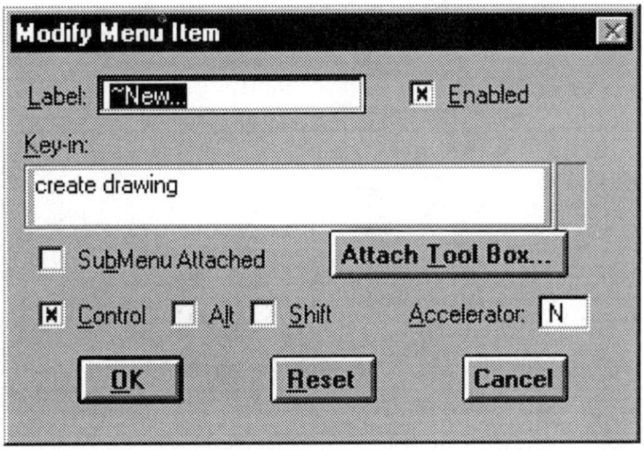

FIGURE 15–50 Modify Menu Item dialog box.

To assign or modify the keyboard accelerator, select [CTRL] alone or with [ALT] or [SHIFT] to indicate the modifier key(s), and type the accelerator key in the Accelerator edit field.

Click the OK button to close the dialog box.

STEP 3: To insert a menu name, first select the entry for the existing menu before which you want to insert the new menu, then click the Insert... button. MicroStation displays an Insert Menu dialog box similar to Figure 15–51.

Key-in the name of the new menu name in the Label edit field, and click the OK button to close the dialog box.

To insert a menu item, first double-click the menu name. MicroStation expands the menu. Select the entry for the existing menu item before which you want to insert the new menu item, then click the Insert... button. MicroStation displays an Insert Menu Item dialog box similar to Figure 15–52.

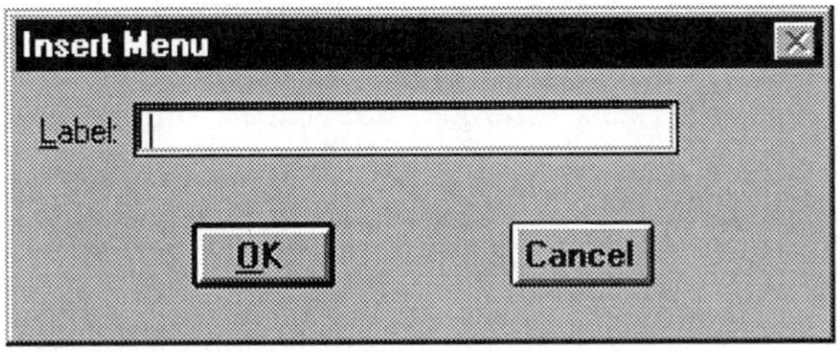

FIGURE 15–51 Insert Menu dialog box.

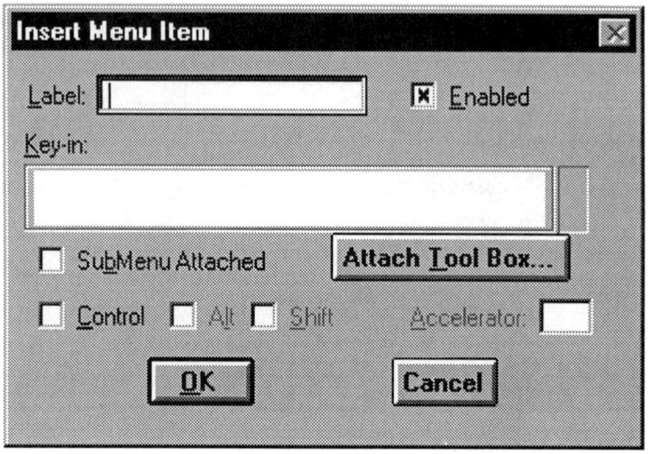

Insert Menu Item

Label: [|]   [X] Enabled

Key-in:

[   ]

☐ SubMenu Attached   **Attach Tool Box...**

☐ Control ☐ Alt ☐ Shift   Accelerator: [   ]

[OK]   [Cancel]

FIGURE 15–52 Insert Menu Item dialog box.

Use the appropriate controls in the Insert Menu Item dialog box to set the menu item, and click the OK button to close the dialog box.

STEP 4: From the available Menu names listed on the Available Menus (left side of the settings box), double-click the Menu name. MicroStation lists the available menu items. Select the menu item you want to insert, and drag and drop it at the appropriate location in the Edit Menu Bar list box.

STEP 5: If necessary, you can rearrange the menu or menu items by dragging and dropping in the Edit Menu Bar list box.

STEP 6: If necessary, you can remove the menu or menu item from the Edit Menu Bar list box. First select the menu or menu item to remove from the list box, then click the Remove button. MicroStation removes the selected menu or menu item from the tool box.

STEP 7: Click the Save button to save the Modification/Addition to Tool Boxes. MicroStation displays the customized version of the pull-down menus.

STEP 8: If no further changes have to be made, close the Customize settings box.

> **NOTE:** To disregard the changes, close the Customize settings box without saving the changes.

FUNCTION KEYS

Each personal computer keyboard has a special set of keys called *function keys*. MicroStation has a utility that assigns menu action strings to the various function keys (F1 through F12). Once the assignment is made, then all you have to do is select the function key, and the menu action string is activated.

There are only 12 functions on the keyboard, but MicroStation allows you to make up to 96 function key assignments by combining a function key with the SHIFT, ALT, and/or CTRL key. So, for instance, you can assign the F1 with the following combinations:

> F1
>
> SHIFT + F1
>
> ALT + F1
>
> CTRL + F1
>
> SHIFT + ALT + F1
>
> SHIFT + ALT + F1
>
> ALT + CTRL + F1
>
> SHIFT + ALT + CTRL + F1

Function key assignments are stored in a special ASCII file, and by default the extension for the function key file is .MNU. This file follows the same concept as the cell library file. Once created, the function key file may be attached to any of your design files to activate the function keys. The default function key menu file is called "funckey.mnu." It is stored under the /USTATION/WSMOD/DEFAULT/DATA/ directory.

Creating and Modifying Function Key Definitions

To create and modify function key definitions, open the Function Keys dialog box from:

Pull-down menu	Workspace > Function Keys... (or ALT + **K**, **F**)

MicroStation displays the Function Keys dialog box, as shown in Figure 15–53.

The title bar identifies the file name of the function key menu. The list box lists currently defined function key combinations and their definitions.

The Shortcut Keys section contains controls for selecting a function key definition to change or for creating a new one. Turn ON the appropriate toggle buttons for CTRL,

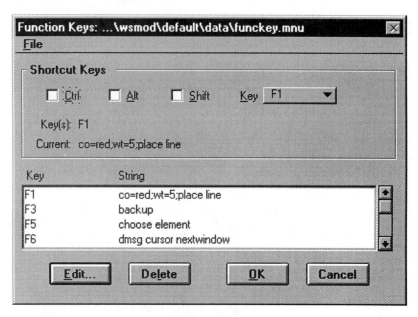

FIGURE 15–53 Function Keys dialog box.

[ALT], and/or [SHIFT] modifiers, and select the function key from the Key option menu to change or to create a new definition. Click the Edit button, and MicroStation opens a Edit Key Definition dialog box similar to Figure 15–54.

Key-in the action string (for example, place line) in the New edit field, then click the OK button to accept the function key definition and close the dialog box.

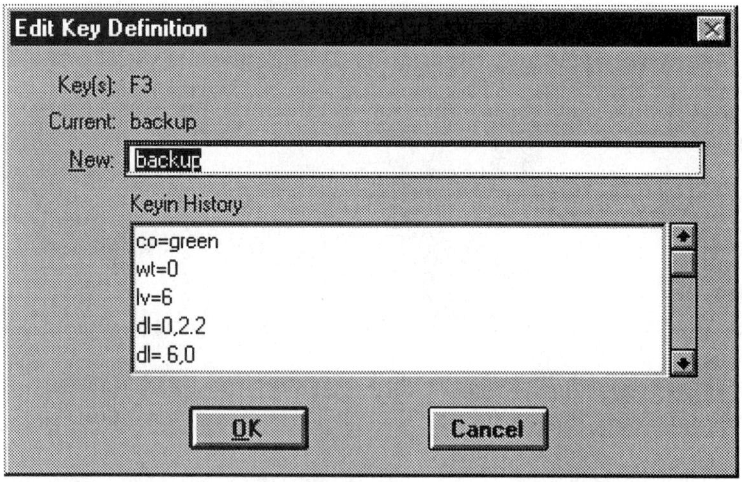

FIGURE 15–54 Edit Key Definition dialog box.

You can also program a function key with multiple action strings (macros) separated by semicolons. For example, the following key-in sets the color to red, the line weight to 2, the active level to 4, and invokes the place line command:

co=red;wt=2;lv=4;place line

In addition, you can also select the action strings from the Keyin History, as shown in Figure 15–54.

To delete a function key definition, first select the function key definition from the list box, then click the Delete button. MicroStation deletes the selected function key definition.

Saving the Function Key Definitions To save the function key definitions, invoke the Save command from:

Pull-down menu (Function Keys dialog box)	File > Save (or ⌨ALT + **F**, **S**)

MicroStation saves the current status of the function key definitions to the function key menu file.

Saving the Function Key Definitions to a Different File To save the function key definitions to a different menu file, invoke the Save As command from:

Pull-down menu (Function Keys dialog box)	File > Save As... (or ⌨ALT + **F**, **A**)

MicroStation opens the Save Function Key Menu As dialog box. Key-in the name of the menu file in the Files edit field and click the OK button.

INSTALLING FONTS

Each time a design file is displayed, a font resource file is used that contains font definitions. Provided the font resource file name has not been changed during workspace definitions, MicroStation, by default, uses a resource file called FONT.RSC. MicroStation allows you to add new fonts to the font resource file via the utility called Font Installer.

The Font Installer dialog box helps you to import fonts from different sources into the MicroStation font library; in addition, you can rename and renumber fonts.

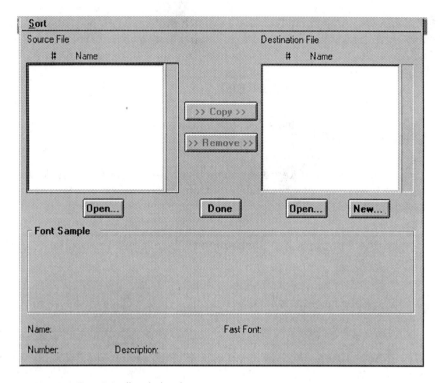

FIGURE 15–55 Font Installer dialog box.

To open the Font Installer dialog box, invoke Install Fonts from:

Pull-down menu	Utilities > Install Fonts (or 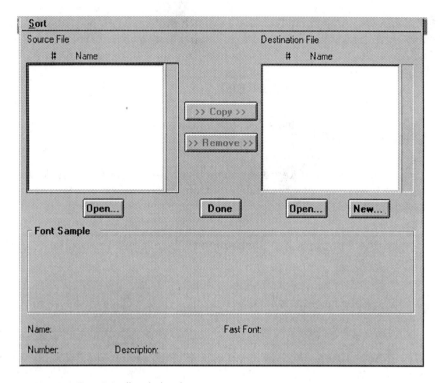 + **U**, **F**)

MicroStation displays the Font Installer dialog box, as shown in Figure 15–55.

Selecting the Source Font Files

To select the source fonts, click the Open... button located below the Source File list box. MicroStation displays an Open Source Font Files dialog box similar to Figure 15–56.

The Type option menu sets the file type from one of the following:

Font Cell Library: MicroStation font cell library, a standard cell library that contains cells that define the characters and symbols in a traditional Micro-Station font and the font's attributes

Font Library: MicroStation Version 5 font library

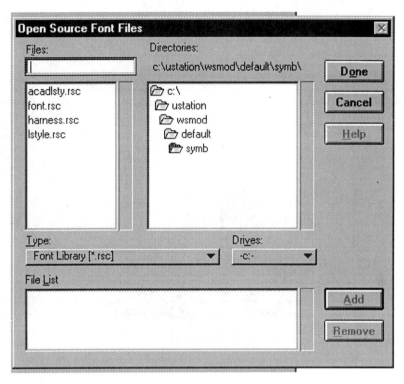

FIGURE 15–56 Open Source Font Files dialog box.

uSTN V4/IGDS Fontlib: Version 4.1 or earlier (or IGDS) font library

PS Type-1: PostScript Type 1 (uncompressed only)

Shape Files (AutoCAD): AutoCAD shape files (.SHX files)

TrueType

Select the font file from the Files list box and click the Add button. You can select multiple files as the source font files. Click the Remove button to remove the font file from the selected list box. Then click the OK button to close the dialog box. Micro-Station lists all the fonts available from the source font file(s)

Selecting the Destination Fonts File

To select the destination fonts file, click the Open... button located beneath the Destination File list box. MicroStation opens the Open Font Library dialog box, similar to Figure 15–57. Select the font library from the Files list box as the destination for the new font insertion, and click the OK button to close the dialog box. MicroStation lists all the available fonts in the Destination File list box.

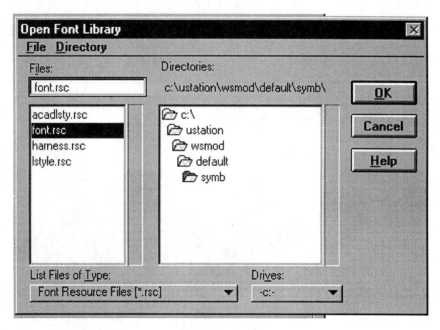

FIGURE 15–57 Open Font Library dialog box.

Importing Fonts

To import the font from the source to the destination file, first select the font in the source file list box, and click the >>Copy>> button. MicroStation copies the selected font into the Destination File list box. To remove the font in the Destination File list box, first select the font to be removed from the list, then click the >>Remove>> button. MicroStation removes the selected font from the Destination File list box.

If necessary, you can change the name of the font, the number of the font, or the description. First select the font in the Destination File list box; MicroStation displays the information in the bottom of the dialog box. Make the necessary changes in the appropriate edit fields.

Click the Done button to close the Font Installer dialog box.

ARCHIVE UTILITY

The Archive utility allows you to select and bundle together the design files you wish to archive, along with all the resources needed to recreate those design files on a different computer system. Following are the classes of resources that can be included in an archive file:

- Design files
- Reference files
- Raster Reference files
- Cell libraries
- Background files (raster images)
- Resource files (line styles, fonts, etc.)
- Material tables
- Material tool boxes
- Materials
- Pattern files
- Bump Map files
- Current workspace files
- All configuration files
- All user interface files

In addition, you can create your own classes to hold additional resource files, such as plotter configuration files, tag templates, and even non-MicroStation files.

Creating a New Archive File

Follow these steps to create a new Archive file:

STEP 1: Invoke the Archive settings box from:

Pull-down menu	Utilities > Archive (or ⌨ + **U, H**)

MicroStation displays an Archive settings box similar to Figure 15–58.

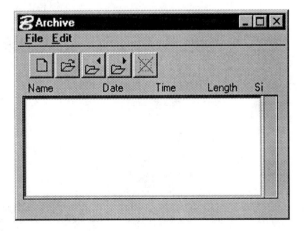

FIGURE 15–58 Archive settings box.

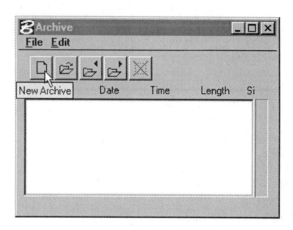

FIGURE 15-59 Invoking the New Archive command.

STEP 2: Invoke the New Archive command from:

Pull-down menu (Archive settings box)	File > New... (or [ALT] + **F, N**)
Archive tool box (Archive settings box)	Select the New Archive tool (see Figure 15–59).

MicroStation displays a Select Archive Classes dialog box similar to Figure 15–60.

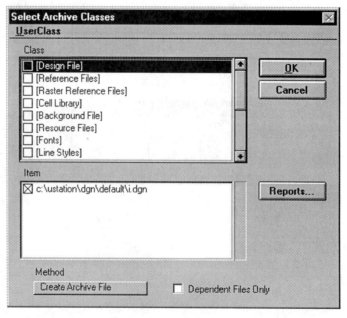

FIGURE 15-60 Select Archive Classes dialog box.

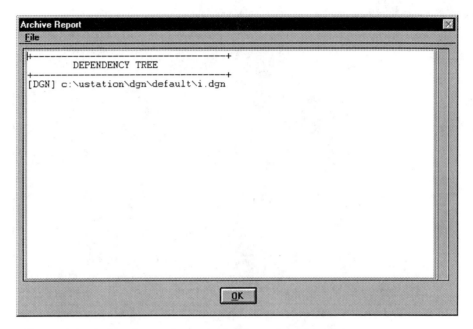

FIGURE 15–61   Archive Report display in the Dependency Tree format.

STEP 3:   Set the toggle button to ON for specific archive classes to include from the Class list box. MicroStation displays any items specifically called for in the design file that will be shown in the Item list box. By default, they are automatically selected for archiving. Click the related option box to select or deselect each file.

STEP 4:   If necessary, click the Reports... button. MicroStation opens the Archive Report dialog box to review the resource file tree used by the current design file. MicroStation provides three different methods by which you can display the report. The methods include Class Summary, Dependency Tree, and File List; you can select one of them from the submenu Style of the pull-down menu File of the dialog box. Figure 15–61 shows the report display in the Dependency Tree format.

STEP 5:   Select Create Archive File from the Method option menu located at the bottom of the Select Archive File dialog box, and click the OK button. MicroStation displays a Create Archive dialog box similar to Figure 15–62.

STEP 6:   If necessary, turn ON the toggle button for the Save Directories option. This will store the file path specification in the archive file. If this option is not selected, only the file names are stored in the archive file.

STEP 7:   If necessary, turn ON the Use Path Filter option. If it is set to ON, then specify the path by clicking the Select... button in the Path Filter section.

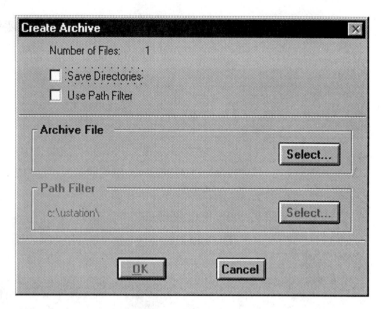

FIGURE 15–62 Create Archive dialog box.

MicroStation will archive all the files not defined in the Path Filter section. This option acts as a filter to remove that part of the path that is unique to a specific system.

STEP 8: Specify the archive file name by clicking the Select... button in the Archive File section.

STEP 9: Click the OK button to create the archive file. A progress indicator is displayed showing the name of the file being processed, as well as the progress of the entire archive process.

Copying a Design File and Its Resources to a New Destination

Follow these steps to copy a design file and its resources to a new destination:

STEP 1: Invoke the Archive settings box from:

Pull-down menu	Utilities > Arc<u>h</u>ive (or + **U, H**)

MicroStation displays an Archive settings box similar to Figure 15–58.

STEP 2: Invoke the New Archive command from:

Pull-down menu (Archive settings box)	File > New... (or ⌨[ALT] + **F, N**)
Archive tool box (Archive settings box)	Select the New Archive tool (see Figure 15–59).

MicroStation displays a Select Archive Classes dialog box similar to Figure 15–60.

STEP 3: Set the toggle button to ON for specific archive classes to include from the Class list box. MicroStation displays any items specifically called for in the design file that will be shown in the Item list box. By default, they are automatically selected for archiving. Click the related option box to select or deselect each file.

STEP 4: If necessary, click the Reports... button. MicroStation opens the Archive Report dialog box to review the resource file tree used by the current design file.

STEP 5: Select Copy Files from the Method option menu located at the bottom of the Select Archive Classes dialog box, and click the OK button. Micro-Station displays a Copy Files dialog box similar to Figure 15–63.

Select a directory to which to copy the selected design files and resource files. Click the OK button to close the dialog box. A progress indicator is displayed.

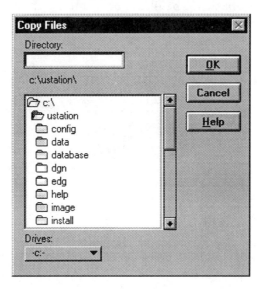

FIGURE 15–63 Copy Files dialog box.

Extracting Files from an Existing Archive

Follow these steps to extract files from an existing archive:

STEP 1: Invoke the Archive settings box from:

Pull-down menu	Utilities > Arc<u>h</u>ive (or <kbd>ALT</kbd> + **U, H**)

MicroStation displays an Archive settings box similar to Figure 15–58.

STEP 2: Invoke the Open Archive command from:

Pull-down menu (Archive settings box)	<u>F</u>ile > <u>O</u>pen (or <kbd>ALT</kbd> + **F, O**)
Archive tool box (Archive settings box)	Select the Open Archive tool (see Figure 15–64).

MicroStation displays an Open Archive File dialog box similar to Figure 15–65.

STEP 3: Select the archive file from which files are to be extracted and click the OK button. The files that constitute the archive file are displayed in the Archive File list box.

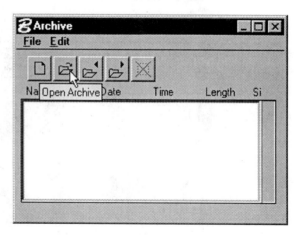

FIGURE 15–64 Invoking the Open Archive tool command.

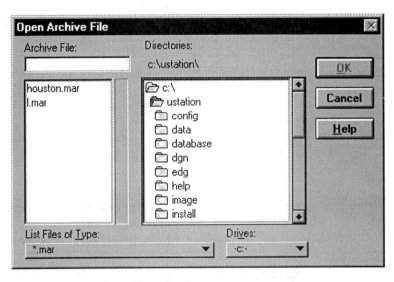

FIGURE 15–65 Open Archive File dialog box.

STEP 4: In the list box, select the files to be extracted. Standard list selection techniques can be used to select more than one file. To select all files in an archive, invoke the Select All item from the pull-down menu Edit.

STEP 5: Invoke the Extract Files command from:

Pull-down menu (Archive settings box)	Edit > Extract... (or [ALT] + **E**, **E**)
Archive tool box (Archive settings box)	Select the Extract Files tool (see Figure 15–66).

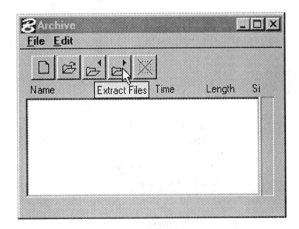

FIGURE 15–66 Invoking the Extract Files command.

MicroStation displays the Extract Archive Files dialog box displaying information about the selected files along with destination options.

STEP 6: If necessary, turn ON the toggle button for the Create Stored Directories option. By selecting this option, you direct the Archive utility to use stored directories as the destination path.

STEP 7: If necessary, turn ON the toggle button for the Overwrite Existing Files option. By selecting this option, the extracted file will overwrite an existing file with the same name.

STEP 8: If necessary, turn ON the toggle button for the Preserve Date/Time option. By selecting this option, the date/time of the extracted file will be copied from the compressed file, preserving its original values.

STEP 9: If necessary, change the target directory by clicking the Select... button in the Extract To section.

STEP 10: Click the OK button to begin the file extraction process.

Adding Files to an Existing Archive

Follow these steps to add files to an existing archive:

STEP 1: Invoke the Archive settings box from:

Pull-down menu	Utilities > Archive (or [ALT] + **U, H**)

MicroStation displays an Archive settings box similar to Figure 15–58.

STEP 2: Invoke the Open Archive command from:

Pull-down menu (Archive settings box)	File > Open (or [ALT] + **F, O**)
Archive tool box (Archive settings box)	Select the Open Archive tool (see Figure 15–64).

MicroStation displays an Open Archive dialog box similar to Figure 15–65.

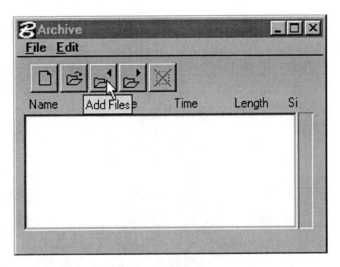

FIGURE 15–67 Invoking the Add Files command.

STEP 3: Select the archive file from which files are to be extracted and click the OK button. The files that constitute the archive file are displayed in the Archive File list box.

STEP 4: Invoke the Add Files command from

Pull-down menu (Archive settings box)	Edit > Add (or [ALT] + E, A)
Archive tool box (Archive settings box)	Select the Add Files tool (see Figure 15–67).

MicroStation displays a Select Files To Add dialog box similar to Figure 15–68.

STEP 5: Select the file from the appropriate directory and click the Add button. The file will appear in the Files list box. Continue selecting files to archive.

STEP 6: Click the Done button after selecting all the files to be archived. MicroStation displays the Add Archive Files dialog box. Make the necessary changes and click the OK button.

MicroStation adds the selected files to the opened archive file.

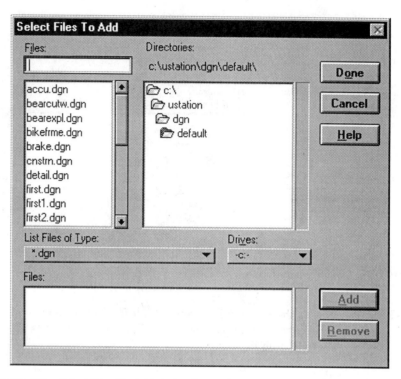

FIGURE 15–68 Select Files To Add dialog box.

SCRIPTS, MACROS, USER COMMANDS

MicroStation has three application software tools that automate often-used command sequences. Depending on the complexity of the operation to be performed, you can choose one of the three application software tools. The tools include scripts, macros, and user commands.

Scripts

A script is the simplest software application in which you create an ASCII file containing the key-in sequence of the MicroStation commands. For example, the following script sets the Active Color, Active Line Weight, and Active Level:

> active color red
> active weight 6
> active level 5

To load and run a script, key-in the following in the Key-in window: @<script_file> and press ⏎. MicroStation executes the command sequence in the order that the script is set.

> **NOTE:** If the script is not in the current directory, script_file must include the full path to the script.

Macros

Macros are BASIC programs that automate often-used, usually short sequences of operation. Many MicroStation-specific extensions have been added to the BASIC language to customize it for the MicroStation environment. Macros select tools and view controls, send key-ins, manipulate dialog boxes, modify elements, and so on.

For detailed information about creating macros, refer to the MicroStation BASIC Guide that comes with the MicroStation software.

Several sample macros are provided with MicroStation. To load and run a macro, invoke the Macro tool from:

Pull-down menu	<u>U</u>tilities > <u>Ma</u>cro (or 🖮 + **U**, **A**)
Key-in window	**Macro** <macro_name> ⏎

MicroStation displays a Macros settings box similar to Figure 15–69. Select the macro from the Macro Name list box, click the Run button, follow the prompts, and provide the appropriate responses.

FIGURE 15–69   Macros settings box.

User Commands

A *user command* is an ASCII text file that groups together "statements" that are executed while in a MicroStation design file. A user command is similar to a macro. The coded statements of a user command follow the rules that are part of the MicroStation User Command Language. This language provides an interface consisting of a set of commands and instructions to automate a task or set of tasks. These instructions are arranged in a logical order that imitates the steps that would be followed if you were performing MicroStation tasks manually. The coded statements are performed one after the other until all have been executed or until a condition is met that causes the user command to exit. Refer to the MicroStation User Manual for a detailed description of user commands.

Several sample user commands are provided with MicroStation. To load and run a user command, invoke the tool from:

Key-in window	**uc=**<name> [ENTER]
Pull-down menu	<u>U</u>tilities > <u>U</u>ser command > <u>R</u>un (or [ALT] + **U, U, R**)

MicroStation displays a Run User Command dialog box similar to Figure 15–70.

Select the User Command file from the Files list box and click the OK button. MicroStation executes the User Command. Then follow the prompts and provide the appropriate responses.

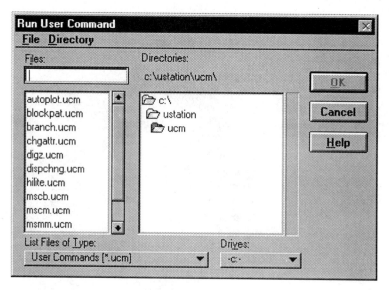

FIGURE 15–70 Run User Command dialog box.

CHAPTER

16

3D DESIGN AND RENDERING

WHAT IS 3D?

In 2D drawings you have been working with two axes, *X* and *Y*. In 3D drawings, in addition to the *X* and *Y* axes, you will be working on the *Z* axis, as shown in Figure 16–1. Plan views, sections, and elevations represent only two dimensions. Isometric, perspective, and axonometric drawings, on the other hand, represent all three dimensions. For example, to create three views of a cube, the cube is simply drawn as a square with thickness. This is referred to as extruded 2D. Only objects that are extrudable can be drawn by this method. Any other views are achieved by simply rotating the viewpoint of the object, just as if one were physically holding the cube. You can also can get an isometric or perspective view by simply changing the viewpoint.

Drawing objects in 3D provides three major advantages:

✓ An object can be drawn once and then can be viewed and plotted from any angle.

✓ A 3D object holds mathematical information that can be used in engineering analysis, such as finite-element analysis and computer numerical control (CNC) machinery.

✓ Shading can be added for visualization.

This chapter provides an overview of the tools and specific commands available for 3D design.

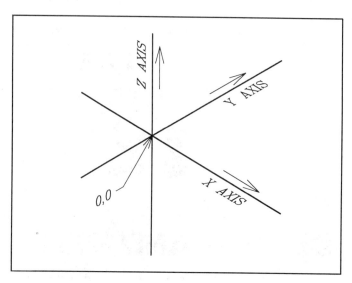

FIGURE 16–1 *X, Y,* and *Z* axes for 3D Design.

CREATING A 3D DESIGN FILE

The procedure for creating a new 3D design file is similar to that for creating a new 2D design file, except you have to use a seed file that is designed specifically for 3D. The same holds good for cell libraries. Invoke the New... command from the pull-down menu File. The Create Design File dialog box opens. Click the Seed button, and MicroStation displays a list of seed files available, as shown in Figure 16–2. Select

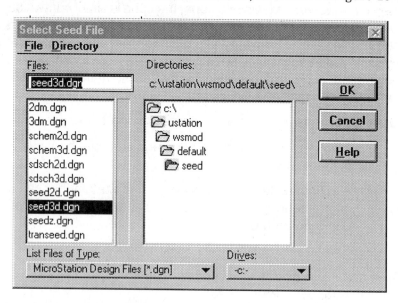

FIGURE 16–2 Select Seed File dialog box.

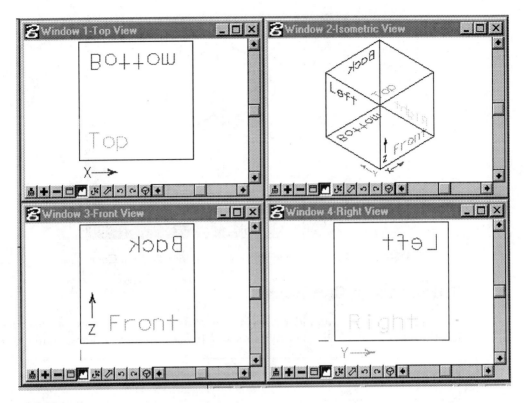

FIGURE 16–3   MicroStation screen display.

one of the 3D seed files from the Files list box and click the OK button. MicroStation by default highlights the name of the file you just created in the Files list box in the Create Design dialog box. To open the new design file, click the OK button and your screen will look similar to the one shown in Figure 16–3. By default, MicroStation displays four view windows, each set for one of the four standard view orientations. As part of the title of the view window, MicroStation displays the name of the view being displayed.

> **NOTE:** The text elements you see displayed when you start a new design are construction elements. You can turn off the display of the construction elements by setting the Constructions toggle button to OFF in the View Attributes settings box.

VIEW ROTATION

There are seven standard view orientations defined in MicroStation: top, bottom, front, back, right, left, and isometric. You can use one of the four tools available in MicroStation to display the standard view orientation in any of the view windows.

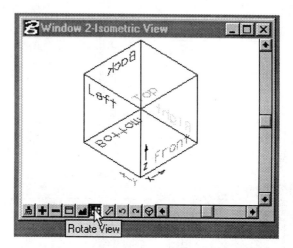

FIGURE 16–4 Invoking the Rotate View command from the View Control bar.

Rotate View Command

The Rotate View command displays one of the standard view orientations. In addition it can rotate the view dynamically. Invoke the Rotate View command from:

View Control bar	Select the Rotate View tool (see Figure 16–4).

Select one of the 10 available options in the Tool Settings window. To position the view to one of the standard view orientations, first select the standard view orientation [Top, Bottom, Front, Back, Right, Left, Isometric (Top, Front, or Left) or Isometric (Top, Front, or Right)]. Then place a data point in the view window where you want to display the view orientation. Selection of the Dynamic option allows you to position the view at any angle around a data point. The three points allow you to rotate the view by defining three data points (origin, direction of the X axis, and a point defining the Y axis).

Changing View Rotation from the View Rotation Settings Box

You can also rotate the view by specifying the angle of rotation in the View Rotation settings box. Open the View Rotation settings box from:

3D View Control tool box	Select the Change View Rotation tool (see Figure 16–5).
Key-in window	**dialog view rotation** (or **di viewro**) [ENTER]

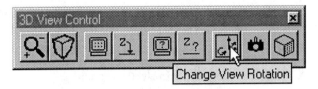

FIGURE 16–5   Invoking the Change View Rotation command from the 3D View Control tool box.

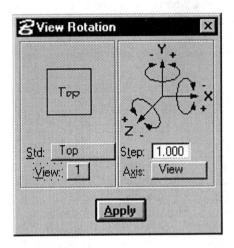

FIGURE 16–6   View Rotation settings box.

MicroStation displays the View Rotation settings box, similar to Figure 16–6.

The view to be manipulated is selected in the View option menu. Key-in the rotation increment in degrees in the Step edit field. Click the "+" control to rotate the view in the positive direction by the Step amount around the specified Axis. Click the "–" to rotate the view in the negative direction by the Step amount around the specified Axis. If you want to reposition the view to one of the standard view orientations, select the view orientation from the Std option menu. Click the Apply button to rotate the selected view to the specified rotation.

Rotating View by Key-in

You can also rotate the view via one of the two key-in commands. Key-in:

Key-in window	**VI**=<name of the view> [ENTER] **Rotate View Absolute=** <xx,yy,zz> [ENTER] or **Rotate View Relative=** <xx,yy,zz> [ENTER]

In the VI key-in, you can specify either one of the standard view rotations (top, bottom, front, back, right, left, or iso) or the name of the saved view.

In the Rotate View Absolute key-in, xx, yy, and zz are the rotations, in degrees, about the view X, Y, and Z axes (by default, 0 for each).

In the Rotate View Relative key-in, xx, yy, and zz are the relative, counter-clockwise rotations, in degrees, about the view X, Y, and Z axes. This key-in follows what is commonly called the "right-hand-rule." For example, if you key-in a positive X rotation and point your right thumb in the view's positive X direction, then the way your fingers curl is the direction of rotation.

DESIGN CUBE

Whenever you start a new two-dimensional design, you get a design plane—the electronic equivalent of a sheet of paper on a drafting table. The two-dimensional design plane is a large, flat plane covered with an invisible matrix grid consisting of 4,294,967,296 (2^{32}) positional units (UOR) along the X and Y axes. In three-dimensional design, you use that same XY plane plus a third-dimension Z axis. The Z axis is the depth in the direction perpendicular to the XY plane. The volume defined by X, Y, and Z is called the *design cube*. Similar to the design plane, the design cube is covered with an invisible matrix grid consisting of 4,294,967,296 (2^{32}) positional units along each of the X, Y, and Z axes. The global origin (0,0,0) is at the very center of the design cube; see Figure 16–7.

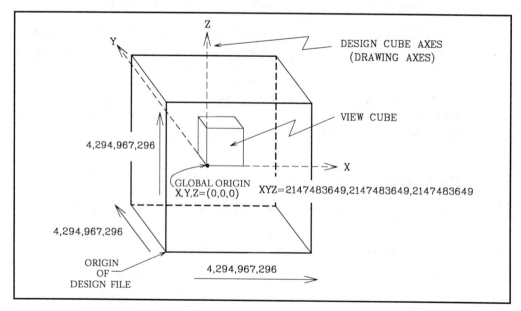

FIGURE 16–7 Design cube.

DISPLAY DEPTH

Display depth enables you to display a portion of your design rather than the entire design. The ability to look at only a portion of the depth comes in handy—especially if the design is complicated. Display depth settings define the front and back clipping planes for elements displayed in a view and is set for each view. Elements not contained in the display depth do not show up on the screen. If you need to work with an element outside the display depth, you must change the display depth to include the element.

Setting Display Depth

To set the display depth, invoke the Set Display Depth command from:

3D View Control tool box	Select the Set Display Depth tool (see Figure 16–8).
Key-in window	**Depth Display** (or **dep d**) [ENTER]

MicroStation prompts:

> Set Display Depth > Select view for display depth *(Place a data point in a view where you want to set the display depth.)*
> Set Display Depth > Define front clipping plane *(Place a data point in any view where you can identify the front clipping plane.)*
> Set Display Depth > Define back clipping plane *(Place a data point in any view where you can identify the back clipping plane.)*

You can also set the display depth by keying-in the distances in MU:SU:PU along the view Z axis by absolute or relative coordinates. To set the display depth by absolute coordinates, key-in:

Key-in window	**dp=<front,back>** [ENTER]

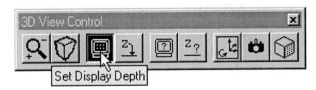

FIGURE 16–8   Invoking the Set Display Depth command from the 3D View Control tool box.

The <front,back> are the distances in MU:SU:PU along the view Z axis from the global origin to the desired front and back clipping planes. MicroStation prompts:

> Set Display Depth > Select view *(Identify the view with a data point to set the display depth.)*

To set the display depth by relative coordinates, key-in:

Key-in window	**dd=**<front,back> [ENTER]

The <front,back> are the distances in MU:SU:PU, and they add the keyed-in values to the current display depth settings. MicroStation prompts:

> Set Display Depth > Select view *(Identify the view with a data point to set the display depth.)*

To determine the current setting for display depth, invoke the Show Display Depth command from:

3D View Control tool box	Select the Show Display Depth tool (see Figure 16–9).
Key-in window	**dp=$** (or **dd=$**) [ENTER]

MicroStation prompts:

> Show Display Depth > Select view *(Place a data point anywhere in the view window.)*

MicroStation displays the current setting of the display depth in the Status bar.

> **NOTE:** When you are setting up the display depth, in all views, you will notice dashed lines, indicating the viewing parameters of the selected view. Both the display volume of the view and the active depth plane are dynamically displayed, with different-style dashed lines.

FIGURE 16–9 Invoking the Show Display Depth command from the 3D View Control tool box.

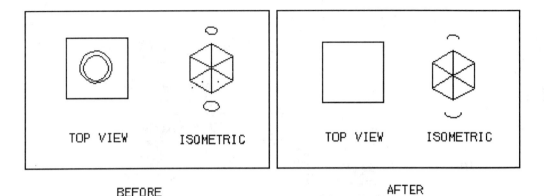

FIGURE 16–10 Example of setting up the display depth.

In Figure 16–10, the display depth is set in such a way that only the square box is displayed but not the circles.

Fitting Display Depth to Design File Elements

A fast way to display the entire design is to invoke the Fit command and select the appropriate view. In two-dimensional design the Fit command adjusts the view window to include all elements in the design file. Similarly, in three-dimensional design the Fit command adjusts both the view window and the display depth to include all the elements in the design file. The Fit command automatically resets the display depth to the required amount to display the entire design file.

ACTIVE DEPTH

MicroStation has a feature that allows you to place an element in front of or behind the XY plane (front and back views), to the left or right of the YZ plane (right and left views), and above or below the XY plane (top and bottom views). This can be done by setting up the *active depth*. The active depth is a plane, parallel to the screen in each view, where elements will be placed by default. Each view has its own active depth plane, which you can change at any time.

Elements are placed at the active depth if you don't either tentative snap to an existing element or use a precision input. In the top and bottom views (XY plane), the depth value is along its Z axis. In the front and back views (XZ plane), the depth value is along its Y axis. And in the case of right and left views (YZ plane), the depth value is along its X axis.

Setting Active Depth

To set the active depth, invoke the Set Active Depth command from:

3D View Control tool box	Select the Set Active Depth tool (see Figure 16–11).
Key-in window	**Depth Active** (or **dep a**) ⏎

MicroStation prompts:

> Set Active Depth > Select view *(Place a data point in a view where you want to set the active depth.)*
> Set Active Depth > Enter active depth point *(Place a data point in a different view where you can identify the location for setting up the active depth.)*

NOTE: When you are setting up the active depth, in all views, you will notice dashed lines, indicating the viewing parameters of the selected view. Both the display volume of the view and the active depth plane are dynamically displayed, with different-style dashed lines.

You can also set the active depth by keying-in the distances in MU:SU:PU along the view Z axis by absolute or relative coordinates. To set the active depth by absolute coordinates, key-in:

Key-in window	**az=<depth>** ⏎

The <depth> is the distance in MU:SU:PU along the view Z axis from the global origin to the desired active depth. MicroStation prompts:

> Set Active Depth > Select view *(Identify the view with a data point to set the active depth.)*

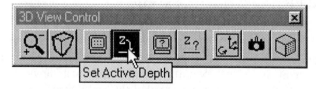

FIGURE 16–11 Invoking the Set Active Depth command from the 3D View Control tool box.

FIGURE 16–12 Invoking the Show Active Depth command in the 3D View Control tool box.

To set the active depth by relative coordinates, key-in:

Key-in window	**dz**=<depth> ⏎

The <depth> is the distance in MU:SU:PU, and it adds the keyed-in values to the current active depth setting. MicroStation prompts:

> Set Active Depth > Select view *(Identify the view with a data point to set the active depth.)*

To determine the current setting for active depth, invoke the Show Active Depth command from:

3D View Control tool box	Select the Show Active Depth tool (see Figure 16–12).
Key-in window	**az=$** (or **dz=$**) ⏎

MicroStation prompts:

> Show Active Depth > Select view *(Place a data point anywhere in the view window.)*

MicroStation displays the current setting of the active depth in the Status bar.

NOTE: Before you place elements, make sure you are working at the appropriate active depth and display depth.

If you set the active depth outside the range of the display depth, then MicroStation displays the following message in the error field:

> Active depth set to display depth

The active depth is set to the value closest to the display depth.

Let's say the current display depth is set to 100,450 and you set the active depth to 525. Since MicroStation sets the active depth to the closest value, in this case the active depth is set to 450. Make sure that MicroStation sets the value for the active depth to the value intended. If necessary, change the display depth and then set the active depth.

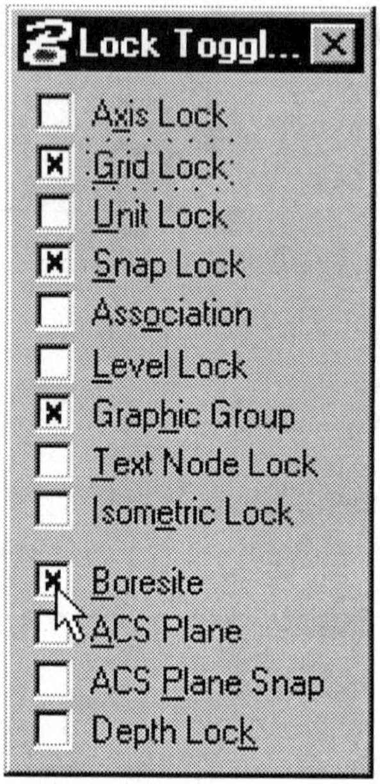

FIGURE 16–13 Lock Toggle settings box.

Boresite Lock

The Boresite lock controls the manipulation of the elements at different depths. If the Boresite lock is set to ON, you can identify or snap to elements at any depth in the view; elements being moved or copied will remain at their original depths. If it is set to OFF, you can identify only those elements at, or very near, the active depth of a view. You can toggle ON or OFF for the Boresite lock from the Lock Toggles settings box, as shown in Figure 16–13.

> **NOTE:** Tentative points override the Boresite lock. You can tentative snap to elements at any depth regardless of the Boresite lock setting.

PRECISION INPUTS

When MicroStation prompts for the location of a point, in addition to providing the data point with your pointing device, you can use precision input commands that allow you to place data points precisely. Similar to two-dimensional placement commands, three-dimensional commands also allow you to key-in by coordinates. MicroStation provides two types of coordinate systems for three-dimensional design: The drawing coordinate system and the view coordinate system.

Drawing Coordinate System

The drawing coordinate system is the model coordinate system fixed relative to the design cube, as shown in Figure 16–14. For example, in the TOP view, X is to the right, Y is up, and Z is out of the screen (right-hand rule). In the RIGHT view, Y is to the right, Z is up, and X is out of the screen, etc. Following are the two key-ins available for the drawing coordinate system:

XY=<X,Y,Z>
DL=<delta_x,delta_y,delta_z>

The XY= key-in places a data point measured from the global origin of the drawing coordinate system. The <X,Y,Z> are the X, Y, and Z values of the coordinates. The view being used at the time has no effect on them. The DL= places a data point to a distance along the drawing axes from a previous data (relative) or tentative point. The <delta_x,delta_y,delta_z> are the relative coordinates in the X, Y, and Z axes relative to the previous data point or tentative point.

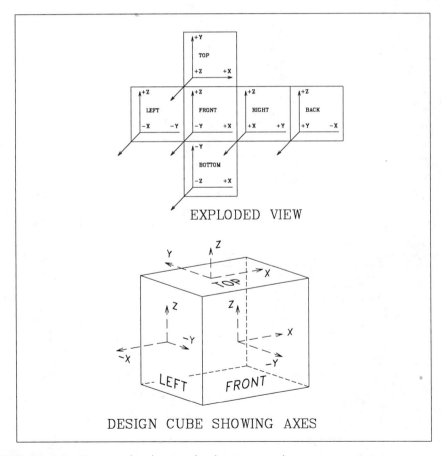

FIGURE 16–14 Design cube showing the drawing coordinate system.

View Coordinate System

The view coordinate system inputs data relative to the screen, where X is to the right, Y is up, and Z comes directly out from the screen in all views, as shown in Figure 16–15. The view coordinate system is view dependent, that is, depends on the orientation of the view for their direction. Following are the two key-ins available for the view coordinate system:

> **DX=**<delta_x,delta_y,delta_z>
> **DI=**<distance,direction>

The DX= key-in places a data point to a distance from the previous data or tentative point (relative) in the same view where the previous point was defined. The <delta_x,delta_y,delta_z> are the relative coordinates in the X, Y, and Z axes relative to the previous data point or tentative point. The DI= key-in places a data point a certain distance and direction from a previous data or tentative point (relative polar)

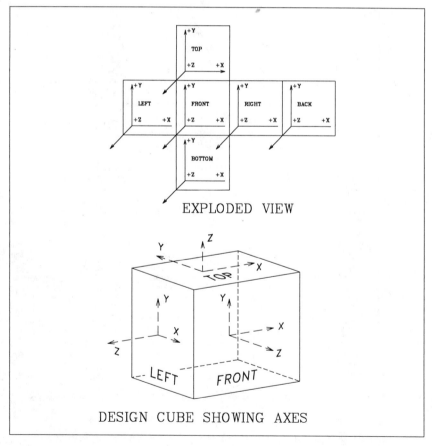

FIGURE 16–15 Design cube showing the view coordinate system.

in the same view where the previous point was defined. The <distance,direction> are specified in relation to the last specified position or point. The distance is specified in current working units (MU:SU:PU), and the direction is specified as an angle, in degrees, relative to the X axis.

> **NOTE:** With key-in precision inputs, MicroStation assumes that the view you want to use is the one you last worked in—that is, the view in which the last tentative or data point was placed. The easiest way to make a view current is to place a tentative point and then press the Reset button. Updating a view is also another way to tell MicroStation that the selected view is the view last worked in.

AUXILIARY COORDINATE SYSTEMS (ACS)

MicroStation provides a set of tools to define an infinite number of user-defined coordinate systems called *auxiliary coordinate systems*. An auxiliary coordinate system allows the user to change the location and orientation of the X, Y, and Z axes to reduce the calculations needed to create 3D objects. You can redefine the origin in your drawing, and establish positive X and Y axes. New users think of a coordinate system simply as the direction of positive X and positive Y. But once the directions X and Y are defined, the direction of Z will be defined as well. Thus, the user only has to be concerned with X and Y. For example, if a sloped roof of a house is drawn in detail using the drawing coordinate system, each end point of each element on the inclined roof plane must be calculated. On the other hand, if the auxiliary coordinate system is set to the same plane as the roof, each object can be drawn as if it were in the plan view. You can define any number of auxiliary coordinate systems, assigning each a user-determined name. But, at any given time, only one auxiliary coordinate system is current with the default system.

MicroStation provides a visual reminder of how the ACS axes are orientated and where the current ACS origin is located. The X, Y, and Z axis directions are displayed using arrows labeled appropriately. The display of the ACS axes is controlled by turning ON/OFF the ACS Triad in the View Attributes settings box, as shown in Figure 16–16.

MicroStation provides you with three types of coordinate systems for defining an ACS: rectangular, cylindrical, and spherical coordinate systems.

Rectangular Coordinate System The rectangular coordinate system is the same one that is available for design cube and is also the default type to define an ACS.

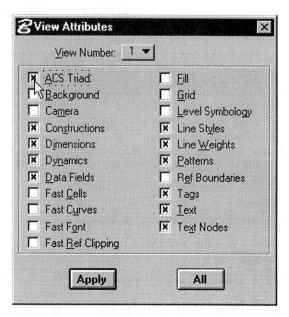

FIGURE 16–16   View Attributes settings box showing the ACS Triad set to ON.

Cylindrical Coordinate System The cylindrical coordinate system is another three-dimensional variant of the polar format. It describes a point by its distance from the origin, its angle in the *XY* plane from the *X* axis, and its *Z* value. For example, to specify a point at a distance of 4.5 units from the origin, at an angle of 35 degrees relative to the *X* axis (in the *XY* plane), and with a *Z* coordinate of 7.5 units, you would enter: **4.5,35,7.5**.

Spherical Coordinate System The spherical coordinate system is another three-dimensional variant of the polar format. It describes a point by its distance from the current origin, its angle in the *XY* plane, and its angle up from the *XY* plane. For example, to specify a point at a distance of 7 units from the origin, at an angle of 60 degrees from the *X* axis (in the *XY* plane), and at an angle 45 degrees up from the *XY* plane, you would enter: **7,60,45**.

Precision Input Key-in Similar to the key-ins available for drawing and view coordinates, MicroStation provides key-ins to input the coordinate in reference to the auxiliary coordinate system. Following are the two key-ins available for the auxiliary coordinate system:

> **AX=**<X,Y,Z>
> **AD=**<delta_x,delta_y,delta_z>

The AX= key-in places a data point measured from the ACS origin and is equivalent to the key-in XY=. The <X,Y,Z> are the *X*, *Y*, and *Z* values of the coordinates. The AD= places a data point to a distance along the drawing axes from a previous data (relative) or tentative point and is equivalent to the key-in DL=. The <delta_x,delta_y,delta_z> are the relative coordinates in the X, Y, and Z axes relative to the previous data point or tentative point.

Defining an ACS

MicroStation provides three different tools to define an ACS. The tools are available in the ACS tool box. Before you select one of the three tools, select the coordinate system you wish to use with the new ACS from the Type option menu in the Tool Settings window. In addition, you can control the ON/OFF toggle buttons for two locks in the Tool Settings window. When the ACS Plane Lock is set to ON, each data point is forced to lie on the active ACS's XY plane (Z=0). When the ACS Plane Snap Lock is set to ON, each tentative point is forced to lie on the active ACS's XY plane (Z=0).

Defining an ACS by Aligning with an Element This option lets you define an ACS by identifying an element where the XY plane of the ACS is parallel to the plane of the selected planar element. The origin of the ACS is at the point of identification of the element. Upon definition, the ACS becomes the active ACS.

To define an ACS aligned with an element, invoke the Define ACS (aligned with element) command from:

ACS tool box	Select the Define ACS (Aligned with Element) tool (see Figure 16–17).
Key-in window	**Define ACS Element** (or **d a e**) [ENTER]

MicroStation prompts:

Define ACS (Aligned with Element) > Identify element *(Identify the element with which to align the ACS and define the ACS origin.)*
Define ACS (Aligned with Element) > Accept/Reject (Select next input) *(Place a data point to accept the element for defining an ACS.)*

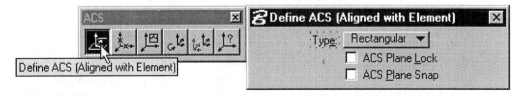

FIGURE 16–17 Invoking the Define ACS (Aligned with Element) command from the ACS tool box.

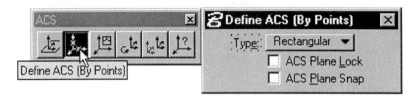

FIGURE 16–18   Invoking the Define ACS (By Points) command from the ACS tool box.

Defining the ACS by Points   This option is the easiest and most used option for controlling the orientation of the ACS. It allows the user to place three data points to define the origin and the directions of the positive X and Y axes. The origin point acts as a base for the ACS rotation; and when a point is selected to define the direction of the positive X axis, the direction of the Y axis is limited because it is always perpendicular to the X axis. When the X and Y axes are defined, the Z axis is automatically placed perpendicular to the XY plane. Upon definition, the ACS becomes the active ACS.

To define an ACS by Points, invoke the Define ACS (By Points) command from:

ACS tool box	Select the Define ACS (By Points) tool (see Figure 16–18).
Key-in window	**Define ACS Points** (or **d a p**) ⏎

MicroStation prompts:

>   Define ACS (By Points) > Enter first point @x axis origin *(Place a data point to define the origin.)*
>   Define ACS (By Points) > Enter second point on x axis *(Place a data point to define the direction of the positive X axis, which extends from the origin through this point.)*
>   Define ACS (By Points) > Enter point to define y axis *(Place a data point to define the direction of the positive Y axis.)*

Defining the ACS by Aligning with a View   In this option, the ACS takes the orientation of the selected view. That is, the ACS axes align exactly with those of the view selected. Upon definition, the ACS becomes the active ACS.

To define an ACS by aligning with a view, invoke the Define ACS (aligning with view) command from:

ACS tool box	Select the Define ACS (Aligned with View) tool (see Figure 16–19).
Key-in window	**Define ACS View** (or **d a v**) ⏎

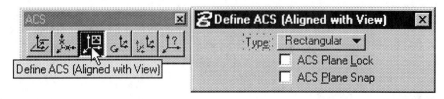

FIGURE 16–19   Invoking the Define ACS (Aligned with View) command from the ACS tool box.

MicroStation prompts:

> Define ACS (Aligned with View) > Select source view *(Place a data point to select the view with which the ACS is to be aligned and define the ACS origin.)*

Rotating the Active ACS

The Rotate Active ACS command rotates the Active ACS. The origin of the ACS is not moved. To rotate the active ACS, invoke the Rotate Active ACS command from:

ACS tool box	Select the Rotate Active ACS tool (see Figure 16–20).
Key-in window	**Rotate ACS** <Absolute/ Relative> [ENTER]

MicroStation displays the Rotate Active ACS dialog box, as shown in Figure 16–21.

Key-in the rotation angles, in degrees, from left to right, for the *X*, *Y*, and *Z* axes. Click the Absolute button to rotate the ACS in relation to the unrotated (top) orientation. Click the Relative button to rotate the ACS in relation to the current orientation. When you are finished, click the DONE button to close the Rotate Active ACS dialog box.

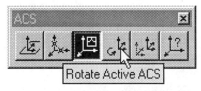

FIGURE 16–20   Invoking the Rotate Active ACS command from the ACS tool box.

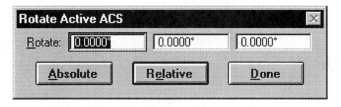

FIGURE 16–21   Rotate Active ACS dialog box.

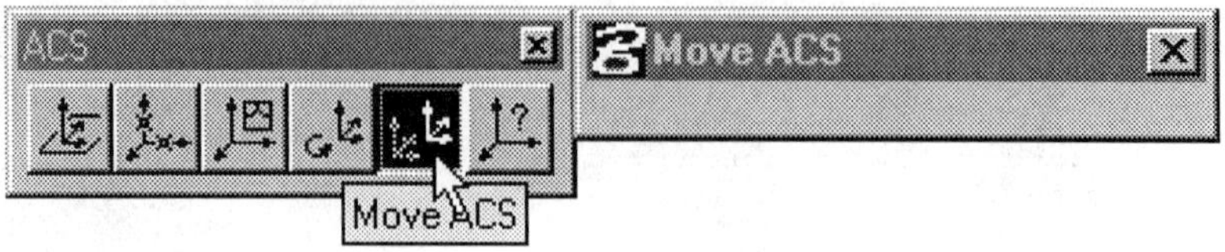

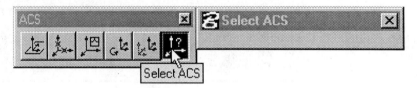

FIGURE 16-22 Invoking the Move ACS command from the ACS tool box.

Moving the Active ACS

The Move ACS command allows you to move the origin of the Active ACS, leaving the directions of the *X*, *Y*, and *Z* axes unchanged. To move the ACS, invoke the Move ACS command from:

ACS tool box	Select the Move ACS tool (see Figure 16–22).
Key-in window	**Move ACS** (or **m a**) [ENTER]

MicroStation prompts:

Move ACS > Define origin *(Place a data point to define the new origin.)*

Selecting the Active ACS

The Select ACS command allows you to identify an ACS for attachment as the active ACS from the saved ACS in each view. To select the ACS, invoke the Select ACS command from:

ACS tool box	Select the Select ACS tool (see Figure 16–23).
Key-in window	**Attach ACS** (**A A**) [ENTER]

MicroStation prompts:

Select ACS > Select auxiliary system @ origin *(Identify the ACS origin from the coordinate triad displayed.)*

FIGURE 16-23 Invoking the Select ACS command from the ACS tool box.

Saving an ACS

You can define any number of ACSs in a design file. Of these, only one can be active at any time. Whenever you define an ACS, you can save it for future use. The Auxiliary Coordinate Systems settings box is used to name, save, attach, or delete an ACS.

Open the Auxiliary Coordinate Systems settings box from:

Pull-down menu	Utilities > Auxiliary Coordinates (or 🄰🄻🄲 + **U**, **X**)

MicroStation displays an Auxiliary Coordinate Systems settings box similar to Figure 16–24.

Key-in the name for the active ACS in the Name edit field. The name is limited to six characters. Select the coordinate system you wish to save with the active ACS from the Type option menu. Key-in the description (optional) of the active ACS in the Description edit field. The description is limited to 27 characters. If necessary, you can change the origin of the active ACS by keying-in the coordinates in the Origin edit field. Click the Save button to save the active ACS for future attachment. MicroStation will display the ACS name, type, and description in the Saved ACS list box.

To attach an ACS as an active ACS, select the name of the ACS from the Saved ACS list box and click the Attach button. To delete an ACS, first highlight the ACS in the Saved ACS list box, then click the Delete button.

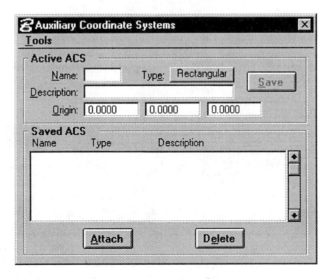

FIGURE 16–24 Auxiliary Coordinate Systems settings box.

> **NOTE:** All the tools that are available in the ACS tool box are also available in the pull-down menu Tools of the Auxiliary Coordinate Systems settings box.

3D PRIMITIVES

MicroStation provides a set of tools to place simple 3D elements that can become the basic building blocks that make up the model. The primitive commands include slab, sphere, cylinder, cone, torus, and wedge.

Place Slab

The Place Slab command places a volume of projection with a rectangular cross section. To place a slab, invoke the Place Slab command from:

3D Primitives tool box	Select the Place Slab tool (see Figure 16–25).
Key-in window	**Place Slab** (or **pl sl**) ⏎

Select the type of surface from the Type option menu in the Tool Settings window. The surface (not capped) option is considered to be open at the base and top, whereas the solid (capped) option is considered to enclose a volume completely.

From the Axis option menu in the Tool Settings window, select the direction in which the height is projected relative to the view or design file axes. If set to Screen X, Screen Y, or Screen Z, the height is projected with the selected screen (view) axis. If set to Drawing X, Drawing Y, or Drawing Z, the height is projected with the selected design file axis.

FIGURE 16–25 Invoking the Place Slab command from the 3D Primitives tool box.

If necessary, turn ON the toggle buttons for Orthogonal, Length, Width, and Height in the Tool Settings window. If Orthogonal is set to ON, the edges are placed orthogonally. If you turn on the constraints for Length, Width, and Height, make sure to key-in appropriate values in the edit fields.

MicroStation prompts:

> Place Slab > Enter start point *(Place a data point or key-in coordinates to define the origin.)*
> Place Slab > Define Length *(Place a data point or key-in coordinates to define the length and rotation angle. If the Length constraint is set to ON, this data point defines the rotation angle.)*
> Place Slab > Define Width *(Place a data point or key-in coordinates to define the width. If the Width constraint is set to ON, this data point accepts the width.)*
> Place Slab > Define Height *(Place a data point or key-in coordinates to define the height. If the Height constraint is set to ON, this data point provides the direction.)*

> **NOTE:** To place a volume of projection with a nonrectangular cross section, use the Construct Surface or Solid of Projection tool in the 3D Free-form Surfaces tool box.

Place Sphere

The Place Sphere command can place a sphere, in which all surface points are equidistant from the center. To place a sphere, invoke the Place Sphere command from:

3D Primitives tool box	Select the Place Sphere tool (see Figure 16–26).
Key-in window	**Place Sphere** (or **pl sp**) ⏎

From the Axis option menu in the Tool Settings window, select the direction of the sphere's axis relative to the view or design file axes. If set to Screen X, Screen Y, or Screen Z, the sphere's axis is set with the selected screen (view) axis. If set to Drawing X, Drawing Y, or Drawing Z, the sphere's axis is set with the selected design file axis.

FIGURE 16–26   Invoking the Place Sphere command from the 3D Primitives tool box.

If necessary, turn ON the toggle button for Radius constraint, and key-in the radius in the Radius edit field.

MicroStation prompts:

> Place Sphere > Enter center point *(Place a data point or key-in coordinates to define the sphere's center.)*
> Place Sphere > Define radius *(Place a data point or key-in coordinates to define the radius. If Radius is set to ON, then the data point accepts the sphere.)*

> **NOTE:** To place a volume of revolution with a noncircular cross section, use the Construct Surface or Solid of Projection tool in the 3D Free-form Surfaces tool box.

Place Cylinder

The Place Cylinder command places a cylinder of equal radius on each end and similar to an extruded circle. To place a cylinder, invoke the Place Cylinder command from:

3D Primitives tool box	Select the Place Cylinder tool (see Figure 16–27).
Key-in window	**Place Cylinder** (or **pl cy**) [ENTER]

Select the type of surface from the Type option menu in the Tool Settings window.

From the Axis option menu in the Tool Settings window, select the direction of the cylinder's axis or its height relative to the view or design file axes. If set to Screen X, Screen Y, or Screen Z, the direction of the cylinder's axis or height is set with the selected screen (view) axis. If set to Drawing X, Drawing Y, or Drawing Z, the direction of the cylinder's axis or height is set with the selected design file axis.

FIGURE 16–27 Invoking the Place Cylinder command from the 3D Primitives tool box.

If necessary, turn ON the toggle buttons for Orthogonal, Radius, and Height in the Tool Settings window. If Orthogonal is set to ON, the cylinder is a right cylinder. If you turn on the constraints for Radius and Height, make sure to key-in appropriate values in the edit fields.

MicroStation prompts:

> Place Cylinder > Enter center point *(Place a data point or key-in coordinates to define the center of the base.)*
> Place Cylinder > Define radius *(Place a data point or key-in coordinates to define the radius. If Radius is set to ON, then the data point accepts the base.)*
> Place Cylinder > Define height *(Place a data point or key-in coordinates to define the height. If Height is set to ON, then the data point accepts the cylinder.)*

Place Cone

The Place Cone command places a cone of unequal radius on each end. To place a cone, invoke the Place Cone command from:

3D Primitives tool box	Select the Place Cone tool (see Figure 16–28).
Key-in window	**Place Cone** (or **pl co**) ⏎

Select the type of surface from the Type option menu in the Tool Settings window.

From the Axis option menu in the Tool Settings window, select the direction of the cone's axis or its height relative to the view or design file axes. If set to Screen X, Screen Y, or Screen Z, the direction of the cone's axis or height is set with the selected screen (view) axis. If set to Drawing X, Drawing Y, or Drawing Z, the direction of the cone's axis or height is set with the selected design file axis.

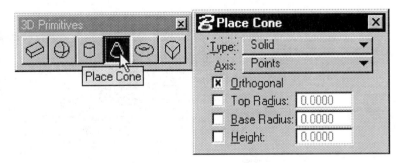

FIGURE 16–28 Invoking the Place Cone command from the 3D Primitives tool box.

If necessary, turn ON the toggle buttons for Orthogonal, Top Radius, Base Radius, and Height in the Tool Settings window. If Orthogonal is set to ON, the cone is a right cone. If you turn on the constraints for Top Radius, Base Radius, and Height, make sure to key-in appropriate values in the edit fields.

MicroStation prompts:

> Place Cone > Enter center point *(Place a data point or key-in coordinates to define the center of the base.)*
> Place Cone > Define radius *(Place a data point or key-in coordinates to define the base radius. If Base Radius is set to ON, then the data point accepts the base.)*
> Place Cone > Define height *(Place a data point or key-in coordinates to define the height and top's center. If Height is set to ON, then the data point defines the top's center; if Orthogonal is set to ON, then the data point defines the direction of the height only.)*
> Place Cone > Define top radius *(Place a data point or key-in coordinates to define the top radius. If Top Radius is set to ON, then the data point accepts the cone.)*

Place Torus

The Place Torus command creates a solid or surface with a donutlike shape. To place a torus, invoke the Place Torus command from:

3D Primitives tool box	Select the Place Torus tool (see Figure 16–29).
Key-in window	**Place Torus** (or **pl to**)

Select the type of surface from the Type option menu in the Tool Settings window.

Select the direction of the axis of revolution relative to the view or design file axes from the Axis option menu in the Tool Settings window. If set to Screen X, Screen Y,

FIGURE 16–29 Invoking the Place Torus command from the 3D Primitives tool box.

or Screen Z, the axis or revolution is set with the selected screen (view) axis. If set to Drawing X, Drawing Y, or Drawing Z, the axis of revolution is set with the selected design file axis.

If necessary, turn ON the toggle buttons for Primary Radius, Secondary Radius, and Angle in the Tool Settings window. If you turn on the constraints for Primary Radius, Secondary Radius, and Angle, make sure to key-in appropriate values in the edit fields.

MicroStation prompts:

> Place Torus > Enter start point *(Place a data point or key-in coordinates to define the start point.)*
> Place Torus > Define center point *(Place a data point or key-in coordinates to define the center point, primary radius, and start angle. If Primary Radius is set to ON, then the data point defines the center and the start angle.)*
> Place Torus > Define angle and secondary radius *(Place a data point or key-in coordinates to define the secondary radius and the sweep angle. If Secondary Radius is set to ON, then the data point defines the sweep angle; if Angle is set to ON, then the data point defines the secondary radius; and if both Secondary Radius and Angle are set to ON, then the data point defines the direction of the sweep angle rotation.)*

Place Wedge

The Place Wedge command creates a wedge—a volume of revolution with a rectangular cross section. To place a wedge, invoke the Place Wedge command from:

3D Primitives tool box	Select the Place Wedge tool (see Figure 16–30).
Key-in window	**Place Wedge** (or **pl w**)

Select the type of surface from the Type option menu in the Tool Settings window.

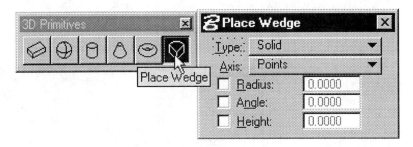

FIGURE 16–30   Invoking the Place Wedge command from the 3D Primitives tool box.

Select the direction of the axis of revolution relative to the view or design file axes from the Axis option menu in the Tool Settings window. If set to Screen X, Screen Y, or Screen Z, the axis of revolution is set with the selected screen (view) axis. If set to Drawing X, Drawing Y, or Drawing Z, the axis of revolution is set with the selected design file axis.

If necessary, turn ON the toggle buttons for Radius, Angle, and Height in the Tool Settings window. If you turn on the constraints for Radius, Angle, and Height, make sure to key-in appropriate values in the edit fields.

MicroStation prompts:

> Place Wedge > Enter start point *(Place a data point or key-in coordinates to define the start point.)*
> Place Wedge > Define center point *(Place a data point or key-in coordinates to define the center point and the start angle. If Radius is set to ON, then the data point defines the start angle.)*
> Place Wedge > Define angle *(Place a data point or key-in coordinates to define the sweep angle. If Angle is set to ON, then the data point defines the direction of the rotation.)*
> Place Wedge > Define Height *(Place a data point or key-in coordinates to define the height. If Height is set to ON, then the data point defines whether the wedge is projected up or down from the start plane.)*

CHANGING THE STATUS—SOLID OR SURFACE

The Change to Active Solid or Surface Status tool can change the status of an element from surface to solid, or vice versa. To change the status, invoke the Change to Active Solid or Surface Status command from:

Modify 3D Surfaces tool box	Select the Change To Active Solid or Surface Status tool (see Figure 16–31).
Key-in window	**Change Surface Cap** (or **chan su c**) [ENTER]

FIGURE 16–31 Invoking the Change to Active Solid or Surface Status command from the Modify 3D Surfaces tool box.

Select the type of surface whose status you wish to change from the Type option menu in the Tool Settings window.

The Tolerance option is used only for B-spline surfaces, in which case two trimmed planes are added as the caps to form the solid.

MicroStation prompts:

> Change to Active Solid or Surface Status > Identify element *(Identify the element whose status is to change.)*
> Change to Active Solid or Surface Status > Accept, change cap/Reject *(Place a data point to accept the change in status, or click the Reset button to reject the operation.)*

USING ACCUDRAW IN 3D

AccuDraw 3D provides the ability to work in a pictorial view rather than the standard, orthogonal views. AccuDraw automatically constrains data points to its drawing plane regardless of its orientation to the view.

Open the AccuDraw window from:

Primary tool box	Select the Start AccuDraw tool (see Figure 16–32).
Key-in window	**Accudraw Activate** (or **acc a**) [ENTER]

The AccuDraw window opens, either as a floating window or docked at the top of the MicroStation workspace.

In 3D, when using rectangular coordinates, the AccuDraw window has an additional field for the *Z* axis. For polar coordinates in 3D, the AccuDraw window has the same two fields as in 2D.

By using AccuDraw keyboard shortcuts you can rotate the drawing plane axes, making it convenient to draw in an isometric view. For example, it is easy with AccuDraw to place a nonplanar complex chain or complex shape in an isometric view in any direction without reverting to an orthogonal view.

FIGURE 16–32 Invoking the Start AccuDraw tool from the Primary tool box.

AccuDraw's ability to adhere to the standard view axes while manipulating your drawing in a pictorial view is so important that it maintains the current orientation from tool to tool.

By default, AccuDraw orients the drawing plane to the view axes, similar to working with 2D design. You can return AccuDraw to this orientation any time the focus is in the AccuDraw window by pressing the **V** key.

To rotate the drawing plane axes to align with the standard top view, focus in the AccuDraw window and press the **T** key. AccuDraw dynamically rotates the compass to indicate the orientation of the drawing plane.

To rotate the drawing plane axes to align with the standard front view, focus in the AccuDraw window and press the **F** key. AccuDraw dynamically rotates the compass to indicate the orientation of the drawing plane.

To rotate the drawing plane axes to align with the standard side (left or right) view, focus in the AccuDraw window and press the **S** key. AccuDraw dynamically rotates the compass to indicate the orientation of the drawing plane.

To rotate the drawing plane axes 90 degrees about an individual axis, focus in the AccuDraw window and press letters **R** and **X** to rotate 90 degrees about the X axis, **R** and **Y** to rotate 90 degrees about the Y axis, and **R** and **Z** to rotate 90 degrees about the Z axis.

To rotate the drawing plane axes interactively, focus in the AccuDraw window and press letters **R** and **A**. Place data points to locate the X axis origin, the direction of the X axis, and the direction of the Y axis.

PROJECTED SURFACES

The Construct Surface or Solid of Projection tool creates a unique three-dimensional object from two-dimensional elements. Line, line string, arc, ellipse, complex chain, complex shape, and B-spline curve are the elements that can be projected to a defined distance. Surfaces formed between the original boundary element and its projection are indicated by straight lines connecting the keypoints.

To project a boundary element, invoke the Construct Surface of Projection command from:

3D Free-Form Surfaces tool box	Select the Construct Surface of Projection tool (see Figure 16–33).
Key-in window	**Construct Surface Projection** (or **constru s p**) ⏎

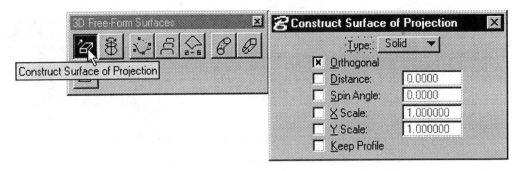

FIGURE 16–33 Invoking the Construct Surface of Projection command from the 3D Free-Form Surfaces tool box.

Select the type of surface from the Type option menu in the Tool Settings window.

If necessary, you can turn ON the toggle buttons for Orthogonal, Distance, Spin Angle, X Scale, Y Scale, and Keep Profile in the Tool Settings window. If Orthogonal is set to ON, the boundary element is projected orthogonally. If you turn on the constraints for Distance, Spin Angle, X Scale, and Y Scale, make sure to key-in appropriate values in the edit fields.

MicroStation prompts:

> Construct Surface Projection > Identify element *(Identify the boundary element.)*
> Construct Surface Projection > Define height *(Place a data point to define the height. If Height is set to ON, then the data point provides the direction.)*

SURFACE OF REVOLUTION

The Construct Surface or Solid of Revolution tool is used to create a unique three-dimensional surface or solid of revolution that is generated by rotating a boundary element about an axis of revolution. Line, line string, arc, ellipse, shape, complex chain, complex shape, and B-spline curve are the elements that can be used in creating a three-dimensional surface or solid. Surfaces created by the boundary element as it is rotated are indicated by arcs connecting the keypoints.

To create a three-dimensional surface or solid of revolution, invoke the Construct Surface of Revolution command from:

3D Free-Form Surfaces tool box	Select the Construct Surface of Revolution tool (see Figure 16–34).
Key-in window	**Construct Surface Revolution** (or **constru s r**) [ENTER]

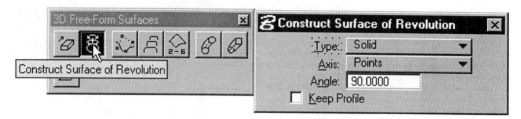

FIGURE 16–34 Invoking the Construct Surface of Revolution command from the 3D Free-Form Surfaces tool box.

Select the type of surface from the Type option menu in the Tool Settings window.

Select the direction of the axis of revolution relative to the view or design file axes from the Axis option menu in the Tool Settings window. If set to Screen X, Screen Y, or Screen Z, the axis of revolution is set with the selected screen (view) axis. If set to Drawing X, Drawing Y, or Drawing Z, the axis of revolution is set with the selected design file axis.

If necessary, turn ON the toggle buttons for Angle and Keep Profile in the Tool Settings window. If you turn on the constraint for Angle, make sure to key-in the appropriate value in the edit field.

MicroStation prompts:

> Construct Surface of Revolution > Identify element *(Identify the boundary element.)*
> Construct Surface of Revolution > Define axis of revolution *(Place a data point or key-in coordinates. If Axis is set to Points, this data point defines one point on the axis of revolution and subsequently MicroStation prompts you for a second data point. If not, this data point defines the axis of revolution.)*
> Construct Surface of Revolution > Accept, continue surface/reset to complete *(Place additional data points to continue, and/or press the Reset button to terminate the sequence.)*

PLACING 2D ELEMENTS

Any two-dimensional elements (such as blocks and circles) that you place with data points without snapping to existing elements will be placed at the active depth of the view. Also, they will be parallel to the screen. Elements that require fewer than three data points to define (such as blocks, circle with radius, circle with diameter/center, polygons) take their orientation from the view being used. The points determine only their dimensions, not their orientation. Elements that require three or more data points to describe (shapes, circle by edge, ellipses, rotated blocks) also provide their planar orientation. Once the first three points have been specified, any further points will fall on the same plane.

CREATING COMPOSITE SOLIDS

MicroStation provides three tools that can create a new composite solid by combining two solids by Boolean operations. There are three basic Boolean operations that can be performed in MicroStation:

> Union
> Intersection
> Difference

Union Operation

The union is the process of creating a new composite solid from two solids. The union operation joins the original solids in such a way that there is no duplication of volume. Therefore, the total resulting volume can be equal to or less than the sum of the volumes in the original solids. The parts of the solids left are determined by their surface normal orientations. These can be changed with the Change Surface Normal tool.

To create a composite solid with the union operation, invoke the Construct Union Between Surfaces command from:

Key-in window	**Boolean Surface Union** (or **bo s u**) ⌨ENTER

MicroStation prompts:

> Construct Union Between Surfaces > Identify first surface *(Identify the first element for union.)*
> Construct Union Between Surfaces > Accept/Reject *(Place a data point to accept the first element for union, or click the Reject button to reject the selection.)*
> Construct Union Between Surfaces > Identify second surface *(Identify the second element for union.)*
> Construct Union Between Surfaces > Accept/Reject *(Place a data point to accept the second element for union, or click the Reject button to reject the union operation.)*

See Figure 16–35 for an example of creating a composite solid by joining two cylinders with the Construct Union Between Surfaces tool.

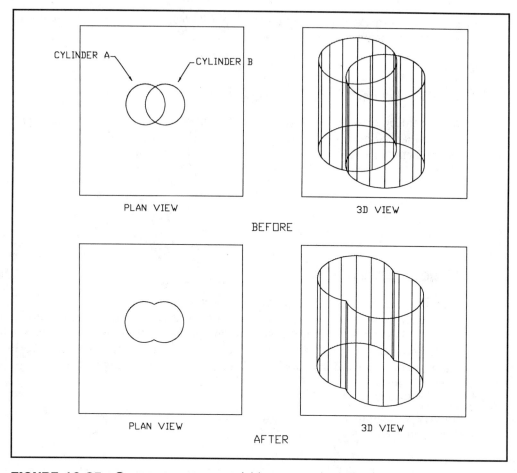

FIGURE 16–35 Creating a composite solid by joining two cylinders via the Construct Union Between Surfaces tool.

Intersection Operation

The intersection is the process of forming a composite solid from only the volume that is common to two solids. The part of each solid that remains is determined by the surface normal orientations. These can be changed with the Change Surface Normal tool.

To create a composite solid with the intersection operation, invoke the Construct Intersection Between Surfaces command from:

Key-in window	**Boolean Surface Intersection** (or **bo s i**) ⏎

MicroStation prompts:

Construct Intersection Between Surfaces > Identify first surface *(Identify the first element for intersection.)*
Construct Intersection Between Surfaces > Accept/Reject *(Place a data point to accept the first element for intersection, or click the Reject button to reject the selection.)*
Construct Intersection Between Surfaces > Identify second surface *(Identify the second element for intersection.)*
Construct Intersection Between Surfaces > Accept/Reject *(Place a data point to accept the second element for intersection, or click the Reject button to reject the intersection operation.)*

See Figure 16–36 for an example of creating a composite solid by joining two cylinders via the Construct Intersection Between Surfaces tool.

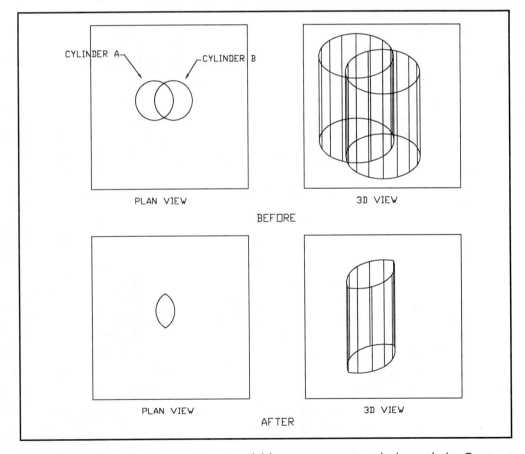

FIGURE 16–36 Creating a composite solid by intersecting two cylinders with the Construct Intersection Between Surfaces tool.

Difference Operation

The difference is the process of forming a composite solid by starting with a solid and removing from it any volume it has in common with a second object. If the entire volume of the second solid is contained in the first solid, then what is left is the first solid minus the volume of the second solid. However, if only part of the volume of the second solid is contained within the first solid, then only the part that is duplicated in the two solids is subtracted. The part of each solid that remains is determined by the surface normal orientations. These can be changed with the Change Surface Normal tool.

To create a composite solid with the difference operation, invoke the Construct Difference Between Surfaces command from:

Key-in window	**Boolean Surface difference** (or **bo s d**) 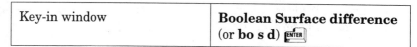

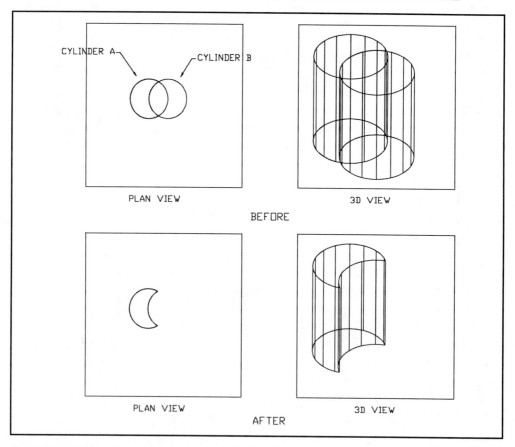

FIGURE 16-37 Creating a composite solid by subtracting Cylinder B from Cylinder A using the Construct Difference Between Surfaces tool.

MicroStation prompts:

> Construct Difference Between Surfaces > Identify first surface *(Identify the first element for the difference operation.)*
>
> Construct Difference Between Surfaces > Accept/Reject *(Place a data point to accept the first element for the difference operations, or click the Reject button to reject the selection.)*
>
> Construct Difference Between Surfaces > Identify second surface *(Identify the second element for the difference operation.)*
>
> Construct Difference Between Surfaces > Accept/Reject *(Place a data point to accept the second element for the difference operation, or click the Reject button to reject the difference operation.)*

See Figure 16–37 for an example of creating a composite solid by joining two cylinders via the Construct Difference Between Surfaces tool.

CHANGE SURFACE NORMAL

The Change Surface Normal tool can change the surface normal direction for a surface. This is useful to control the way the elements are treated while performing the Boolean operations.

To change the surface normal of an element, invoke the Change Surface Normal command from:

Modify 3D Surfaces tool box	Select the Change Surface Normal tool (see Figure 16–38).
Key-in window	**Change surface normal** (or **chan s n**) ⏎

MicroStation prompts:

> Change Surface Normal > Identify element *(Identify the element; surface normals are displayed.)*
>
> Change Surface Normal > Reverse normals, or RESET *(Place a data point to accept the change in the normal direction.)*

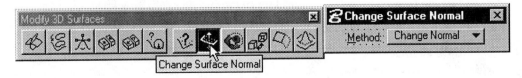

FIGURE 16–38 Invoking the Change Surface Normal command from the Modify 3D Surfaces tool box.

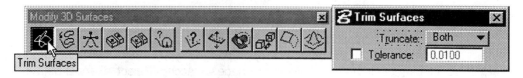

FIGURE 16-39 Invoking the Trim Surfaces command from the Modify 3D Surfaces tool box.

TRIM SURFACES

The Trim Surfaces tool lets you trim two elements (surface of projection or revolution, cones, or B-spline surfaces) to their common intersection or trim just one element. To trim two elements to their common intersection, invoke the Trim Surfaces command from:

Modify 3D Surfaces tool box	Select the Trim Surfaces tool (see Figure 16–39).
Key-in window	**Trim Surface** (or **tri s**) (ENTER)

Select one of the three options available from the Truncate option menu in the Tool Settings window. Selection of Both trims both surfaces to their command intersection. The Single selection trims the first surface to its intersection with the second element. And the None selection will not trim either surface.

MicroStation prompts:

Trim Surfaces > Identify first surface *(Identify the first surface.)*
Trim Surfaces > Identify second surface *(Identify the second surface.)*
Trim Surfaces > Accept/Reject *(Place a data point to accept the trim, or click the Reject button to cancel the operation.)*

CONSTRUCT FILLET BETWEEN SURFACES

The Construct Fillet Between Surfaces tool helps you construct a 3D fillet between two surfaces. The fillet is placed by sweeping an arc with a specified radius (constant radius), or two arcs with different radii (variable radius), along the common intersection curve. The fillet is created in the area pointed to by the surface normals of both surfaces.

To fillet between surfaces, invoke the Construct Fillet Between Surfaces command from:

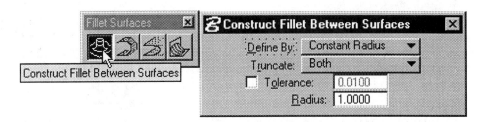

FIGURE 16–40 Invoking the Construct Fillet Between Surfaces command from the Fillet Surfaces tool box.

Fillet Surfaces tool box	Select the Construct Fillet Between Surfaces tool (see Figure 16–40).
Key-in window	**Fillet Surface (or fill su)** [ENTER]

Select one of the two available options (Constant Radius or Variable Radius) from the Define By option in the Tool Settings window. With Constant Radius, the fillet is drawn with a fixed radius; with Variable Radius, the fillet sweeps from the first radius to the second. For Constant Radius, key-in the Radius of the fillet to be drawn. In the case of Variable Radius, key-in both the initial and the final radius.

The Truncate option menu sets which surface(s) are truncated at the point of tangency with the fillet.

MicroStation prompts:

> Construct Fillet Between Surfaces > Identify first surface *(Identify the first surface.)*
> Construct Fillet Between Surfaces > Accept/Reject *(Click the Data button to accept the first surface selection.)*
> Construct Fillet Between Surfaces > Identify second surface *(Identify the second surface.)*
> Construct Fillet Between Surfaces > Accept/Reject *(Click the Data button to accept the second surface selection.)*
> Construct Fillet Between Surfaces > Accept/Reject *(Click the Data button to accept the fillet, or click the Reject button to cancel the operation.)*

CONSTRUCT CHAMFER BETWEEN SURFACES

The Construct Chamfer Between Surfaces tool enables you to construct a 3D chamfer between two surfaces by a specified length along the common intersection curve. The chamfer is created in the area pointed to by the surface normals of both surfaces.

FIGURE 16–41 Invoking the Construct Chamfer Between Surfaces command from the Fillet Surfaces tool box.

To chamfer between surfaces, invoke the Construct Chamfer Between Surfaces command from:

Fillet Surfaces tool box	Select the Construct Chamfer Between Surfaces tool (see Figure 16–41).
Key-in window	**Chamfer Surface** (or **chamf su**) ![ENTER]

The Truncate option menu sets which surface(s) are truncated at the point of tangency with the chamfer.

Key-in the Chamfer length in the Chamfer Length edit field.

MicroStation prompts:

> Construct Chamfer Between Surfaces > Identify first surface *(Identify the first surface.)*
> Construct Chamfer Between Surfaces > Accept/Reject *(Click the Data button to accept the first surface selection.)*
> Construct Chamfer Between Surfaces > Identify second surface *(Identify the second surface.)*
> Construct Chamfer Between Surfaces > Accept/Reject *(Click the Data button to accept the second surface selection.)*
> Construct Fillet Between Surfaces > Accept/Reject *(Click the Data button to accept the chamfer, or click the Reject button to cancel the operation.)*

PLACING TEXT

MicroStation provides two options to place text in a 3D design: (1) placing text (view-dependent) in such a way that it appears planar to the screen in the view in which the data point is placed but rotated in the other views, or (2) placing text (view-independent) in such a way that it appears planar to the screen in all views.

To place text (view-dependent), click the Place Text icon in the Text tool box, select By Origin from the Method option menu, and follow the prompts. To place text (view-independent), click the Place Text icon in the Text tool box, select View Ind from the Method option menu, and follow the prompts. Text parameters are set up in the same way as in the 2D design.

FENCE MANIPULATIONS

Fences are used in a three-dimensional design in much the same way as in a two-dimensional design (see Chapter 5). The difference is that a three-dimensional fence defines a volume. The volume is defined by the fenced area and the display depth of the view in which the fence is placed. The Fence lock options work the same way as in a two-dimensional design.

CELL CREATION AND PLACEMENT

The procedure for creating and placing cells in 3D design is the same as in 2D design (see Chapter 10). Before you create a 3D cell, make sure the display depth is set to include all elements to be used in the cell and the origin is defined at an appropriate active depth. If a normal cell was created in the top view and then placed in the front view, it will appear as it did in the top view and rotated in other views. In other words, the normal cell is placed as view-dependent, whereas a point cell when placed will appear planar to the screen in all views. A point cell is placed view-independent.

You can attach a 2D cell library to a 3D design file, but the cells will have no depth and will be placed at the active depth of the view in which you are working. However, you cannot create 3D cells and store them in a 2D cell library.

> **NOTE:** You cannot attach a 3D cell library to a 2D design file.

DIMENSIONING

The procedure for dimensioning setup and placement in 3D design is similar to that for 2D design (see Chapter 8). The main difference is that you have to consider on which plane you want the dimensioning to be located. Before you place dimensions in a 3D design, make sure the appropriate option is selected from the Alignment option menu in the Linear Dimension tool box. The view measurement axis measures the projection of the element along the view's horizontal or vertical axis. The true measurement axis measures the actual distance between two points, not the projected distance. And the drawing measurement axis measures the projection of an element along the design cube coordinate system's axis.

RENDERING

Shading, or rendering, can turn your 3D model into a realistic, eye-catching image. MicroStation's rendering options give you complete control over the appearance of your final images. You can add lights and control lighting in your design and also define the reflective qualities of individual surfaces in your design, making objects appear dull or shiny. You can create the rendered image of your three-dimensional model entirely within MicroStation. This section provides an overview of the various options available for rendering. Refer to the *MicroStation Reference Guide* for a more detailed description of various options.

Setting Up Cameras

In establishing a viewing position in MicroStation, the assumption you must make is that you are, as it were, looking through a camera to see the image. By default, MicroStation places the camera at a right angle to a view's *XY* plane. If necessary, you can move or reposition the camera to view the model from a different viewing angle.

To enable or disable the default camera setting and make changes to the camera setup, invoke the Camera Settings tool from:

3D View Control tool box	Select the Camera Settings tool (see Figure 16–42).

Select one of the available options from the Camera Settings option menu in the Tool Settings window.

- Turn On: Turns on the camera in a view or views
- Turn Off: Turns off the camera in a view or views
- Set Up: Turns on the camera in a view and sets the camera target and position. The target is the focal point (center) of a camera view. The position is the design cube location from which the model is viewed with the camera. Objects beyond the

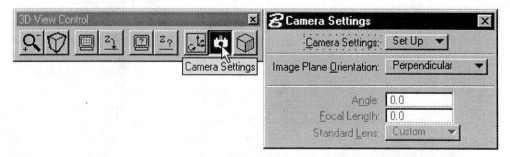

FIGURE 16–42   Invoking the Camera Settings tool from the 3D View Control tool box.

camera target appear smaller; objects in front of the camera target appear larger and may be outside of the viewing pyramid.
- Move: Moves the camera position
- Target: Moves the target

Select one of the available options from the Image Plane Orientation option menu in the Tool Settings window:

- Perpendicular: Perpendicular to the camera direction
- Parallel to X axis: Parallel to the view X axis; analogous to a bellows camera
- Parallel to Y axis: Parallel to the view Y axis; analogous to a bellows camera
- Parallel to Z axis: Parallel to the view Z axis; all vertical lines (along the axis) appear parallel

Set the lens angle in degrees and the lens focal length in millimeters in the Angle and Focal Length edit fields, respectively.

Select one of the available options from the Standard Lens option menu if you wish to use the standard lens type commonly used by photographers. MicroStation sets the appropriate lens angle and focal length.

MicroStation prompts depend on the options selected in the Tool Settings window.

Placement of Light Sources

The lighting setup is equally as important as setting the camera angle for producing a high-quality rendered image. MicroStation allows you four types of lighting:

Ambient lighting
Flashbulb lighting
Solar lighting
Source lighting, including point, spot, and distant

Ambient lighting is a uniform light that surrounds your model. *Flashbulb lighting* is a localized, intense light that appears to emanate from the camera position. *Solar lighting* is sunlight. By defining your location on the earth in latitude, longitude, day, month, and time, you can simulate lighting for most exterior architectural projects. Ambient, flashbulb, and solar lighting are set in the Global settings box invoked from the Rendering submenu of the pull-down menu Settings.

Source lighting is achieved by placing light sources in the form of cells. The Micro-Station program comes with three light source cells (point lights—PNTLT; spot lights—SPOTLT; and distant lights—DISTLT) provided in the LIGHTING.CEL cell library.

Point light can be thought of as a ball of light. It radiates beams of light in all directions. Such a light also has more natural characteristics. Its brilliance may be diminished as an object moves away from the source of light. An object that is near a point light will appear brighter; an object that is farther away will appear darker.

Spot lights are very much like the kind of spotlight you might be accustomed to seeing at a theater or auditorium. Spot lights produce a cone of light toward a target that you specify.

Distant light gives off a fairly straight beam of light that radiates in one direction, and its brilliance remains constant so that an object close to the light will receive as much light as a distant object.

Before you place the light cells, adjust the settings in the Source Lighting settings box invoked from the Rendering submenu of the pull-down menu Settings. Micro-Station provides various options under the pull-down menu Tool, in the Settings box.

Rendering Methods

MicroStation provides seven different tools to render a view. Depending on the needs and availability of the hardware, you can choose one of the seven tools to render the model.

To render a view, invoke the Render command from:

3D View Control tool box	Select the Render tool (see Figure 16–43).

Select the type of area or element to be rendered from the Target option menu in the Tool Settings window. The available options include View, Fence (contents), and Element.

Select one of the available options (Wiremesh, Hidden Line, Filled Hidden Line, Constant, Smooth, or Phong) from the Shading Mode option menu in the Tool Settings window. The Shading Mode option menu sets the rendering method.

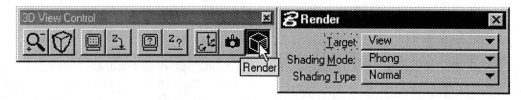

FIGURE 16–43   Invoking the Render command from the 3D View Control tool box.

- Wiremesh: Similar to the default wireframe display, all elements are transparent and do not obscure other elements.
- Hidden Line: Displays only the element parts that would actually be visible.
- Filled Hidden Line: Identical to a Hidden Line option display except that the polygons are filled with the element color.
- Constant: Displays each element as one or more polygons filled with a single (constant) color. The color is computed once for each polygon, from the element color, material characteristics, and lighting configurations.
- Smooth: Displays the appearance of curved surfaces more realistically than in constant shaded models because polygon color is computed at polygon boundaries and color is blended across polygon interiors.
- Phong: Displays the image after recomputing the color of each pixel. Phong shading is useful for producing high-quality images when speed is not critical.
- Phong Anti-alias: Displays the image with reduced jagged edges that are particularly noticeable on low-resolution displays. The additional time required for anti-aliasing is especially worthwhile when saving images for presentation, publication, or animated sequences.
- Phong Stereo: Renders a view with a stereo effect that is visible when seen through 3D (red/blue) glasses. Stereo Phong shading takes twice as long as Phong because two images—one each from the perspective of the right and left eyes—are rendered and combined into one color-coded image.

DRAWING COMPOSITION

One of MicroStation's useful features is the ability to compose multiple views (standard and saved) on a drawing sheet. This will allow you to plot multiple views on one sheet of paper—what-you-see-is-what-you-get (WYSIWYG). The Drawing Composition settings box automates the process of attaching the views of the model. The views are attached as reference files. An attached view in a sheet file can be any standard (top, bottom, right, left, front, back, or isometric), fitted view, or any saved view of a model file. Standard views can be clipped or set to display only certain levels. A view of the model file can be attached in any position at any scale. MicroStation provides a tool that allows you to group a set of views. A group of attached views can be moved, scaled, or detached as one. If necessary, you can remove or add a view to a group. In addition, MicroStation provides a tool that allows you to attach a view by folding an attached view about an orthogonal axis or a line defined by two data points. A folded view is automatically aligned and grouped with the attached view from which it is folded.

Open the Drawing Composition settings box from:

Pull-down menu	File > Drawing Composition (or ![ALT] + **F**, **D**)

MicroStation displays a Drawing Composition settings box similar to Figure 16–44.

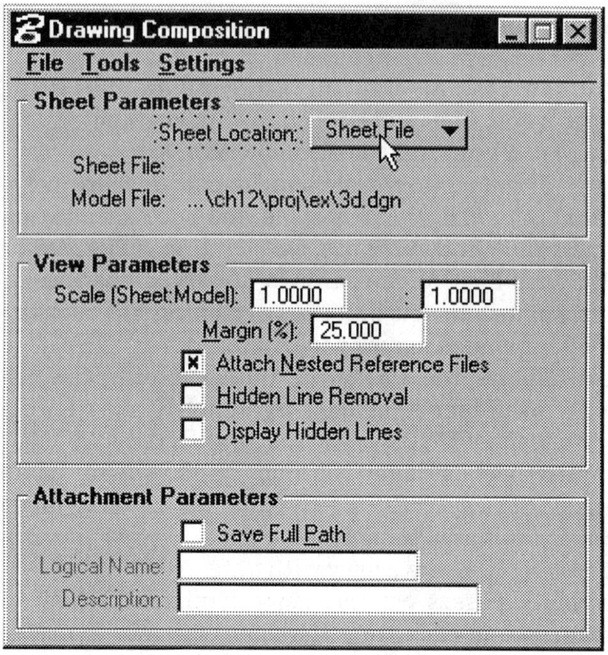

FIGURE 16–44 Drawing Composition settings box.

MicroStation provides two different methods by which you can place the model on the sheet. Method 1 consists of creating or opening a sheet and placing the model (standard views or saved views). In Method 2, you designate one of the view windows in the model design for drawing composition, open an existing border file as a reference file, then place the model (standard views or saved views).

Method 1

Select Sheet File from the Sheet Location option menu located in the Sheet Parameters area, as shown in Figure 16–44.

Creating a New Sheet File To create a new sheet file, open the Create Sheet File dialog box from:

Drawing Composition settings box	File > New > Sheet... (or [ALT] + F, N, S)

MicroStation displays the Create Sheet File dialog box. The default sheet seed file is the SEED.SHT. If necessary, change the seed file by clicking the Seed button. MicroStation displays the Select Sheet File dialog box. Select the appropriate seed file, and click the OK button to close the dialog box. Table 16-1 lists the seed sheet files delivered with the MicroStation program.

Table 16–1.   Seed Sheet Files That Come with MicroStation

SEED FILE	SIZE
Seed.sht	11 × 17
Seedah.sht	A (horizontal orientation)
Seedav.sht	A (vertical orientation)
Seedb.sht	B
Seedc.sht	C
Seedd.sht	D
Seede.sht	E
Seedf.sht	F

Key-in the name of the new sheet file in the Files edit field, and click the OK button. MicroStation displays the name of the newly created sheet file in the Drawing Composition settings box.

Opening an Existing Sheet File   To open an existing sheet file, open the Open Sheet File dialog box from:

Drawing Composition settings box	File > Open > Sheet... (or [ALT] + **F, O, S**)

MicroStation displays the Open Sheet File dialog box. Select the appropriate sheet file and click the OK button. MicroStation displays the name of the opened sheet file in the Drawing Composition settings box.

Opening a Design File to Place the Views   To open a design file to place the views on the active sheet file, open the Open Model File dialog box from:

Drawing Composition settings box	File > Open > Model... (or [ALT] + **F, O, M**)

MicroStation displays the Open Design File dialog box. Select the appropriate design file and click the OK button. MicroStation displays the name of the opened design file in the Drawing Composition settings box.

Use one of the tools provided in the pull-down menu Tools in the Drawing Composition settings box to attach the views of the model. Refer to the section on "Attaching Views" for a detailed description of various methods of attaching the views.

Method 2

Create a new design file or open an existing design file. Select Sheet View from the Sheet Location option menu located in the Sheet Parameters area of the Drawing Composition settings box as shown in Figure 16–45.

The levels used for text and dimensions in the sheet view are set in the Sheet Parameters section of the settings box. The View Annotation Level edit field sets the level for dimensions and text that are to be displayed only in one sheet view (level 63 is the default). The Sheet Annotation Level edit field sets the level for any annotations to be displayed in the drawing sheet (level 62 is the default).

Designate a view window as a sheet view from:

Drawing Composition settings box	Tools > Open Sheet View > <number of the view>

If necessary, set the Scale in the View Parameters section of the Drawing Composition settings box.

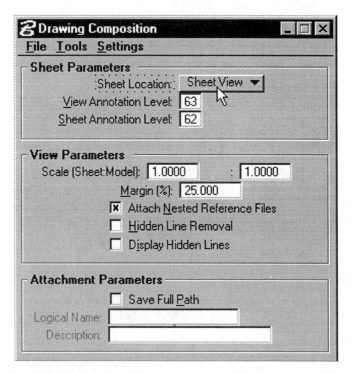

FIGURE 16–45 Drawing Composition settings box with Sheet View selected.

Attaching a Border Open the Attach Border File dialog box from:

Drawing Composition settings box	Tools > Attach Border > Fitted (or ⌨ + **T, B, F**)

MicroStation opens the Attach Border File dialog box. Select the border file and click the OK button.

You can also attach the saved view of a border file by invoking the Saved View... option under the Attach Border menu.

Invoke one of the tools provided in the pull-down menu Tools in the Drawing Composition settings box to attach the views of the model. Refer to the next section, on "Attaching Views," for a detailed description of various methods of attaching the views.

Attaching Views

Following are the available methods by which you can attach views of the model onto a sheet.

Attaching a Standard, Fitted View of the Model To attach one of the standard views (top, bottom, left, right, front, back, isometric, or right isometric), invoke the Attach Standard View command from:

Drawing Composition settings box	Tools > Attach Standard > (select one of the standard views)

MicroStation prompts:

> Attach Standard View > Identify view center *(Identify the view center to place the view.)*

MicroStation places the selected standard view. Before you place the view, if necessary you can change the scale factor in the View Parameters section of the Drawing Composition settings box.

Attaching Saved Views To attach saved views, invoke the Attach Saved View command from:

Drawing Composition settings box	Tools > Attach Saved View (or ⌨ + **T, S**)

MicroStation prompts:

> Attach Saved View > Identify view center *(Identify the view center to place the view.)*

MicroStation places the selected saved view. Before you place the view, if necessary you can change the scale factor in the View Parameters section of the Drawing Composition settings box.

Attaching a Copy of the View To attach a copy of the view, invoke the Attach the Copy of Existing Attachment command from:

Drawing Composition settings box	Tools > Attach Copy (or ⌨ + T, C)

MicroStation prompts:

> Attach the Copy of Existing Attachment > Identify attachment *(Identify an element in the attached view to be copied.)*
> Attach the Copy of Existing Attachment > Accept/Copy attachment *(Place a data point where you want to place the copy of the attached view.)*

Attaching a View by Folding It Orthogonally To attach a view of the model by folding it orthogonally about the edge of an attached view, invoke Attach Auxiliary By Orthogonal Fold command from:

Drawing Composition settings box	Tools > Attach Folded > Orthogonal (or ⌨ + T, F, O)

MicroStation prompts:

> Attach Auxiliary By Orthogonal Fold > Identify principle attachment *(Identify an element in an attached view from which to fold the new attached view.)*
> Attach Auxiliary By Orthogonal Fold > Accept @ fold line *(Identify the edge of the attached view about which the new attached view is to be folded.)*
> Attach Auxiliary By Orthogonal Fold > Identify view center *(Place a data point to position the view.)*
> Attach Auxiliary By Orthogonal Fold > *(Continue identifying the fold line to place additional views, or click the Reset button to terminate the command sequence.)*

Attaching a View by Folding It from an Attached View To attach a view of the model by folding it from an attached view about a line defined by two points, invoke the Auxiliary View By Fold Line command from:

Drawing Composition settings box	<u>T</u>ools > Attach <u>F</u>olded > <u>A</u>bout Line (or 🔲 + **T, F, A**)

MicroStation prompts:

> Auxiliary View By Fold Line > Identify principle attachment *(Identify an element in an attached view from which to fold the new attached view.)*
>
> Auxiliary View By Fold Line > Accept at fold line end point *(Place a data point to define one end point of the line about which the new attached view will be folded.)*
>
> Auxiliary View By Fold Line > Identify fold line end point *(Place a data point to define the other end point of the line about which the new attached view will be folded.)*
>
> Auxiliary View By Fold Line > Identify fold line end point *(Continue identifying the fold line to place additional views, or click the Reset button to terminate the command sequence.)*

Additional Tools for Manipulating Views

Following are the additional tools available in the pull-down menu Tools.

Group The Group option allows you to add to or remove attached view(s) to or from a group.

Clip The Clip option allows you to clip a portion of the attached view. Refer to Chapter 12 on Reference Files for a detailed explanation on Clipping.

Move The Move option allows yout to move an attached view of the model, a group of views, or all attached views.

Scale The Scale option allows you to set the scale (Master Scale:Reference Scale) of an attached view of the model, a group of views, or all attached views.

Detach The Detach option allows you to detach a view of the model, a group of views, or all attached views.

Once you set up all the views, add any annotations and title block information. Invoke the Plot... command and plot the design.

DRAWING EXERCISES 16–1 THROUGH 16–5

Lay out the objects shown in 3D form. Create the design to the given dimensions.

Exercise 16–1

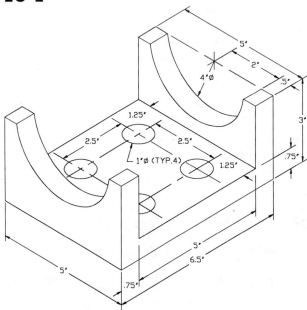

Exercise 16–2

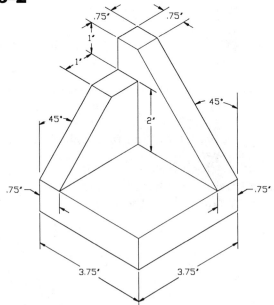

Exercise 16–3

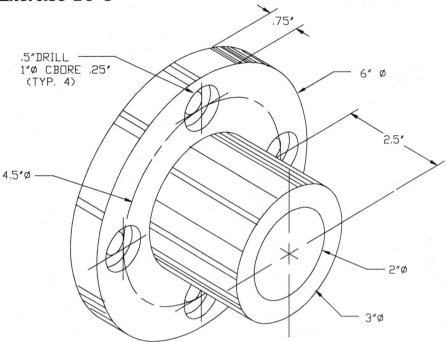

.5"DRILL
1"Ø CBORE .25'
(TYP. 4)

.75'

6" Ø

2.5'

4.5'Ø

2"Ø

3"Ø

Exercise 16–4

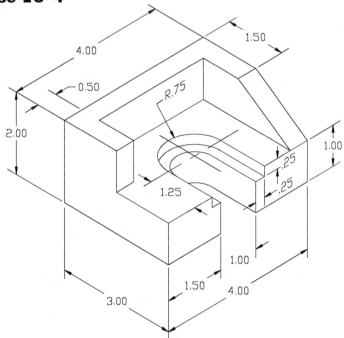

4.00

1.50

0.50

R.75

2.00

1.00

.25

.25

1.25

1.00

1.50

1.50

3.00

4.00

Exercise 16–5

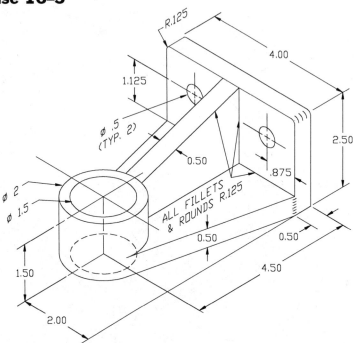

A

MICROSTATION PULL-DOWN MENU LAYOUT AND TOOL BOXES

• • • • • • • • • • • • • • • •

(See tear-out sheet in back of book.)

APPENDIX

B

TABLET MENU

(See figure on following page.)

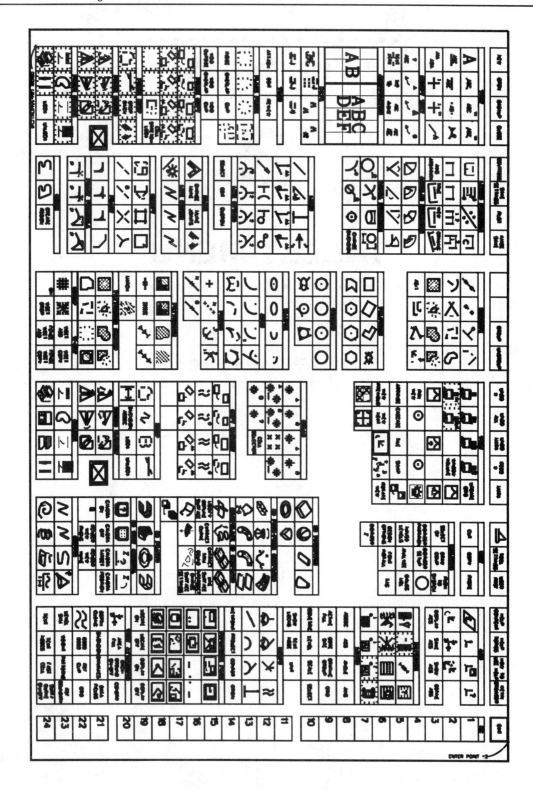

APPENDIX

C

DOS AND FILE HANDLING

This section of the appendix briefly explains the DOS-related features, commands, and terms that are useful to the operator of the MicroStation program.

DISKS

Floppy disks are the media on which software is stored. The software is in the form of files. Once properly formatted, a floppy disk is addressed simply by the name of the drive in which it is inserted.

Usually floppy disk drives are labeled drive A and (if there is a second floppy drive) drive B. Important uses of the floppy disk are:

1. Safe backup storage of files.
2. Transfer of files from one computer to another.
3. Temporary repository of files for support or editing without copying them onto the fixed disk.

The fixed disk (or hard disk drive), like the floppy disk, stores software in the form of files. As its name says, it is fixed and not removable for the purpose of transferring files to another computer. The main advantage is its large capacity, being equal to that of hundreds of floppy disks. Fixed drives are usually labeled drive C and (if a second fixed drive is installed) drive D. The fixed drive is where the main Micro-Station program files are stored. Because of the risk of fixed disk failure (beyond recoverability of files), all important files on a fixed disk should also be stored on backup floppy disks or backup tapes. These backup files are not the same as the files that are created automatically by some programs and have the file extension .BAK. Backup files that are copied to floppy disks for purpose of safekeeping usually have the same name and file extension as the file they back up.

FILES

File specifications (or filespecs) include the drive label, the file name, and an optional extension. The directory path is sometimes included when accessing a file. The drive label and directory path do not always have to be included, as will be explained later.

A file contains data and is stored under a particular file name. The data on the file may be a simple two-line batch file, a ten-page letter, or a large, encrypted and compiled executable program like MicroStation's MGDS.EXE file or one of your larger design files with the file extension of .DGN. When DOS commands operate on a file, they usually operate on the whole file as a unit. Programs like MicroStation, line editors, word processors, and data base manipulators (which are all program files themselves) create or open data files, edit them, and close them. Being able to create files and knowing how and when to address them are skills necessary to do advanced file editing and manipulation.

DRIVES AND DIRECTORIES

Drives and directories are established for the purpose of storing files. The combination of a fixed drive and a floppy drive is like a warehouse with a railroad loading dock attached. DOS is the warehouse manager, and does the following when properly instructed by the user:

1. Moves the files into and out of storage.
2. Takes you to a program file that can operate on a data file (reading, editing, and printing are all done by means of a program file).
3. Takes you to a data file and opens it for you to read, edit, or print a copy of the file.
4. Closes the file when you are through and takes you to another set of program and data files.

The main warehouse is the fixed drive. You may have the manager, DOS, store all the files in the open space, known as the *root directory*. But when enough files start to fill the root directory, it becomes unwieldy. Just listing all the files causes the screen to fill and scroll, making it cumbersome to locate and identify particular files. Therefore, DOS can create storerooms in the warehouse called subdirectories, which conveniently allow you to store groups of related files apart from other groups of files.

A subdirectory may even have its own sub-subdirectories, like storerooms within the storerooms in the warehouse.

It is advisable to keep the root directory (the area of the warehouse outside of all storerooms) as free as possible. Only the needed DOS command files and batch files (to be explained later) should be stored in the root directory. All other data and program files should be stored in subdirectories created especially for them. It is also advisable to use short names for the subdirectories. They will have to be keyed-in from the keyboard as part of the path to the files. Keep them as short as possible and still have them identifiable. If you have created a directory named User-Com, you will be surprised how quickly you will get tired of keying-in "User-Com," or even "User," every time you key-in the path to your file. You will soon get used to remembering "UC" or just "U" as the name of the directory that your files are stored in, and it is much easier to key-in. However, if most of your file manipulations are done with the help of a utility program such as Norton Utilities™, PCTOOLS™, or XTREE™, then longer, more recognizable directory names are easily accessed without the burden of keying-in.

The floppy drive is like the railroad loading dock. The disk inserted in the drive is like a railroad car parked at the loading dock. It is accessible through the label for the drive it is in.

It is possible, though not as commonly done as on the fixed drive, to create subdirectories on the floppy disk while it is parked in the floppy drive. These subdirectories are like storerooms and rooms in the main warehouse. They stay with that diskette and when it leaves the dock (the floppy drive), the subdirectories go with it. A new car (floppy diskette) brings its own rooms (subdirectories) with it if they have been created previously by DOS.

As an experienced MicroStation operator, you will soon learn your way around drives and directories in order to get to appropriate files. The most common arrangement is to have the computer start up (boot-up) with the floppy drive door open. The computer, after memory check, looks at drive A (floppy) first, finds it inaccessible, redirects itself to the fixed drive, looking for the disk operating system on a file called COMMAND.COM. When the boot-up is complete, you are automatically logged on to the fixed drive (usually labeled C) and a C:\> or C> prompt appears on the display screen. Failure to keep the A drive (floppy) open during boot-up will cause a message to appear regarding a "nonsystem disk...". However, if the A drive contains a diskette with the COMMAND.COM file on it, an A:> or A> prompt would appear, indicating that you were "logged on" to the A drive. This would be your current drive until you invoked the DOS command to change drives.

Should the "nonsystem disk..." message appear, simply open the floppy drive door and press any key. The redirection to drive C should proceed without further problems.

CHANGING DRIVES

To change from one drive to another, simply enter the new drive letter followed by a colon. For example, while on drive A the prompt reads:

> A>

After you key-in **C:**, the prompt reads:

> A>C:

After you press ⌨, the prompt reads:

> C>

You are now logged on to drive C. It is your current drive. Reversing the above: **C>A:** produces A> and logs you back on to drive A, the floppy drive.

LOGGING ON TO A DRIVE AND DIRECTORY

The importance of being logged on to a particular drive and directory depends on the type of file you are operating with. As mentioned before, some files just contain data to be operated on by other programs. These data files are letters, designs, or lists of items, such as a phone list or bill of materials. Other files are, of course, the programs themselves.

If you decide to delve into customizing MicroStation, one of the first files you become involved with is the MENU file (with the extension .MNU). It is an excellent example of a file that, while being created or edited is a data file, but when completed becomes a program file. Note with care which drive and directory you are currently logged onto and which drive and subdirectory the program and data files are on at the time a command is invoked. It is possible that four different locations (drives and directories) could be involved at the same time during one command.

As mentioned previously, diskettes and fixed disks are addressed through their drive label. To access or operate on a file stored on a floppy disk in drive A (when drive A is not the current drive), you must prefix the file specification with "A:" For example:

> C>**TYPE A:MYNEW.UCM**

In order for the DOS command called TYPE to operate on the file called MYNEW.UCM, you must address MYNEW.UCM through its drive label, followed by a colon if you are not logged onto drive A. If you are logged onto drive A you may address the file without using the drive label prefix, as follows:

> A:>**TYPE MYNEW.UCM**

Three things must be taken into consideration concerning drives when operating on files:

1. **Current Drive**—You need to know which drive you are presently logged onto.
2. **Source and Target Drives**—You need to know the drive(s) where the source file and the target are. For instance, in using the DOS COPY command, the *source* is where the file is stored before the command is used and the *target* is where the new copy of the file will reside.
3. **Internal or External DOS Command**—It is advisable to study the list of the particular DOS commands you will be using in order to know if they are internal or external commands. For example, the DOS commands COPY and TYPE are internal commands. They reside within the COMMAND.COM program file and can be invoked from any directory while logged on any drive because COMMAND.COM was loaded into RAM when the computer was booted up.

FIRST THE RULE

The DOS command PRINT is an external command. It requires access to the program file called PRINT.COM. In versions of DOS prior to 3.0, it can be invoked only when the directory that it is stored on is the current directory of its drive. The commands with the extension of .COM, .EXE, or .BAT are accessed in a similar manner.

In DOS version 3.0 and later, accessing files on drives other than the current one can be done in an easier fashion than before. If the computer environment has previously been setup with a PATH to the .COM, .EXE, or .BAT file, then they can be invoked from another directory than their own. For example, PRINT.COM is on the directory named DOSX. When the computer is booted up enter the following:

PATH=\DOSX

Then while in the USTATION directory you may simply enter:

PRINT MYNEW.MNU

and DOS will go to the DOSX and use the PRINT command to print the file on the USTATION directory named MYNEW.MNU.

The "PATH=" entry is best included in the AUTOEXEC.BAT file.

By studying carefully and understanding the following examples, the novice can apply the same approach to other file handling procedures and programs, including his or her own custom programs that involve file handling. Even the moderately experienced DOS user can get into some procedure habits that might be improved upon.

Example 1

Objective: *Print the file named MYNEW.UCM*
Current Drive: **A**
Current Directory: *Root directory (of Drive A)*
Drive where MYNEW.UCM is stored: **C**
Directory where MYNEW.UCM is stored: **\USER**
Drive where PRINT.COM is stored: **C**
Directory where PRINT.COM is stored: **\DOS**

Entering the following will work under one condition:

A>C:PRINT C:\USER\MYNEW.UCM

Even though the path to the file is correct, the path to the DOS command PRINT will work only if, when you changed from drive C, the current directory on drive C was \DOS (in older versions of DOS) or the PATH= \DOS\ has been entered previously. Otherwise, if you had been in the root directory or in the \USER directory when you left drive C (by entering A: to get to drive A), then the path "C:" to PRINT.COM would not work.

Example 2

Objective: *Print the file named MYNEW.UCM*
Current Drive: **C** *(Changed from Example 1)*
Current Directory: **\USER** *(Changed from Example 1)*
Drive where MYNEW.UCM is stored: **C**
Directory where MYNEW.UCM is stored: **\USER**
Drive where PRINT.COM is stored: **C**
Directory where PRINT.COM is stored: **\DOS**

Entry 1:

C>CD\DOS

This logs you onto the DOS directory, where the program file called PRINT.COM is stored. It is an external DOS command.

Entry 2:

C>PRINT \USER\MYNEW.UCM

This will work now.

Review

Files may be accessed through their paths no matter which drive and directory you are logged onto. The drive label and/or directory path may be omitted when you are logged onto the same drive and/or directory as the file you are accessing.

Internal DOS commands may be invoked from any drive and directory—but not at all times. While a program is running, DOS may or may not be accessible, depending on the program.

External DOS commands require one of three things: One option is to be logged on to the same directory as the DOS program file for that command. Another option: If you are on another drive, then the drive on which the DOS command program file is stored must have as its current directory the one on which the DOS program file is stored (this applies to older versions of DOS with or without the PATH= entry). The third option is to have entered a "PATH=" command so that DOS will seek out the .COM, .EXE, or .BAT file from any directory.

NOW THE EXCEPTION—PATH

The following example is a method of using external DOS commands from a directory other than the one on which they are stored. This shows how to set up a PATH to their directory. Care must be taken in doing this. If the computer environment has already had a PATH set up to include other directories, then arbitrarily using the DOS command called PATH might nullify the other preset paths. It is best to include the path to external DOS commands with the path to other necessary directories in the PATH command in the AUTOEXEC.BAT file, as mentioned previously. An example would be as follows:

Objective: *Provide access to files in the USTATION directory, to certain digitizer files in the DIGI directory, and to the EXTERNAL DOS commands in the DOSX directory.*

Context: **PATH=C:\USTATION;\DIGI;\DOSX;**

Because the DOS command PATH is an internal command, the above can be entered from any directory or drive.

DIRECTORY COMMANDS

While logged onto the root directory of drive C, the prompt should show only the C or C:\ without any subdirectory name displayed. It would be advisable to key-in **CD** to be sure that you are on the root directory. Depending on the boot-up parameters for the prompt, it is possible for you to be logged onto a subdirectory and not have it show in the prompt area. Under certain prompt parameter settings, if you were logged onto the subdirectory named USTATION on drive C, the prompt might display C:\USTATION.

Making Directories

You may use the MKDIR or MD command to create a new directory as a branch of any directory, including the root directory. A subdirectory called MENU is created as follows:

    C:\>**MD\MENU**

This creates a subdirectory to the root directory. This only creates the subdirectory, and does not log you onto it. Another command is used for that purpose.

> **NOTE:** Note the use of the "\" (backslash) for specifying a directory. Any time you are logged onto a directory other than the root directory or the one whose path you wish to specify, you must prefix the name of the target directory with the "\" symbol. The root directory is the "NO NAME" directory, therefore when specifying a path to it from some other directory, you must use the "\" symbol without a directory name.

For simplicity, from here on, directories and subdirectories will primarily be referred to as just directories. The distinction between directories and subdirectories is mostly technical and not critical as long as one learns the correct path to any file.

Searching Directories

It is useful to be able to display on the screen a list of all the files that are stored in a directory. This is accomplished with the DOS command called DIRECTORY or DIR. This command will display the files and also any directories created as a part of the particular directory you are searching. A search of the root directory can be entered as follows:

    C:\>**DIR**

The following might be displayed:

```
Volume in drive C has no label
Directory of C:\
COMMAND  COM      23456      1-23-93
DOS               <DIR>      1-23-93
AUTOEXEC BAT        128      2-13-93
USTATION BAT         28      3-21-93
USTATION          <DIR>      3-21-93
PIPESTAR          <DIR>      4-12-93
SIDEKICK          <DIR>      4-30-93
```

After having used the MD\MENU command the DIR command would display:

```
Volume in drive C has no label
Directory of C:\
COMMAND  COM       23456       1-23-93
DOS               <DIR>        1-23-93
AUTOEXEC BAT        128        2-13-93
USTATION BAT         28        3-21-93
USTATION          <DIR>        3-21-93
PIPESTAR          <DIR>        4-12-93
SIDEKICK          <DIR>        4-30-93
MENU              <DIR>        (the current date is displayed)
```

An additional convenience of the DIR command is to be able to list the files across the screen in a wide fashion. This is done by adding a "/W" to the DIR command:

C:\>**DIR/W**

The display would be as follows:

```
Volume in drive C has no label
Directory of C:\
COMMAND COM     [DOS]     AUTOEXEC BAT     USTATION BAT
[USTATION]     [PIPESTAR]     [SIDEKICK]     [MENU]
```

The sizes and dates of files are not displayed when the "/W" parameter is added to the DIR command. Another handy feature is the "/P" either with or without the "/W" following the DIR command. "/P" causes the scrolling to pause each time the screen is filled with a display of the list of files and directories. Of course, it is only needed when the list is longer than one screen can display.

When a directory has been created, there are two unnamed hidden files created at the same time. Their presence is indicated by the "." and the ".." symbols displayed when the DIR command is used. These are of no special concern to the average operator. An effort to delete them, however, might play havoc with DOS, so they are best left alone.

Changing Directories

Logging on to another directory on the same drive is done via the DOS command called CHDIR or CD. It requires the "\" (backslash) prefix in the following manner:

C:\>**CD\MENU**

This will log you on to the directory called MENU. In the later versions of DOS, logging on to (or accessing) another directory from the root directory can be done without the backslash, as follows:

C:\>**CD MENU**

Getting Back to the Root Directory

Because the root directory has no name, enter the following:

   C>**CD**

This will return you to the root directory.

Drive and Directory Specifiers

It is possible (but not advisable at this time) to create a subdirectory inside the MENU directory. It may be done in three different ways, depending on which is the current drive and directory. This example is for the purpose of illustrating the use of the ":" symbol for the drive specifier and the "\" symbol for the directory specifier.

Example 3

   Objective: *Create a subdirectory named USERMENU to the directory named "MENU," which is itself a subdirectory of the root directory of drive C.*
   Current Drive: **A** *(Same as Example 1)*
   Current Directory: *(Root of A) (Same as Example 1)*

Enter the following:

   A>**MD C:\MENU\USERMENU**

Example 4

   Objective: *(Same as Example 3)*
   Current Drive: **C** *(Changed from Example 3)*
   Current Directory: *(Root of C) (Changed from Example 3)*

Enter the following:

   C>**MD \MENU\USERMENU**

FORMATTING THE DISK

Before you can write information onto a new disk, you must prepare the diskette so that you can store information. This can be done by a program called FORMAT.COM. The formatting program is located on your DOS directory. You only need to format a disk once. Log on to the directory that has the FORMAT program or if you have a path for the directory that has the FORMAT program, then you can type the command at any DOS prompt.

Example 5

Current Drive: **C**
Current Directory: *Root directory*
Drive where FORMAT.COM is stored: **C:**
Disk to be formatted is in drive A

A suggested sequence would be as follows:

C:\format a:

The following message will appear:

Insert new diskette for drive A:
and strike ENTER when ready

Insert a new diskette and press [ENTER].

You will see the message:

Formatting...

After a few minutes, the clanking sound stops and the following message appears:

Format complete
Format another (Y/N):

If you want to format another disk, take out the newly formatted disk and replace it with another new disk. Then press **Y** and [ENTER]. If you do not want to format another disk, press **N** and [ENTER] to terminate the program. Remember, you only have to format a disk once, even if you later erase the information on it.

> **NOTE:** To format a low-density diskette (360KB), you have to add switch /4 to the format command, as follows:
>
>   c:>**format a:/4**

COPYING FILES

It is sometimes necessary to copy files from one location to another. The only case where a file can be copied to its same drive and directory is if the name is changed in the process. This would produce two identical files with different names.

An example of a need to copy a file would be if you created a custom menu on a directory containing a word processing program and wanted to transfer it to the USTATION directory for use in MicroStation. This is not the most efficient way to write and test programs, but it does illustrate the DOS command called COPY.

Example 6

Objective: *Copy the file named TRIAL.MNU from the directory called WRDPRCSR to the directory called USTATION*
Current Drive: **C**
Current Directory: *Root directory*

A suggested sequence would be as follows:

C>COPY \WRDPRCSR\TRIAL.MNU \USTATION\TRIAL.MNU

Example 7

Objective: *(Same as Example 6)*
Current Drive: **C**
Current Directory: **\WRDPRCSR**

A suggested sequence would be as follows:

C>COPY TRIAL.MNU \USTATION\TRIAL.MNU

Example 8

Objective: *(Same as Example 6)*
Current Drive: **C**
Current Directory: **B\USTATION**

A suggested sequence would be as follows:

C>COPY \WRDPRCSR\TRIAL.MNU

Copying Between Drives

Another common need for copying files is from floppy drives to fixed drives (or vice versa). This method also facilitates transferring files from one computer station to another.

Example 9

Objective: *Copy the file named TRIAL.MNU from a floppy disk in drive A to the USTATION directory on the fixed drive.*
Current Drive: **C**
Current Directory: *Root directory*

A suggested sequence would be as follows:

C>COPY A:TRIAL.MNU \USTATION\TRIAL.MNU

Example 10

Objective: *(Same as Example 9)*
Current Drive: **A**
Current Directory: *Root directory*

A suggested sequence would be as follows:

A>COPY TRIAL.MNU C:\USTATION\TRIAL.MNU

Example 11

Objective: *(Same as Example 9)*
Current Drive: **C**
Current Directory: **USTATION**

A suggested sequence would be as follows:

C>COPY A:TRIAL.MN

Example 12   (Use of the global symbol "*")

Objective: *Copy all files with the file EXTENSION .MNU from drive A to the USTATION directory on drive C.*
Current Drive: **C**
Current Directory: **USTATION**

A suggested sequence would be as follows:

C>COPY A:*.MNU

Example 13   (Use of the global symbol "*")

Objective: *Copy all files on drive A to the USTATION directory on drive C.*
Current Drive: **C**
Current Directory: **USTATION**

A suggested sequence would be as follows:

C>COPY A:*.*

or

C>COPY A:.

As you can see, like in programming, DOS commands can be made easier with a little planning.

DELETING A FILE OR GROUP OF FILES

The storage space on a disk is limited, and all of it may eventually be occupied by files. Therefore, it is sometimes necessary to delete files you no longer need. The built-in command ERASE and its shorter form DEL can delete a single file or a group of files. Both commands do exactly the same thing and work the same way. You can use whichever command you prefer.

Example 14

Objective: *Delete the file XMPL.BAK.*
Current Drive: **C**
Current Directory: *Root directory*
Drive where XMPL.BAK is stored: **C**
Directory where XMPL.BAK is stored: **\USTATION\DGN**
   (Note that \DGN\ is a subdirectory of \USTATION\)

A suggested sequence would be as follows:

   A:\>**ERASE C:\USTATION\DGN\XMPL.BAK**

Example 15

Objective: *Delete all the files with extension .BAK in drive A.*
Current Drive: **C**
Current Directory: *Root directory*

A suggested sequence would be as follows:

   C:\>**erase a:*.BAK**

Example 16

Objective: *Delete all the files in the directory DGN.*
Current Drive: **C**
Current Directory: **c:\dgn**

A suggested sequence would be as follows:

   C:\dgn>**erase *.***
or
   C:\dgn>**erase .**

The following message will appear:

    Are you sure (Y/N)?

You must answer **Y** if you want DOS to continue. Otherwise, the operation is terminated without further action.

DOS REFERENCE BOOKS

A variety of books are available that discuss the MS-DOS operating system. Read any one of the available books for detailed information about the operating system and system management.

> **NOTE:** MicroStation is not case-sensitive. That is, key-ins can be uppercase or lowercase, or even a mixture of the two, and MicroStation will still understand the key-ins in the same way.

TOOL NAME	KEY-IN
Add to Graphic Group	GROUP ADD
Attach Active Entity	ATTACH AE
Attach Active Entity to Fence Contents	FENCE ATTACH
Attach Displayable Attributes	ATTACH DA
Attach Reference File	REFERENCE ATTACH (RF=)
Automatic Create Complex Chain	CREATE CHAIN AUTOMATIC
Automatic Create Complex Shape	CREATE SHAPE AUTOMATIC
Automatic Fill in Enter Data Fields	EDIT AUTO
B-spline Polygon Display On/Off	MDL LOAD SPLINES; CHANGE BSPLINE POLYGON
Chamfer	CHAMFER
Change B-spline Surface to Active U-Order	MDL LOAD SPLINES; CHANGE BSPLINE UORDER
Change B-spline Surface to Active U-Rules	MDL LOAD SPLINES; CHANGE BSPLINE URULES

TOOL NAME	KEY-IN
Change B-spline Surface to Active V-Order	MDL LOAD SPLINES; CHANGE BSPLINE VORDER
Change B-spline Surface to Active V-Rules	MDL LOAD SPLINES; CHANGE BSPLINE VRULES
Change B-spline to Active Order	MDL LOAD SPLINES; CHANGE BSPLINE ORDER
Change Element to Active Class	CHANGE CLASS
Change Element to Active Color	CHANGE COLOR
Change Element to Active Level	CHANGE LEVEL
Change Element to Active Line Style	CHANGE STYLE
Change Element to Active Line Weight	CHANGE WEIGHT
Change Element to Active Symbol	CHANGE SYMBOLOGY
Change Fence Contents to Active Color	FENCE CHANGE COLOR
Change Fence Contents to Active Level	FENCE CHANGE LEVEL
Change Fence Contents to Active Style	FENCE CHANGE STYLE
Change Fence Contents to Active Symbology	FENCE CHANGE SYMBOLOGY
Change Fence Contents to Active Weight	FENCE CHANGE WEIGHT
Change Fill	CHANGE FILL
Change Text to Active Attributes	MODIFY TEXT
Circular Fillet (No Truncation)	FILLET NOMODIFY
Circular Fillet and Truncate Both	FILLET MODIFY
Circular Fillet and Truncate Single	FILLET SINGLE
Closed Cross Joint	MDL LOAD CUTTER; JOIN CROSS CLOSED
Closed Tee Joint	MDL LOAD CUTTER; JOIN TEE CLOSED
Complete Cycle Linear Pattern	PATTERN LINE SCALE
Construct Active Point at Distance Along an Element	CONSTRUCT POINT DISTANCE
Construct Active Point at Intersection	CONSTRUCT POINT INTERSECTION
Construct Active Points Between Data Points	CONSTRUCT POINT BETWEEN
Construct Angle Bisector	CONSTRUCT BISECTOR ANGLE
Construct Arc Tangent to Three Elements	CONSTRUCT TANGENT ARC 3
Construct B-spline Curve by Least Squares	MDL LOAD SPLINES; CONSTRUCT BSPLINE CURVE LEAST SQUARE
Construct B-spline Curve by Points	MDL LOAD SPLINES; CONSTRUCT BSPLINE CURVE POINTS
Construct B-spline Curve by Poles	MDL LOAD SPLINES; CONSTRUCT BSPLINE CURVE POLES

TOOL NAME	KEY-IN
Construct B-spline Surface by Cross-Section	MDL LOAD SPINES; CONSTRUCT BSPLINE SURFACE CROSS
Construct B-spline Surface by Edges	MDL LOAD SPLINES; CONSTRUCT BSPLINE SURFACE EDGE
Construct B-spline Surface by Least Squares	MDL LOAD SPLINES; CONSTRUCT BSPLINE SURFACE LEAST SQUARE
Construct B-spline Surface by Points	MDL LOAD SPLINES; CONSTRUCT BSPLINE SURFACE POINTS
Construct B-spline Surface by Poles	MDL LOAD SPLINES; CONSTRUCT BSPLINE SURFACE POLES
Construct B-spline Surface by Skin	MDL LOAD SPLINES; CONSTRUCT BSPLINE SURFACE SKIN
Construct B-spline Surface by Tube	MDL LOAD SPLINES; CONSTRUCT BSPLINE SURFACE TUBE
Construct B-spline Surface of Projection	MDL LOAD SPLINES; CONSTRUCT BSPLINE SURFACE PROJECTION
Construct B-spline Surface of Revolution	MDL LOAD SPLINES; CONSTRUCT BSPLINE SURFACE REVOLUTION
Construct Circle Tangent to Element	CONSTRUCT TANGENT CIRCLE 1
Construct Circle Tangent to Three Elements	CONSTRUCT TANGENT CIRCLE 3
Construct Line at Active Angle from Point (key-in)	CONSTRUCT LINE AA 4
Construct Line at Active Angle from Point	CONSTRUCT LINE AA 3
Construct Line at Active Angle to Point (key-in)	CONSTRUCT LINE AA 2
Construct Line at Active Angle to Point	CONSTRUCT LINE AA 1
Construct Line Bisector	CONSTRUCT BISECTOR LINE
Construct Line Tangent to Two Elements	CONSTRUCT TANGENT BETWEEN
Construct Minimum Distance Line	CONSTRUCT LINE MINIMUM
Construct Perpendicular from Element	CONSTRUCT PERPENDICULAR FROM
Construct Perpendicular to Element	CONSTRUCT PERPENDICULAR TO
Construct Points Along Element	CONSTRUCT POINT ALONG
Construct Surface/Solid of Projection	SURFACE PROJECTION
Construct Surface/Solid of Revolution	SURFACE REVOLUTION
Construct Tangent Arc by Keyed-in Radius	CONSTRUCT TANGENT ARC 1
Construct Tangent from Element	CONSTRUCT TANGENT FROM
Construct Tangent to Circular Element and Perpendicular to Linear Element	CONSTRUCT TANGENT PERPENDICULAR

TOOL NAME	KEY-IN
Construct Tangent to Element	CONSTRUCT TANGENT TO
Convert Element to B-spline (Copy)	MDL LOAD SPLINES; CONSTRUCT BSPLINE CONVERT COPY
Convert Element to B-spline Original	MDL LOAD SPLINES; CONSTRUCT BSPLINE CONVERT ORIGINAL
Copy Fence Content	FENCE COPY
Copy Parallel by Distance	COPY PARALLEL DISTANCE
Copy Parallel by Key-in	COPY PARALLEL KEYIN
Corner Joint	MDL LOAD CUTTER; JOIN CORNER
Create Complex Chain	CREATE CHAIN MANUAL
Create Complex Shape	CREATE SHAPE MANUAL
Crosshatch Element Area	CROSSHATCH
Cut All Component Lines	MDL LOAD CUTTER; CUT ALL
Cut Single Component Line	MDL LOAD CUTTER; CUT SINGLE
Define ACS (Aligned with Element)	DEFINE ACS ELEMENT
Define ACS (Aligned with View)	DEFINE ACS VIEW
Define ACS (By Points)	DEFINE ACS POINTS
Define Active Entity Graphically	DEFINE AE
Define Cell Origin	DEFINE CELL ORIGIN
Define Reference File Back Clipping Plane	REFERENCE CLIP BACK
Define Reference File Clipping Boundary	REFERENCE CLIP BOUNDARY
Define Reference Clipping Mask	REFERENCE CLIP MASK
Define Reference File Front Clipping Plane	REFERENCE CLIP FRONT
Define True North	DEFINE NORTH
Delete Element	DELETE ELEMENT
Delete Fence Contents	FENCE DELETE
Delete Part of Element	DELETE PARTIAL
Delete Vertex	DELETE VERTEX
Detach Database Linkage	DETACH
Detach Database Linkage from Fence Contents	FENCE DETACH
Detach Reference File	REFERENCE DETACH
Dimension Angle Between Lines	DIMENSION ANGLE LINES
Dimension Angle from X-Axis	DIMENSION ANGLE X
Dimension Angle from Y-Axis	DIMENSION ANGLE Y
Dimension Angle Location	DIMENSION ANGLE LOCATION
Dimension Angle Size	DIMENSION ANGLE SIZE
Dimension Arc Location	DIMENSION ARC LOCATION
Dimension Arc Size	DIMENSION ARC SIZE

TOOL NAME	KEY-IN
Dimension Diameter	DIMENSION DIAMETER
Dimension Diameter (Extended Leader)	DIMENSION DIAMETER EXTENDED
Dimension Diameter Parallel	DIMENSION DIAMETER PARALLEL
Dimension Diameter Perpendicular	DIMENSION DIAMETER PERPENDICULAR
Dimension Diameter	DIMENSION DIAMETER
Dimension Element	DIMENSION ELEMENT
Dimension Location	DIMENSION LOCATION SINGLE
Dimension Location (Stacked)	DIMENSION LOCATION STACKED
Dimension Ordinates	DIMENSION ORDINATE
Dimension Radius	DIMENSION RADIUS
Dimension Radius (Extended Leader)	DIMENSION RADIUS EXTENDED
Dimension Size (Custom)	DIMENSION LINEAR
Dimension Size with Arrow	DIMENSION SIZE ARROW
Dimension Size with Strokes	DIMENSION SIZE STROKE
Display Attributes of Text Element	IDENTIFY TEXT
Drop Association	DROP ASSOCIATION
Drop Complex Status	DROP COMPLEX
Drop Complex Status of Fence Contents	FENCE DROP
Drop Dimension	DROP DIMENSION
Drop from Graphic Group	GROUP DROP
Drop Line String/Shape Status	DROP STRING
Drop Text	DROP TEXT
Edit Text	EDIT TEXT
Element Selection	CHOOSE ELEMENT
Extend 2 Elements to Intersection	EXTEND ELEMENT 2
Extend Element to Intersection	EXTEND ELEMENT INTERSECTION
Extend Line	EXTEND LINE DISTANCE
Extend Line By Key-in	EXTEND LINE KEYIN
Extract Bspline Surface Boundary	MDL LOAD SPLINES; EXTRACT BSPLINE SURFACE BOUNDARY
Fence Stretch	FENCE STRETCH
Fill in Single Enter Data Field	EDIT SINGLE
Freeze Element	FREEZE
Freeze Elements in Fence	FENCE FREEZE
Generate Report Table	FENCE REPORT
Global Origin	ACTIVE ORIGIN (GO=)
Group Holes	GROUP HOLES

TOOL NAME	KEY-IN
Hatch Element Area	HATCH
Horizontal Parabola (No Truncation)	PLACE PARABOLA HORIZONTAL NOMODIFY
Horizontal Parabola and Truncate Both	PLACE PARABOLA HORIZONTAL MODIFY
Identify Cell	IDENTIFY CELL
Impose Bspline Surface Boundary	MDL LOAD SPLINES; IMPOSE BSPLINE SURFACE BOUNDARY
Insert Vertex	INSERT VERTEX
Label Line	LABEL LINE
Load Displayable Attributes	LOAD DA
Load Displayable Attributes to Fence Contents	FENCE LOAD
Match Pattern Attributes	ACTIVE PATTERN MATCH
Match Text Attributes	ACTIVE TEXT
Measure Angle Between Lines	MEASURE ANGLE
Measure Area	MEASURE AREA
Measure Area of Element	MEASURE AREA ELEMENT
Measure Distance Along Element	MEASURE DISTANCE ALONG
Measure Distance Between Points	MEASURE DISTANCE POINTS
Measure Minimum Distance Between Elements	MEASURE DISTANCE MINIMUM
Measure Perpendicular Distance From Element	MEASURE DISTANCE PERPENDICULAR
Measure Radius	MEASURE RADIUS
Merged Cross Joint	MDL LOAD CUTTER; JOIN CROSS MERGE
Merged Tee Joint	MDL LOAD CUTTER; JOIN TEE MERGE
Mirror Element About Horizontal (Copy)	MIRROR COPY HORIZONTAL
Mirror Element About Horizontal (Original)	MIRROR ORIGINAL HORIZONTAL
Mirror Element About Line Copy	MIRROR COPY LINE
Mirror Element About Line (Ordinal)	MIRROR ORIGINAL LINE
Mirror Element About Vertical (Copy)	MIRROR COPY VERTICAL
Mirror Element About Vertical (Original)	MIRROR ORIGINAL VERTICAL
Mirror Fence Contents About Horizontal (Copy)	FENCE MIRROR COPY HORIZONTAL

TOOL NAME	KEY-IN
Mirror Fence Contents About Horizontal (Original)	FENCE MIRROR ORIGINAL HORIZONTAL
Mirror Fence Contents About Line (Copy)	FENCE MIRROR COPY LINE
Mirror Fence Contents About Line (Original)	FENCE MIRROR ORIGINAL LINE
Mirror Fence Contents About Vertical (Copy)	FENCE MIRROR COPY VERTICAL
Mirror Fence Contents About Vertical (Original)	FENCE MIRROR ORIGINAL VERTICAL
Mirror Reference File About Horizontal	REFERENCE MIRROR HORIZONTAL
Mirror Fence About Vertical	REFERENCE MIRROR VERTICAL
Modify Arc Angle	MODIFY ARC ANGLE
Modify Arc Axis	MODIFY ARC AXIS
Modify Arc Radius	MODIFY ARC RADIUS
Modify Element	MODIFY ELEMENT
Modify Fence	MODIFY FENCE
Move ACS	MOVE ACS
Move Element	MOVE ELEMENT
Move Fence Block/Shape	MOVE FENCE
Move Fence Contents	FENCE MOVE
Move Reference File	REFERENCE MOVE
Multi-Cycle Segment Linear Pattern	PATTERN LINE MULTIPLE
Open Cross Joint	MDL LOAD CUTTER; JOIN CROSS OPEN
Open Tee Joint	MDL LOAD CUTTER; JOIN TEE OPEN
Pattern Element Area	PATTERN AREA ELEMENT
Pattern Fence Area	PATTERN AREA FENCE
Place Active Cell	PLACE CELL ABSOLUTE
Place Active Cell (Interactive)	PLACE CELL INTERACTIVE ABSOLUTE
Place Active Cell Matrix	MATRIX CELL (CM=)
Place Active Cell Relative	PLACE CELL RELATIVE
Place Active Cell Relative (Interactive)	PLACE CELL INTERACTIVE RELATIVE
Place Active Line Terminator	PLACE TERMINATOR
Place Active Point	PLACE POINT
Place Arc by Center	PLACE ARC CENTER
Place Arc by Edge	PLACE ARC EDGE
Place Arc by Keyed-in Radius	PLACE ARC RADIUS

TOOL NAME	KEY-IN
Place B-spline Curve by Least Squares	MDL LOAD SPLINES; PLACE BSPLINE CURVE LEASTSQUARE
Place B-spline Curve by Points	MDL LOAD SPLINES; PLACE BSPLINE CURVE POINTS
Place B-spline Curve by Poles	MDL LOAD SPLINES; PLACE BSPLINE CURVE POLES
Place B-spline Surface by Least Squares	MDL LOAD SPLINES; PLACE BSPLINE SURFACE LEASTSQUARES
Place B-spline Surface by Points	MDL LOAD SPLINES; PLACE BSPLINE SURFACE POINTS
Place B-spline Surface by Poles	MDL LOAD SPLINES; PLACE BSPLINE SURFACE POLES
Place Block	PLACE BLOCK ORTHOGONAL
Place Center Mark	DIMENSION CENTER MARK
Place Circle by Center	PLACE CIRCLE CENTER
Place Circle by Diameter	PLACE CIRCLE DIAMETER
Place Circle by Edge	PLACE CIRCLE EDGE
Place Circle by Keyed-in Radius	PLACE CIRCLE RADIUS
Place Circumscribed Polygon	PLACE POLYGON CIRCUMSCRIBED
Place Ellipse by Center and Edge	PLACE ELLIPSE CENTER
Place Ellipse by Edge Points	PLACE ELLIPSE EDGE
Place Fence Block	PLACE FENCE BLOCK
Place Fence Shape	PLACE FENCE SHAPE
Place Fitted Text	PLACE TEXT FITTED
Place Fitted View Independent Text	PLACE TEXT VI
Place Half Ellipse	PLACE ELLIPSE HALF
Place Helix	MDL LOAD SPLINES; PLACE HELIX
Place Inscribed Polygon	PLACE POLYGON INSCRIBED
Place Isometric Block	PLACE BLOCK ISOMETRIC
Place Isometric Circle	PLACE CIRCLE ISOMETRIC
Place Line	PLACE LINE
Place Line at Active Angle	PLACE LINE ANGLE
Place Line String	PLACE LSTRING POINT
Place Multi-line	PLACE MLINE
Place Note	PLACE NOTE
Place Orthogonal Shape	PLACE SHAPE ORTHOGONAL
Place Parabola by End Points	MDL LOAD SPLINES; PLACE PARABOLA ENDPOINTS
Place Point Curve	PLACE CURVE POINT
Place Polygon by Edge	PLACE POLYGON EDGE
Place Quarter Ellipse	PLACE ELLIPSE QUARTER
Place Right Cone	PLACE CONE RIGHT
Place Right Cone by Keyed-in Radius	PLACE CONE RADIUS

TOOL NAME	KEY-IN
Place Right Cylinder	PLACE CYLINDER RIGHT
Place Right Cylinder by Keyed-in Radius	PLACE CYLINDER RADIUS
Place Rotated Block	PLACE BLOCK ROTATED
Place Shape	PLACE SHAPE
Place Skewed Cone	PLACE CONE SKEWED
Place Skewed Cylinder	PLACE CYLINDER SKEWED
Place Slab	PLACE SLAB
Place Space Curve	PLACE CURVE SPACE
Place Space Line String	PLACE LSTRING SPACE
Place Sphere	PLACE SPHERE
Place Spiral By End Points	MDL LOAD SPLINES; PLACE SPIRAL ENDPOINTS
Place Spiral By Length	MDL LOAD SPLINES; PLACE SPIRAL LENGTH
Place Spiral by Sweep Angle	MDL LOAD SPLINES; PLACE SPIRAL ANGLE
Place Stream Curve	PLACE CURVE STREAM
Place Stream Line String	PLACE LSTRING STREAM
Place Text	PLACE TEXT
Place Text Above Element	PLACE TEXT ABOVE
Place Text Along Element	PLACE TEXT ALONG
Place Text Below Element	PLACE TEXT BELOW
Place Text Node	PLACE NODE
Place Text On Element	PLACE TEXT ON
Place View Independent Text	PLACE TEXT VI
Place View Independent Text Node	PLACE NODE VIEW
Polar Array	ARRAY POLAR
Polar Array Fence Contents	FENCE ARRAY POLAR
Project Active Point Onto Element	CONSTRUCT POINT PROJECT
Rectangular Array	ARRAY RECTANGULAR
Rectangular Array Fence Contents	FENCE ARRAY RECTANGULAR
Reload Reference File	REFERENCE RELOAD
Replace Cell	REPLACE CELL
Review Database Attributes of Element	REVIEW
Rotate ACS Absolute	ROTATE ACS ABSOLUTE
Rotate ACS Relative	ROTATE ACS RELATIVE
Rotate Element Active Angle Copy	ROTATE COPY
Rotate Element Active Angle Original	ROTATE ORIGINAL
Rotate Fence Contents by Active Angle (Copy)	FENCE ROTATE COPY
Rotate Fence Contents by Active Angle (Original)	FENCE ROTATE ORIGINAL
Rotate Reference File	REFERENCE ROTATE .

TOOL NAME	KEY-IN
Scale Element (Copy)	SCALE COPY
Scale Element (Original)	SCALE ORIGINAL
Scale Fence Contents (Copy)	FENCE SCALE COPY
Scale Fence Contents (Original)	FENCE SCALE ORIGINAL
Scale Reference File	REFERENCE SCALE
Select ACS	ATTACH ACS
Select and Place Cell	SELECT CELL ABSOLUTE
Select and Place Cell (Relative)	SELECT CELL RELATIVE
Set Active Depth	DEPTH ACTIVE
Show Active Depth	SHOW DEPTH ACTIVE
Show Active Entity	SHOW AE
Show Linkage Mode	ACTIVE LINKAGE
Show Pattern Attributes	SHOW PATTERN
Single Cycle Segment Linear Pattern	PATTERN LINE SINGLE
Spin Element (Copy)	SPIN COPY
Spin Element (Original)	SPIN ORIGINAL
Spin Fence Contents (Copy)	FENCE SPIN COPY
Spin Fence Contents (Original)	FENCE SPIN ORIGINAL
Symmetric Parabola (No Truncation)	PLACE PARABOLA NOMODIFY
Symmetric Parabola and Truncate Both	PLACE PARABOLA MODIFY
Thaw Element	THAW
Thaw Elements in Fence	FENCE THAW
Truncated Cycle Linear Pattern	PATTERN LINE ELEMENT
Uncut Component Lines	MDL LOAD CUTTER; UNCUT

APPENDIX

E

ALTERNATE KEY-INS

NOTE: MicroStation is not case-sensitive. That is, key-ins can be uppercase or lowercase, or even a mixture of the two, and MicroStation will still understand the key-ins in the same way.

AA = ACTIVE ANGLE   set active angle
AC = ACTIVE CELL   set active cell; place absolute
AD = POINT ACSDELTA   data point—delta ACS
AE = ACTIVE ENTITY   define active entity
AM = ATTACH MENU   activate menu
AP = ACTIVE PATTERN CELL   set active pattern cell
AR = ACTIVE RCELL   set active cell; place relative
AS = ACTIVE SCALE   set active scale factors
AT = TUTORIAL   activate tutorial
AX = POINT ACSABSOLUTE   data point absolute ACS
AZ = ACTIVE ZDEPTH ABSOLUTE   set active depth

CC = CREATE CELL   create cell
CD = DELETE CELL   delete cell from cell library
CM = MATRIX CELL   place active cell matrix
CO = ACTIVE COLOR   set active color
CR = RENAME CELL   rename cell
CT = ATTACH COLORTABLE   attach color table

DA = ACTIVE DATYPE   set active displayable attribute type
DB = ACTIVE DATABASE   attach control file to design file
DD = SET DDEPTH RELATIVE   set display depth (relative)
DF = SHOW FONT   open Fonts settings box
DI = POINT DISTANCE   data point—distance, direction
DL = POINT DELTA   data point—delta coordinates
DP = DEPTH DISPLAY   set display depth
DR = TYPE   display text file
DS = SEARCH   specify fence filter
DV = VIEW   delete saved view
DX = POINT VDELTA   data point—delta view coordinates
DZ = ZDEPTH RELATIVE   set active depth (relative)

EL = ELEMENT LIST   create element list file

FF = FENCE FILE   copy fence contents to design file
FI = FIND   set database row as active entity
FT = ACTIVE FONT   set active font

GO = ACTIVE ORIGIN   Global Origin
GR = ACTIVE GRIDREF   set grid reference spacing
GU = ACTIVE GRIDUNIT   set horizontal grid spacing

KY = ACTIVE KEYPNT   set Snap divisor

LC = ACTIVE STYLE   set active line style
LD = DIMENSION LEVEL   set dimension level
LL = ACTIVE LINE LENGTH   set active text line length
LS = ACTIVE LINE SPACE   set active text node line spacing
LT = ACTIVE TERMINATOR   set active terminator
LV = ACTIVE LEVEL   set active level

NN = ACTIVE NODE   set active text node number

OF = SET LEVELS <level list> OFF   set level display off
ON = SET LEVELS <level list> ON   set level display on
OX = ACTIVE INDEX   retrieve user command index

PA = ACTIVE PATTERN ANGLE   set active pattern angle
PD = ACTIVE PATTERN DELTA   set active pattern delta (distance)
PS = ACTIVE PATTERN SCALE   set active pattern scale
PT = ACTIVE POINT   set active point
PX = DELETE ACS   delete ACS

RA = ACTIVE REVIEW   set attribute review selection criteria
RC = ATTACH LIBRARY   open cell library

RD = NEWFILE   open design file
RF = REFERENCE ATTACH   attach reference file
RS = ACTIVE REPORT   name report table
RV = ROTATE VIEW   rotate view (relative)
RX = ATTACH ACS   select ACS

SD = ACTIVE STREAM DELTA   set active stream delta
SF = FENCE SEPARATE   move fence contents to design file
ST = ACTIVE STREAM TOLERANCE   set active stream tolerance
SV = SAVE VIEW   save view
SX = SAVE ACS   save auxiliary coordinate system

TB = ACTIVE TAB   set tab spacing for importing text
TH = ACTIVE TXHEIGHT   set active text height
TI = ACTIVE TAG   set copy and increment value
TS = ACTIVE TSCALE   set active terminator scale
TV = DIMENSION TOLERANCE   set dimension tolerance limits
TW = ACTIVE TXWIDTH   set active text width
TX = ACTIVE TXSIZE   set active text size (height/width)

UC = USERCOMMAND   activate user command
UCC = UCC   compile user command
UCI = UCI   user command index
UR = ACTIVE UNITROUND   set unit distance

VI = VIEW   attach named view

WO = WINDOW ORIGIN   Window Orgin
WT = ACTIVE WEIGHT   set active line weight

XD = EXCHANGEFILE   open design file; keep view config.
XS = ACTIVE XSCALE   set active X scale
XY = POINT ABSOLUTE   data point absolute coordinates

YS = ACTIVE YSCALE   set active Y scale

ZS = ACTIVE ZSCALE   set active Z scale

APPENDIX

F

PRIMITIVE COMMANDS

NOTE: MicroStation is not case-sensitive. That is, key-ins can be uppercase or lowercase, or even a mixture of the two, and MicroStation will still understand the key-ins in the same way.

NAME OF THE COMMAND	PRIMITIVE COMMAND
ACTIVE ANGLE PT2	/ACTAN2
ACTIVE ANGLE PT3	/ACTAN3
ACTIVE CAPMODE OFF	/WOCMDE
ACTIVE CAPMODE ON	/CAPMDE
ACTIVE SCALE DISTANCE	/ACTSCA
ACTIVE TNJ CB	/TJST#
ACTIVE TNJ CC	/TJST7
ACTIVE TNJ CT	/TJST6
ACTIVE TNJ LB	/TJST2
ACTIVE TNJ LC	/TJST]
ACTIVE TNJ LMB	/TJST5
ACTIVE TNJ LMC	/TJST4
ACTIVE TNJ LMT	/TJST3
ACTIVE TNJ LT	/TJSTO
ACTIVE TNJ RB	/TJST14
ACTIVE TNJ RC	/TJST13
ACTIVE TNJ RMB	/TJST1 1

NAME OF THE COMMAND	PRIMITIVE COMMAND
ACTIVE TNJ RMC	/TJST 1 0
ACTIVE TNJ RMT	/TJST9
ACTIVE TNJ RT	/TJSTl 2
ACTIVE TXHEIGHT PT2	/TXTHGT
ACTIVE TXJ CB	/TXJS8
ACTIVE TXJ CC	/TXJS7
ACTIVE TXJ CT	/TXJS6
ACTIVE TXJ LB	/TXJSZ
ACTIVE TXJ LC	/TXJSl
ACTIVE TXJ LT	/TXJSO
ACTIVE TXJ RB	/TXJS14
ACTIVE TXJ RC	/TXJS13
ACTIVE TXJ RT	/TXJSlz
ACTIVE TXWIDTH PT2	/TXTWDT
ALIGN	/ALIGN
ATTACH AE	/ATCPTO
CHANGE COLOR	/CELECR
CHANGE STYLE	/CELELS
CHANGE SYMBOLOGY	/CELESY
CHANGE WEIGHT	/CELEWT
CONSTRUCT BISECTOR ANGLE	/ANGBIS
CONSTRUCT BISECTOR LINE	/PERBIS
CONSTRUCT LINE AA 1	/CNSAA1
CONSTRUCT LINE AA 2	/CNSAA2
CONSTRUCT LINE AA 3	/CNSAA3
CONSTRUCT LINE AA 4	/CNSAA4
CONSTRUCT LINE MINIMUM	/MDL2EL
CONSTRUCT POINT	/CNSINT
CONSTRUCT POINTALONG	/NPAE
CONSTRUCT POINT BETWEEN	/NPNTS
CONSTRUCT POINT DISTANCE	/PPAE
CONSTRUCT POINT PROJECT	/PRJPNT
CONSTRUCT TANGENT	/LNTNNR
CONSTRUCT TANGENT ARC 1	/PTARCC
CONSTRUCT TANGENT ARC 3	/ATN3EL
CONSTRUCT TANGENT BETWEEN	/LTZELP
CONSTRUCT TANGENT CIRCLE 1	/CTNlEL
CONSTRUCT TANGENT CIRCLE 3	/CTN3EL
CONSTRUCT TANGENT FROM	/PTFROM
CONSTRUCT TANGENT TO	/PITO
COPY ED	/EDCOPY
COPYELEMENT	/CPELE
COPY PARALLEL DISTANCE	/CPYPP

NAME OF THE COMMAND	PRIMITIVE COMMAND
COPY PARALLEL KEYIN	/CPYPK
COPY VIEW	/COPY
CREATE CHAIN MANUAL	/CONNST
CREATE SHAPE MANUAL	/CPXSHP
DEFINE ACS ELEMENT	/AUXELE
DEFINE ACS POINTS	/AUX3PT
DEFINE ACS VIEW	/AUXVW
DEFINE AE	/DEFPTO
DEFINE CELL ORIGIN	/DOCELL
DELETE ELEMENT	/DLELEM
DELETE PARTIAL	/DLPELE
DELETE VERTEX	/DVERTX
DEPTH ACTIVE PRIMITIVE	/ADEPTH
DEPTH DISPLAY PRIMITIVE	/DDEPTH
DIMENSION ANGLE LINES	/ANGLIN
DIMENSION ANGLE LOCATION	/PITLOC
DIMENSION ANGLE SIZE	/PTSIZ
DIMENSION ARC LOCATION	/ARCLOC
DIMENSION ARC SIZE	/ARCSIZ
DIMENSION AXIS DRAWING	/ACTAXD
DIMENSION AXIS TRUE	/ACTAXP
DIMENSION AXIS VIEW	/ACTAXV
DIMENSION DIMAETER PARALLEL	/DIAPAR
DIMENSION DIAMETER PERPENDICULAR	/DIAPER
DIMENSION DIAMETER POINT	/DIACIR
DIMENSION FILE ACTIVE	/MEAACT
DIMENSION FILE REFERENCE	/MEAREF
DIMENSION JUSTIFICATION CENTER	/JUSC
DIMENSION JUSTIFICATION LEFT	/JUSL
DIMENSION JUSTIFICATION RIGHT	/JUSR
DIMENSION LOCATION SINGLE	/LOCSNG
DIMENSION LOCATION STACKED	/LOCSTK
DIMENSION PLACEMENT AUTO	/ADMAUT
DIMENSION PLACEMENT MANUAL	/PADMAU
DIMENSION RADIUS POINT	/RADRAD
DIMENSION SIZE ARROW	/SIZARW
DIMENSION SIZE STROKE	/SIZOBL
DIMENSION UNITS DEGREES	/UNITDG
DIMENSION UNITS LENGTH	/UNITLN
DIMENSION WITNESS OFF	/WITLOF
DIMENSION WITNESS ON	/WITLON
DROP COMPLEX	/DRCMPX

NAME OF THE COMMAND	PRIMITIVE COMMAND
EDIT AUTO	/EDAUTO
EDIT SINGLE	/EDSING
EDIT TEXT	/EDTEXT
EXTEND ELEMENT 2	/EXLIN2
EXTEND ELEMENT INTERSECTION	/EXLNIN
EXTEND LINE DISTANCE	/EXLIN
EXTEND LINE KEYIN	/EXLINK
FENCE ATTACH	/AAEFCN
FENCE CHANGE STYLE	/CFNCLS
FENCE CHANGE SYMBOLOGY	/CFNCSY
FENCE COPY	/CPFNCC
FENCE DELETE	/DLFNCC
FENCE DETACH	/RATFCN
FENCE LOCATE	/FNCLOC
FENCE MIRROR COPY HORIZONTAL	/MHCPFC
FENCE MIRROR COPY LINE	/MLCPFC
FENCE MIRROR COPY VERTICAL	/MVCPFC
FENCE MIRROR ORIGINAL	/MFVERT
FENCE MIRROR ORIGINAL HORIZONTAL	/MFHRIZ
FENCE MIRROR ORIGINAL LINE	/MFLINE
FENCE MOVE	/MVFNCC
FENCE REPORT	/RPTACT
FENCE ROTATE COPY	/RTCPFC
FENCE ROTATE ORIGINAL	/RFNCC
FENCE SCALE COPY	/SCCPFC
FENCE SCALE ORIGINAL	/SCFNCC
FENCE TRANSFORM	/TRSFCC
FENCE WSET ADD	/ADWSFN
FENCE WSET COPY	/ADWSFC
FILE DESIGN	/FILDGN
FILLET MODIFY	/PFILTM
FILLET NOMODIFY	/PFILTN
FILLET SINGLE	/FILTRM
FIT ACTIVE	/FIT1
GROUP ADD	/ADDGG
GROUP DROP	/DRFGG
IDENTIFY CELL	/IDCELL
IDENTIFY TEXT	/TXNODA
INCREMENT ED	/CIDATA
INCREMENT TEXT	/CITEXT
INSERT VERTEX	/IVERTX

NAME OF THE COMMAND	PRIMITIVE COMMAND
JUSTIFY CENTER	/EDCJST
JUSTIFY LEFT	/EDLJST
JUSTIFY RIGHT	/EDRJST
LABEL LINE	/LABLN
LABEL LINE	/LBLINE
LOCELE	/LOCELE
LOCK ACS [OFF | ON | TOGGLE]	/CPLOCK
LOCK ANGLE [OFF | ON | TOGGLE]	/ANGLLK
LOCK AXIS [OFF | ON | TOGGLE]	/AXLKFF
LOCK BORESITE [OFF | ON | TOGGLE]	/BORSIT
LOCK FENCE CLIP	/CLIP
LOCK FENCE INSIDE	/INSIDE
LOCK FENCE OVERLAP	/OVRLAP
LOCK GGROUP [OFF | ON | TOGGLE]	/GGLOCK
LOCK GRID [OFF | ON | TOGGLE]	/GRIDLK
LOCK SCALE [OFF | ON | TOGGLE]	/SCALLK
LOCK SNAP KEYPOINT	/KEYSNP
LOCK SNAP [OFF | ON]	/SNPOFF
LOCK SNAP PROJECT	/SNAPLK
LOCK TEXTNODE [OFF | ON]	/TXTNLK
LOCK UNIT [OFF | ON]	/UNITLK
MEASURE ANGLE	/LINANG
MEASURE AREA	/AREAPT
MEASURE AREA ELEMENT	/AREAEL
MEASURE DISTANCE ALONG	/MDAE
MEASURE DISTANCE PERPENDICULAR	/PRPND
MEASURE DISTANCE POINTS	/PERIM
MEASURE RADIUS	/RADIUS
MIRROR COPY HORIZONTAL	/MHCPEL
MIRROR COPY LINE	/MLCPEL
MIRROR COPY VERTICAL	/MVCPEL
MIRROR ORIGINAL HORIZONTAL	/MEHRIZ
MIRROR ORIGINAL LINE	/MELINE
MIRROR ORIGINAL VERTICAL	/MEVERT
MODIFY ARC ANGLE	/MDARCA
MODIFY ARC AXIS	/MDARCX
MODIFY ARC RADIUS	/MDARCR
MODIFY ELEMENT	/MDELE
MODIFY FENCE	/MDFNC
MODIFY TEXT	/TXNODC
MOVE ACS	/AUXORC
MOVE ELEMENT	/MVELEM
MOVE FENCE	/MVFNC

NAME OF THE COMMAND	PRIMITIVE COMMAND
NULL	/NULCMD
PLACE ARC CENTER	/PARCC
PLACE ARC EDGE	/PARCE
PLACE ARC RADIUS	/PARCR
PLACE ARC TANGENT	/PTARCC
PLACE BLOCK ORTHOGONAL	/PBLOCK
PLACE BLOCK ROTATED	/PRBLOC
PLACE CELL ABSOLUTE	/PACELL
PLACE CELL ABSOLUTE TMATRX	/PACMTX
PLACE CELL RELATIVE	/PACELR
PLACE CELL RELATIVE TMATRX	/PACRMX
PLACE CIRCLE CENTER	/PCIRC
PLACE CIRCLE DIAMETER	/PCIRD
PLACE CIRCLE EDGE	/PCIRE
PLACE CIRCLE RADIUS	/PCIRR
PLACE CONE RADIUS	/PRCONR
PLACE CONE RIGHT	/PRCONE
PLACE CONE SKEWED	/PCONE
PLACE CURVE POINT	/PPTCRV
PLACE CURVE SPACE	/PSPCRV
PLACE CURVE STREAM	/PSTCRV
PLACE CYLINDER RADIUS	/PRCYLR
PLACE CYLINDER RIGHT	/PRCYL
PLACE CYLINDER SKEWED	/PCYLIN
PLACE ELLIPSE CENTER	/PELL1
PLACE ELLIPSE EDGE	/PELL2
PLACE ELLIPSE HALF	/PPELL1
PLACE ELLIPSE QUARTER	/PPELL2
PLACE FENCE BLOCK	/PFENCB
PLACE FENCE SHAPE	/PFENCE
PLACE LINE	/PLINE
PLACE LINE ANGLE	/PLINAA
PLACE LSTRING POINT	/PPTLST
PLACE LSTRING SPACE	/PSPLST
PLACE LSTRING STREAM	/PSTLST
PLACE NODE	/PTEXTN
PLACE NODE TMATRX	/PTNMTX
PLACE NOTE VIEW	/PVITXN
PLACE PARABOLA HORIZONTAL MODIFY	/PPARMD
PLACE PARABOLA HORIZONTAL NOMODIFY	/PPARNM
PLACE POINT	/PLPNT
PLACE POINT STRING	/PDPTST
PLACE POINT STRING DISJOINT	/PCPTST

NAME OF THE COMMAND	PRIMITIVE COMMAND
PLACE SHAPE	/PSHAPE
PLACE SHAPE ORTHOGONAL	/POSHAP
PLACE TERMINATOR	/PTERM
PLACE TEXT	/PTEXT
PLACE TEXT ABOVE	/PTXTA
PLACE TEXT ALONG	/PTAE
PLACE TEXT BELOW	/PTXTB
PLACE TEXT FITTED	/PFTEXT
PLACE TEXT FVI	/PVIFTX
PLACE TEXT ON	/PTOE
PLACE TEXT TMATRX	/PTXMTX
PLACE TEXT VI	/PVITXT
REFERENCE CLIP BACK	/RFCBCK
REFERENCE CLIP BOUNDARY	/RFCBND
REFERENCE CLIP FRONT	/RFCFRO
REFERENCE DETACH	/RFDTCH
REFERENCE DISPLAY OFF	/RFDISO
REFERENCE DISPLAY ON	/RFDIS1
REFERENCE LEVELS OFF	/RFLEVO
REFERENCE LEVELS ON	/RFLEV1
REFERENCE LOCATE OFF	/RFLOCO
REFERENCE LOCATE ON	/RFLOC1
REFERENCE MOVE	/RFMOVE
REFERENCE ROTATE	/RFROT
REFERENCE SCALE	/RFSCAL
REFERENCE SNAP OFF	/RFSNPO
REFERENCE SNAP ON	/RFSNP1
REPLACE CELL	/RPCELL
REVIEW	/RVWATR
ROTATE 3PTS	/VIEWPL
ROTATE COPY	/RTCPEL
ROTATE ORIGINAL	/ROTELE
ROTATE VIEW POINTS	/VIEWPL
ROTATE VMATRX	/VMATRX
SCALE COPY	/SCCPEL
SCALE ORIGINAL	/SCAELE
SELECT CELL ABSOLUTE	/PSCELL
SELECT CELL ABSOLUTE MATRX	/PSCMTX
SELECT CELL RELATIVE	/PSCELR
SELECT CELL RELATIVE TMATRX	/PSCRMX
SET CONSTRUCT [OFF|ON|TOGGLE]	/CONST1
SET CURVES [FAST|SLOW|OFF|ON|TOGGLE]	/FCURV1

NAME OF THE COMMAND	PRIMITIVE COMMAND
SET DELETE [OFF | PN | TOGGLE]	/DLENSW
SET DIMENSION [OFF | PN | TOGGLE]	/DIMEN1
SET DYNAMIC [FAST | SLOW | OFF | ON | TOGGLE]	/DRAG
SET ED [OFF | ON | TOGGLE]	/UNDLI1
SSET FONT [FAST | SLOW | OFF | ON | TOGGLE]	/FFONT1
SET GRID [OFF | ON | TOGGLE]	/GRID1
SET NODES [OFF | ON | TOGGLE]	/TXNOD1
SET PATTERN [OFF | ON | TOGGLE]	/PATRN1
SET TEXT [OFF | ON | TOGGLE]	/TEEXT1
SET TPMODE ACSDELTA	/AXDTEN
SET TPMODE ACSLOCATE	/AXXTEN
SET TPMODE DELTA	/MDELTA
SET TPMODE DISTANCE	/MANGL2
SET TPMODE LOCATE	/LOCATE
SET TPMODE VDELTA	/MDLTVW
SET WEIGHT [OFF | ON]	/DWGHT1
SHOW HEADER	/HEADER
SURFACE PROJECTION	/PRJELE
SURFACE REVOLUTION	/SURREV
SWAP SCREEN	/SWAP
TRANSFORM	/TRSELE
UPDATE1...UPDATE8	/UPDATE
UPDATE BOTH	/UPDBTH
UPDATE LEFT	/UPDAT2
UPDATE RIGHT	/UPDAT1
UPDATE VIEW	/UPDATV
VIEW OFF	/VIEWOF
WINDOW AREA	/WINDA1
WINDOW CENTER	/WINDC1
WINDOW VOLUME	/WINVOL
WSET ADD	/ADWSEL
WSET COPY	/ADWSEC
WSET DROP	/WSDROP
ZOOM IN 2	/HALF1
ZOOM OUT 2	/DOUBL1

APPENDIX

G

SEED FILES

NAME OF THE SEED FILE	WORKING UNITS			VIEW ATTRIBUTES	TEXT PARAMETERS
	MU	SU	RESOLUTION		
USTATION/WSMOD/DEFAULT/ SEED/SCHEM2D.DGN	MM	TH	1MM=100TH 1TH=1000PU	SEE NOTE	TX=0.5000 LS=0.0500
USTATION/WSMOD/DEFAULT/ SEED/SCHEM3D.DGN	MM	TH	1MM=100TH 1TH=1000PU	SEE NOTE GRID DISPLAY OFF	TX=0.0100 LS=0.0500
USTATION/WSMOD/DEFAULT/ SEED/SDSCH2D.DGN	IN	TH	1IN=10TH 1TH=1000PU	SEE NOTE GRID DISP. OFF	TX=6.0000 LS=0.5000
USTATION/WSMOD/DEFAULT/ SEED/SDSCH3D.DGN	IN	TH	1MM=100TH 1TH=1000PU	SEE NOTE GRID DISP. OFF	TX=0.1250 LS=0.5000
USTATION/WSMOD/DEFAULT/ SEED/SEED2D.DGN	MU	SU	1MU=10TH 1SU=1000PU	SEE NOTE	TX=1.0000 LS=0.5000
USTATION/WSMOD/DEFAULT/ SEED/SEED3D.DGN	MU	SU	1MU=10TH 1SU=1000PU	SEE NOTE GRID DISP. OFF	TX=0.1250 LS=0.5000
USTATION/WSMOD/DEFAULT/ SEED/SEEDZ.DGN	MU	SU	1MU=10TH 1SU=1000PU	SEE NOTE GRID DISP. OFF	TX=0.1250 LS=0.5000
USTATION/WSMOD/DEFAULT/ SEED/TRANSEED.DGN	MU	SU	1MU=10TH 1SU=1000PU	SEE NOTE	TX=1.0000 LS=0.5000
USTATION/WSMOD/ARCH/ SEED/ARCHSEED.DGN	'	"	1'=12" 1"=8000PU	SEE NOTE FILL DISP. ON	TX=1.0000 LS=0.5000
USTATION/WSMOD/ARCH/ SEED/SDARCH2D.DGN	'	"	1'=12" 1"=8000PU	SEE NOTE	TX=0:9000 LS=0.3000

SEED FILES *(concluded)*

NAME OF THE SEED FILE	WORKING UNITS			VIEW ATTRIBUTES	TEXT PARAMETERS
	MU	SU	RESOLUTION		
USTATION/WSMOD/ARCH/ SEED/SDARCH3D.DGN	'	"	1'=12" 1"=8000PU	SEE NOTE GRID DISP. OFF	TX=1.0000 LS=0.3000
USTATION/WSMOD/CIVIL/ SEED/CIV2D.DGN	FT	TH	1'=10TH 1TH=100PU	SEE NOTE	TX=1:5000 LS=5:0000
USTATION/WSMOD/CIVIL/ SEED/CIV3D.DGN	FT	TH	1'=10TH 1TH=100PU	SEE NOTE GRID DISP. OFF	TX=25.4 LS=25.4
USTATION/WSMOD/MAPPING/ SEED/MAP2D.DGN	FT	TH	1'=10TH 1TH=100PU	SEE NOTE	TX=2:5.00 LS=5:0.00
USTATION/WSMOD/MAPPING/ SEED/MAP3D.DGN	FT	TH	1'=10TH 1TH=100PU	SEE NOTE	TX=2:5.00 LS=5:0.00
USTATION/WSMOD/MAPPING/ SEED/SDMAP2D.DGN	FT	TH	1'=10TH 1TH=100PU	SEE NOTE GRID DISP. OFF	TX=1.0000 LS=0.5000
USTATION/WSMOD/MAPPING/ SEED/SDMAP3D.DGN	FT	TH	1'=10TH 1TH=100PU	SEE NOTE GRID DISP. OFF	TX=1.000 LS=5:000
USTATION/WSMOD/MAPPING/ SEED/SDMAPM2D.DGN	M	MM	1M=1000MM 1MM=10PU	SEE NOTE GRID DISP. OFF	TX=2.0000 LS=3.0002
USTATION/WSMOD/MAPPING/ SEED/SDMAPM3D.DGN	M	MM	1M=1000MM 1MM=10PU	SEE NOTE GRID DISP. OFF	TX=6.0000 LS=3.0001
USTATION/WSMOD/MECHDRAF/ SEED/MECHDET.DGN	IN	TH	1IN=1000TH 1TH=254PU	SEE NOTE GRID & NODES DISP. OFF	TX=0.0047 LS=0.0295
USTATION/WSMOD/MECHDRAF/ SEED/MECHDETM.DGN	MM		1MM=1000 1=100PU	SEE NOTE GRID DISP. OFF	TX=0.0300 LS=0.0150
USTATION/WSMOD/MECHDRAF/ SEED/MECHLAY.DGN	IN	TH	1IN=1000TH 1TH=254PU	SEE NOTE GRID & NODES DISP. OFF	TX=0.0047 LS=0.0295
USTATION/WSMOD/MECHDRAF/ SEED/MECHLAYM.DGN	MM		1MM=1000 1=100PU	SEE NOTE GRID DISP. OFF	TX=0.0300 LS=0.0150
USTATION/WSMOD/MECHDRAF/ SEED/SDMECH2D.DGN	IN	TH	1IN=1000TH 1TH=254PU	SEE NOTE GRID DISP. OFF	TX=2.0000 LS=0.5000
USTATION/WSMOD/MECHDRAF/ SEED/SDMECH3D.DGN	IN	TH	1IN=1000 1TH=254PU	SEE NOTE GRID DISP. OFF	TX=0.1000 LS=0.0295
USTATION/WSMOD/MECHDRAF/ SEED/SDMENG2D.DGN	MM	SU	1MM=1000SU 1SU=100PU	SEE NOTE GRID DISP. OFF	TX=2.0000 LS=0.0500
USTATION/WSMOD/MECHDRAF/ SEED/SDMENG3D.DGN	MM	SU	1MM=1000SU 1SU=100PU	SEE NOTE GRID DISP. OFF	TX=0.0100 LS=0.0500

Note: Following are the Display Attributes turned on by default unless noted differently in the table:

CONSTRUCTIONS   LINE STYLES
DATA FIELDS   LINE WEIGHTS
DIMENSIONS   PATTERNS
DYNAMICS   TEXT
GRID   TEXT NODES

INDEX

Note: Page numbers in **bold type** reference non-text materials.